RANDOM
HOUSE

LARGE
PRINT

ALSO BY JON MEACHAM
Available from Random House Large Print

American Gospel:
God, the Founding Fathers, and
the Making of a Nation

Franklin and Winston:
An Intimate Portrait of an Epic Friendship

American Lion:
Andrew Jackson in the White House

Th Jefferson

THOMAS JEFFERSON THE ART OF POWER

Jon Meacham

RANDOM HOUSE
LARGE PRINT

Grateful acknowledgment is made to the following for permission to reprint previously
published material:

Alfred A. Knopf, a division of Random House, Inc.: Excerpts from Origins of American
Politics by Bernard Bailyn, copyright © 1968 by Bernard Bailyn. Used by permission of Alfred
A. Knopf, a division of Random House, Inc.
Oxford University Press, Ltd.: Excerpts from "Thomas Jefferson Through the Eyes of a New
Hampshire Politician" by Lynn W. Turner from Mississippi Valley Historical Review 30,
no. 2 (September 1943): 206, 210, 211, copyright 1943. Reprinted by permission of Oxford
University Press, Ltd.
Rowman & Littlefield Publishing Group: Excerpt from Jefferson's America, 1760–1815, Third
Edition by Norman K. Risjord, copyright © 2010 by Rowman & Littlefield Publishers, Inc.
Reprinted with the permission of the Rowman & Littlefield Publishing Group.
Scribner, a division of Simon & Schuster, Inc.: Excerpts from "Jouette Outrides Tarleton and
Saves Jefferson from Capture" by Virginius Dabney from Scribner's Magazine (June 1928):
691–692, 697. Copyright 1928 by Charles Scribner's Sons. Reprinted with the permission of
Scribner, a division of Simon & Schuster, Inc.
The Thomas Jefferson Foundation: Excerpt from "Assessment of Possible Paternity of Other
Jeffersons" from Report of the Research Committee on Thomas Jefferson and Sally Hemings
(the Thomas Jefferson Foundation, January 2000); excerpt as quoted at the Thomas Jefferson
Foundation, www.monticello.org/site/research-andcollections/jefferson- conversation. Reprinted
by permission of the Thomas Jefferson Foundation, www.monticello.org.
University of North Carolina Press: Excerpts from correspondence from Lester J. Cappon (ed.),
The Adams-Jefferson Letters: The Complete Correspondence between Thomas Jefferson and
Abigail and John Adams, copyright © 1959 by the University of North Carolina Press, renewed
1987 by Stanley B. Cappon; excerpts from correspondence from The Papers of John Marshall,
Volume VI, edited by Herbert A. Johnson, et al. Copyright © 1990 by the University of North
Carolina Press. Published for the Omohundreo Institute of Early American History and
Culture; excerpts from The Stamp Act Crisis: Prologue to Revolution by Edmund S. Morgan
and Helen M. Morgan, copyright 1953 by the University of North Carolina Press, renewed ©
1981 by Edmund S. Morgan and Helen M. Morgan.Used by permission of the publisher, www
.uncpress.unc.edu.

Cover design: Tom McKeveny
Cover painting: Rembrandt Peale, portrait of Thomas Jefferson (detail), 1800 (Gift of Mr.
and Mrs. Paul Mellon/White House Historical Association/White House Collection)
Endpapers: An early sketch of Monticello, Jefferson's plantation house in Albemarle County,
Virginia.
Title Page: An 1825 watercolor of the West Front of Monticello by Jane Pitford Braddick
Peticolas.

The Library of Congress has established a Cataloging-in-Publication record for this title.

ISBN: 978–0-307–99087–7

www.randomhouse.com/largeprint

FIRST LARGE PRINT EDITION

Printed in the United States of America

10 9 8 7 6 5 4 3 2 1

This Large Print edition published in accord with the standards of the N.A.V.H.

TO HERBERT WENTZ

And, as ever, for Mary, Maggie, Sam, and Keith

A few broad strokes of the brush would paint the portraits of all the early Presidents with this exception. . . . Jefferson could be painted only touch by touch, with a fine pencil, and the perfection of the likeness depended upon the shifting and uncertain flicker of its semi-transparent shadows.

—HENRY ADAMS, **History of the United States of America During the Administrations of Thomas Jefferson**

I think this is the most extraordinary collection of talent, of human knowledge, that has ever been gathered together at the White House, with the possible exception of when Thomas Jefferson dined alone.

—PRESIDENT JOHN F. KENNEDY, at a dinner in honor of all living recipients of the Nobel Prize, 1962

CONTENTS

A NOTE ON THE TEXT   xv

PROLOGUE · The World's Best Hope   xvii

PART I ‖ THE SCION · **Beginnings to Spring 1774**

ONE · A Fortunate Son   3

TWO · What Fixed the Destinies of My Life   23

THREE · Roots of Revolution   40

FOUR · Temptations and Trials   61

FIVE · A World of Desire and Denial   77

PART II ‖ THE REVOLUTIONARY · **Spring 1774 to Summer 1776**

SIX · Like a Shock of Electricity   99

SEVEN · There Is No Peace   115

EIGHT · The Famous Mr. Jefferson   125

NINE · The Course of Human Events   146

TEN · The Pull of Duty   162

PART III ‖ REFORMER AND GOVERNOR · **Late 1776 to 1782**

ELEVEN · An Agenda for Liberty   177

TWELVE · A Troublesome Office   192

THIRTEEN · Redcoats at Monticello   203

FOURTEEN · To Burn on Through Death   214

PART IV || THE FRUSTRATED
CONGRESSMAN · **Late 1782 to
Mid-1784**

FIFTEEN · Return to the Arena   225

SIXTEEN · A Struggle for Respect   238

SEVENTEEN · Lost Cities and Life
Counsel   245

PART V || A MAN OF THE WORLD ·
1785 to 1789

EIGHTEEN · The Vaunted Scene
of Europe   265

NINETEEN · The Philosophical World   278

TWENTY · His Head and His Heart   291

TWENTY-ONE · Do You Like Our
New Constitution?   304

TWENTY-TWO · A Treaty in Paris   322

PART VI || THE FIRST SECRETARY OF
STATE · **1789 to 1792**

TWENTY-THREE · A New Post in
New York   343

TWENTY-FOUR · Mr. Jefferson Is
    Greatly Too Democratic   366
TWENTY-FIVE · Two Cocks in the Pit   385
TWENTY-SIX · The End of a Stormy
    Tour   404

PART VII ‖ THE LEADER OF THE
            OPPOSITION · 1793 to 1800
TWENTY-SEVEN · In Wait at Monticello   421
TWENTY-EIGHT · To the Vice
    Presidency   445
TWENTY-NINE · The Reign of Witches   463
THIRTY · Adams vs. Jefferson Redux   479
THIRTY-ONE · A Desperate State
    of Affairs   497

PART VIII ‖ THE PRESIDENT OF THE
             UNITED STATES · 1801 to 1809
THIRTY-TWO · The New Order of
    Things Begins   517
THIRTY-THREE · A Confident President   538
THIRTY-FOUR · Victories, Scandal,
    and a Secret Sickness   557
THIRTY-FIVE · The Air of Enchantment!   574
THIRTY-SIX · The People Were
    Never More Happy   591

THIRTY-SEVEN · A Deep, Dark,
and Widespread Conspiracy   623

THIRTY-EIGHT · This Damned
Embargo   639

THIRTY-NINE · A Farewell to
Ultimate Power   656

PART IX || THE MASTER OF MONTICELLO ·
1809 to the End

FORTY · My Body, Mind, and Affairs   669

FORTY-ONE · To Form Statesmen,
Legislators and Judges   696

FORTY-TWO · The Knell of the Union   715

FORTY-THREE · No, Doctor,
Nothing More   740

EPILOGUE · All Honor to Jefferson   751

AUTHOR'S NOTE AND
ACKNOWLEDGMENTS   765

NOTES   779

BIBLIOGRAPHY   1181

ILLUSTRATION CREDITS   1271

INDEX   1283

A NOTE ON THE TEXT

THOMAS JEFFERSON LEFT POSTERITY an immense correspondence, and I am particularly indebted to **The Papers of Thomas Jefferson,** published by Princeton University Press and first edited by Julian P. Boyd. I am, moreover, grateful to the incumbent editors of the **Papers,** especially general editor Barbara B. Oberg, for sharing unpublished transcripts of letters gathered for future volumes. The goal of the Princeton edition was, and continues to be, "to present as accurate a text as possible and to preserve as many of Jefferson's distinctive mannerisms of writing as can be done." To provide clarity and readability for a modern audience, however, I have taken the liberty of regularizing much of the quoted language from Jefferson and from his contemporaries. I have, for instance, silently corrected Jefferson's frequent use of "it's" for "its" and "recieve" for "receive," and have, in most cases, expanded contractions and abbreviations and followed generally accepted practices of capitalization.

THE WORLD'S BEST HOPE

Washington, D.C., Winter 1801

H E WOKE AT FIRST LIGHT. Lean and loose-limbed, Thomas Jefferson tossed back the sheets in his rooms at Conrad and Mc-Munn's boardinghouse on Capitol Hill, swung his long legs out of bed, and plunged his feet into a basin of cold water—a lifelong habit he believed good for his health. At Monticello, his plantation in the Southwest Mountains near the Blue Ridge of Virginia, the metal bucket brought to Jefferson every morning wore a groove on the floor next to the alcove where he slept.

Six foot two and a half, Jefferson was nearly fifty-eight years old in the Washington winter of 1800–1801. His sandy hair, reddish in his youth, was graying; his freckled skin—always susceptible to the sun—was wrinkling a bit. His eyes were penetrating but elusive, alternately described as blue, hazel, or brown. He had great teeth.

It was early February 1801. The capital, with its muddy avenues and scattered buildings, was in chaos, and had been for weeks. The future of the presidency was uncertain, the stability of the Constitution in question, and, secluded inside Conrad and McMunn's on New Jersey Avenue—a new establishment with stables for sixty horses just two hundred paces away from the unfinished Capitol building—Jefferson was in a quiet agony.

He soaked his feet and gathered his thoughts. After a vicious election in which he had challenged the incumbent president, John Adams, it turned out that while Jefferson had defeated Adams in the popular vote, the tall Virginian had received the same number of electoral votes for president as the dashing, charismatic, and unpredictable Aaron Burr of New York, who had been running as Jefferson's vice president. Under the rules in effect in 1800, there was no way to distinguish between a vote for president and one for vice president. What was supposed to have been a peaceful transfer of power from one rival to another—from Adams to Jefferson—had instead produced a constitutional crisis.

Anxious and unhappy, Jefferson was, he wrote to his eldest daughter, "worn down here with pursuits in which I take no delight, surrounded by enemies and spies catching and perverting every word which falls from my lips or flows from my pen, and inventing where facts fail them." His fate was in the hands of other men, the last place he wanted it to be. He hated the waiting, the whispers, the **not knowing**.

But there was nothing he could do. And so Thomas Jefferson waited.

The election, Jefferson said, was "the theme of all conversation." The electoral tie between Jefferson and Burr, with Adams not so far behind, threw the contest to the House of Representatives—and no one knew what would happen. It was suddenly a whole new election, taking place in the House where each of the sixteen state delegations had one vote to cast. Whoever won nine of those votes would become president. "THE CRISIS is momentous . . . !" the **Washington Federalist** newspaper declared in the second week of February. Could Burr, who admitted that he thought of politics as "fun and honor and profit," be made president by mischievous Federalists, taking the election from Jefferson, a fellow Republican? Or could Jefferson's foes elect an interim president, denying Jefferson and his Republicans ultimate power?

In the claustrophobic atmosphere of Washington, anything seemed possible—and Jefferson, who liked to cultivate the air of a philosopher who was above the merely political, found himself in a struggle to secure his own election and, in his mind, rescue the nation from the allegedly monarchical tendencies of the Federalist Party. As a young man in 1776 he had hazarded all for the American experiment in liberty. Now, a quarter of a century later, Jefferson believed that the United States as he knew it and loved it might not long endure. During the 1800 campaign, the patriot-physician Benjamin Rush told Jefferson that he had "heard a member of Congress lament our separation from Great Britain and express his sincere wishes that we were again dependent on her."

Such thoughts terrified Jefferson, who confessed that he felt bound to protect the principles of '76 he had articulated in the Declaration of Independence. If he—the choice of the majority of the electorate—lost the presidency, then what had Americans been fighting for all these years? So much was at stake. An old Revolutionary ally from Massachusetts, Elbridge Gerry, said Jefferson's foes were acting from "a desire to promote . . . division among the people, which they have excited and nourished as the germ of a civil war."

There had been a rumor that John Marshall, the secretary of state who had just been named chief justice, might be appointed president, blocking Jefferson from the office. "If the union could be broken, that would do it," said Virginia governor James Monroe, who was told that twenty-two thousand men in Pennsylvania were "prepared to take up arms in the event of extremities."

Disorder, which Jefferson hated, threatened harmony, which he loved.

In the end, after a snowstorm struck Washington, Jefferson narrowly prevailed on the thirty-sixth ballot in the House to become the third president of the United States. And so began the Age of Jefferson, a political achievement without parallel in American life. George Washington, John Adams, and Alexander Hamilton are sometimes depicted as wiser, more practical men than the philosophical master of Monticello. Judged by the raw standard of the winning and the keeping of power, however, Thomas Jefferson was the most successful political figure of the first half century of the American republic. For thirty-six of the forty years between 1800 and 1840, either Jefferson or a self-described adherent of his served as president of the United States: James Madison, James Monroe, Andrew Jackson, and Martin Van Buren. (John Quincy Adams, a one-term president, was the single exception.) This unofficial and little-noted Jeffersonian dynasty is unmatched in American history.

He had a defining vision, a compelling goal—the survival and success of popular government in America. Jefferson believed the will of an educated, enlightened majority should prevail. His opponents had less faith in the people, worrying that the broad American public might be unequal to self-government. Jefferson thought that same public was the salvation of liberty, the soul of the nation, and the hope of the republic.

In pursuit of his ends, Jefferson sought, acquired, and wielded power, which is the bending of the world to one's will, the remaking of reality in one's own image. Our greatest leaders are neither dreamers nor dictators: They are, like Jefferson, those who articulate national aspirations yet master the mechanics of influence and know when to depart from dogma. Jefferson had a remarkable capacity to marshal ideas and to move men, to balance the inspirational and the pragmatic. To realize his vision, he compromised and improvised. The willingness to do what he needed to do in a given moment makes him an elusive historical figure. Yet in the real world, in real time, when he was charged with the safety of the country, his creative flexibility made him a transformative leader.

America has always been torn between the ideal and the real, between noble goals and inevitable compromises. So was Jefferson. In his head and in his heart, as in the nation itself, the perfect warred with the good, the intellectual with the visceral. In him as in America, that conflict was, and is, a war without end. Jefferson's story resonates not least because he embodies an eternal drama: the struggle of the leadership of the nation to achieve greatness in a difficult and confounding world.

More than any of the other early presidents—more than Washington, more than Adams—Jefferson believed in the possibilities of humanity. He dreamed big but understood that dreams become reality only when their champions are strong enough and wily enough to bend history to their purposes. Broadly put, philosophers think; politicians maneuver. Jefferson's genius was that he was both and could do both, often simultaneously. Such is the art of power.

He loved his wife, his books, his farms, good wine, architecture, Homer, horseback riding, history, France, the Commonwealth of Virginia, spending money, and the very latest in ideas and insights. He believed in America, and in Americans. The nation, he said in his first inaugural address in 1801, was "the world's best hope." He thought Americans themselves capable of virtually anything they put their minds to. "Whatever they can, they will," Jefferson said of his countrymen in 1814.

A formidable man, "Mr. Jefferson was as tall, straight-bodied [a] man as ever you see, right square-shouldered," said Isaac Granger Jefferson, a Monticello slave. "Neat a built man as ever was seen . . . a straight-up man, long face, high nose." Edmund Bacon, a Monticello overseer, said that Jefferson "was like a fine horse; he had no surplus flesh. . . . His countenance was always mild and pleasant."

To be tall and forbidding might command respect for a time, but not affection. To be overly familiar might command affection for a time, but not respect. Jefferson was the rare leader who stood out from the crowd without intimidating it. His bearing gave him unusual opportunities to make the thoughts in his head the work of his hands, transforming the world around him from what it was to what he thought it ought to be.

A philosopher and a scientist, a naturalist and a historian, Jefferson was a man of the Enlightenment, always looking forward, consumed by the quest for knowledge. He adored detail, noting the temperature each day and carrying a tiny, ivory-leaved notebook in his pocket to track his daily expenditures. He drove his horses hard and fast and considered the sun his "almighty physician." Jefferson, an inveterate walker, was fit and virile. He drank no hard liquor but loved wine, taking perhaps three glasses a day. He did not smoke. When he received gifts of Havana cigars from well-wishers, he passed them along to friends.

Jefferson never tired of invention and inquiry, designing dumbwaiters and hidden mechanisms to open doors at Monticello. He delighted in archaeology, paleontology, astronomy, botany, and meteorology, and once created his own version of the Gospels by excising the New Testament passages he found supernatural or implausible and arranging the remaining verses in the order he believed they should be read. He drew sustenance from music and found joy in gardening. He bought and built beautiful things, creating Palladian plans for Monticello and designing the Roman-inspired capitol of Virginia, which he conceived after seeing an ancient temple in Nîmes, in the south of France. He was an enthusiastic patron of pasta, took the trouble to copy down a French recipe for ice cream, and enjoyed the search for the perfect dressing for his salads. He kept shepherd dogs (two favorites were named Bergere and Grizzle). He knew Latin, Greek, French, Italian, and Spanish.

He was also a student of human nature, a keen observer of what drove other men, and he loved knowing the details of other lives. He admired the letters of Madame de Sévigné, whose correspondence offered a panoramic view of the France of Louis XIV, and Madame de Staël's **Corinne, or Italy,** a romantic picaresque novel. In his library at Monticello was a collection of what a guest called "regal scandal" that Jefferson had put together under the title **The Book of Kings.** It included the **Mémoires de la Princesse de Bareith** (by the princess royal of Prussia, sister of Frederick the Great); **Les Mémoires de la Comtesse de la Motte** (by a key figure in a scandal involving a diamond necklace and Marie-Antoinette); and an account of the trial of the Duke of York, the commander in chief of the British army who had been forced to resign amid charges that he had allowed his mistress to sell officer commissions. Jefferson spoke of these tales, his guest recalled, "with a satisfaction somewhat inconsistent with the measured gravity he claims in relation to such subjects generally."

A guest at a country inn was said to have once struck up a conversation with a "plainly-dressed and unassuming traveler" whom the stranger did not recognize. The two covered subject after subject, and the unremarkable traveler was "perfectly acquainted with each." Afterward, "filled with wonder," the guest asked the landlord who this extraordinary man was. When the topic was the law, the traveler said, "he thought he was a lawyer"; when it was medicine, he "felt sure he was a physician"; when it was theology, "he became convinced that he was a clergyman."

The landlord's reply was brief. "Oh, why I thought you knew the Squire."

To his friends, who were numerous and devoted, Jefferson was among the greatest men who had ever lived, a Renaissance figure who was formidable without seeming overbearing, sparkling without being showy, winning without appearing cloying.

Yet to his foes, who were numerous and prolific, Jefferson was an atheist and a fanatic, a demagogue and a dreamer, a womanly Francophile who could not be trusted with the government of a great nation. His task was to change those views as best he could. He longed for affection and for approval.

A master of emotional and political manipulation, sensitive to criticism, obsessed with his reputation, and devoted to America, he was drawn to the world beyond Monticello, endlessly at work, as he put it, "to see the standard of reason at length erected after so many ages during which the human mind has been held in vassalage by kings, priests, and nobles." As a planter, lawyer, legislator, governor, diplomat, secretary of state, vice president, and president, Jefferson spent much of his life seeking control over himself and power over the lives and destinies of others. For Jefferson, politics was not a dispiriting distraction but an undertaking that made everything else possible.

Inspired by his own father's example, he long sought to play the part of a patriarch, accepting—even embracing—the accompanying burdens of responsibility. He was the father of the ideal of individual liberty, of the Louisiana Purchase, of the Lewis and Clark expedition, of the American West. He led the first democratic movement in the new republic to check the power and influence of established forces. And perhaps most important, he gave the nation the idea of American progress—the animating spirit that the future could be better than the present or the past. The greatest American politicians since have prospered by projecting a Jeffersonian vision that the country's finest hours lay ahead.

The story of Jefferson's life fascinates still in part because he found the means to endure and, in many cases, to prevail in the face of extreme partisanship, economic uncertainty, and external threat. Jefferson's political leadership is instructive, offering us the example of a president who can operate at two levels, cultivating the hope of a brighter future while preserving the political flexibility and skill to bring the ideal as close as possible to reality.

He has most commonly been thought of as the author or designer of America: a figure who articulated a vision of what the country could be but was otherwise a kind of detached dreamer. Yet Jefferson did not rest once his words were written or his ideas entered circulation. He was a builder and a fighter. "What is practicable must often control what is pure theory," he said during his presidency; moreover, "the habits of the governed determine in a great degree what is practicable."

Jefferson fought for the greatest of causes yet fell short of delivering justice to the persecuted and the enslaved. In the end, for all the debate and the division and the scholarship and the symposia, there may be only one thing about Thomas Jefferson that is indisputable: that the man who lived and worked from 1743 to 1826 was a breathing human being who was subject to the passion and prejudice and pride and love and ambition and hope and fear that drive most other breathing human beings. Recovering a sense of that mortal Jefferson—the Jefferson who sought office, defined human rights for a new age, explored expanding frontiers in science and philosophy, loved women, owned slaves, and helped forge a nation—is my object in the following pages.

He is not a man of our time but of his own, formed by the historical realities of the eighteenth and nineteenth centuries. He must be seen in context. It is also true, however, that many of his concerns were universal. His was a particular life of perennial significance.

And the world—or at least much of it—found him charming, brilliant, and gracious. Engaged in a constant campaign to win the affection of whoever happened to be in front of him at a given moment, Jefferson flirted with women and men alike. "It is a charming thing to be loved by everybody," he told his grandchildren, "and the way to obtain it is, never to quarrel or be angry with anybody." He hated arguing face-to-face, preferring to smooth out the rough edges of conversation, leading some people to believe Jefferson agreed with them when, in fact, he was seeking to avoid conflict. He paid a price for this obsession with congeniality among those who mistook his reticence for duplicity.

Yet women in particular loved him. Calling on Samuel Harrison Smith, the Republican publisher of the Washington **National Intelligencer,** Jefferson was shown into the Smiths' parlor, where he spent a few minutes alone with Smith's wife, Margaret, a writer and hostess. The child of a Federalist family, Mrs. Smith did not at first realize who Jefferson was, and found herself "somewhat checked by the dignified and reserved air" of the caller. What she experienced as a "chilled feeling," however, passed almost instantly. Offered a chair, the stranger assumed "a free and easy manner, and, carelessly throwing his arm on the table near which he sat, he turned towards me with a countenance beaming with an expression of benevolence and with a manner and voice almost femininely soft and gentle." Gifted in the arts of the morning call, he "entered into conversation on the commonplace topics of the day," Mrs. Smith said, "from which, before I was conscious of it, he had drawn me into observations of a more personal and interesting nature."

Such was his charm that though she did not know quite why, here she was, saying things she had not meant to say. "There was something in his manner, his countenance and voice that at once unlocked my heart." The caller was in a kind of control, reversing the usual order of things in which the host, not the hosted, set the terms and conditions of conversation. "I found myself frankly telling him what I liked or disliked in our present circumstances and abode," Mrs. Smith said. "I knew not who he was, but the interest with which he listened to my artless details . . . put me perfectly at my ease; in truth, so kind and conciliating were his looks and manners that I forgot he was not a friend of my own."

At this point the door to the parlor opened, and Mr. Smith walked in. Learning that the caller was "**Mr. Jefferson,**" Mrs. Smith was at once thrilled and embarrassed. "I felt my cheeks burn and my heart throb, and not a word more could I speak while he remained." She was struck by the gulf between the image and the man. "And is this the violent democrat, the vulgar demagogue, the bold atheist and profligate man I have so often heard denounced by the Federalists?" she asked. "Can this man so meek and mild, yet dignified in his manners, with a voice so soft and low, with a countenance so benignant and intelligent, can he be that daring leader of a faction, that disturber of the peace, that enemy of all rank and order?" Taking his leave, Jefferson "shook hands cordially with us . . . and in a manner which said as plain as words could do, 'I am your friend.' "

Jefferson did not limit his sensuous appetites to the beauties of art, the power of music, or the splendor of landscapes. He pursued two women before he met his future wife; his marriage was the source of more than a decade of domestic happiness. Her death devastated him into insensibility, and he wandered the woods of Monticello in a grief that led him to thoughts of suicide.

He had promised his dying wife he would never remarry. He kept his word but embarked on a love affair with one woman, the beautiful (and married) Maria Cosway. Finally, Jefferson maintained a decades-long liaison with Sally Hemings, his late wife's enslaved half sister who tended to his personal quarters at Monticello. They produced six children (four of whom lived) and gave rise to two centuries of speculation about the true nature of the affair. Was it about love? Power? Both? And if both, how much was affection, how much coercion? Jefferson's connection with Sally Hemings lasted from about 1787 to Jefferson's death in 1826—almost forty years.

The power of America's founding myth—or myths, if one divides the stories into a seventeenth-century one of Jamestown and Plymouth and an eighteenth-century one of the Revolution—is such that it is difficult to envision the story of the country as it actually unfolded. By force of nearly two and a half centuries of habit, we tend to view our history as an inevitable chain of events leading to a sure conclusion. There was, however, nothing foreordained about the American experiment. To treat it as a set piece pitting an evil empire of Englishmen against a noble band of Americans does a disservice to both, for it caricatures Britain and minimizes the complexities that Jefferson and his contemporaries faced in choosing accommodation or rebellion.

Most Americans were, after all, of British descent, and American culture in the decades leading up to the Revolution was deferential to—and even celebratory of—the monarchy. The whole structure of the lives of Jefferson's American ancestors and of his generation was built around membership in the

British Empire. For many if not most Americans, the hatred of King George III that marked the active Revolutionary period was the exception, not the rule.

Jefferson lived and worked in a time when nothing was certain. He knew—he **felt**—that America's enemies were everywhere. The greatest of these was Britain, and not only during the struggle for independence. Rather than recalling the Revolutionary War in its traditional way—as the armed struggle that lasted from Lexington and Concord in 1775 until the British defeat at Yorktown in 1781—it is illuminating in considering Jefferson to think of the struggle against Great Britain and its influence in American life as one that opened in 1764 and did not end until the Treaty of Ghent and the Battle of New Orleans brought the War of 1812 to a close in 1815.

Seen this way—which is how Jefferson saw it, or at least implicitly experienced it—Jefferson lived and governed in a Fifty Years' War. It was a war that was sometimes hot and sometimes cold, but was always unfolding. It took different forms. There were traditional battlefield confrontations from 1775 to 1783 and again from 1812 to 1815. There were battles by proxy with Loyalists and British allies among the Indians. There were commercial strikes and counterstrikes. There were fears of political encroachment within the United States that could be aided by British military movements from Canada, Nova Scotia, or Britain's western posts (posts they declined to surrender after the Revolution). There were anxieties about disunionist sentiment in New England and New York. There were terrors about monarchical tendencies within American life and government.

Anything that happened in either foreign or domestic politics was interpreted through the prism of the ongoing conflict with Britain. Even talk of potential alliances with London in the event of war with France was driven not by affection for Britain but by calculations of national interest. Jefferson did not trust the old mother country, and he did not trust those Americans who maintained even imaginative ties to monarchy and its trappings—aristocracy of birth, hereditary executives, lifetime legislatures, standing armies, large naval establishments, and grand, centralized financial systems. When Jefferson sensed any trend in the general direction of such things, he reacted viscerally, fearing that the work of the Revolution and of the Constitutional Convention was at risk. The proximity of British officials and troops to the north of the United States and the strength of the British fleet exacerbated these anxieties.

Was Jefferson paranoid about such possibilities, especially in the period from the Treaty of Paris in 1783, which marked the end of the Revolutionary

War, through his presidency, which ended in 1809? Perhaps. Was he engaging in conspiracy mongering? Yes. But sometimes paranoids have enemies, and conspiracies are only laughable when they fail to materialize. Jefferson's fevered fears about a return of monarchy, which was often his shorthand for a restoration of British influence and an end to the uniquely American enterprise in self-government, were dismissed as fanciful by no less a figure than George Washington. But in the climate of the time—a time of revolution, of espionage, and of well-founded worries that the American republic might meet the dismal fate all other republics had ever met—Jefferson's sense of Britain as a perennial foe is unsurprising and essential to understand. He thought he was in a perennial war. And if we are to understand what he was like, and what life was like for him, then we must see the world as he saw it, not as how we know it turned out.

To Jefferson, little in America was secure, for the military success of the Revolution had marked only the end of one battle in a larger, half-century war. From Alexander Hamilton's financial program to John Adams's weakness for British forms to the overt New England hostility toward his presidency, he judged political life in the context of the British threat to democratic republicanism. In retrospect, Jefferson's fears about the British may seem overheated—they surely did to some who lived through the same years and the same pressures—but they were real to him.

Jefferson hungered for greatness, and the drama of his age provided him a stage which he never really left. Writing his William and Mary schoolmate and Revolutionary colleague John Page in 1803—Page was governor of Virginia, Jefferson president of the United States—Jefferson said: "We have both been drawn from our natural passion for study and tranquility, by times which took from us the freedom of choice: times however which, planting a new world with the seeds of just government, will produce a remarkable era in the history of mankind. It was incumbent on those therefore who fell into them, to give up every favorite pursuit, and lay their shoulder to the work of the day."

In his retirement at Monticello, he looked back over the years, through the haze of war and struggle and peril, and knew that he had done his duty. "The circumstances of our country at my entrance into life," he remarked to a visitor, "were such that every honest man felt himself compelled to take a part, and to act up to the best of his abilities." He could have done no other. The Revolution, Jefferson once said, had been nothing less than a "bold and doubtful election . . . for our country, between submission, or the sword."

The point of departure for understanding Jefferson lies not at Conrad and McMunn's, nor at the

President's House nor even at Jefferson's beloved plantation on the hill. Before Monticello there was another house in the woods of the Southwest Mountains of Virginia. The search for Thomas Jefferson must begin there, on the banks of the Rivanna River, a tributary of the James, at a vanished plantation called Shadwell.

PART I
THE SCION

BEGINNINGS to SPRING 1774

The public or political character of the
Virginians corresponds with the private
one: they are haughty and jealous of
their liberties, impatient of restraint and
can scarcely bear the thought of being
controlled by any superior power.

—ANDREW BURNABY, an English
traveler who visited the middle colonies
in America in 1759–60

A MAP of
the most INHABITED part of
VIRGINIA
containing the whole PROVINCE of
MARYLAND
with Part of
PENSILVANIA, NEW JERSEY and NORTH CAROLINA
Drawn by
Joshua Fry & Peter Jefferson
in 1775.

To the Right Honourable George Dunk Earl of Halifax, First Lord Commissioner and to the Rest of the Right Honourable and Honourable Commissioners for TRADE and PLANTATIONS This Map is most humbly Inscribed to their Lordships, Most Obedient & most Humble Serv. Jos. Jeffers.

In 1752, Peter Jefferson, Thomas Jefferson's father, published the results of collaboration with a fellow surveyor, Joshua Fry, to fix the boundaries of Virginia and draw a map of the colony.

ONE

A Fortunate Son

*It is the strong in body who are both the
strong and free in mind.*

—PETER JEFFERSON, the father of
Thomas Jefferson

HE WAS THE KIND OF MAN people noticed.
An imposing, prosperous, well-liked farmer
known for his feats of strength and his
capacity for endurance in the wilderness, Peter Jefferson had amassed large tracts of land and scores
of slaves in and around what became Albemarle
County, Virginia. There, along the Rivanna, he built
Shadwell, named after the London parish where his
wife, Jane, had been baptized.

The first half of the eighteenth century was a
thrilling time to be young, white, male, wealthy,
and Virginian. Money was to be made, property to
be claimed, tobacco to be planted and sold. There
were plenty of ambitious men about—men with the
boldness and the drive to create farms, build houses,

and accumulate fortunes in land and slaves in the wilderness of the mid-Atlantic.

As a surveyor and a planter, Peter Jefferson thrived there, and his eldest son, Thomas, born on April 13, 1743, understood his father was a man other men admired.

Celebrated for his courage, Peter Jefferson excelled at riding and hunting. His son recalled that the father once single-handedly pulled down a wooden shed that had stood impervious to the exertions of three slaves who had been ordered to destroy the building. On another occasion, Peter was said to have uprighted two huge hogsheads of tobacco that weighed a thousand pounds each—a remarkable, if mythical, achievement.

The father's standing mattered greatly to the son, who remembered him in a superlative and senti-mental light. "The tradition in my father's family was that their ancestor came to this country from Wales, and from near the mountain of Snowden, the highest in Great Britain," Jefferson wrote. The connection to Snowdon (the modern spelling) was the only detail of the Jeffersons' old-world origins known to pass from generation to generation. Everything else about the ancient roots of the paternal clan slipped into the mists, save for this: that they came from a place of height and of distinction—if not of birth, then of strength.

Thomas Jefferson was his father's son. He was raised to wield power. By example and perhaps explicitly he was taught that to be great—to be heeded—one had to grow comfortable with authority and with responsibility. An able student and eager reader, Jefferson was practical as well as scholarly, resourceful as well as analytical.

Jefferson learned the importance of endurance and improvisation early, and he learned it the way his father wanted him to: through action, not theory. At age ten, Thomas was sent into the woods alone, with a gun. The assignment—the **expectation**—was that he was to come home with evidence that he could survive on his own in the wild.

The test did not begin well. He killed nothing, had nothing to show for himself. The woods were forbidding. Everything around the boy—the trees and the thickets and the rocks and the river—was frightening and frustrating.

He refused to give up or give in. He soldiered on until his luck finally changed. "Finding a wild turkey caught in a pen," the family story went, "he tied it with his garter to a tree, shot it, and carried it home in triumph."

The trial in the forest foreshadowed much in Jefferson's life. When stymied, he learned to press forward. Presented with an unexpected opening, he figured out how to take full advantage. Victorious, he enjoyed his success.

Jefferson was taught by his father and mother, and later by his teachers and mentors, that a gentleman owed service to his family, to his neighborhood, to his county, to his colony, and to his king. An eldest son in the Virginia of his time grew up expecting to lead—and to be followed. Thomas Jefferson came of age with the confidence that controlling the destinies of others was the most natural thing in the world. He was born for command. He never knew anything else.

The family had immigrated to Virginia from England in 1612, and in the New World they had moved quickly toward prosperity and respectability. A Jefferson was listed among the delegates of an assembly convened at Jamestown in 1619. The future president's great-grandfather was a planter who married the daughter of a justice in Charles City County and speculated in land at Yorktown. He died about 1698, leaving an estate of land, slaves, furniture, and livestock. His son, the future president's grandfather, rose further in colonial society, owning a racehorse and serving as sheriff and justice of the peace in Henrico County. He kept a good house, in turn leaving his son, Peter Jefferson, silver spoons and a substantial amount of furniture. As a captain of the militia, Thomas Jefferson's grandfather once hosted Colonel William Byrd II, one of Virginia's greatest men, for a dinner of roast beef and persico wine.

Born in Chesterfield County in 1708, Peter Jefferson built on the work of his fathers. Peter, with Joshua Fry, professor of mathematics at the College of William and Mary, drew the first authoritative map of Virginia and ran the boundary line between Virginia and North Carolina, an achievement all the more remarkable given Peter Jefferson's intellectual background. "My father's education had been quite neglected; but being of a strong mind, sound judgment and eager after information," Thomas Jefferson wrote, "he read much and improved himself." Self taught, Peter Jefferson became a colonel of the militia, vestryman, and member of the Virginia House of Burgesses.

On that expedition to fix the boundary between Virginia and North Carolina, the father proved himself a hero of the frontier. Working their way across the Blue Ridge, Peter Jefferson and his colleagues fought off "the attacks of wild beasts during the day, and at night found but a broken rest, sleeping—as they were obliged to do for safety—in trees," as a family chronicler wrote.

Low on food, exhausted, and faint, the band faltered—save for Jefferson, who subsisted on the raw flesh of animals ("or whatever could be found to sustain life," as the family story had it) until the job was done.

Thomas Jefferson grew up with an image—and, until Peter Jefferson's death when his son was fourteen, the reality—of a father who was powerful, who could do things other men could not, and who, through the force of his will or of his muscles or of both at once, could tangibly transform the world around him. Surveyors defined new worlds; explorers conquered the unknown; mapmakers brought form to the formless. Peter Jefferson was all three and claimed a central place in the imagination of his son, who admired his father's strength and spent a lifetime recounting tales of the older man's daring. Thomas Jefferson, a great-granddaughter said, "never wearied of dwelling with all the pride of filial devotion and admiration on the noble traits" of his father's character. The father had shaped the ways other men lived. The son did all he could to play the same role in the lives of others.

Peter Jefferson had married very well, taking a bride from Virginia's leading family. In 1739, he wed Jane Randolph, a daughter of Isham Randolph, a planter and sea captain. Born in London in 1721, Jane Randolph was part of her father's household at Dungeness in Goochland County, a large establishment with walled gardens.

The Randolph family traced its colonial origins to Henry Randolph, who emigrated from England in 1642. Marrying a daughter of the Speaker of the House of Burgesses, Henry Randolph thrived in Virginia, holding office in Henrico County and serving as clerk of the House of Burgesses. Returning home to England in 1669, he apparently prevailed on a young nephew, William, to make the journey to Virginia.

William Randolph, Thomas Jefferson's great-grandfather, thus came to the New World at some point between 1669 and 1674; accounts differ. He, too, rose in Virginia with little delay, taking his uncle's place as Henrico clerk and steadily acquiring vast acreage. An ally of Sir William Berkeley, the British governor, William Randolph soon prospered in shipping, raising tobacco, and slave trading.

William became known for his family seat on Turkey Island in the James River, which was described as "a splendid mansion." With his wife, Mary Isham Randolph, the daughter of the master of a plantation called Bermuda Hundred, William had ten children, nine of whom survived. The Randolphs "are so numerous that they are obliged, like the clans of Scotland, to be distinguished by their places of residence," noted Thomas Anburey, an English visitor to Virginia in 1779–80. As the Randolph historian Josephus Daniels noted, there was William of Chatsworth; Thomas of Tuckahoe; Sir John of Tazewell Hall, Williamsburg; Richard of Curles Neck; Henry of Longfield; Edward of Bremo. And there was Isham of Dungeness, who was Jefferson's maternal grandfather.

As a captain and a merchant, Jefferson's grandfather moved between the New and Old Worlds. About 1717, he married an Englishwoman, Jane Rogers, who was thought to be a "pretty sort of woman." They lived in London and at their Goochland County estate in Virginia.

In 1737, a merchant described Thomas Jefferson's

grandfather's family as "a very gentle, well-dressed people." Jefferson's mother, Jane, was a daughter of this house and had an apparent sense of pride in her British ancestry. She was said to have descended from "the powerful Scotch Earls of Murray, connected by blood or alliance with many of the most distinguished families in the English and Scotch peerage, and with royalty itself."

The family of William Byrd II—he was to build Westover, a beautiful Georgian plantation mansion on the James River south of Richmond—had greater means than the Jeffersons, but the description of a typical day for Byrd in February 1711 gives a sense of what life was like for the Virginia elite in the decades before the birth of Thomas Jefferson.

> I rose at 6 o'clock and read two chapters in Hebrew and some Greek in Lucian. I said my prayers and ate boiled milk for breakfast. I danced my dance [exercised] and then went to the brick house to see my people pile the planks and found them all idle for which I threatened them soundly but did not whip them. The weather was cold and the wind at northeast. I wrote a letter to England. Then I read some English till 12 o'clock when Mr. Dunn and his wife came. I ate boiled beef for dinner. In the afternoon Mr. Dunn and I played at billiards. Then we took a long walk about the plantation

and looked over all my business. . . . At night I
ate some bread and cheese.

Whether in the Tidewater regions closer to the Atlantic or in the forested hills of the Blue Ridge, the
Virginia into which Jefferson was born offered lives
of privilege to its most fortunate sons.

Visiting Virginia and Maryland, an English traveler
observed "the youth of these more indulgent settlements . . . are pampered much more in softness and
ease than their neighbors more northward." Children were instructed in music and taught to dance,
including minuets and what were called "country-
dances." One tutor described such lessons at Nomini
Hall, the Carter family estate roughly one hundred
miles east of Albemarle. The scene of young Virginians dancing, he said, "was indeed beautiful to admiration, to see such a number of young persons, set
off by dress to the best advantage, moving easily, to
the sound of well-performed music, and with perfect
regularity."

Thomas Jefferson was such a youth, and he grew
up as the eldest son of a prosperous, cultured,
and sophisticated family. They dined with silver,
danced with grace, entertained constantly.

His father worked in his study on the first floor of
the house—it was one of four rooms on that level—
at a cherry desk. Peter Jefferson's library included

Shakespeare, Jonathan Swift, Joseph Addison, and Paul de Rapin-Thoyras's **History of England**. "When young, I was passionately fond of reading books of history, and travels," Thomas Jefferson wrote. Of note were George Anson's **Voyage Round the World** and John Ogilby's **America,** both books that offered the young Jefferson literary passage to larger worlds. A grandson recalled Jefferson's saying that "from the time when, as a boy, he had turned off wearied from play and first found pleasure in books, he had never sat down in idleness."

It was a world of leisure for well-off white Virginians. "My father had a devoted friend to whose house he would go, dine, spend the night, dine with him again on the second day, and return to Shadwell in the evening," Jefferson recalled. "His friend, in the course of a day or two, returned the visit, and spent the same length of time at his house. This occurred once every week; and thus, you see, they were together four days out of the seven." The food was good and plentiful, the drink strong and bracing, the company cheerful and familiar.

Jefferson believed his first memory was of being handed up to a slave on horseback and carried, carefully, on a pillow for a long journey: an infant white master being cared for by someone whose freedom was not his own. Jefferson was two or three at the time. On that trip the family was bound for Tuckahoe, a Randolph estate about fifty miles east of

Shadwell. Tuckahoe's master, Jane Randolph Jefferson's cousin William Randolph, had just died. A widower, William Randolph had asked Peter Jefferson, his "dear and loving friend," to come to Tuckahoe in the event of his death and raise Randolph's three children there, and Peter Jefferson did so. (William Randolph and Peter Jefferson had been so close that Peter Jefferson had once purchased four hundred acres of land—the ultimate site of Shadwell—from Randolph. The price: "Henry Weatherbourne's biggest bowl of arrack [rum] punch!")

The Jeffersons would stay on the Randolph place for seven years, from the time William Randolph died, when Thomas was two or three, until Thomas was nine or ten.

Peter Jefferson, who apparently received his and his family's living expenses from the Randolph estate (which he managed well), used the years at Tuckahoe to discharge his duty to his dead friend while his own Albemarle fields were being cleared. This was the era of many of Peter Jefferson's expeditions, which meant he was away from home for periods of time, leaving his wife and the combined Randolph and Jefferson families at Tuckahoe.

The roots of the adult Jefferson's dislike of personal confrontation may lie partly in the years he spent at Tuckahoe as a member of a large combined family. Though the eldest son of Peter and Jane Jefferson, Thomas was spending some formative years in a house not his own. Thomas Mann Randolph was two years older than he was, and this Thomas Randolph was the heir of the Tuckahoe property. Whether such distinctions manifested themselves when the children were so young is unknowable, but Jefferson emerged from his childhood devoted to avoiding conflict at just about any cost. It is possible his years at Tuckahoe set him on a path toward favoring comity over controversy in face-to-face relations.

It was also at Tuckahoe that Thomas Jefferson, as he grew into childhood, first consciously encountered the complexities of life in slave-owning Virginia. Decades later, in **Notes on the State of Virginia,** he wrote: "The whole commerce between master and slave is a perpetual exercise of the most boisterous passions, the most unremitting despotism on the one part, and degrading submissions on the other. Our children see this, and learn to imitate it; for man is an imitative animal. . . . The parent storms, the child looks on, catches the lineaments of wrath, puts on the same airs in the circle of smaller slaves, gives a loose to his worst of passions, and thus nursed, educated, and daily exercised in tyranny, cannot but be stamped by it with odious peculiarities."

Tuckahoe was the scene of another small childhood moment. Anxious for school to be over, Thomas slipped away, hid, and repeated the Lord's Prayer in hopes of hastening the end of school. His prayer went unanswered. He would come to believe that orthodox Christianity was not all it was said to be.

In 1752, the Jeffersons moved back to Shadwell. Five years later, in 1757, Peter Jefferson died. The father was 49, and Thomas, fourteen, was propelled into the role, if not the reality, of man of the house. He did not recall the sudden transition fondly. "At 14 years of age the whole care and direction of myself was thrown on my self entirely, without a relative or friend qualified to advise or guide me," he later wrote to a grandson.

There would be no more evenings spent in the first-floor study, looking over maps, listening to tales of brave expeditions, tinkering with the tools of surveying, discussing Shakespeare or **The Spectator**. Those hours with his father were now to live only in memory, with the image of Peter Jefferson before him, inspiring and daunting.

Shadwell was to be dominated by Thomas's mother, Jane Randolph Jefferson, who almost certainly exerted as great an influence on her eldest son as the legend of Peter Jefferson did—but in subtler ways.

To all appearances, Jane ran things as she saw fit. Literate, social, fond of cultivated things—from fancy plate and crockery to well-made furniture to fine clothing—she was to endure the death of a husband, cope with the deaths of children, and remain in control to the end, immersed in the universe around her and in the lives of those she loved.

That her eldest son grew to become just such an unflinching, resilient aristocrat is no surprise.

Thomas Jefferson's bravery in the face of domestic tragedy and his determination to have his own way on his own land among his own people could owe something to the example of a mother from whom he learned much about negotiating the storms of life.

On the death of her husband Jane Jefferson became both mistress and master at Shadwell. At the age of thirty-seven she was the mother of eight surviving children—the oldest, Jane, was seventeen; Thomas was fourteen; the youngest were two-year-old twins. Her great-great-granddaughter later reported a family tradition that Mrs. Jefferson was "a woman of a clear and strong understanding." She would have to have been in order to manage her children and the complexities of Shadwell, with its sixty-six slaves and at least 2,750 acres (which included the thousand-acre tract that became Monticello). From the family Bible that has survived from Shadwell, Jane Jefferson emerges as a meticulous record keeper (a habit her son inherited).

There was death and fire and family tragedy. One of Jane's eight children—Thomas's sister Elizabeth—appears to have been disabled. "The most fortunate of us all in our journey through life frequently meet with calamities and misfortunes which may greatly afflict us," Jefferson once wrote, and "to fortify our minds against the attacks of these calamities and misfortunes should be one of the principal studies and endeavors of our lives."

As a woman wielding authority over her family, her hired laborers, and her slaves, Mrs. Jefferson probably developed a fine tactical sense. "She was an agreeable, intelligent woman, as well educated as the other Virginia ladies of the day, of her own elevated rank in society . . . and . . . she was a notable housekeeper," wrote a great-granddaughter. "She possessed a most amiable and affectionate disposition, a lively, cheerful temper, and a great fund of humor. She was fond of writing, particularly letters, and wrote readily and well."

Jane Jefferson came from a family that did not doubt its place, and her husband had often been away when he was alive, leaving her to run things in his absence at both Tuckahoe and Shadwell. That Jane Jefferson was a determined woman can be further deduced from the fact that she rebuilt Shadwell after it burned in 1770 rather than moving. It was her world in the way Monticello became her son's, and she sought to arrange reality as she wanted it to be.

In an autobiographical sketch he began when he was seventy-seven, Jefferson talked of his mother only in relation to his father. Of Peter Jefferson, Thomas wrote: "He was born February 29th, 1708, and intermarried 1739 with Jane Randolph, of the age of 19, daughter of Isham Randolph, one of the seven sons of that name and family settled at Dungeness in Goochland." After describing his father's surveying and mapmaking, Thomas wrote:

"He died August 17th, 1757, leaving my mother a widow who lived till 1776, with six daughters and two sons, myself the elder."

Except for a brief mention in a letter to a Randolph relative in England several months after her death and for a notation of his paying a clergyman for conducting her funeral, Mrs. Jefferson is absent from the surviving written record of her son's life.

Letters between the two burned in the Shadwell fire of 1770, and Jefferson apparently destroyed any subsequent correspondence. Generations of biographers have speculated that Jefferson and his mother were somehow estranged. Yet Jefferson chose to live in proximity to her for many of the nineteen years that she survived her husband—long into Jefferson's adulthood. Mrs. Jefferson did not die until 1776, the year her son, at age thirty-three, authored the Declaration of Independence. Jefferson made his home at Shadwell while he was away at school and during his early years of law practice. The first was to be expected, but to have headquartered himself after college, as a young lawyer, in what he called "my mother's house," is a sign that things between them were not hopelessly hostile, and may not have been hostile at all. He did not move to Monticello, his "little mountain," until November 1770, when the Shadwell fire upended the family's domestic arrangements. The rebuilt house at Shadwell would be much smaller than the original.

———

Jefferson, in any event, always enjoyed the company of women. His most intimate friend among his siblings was his elder sister, also named Jane. Born in 1740, the first child of Peter and Jane, the younger Jane was reported to have been her younger brother's "constant companion when at home, and the confidant of all his youthful feelings."

They indulged common passions for the woods and for music. Jane sang hymns for her brother, and together they would sing psalms, and "many a winter evening, round the family fireside, and many a soft summer twilight, on the wooded banks of the Rivanna, heard their voices, accompanied by the notes of his violin, thus ascending together." He paid her the highest of compliments: "He ever regarded her as fully his own equal in understanding."

At nine years old, Thomas was sent to study classics and French with the Reverend William Douglas, rector of St. James Northam Parish near Tuckahoe in Goochland County. For five years, excepting only the summers, Thomas lived with Douglas. The mature Jefferson later thought Douglas "but a superficial Latinist, less instructed in Greek, but with the rudiments of these languages he taught me French."

Later Jefferson boarded with the Reverend James Maury, whom he described as "a correct classical scholar." Maury did splendidly by Jefferson, grounding him in the classics and giving him a sense of order. Jefferson warmly recalled his years with Maury, both at study and at play. Much later in life, in a letter to Maury's son, Jefferson said that should they meet again they "would beguile our lingering hours with talking over our youthful exploits, our hunts . . . and feel, by recollection at least, a momentary flash of youth."

One source of his happiness at Maury's school was Dabney Carr, a fellow student who became the central friend of Jefferson's youth. Born in 1743—the same year as Jefferson—Carr came from Louisa County. The two young men shared a love of literature, learning, and the landscape of their Virginia neighborhood. When at Shadwell, they took the books they happened to be reading and climbed through the woods of the mountain Jefferson later called Monticello, talking and thinking together, coming to rest at the base of an oak near the summit. There, Jefferson and Carr read their books and spoke of many things. To Jefferson, Dabney Carr was the best of friends, and their minds took flight with each other. No man, Jefferson recalled later, had "more of the milk of human kindness, of indulgence, of softness, of pleasantry of conversation and conduct." In the way of young friendships, there was an intensity and a seriousness—a sense that their lives were linked, their shared hours sacred. They made a pact. Whoever survived the other was to bury the one to die first beneath the favored oak.

———

At school James Maury cultivated Jefferson's engagement with the literature, history, and philosophy of the ancients. In a **Dissertation on Education** written in 1762, Maury explained that the classics were not for everyone—but they were for a young man like Jefferson. "An acquaintance with the languages, anciently spoken in Greece and Italy, is necessary, absolutely necessary, for those who wish to make any reputable figure in divinity, medicine, or law," Maury wrote. Greek and Latin were also critical for men who might take places in society "to which the privilege of birth, the voice of their country, or the choice of their prince may call them."

Jefferson valued his education—and education in general—above all things, remarking that, given the choice, he would take the classical training his father arranged for him over the estate his father left him.

Thomas Jefferson was nearly seventeen when he arrived for the 1759–60 holidays at Chatsworth, his mother's cousin Peter Randolph's house on the James near the ancestral Turkey Island plantation. During the visit, Peter Randolph advised Jefferson to enroll at the College of William and Mary in Williamsburg, the wisest step beyond the Reverend Maury's tutelage in classical studies. "By going to the College," Jefferson wrote, "I shall get a more universal acquaintance which may hereafter be serviceable to me. . . . [and] I can pursue my studies in the Greek and Latin as well there as here, and likewise learn something of the mathematics."

The standards for admission to William and Mary were not onerous. According to the college, the test for potential students was "whether they have made due progress in their Latin and Greek. . . . And let no blockhead or lazy fellow in his studies be elected."

Jefferson was neither, and so he left Albemarle County in 1760, bound for Williamsburg. The capital of Virginia, it was home to the House of Burgesses, to theaters, to taverns—and to a circle of men who would change Jefferson's life forever.

TWO

What Fixed the Destinies of My Life

Enlightenment is man's emergence from his self-imposed immaturity. . . . Nothing is required for this enlightenment . . . except freedom; and the freedom in question is the least harmful of all, namely, the freedom to use reason publicly in all matters.

—IMMANUEL KANT, "What Is Enlightenment?"

The best news I can tell you is that Williamsburg begins to brighten up and look very clever.

—PEYTON RANDOLPH

WILLIAMSBURG, THE COLONIAL CAPITAL, suited Jefferson wonderfully. It had an intellectual climate informed by the very latest in books and a social swirl that included Virginia's most charming women and most prominent men. It had the professor William Small, the lawyer

George Wythe, the royal governor Francis Fauquier, and the statesman Peyton Randolph, all of whom became critical in Jefferson's life. It had lively distractions. Jefferson gambled on horses and hunted foxes; he gossiped and courted and danced. Above all, Williamsburg had an ethos that was to enthrall Jefferson: the drama and glamour of politics.

To Jefferson, this was the great world, and the college was an integral part of Virginia life. George Washington received his surveying certificate from William and Mary; other alumni included future chief justice John Marshall, future president James Monroe, and some seventeen governors of Virginia. There were also reminders of the grim facts of life in the colony. In the mid-1760s a French traveler in Williamsburg saw "three Negroes hanging at the gallows" for robbery.

Jefferson was enrolled in William and Mary from the time he was seventeen until he was nineteen. He was then in and out of the city for an additional five years as he studied law. Williamsburg had as lasting an influence on the man Jefferson became as Shadwell did. In decades to come, in moments of crisis and of calm, he returned there in his mind's eye, finding direction in the political lessons he learned and guidance in the ideas he explored.

College life centered on the Wren Building, which was, in 1760, a three-and-a-half-story, brick-walled structure topped by a cupola. A chapel and crypt had been added in the previous thirty years. Three blocks east along Duke of Gloucester Street was Bruton Parish Church on the left, followed by the Palace Green leading to the Governor's Palace. Farther down Duke of Gloucester sat the brick capitol, home to the House of Burgesses and the General Court. There, then, in not quite half a square mile, no one landmark more than a few minutes' walk—or an even briefer ride in one of the carriages that were so prominent when Williamsburg was full and busy with the public business—was the whole structure of public power in Jefferson's Virginia. No one could have loved it all more than Jefferson himself.

For Jefferson, William and Mary was largely about what university life is supposed to be about: reading books, enjoying the company of the like-minded, and savoring teachers who seem to be ambassadors from other, richer, brighter worlds. Jefferson believed Williamsburg "the finest school of manners and morals that ever existed in America."

The man who put him on the path toward that hyperbolic but heartfelt conclusion was Dr. William Small, a Scottish layman and professor who brought an Enlightenment worldview to Williamsburg. It was fortuitous that Jefferson encountered Small at all, for Small's stay on the faculty at William and Mary lasted only six years, from 1758 to 1764—the right period to overlap with Jefferson, who revered him. "It was my great good fortune, and what probably fixed the destinies of my life, that Dr. William

Small of Scotland, was then professor of mathematics, a man profound in most of the useful branches of science, with a happy talent of communication, correct and gentlemanly manners, and an enlarged and liberal mind," Jefferson said.

Born in Scotland in 1734—he was less than a decade older than Jefferson—Small was, in addition to professor of mathematics at the college, the interim professor of moral philosophy. Described by a contemporary as a "polite, well-bred man," Small lived in two rooms in the college. The accommodations, it was said, were "by no means elegant," but Small and his colleagues were "very well satisfied with the homeliness of their appearance, though at first sight [they were] rather disgusting."

A bit more care seems to have been taken with clothing than with interior decoration. Faculty were expected to have a suit of "handsome full-dressed silk clothes to wear on the King's birthday at the Governor's," where it was "expected that all English gentlemen attend and pay their respects."

Small taught ethics, rhetoric, and belles lettres as well as natural philosophy—what we think of as the sciences—and mathematics, lecturing in the mornings and holding seminar-like sessions in the afternoons in which the professor and his students discussed the material. Conversant with the thought of Bacon, Locke, Newton, Adam Smith, and the philosophers of the Scottish Enlightenment, Small introduced Jefferson to the key insight of the new intellectual age: that reason, not revelation or unquestioned tradition or superstition, deserved pride of place in human affairs.

Under Small's influence Jefferson came to share Immanuel Kant's 1784 definition of the spirit of the era: "Enlightenment is man's emergence from his self-imposed immaturity," Kant wrote. "Immaturity is the inability to use one's understanding without guidance from another. This immaturity is self-imposed when its cause lies not in lack of understanding, but in lack of resolve and courage to use it without guidance from another."

This was Small's message to his charges at William and Mary. Jefferson was entranced, later giving Small the noblest of accolades when he recalled that Small was "to me . . . a father."

It was said that Jefferson studied fifteen hours a day, rising at dawn and reading until two o'clock each morning. At twilight in Williamsburg he exercised by running to a stone a mile from town; at Shadwell, he rowed a small canoe of his own across the Rivanna River and climbed the mountain he was to call Monticello. For Jefferson laziness was a sin. "Of all the cankers of human happiness, none corrodes it with so silent, yet so baneful, a tooth, as indolence," he told one of his daughters. Time spent at study was never wasted. "Knowledge," Jefferson said, "indeed is a desirable, a lovely possession."

Like his father, he believed in the virtues of riding

and of walking, holding that a vigorous body helped create a vigorous mind. "Not less than two hours a day should be devoted to exercise, and the weather should be little regarded," Jefferson once said. In fact, Jefferson believed the rainier and the colder the better. "A person not sick will not be injured by getting wet," he said. "It is but taking a cold bath, which never gives a cold to any one. Brute animals are the most healthy, and they are exposed to all weather, and of men, those are healthiest who are the most exposed."

Aspiring attorneys, he said, should devote their mornings to the law, but variety was key. "Having ascribed proper hours to exercise, divide what remain (I mean of your vacant hours) into three portions. Give the principal to History, the other two, which should be shorter, to Philosophy and Poetry."

Jefferson was always asking questions. With "the mechanic as well as the man of science," a descendant recalled, Jefferson learned all he could, "whether it was the construction of a wheel or the anatomy of an extinct species of animals," and then went home to transcribe what he had heard. He would soon be known as a "walking encyclopedia."

Jefferson could play as hard as he worked. Worrying that he had spent too much money in his first year in what the nineteenth-century biographer Henry Randall called "a little too showy style of living—particularly in the article of fine horses"—Jefferson wrote a guardian offering to charge the whole of his bills to his separate share of the estate. (More amused than alarmed, the guardian declined Jefferson's offer.) Later in life, Jefferson wrote: "I was often thrown into the society of horse racers, and card players, fox hunters, scientific and professional men. . . . Many a time have I asked myself, in the enthusiastic moment of the death of a fox, the victory of a favorite horse, the issue of a question eloquently argued at the bar . . . Well, which of these kinds of reputation should I prefer? That of a horse jockey? A fox hunter? An orator? Or the honest advocate of my country's rights?"

In truth these things are not mutually exclusive, which Jefferson knew. He spent his Williamsburg years in ways that suggest he understood that the pursuit of knowledge could coexist with the pursuit of pleasure. The motto at Williamsburg's popular Raleigh Tavern had it right: "Jollity, offspring of wisdom and good living."

It was in the Governor's Palace, not at the Raleigh, that Jefferson's most intensive tutorial in the art of living well—as measured in elegance and conversation, two things he cherished—took place.

Francis Fauquier, the royal governor of the colony of Virginia, held frequent gatherings with William Small and George Wythe, one of Virginia's greatest lawyers. (Fauquier's formal title was lieutenant governor; the official royal governor delegated the actual work of the post.) Thomas Jefferson made a fourth at what Jefferson called Fauquier's "familiar table." There was dinner, conversation, and music. The older men nurtured Jefferson's passion for the violin, and Jefferson was invited to join Fauquier on the governor's musical evenings, performing in the palace.

Fauquier was born in 1703, only five years before Peter Jefferson, and so was roughly the age Jefferson's father would have been had Peter Jefferson survived. The governor loved science, fine food, good music, and spirited card playing.

No dry philosopher, Fauquier also had a worldly, even rakish air. The story was told that he came to office in the New World through the good grace of Lord Anson, the British admiral who had circumnavigated the globe, after Fauquier lost everything he had to Anson in a single night of cards. However embellished that tale, its currency shows that the man Jefferson encountered at this impressionable age led a life in which the pursuits of pleasure, power, and erudition unfolded simultaneously.

Fauquier's father was a Huguenot physician who worked with Sir Isaac Newton at the Royal Mint and became a director of the Bank of England. The son, too, was interested in science and became a fellow of the Royal Society as well as a director of the South Sea Company—evidence of his keeping a hand in both the world of ideas and of practical power, something the young Jefferson may have noticed.

Fauquier was energetic. Within weeks of his arrival in Virginia in 1758, there was an unusual July hailstorm. The ice smashed the windows on the north side of the Governor's Palace. Fascinated, Fauquier wrote a scientific paper about the phenomenon and dispatched it to his brother, who presented it to the Royal Society in London.

Born in 1726 in Elizabeth City County, Virginia, the lawyer George Wythe was also a noted statesman. Hawk-nosed and, in Jefferson's description, "of the middle size, well formed and proportioned," Wythe was wise, intellectually curious, and probably had more direct influence on Jefferson's thinking than Small simply by virtue of longevity. Wythe taught Jefferson in the law and other subjects for five years, an unusually long period of time. The older man lived in a house near Bruton Parish Church, in the center of Williamsburg. "Mr. Wythe continued to be my faithful and beloved mentor in youth, and my most affectionate friend through life," Jefferson recalled.

In Wythe, the man with whom Jefferson spent the most time in the period from roughly 1765 to 1772, Jefferson had a teacher in both liberty and luxury. The older man had expensive tastes, sending to London for satin cloaks for his wife, velvet breeches and black silk stockings for himself, and, for them both, "an elegant set of table and tea china, with bowls of the same of different sizes, decanters and drinking glasses, a handsome service of glass for a dessert, four middle-sized and six lesser dishes, and . . . a handsome well-built chariot." The Wythes also loved to entertain. "Mrs. Wythe puts 1/10 very rich Malmsey to a dry Madeira and makes a fine wine," Jefferson once noted appreciatively.

In a literary commonplace book in which he copied passages that struck him as important, Jefferson quoted Euripides during the years with Wythe: "There is nothing better than a trusty friend, neither wealth nor princely power; mere number is a senseless thing to set off against a noble friend."

In 1767, Wythe introduced Jefferson to the practice of law at the bar of the General Court, inaugurating Jefferson's legal career—a phase of Jefferson's life that consumed him from 1767 until 1774, when the work of the Revolution drew him into politics and diplomacy.

When those close to Jefferson surveyed his life and career, they returned to the Governor's Palace and to the influence of the bright men who moved through those elegant, high-ceilinged rooms. "Apart from the intellectual improvement derived from such an intercourse," wrote Henry Randall, "Mr. Jefferson, it is said, owed that polish of manner which distinguished him through life, to his habitual mingling with the elegant society which Governor Fauquier collected about him."

For the rest of his life Jefferson sought to replicate the spirit and substance of these long Williamsburg nights. At his round dining table at Monticello, in the salons of Paris, and in the common rooms of boardinghouses and taverns in Philadelphia and New York, and finally at the President's House in Washington, D.C., Jefferson craved talk of the latest in science and the arts and adored conversation with the beautiful women, politicians, and men of affairs who made the world run on both sides of the Atlantic.

In this elite number Jefferson also included his cousin Peyton Randolph, attorney general of Virginia, Speaker of the House of Burgesses, and the first president of the Continental Congress. Born in 1721, Randolph was at once convivial and imposing. On meeting him, Silas Deane of Connecticut wrote that Peyton Randolph was "of an affable, open and majestic deportment, large in size, though not out of proportion"; he also "commands respect and esteem by his very aspect, independent of the high character he sustains."

Small, Wythe, Fauquier, and Peyton Randolph established the standards by which Jefferson judged everyone else. They represented a love of engaging company, a devotion to the life of the mind, and a commitment to the responsible execution of political duties for the larger good. "Under temptations and difficulties," he told a grandson, "I would ask myself—what would Dr. Small, Mr. Wythe, Peyton Randolph do in this situation? What course in it will ensure me their approbation?"

Jefferson was to be always guided by experience

and example, thinking about what men of the world—men he respected and loved—might do, for in their day their decisions had given them, in Jefferson's words, "very high standing," standing that Jefferson felt "the incessant wish" to match, and surpass.

In pursuit of that standing, Jefferson never cut himself off from the social and cultural currents of his time. When on holiday from Williamsburg, he played his part in the rites of Virginia hospitality, often hosting others at Shadwell or visiting friends at their plantations.

On a visit one winter to Colonel Nathaniel Dandridge's place in Hanover County, Jefferson met Patrick Henry, a young man living in Louisa County. Jefferson recalled that the two "passed perhaps a fortnight together at the revelries of the neighborhood and season. His manners had something of the coarseness of the society he had frequented; his passion was fiddling, dancing and pleasantry. He excelled in the last, and it attached every one to him."

Jefferson conceived of life in social terms, and he believed that his own identity was bound up with the world around him. A slave was always in attendance. Family, neighbors, and callers were more or less constant presences. "I am convinced our own happiness requires that we should continue to mix with the world, and to keep pace with it as it goes," he once wrote to one of his daughters.

He was a political man in the purest sense of the term. He lived among others, engaged in the business of living in community, and enjoyed being at the center of everything no matter what the everything was: He was a happy member of the FHC (or Flat Hat Club) at William and Mary, a secret society that, as Jefferson put it, "had no useful object."

Even the bustle of a plantation paled in contrast to the charms of Williamsburg. When away from the capital, he longed for intelligence about what he might be missing. "If there is any news stirring in town or country, such as deaths, courtships and marriages in the circle of my acquaintance let me know it," Jefferson wrote his college friend John Page.

For a time in the early 1760s, Jefferson was in love—passionately if ineffectually—with a young woman named Rebecca Lewis Burwell, the sister of his classmate Lewis Burwell, Jr., of Gloucester County. His letters on the subject are about what one would expect of a young man not quite twenty years old: overstated, breathless, self-serious, and melodramatic. His attempts at humor and self-mockery in his correspondence about Rebecca Burwell fall largely flat, and the episode is chiefly interesting for the light it sheds on Jefferson's sensitivity to rejection, disorder, and criticism.

Little about the courtship went well. Even rats and rain seemed to conspire against him. On Christmas

Eve 1762, at Fairfields, a brother-in-law's place in Goochland County, Jefferson went to bed as usual, leaving his pocketbook, garters, and watch in his room. The watch held a paper drawing of Rebecca Burwell, the single token Jefferson appears to have had of the object of his affections.

Awaking on Christmas morning, Jefferson discovered not only that rats had gotten into his room and gnawed at his pocketbook and garters—the rodents spent part of the night only inches from Jefferson's head—but that rain in the night had leaked into the house, soaking the watch and destroying the image of his beloved. To the lovesick Jefferson the accidents seemed terrible omens.

In this season he compared himself to Job and wondered, "Is there any such thing as happiness in this world?" His answer: "No." About a month later, in January 1763, writing from Shadwell, Jefferson was still gloomy. "All things here appear to me to trudge on in one and the same round: we rise in the morning that we may eat breakfast, dinner and supper and go to bed again that we may get up the next morning and do the same: so that you never saw two peas more alike than our yesterday and to-day," he wrote John Page.

Jefferson always wanted some level of control, too, and he savored secrecy. "We must fall on some scheme of communicating our thoughts to each other, which shall be totally unintelligible to everyone but to ourselves," he wrote Page as they shared gossip about courtships, dances, and lovers' maneuverings.

His feelings for Rebecca grew stronger as the year wore on. Nine months later, on Thursday, October 6, 1763, Jefferson decided to declare himself. There was a dance that evening in the Apollo Room of the Raleigh Tavern in Williamsburg, with its brightly lit banqueting hall.

In this elegant setting Jefferson believed his hour had come. "I was prepared to say a great deal: I had dressed up in my own mind such thoughts as occurred to me, in as moving language as I knew how, and expected to have performed in a tolerably creditable manner," Jefferson wrote the next day. He was dancing with Rebecca in an "agreeable company." Everything appeared set.

He tried to speak, and it all fell apart. "But, good God!" Jefferson wrote afterward. "When I had an opportunity of venting them, a few broken sentences, uttered in great disorder, and interrupted with pauses of uncommon length, were the too visible signs of my strange confusion!"

His humiliation was nearly complete. Yet he did not capitulate totally, not without one additional attempt: a conversation in which Jefferson "opened my mind more freely and more fully." He had plans (not then realized) to travel to England, but his heart was Rebecca's if she would have it—sort of.

As Jefferson told the story to his friend John Page

in January 1764, he made his intentions clear to Rebecca without committing himself, which gave Jefferson a degree of dignity and control: "I asked no question which would admit of a categorical answer, but assured [her] that such questions would one day be asked." In the end there were no further questions—there were, in fact, no further interviews of any kind between the two. Defeated, he made his retreat. After he was rejected by Rebecca, Jefferson experienced what may have been the first instance of an ailment that was to recur at times of stress: a painful prolonged headache.

Characterizing himself as "abominably indolent" in a letter to a friend written late on a March evening, Jefferson said that his "scheme" to marry Rebecca was now "totally frustrated" by her impending marriage to the wealthy Jacquelin Ambler of Yorktown, which took place in May 1764.

Then, in an apparent allusion to prostitution or to sexual activity with enslaved women or with women in the servant class—it is unclear which, but these seem the likeliest possibilities—Jefferson wrote: "Many and great are the comforts of a single state, and neither of the reasons you urge can have any influence with an inhabitant and a young inhabitant too of Williamsburg. For St. Paul only says that it is better to be married than to burn. Now I presume that if that apostle had known that providence would at an after day be so kind to any particular set of people as to furnish them with other means of extinguishing their fire than those of matrimony, he would have earnestly recommended them to their practice."

It was nearing midnight as he wrote these words. He was suffering from his headache as the candle burned down and Jupiter, his personal slave, fell asleep. Perhaps it was the intimacy of the hour that encouraged his candor; perhaps he was boasting vainly. But Jefferson had some reason to say that "providence" had given men like himself the "means" to satisfy his sexual appetites—means he appears to have made use of. This much was clear: Jefferson needed to get his mind off his lost love. Fortunately for him, he was a man of wide interests—interests his teachers and mentors were nurturing as his love-sickness faded.

THREE

Roots of Revolution

> Our minds were circumscribed within narrow limits by an habitual belief that it was our duty to be subordinate to the mother country.
> —THOMAS JEFFERSON

FOR THOMAS JEFFERSON, politics were ubiquitous. They were the air he breathed. "May we outlive our enemies," Jefferson once wrote in a private note to himself. On the same page of a memorandum book on which he noted that he had sent to London for summer clothes for his slave Jupiter and scarlet cloth for his own waistcoats, he added an aphorism: "No liberty, no life."

To follow Jefferson in the 1760s and early 1770s is to see how the American Revolution took shape, and why. The definition of liberty and the nature of representative government—fundamental human questions—were consuming concerns in the America of Jefferson's young adulthood. In these decades, London held power over the American colonies. The

British Navigation Acts controlled trade and transportation; merchants in Philadelphia or farmers in Albemarle County were subject to an economic system in which they had no real political voice. Royal governors could convene colonial assemblies such as the Virginia House of Burgesses. The governors could also veto any legislation and were empowered to dissolve the sessions at will. No directly elected representatives of the British in North America sat in the British Parliament.

Such issues were to grow in scope and significance as Jefferson himself grew older. In 1754, when Jefferson was not yet twelve years old, at a convention in Albany, New York, the American colonists made a proposal, known as the Albany Plan of Union. It was a bid to become a largely self-governing province under a national royal governor. Its author, Benjamin Franklin, noted that the plan collapsed because Americans thought it too autocratic and the British found it too democratic.

When Jefferson was fourteen, he inherited his father's edition of Paul de Rapin-Thoyras's history of England—a book that sheds light on the roots of the American Revolution, for the American story of the eighteenth and nineteenth centuries was inextricably linked with the story of England in the seventeenth.

Americans who knew their British history—and since most Americans were provincial Britons, most of them did—understood political life to be a constant struggle to preserve individual liberty from encroachments of Crown and courtier.

With the British politician and writer Henry St. John, Viscount Bolingbroke, Jefferson believed history was "philosophy teaching by examples." History, then, mattered enormously, for it could repeat itself at any time in any generation. And if that history brought tyranny, it was to be fought at all costs.

First published in 1723, Rapin's book held that the story of England (and thus of English peoples such as the Americans) was the story of the battle between monarchical and (relatively) popular authority. Whigs were oriented more toward the Parliament and the people, Tories toward the king. Jefferson took this way of thinking about politics seriously, later arguing that all societies were likely to be divided into such camps.

The drama of the English Civil War, the Restoration, and the Glorious Revolution had shaped the American view of life and politics. In books by Rapin, Bolingbroke, and others, history was depicted as a war between the few and the many for ultimate power. In Britain in the seventeenth century, the people, including many aristocrats, had rebelled against the absolutist tendencies of the Stuart kings, leading to chaos. There was the execution of Charles I, the commonwealth under Oliver Cromwell, the Restoration of the Stuarts (which led to more political and religious strife), and finally the Glorious Revolution of 1688, when William of Orange and his wife, Mary, were crowned to preside over a balanced constitution. As a condition of kingship, William and Mary agreed to uphold an English Declaration of Rights that limited the monarchy's power to abuse the rights of individuals and of Parliament. Through the Constitutional Settlement of 1689–1701, England achieved order and protected liberty with a balance of powers.

Americans of Jefferson's time lived in an atmosphere in which life was viewed in the context of the episodic tyranny that had roiled the mother country in the previous century. Security could be found only in a mixed government in which the executive—the monarchy, in Britain's case—was checked by a bicameral legislature made up of Commons and Lords. (An independent judiciary also played a key role.) The history Americans wanted was that of a balanced constitution. The history they would go to war against was that of anything less than a government they judged fair and representative.

By virtue of his birth and education, Jefferson was disposed to support the American cause. The inclusion of Rapin's multivolume history of England in Peter Jefferson's library suggests an ancestral sympathy for the worldview Thomas Jefferson would help propel to the center of the Atlantic world. Henry Randall, the early Jefferson biographer, reported that Peter Jefferson was "a staunch Whig, and he adhered to certain democratic (using the word in its broad, popular sense) notions and maxims, which descended to his son."

Ever curious, Thomas Jefferson went further into the matter than most. He read Tacitus's **Germania** and became an adherent of the theory that England was initially populated by freedom-loving Saxons who were subjugated by the monarchical and feudal forces of William the Conqueror. According to this view, Americans were now heirs of the Saxon tradition of individual freedom, a tradition long under siege.

Jefferson and his fellow American Revolutionaries took the positions they did—positions that led to war in 1775 and the Declaration of Independence in 1776—partly because they saw themselves as Englishmen who were being denied a full share of the benefits of the lessons of English life. In the decade between 1764 and 1774—between a protest over taxation to the eve of revolution—Jefferson and like-minded Americans were guarding against the abridgement of the personal liberties or of the representation Englishmen had won for themselves as a result of the Glorious Revolution. Every proposal from London, every thought of a tax, every sign of imperial authority, raised fears of tyranny in America, for such proposals, taxes, and expressions of authority in the seventeenth century had produced such tyranny in the mother country during the Civil War and the Restoration.

The arguments over taxation and representation—which were really arguments, of course, about liberty and control—gained fresh force at the conclusion of the French and Indian War, also known as the Seven Years' War or the Great War for the Empire.

The conflict of arms had ended in 1759 on the Plains of Abraham, but the fighting between the French and their Indian allies on the one hand and the British and the Americans on the other led to a cold war over money and power between the Old and New Worlds.

Empires are expensive, and the one London controlled at the end of the Seven Years' War was of remarkable scope. Simply put, London needed revenue and believed the American colonies should bear more of the cost of maintaining the British dominions. About ten thousand British troops were to remain in North America; the redcoats represented a pervasive sense of threat. Armies that could liberate and protect could also conquer and subjugate.

The imperial authorities were now reaching ever more deeply into the lives and fortunes of Americans—Americans who watched such assertions of power warily, fearful that despotism was at hand. Before the French and Indian War, London had not exercised strict control over grants of the western lands beyond the Appalachian Mountains. After the war, and after an uprising of Ohio Valley Indian tribes against British posts, London sought to give the king the power to decide the fate of the western lands, a move that particularly alienated Virginians accustomed to speculating freely there. Before the war, London had not been especially rigorous in its enforcement of Navigation Acts to regulate trade. After the war, London opened a campaign to use "writs of assistance" to board and search colonial vessels, enraging Boston in particular.

The South and West were angry about the lands and the Indians; the Northeast was uneasy about the writs of assistance. And the whole of the colonies was infuriated by what was known as the Sugar Act of 1764, which included mechanisms for strict enforcement. Though the bill actually lowered the tax on molasses, it imposed duties on other items (including Madeira wine, a favorite of the young Jefferson). The Sugar Act was also an attempt to establish a principle and a precedent in these post–Seven Years' War days: that, in the words of the legislation, it was "just and necessary that a revenue be raised in your Majesty's said dominions in America."

In the House of Commons on Friday, March 9, 1764, Prime Minister George Grenville, a Whig politician who served as head of government from 1763 to 1765, had risen to announce the Sugar Act and the prospect of a colonial stamp tax (a tax on documents and things made of paper, including newspapers and playing cards). Grenville told the

House that he "hoped that the power and sovereignty of Parliament, over every part of the British dominions, for the purpose of raising or collecting any tax, would never be disputed."

Yet disputed it was, and would be. Americans were avidly reading the Massachusetts lawyer James Otis's **Rights of the British Colonies Asserted and Proved,** a kind of forerunner to Thomas Paine's **Common Sense,** the 1776 pamphlet that made a compelling case for the American cause.

Otis's views were abroad in the colonies in the autumn of 1764, when, in Williamsburg, George Wythe drafted a petition to the House of Commons protesting taxation. His language, however, was considered too strong by some burgesses, even treasonable, which suggests that Wythe—the man closest to Jefferson, and whom Jefferson idolized— held decided opinions on the questions that led to revolution.

The essence of the anti-British position was summed up in a 1764 resolution that Virginia sent to the king and to Parliament: "that the People are not [to be] subject to any taxes but such as are laid on them by their own consent, or by those who are legally appointed to represent them." Virginia's resolutions had no effect on the outcome in London. Parliament did not even consider them, and the Stamp Act passed on Friday, March 22, 1765.

The subsequent drama offered Jefferson his first intimate glimpse of politics. The Virginia debates

over how to respond to the Stamp Act had a bit
of everything: emotional rhetoric, imperial tension, generational division, and legislative sleight of
hand. There were principles at stake and ideas to
be refined and applied to the real world—and there
were raw political and human calculations. It was a
perfect laboratory for the struggles that concerned
Jefferson for the rest of his life.

A significant number of the members of the Virginia House of Burgesses wanted to take a stand
against Parliament's assertion of power. But how far
should the Americans push the Whig interpretation
of the rights of the colonies and of individuals? At
this point, in 1765, the notion of a full clash of arms
with Great Britain was remote, even to men like
Patrick Henry, whom Jefferson watched speak in
the House on Thursday, May 30, 1765.

It was already late in the House of Burgesses' spring
session. Many members had left Williamsburg for
home. Jefferson, "yet a student," as he recalled, was
there to watch the action. A number of anti–Stamp
Act resolutions—seven in all—were in play. On
the floor, Patrick Henry, the self-taught lawyer and
charmer whom Jefferson had first met at Nathan
Dandridge's house, was pressing for the boldest of
the measures.

Jefferson stood at the door of the House, listening to Henry in wonder. With eloquence Jefferson

believed "great indeed," Henry said Tarquin and
Caesar had had their Brutus, Charles his Cromwell,
and Henry, according to the single contemporaneous account of the debate, "did not doubt but some
good American would stand up in favor of his country." Jefferson was swept away. "He appeared to me
to speak as Homer wrote," Jefferson said of Henry.

A French traveler who was watching with Jefferson recorded that the Speaker of the House, hearing Henry invoke Brutus and Cromwell, said that
Henry had "spoke treason."

Henry backed down. According to the French
observer, Henry said "he was ready to ask pardon,
and he would show his loyalty to His Majesty King
George III at the expense of the last drop of his
blood, but what he had said must be attributed to
the interest of his country's dying liberty which he
had at heart."

With Henry's rhetorical flight ending, a divided
House took up the resolutions. The struggle on the
floor, Jefferson said, was "most bloody." Records of
the deliberations are scant, but the formulation at
issue seems to have been this, which was apparently
framed as the "Fifth Resolution" put forward by
Henry:

Resolved Therefore that the General Assembly of
this colony have the only and sole exclusive right
and power to lay taxes and impositions upon the

inhabitants of this colony and that every attempt to vest such power in any other person or persons whatsoever other than the General Assembly aforesaid has a manifest tendency to destroy British as well as AMERICAN FREEDOM.

Men such as Peyton Randolph wanted to strike a more moderate tone for the moment, but the stronger language passed by the narrowest of margins, 20–19. "By God, I would have given 500 guineas for a single vote," Randolph said afterward. One more vote against the resolution would have tied the count, and the Speaker, John Robinson, would have voted no, defeating it.

Instead, the radicals had won. Going on record against London was, itself, not as disturbing to the more moderate members as was the sense that they had lost control. Patrick Henry had taken on the establishment and succeeded.

As night fell in Williamsburg, a triumphant Henry left the capital. He had won. Or so he thought.

The next morning—it was now Friday, May 31, 1765—Jefferson could not wait to return to the House. Intrigued by the cut and thrust, he arrived at the chamber early. Once there he discovered another Randolph cousin, Peter Randolph, already at work. Randolph was examining the records of the House to find a precedent for what the leadership hoped to accomplish once the bell rang the burgesses into session: rescind the Fifth Resolution, undoing Henry's victory and regaining command of the field.

Jefferson was therefore witness to a bid to overturn the previous day's result. An hour or so later, the House took up the matter and reversed itself from the day before. Henry's departure had given his foes an opportunity they did not fail to exploit. Though the records of the House are silent about the Stamp Act on May 31, Governor Francis Fauquier wrote the Board of Trade that after "a small alteration in the House"—presumably Henry's departure—"there was an attempt to strike all the Resolutions off the Journals. The 5th which was thought the most offensive was accordingly struck off."

The lesson for Jefferson, the man who would come to be seen as the great democrat, tribune of liberty, and scourge of elite authority? Never give up the political fight and never shy away from using any and all means to carry the day. Only six weeks after his twenty-second birthday, Jefferson had been given a tutorial in the intricacies of power. On Thursday he had been thunderstruck by Homeric oratory evoking the glories of liberty and asserting that to give Parliament any control over Virginia or her sister colonies would do nothing less than "destroy AMERICAN FREEDOM."

Then on Friday, he watched the prior day's defeated faction become today's victors through resilience and opportunism. Unwilling to give up,

Henry's foes were vigilant and resourceful, seeing their chance in his departure and taking steps to find precedent to give their course of action the color of authority. Important, too, was mastery of the means (in this case, the legislative process) to give oneself the ability to achieve the desired end. In later years, whenever Jefferson was able to seize unexpected political moments and turn them to his advantage, he appreciated the role of tactical skill. He had seen it all demonstrated late in a Williamsburg May.

Fauquier saw, too, that things were changing. On the following Tuesday, June 4, 1765, he hosted the annual birth-night ball in honor of George III, usually a spectacular occasion in Williamsburg. Not this year. "I went there in expectation of seeing a great deal of company," wrote the anonymous French traveler, "but was disappointed for there was not above a dozen of people. I came away before supper."

As the Stamp Act debates unfolded, Jefferson's own first significant public act, the memory of which he cherished, was an elaborate attempt to bend the natural world to his purposes. To do so he used his mind and the arts of quiet persuasion.

The Rivanna was not navigable for boats carrying crops from Albemarle farmers to market. Climbing into a canoe, Jefferson set out to learn whether anything could be done.

Paddling along the river his friend Margaret Bayard Smith once described as "wild and romantic," Jefferson discovered that the removal of rocks below Milton Falls could transform the Rivanna into a vital route for his and his neighbors' crops. Jefferson raised private money to undertake the project, successfully making the case to individual investors. In October 1765, the colonial assembly praised Jefferson's "laudable and useful" work, and authorized the "clearing the great falls of [the] James River, the river Chickahominy and the north branch of [the] James River."

Jefferson was thrilled. He was working in the tradition of his father, bringing order to the wilderness and—no small thing—being recognized and honored for it.

For Jefferson, the eleven years between the Stamp Act battle in Williamsburg and the Rivanna work in 1765 and the formal Declaration of Independence in Philadelphia in 1776 was a time of steady maturation—intellectually, politically, and emotionally. Like many Americans, he was an unlikely revolutionary. His journey from loyal subject to leading rebel reveals Jefferson to be a pragmatist as well as an idealist, a man who understood the importance of using philosophy and history to create emotional appeals to shape broad public sentiment.

Leadership, Jefferson was learning, meant knowing how to distill complexity into a comprehensible message to reach the hearts as well as the minds of the larger world. In 1766, Jefferson helped bring a Maryland publisher, William Rind, to Williamsburg to create a **Virginia Gazette** to rival the one that was controlled by Joseph Royle, John Dixon, and Alexander Purdie. "Until the beginning of our revolutionary disputes," recalled Jefferson, "we had but one press, and that having the whole business of the government, and no competitor for public favor, nothing disagreeable to the governor could be got into it."

Fascinated with how to marshal men, he studied the political arts not only in books but in Williamsburg and Albemarle County. A poor public speaker himself, he admired gifted orators such as Patrick Henry. Shadwell, a convenient stopping place for those making their way to and from Williamsburg, was open to all sorts and conditions of travelers, including Ontassete, the Cherokee chief who crossed the Atlantic in 1762 for a celebrated visit to George III. "The moon was in full splendor," Jefferson recalled, "and to her he seemed to address himself in his prayers for his own safety on the voyage, and that of his people during his absence: His sounding voice, distinct articulation, animated actions, and the solemn silence of his people at their several fires, filled me with awe and veneration, although I did not understand a word he uttered."

When it came to the spoken word, Jefferson knew that he could not compete in such arenas with such men. Armed with this insight, he cultivated alternative means of influencing others. He studied the folkways of deliberative bodies. He learned to write with grace, with conviction, and—important in a revolutionary time—with speed.

He immersed himself in the subtle skills of engaging others, chiefly by offering people that which they value most: an attentive audience to listen to their own visions and views. Politicians often talk too much and listen too little, which can be self-defeating, for in many instances the surer route to winning a friend is not to convince them that you are right but that you care what they think. Everyone wants to believe that what they have to say is fascinating, illuminating, and possibly even epochal. The best political figures create the impression that they find everyone they encounter to be what Abigail Adams said Jefferson was: "one of the choice ones of the earth."

A grandson described Jefferson's tactical approach to personal exchanges. "His powers of conversation were great, yet he always turned it to subjects most familiar to those with whom he conversed, whether laborer, mechanic, or other."

There was a method to this habit beyond the acquisition of information. Henry Randall tells the story of a "most intelligent and dignified Virginia matron of the old school" who often hosted Jefferson at her table. She was, Randall reported, "wont to boast that [Jefferson] never failed to inquire with great particularity how her best dishes were compounded and cooked." Though she suspected that charm was at work—even flattery—she was also convinced by the apparent sincerity of Jefferson's manner of listening. "I know this was half to please me," she allowed, "but he's a nice judge of things, and you may depend upon it, he won't throw away anything he learns worth knowing." With her, as with so many others, Jefferson knew what he was doing.

The autumn of 1765 should have been a heady time for Jefferson. In July his sister Martha had married his friend Dabney Carr, an alliance that pleased Jefferson beyond measure. The Carrs set up housekeeping in Goochland County, at a place called Spring Forest that was along Jefferson's route to and from Williamsburg.

Young and bright, beloved and respected by his teachers in Williamsburg, popular in the aristocratic circles of Virginia, and with the Rebecca Burwell debacle fading from his memory, Jefferson thought the world a largely happy place.

Then, on Tuesday, October 1, 1765, his sister Jane died, reminding him anew, in the manner of his father's death and of the failed romance with Burwell, of the fragility of life.

He had loved Jane, and his grief as the autumn of 1765 gave way to the new year was so deep that it endured in family lore. "The loss of such a sister to such a brother was irreparable," a great-granddaughter wrote. Drawing on the works of the English poet William Shenstone, a writer much interested in mourning and in the virtues of rural seclusion, Jefferson composed an epitaph in Latin for Jane, which reads in translation:

Ah, Joanna, best of girls.
Ah, torn away from the bloom of vigorous age.
May the earth be light upon you.
Farewell, forever and ever.

In the last week of March 1766, nearly six months after Jane died, Jefferson began his garden book, an episodic record of the lives—and deaths—of flowers and vegetables. He longed for spring. "Purple hyacinth begins to bloom," he wrote on Sunday, March 30, 1766. "Narcissus and Puckoon open," he noted on April 6. The "puckoons," or bloodroot, were not long for this world. A week later, on his birthday, the "Puckoon flowers fallen."

Still mourning Jane, he was torn between home and the larger world. As the weeks fell away, he planned an excursion north. His first journey outside Virginia foreshadowed much in his life: his ability to conceal anxiety beneath a cool veneer and his urge to engage the world of politics. Setting out in the spring of 1766, Jefferson, always concerned with combating and controlling diseases, stopped at Philadelphia to see Dr. William Shippen, Jr., to be inoculated against smallpox. Jefferson continued on to New York, where, in a sign of the intimacy of the American elite, he boarded in a house along with Elbridge Gerry of Massachusetts, a future Revolutionary friend and ally.

It was a perilous trip. Twice on the first day Jefferson's horse broke away from him, "greatly endanger[ing] the breaking [of] my neck." The second day brought terrible rains, and Jefferson could find no shelter on the road. The third day he was fording a stream and was nearly swamped by unexpectedly deep water. He was among strangers, too, for the first time in his life, seeing "no face known to me before."

Stopping in Annapolis, which he found "extremely beautiful" and whose houses he thought rather better than those in Williamsburg, Jefferson was drawn to the Maryland colonial assembly. His descriptions of the chambers, which he found wanting, and of the lawmakers, whom he also found wanting, are rich in detail. He was not impressed by the appearance and the seriousness of the Maryland legislators.

He was snobbish about his fellow colonists. "I was surprised on approaching it to hear as great a hubbub as you will usually observe at a public meeting of the planters in Virginia," Jefferson told John Page. He noted that the Speaker's wig was yellowed, and, to the young Virginian, the man had "very little the air of a speaker." The close cataloging of the assembly suggests his interest in the workings of power. It was natural for Jefferson, now a son of Williamsburg, to document his impressions of the seat of a neighboring colony. The spirit of the hour, meanwhile, was momentous: "I would give you an account of the rejoicings here on the repeal of the Stamp Act but this you will probably see in print before my letter can reach you."

In London, Parliament had stood down from the stamp duties, but passed the Declaratory Act asserting its view that it possessed the power to levy taxes on its colonies "in all cases whatsoever." For Jefferson, the story of the Stamp Act had begun in the lobby of the House of Burgesses. That it ended for him when he was on the road gave him his first tactile evidence that the American story, and the American cause, was larger than Williamsburg and larger than Virginia. His conception of the American nation may owe something to the celebrations he watched on the Maryland shore.

In 1767, Jefferson was admitted to the bar of the General Court of Virginia after his study with George Wythe. He lived at Shadwell with his mother but traveled often. Cases took him to courthouses from Staunton to Winchester. His sister Martha wrote him a report from the garden in early June, noting that his carnations were in bloom, seventy-one days after being planted. His interest in the garden and the farm was practical as well as ornamental. In late November 1767, he calculated how much hay he would need to store up to feed his horses through the winter nights.

Contemporaries recalled Jefferson as a bright, enthusiastic, and intellectually curious lawyer. His practice was eclectic. One case involved the theft of a bottle of whiskey and a shirt, another a charge of slander in which a David Frame sued a man for saying "he saw [Frame] who is a married man in bed with Elizabeth Burkin, etc."

Jefferson's friends loved him, his clients appreciated him, his elders admired him. He was the kind of man other men thought well of and believed they could trust—unless, as one of his best friends was to discover, a beautiful young wife was in the picture.

FOUR

Temptations and Trials

You will perceive that I plead guilty to one of
their charges, that when young and single I offered love to a handsome lady.

—JEFFERSON, in an 1805
acknowledgment of his infatuation
with Elizabeth Moore Walker

Under the law of nature, all men are born free
[and] everyone comes into the world with the
right to his own person which includes the liberty of moving and using it at his own will.

—JEFFERSON
in the **Howell** slavery case, 1770

IT WOULD HAVE BEEN ADULTERY, but Jefferson
was too much in love (or thought he was) to
care. Attractive and virile, a powerful and charismatic man, he wanted what he wanted, and he did
not give up easily.

Elizabeth Walker was what he wanted. She was
the bride of his friend John Walker, a man he had

known virtually all his life. The connections between the two men were old and deep. Peter Jefferson had made Walker's father one of his own executors: Dr. Thomas Walker of Castle Hill was among those who had watched over young Thomas. The two boys followed a similar path, boarding at James Maury's school before going to the College of William and Mary. "We had previously grown up together at a private school and our boys' acquaintance was strengthened at college," John Walker recalled of his friendship with Jefferson. "We loved (at least I did sincerely) each other."

Elizabeth Moore, known as Betsy, was a granddaughter of a royal governor and daughter of Bernard Moore, the master of Chelsea, a Tidewater plantation in King William County. Two of her brothers attended William and Mary with Jefferson and her future husband. In January 1764—a period in which he remained gloomy about Rebecca Burwell—Jefferson had reported his friend's impending marriage. "Jack Walker is engaged to Betsy Moore," Jefferson wrote John Page from Williamsburg, "and desired all his brethren might be made acquainted with his happiness."

There is irony in the phrasing, and perhaps envy. Still smarting from his rejection by Rebecca, Jefferson was in no mood to celebrate another man's romantic good fortune. His melancholy was exacerbated by the absence of his horses, which he had sent "up the country." Without them he felt marooned, he said, for it was now "out of my power to take even an airing on horseback at any time." The letter to John Page was dated from "Devilsburg," Jefferson's dark rendering of a Williamsburg that had not given him the bride he thought he wanted. The world seemed bleak. Even poor John Walker, Jefferson thought, would have to forgo the joys of a pretty wife for a while longer: "But I hear he will not be married this year or two."

Jefferson was wrong. Less than five months later, in the first week of June 1764, Betsy Moore and John Walker were married at her home at Chelsea. Jefferson was in attendance, John Walker recalled, as "the friend of my heart" and as a groomsman. By 1768 the Walkers were living, with an infant daughter, in a house known as Belvoir only five or so miles from Shadwell. Like Jefferson, Walker was a rising man in Virginia politics. Soon Walker agreed to join a delegation bound for Fort Stanwix, in New York, for Indian negotiations.

In the will John Walker made before he left, he appointed "Mr. Jefferson . . . my neighbor and fast friend" as "first among my executors." Walker's delegation departed for New York in early summer.

Jefferson had just turned twenty-five, and Betsy Walker was about two years younger. In the warm months of 1768, in visits to Belvoir, he found himself in her exclusive company, and he seems to have fallen in love with his old friend's new wife.

Given the risks he was taking, the intensity of

the passion Jefferson felt must have been acute. The young wife resisted, but Jefferson did not give up the chase. And though she kept Jefferson's advances secret, she allowed her anxiety to manifest itself to her husband indirectly. As John Walker recalled, his wife began to object to Jefferson's serving as Walker's executor, "telling me that she wondered why I could place such confidence in him."

Over the next few years Jefferson kept up his quiet campaign. On a visit of the Walkers to Shadwell, Jefferson "renewed his caresses" toward Betsy, slipping a note into the cuff of the sleeve of her gown. The letter, John Walker later recalled, was "a paper tending to convince her of the innocence of promiscuous love."

Perhaps from the hour of his humiliation in the Apollo Room with Rebecca Burwell, Jefferson knew he expressed himself better in writing. To write Mrs. Walker an argued love letter—one attempting to change her mind, "to convince her"—was in character. The ploy failed on this occasion: Mrs. Walker said that she "on the first glance tore [Jefferson's note] to pieces."

Later, at a house party at the plantation of a mutual friend, John Coles, a noted hunter, Jefferson watched for a chance to steal a few moments with Betsy. One evening when the women retired for the night, Jefferson saw his opportunity. "He pretended to be sick, complained of a headache and left the gentlemen among whom I was," John Walker recalled.

Slipping away, Jefferson found Betsy's room, where, her husband said, "my wife was undressing or in bed." Jefferson failed again. "He was repulsed with indignation and menaces of alarm and ran off," said John Walker.

Decades later, Jefferson confirmed the Walker story. It had come to light after a political break between Jefferson and John Walker, who had learned in the intervening years of his friend's pursuit of his wife. It had been, Jefferson said, an incorrect thing to do.

Frustrated by his failure with Mrs. Walker, Jefferson took solace in a glorious autumn of plays and politics in Williamsburg in 1768. Some years before, the Reverend Samuel Davies, a Presbyterian clergyman, had chastised Virginia for its love of drama, saying "plays and romances" were "more read than the history of the blessed Jesus." Offerings in the capital in the spring had included Joseph Addison's **Drummer**, Shakespeare's **Merchant of Venice**, John Gay's **Beggar's Opera**, and Thomas Otway's **Venice Preserved** and **The Orphan**. Now Jefferson watched performances by William Verling's Virginia Company of Comedians and of John Home's **Douglas** and Henry Carey's farce **The Honest Yorkshireman**. Meanwhile, Jefferson was playing the part of patron to the arts, bringing the Italian musician Francis Alberti from Williamsburg to Albemarle; Alberti taught Jefferson on the violin.

The Wythe-Jefferson circle lost its most powerful member when Francis Fauquier died at the Governor's Palace in March 1768. In his will, Fauquier expressed regret that his slaves would have to be sold after his death, and he took the then-unusual step of allowing his dozen adult slaves to choose their new masters and stipulating that the women were not to be separated from their children. A man of the Enlightenment to the end, he also suggested that his body be autopsied should the cause of death be uncertain. His hope, he said in his will, was that he "may become more useful to my fellow creatures by my death than I have been in my life."

Fauquier's burial five days later in the north aisle of Bruton Parish Church, not far from Wythe's house, marked the end of an era for Jefferson, Wythe, and the other Fauquier intimates at the Palace—the guests who had enjoyed the royal governor's hospitality and listened with pleasure to Jefferson's performances on the violin in the big rooms—as well as the end of a period of temperate local imperial governance. In later years Jefferson came to think of Fauquier as "the ablest man who had ever filled that office."

Norborne Berkeley, 4th Baron Botetourt—popularly referred to as Lord Botetourt—succeeded Fauquier as governor, and he was determined to make himself pleasant. A family of Jefferson's friends were spending an evening singing on the steps to their

Williamsburg house when they heard a passerby call out: "Charming, charming! Proceed for God's sake, or I will go home directly." It was Botetourt, who happily joined them.

The good cheer could not last. On the same day **The Virginia Gazette** reported Fauquier's death, the paper published the ninth installment of a series of Farmer's Letters by John Dickinson, a Pennsylvanian who argued that should London ignore American concerns, "let us then take **another step,** by withholding from **Great Britain** all the advantages she has been used to receive from us. . . . Let us all be united with one spirit, in one cause."

With Fauquier dead, one world was beginning to end, and another was being born.

At the same time Jefferson was creating chaos at Belvoir and living a cosmopolitan life in Williamsburg, he was building a new home for himself two miles—or less than a half hour's ride—from his mother's house. He named it Monticello, Italian for "little mountain." On Monday, August 3, 1767, Jefferson noted the grafting of cherry trees on the property; on Sunday, May 15, 1768, he reached an agreement to "level 250 ft. square on the top of the mountain at the N.E. end by Christmas" in exchange for 180 bushels of wheat and 24 bushels of corn (12 of those would not be due until the corn was harvested). If solid rock had to be dug, Jefferson noted in his garden book, then they would ask "indifferent men to settle that part between us"—"indifferent" in this context meaning "impartial." What is striking about Jefferson's attention to the possibility of hitting what he called "solid rock" is not that it might present insuperable obstacles but that he was prepared to do whatever it took to have his way. He had decided to build there, and build he would.

The Virginia Gazette of Thursday, December 15, 1768, reported Thomas Jefferson's election to represent Albemarle County in the House of Burgesses. He was twenty-five years old.

He would serve with Dr. Thomas Walker, John Walker's father and Betsy Walker's father-in-law. The campaign consisted largely of buying drinks and cakes for the landowners who had the suffrage. Over the next forty-one years Jefferson was rarely out of public office. Even without formal duties, he was never far from the contentions of his times.

Since the Stamp Act debates and repeal, Parliament had, beginning in 1767, passed the Townshend Acts, taxes and duties named in honor of the chancellor of the exchequer, Charles Townshend. Massachusetts led the opposition for the colonies. In Boston in February 1768 the Massachusetts legislature approved a circular letter protesting the acts and calling on other colonies to follow suit. This was the political climate when the Burgesses first sat with Jefferson as a member on Monday, May 8, 1769.

There was a sense of urgency in Williamsburg. London had ordered Botetourt to dissolve the House if the Burgesses joined Massachusetts in protesting the Townshend Acts. Within days Botetourt had the opportunity to obey the imperial command.

The colonial lawmakers had passed a resolution in support of Massachusetts. At noon on Wednesday, May 17, 1769, therefore, Botetourt summoned the Burgesses to the Council Chamber. "I have heard of your resolves, and augur ill of their effect," Botetourt told them. "You have made it my duty to dissolve you; and you are dissolved accordingly."

Jefferson had been seated in the House for not quite ten days. The very opening hours of his elective career, then, were suffused with conflict, crisis, and a creative search for a path forward that gave Americans, rather than distant authorities, control over their lives.

With his colleagues he left the Council Chamber and walked to the Apollo Room of the Raleigh Tavern, the same place where he had once stammered before Rebecca Burwell. As the Burgesses passed beneath the lead bust of Sir Walter Raleigh above the front door of the two-story tavern, they were, in the words of the **Journal** of the House, to decide which "measures should be taken in their distressed situation for preserving the true and essential interests of the colony." By the next day the Virginians had a plan. They would not import or consume anything from Great Britain.

When Jefferson left Williamsburg after his inaugural session, he was already steeped in the politics of protest and of power.

On Thursday, February 1, 1770, Jefferson was playing his accustomed role as head of the family, accompanying his mother on a visit to a neighbor, when word of disaster reached them: Shadwell had burned.

Jefferson was devastated. His first question to the slave who brought the news was whether his library had been rescued from the flames. The books were all burned, the slave replied, adding: "But, ah! we saved your fiddle!"

For a man who prized physical objects—he was to prove an inveterate collector, a tangible manifestation of his curious mind—the ash and the smoke and the ruins were especially galling and dispiriting. Fire was a reminder of those things—those many things—that lay beyond human control. Jefferson had spent almost a decade in the study and the practice of law, an undertaking based on the premise that men could, with some limitations, construct an order that enabled them to exert some power over the affairs of the world. The destruction of Shadwell was an example of how little control Jefferson—or any man—really had.

Nearly everything was gone. The burned books amounted to £200, Jefferson guessed, but that did not bother him so much. "Would to God it had been the money . . . [that would have] never cost me a sigh!" he wrote to John Page.

The real pain came from the loss of his books and his legal papers, including notes he had prepared for his work as a lawyer during the coming court term. Without them he was no longer master of the work at hand. He was desperate, even frantic, dispatching news of the fire and pleas for advice and reassurance. He contemplated moving from the neighborhood altogether—a remarkable thought for a man so engaged by his sense of place.

Another measure of Jefferson's grief at the fire is that the loss of his notes evoked a speech of Prospero's in **The Tempest,** one of the landmark tragic set pieces in Shakespeare, whom Jefferson had first encountered in his father's now-charred library. He bleakly alluded to it in the wake of the Shadwell disaster:

Our revels now are ended. These our actors,
As I foretold you, were all spirits and
Are melted into air, into thin air:
And, like the baseless fabric of this vision,
The cloud-capp'd towers, the gorgeous palaces,
The solemn temples, the great globe itself,
Yea, all which it inherit, shall dissolve
And, like this insubstantial pageant faded,
Leave not a rack behind. We are such stuff
As dreams are made on, and our little life
Is rounded with a sleep.

It was a time of testing for the young scholar and aspiring statesman. It was easy enough to read of tragedy and to explore it philosophically, turning over the problems of the spirit and the nature of things with glasses of wine in hand at warm hearths. The ability to apply what one **thought** in order to shape how one **felt**, however, was another, more difficult thing. Thomas Jefferson had this ability: His head and his heart were contiguous regions of his character with open borders. Plenty of philosophical men live in abstract regions, debating types and shadows. The rarer sort is the reader and thinker who can see the world whole. In the ashes of Shadwell, Jefferson managed to do just that.

He turned to the future, which to him meant Monticello. The summit of his mountain was now cleared. On the southeastern hillside he created an orchard of pears, apples, nectarines, pomegranates, and figs. "You bear your misfortune so becomingly," George Wythe wrote his pupil, "that, as I am convinced you will surmount the difficulties it has plunged you into, so I foresee you will hereafter reap advantages from it several ways." Wythe added a tag from Virgil: "**Durate, et vosmet rebus servate secundis.**" The line means "Carry on, and preserve yourselves for better times."

In an advertisement Jefferson placed in **The Virginia Gazette** for a runaway slave in 1769, he wrote:

RUN away from the subscriber
in **Albemarle**, a Mulatto slave called **Sandy**,
about 35 years of age, his stature is rather low,
inclining to corpulence, and his complexion light;
he is a shoemaker by trade, in which he uses his
left hand principally, can do coarse carpenters
work, and is something of a horse jockey; he is
greatly addicted to drink, and when drunk is insolent and disorderly, in his conversation he swears
much, and his behaviour is artful and knavish.
He took with him a white horse, much scarred
with traces, of which it is expected he will
endeavour to dispose; he also carried his
shoe-makers tools, and will probably endeavour
to get employment that way. Whoever conveys
the said slave to me in **Albemarle**, shall have 40 s.
[shillings] reward, if taken up within the county,
4 l. [pounds] if
elsewhere within the colony, and 10 l. if in any
other colony, from

THOMAS JEFFERSON.

From about this period until his death, according
to the historian Lucia Stanton's research, Thomas
Jefferson would own more than 600 slaves. He inherited 150 (from his father and his father-in-law)
and bought roughly 20; most of the others were
born into slavery on his lands. From 1774 to 1826,
Jefferson tended to have about 200 slaves at any
one time (the range ran from 165 to 225). When

he served at the highest levels as a diplomat, as a member of George Washington's cabinet, as vice president, as president, and, in his retirement at Monticello, as an American sage, Jefferson was to embody the slave-owning interest.

In the beginning of his public career, though, Jefferson was more willing to work to reform slavery than he was to prove in later decades. In 1769 in the House of Burgesses, Jefferson recalled, "I made one effort in that body for the permission of the emancipation of slaves, which was rejected." Two words in Jefferson's recollection are key: He was making an effort for the "permission of" emancipation, not for the kind of broad emancipation that Abraham Lincoln would declare nine decades later.

For Jefferson, it was a question of power. In that first session, in 1769, he crafted a bill that shifted control of emancipation from the General Court to slave owners themselves. The legislation would have given the individual Virginia slave owner the unilateral authority to free a slave.

In his mind's eye, Jefferson envisioned a Virginia in which he and others like him were beyond the reach of the governor and council who, under current law, decided requests for emancipation based on how they—not the planter, but the judges—chose to define "meritorious services." Jefferson asked Richard Bland, a cousin, to take the lead on the legislation. The reaction from the House was swift and certain. Bland, Jefferson recalled, was "treated with the grossest indecorum."

Very shortly thereafter, Jefferson argued the case of **Samuel Howell** v. **Wade Netherland**. At issue was a matter of perennial concern to the planter class: To what extent were the descendants of mixed-race parents bound into servitude? Jefferson argued that his client, Samuel Howell, a grandson of a white woman and a black man, should be free despite Virginia statutes that said he should be held in servitude until the age of thirty-one.

Jefferson took the occasion to make a natural-law argument, writing that "everyone comes into the world with a right to his own person and using it at his own will," Jefferson said. "This is what is called personal liberty, and is given him by the author of nature, because it is necessary for his own sustenance." He lost the case.

At different moments in his legislative and public life, Jefferson said things or proposed courses of action that could conceivably have led to the end of a slave society. The **Howell** brief suggests a Jeffersonian openness to such an eventuality, but for him abolition was always to be an eventuality for future generations, not a reality that he would ever see. The reaction to the Bland bill and of the court in **Howell** could not have failed to leave an impression, too, on the young lawyer-legislator so anxious for popularity. Wounded by the defeats of his progressive efforts on slavery, Jefferson was finally to retreat to a more conventional position.

Jefferson sought refuge from the anxieties of the Shadwell fire, the toll of trial work, and the capturing of runaways in a familiar pastime: flirting. "I reflect often with pleasure on the philosophical evenings I passed at Rosewell in my last visits there," Jefferson wrote in a section of a letter addressed to his friend and classmate John Page's wife. "I was always fond of philosophy even in its drier forms, but from a ruby lip it comes with charms irresistible." Writing about another friend in love, Jefferson said: "I do not mean, madam, to advise him against it. On the contrary I am become an advocate for the passion: for I too am **coelo tactus**." The last Latin phrase translates as "struck by."

Jefferson, it seemed, was also in love.

FIVE

A World of Desire and Denial

Harmony in the marriage state is the very first object to be aimed at.

—THOMAS JEFFERSON

THE WOMAN IN QUESTION was a rich widow. Accomplished and intelligent, with what family tradition held to be "a lithe and exquisitely formed figure," Martha Wayles Skelton had been born at a plantation called the Forest, in Charles City County, Virginia, in 1748. She was five and a half years younger than Jefferson.

Known to intimates as Patty, she was beautiful, musical, and well-read—and Jefferson adored her. She was said to be striking looking. "Her complexion was brilliant—her large expressive eyes of the richest shade of hazel—her luxuriant hair of the finest tinge of auburn," Henry Randall wrote after interviewing her descendants. She was, a contemporary said, a woman of "good sense and good nature." Patty and Thomas shared tastes in literature and in wide-ranging conversation. One kinsman

thought the Jeffersons "a couple . . . well calculated and disposed to communicate knowledge and
pleasure." Patty taught her children and her nieces
and nephews what tradition calls "the beginnings
of knowledge," suggesting an interest in education
similar to Jefferson's.

In her, Jefferson found the most congenial of
companions, a woman who spoke his language.
Their nights were filled with music and wine and
talk—talk of everything. They seem to have fully
shared their lives with each other. He confided in
her about politics. A granddaughter recalled Patty's "passionate attachment" to Jefferson and her
"exalted opinion of him." For his part, Jefferson's
"conduct as a husband had been admirable in its
ensemble, charming in its detail."

Patty once complained that some instance of Jefferson's generosity had gone unappreciated by its
recipient. "But it was always so with him," Mrs.
Jefferson is said to have remarked. "He is so good
himself, that he cannot understand how bad other
people may be."

Smart and strong willed, Patty liked having her
way. She was insistent on discipline. Jefferson once
gently rebuked her for reminding their eldest daughter, Patsy, of an old childhood crime. "My dear, a
fault in so young a child once punished should be
forgotten," Jefferson said to Patty. (Patsy recalled
feeling a "warm gush of gratitude" for her father's
support.)

Patty was not a woman of retiring nature or of quiet views. She had a mind of her own and could be assertive and acerbic. "My grandmother Jefferson had a vivacity of temper which might sometimes border on tartness, but which, in her intercourse with her husband, was completely subdued by her exceeding affection for him," said Ellen Randolph Coolidge, a Jefferson granddaughter.

Perhaps not always, however. Jefferson may have been speaking from marital experience when he advised a daughter: "Much better . . . if our companion views a thing in a light different from what we do, to leave him in quiet possession of his view. What is the use of rectifying him if the thing be unimportant; and if important let it pass for the present, and wait a softer moment and more conciliatory occasion of revising the subject together."

Yet Patty could reassure and calm her husband, who was given to worry and restlessness. Easing Thomas Jefferson's emotional tensions was a difficult task. He was acutely sensitive. At first blush, the fact that such a man was drawn to politics—where approval is fleeting and criticism constant—may seem contradictory. The connection between Jefferson's interior and exterior lives, however, follows a familiar pattern found in politicians from age to age. Ambition creates a hunger for action and acclaim, and those who crave applause have a particular aversion to criticism. His wife appears to have been one of the few people who could soothe him.

Patty Wayles Jefferson was the daughter of a man who had risen far in Virginia. Born to a poor, undistinguished family in Lancaster, England, John Wayles made his fortune in America as a lawyer, debt collector, slave trader, and planter. John Wayles's first wife, Martha Eppes, was the daughter of Francis Eppes of the Bermuda Hundred plantation. They had married in 1746. In the autumn of 1748, a daughter named Martha, called Patty, was born. The child lived but the mother did not. John Wayles married twice more, producing four other daughters, three of whom survived.

Patty Wayles grew up, then, in an uncertain household. She never knew her own mother, and two stepmothers came and went. Her experience with her father's wives was unhappy enough that she never wanted her own children to face the possibility of having a stepmother. On her deathbed she reportedly extracted a promise from Jefferson never to marry again. From the loss of her mother to the shifting cast of characters in the domestic life of the Forest, Patty learned early that the world was perilous and changeable.

Her father's livelihood partly depended on precariousness in the lives of others. As what was called an "agent" for Farrell and Jones, a British merchant house, John Wayles was a debt collector—a detail Jefferson neglected to mention in his description of his father-in-law in his **Autobiography**. "Mr.

Wayles was a lawyer of much practice, to which he was introduced more by his great industry, punctuality and practical readiness, than to eminence in the science of his profession," Jefferson wrote of his father-in-law. "He was a most agreeable companion, full of pleasantry and good humor, and welcomed in every society."

There are notes of both condescension and insecurity in Jefferson's account of his father-in-law. The assessment of Wayles's legal career is that of a much more learned lawyer, as Jefferson was. More interesting still is the phrase "welcomed into every society"—why assert a man's **inclusion** in social circles unless **exclusion** was a threat or even an occasional reality? The point accomplishes the opposite of what Jefferson intended, for it raises the question of Wayles's standing in colonial society.

That standing was at risk in the circles in which Jefferson moved, for Wayles embodied one of the two worst fears of any planter. If slave insurrections ranked first, being made to pay one's (usually enormous) debts was a near second. The sight of Wayles coming into view provoked anxiety among the planters, many of whom appear to have taken steps to avoid his collection calls.

A mocking poem in **The Virginia Gazette** of Thursday, January 1, 1767, refers to John Wayles as "ill bred." The context of the remark was a controversial murder trial in Williamsburg. Wayles, who was representing the accused, had been charged with lying in a deposition. That Patty's father was not a man as established as, say, a Randolph, suggests there was more love than calculation in Jefferson's decision to take his chances with the man's daughter.

Jefferson undertook legal work for Wayles beginning in 1768. Two years before, in November 1766, Patty, who had just turned eighteen, married Bathurst Skelton. She bore him a son, John, a year later. Patty lost her husband in September 1768, and their son, John, died in the summer of 1771.

The bereaved Mrs. Skelton had returned to the Forest, her father's house, where, as an attractive widow, she had no want of company. Suitors lurked about, hoping they might succeed the late Mr. Skelton.

Patty Wayles Skelton was, taken on her own, immensely appealing to a man like Jefferson. He was her elder, but she had seen and experienced much. There would have been little frivolity in her manner. No coquette, she had more in common with Betsy Walker than with Rebecca Burwell. Patty was a woman who had lost her mother, her husband, her son, and who understood what it took to run complex households.

One of the chief complexities of domestic life on Virginia's plantations—a complexity Patty knew well—lay in negotiating the questions of

blood, sex, and dominion that bound white and enslaved families in largely unspoken ways.

The Forest was rife with such issues. Around 1735,
a man named Hemings, the white English captain
of a trading ship, fathered a daughter with a "full-
blooded African" woman. The African woman's child
was named Elizabeth, also known as Betty. (The details come from the account of Madison Hemings,
a great-grandson of Captain Hemings and of the
African woman.) Mother and daughter ended up as
slaves of the Eppes family of Bermuda Hundred—
the Eppes family from which John Wayles would
take his first bride, Martha, who died in childbirth.
By 1746—the year Wayles married Martha Eppes—
Elizabeth Hemings, then about eleven years old,
moved to the Forest. There, beginning at age eighteen, she gave birth to several children.

Wayles, meanwhile, outlived his daughter's two
stepmothers. After the third Mrs. Wayles died in February 1761, Elizabeth Hemings, now about twenty-
six years old, was "taken by the widower Wayles as
his concubine," said Madison Hemings. Beginning
in 1762, Elizabeth Hemings bore five children to
Thomas Jefferson's father-in-law: Robert, James,
Thenia, Critta, and Peter. In 1773 came a sixth:
Sarah, who was to be known by the nickname Sally.

Such arrangements were not uncommon in slave-
owning states. In the nineteenth century, South
Carolinian Mary Boykin Chestnut noted some-

thing about white women that was equally true in the eighteenth: "Any lady is able to tell who is the father of all the mulatto children in everybody's household but their own. Those she seems to think drop from the clouds."

It was a world of desire and denial. Sex across the color line—sex between owner and property—was pervasive yet rarely directly addressed or alluded to. The strange intermingling of blood and affection and silence suffused the world of the Forest that Jefferson came to know in 1770, the year he turned up as one of the candidates for Patty's hand. It was to suffuse Monticello, too, in the fullness of time.

Jefferson's success in wooing the Widow Skelton was not assured, which may have made him work all the harder. By the first months of 1771, Jefferson was in full pursuit. He wrote a "romantic, poetical" description of her to a correspondent in Williamsburg named Mrs. Drummond, an elderly woman who was friendly with the George Wythes. "No pen but yours could surely so beautifully describe" Patty, wrote Mrs. Drummond, who praised Jefferson's (now lost) "Miltonic" lines and said she did not know whether Patty's heart was "engaged already."

How to capture her? Music was one means, books another. In family lore, Jefferson and Patty were destined for each other. A pair of competing suitors once arrived at the Forest, where they heard Patty and Jefferson playing and singing beautifully together. Looking at each other, the two callers were said to have recognized the inevitable and departed without announcing themselves.

As always, music was Jefferson's ally. To him singing or the playing of the violin or the pianoforte was more than entertainment, more than the means of passing the hours when time grew heavy. Music, rather, offered a window into a man's soul—or into a woman's. In his literary commonplace book Jefferson transcribed these lines from Shakespeare's **Merchant of Venice:**

The Man who has not Music in his Soul,
Or is not touch'd with Concord of sweet Sounds,
Is fit for Treason, Stratagems, and Spoils,
The Motions of his Mind are dull as Night,
And his Affections dark as Erebus:
Let no such man be trusted.

Jefferson's mind was considering the defining human themes, always returning to the central question of politics: How is a man, as an intrinsically social animal, to live in relative peace and charity with his neighbors in a world given to passion and conflict? There was no single answer, only the enduring effort to bring clashing elements into harmony—and perhaps the most significant decision a man could make in fighting this lifelong battle was whom to marry. Jefferson needed a woman who shared his passion for music and all that music represented—sophistication, transcendence, and the life of the imagination and the heart, as well as that of flesh and blood. Patty Wayles Skelton was such a woman.

Jefferson was determined to have her and to give her the best of everything. He was even briefly interested in his own aristocratic heritage in the Old World. "I have what I have been told were the family arms, but on what authority I know not," Jefferson wrote his English agent, Thomas Adams. "It is possible there may be none. If so, I would with your assistance become a purchaser, having Sterne's word for it that a coat of arms may be purchased as cheap as any other coat." He usually affected an air of indifference about his mother's ancestry and, with the allusion to the novelist Laurence Sterne's dismissive remark about heraldry, managed to poke fun at his own request even as he was making it. Yet the inquiry was a sign of curiosity if nothing else.

Jefferson was more interested in buying his bride larger things. He ordered a clavichord (from Hamburg, he said, "because they are better made there, and much cheaper"), but soon fell in love with a pianoforte that he had to have. He was, he told his British agent, "charmed" by the pianoforte, and he canceled the clavichord request. The pianoforte was the thing, and he wanted it right away. "Let the case be of fine mahogany, solid, not veneered. The compass from Double G. to F. in alt. a plenty of spare strings; and the workmanship of the whole very handsome, and worthy [of] the acceptance of a lady for whom I intend it." He also needed a half-dozen white silk cotton stockings and a very particular umbrella—"large . . . with brass ribs covered with green silk, and neatly finished"—but the instrument was crucial. He was, he said, "very impatient" to have it by October. If it made it, it would be just in time for the wedding.

Thomas Jefferson married Martha Wayles Skelton on New Year's Day 1772. He was twenty-eight; she was twenty-three.

It was a winter Wednesday. The Anglican ceremony, conducted by the Reverend William Coutts, was held at her father's house, and the celebrations ran for several days. (Jefferson paid the clergyman £5 and tipped Elizabeth Hemings—Sally's mother's first appearance in his account books.) On January 2, **The Virginia Gazette** reported the marriage: "**Thomas Jefferson,** Esquire, one of the Representatives for Albemarle, to Mrs. **Martha Skelton,** Relict of Mr. **Bathurst Skelton**."

The Skelton connection was not something Jefferson thought much about. Captivated by visions of their new life together, he had unconsciously edited Patty's first husband out of the picture in his preparations for the wedding. In his bond for a marriage license, dated December 30, 1771, Jefferson mistakenly referred to her as a "spinster." On the document, another hand crossed it out and inserted "Widow."

Her widowhood is more than an incidental detail. Though younger, Patty already knew more of marriage and its consolations and demands than Jefferson did—a fact that may have given her more confidence in herself as she embarked on a new life.

In the depths of the first weeks of the snowy winter of 1772, Jefferson was a satisfied man. Given his wife's numerous pregnancies in the following years, there was no shortage of physical passion between them. Their first child, Martha, nicknamed Patsy, was born at one o'clock in the morning of Sunday, September 27, 1772—nine months and twenty-six days after the marriage at the Forest.

After their wedding, the Jeffersons remained at the Forest for some days before setting out for Monticello through ever-worsening snowy weather. As they approached Shadwell and Monticello, the snow had grown too deep for their phaeton to continue. He and Patty then got on horseback and pressed on through the forests and the wind and the snow and the ice and, as the shadows lengthened, through the gathering darkness.

At sunset, they began their ascent, slowly and miserably taking the mountain's 867 feet. The trees along the path up to Monticello were likely weighed down by ice and snow. The Jeffersons may have had to pass through thickets of frozen branches hanging low across the trail.

When they arrived, they found themselves on a lonely mountaintop, cold and unexpected. The fires were out and the slaves were elsewhere. "The horrible dreariness of such a house, at the end of such a journey, I have often heard both relate," said their daughter Patsy.

The Jeffersons discovered part of a bottle of wine, and the night was, according to tradition, "lit up with song, and merriment, and laughter!" After a week or so they moved on to Elk Hill, a plantation in Goochland County along the James River and Byrd Creek. Elk Hill belonged to Patty—she had lived there with her first husband—and the Jeffersons made much use of the house and the land (at its peak Elk Hill was 669 acres).

A subject of particular interest in their private hours was James Macpherson's popular translation of the poetry of Ossian, said to be a third-century legendary Celtic bard. (He was not; the poems were, in fact, written largely by Macpherson and passed off as ancient verse.) "The tender and the sublime emotions of the mind were never before so finely wrought up by human hand," Jefferson said in 1773. "I am not ashamed to own that I think this rude bard of the North the greatest poet that has ever existed."

Monticello is often seen as Jefferson's retreat from the world. He himself spoke of it in such terms. The house on the hill was also an imaginative redoubt, a fortress in which the master could not only seek shelter but also gather himself and his forces to fight great battles. He may well have found in Ossian's epic imagery a poetic model for what he wanted his own world to be like. In his commonplace book, he copied a section that spoke to height and power and fame and adventure:

> **As two dark streams from high rocks meet, and mix and roar on the plain; loud, rough, and dark in battle meet Lochlin and Innis-fail: chief mixed his strokes with chief, and man with man; steel clanging sounded on steel, helmets are cleft on high; blood bursts and smokes around. Strings murmur on the polished yews. Darts rush along the sky. Spears fall like the circles of light that gild the stormy face of the night. As the troubled noise of the ocean when roll the waves on high; as the last peal of the thunder of heaven, such is the noise of the battle. . . . For many were the falls of the heroes; and wide poured the blood of the valiant.**

Patty Jefferson was a careful housekeeper, taking steps to ensure that her husband's private world ran smoothly. She saw to fresh supplies of meat, eggs, butter, and fruit and supervised the making of beer and of soap. She personally directed the work of the kitchen on more sophisticated foods. "Mrs. Jefferson would come out there with a cookery book in her hand and read out of it to Isaac's mother how to make cakes, tarts, and so on," recalled Isaac Granger

Jefferson, a slave who left a memoir of life at Monticello among the Jeffersons.

A caller at Monticello, a German officer, found the Jeffersons charming and engaging. He admired Jefferson's "copious and well-chosen library" and the Monticello project itself, saluting his host's "noble spirit of building." He also noted that Jefferson was designing a compass for the parlor ceiling, to track the strength and direction of the wind.

What the Jeffersons did together made perhaps the greatest impression. "As all Virginians are fond of music, he is particularly so," the visitor said. "You will find in his house an elegant harpsichord piano forte and some violins. The latter he performs well upon himself, the former his lady touches very skillfully and who is in all respects a very agreeable, sensible and accomplished lady."

It is a warm portrait of a harmonious and happy life on the little mountain, a life of ideas, invention, and the making of music. It was the life Jefferson had long hoped for—the kind of life his father had built and his mother had maintained, and which he now gave his own family at his chosen summit.

On Sunday, May 16, 1773, in a keen personal loss for Jefferson, his friend and brother-in-law Dabney Carr died of a "bilious fever," leaving Jefferson's sister Martha to raise six children.

Jefferson's instinctive reaction was that of a father.

He did whatever was within his power to bring stability to his sister's family by offering order, shelter, and love in the midst of his own sadness over losing the beloved friend of his youth. His grief seems to have surpassed that of his reaction to his sister Jane's death. For Carr, whom he buried at Monticello, he could not, at first, settle on a single epitaph, sketching out his plans for his friend's grave on a sheet of paper:

INSCRIPTION ON MY FRIEND D. CARR'S TOMB.

Lamented shade, whom every gift of heaven
Profusely blest; a temper winning mild;
Nor pity softer, nor was truth more bright.
Constant in doing well, he neither sought
Nor shunned applause. No bashful merit sighed
Near him neglected: sympathizing he
Wiped off the tear from Sorrow's clouded eye
With kindly hand, and taught her heart to smile.
                                    MALLET'S Excursion.

Send for a plate of copper to be nailed on the tree at the foot of his grave, with this inscription:

Still shall thy grave with rising flowers be dressed
And the green turf lie lightly on thy breast;
There shall the morn her earliest tears bestow,
There the first roses of the year shall blow,
While angels with their silver wings o'ershade
The ground now sacred by thy reliques made.

On the upper part of the stone inscribe as follows:

Here lie the remains of
Dabney Carr,
Son of John and Jane Carr, of Louisa County,
Who was born ———, 1744.
Intermarried with Martha Jefferson, daughter
  of Peter
and Jane Jefferson, 1765;
And died at Charlottesville, May 16, 1773,
Leaving six small children.
To his Virtue, Good Sense, Learning, and
 Friendship
this stone is dedicated by Thomas Jefferson,
  who, of all men living,
loved him most.

While Jefferson struggled to absorb Carr's loss, Patty mourned her father. On Friday, May 28, 1773, John Wayles died, leaving a heavily indebted estate. Patty Jefferson did not hesitate to move Elizabeth Hemings and the Hemings-Wayles children—Patty's half siblings—from the Forest to Monticello in the wake of her father's death.

We do not know how Patty really felt about her father's liaison with Elizabeth Hemings and about their children. Within the limitations of the world in which she lived, however, we do know that Patty chose to protect the Hemings family by keeping them together after Wayles's death and by bringing them into the domestic sphere she shared with her husband and child.

The Hemings family was to be forever intertwined with the Jeffersons and with Monticello. Elizabeth Hemings's son Robert, whom Jefferson called Bob, replaced Jupiter as Jefferson's body servant until Jefferson left for France in the 1780s. Elizabeth's son James Hemings traveled with him to Paris and worked as Jefferson's chef. Another son, John Hemings (often spelled Hemmings), became an accomplished joiner and cabinetmaker, crafting furniture, interior moldings, and a landau (four-wheeled) carriage of Jefferson's design.

Jefferson now had charge over three branches of his or his wife's family. There was his own wife, Patty, and their infant daughter. There was his sister and his nieces and nephews. And, in a connection no one could acknowledge, there was his wife's father's concubine, Elizabeth Hemings, and his wife's half siblings, including Sally Hemings.

One man, Thomas Jefferson, stood at the center of this eclectic universe. He was the master of Monticello, a burgess of Virginia, a lawyer of note. And he was about to become a central leader and defining voice of a revolutionary nation in armed rebellion against the world's greatest empire.

PART II

THE REVOLUTIONARY

SPRING 1774 to SUMMER 1776

The Americans have made a discovery, or think they have made one, that we mean to oppress them. We have made a discovery, or think we have made one, that they intend to rise in rebellion. . . . We know not how to advance; they know not how to retreat.

—The British statesman
EDMUND BURKE

John Trumbull's reimagining of the
presentation of the draft of the Declaration of
Independence in the summer of 1776.

SIX

Like a Shock of Electricity

Things seem to be hurrying to an alarming
crisis, and demand the speedy, united councils
of all those who have a regard for the common
cause.

—Letter of the Virginia House of
Burgesses, May 31, 1774

IT WAS A BIZARRE SEASON at Monticello. In the
early afternoon hours of Monday, February 21,
1774, the first recorded earthquake in the history of Virginia struck with strength in Albemarle
County. In the furor, Elizabeth Jefferson, Thomas's
reputedly mentally disabled sister, disappeared from
Shadwell. She was found, dead, three days later,
after apparently drowning in the Rivanna.

In the middle of the first week of May, a springtime
snowstorm left the Blue Ridge covered in white. The
next day brought a terrible frost that killed "almost
everything," Jefferson said: leaves, vines, wheat, rye,
corn, and a good deal of tobacco. "This frost was
general and equally destructive through the whole

country and the neighboring colonies," Jefferson wrote in his garden book. Only half of Monticello's fruit survived.

Yet there was also joy on Jefferson's mountain: Patty Jefferson gave birth to a second daughter on Sunday, April 3, 1774. Called Jane Jefferson, the baby bore the name of both Jefferson's mother and of his late sister. It was Patty Jefferson's second delivery in nineteen months. She had been pregnant for all but about nine or so months of her twenty-seven-month-old marriage. Even among the elite, childbirth was dangerous and could be fatal to both mother and infant. Jefferson was to learn this well: All but two of the six children born to Patty and Thomas Jefferson were fated to die in infancy or childhood.

Self-evidently an ardent lover, Jefferson also proved an attentive husband and father. His memorandum book notes the purchase of "breast pipes," glass devices that facilitated the breastfeeding of infants.

Political duty, however, always called. The House of Burgesses was set to meet in Williamsburg in the spring of 1774. There was much to discuss. And Jefferson had to be there.

Leaving his wife and his two infant daughters—the newborn Jane and the toddler Patsy—Jefferson reached Williamsburg on the eve of confrontation with Britain.

These had been—and would continue to be—years of crisis. Beginning in his first session as a member of the House of Burgesses in May 1769, Jefferson had served in the midst of conflicts with Britain of varying degrees of severity. A pattern took hold. The British Parliament imposed new taxes to raise revenue from British America. Colonists in their sundry capitals (Boston, Annapolis, Philadelphia, Williamsburg, and so on) resisted to a greater or lesser degree depending on the moment. The royal governments in the New World and the establishment in Britain grew yet more impatient with what they saw as a continent populated by the recalcitrant, the unreasonable, and the ungrateful.

From the time of the Townshend Acts to the Boston Tea Party (a protest over duties on tea), London attempted to exert control. The American colonists fought back by various means. There were nonimportation agreements in the colonies to keep British goods off the American market. There were objections to the possible arrest of Americans who would then be tried in England. There were committees of correspondence to establish communication among the colonies.

In Virginia, Thomas Jefferson sensed a sort of tragic stasis. Independence was a possibility, but not a certain one. As late as May 1772, for example, George Wythe was still committed to the maintenance of at least the appearance of the status quo. Writing to London, he ordered a "robe, such as is worn by the clerk of the House of Commons, but better than the one I had before . . . which indeed was scandalous." Even allowing for irony in his manner of expression, Wythe clearly did not yet envision a new world of republican simplicity.

A remark of Jefferson's father-in-law's illuminated the ethos of the time for many of the colonists. Writing in Williamsburg in October 1772, John Wayles had reported: "Our sale of slaves goes on slowly so 'tis uncertain when we shall be down, but I suppose before the Rebel party leaves town." The "Rebel party" was still only a movement to be alluded to in passing.

To protest was one thing, to rebel quite another. There were Virginians of Jefferson's class who chose to remain loyal to London rather than take the path of revolution. Jefferson's cousin John Randolph of Tazewell Hall was to become known as John Randolph "The Tory" for his allegiance to the Crown—an allegiance that led him to return to England as revolutionary sentiment grew. Overall, about a fifth of white American colonists in these years, or 20 percent, sided with England.

Still, a notation in Jefferson's memorandum book suggests his own musings were more expansive. **"Non solum nobis, sed patriae"**: "Not for ourselves only, but for our country."

For the elite, revolution was the shrewdest economic choice. London had already stymied landownership in the West, restricting those with capital (or those capable of borrowing capital) from acquiring coveted acres. Virginia's public finances were a mess; there was no way for the colony to honor the paper money issued during the Seven Years' War, which alienated most of the holders of the paper. And there was the inescapably personal issue of the money that planters owed creditors in Britain. In Jefferson's words, such debts were now "hereditary from father to son for many generations, so that the planters were a species of property annexed to certain mercantile houses in London." Virginians owed at least £2.3 million to British merchants, nearly half the total owed by all the American colonies. In May 1774, Jefferson and Patrick Henry had proposed suspending payments of such debts.

Only weeks earlier Jefferson had made a personal financial decision with perilous consequences. When John Wayles died in 1773, he left an estate worth £30,000, but one that was also heavily indebted, with £11,000 owed to his largest creditor, Farell and Jones in Bristol. In January 1774, Jefferson and Wayles's two other sons-in-law decided to break up the jointly held estate among themselves, with a fateful result: Jefferson's liability for his portion of the Wayles debt now extended to his personal property.

For the colonists, the decision to revolt was not solely economic, but it was surely informed by concerns over money. In Virginia the impetus to rebel came from the propertied elements of society; the middle and lower classes were slower to follow the lead of men such as Jefferson. It was a rich man's revolution, and Jefferson was a rich man. It was a philosophical revolution, and Jefferson was a philosophical man.

The intersection of economic and ideological forces created a climate in which well-off, educated Virginians saw a clearer, more compelling, and more attractive future if they could successfully separate themselves from London.

In Jefferson's political imagination, any move that could be interpreted as an encroachment on liberty was interpreted in just that way. Taxes, the presence of British troops, trade regulations, the disposition of western lands, and relations with Indian tribes, among other matters, were all seen as grasps for power by London, power that Jefferson and others believed rightly belonged to them (or at least to them within a constitution in which they played a much larger role). Absolutism was always just a step away; subjugation an imminent possibility. The Americans were not wrong to think this way, for the history they knew—and the politics they were experiencing—tended to favor the Crown and its adherents rather than the people as more broadly defined.

As a Virginian and a burgess, Jefferson had an acute sense of the tightening of royal authority. Before 1729, no royal governor in Virginia had suspended an act of the colonial legislature. In the ensuing thirty-five years, until 1764, governors intervened fewer than sixty times, or less than twice a year. Then, in the nine years between 1764 and 1773, there were seventy-five such suspensions—a steady, and infuriating, rate of increase that the most powerful Virginians, those in the House of Burgesses, felt directly and ever more often.

On Thursday, May 19, 1774, Virginia newspapers announced the Boston Port Act. Enacted by Parliament, the law closed the city's port until restitution was made for the losses incurred by the East India Company in the Boston Tea Party the previous December.

The legislation infuriated Jefferson's circle. (It was one of what became known as the Intolerable Acts of 1774.) Jefferson said he was among the burgesses who agreed "we must boldly take an unequivocal stand in the line with Massachusetts."

Patrick Henry, Richard Henry Lee, and four or five other members joined Jefferson in the capitol's Council Chamber, home to a library of parliamentary and legislative precedents that included documents edited by John Rushworth, an antimonarchical historian who had fought in the English Civil War. "We were under [the] conviction of the necessity of arousing our people from the lethargy into which they had fallen as to passing events," Jefferson recalled, "and thought that the appointment of a day of general fasting and prayer would be most likely to call up and alarm their attention."

The Day of Fasting and Prayer resolution of Tuesday, May 24, 1774, was one in a series of lessons in the politics of revolution that, from the unseasonably frosty May of 1774 through June and July of 1776, offered Jefferson opportunities to manage and marshal the American mind. He had learned the art of pragmatism during the Stamp Act debates, watching more experienced lawmakers find ways to exert their will against that of Patrick Henry. Now Jefferson turned his attention from the chambers of Williamsburg to the broad countryside, from the mechanics of legislation to the leadership of a mass movement. Jefferson's role in the adoption and promotion of the Day of Fasting and Prayer resolution illustrated his growing understanding of the importance of engaging the emotions of one's followers.

For Jefferson, the decision to base a revolutionary appeal on religious grounds was expedient, reflecting more an understanding of politics than a belief that the Lord God of Hosts was about to intervene in British America. Though not a conventional Christian, Jefferson appreciated the power of spiritual appeals. To frame an anti-British argument in the language of faith took the rhetorical fight to the enemy in a way that was difficult to combat. Jefferson and his colleagues could argue that they were only humbling themselves before the Lord, calling on a largely religious populace to fast and pray, not to resist authority.

The wording itself came after Jefferson and his

comrades "rummaged" through Rushworth's collection of "revolutionary precedents and forms of the Puritans of that day." In Jefferson's telling, his group "cooked up a resolution" on Monday, May 23, 1774. It asked Virginians to pray for deliverance from "the evils of civil war."

The House of Burgesses, meanwhile, considered joining a full boycott of all British goods and supporting calls for a Continental Congress. Reading the messages from the North and feeling the anxiety in the city, the colonial leadership in Williamsburg was aware of the stakes. A reckoning could not be far off.

Monticello's cherries had ripened in the interval between Jefferson's departure for Williamsburg in May and his return to Albemarle County by July. He was home to do business. In a letter to their constituents, he and John Walker announced the Day of Fasting and Prayer, a reaction, they wrote, to "the dangers impending over British America from the hostile invasion of a sister colony." Their language was martial and grave; echoing the burgesses' resolution, he and Walker argued there was a threat of "civil war."

To execute this strategy Jefferson turned to his friend the Reverend Charles Clay, the clergyman who had buried Jefferson's sister Elizabeth after she drowned earlier in the year. Clay was to preach the sermon in the parish of St. Anne's in "the new church" on the Hardware River. The location itself was chosen to make the greatest impression, for it was the "place . . . thought the most centrical to the parishioners in general."

Services were held on different days in different counties. The St. Anne's ceremony fell on Saturday, July 23, 1774. Jefferson was struck by the human element of the experience, writing; "The people met generally, with anxiety and alarm in their countenances, and the effect of the day[s] through the whole colony was like a shock of electricity, arousing every man and placing him erect and solidly on his center."

Three days later, the freeholders of Albemarle gathered at the courthouse in Charlottesville to elect Jefferson and Walker to the special August meeting in Williamsburg. The voters also adopted the Resolutions of the Freeholders of Albemarle County that denounced the Boston Port Act. Composed by Jefferson, the resolutions spoke of "the common rights of mankind," promising "we will ever be ready to join with our fellow subjects . . . in exerting all those rightful powers which God has given us, for the re-establishing and guaranteeing such their constitutional rights when, where, and by whomsoever invaded." They called for an immediate ban on British imports and set a more distant date—October 1, 1775, fifteen months away—for an end to exports unless American grievances were redressed.

A t Monticello, working fast, enjoying fresh cucumbers and lettuce, Jefferson hurried to compose instructions to the delegates who were to attend the larger national Continental Congress, scheduled for September 5, 1774, in Philadelphia.

Entitled **A Summary View of the Rights of British America,** Jefferson's midsummer work was his first substantial state paper. With these pages—the instructions ran roughly 6,700 words—he invested the American cause with universal themes, linking the claims of the New World with the Whig story of the march of liberty in the Old.

He was writing, he said, to remind George III

that our ancestors, before their emigration to America, were the free inhabitants of the British dominions in Europe, and possessed a right which nature has given to all men, of departing from the country in which chance, not choice, has placed them. . . . That their Saxon ancestors had, under this universal law, in like manner left their native wilds and woods in the North of Europe, had possessed themselves of the island of Britain, then less charged with inhabitants, and had established there that system of laws which has so long been the glory and protection of that country.

He concluded with a passage on the nature of politics and governing:

Let those flatter, who fear; it is not an American art. To give praise which is not due might be well from the venal, but would ill beseem those who are asserting the rights of human nature. . . . Open your breast, sire, to liberal and expanded thought. Let not the name of George the third be a blot in the page of history. . . . The whole art of government consists in the art of being honest. Only aim to do your duty, and mankind will give you credit where you fail. No longer persevere in sacrificing the rights of one part of the empire to the inordinate desires of another; but deal out to all equal and impartial right. . . . This is the important post in which fortune has placed you, holding the balance of a great, if a well poised empire.

And a claim of ultimate, if conditional, loyalty: "It is neither our wish nor our interest to separate from" Great Britain. Yet the demands were great. "Still less let it be proposed that our properties within our own territories shall be taxed or regulated by any power on earth but our own. The God who gave us life gave us liberty at the same time; the hand of force may destroy, but cannot disjoin them."

The author intended to carry the draft to Williamsburg himself. On the road, however, Jefferson was stricken with dysentery. Incapacitated, he sent his enslaved personal servant Jupiter to Williamsburg with two copies of the document: one for

Peyton Randolph and the other for Patrick Henry. His words now on their way into the hands of other men, he returned to Monticello.

Thanks to Jupiter, Jefferson's paper reached Williamsburg; and thanks to Clementina Rind, the widow of William Rind, the printer with offices on North England Street, the piece was published, winning audiences in the rest of the colonies and in London.

The assembled burgesses applauded when the **Summary View** was read aloud at Peyton Randolph's house. To widen its reach, Mrs. Rind used her hand-pulled press to publish the **Summary View** from the newspaper's offices in the Ludwell-Paradise House in Williamsburg. In a preface, the printer wrote: "Without the knowledge of the author, we have ventured to communicate his sentiments to the public; who have certainly a right to know what the best and wisest of their members have thought on a subject in which they are so deeply interested." Either she or another editor chose a motto from Cicero to affix to the opening of the pamphlet: "It is the indispensable duty of the supreme magistrate to consider himself as acting for the whole community, and obliged to support its dignity, and assign to the people, with justice, their various rights, as he would be faithful to the great trust reposed in him."

On Saturday, August 6, 1774, George Washington paid 3s 9d for several copies of what he called "Mr. Jefferson's Bill of Rights." Thomas Walker, one of Jefferson's guardians from Peter Jefferson's will, loaned his to William Preston, a burgess and colonel of the militia, urging him to read "the enclosed piece" and trusting that "your care of it I can depend on as I have no other copy."

The **Summary View** framed the issue starkly—too starkly for some at that hour. However far the mind might range in the direction of independence and war, thinking about the intellectual justifications for revolution and taking up arms were very different things. "Tamer sentiments were preferred, and I believe, wisely preferred; the leap I proposed being too long as yet for the mass of our citizens." In the Virginia of the time, there was, he said, an "inequality of pace" among the people, and "prudence" was "required to keep front and rear together."

With the **Summary View** Jefferson moved toward the front ranks of the cause, taking an advanced position. There were even rumors that Jefferson had been added to a bill of attainder in London, which would have declared him guilty, presumably of treason—a capital offense.

In the Day of Fasting and Prayer resolution, the Albemarle resolves, and the **Summary View,** Jefferson had appealed to his audience's sense of justice, which one would expect in the litigation of grievances, but also to its sense of destiny. In his rhetoric he deployed both the particular and the universal. He simultaneously made the most specific of allegations of British wrongdoing (some of which were obscure even to contemporary readers and listeners) and sketched out a vision of history in which the struggles of the hour were indelible chapters in the long story of freedom. In so doing Jefferson mastered the art of rhetorical political leadership by appearing at once concerned about the needs of his people and attentive to their innate need to be part of a larger drama that imbues daily life with mythic stakes.

The work of his conscious life had been the accumulation of knowledge, the broadening of his mind, and the formation of ideas about liberty, law, and how one ought to live. Under William Small, under George Wythe, alongside Dabney Carr and John Page, Jefferson had come to believe that reason, not hereditary right, should govern human affairs. Tyranny was tyranny, whether practiced by kings or priests.

He knew, too, that he was risking everything—and everything of his young family's. In his commonplace book he had copied down these lines from Pope's translation of Homer:

> Death is the worst; a Fate which all must try;
> And, for our Country, 'tis a Bliss to die,
> The gallant Man tho' slain in Fight he be,
> Yet leaves his Nation safe, his children free,
> Entails a debt on all the grateful State;
> His own brave Friends shall glory in his Fate;
> His wife live Honour'd, all his Race succeed;
> And late Posterity enjoy the Deed.

America was still twenty-three months from declaring independence when Thomas Jefferson gave the Atlantic world the **Summary View.** His celebrity grew as his pamphlet circulated. John Adams thought it "a very handsome public paper" that demonstrated "a happy talent for composition."

Because of the play of his mind and the formation of his convictions, Jefferson was something of a prophet in the summer and fall of 1774, a figure who, from a mountaintop, looked deep into the nature of things and told his countrymen what he had seen. The **Summary View** was an act of courage driven by conviction offered to a people in search of a creed.

As 1774 drew to a close, Jefferson—at thirty-one years old, a husband, father, lawyer, planter, legislator, and thinker—had moved to a new, higher rank of political skill. The **Summary View** and his other pieces demonstrated a capacity to reflect and advance the sentiments of his public simultaneously, giving his audience both a vision of the future and a concrete sense that he knew how to bring the distant closer to hand, and dreams closer to reality.

SEVEN

There Is No Peace

Blows must decide whether they are to be subject to this country or independent.

—KING GEORGE III,
on the American colonies

AT MONTICELLO THE PEACH TREES were blossoming. It was early March 1775, and Jefferson was preparing to leave for Richmond to attend the Virginia Convention, a meeting of revolutionary leaders to be held at St. John's, a hilltop wooden Anglican church. The building was the largest structure in Richmond, and every bit of space was needed: Organizers expected one hundred or so delegates to make their way to St. John's through the springtime mud. The president of the convention sat behind the communion rail. Delegates filled the pews, and eager spectators took up the remaining seating. The overflow from the daily crowds stood outside the open windows in the walled churchyard, listening.

The work of the convention was intense, Jefferson's range of tasks wide. Virginia's revolutionary leaders had to make decisions about military preparations, taxes, and trade—formulating policy in the expectation of war while British officials in the colony were themselves taking a stronger stand against Jefferson and his colleagues.

John Murray, 4th Earl of Dunmore, the tough-minded, Scottish-born royal governor who had succeeded Botetourt, had forbidden Virginians to import arms and powder from Britain. London had also ordered the seizure of any munitions that arrived in America, stipulating that the royal representatives were to prevent elections to the Second Continental Congress. Neither side showed any inclination to back down.

At St. John's, Jefferson threw himself into whatever came his way. He was hardheaded, not theoretical. He believed the hour called for action, not rhetoric.

On March 23, 1775—a springtime Thursday warm enough for the windows of the church to be left open—Patrick Henry called on Virginia to move its militia "into a posture of defense." Standing in pew 47 in the eastern aisle of the nave of the church, Henry spoke brilliantly. "Gentlemen may cry, Peace, Peace—but there is no peace," Henry said. "The war is actually begun!" In a transporting climax, Henry cried: "I know not what course others may take; but as for me—give me liberty, or give me death!"

To Jefferson, Henry was essentially a magician. "His eloquence was peculiar; if indeed it should be called eloquence, for it was impressive and sublime beyond what can be imagined," Jefferson later said. "Although it was difficult, when he had spoken, to tell what he had said, yet while he was speaking, it always seemed directly to the point."

Afterward it fell to a committee that included Jefferson to work out the actual plans for colonial defense. The committee resolved:

> That each troop of horse consist of thirty exclusive of officers: that every horseman be provided with a good horse, bridle, saddle with pistols and holsters, a carbine or other short firelock with a bucket, a cutting sword or tomahawk, one pound of gunpowder and four pound of ball at the least, and use the utmost diligence in training and accustoming his horse to stand the discharge of firearms, and in making himself acquainted with the military exercise for cavalry.

There were possible fissures within the colonies. New York had reportedly voted against electing representatives to the Second Continental Congress scheduled for May. Did that decision, Jefferson asked, mean New York had "deserted the Union"?

Weapons, militiamen, unity: In Richmond, Jefferson was at work in the cause of defense. Away from his committee duties and the action on the floor, he tried to enjoy himself in Richmond, drinking at Mrs. Younghusband's tavern, dining at Gunn's rival establishment, and buying book muslin for his library from Mrs. Ogilvie. The next political act, however, was already scheduled. On Monday, March 27, 1775, Jefferson was elected as a deputy to the Second Continental Congress.

The first Congress had been called in the wake of the Boston Port Act and the other so-called Coercive Acts. Gathering from September to October 1774—shortly after Jefferson wrote the **Summary View,** then fell ill—the Congress had issued a list of grievances against the British government, called for a continued boycott of British goods (as well as enforcement of that boycott), and agreed to meet again if necessary.

And necessary it was. The threat of war seemed to grow in the autumn of 1774. In New England, British troops took control of powder magazines and cannons to secure them from colonial militias and asked London for more troops in expectation that bloodshed was at hand. London's response to this request, and to the First Continental Congress, was to offer the British military commander in North America, General Thomas Gage, a clear instruction: "Force," the government advised Gage, "should be repelled by force."

There was to be no negotiation. There was to be war. The Second Continental Congress was therefore to take on an even more daunting task than the first: the management of an aspiring nation undertaking an armed revolution.

In Richmond, Jefferson's committee's resolution on preparing the militia noted that a failure to prepare militarily would leave Virginia in "evident danger . . . in case of invasion or insurrection." Both possibilities—invasion from without or insurrection from within—felt more likely after the third week of April 1775.

In Massachusetts, British troops and American colonists clashed at Lexington and Concord on Wednesday, April 19, 1775. By the end of the day, after gunfire along a shifting sixteen-mile front, there were 273 British and 95 American casualties. The exact sequence of the battle is unclear, but the meaning of the bloodshed was unmistakable. As Jefferson wrote after hearing the reports, any "last hopes of reconciliation" were now gone. "A frenzy of revenge," he added, "seems to have seized all ranks of people."

The painter John Singleton Copley wrote his half brother: "The flame of civil war is now broke out in America, and I have not the least doubt it will rage with a violence equal to what it has ever done in any other country at any time."

In Virginia, elite whites were contending with slave violence both rumored and real and with the seizure, by Lord Dunmore, of the supplies of gunpowder at Williamsburg. In the middle of April in Chesterfield County, not far from Albemarle, whites were "alarmed for an insurrection of the slaves." In Northumberland County two slaves set fire to a militia officer's house "with a parcel of straw fixed to the end of a pole." Dunmore decided that the enemy of his enemy was his friend—that the slaves whom the whites often feared were Britain's natural allies in Virginia.

As Thursday, April 20, 1775, became Friday, April 21, royal marines removed fifteen half barrels of gunpowder from the public magazine at Williamsburg to the HMS **Magdalen,** effectively disarming the Virginians. A furious crowd of colonists gathered outside the Governor's Palace, ready for anything.

At the Palace, Dunmore announced that he was simply securing the powder in the event of a slave insurrection, but the royal governor barely concealed his fury and contempt, later calling the crowd "one of the highest insults, that could be offered to the authority of his majesty's government." Dunmore was especially angry about the presence of militia in Williamsburg, noting that the colonists were treating with him "under the muskets of their independent company which they left only at a little distance from my house." Two days later Dunmore arrested two of the company's leaders. It was then that he truly struck.

On Saturday, April 22, 1775, Dunmore announced that "by the living God" he would "declare freedom to the slaves, and reduce the city of Williamsburg to ashes" should there be further "injury or insult" to the royal establishment.

Reaction was swift and predictable. From Pennsylvania, a colonist wrote a friend overseas: "Hell itself could not have vomited anything more black than his design of emancipating our slaves." Colonists with slaveholding sympathies either began or accelerated their preparations for war, Jefferson among them.

Jefferson was obsessed with politics of the continental crisis. In a Sunday, May 7, 1775, letter to his old teacher William Small in England, Jefferson interrupted himself at one point to say: "But for God's sake where am I got to? Forever absorbed in the distresses of my country I cannot for three sentences keep clear of its political struggles."

Yet he could not help himself. "Within this week," he wrote to Small, "we have received the unhappy news of an action of considerable magnitude between the king's troops and our brethren of Boston." The fact that blood was shed under such circumstances, Jefferson said, seemed to doom prospects for a peaceful resolution. (Small died in Birmingham, England, before Jefferson's letter reached him.)

Dunmore's seizure of the gunpowder and his statements about the slaves inflamed matters in Jefferson's immediate world. In Albemarle County, the militia declared they wanted "to demand satisfaction of Dunmore for the powder, and his threatening to fix his standard and call over the Negroes."

To Jefferson, Dunmore was the particular manifestation of a universal truth. The British were unbending, apparently uninterested in even affecting an air of respect toward the Americans. The bolder the Americans grew, the surlier the British seemed. Ever sensitive to slights and conscious of the alchemy of human relationships in which respect, rivalry, affection, and deference were bound together in varying and changing proportions, Jefferson was able to detect such shifts in the political realm as well as in his personal one.

He offered an astute analysis of the British approach: "A little knowledge of human nature and attention to its ordinary workings might have foreseen that the spirits of the people here were in a state in which they were more likely to be provoked than frightened by haughty deportment."

Jefferson's political education continued during a spirited session when the House of Burgesses met in Williamsburg in June 1775. While the House considered conciliatory proposals from London, three Virginia colonists trying to break into the powder magazine were wounded by a shotgun rigged to fire if the magazine were tampered with. Dunmore felt the situation so precarious—and his security so tenuous—that he and his family left Williamsburg, seeking refuge aboard the HMS **Fowey.**

Around Saturday, June 10, 1775, Jefferson replied to London's conciliatory proposal on behalf of Virginia. Despite the passions of the hour—a fleeing royal governor, skirmishes over gunpowder, and the fear of slave rebellion—Jefferson took a measured tone, saying that the Virginians had "examined it minutely; we viewed it in every point of light in which we were able to place it; and with pain and disappointment we must ultimately declare it only changes the form of oppression, without lightening its burden."

Others in Virginia were not so certain. As Jefferson recalled it, Robert Carter Nicholas and James Mercer, a lawyer from Stafford County, were more open to talk of reconciliation with London than was either Jefferson or, more important, Peyton Randolph, who believed Virginia should take a stronger revolutionary stance.

In a sign of his standing with Peyton Randolph, Jefferson was asked to draft the House's response, for Randolph "feared that Mr. Nicholas, whose mind was not yet up to the mark of the times, would undertake the answer." With Jefferson's text as the starting point, Randolph was able to exert a greater level of control than if Nicholas had been the initial author.

It was still a contentious argument. Even after the Boston Tea Party, even after Lexington and Concord, even after Dunmore and the Gunpowder Affair and the talk of arming slaves, a permanent separation from Great Britain was a matter of intense debate for Jefferson and his contemporaries.

Divided opinion was a recurring fact of life for Jefferson in these years of political formation. He came of age amid conflict, not certitude. To him statecraft was always a struggle between passionately held points of view. Smooth marches of like minds to glorious conclusions may have been the stuff of his dreams, but reality was far different—and it was reality that concerned him most.

Randolph shepherded Jefferson's draft through the assembly. There were, Jefferson said, "long and doubtful scruples from Mr. Nicholas and James Mercer, and a dash of cold water on it here and there, enfeebling it somewhat," but it finally passed. For Jefferson and Randolph the key point was unity among the colonies.

Such unity was on Jefferson's mind, for he was to take his place on the national stage at last. He left Williamsburg for the Second Continental Congress in Philadelphia on Sunday, June 11, 1775. A larger world beckoned.

EIGHT

The Famous Mr. Jefferson

> As our enemies have found we can reason like men, so now let us show them we can fight like men also.
>
> —Thomas Jefferson, July 5, 1775

> The present crisis is so full of danger and uncertainty that opinions here are various.
>
> —Thomas Jefferson,
> from Philadelphia, 1775

LODGING ON CHESTNUT between Third and Fourth streets in Philadelphia, where the Continental Congress was meeting at the Pennsylvania State House (later known as Independence Hall), Jefferson effortlessly entered the flow of things. He sent accounts of the military situation to Virginia. He looked over Benjamin Franklin's proposal for "Articles of confederation and perpetual Union." He recorded the "Financial and Military Estimates for Continental Defense."

In a way, he had been preparing for this hour and for this work since he first stood in the lobby of the House of Burgesses in Williamsburg, listening, rapt, to Patrick Henry a decade before. There had been the glittering evenings in Fauquier's Palace, full of music and ideas; the golden years in the Wythe house, immersed in law and history; the apprenticeship in politics under Peyton Randolph in the Raleigh Tavern, watching and learning. The Jefferson style—cultivate his elders, make himself pleasant to his contemporaries, and use his pen and his intellect to shape the debate—armed him well for the national arena. He was no longer in Williamsburg or Richmond, but he felt at home.

In Virginia, Jefferson had known everything and everyone. In sessions of the Congress in Philadelphia and in hours of walking the city, he encountered new ideas, new people, new forces.

Philadelphians, said the Anglican clergyman William Smith, were "a people, thrown together from various quarters of the world, differing in all things—language, manners, and sentiment." Another clergyman, Jacob Duché, said, "The poorest laborer upon the shore of the Delaware thinks himself entitled to deliver his sentiments in matters of religion and politics with as much freedom as the gentleman or the scholar. . . . For every man expects one day or another to be upon a footing with his wealthiest neighbor."

In Philadelphia, Jefferson was caught up in a whirlwind of war and the rumors of war. John Adams of Massachusetts had proposed the appointment of George Washington of Virginia as commanding general for the Continental forces, a choice the Congress approved on Thursday, June 15, 1775. Two days later came the battle at Bunker Hill in Boston.

What Jefferson had heard Patrick Henry assert in the nave of St. John's Church 250 miles south of Philadelphia in March was now fact. There was no peace.

Jefferson's arrival in Philadelphia was an occasion of note among the delegates. Samuel Ward of Rhode Island recorded seeing "the famous Mr. Jefferson," and said the Virginian "looks like a very sensible spirited fine fellow and by the pamphlet which he wrote last summer [the **Summary View**] he certainly is one." Later in the year John Adams reported a fellow delegate's view that "Jefferson is the greatest Rubber off of Dust that he has ever met with, that he has learned French, Italian, Spanish and wants to learn German."

Adams and Jefferson could hardly have appeared less alike. Adams was eight years older and about five inches shorter, as thoroughgoing a New Englander as Jefferson was a Virginian. Adams had difficulty holding his tongue or his temper; Jefferson was a master of keeping his emotions in check. Yet the two men—and, in time, Abigail, Adams's wonderful wife—were to forge one of the greatest and most complicated alliances in American history.

Born in Braintree, Massachusetts, in 1735, John Adams was the son of a farmer and public servant. Like Peter Jefferson, John Adams, Sr., loomed large to his son. Young Adams was educated at Harvard, considered but decided against becoming a Congregational minister, and made his mark as a lawyer in Boston in the tumultuous years leading to the American Revolution.

From 1775 until the politics of the first Washington administration drove them apart, Adams and Jefferson worked together often and well, particularly in their years as fellow American diplomats in Europe. Their falling-out over the direction of the nation in the 1790s and the first decade or so of the nineteenth century was profound, for their disagreements were deep. Yet after both men retired they would revive the friendship they formed in these early Philadelphia days. "I consider you and him as the North and South Poles of the American Revolution," their fellow Revolutionary Benjamin Rush wrote Adams in February 1812. "Some talked, some wrote, and some fought to promote and establish it, but you and Mr. Jefferson **thought** for us all."

Jefferson's proximity to the action and his new connections to delegates from the northern colonies, particularly Adams, grew into an intense admiration for New England. To read of valor is one thing. To live among those who are following the news of bloodshed in their homes, who have a direct stake in the outcome, is to experience conflict at a more fundamental level. The ethos of war was all around him.

One week after Jefferson came to the city the Congress authorized an invasion of Canada—a dramatic move that helped fix Canada's place firmly in Jefferson's political and military imaginations. Since the end of the French and Indian War in 1763, the British had occupied large sections of Canada, once known as New France. In the face of American invasion in 1775, Montreal surrendered but Quebec held out. The failure to conquer the whole territory effectively left it in British hands, and Canada became a haven for Loyalists. After the war, Canada was, in the American mind, a possible staging ground for a reassertion of British force and influence in the new United States.

Jefferson found an infectious courage in Philadelphia in 1775. "Nobody now entertains a doubt but that we are able to cope with the whole force of Great Britain, if we are but willing to exert ourselves," he wrote in July. They were high hopes, but Jefferson was in a noble frame of mind, believing the Americans capable of vigor and virtue.

Jefferson and John Dickinson, the author of **Letters from a Farmer in Pennsylvania,** consulted in these weeks at Dickinson's Fairhill estate outside Philadelphia on the Germantown Road. The result:

a Declaration of the Causes and Necessity for Taking Up Arms, which was adopted by the Congress on Thursday, July 6, 1775.

The next day, Jefferson slipped away from the Congress and rode the ferry to the Woodlands, the botanist William Hamilton's estate on the Schuylkill River. Hamilton and Jefferson shared a passion for landscape gardening. Walking the Woodlands on this summer's day, Jefferson was likely imaginatively engaged by visions of creation, of bringing the natural world into harmony with the human. He also made a trip to the falls of the Schuylkill for an outing and dinner.

Such excursions offered welcome, if brief, respites from politics and from war. On Saturday, July 8, 1775, having made the case for armed resistance with Dickinson and Jefferson's Declaration of Causes, the Congress extended its hand to the king, dispatching an "Olive Branch Petition" to London.

Nothing came of it.

Jefferson rarely spoke in large assemblies, preferring to make his mark in different ways. As accomplished a student of politics and of history as John Adams believed Jefferson benefited enormously from holding his tongue in debate. From all that Adams had read and all that he had experienced firsthand, he had learned, he said, "eloquence in public assemblies is not the surest road to fame and preferment, at least unless it be used with great caution, very rarely, and with great reserve." Classing Jefferson with George Washington and Benjamin Franklin, both of whom were also reluctant to speak at length in public, Adams said, "A public speaker who inserts himself, or is urged by others into the conduct of affairs, by daily exertions to justify his measures and answer the objections of opponents, makes himself too familiar with the public, and unavoidably makes himself enemies."

To write public papers or to negotiate quietly, away from the floor of an assembly or even away from a largish committee, enabled a politician to exert his will with less risk of creating animosity. "Few persons can bear to be outdone in reasoning or declamation or wit, or sarcasm or repartee or satire, and all these things are very apt to grow out of public debate," said Adams. "In this way in a course of years, a nation becomes full of a man's enemies, or at least of such as have been galled in some controversy, and take a secret pleasure in assisting to humble and mortify him."

Jefferson was reflective yet practical, confident yet realistic in the middle of the maelstrom of 1775. "The continuance and the extent of this conflict we consider as among the secrets of providence; but we also reflect on the propriety of being prepared for the worst events, and, so far as human foresight can provide, to be guarded against probable evils at least," he said. Perhaps "a few gentlemen of genius and spirit" should be sent to train under General Washington to learn the "necessary art" of war.

So much was unknowable, but the political language of war had to celebrate what had been done and offer hope for darker moments. Jefferson was mastering this complex vocabulary. He knew, clearly, that Virginia faced a "deficiency" of military skill—a skill that "in these days of rapine can only be relied upon for public safety." The use of "rapine" came from the lawyer in Jefferson. It was an ancient legal term for violent seizure of property, a rhetorical touch underscoring the view that anyone with property had a stake in the struggle.

After a visit to Robert Bell's shop on Third Street to buy a copy of James Burgh's book **Political Disquisitions**, Jefferson left Philadelphia for Virginia on Tuesday, August 1, 1775. He stopped along the road at Mrs. Clay's inn at New Castle, Delaware, then continued onward to Chestertown, Annapolis, and Port Royal en route home to Monticello.

In the absence of any surviving letters between Jefferson and his wife—the assumption is that he destroyed their correspondence in the interests of privacy—we can only guess about the tone they used with each other when apart. Given Jefferson's letters to his family and friends throughout his life, though, it is likely that he wrote to Patty in rather the way his contemporary Theodorick Bland, Jr., wrote his own wife. Bland was a Virginian, a physician, a politician, and a revolutionary. Writing his wife, also named Martha, from the front in New Jersey in 1777, Bland said: "For God's sake, my dear, when you are writing, write of nothing but yourself, or at least exhaust that dear, ever dear subject, before you make a transition to another; tell me of your going to bed, of your rising, of the hour you breakfast, dine, sup, visit, tell me of anything, but leave me not in doubt about your health. . . . Fear not . . . yes, 'you will again feel your husband's lips flowing with love and affectionate warmth.' Heaven never means to separate two who love so well, so soon; and if it does, with what transport shall we meet in heaven?"

With Patty, Jefferson had built the kind of marriage and life he wanted on the mountain. Music and dancing were essential. Jefferson never stopped humming, ordered an Aeolian harp, and paid £5 for a new violin. In memory he could hear his sister Jane's voice, singing. And in the moment he could sit and listen to Patty play the pianoforte or the harpsichord.

"Mrs. Jefferson was small," said the slave Isaac Granger Jefferson, and "pretty." She was also busy, both bearing children and presiding over the plantation during her husband's absences. Her account book tracks her daily work, including supervising the slaughter of ducks, turkeys, hogs, sheep, and lambs. She also managed the slaves in the house.

The "first" Monticello—Jefferson eventually tore down the house and started anew in the 1790s—was smaller than the second and final version, but it was still a grand place. "The house was built quite recently, in the latest **Italian** style," a visitor wrote of the first Monticello. "There is a colonnade around the structure and the frieze is very charmingly decorated with all kinds of sculptures drawn from mythology." He acquired a chessboard and pieces, a backgammon table, a refracting telescope, eight Venetian blinds, and Scotch carpet: He was always on the watch for lovely things—and always, always books. Even the first Monticello had, a visitor noted, "a copious and well-chosen library."

The house itself—"an elegant building," the visitor recalled—was only the most vivid expression of Jefferson's wide-ranging mind. From books to languages to music to entertaining to art to architecture, he was constantly learning, experiencing, experimenting, tasting, **living**: At Shadwell and at the Governor's Palace in Williamsburg he had been taught that there was a vast world to engage and shape.

His architectural sense was informed by, among other works, James Gibbs's **Rules for Drawing the Several Parts of Architecture** and an edition of **The Architecture of A. Palladio**. He mused on the painting scheme for his dining room, ordered a copy of Hannah Glasse's **Art of Cookery Made Plain and Easy,** and sent for a clothespress.

Jefferson had joined the Philosophical Society for the Advancement of Useful Knowledge, founded by Virginians (including his friend John Page) on the model of the American Philosophical Society, to which Jefferson was elected in 1780. In 1772, James McClurg, the future director of hospitals for Virginia during the Revolutionary War, published a book entitled **Experiments upon the Human Bile**. Jefferson bought a copy.

Following in the tradition of his kinsman John Randolph, the attorney general who lived in a beautiful house, Tazewell Hall, on a ninety-nine-acre estate on South England Street in Williamsburg, Jefferson was fascinated by gardening. Randolph, a Loyalist, owned perhaps the best violin in Virginia—Jefferson long envied it—and had written a book, **A Treatise on Gardening by a Citizen of Virginia**. The works of Philip Miller, Bernard McMahon, and Thomas Whately also influenced Jefferson's understanding of gardening and landscaping—an understanding centered on the idea of creating and controlling the illusion of wildness and of the natural.

In the summer of 1775, his Loyalist cousin John Randolph was on Jefferson's mind for reasons other than gardening. Writing to Randolph that August, Jefferson opened pleasantly, expressing regret that Randolph was leaving America for England and reminding him of his enduring admiration for Randolph's violin.

Then Jefferson moved to the real business of the letter: enlisting Randolph as an asset for the American cause. The British, Jefferson believed, were suffering from two fundamental misunderstandings of the American position. The first was that the discontent was concentrated within "a small faction" and was not shared by the broader population. Here Jefferson was shaping reality to suit his purposes. The American movement, while not limited to the elite, was still working its way through the social ranks.

The second matter on Jefferson's mind was visceral. "They have taken it into their heads too that we are cowards and shall surrender at discretion to an armed force," he said, adding, with a reserved pride, "The past and future operations of the war must confirm or undeceive them on that head." In sum, Jefferson wanted Randolph to present the colonists as a broad, united, and brave force that deserved more respect from London.

Jefferson was thinking in plain political terms. If America were thought to be divided and cowardly, then the British would have no incentive to negotiate. Weakness in the New World would create contempt in the Old.

Jefferson drafted but deleted an interesting threat from the Randolph letter. If Britain were to come to dominate the seaboard colonies militarily, Jefferson mused, there was another option. Perhaps the hardiest of Virginians might move "beyond the mountains," which suggested that Jefferson had been party to conversations about an extreme scenario in which the colonists devoted to the American cause might move to the interior of the continent.

It is an early example in Jefferson's papers of his envisioning the West as a source of liberty and a theater for reinvention. The specificity of the suggestion in the crisis of 1775 shows that he was thinking hard about the practical implications of rebellion and was open to the most dire contingencies should things go badly.

He did not want to leave Randolph with angry words. That would defeat the purpose of the letter, which was to use his departing kinsman as a conduit to influential people in London. In closing, Jefferson parted on a warm note: "My collection of classics and of books of parliamentary learning particularly is not so complete as I could wish. As you are going to the land of literature and of books you may be willing to dispose of some of yours here and replace them there in better editions. I should be willing to treat on this head with anybody you may think proper to empower for that purpose."

The subtext: We may be political opponents, but we are men of culture who share a love of common things. It was a shrewd touch of Jefferson's. The opening about the violin and the conclusion about the books made the intervening political assessments and assertions appear to be part of a natural conversation.

John Randolph read it as such. "Though we **may politically** differ in sentiments, yet I see no reason why **privately** we may not cherish the same esteem for each other which formerly I believe subsisted between us," Randolph wrote Jefferson on August 31, 1775. "Should any coolness happen between us, I'll take care not to be the first mover of it. We both of us seem to be steering opposite courses; the success of either lies in the womb of time."

Jefferson's letter served its purpose, finding its way from John Randolph to William Legge, 2nd Earl of Dartmouth, the British secretary of state for the colonies. Jefferson had accomplished what he had set out to achieve: present his views to the imperial powers in London.

Jefferson spent much of September 1775 at Monticello with his family. The interlude was tragic: His daughter Jane, only a year and a half old, died. After her loss his letters home while he was away were marked by an obsessive concern for Patty and for little Patsy, now his only living child.

The demands of his sense of public obligation, however, were great. He left the mountain for the Congress in Philadelphia on Monday, September 25, 1775.

Boarding again on Chestnut Street, Jefferson returned to the work of the Congress, but his mind was on Patty and Monticello. He depended on his wife, confiding in her on political matters. He wrote to her, too, of military affairs. Yet for him there was nothing but silence from home in this Philadelphia autumn. She was ill.

By Tuesday, October 31, 1775, he was even more worried about Patty. "I have set apart nearly one day in every week since I came here to write letters," he told his friend John Page. "Notwithstanding this I have never received the scrip of a pen from any mortal breathing."

Eight days later he was more desperate. "I have never received the scrip of a pen from any mortal in Virginia since I left it, nor been able by any enquiries I could make to hear of my family," he wrote a brother-in-law. "The suspense under which I am is too terrible to be endured. If anything has happened, for God's sake let me know it."

Jefferson's anxiety about his personal world extended to the political one as well. There were reports of gathering British strength—cannons en route from the Tower of London, two thousand troops from Ireland, frigates bound for the middle colonies. One target: Virginia.

And more specifically, Virginia planters. The naval forces, Jefferson said, were coming "at the express and earnest intercessions of Lord Dunmore, and the plan is to lay waste all the plantations of our river sides."

Little seemed cheering. On Sunday, October 22, 1775, an invitation for Jefferson to dine at Roxborough, the country house of the Philadelphia wine merchant Henry Hill, may have promised some shelter from the storms. It was a congenial company, headed by Peyton Randolph, whom Jefferson adored.

At Roxborough around four o'clock, Peyton Randolph suffered a stroke—Jefferson called it "apoplexy"—and lingered about five hours, dying at the Hills' at nine o'clock that evening.

For Jefferson, the emblem of a whole world—a world Jefferson had known forever and which he aspired to lead—was dead at an hour of great danger. Peyton Randolph had dominated Virginia from the House of Burgesses to the Raleigh Tavern to St. John's Church to the Pennsylvania State House. Jefferson always kept Randolph's example in mind, admiring the blend of conviction and amiability that enabled the man Jefferson called "our most worthy Speaker" to survive and thrive in the arena.

Peyton Randolph was dead, Patty Jefferson was sick, and a daughter had died: Jefferson was beset from seemingly every side. Then, in late October 1775, at Hampton, near Norfolk, Virginia, the British tried to land armed parties from British vessels to burn the town. Dunmore was in command of Norfolk, which gave the British a strategic base in a critical point of access. To the north, colonial troops under Benedict Arnold and Richard Montgomery were undertaking expeditions against

Canada. And in Virginia, the Virginia Convention, which was governing in the wake of Dunmore's dissolution of the House of Burgesses, created a Committee of Safety, a civilian body to oversee the state's military.

All that Jefferson loved was in peril. The eleven months preceding the Declaration of Independence were a contentious time in which nothing was certain in his family except Patty's ill health and in politics except conflict with overwhelming British force.

In Philadelphia, Jefferson absorbed account after account, written by his most intimate friends, of the depredations of a superior military force against Virginia. "We care not for our towns, and the destruction of our houses would not cost us a sigh," John Page wrote Jefferson, unconsciously echoing Jefferson's remark to him five years earlier after the Shadwell fire. "I have long since given up mine as lost."

Jefferson's political colleagues in the Pennsylvania State House were suffering the same fears over events in their own states. The human element of Jefferson's service in Philadelphia is sometimes minimized, with more attention paid to textual investigations of his resonant state papers. Yet the personal and the philosophical were intimately connected: The Jefferson of the summer of 1776 was shaped by the tensions and contests of 1775. What he read of the deteriorating relations with Dunmore and of the bloodshed and fears in Virginia steeled him for the war ahead.

November 7, 1775, is a forgotten date in the popular memory of the American Revolution, but the events of that autumn Tuesday in Virginia had much to do with those that culminated in the passage of the Declaration of Independence in Philadelphia the next year.

From his shipboard quarters at Norfolk, Dunmore declared martial law and directly challenged white Virginia, ordering that any slave or indentured servant who took up arms against the American Revolutionaries would be granted their freedom. Frightened white Virginians—and sympathetic whites in other colonies—suddenly saw their most fevered visions of slaves turning against masters threatening to become real. The announcement drove a number of those who had been previously lukewarm about independence into the Revolutionary camp.

Jefferson thought instantly of his family. If Dunmore succeeded in inspiring an army of slaves and indentured servants, then Monticello might not be safe. Jefferson made plans for Patty and his family to escape in the event of violence, plans that included his joining them in presumably safe territory. "I have written to Patty a proposition to keep yourselves at a distance from the alarms of Lord Dunmore," he wrote a brother-in-law in November.

As Jefferson crafted emergency measures for his family, word of Dunmore's strike swept up and down the eastern coast. In late November, John Page was both defiant and pleading. "For God's sake endeavor to procure us arms and ammunitions," Page wrote Jefferson from Virginia. Page feared the British—and he feared "an insurrection of the negroes."

There was something else, too: the sense that the property of Virginia's elites would fall into the hands of the British. "Some rascals, all **foreigners**, are already looking out for places and handsome seats," Virginia statesman Robert Carter Nicholas wrote Jefferson in late 1775. "No country ever required greater exertions of wisdom than ours does at present," Nicholas wrote Jefferson on November 25, 1775. "I fear no time is to be **lost**."

As the session of the Congress drew to a close, Jefferson was named to a committee "to Ascertain Unfinished Business before Congress." He found twenty-seven separate matters that required attention, from reports on currency and Indian affairs to the making of salt. A second Jefferson task: service on a panel charged with planning the powers of a proposed committee to govern during the congressional recess.

It was an instructive exercise, for it required Jefferson to analyze the role the Congress had been playing and discern which functions were essential. In a draft dated December 15, 1775, he listed nineteen duties he saw as crucial, ranging from supplying "the Continental forces by sea and land" to gathering "intelligence of the condition and designs of the enemy" to ensuring "the defense and preservation of forts and strong posts and to prevent the enemy from acquiring new holds." The emphasis on practical military matters was consistent with what had chiefly occupied Jefferson for months.

With even his own family in possible danger, he wanted to make it clear that the Americans were ready to exact an eye for an eye. Responding to reports that the American officer Ethan Allen had been captured in the Canadian campaign and was to be "sent to Britain in **irons,** to be **punished** for pretended treasons," Jefferson, in a draft declaration for Congress, said British prisoners would be held accountable for anything that happened to Allen. "We deplore the event which shall oblige us to shed blood for blood, and shall resort to retaliation but as the means of stopping the progress of butchery," he said—but Americans would do what had to be done.

In the end, though the Congress deferred any decision to George Washington, the threatening draft shows that Jefferson saw the world as it was.

Leaving Philadelphia on Thursday, December 28, 1775, he reached Monticello in the middle of

January. It was a new year when he rode up the mountain.

There were outward signs of life as usual. He opened a cask of 1770 Madeira and began to think about taking his wife back with him to Philadelphia to be inoculated against smallpox. But the enveloping crisis could not be kept at bay. On Sunday, February 4, 1776, he was sent a new pamphlet entitled **Common Sense.** "The cause of America is, in a great measure, the cause of all mankind," wrote Thomas Paine. Jefferson could not have agreed more.

NINE

The Course of Human Events

For God's sake declare the colonies independent at once, and save us from ruin.
—JOHN PAGE to Thomas Jefferson,
spring 1776

The bells rung all day and almost all night.
Even the chimers chimed away.
—JOHN ADAMS, describing the reaction
to the Declaration of Independence
in Philadelphia, 1776

AT ABOUT SEVEN O'CLOCK on the morning of
Sunday, March 31, 1776, Jefferson's mother,
Jane, fifty-five years old, was stricken with a
stroke and succumbed within an hour.

Jefferson asked the Reverend Charles Clay to preside over the funeral. Jane Randolph Jefferson was
buried at Monticello. In seeing that his mother was
put in ground he held sacred, near others he loved,
Jefferson made certain that she would always be
part of his home, and part of him.

Jane's death disoriented her son. Already immersed in the most difficult and fearful of political enterprises—revolution and the creation of a new form of government—Jefferson was brought face-to-face with one of the deepest personal crises a man can experience. In their parents, children ideally have sources of protection and comfort and love. Parents can also be sources of irritation, fear, and anxiety. Their deaths thus represent both loss and liberation.

The mix of the two emotions can be changeable depending on the hour or the year, but one thing is constant: The parent is gone, which means the child himself, at whatever age, is compelled to assume a measure of the weight of the world commensurate with the passing of time and the increase in responsibility. Though living a crowded and consequential life, Jefferson may have been a lonelier man on the day his mother died than he had ever been.

As he turned away from the graveyard, he was not leaving his mother behind. At moments of intense emotional distress Jefferson often suffered what he would call an "attack of my periodical headache," a migraine headache so debilitating and vicious that he once said he was "obliged to avoid reading, writing, and almost thinking." Before 1776, his last known bout had come in the wake of his heartbreak over Rebecca Burwell. With the death of Jane Randolph Jefferson, the blood and nerves in his brain gave him nothing but anguish. The force of her death was almost more than he could stand. The pain would not stop.

It was a strange time for Jefferson, who lived with the headache, the mourning, and the uncertainty about America's next step. He tried to stay engaged in the life of the plantation, paying a midwife to deliver Elizabeth Hemings's son John. He tried, too, to stay engaged in life beyond Monticello, collecting money for powder for Virginia and for the relief of the poor of Boston.

He left Monticello for Philadelphia on Tuesday, May 7, 1776, arriving seven days later. Patty stayed in Virginia. "I am here in the same uneasy anxious state in which I was the last fall without Mrs. Jefferson who could not come with me," Jefferson told his fellow Virginia politician Thomas Nelson, Jr. On May 23 he took quarters at a three-story house owned by the bricklayer Jacob Graff, Jr., on the southwest corner of Seventh and Market streets in Philadelphia.

He initially felt out of phase with the other delegates. They were speaking of matters he had missed while he had been in mourning at Monticello.

But he soon found himself at the center of everything.

At the end of the first week of June 1776, Richard Henry Lee of Virginia moved that the "United Colonies" were "absolved from all allegiance to the British Crown, and that all political connection between them and the state of Great Britain is, and ought to be, totally dissolved."

At last, the hour of decision was at hand. The debate over independence began the next day.

Congress was not chiefly concerned about the rights of man or even the shape of an American polity. History's trumpets were sounding, but only in the distance. The clatter that dominated the Pennsylvania State House in Philadelphia was about domestic politics and international relations at their most practical.

Some representatives argued that a precipitous declaration of independence might provoke some if not all of the middle colonies (Pennsylvania, Maryland, Delaware, and New York) to secede from the American cause. If there were such a domestic crack-up, Jefferson reported, "foreign powers would either refuse to join themselves to our fortunes, or having us so much in their power . . . they would insist on terms proportionately more hard and prejudicial."

John Adams, Richard Henry Lee, George Wythe, and others marshaled the evidence in favor of declaring independence. First, they noted that "no gentleman had argued against the policy or the right of separation from Britain, nor had supposed it possible we should ever renew our connection: that they had only opposed its being now declared."

A compromise was proposed. New York, New Jersey, Pennsylvania, Delaware, Maryland, and South Carolina were "not yet matured for falling from the parent stem," Jefferson said, and "it was thought most prudent to wait a while for them."

But not too long. A vote was put off three weeks, until the first of July. In the interim, so "that this might occasion as little delay as possible," Jefferson said, committees were appointed to draft a declaration, prepare a plan for the new government, and set guidelines for the negotiation of foreign alliances.

But who was best to draft the declaration, which was due for consideration and a vote in fewer than three weeks?

John Adams thought Jefferson should do it, a decision with roots in a secret conversation that had taken place two years before. In 1774, on the eve of the First Continental Congress, Benjamin Rush and a few other delegates had met the Massachusetts contingent on the outskirts of Philadelphia. Taking tea in a private room at an inn in Frankford, Pennsylvania, six miles from the city, Rush and his colleagues offered Adams and company some practical political counsel. "We were all suspected of having independence in view," Adams recalled long afterward, and Massachusetts seemed ahead of much of the rest of America. Adams continued:

Now, said they, you must not utter the word independence, nor give the least hint or insinuation of the idea, neither in Congress or any private conversation; if you do, you are undone;

for the idea of independence is as unpopular in Pennsylvania and in all the Middle and Southern States as the Stamp Act itself. No man dares to speak of it. Moreover, you are the representatives of the suffering state. Boston and Massachusetts are under a rod of iron. British fleets and armies are tyrannizing over you; you yourselves are personally obnoxious to them and all the friends of government; you have been long persecuted by them all; your feelings have been hurt, your passions excited; you are thought to be too warm, too zealous, too sanguine. You must be, therefore, very cautious. You must not come forward with any bold measures, you must not pretend to take the lead. You know Virginia is the most populous State in the Union. They are very proud of their ancient dominion, they call it; they think they have a right to take the lead, and the Southern States and Middle States too, are too much disposed to yield it to them.

Adams appreciated the straight talk. "This was plain dealing . . . and I must confess that there appeared so much wisdom and good sense in it, that it made a deep impression on my mind, and it had an equal effect on all my colleagues," he recalled.

Two years later, meeting with Jefferson in the early summer of 1776, Adams had what he called "the Frankfort advice" (the town was actually Frankford) in mind. To a correspondent who wondered why Jefferson had been invested with such responsibility, Adams wrote:

You inquire why so young a man as Mr. Jefferson was placed at the head of the committee for preparing a Declaration of Independence? I answer: It was the Frankfort advice, to place Virginia at the head of everything. . . . There were three committees appointed at the same time, one for the Declaration of Independence, another for preparing articles of confederation, and another for preparing a treaty to be proposed to France. Mr. Lee was chosen for the Committee of Confederation, and it was not thought convenient that the same person should be upon both. Mr. Jefferson came into Congress in June, 1775, and brought with him a reputation for literature, science, and a happy talent of composition. Writings of his were handed about, remarkable for the peculiar felicity of expression. Though a silent member in Congress, he was so prompt, frank, explicit, and decisive upon committees and in conversation—not even Samuel Adams was more so—that he soon seized upon my heart; and upon this occasion I gave him my vote, and did all in my power to procure the votes of others. I think he had one more vote than any other, and that placed him at the head of the committee. I had the next highest number, and that placed me the second. The committee met, discussed the subject, and then appointed Mr. Jefferson and me to make the draft, I suppose because we were the two first on the list.

As Adams recalled the ensuing conversation with Jefferson, the Virginian suggested that Adams himself write the draft.

"I will not," Adams said.

"You should do it," Jefferson said.

"Oh! no."

"Why will you not? You ought to do it."

"I will not."

"Why?"

"Reasons enough."

"What can be your reasons?"

"Reason first, you are a Virginian, and a Virginian ought to appear at the head of this business. Reason second, I am obnoxious, suspected, and unpopular. You are very much otherwise. Reason third, you can write ten times better than I can."

"Well, if you are decided, I will do as well as I can."

"Very well. When you have drawn it up, we will have a meeting."

In drafting the Declaration of Independence, Jefferson was to be both poetic and prosaic, creating sympathy for the larger cause while condemning Britain in compelling terms. His purpose, he said, was "not to find out new principles, or new arguments, never before thought of . . . but to place before mankind the common sense of the subject; in terms so plain and firm as to command their assent, and to justify ourselves in the independent stand we were compelled to take."

As he sat to write the declaration at Jacob Graff's house—he slept in one room and wrote in a private parlor across the stairs—Jefferson knew what had to be done, and he knew how to do it. He had thought much about the ends and means of independence. The document he wrote on a small wooden desk he designed flowed naturally from his character and his convictions. He later wrote: "Neither aiming at originality of principle or sentiment, nor yet copied from any particular and previous writing, it was intended to be an expression of the American mind, and to give to that expression the proper tone and spirit called for by the occasion."

The words of the declaration came to Jefferson amid the hectic pace of legislative life in a time of worry over war. Distilling an Enlightenment vision about the sanctity and centrality of the individual, he argued that self-government was part of the nature of things.

When in the course of human events it becomes necessary for one people to dissolve the political bands which have connected them with another, and to assume among the powers of the earth the separate and equal station to which the laws of nature and of nature's God entitle them, a decent respect to the opinions of mankind requires that they should declare the causes which impel them to the separation.

We hold these truths to be self-evident: that all men are created equal; that they are endowed by their creator with inalienable rights; that among these are life, liberty and the pursuit of happiness: that to secure these rights, governments are instituted among men, deriving their just powers from the consent of the governed; that whenever any form of government becomes destructive of these ends, it is the right of the people to alter or to abolish it, and to institute new government, laying its foundation on such principles, and organizing its powers in such form, as to them shall seem most likely to effect their safety and happiness.

He had the best of editors in private: "self-evident" was Benjamin Franklin's. In sum, Jefferson's draft was a political undertaking with a philosophical frame. It was produced in a particular moment by a politician to satisfy particular concerns for a particular complex of audiences: undecided Americans, soldiers in arms, and potential global allies.

He worked away in these summer days of 1776, dividing his time between writing in his quarters and executing congressional business. Congress ordered that the declaration be sent "to the several assemblies, conventions, and committees, or councils of safety, and to the several commanding officers of the continental troops; that it be proclaimed in each of the United States, and at the head of the army." Constituencies included readers in all of the colonies (especially in regions where opinion still tended against independence) and those in the armed service of the American cause. Hence Jefferson included a lengthy list of charges against King George III, some of which were obscure even to contemporaries.

Jefferson's influences were manifold. Locke, Montesquieu, and the philosophers of the Scottish Enlightenment were among them, as was James Wilson's pamphlet **Considerations on the Nature and Extent of the Authority of the British Parliament** and George Mason's Declaration of Rights, written for the Virginia constitution.

Jefferson had consulted, too, with Franklin and Adams. ("The enclosed paper has been read and with some small alterations approved of by the committee," Jefferson wrote in a note to Franklin, whose gout and boils were keeping him confined to his lodgings. "Will Doctor Franklin be so good as to peruse it and suggest such alterations as his more enlarged view of the subject will dictate?")

Jefferson spared nothing in his attacks on England and on George III, including harsh language condemning the slave trade. Despite his defeats on antislavery measures in Virginia, both in court and in the House of Burgesses, Jefferson tried once more to lead an American institution—in this case, the Continental Congress—to a relatively progressive position on slavery.

Yet he failed again. Adams long remembered these passages of Jefferson's.

> A meeting we accordingly had, and conned the paper over. I was delighted with its high tone and the flights of oratory with which it abounded, especially that concerning Negro slavery, which, though I knew his Southern brethren would never suffer to pass in Congress, I certainly never would oppose. . . .
>
> We reported it to the committee. . . . We were all in haste. Congress was impatient, and the instrument was reported, as I believe, in Jefferson's handwriting, as he first drew it. Congress cut off about a quarter of it, as I expected they would; but they obliterated some of the best of it, and left all that was exceptionable, if anything in it was.

The declaration was introduced on Friday, June 28, 1776, and debate began on Monday, July 1. As Adams remembered, large passages were cut, irritating Jefferson. "The pusillanimous idea that we had friends in England worth keeping terms with, still haunted the minds of many," he said. "For this reason those passages which conveyed censures on the people of England were struck out, lest they should give them offense."

The denunciation of slavery was also eliminated. "The clause, too, reprobating the enslaving [of] the inhabitants of Africa, was struck out in complaisance to South Carolina and to Georgia, who had never attempted to restrain the importation of slaves, and who on the contrary still wished to continue it," said Jefferson. "Our Northern brethren also I believe felt a little tender under those censures; for though their people have very few slaves themselves yet they had been pretty considerable carriers of them to others." He had tried anew on slavery and fallen short anew. His political instinct to fight only those battles he believed he could win now took even firmer hold.

Jefferson hated being edited by such a large group. He fairly writhed as he sat in the Pennsylvania State House, listening to member after member offering his thoughts, wanting to change this and cut that. Benjamin Franklin had sufficiently conquered his gout to attend the sessions. Sympathetic about Jefferson's evident distress, Franklin tried to soothe his young colleague, to whom every suggestion and demand on the floor was a fresh agony, as though each objection was directed not at the document but at Jefferson himself. As Franklin told Jefferson, "I have made it a rule, whenever in my power, to avoid becoming the draughtsman of papers to be reviewed by a public body." Yet for all his momentary discomfort, Jefferson exercised an extraordinary measure of power by taking on drafting duties: However many changes came in, it was still his voice at the core of the enterprise. And the author of the document saw his words as sacred. Describing the desk on which he wrote the declaration, Jefferson later said: "Politics as well as religion has its superstitions. These gaining strength with time may one day give imaginary value to this relic for its association with the birth of the Great Charter of our Independence."

On Tuesday, July 2, 1776, the delegates voted to adopt the resolution for independence. Two days later, on a pleasant summertime Thursday—at midday the temperature was 76 degrees—they ratified the declaration. (Jefferson recorded purchases he managed to make on the 4th: seven pairs of ladies' gloves and a thermometer.) Overnight the Philadelphia printer John Dunlap produced the approved text on broadside, creating the first set of published copies; on July 6, Benjamin Towne, publisher of **The Pennsylvania Evening Post**, ran the declaration on his front page.

The following Monday, July 8, the news was announced in Philadelphia in front of the State House; the crowd cheered, "God bless the free states of North America!"

It was a nervous time. The delegates knew they had committed themselves to a treasonous course. They relieved the tension where they could, in small moments of grim levity. Horseflies buzzed through the Pennsylvania State House from a nearby stable, Jefferson said in later years, bedeviling what James Parton called "the silk-stockinged legs of honorable members. Handkerchief in hand, they lashed the flies with such vigor as they could command . . . but the annoyance became at length so extreme as to render them impatient of delay, and they made haste to bring the momentous business to a conclusion."

Jefferson loved the story of an exchange between the fat Benjamin Harrison of Virginia and the wispy Elbridge Gerry of Massachusetts. "Gerry, when the hanging comes, I shall have the advantage; you'll kick in the air half an hour after it is all over with me!"

In later years there was much back-and-forth over the declaration and its significance, with John Adams, jealous of Jefferson's authorial fame, complaining that the declaration was "a theatrical show," not a substantive document. "Jefferson ran away with all the stage effect of that, i.e. all the glory of it," Adams remarked in 1811.

The revolutionary nature of Jefferson's words was, nevertheless, clear from the beginning. With the power of the pen, he had articulated a new premise for the government of humanity: that all men were created equal. He basically meant all white men, especially propertied ones, but the English philosopher Jeremy Bentham, for one, recognized the import of the document adopted in Philadelphia. Attacking the declaration from London, Bentham scoffed at the idea that every man had a natural, God-given right to "life, liberty, and the pursuit of happiness"; such assertions, Bentham said, were "absurd and visionary," and he likened the American political thinking to the old New England fury over witchcraft.

" 'All men,' they tell us, 'are created equal,' " Bentham wrote. "This surely is a new discovery; now, for the first time, we learn, that a child, at the moment of his birth, has the same quantity of natural power as the parent, the same quantity of political power as the magistrate."

Ultimately, though, this was the essential American view. Bentham had read Jefferson right. Jefferson's pride in authorship, meanwhile, was contemporaneous and clear. He dispatched copies of his original version to friends. "You will judge whether it is the better or worse for the critics," he wrote a colleague. His friend John Page reassured Jefferson by complimenting him, and then Page suggested, gently, that the event of independence transcended the querulous editors of the Pennsylvania State House. "I am highly pleased with your Declaration," said Page. "God preserve the United States. We know the race is not to the swift nor the battle to the strong. Do you not think an angel rides in the whirlwind and directs this storm?"

TEN

The Pull of Duty

I pray you to come. I am under a sacred obligation to go home.

—THOMAS JEFFERSON to
Richard Henry Lee, 1776

Rebellion to tyrants is obedience to God.
—American motto suggested by Jefferson

IN 1776, WITH JEFFERSON at work in the cause
of the nation in Philadelphia, Patty suffered a
disastrous miscarriage. In the same days and
weeks in which he drafted the Declaration of Independence, Jefferson could not rest easy about his
wife, desperately watching out for letters from her
hand. "I wish I could be better satisfied on the point
of Patty's recovery," he wrote a brother-in-law in July
1776. "I had not heard from her at all for two posts
before, and no letter from herself now."

Jefferson hated not hearing, and he feared the

worst. His 1772 marriage had proved an enviable one; Patty Jefferson was a good and loving wife. She was, a granddaughter wrote, "a favorite with her husband's sisters (we all know that this is a delicate and difficult relation), with his family generally, and with her neighbors. . . . She commanded his respect by her good sense and domestic virtues, and his admiration and love by her wit, her vivacity, and her agreeable person and manners."

Jefferson knew that it was his duty to remain in Philadelphia, and he felt inescapably drawn to political life. Still, he longed to be home with his wife and family.

When we think of Jefferson in Philadelphia in the summer of 1776, we think of a philosopher at work with a quill pen and an agile mind shaped by, and suffused with, Enlightenment ideas about the rights of man. The drafting of the Declaration of Independence, however, was only one of many things that Jefferson did and that happened around him in those critical months. The onslaught of military reports, wartime supply issues, and intelligence and rumor about subversion from within taught him about the centrality of national security, the dangers of conspiracy, and the eternal need to manage public opinion.

The work was exhausting. The politics of the moment were fraught with fears over conspiracies, of

Loyalists plotting at home, and of Indian attacks on the frontier. Nothing—and no one—was to be counted on.

It was a season of schemes and secrets. In late June came word of a Loyalist plot in New York within the Continental army to kill George Washington and desert the American cause. The mayor of New York was said to be part of the conspiracy. A member of Washington's personal bodyguard detail was condemned to death. The British, meanwhile, were gathering force.

Depressed and harried, Jefferson could find little good news. "Our camps recruit slowly, amazing slowly," he told Richard Henry Lee in July. "God knows in what it will end."

In the context of the time—the drafting of the declaration, which was treason, and the ongoing, not particularly successful military operations—the atmosphere in America was charged. On learning that he had received the fewest votes of any Virginia incumbent in his reelection to the Continental Congress, Jefferson assumed that he had been criticized and undermined at home. "It is a painful situation to be 300 miles from one's country, and thereby open to secret assassination without a possibility of self-defense," he said.

Jefferson believed the work of his hands would vindicate him. "If any doubt has arisen as to me, my country will have my political creed in the form of a 'Declaration etc' which I was lately directed to draw."

Virginians were particularly frustrated by a war with the Cherokees. Jefferson's views of Native Americans were a bit more nuanced than those of many of his fellow white contemporaries, but only a bit. Fascinated by Indian language and culture, Jefferson often sought artifacts and information to satisfy a genuine curiosity about America's original inhabitants. He believed Indians a noble race. At his core, though, Jefferson shared the prevailing views of white landowners: that Indian lands were destined to belong to whites, and the Indians themselves should be inculcated in the ways of the whites.

Tribes who allied with Britain (or with any of the other European powers) were direct threats to the Revolutionary enterprise. In August 1776, Jefferson reacted viscerally to word of Cherokee assaults to the south. "Nothing will reduce those wretches so soon as pushing the war into the heart of their country," Jefferson wrote. "But I would not stop there. I would never cease pursuing them while one of them remained on this side of the Mississippi." It was a telling reaction, one that foreshadowed the fate of a race.

In the summer of 1776 Jefferson spent time planning for the difficult work of government. In one case he wrote a proposed constitution for Virginia. In another, he closely followed the Congress's debates over a national government and the content of what Jefferson referred to as "the articles of confederation."

Jefferson also helped draft rules of procedure for the Congress. His suggestions speak to a hunger for order and the appearance of civility: "No Member shall read any printed paper in the House during the sitting thereof without Leave of the Congress." Another: "No Member in coming into the House or in removing from his Place shall pass between the President and the Member then speaking." And another: "When the House is sitting no Member shall speak [or whisper] to another as to interrupt any Member who may be speaking in the Debate."

Jefferson believed civility an important political virtue, and he largely practiced what he preached. He and John Adams once disagreed on the floor over a proposal to call for a day of prayer. Though he had seen the good uses of public appeals to religious sentiments in Virginia, Jefferson grew ever more uncomfortable with frequent political resorts to orthodox belief. "You rose and defended the motion, and in reply to Mr. Jefferson's objections to Christianity you said you were sorry to hear such sentiments from a gentleman whom you so highly respected and with whom you agreed upon so many subjects, and that it was the only instance you had ever known of a man of sound sense and real genius that was an enemy to Christianity," Benjamin Rush recalled to Adams years later. "You suspected, you told me, that you had offended him, but that he soon convinced you to the contrary by crossing the room and taking a seat in the chair next to you."

Jefferson understood a timeless truth: that politics is kaleidoscopic, constantly shifting, and the morning's foe may well be the afternoon's friend.

His wife's health remained such a concern that Jefferson sought to leave Philadelphia to return to Patty in Virginia. "I receive by every post such accounts of the state of Mrs. Jefferson's health, that it will be impossible for me to disappoint her expectation of seeing me at the time I have promised, which supposed my leaving this place on the 11th of next month," he wrote Richard Henry Lee. The letter finished, Jefferson added a postscript begging Lee to come relieve him.

Yet Jefferson had to stay to keep Virginia's quorum. He hated it. "I am under the painful necessity of putting off my departure, notwithstanding the unfavorable situation of Mrs. Jefferson's health," he told John Page in August.

There is no mistaking how significant Jefferson and his colleagues believed the scale of the American struggle to be. One of Jefferson's duties in Philadelphia was the design of a seal for the new nation, a task he shared with Benjamin Franklin and John Adams.

Reacting to a proposal of Franklin's that invoked the parting of the Red Sea, Jefferson suggested: "Pharaoh sitting in an open chariot, a crown on his head and a sword in his hand passing through the divided waters of the Red Sea in pursuit of the Israelites: rays from a pillar of fire in the cloud, expressive of the divine presence, and command, reaching to Moses who stands on the shore and, extending his hand over the sea, causes it to overwhelm Pharaoh. Motto: Rebellion to tyrants is obedience to God." The Founders were Moses; George III was Pharaoh; Americans were the Israelites being led from bondage.

In truth the British demands on the colonists were hardly outrageous. The expense of defending the borders was considerable; American wealth was substantial; and Edmund Burke made a compelling case in London for "virtual representation"—the argument that the king and Parliament were stewards of the whole empire whether particular colonists could vote for members of the House of Commons or not.

So why did the colonists take such extreme steps—arming themselves and putting their lives and their families' lives at risk? There is no single answer. The intellectual and political legacy of the English Civil War was vital, for it was both a beacon and a warning. John Locke and others articulated what became known as the liberal tradition—the collection of insights and convictions that emphasized individual freedom in civic, economic, and religious life. The classical republican ethos that centered on virtue, harmony, balance, and fear of corruption had come to the Anglo-American world through Renaissance Florence, where Machiavelli and others sought to preserve the best of the ancient republics. The revivals of the First Great Awakening were critical, too, for the preaching of the mid-eighteenth century tended to focus on the centrality of the individual soul in relation to God. It was a Protestant movement, and for all its variations, Protestantism was largely about the importance of all believers, not the importance of priests and bishops and ecclesiastical systems. Then there was capitalism and its discontents. Americans were blessed with enormous natural resources and endless economic energy, yet many—including Jefferson—found themselves in perpetual debt to British creditors.

Succeeding generations have sometimes tried to isolate one of these phenomena as the origin of the Revolution. It seems most convincing, though, to think of Lockean liberalism, classical republicanism (via the Renaissance), the Great Awakening, the promise of capitalism, and the hatred of debt (and the British merchants and banks who were owed the debts) as tributaries that all helped form the larger rushing river of the American Revolution.

The debate over declaring independence took on such significance in part because a permanent break with London was not foreordained. For years colonists chose to believe that the monarchy was in the hands of nefarious, anti-American ministers. The hope from the 1750s to 1776 was that somehow the sovereign would put things to rights. It is a measure of the confidence Jefferson had in this possibility, for instance, that he maintained a tone of respect and deference to George III in his 1774 **Summary View**. And it is a measure of the depth of his sense of betrayal and disappointment in the king that the Declaration of Independence struck such virulent antimonarchical notes.

Jefferson's service in the Congress in 1776 left him thoroughly versed in the ways and means of politics. He had defined an ideal in the declaration, using words to transform principle into policy, and he had lived with the reality of managing both a war and a fledgling government. A politician's task was to bring reality and policy into the greatest possible accord with the ideal and the principled. It was a task that Jefferson, at the age of thirty-three, had found that he liked. He had found out something else, too. He was good at it.

The leaves were just beginning to turn as Jefferson rode from Philadelphia to Monticello in the early autumn of 1776. At home on the mountaintop, he was relieved to be with his wife and with little Patsy, who celebrated her fourth birthday in the last week of September.

The action, though, was elsewhere—in Philadelphia, of course, and in Williamsburg, where state delegates were at work on creating a new government for Virginia. Jefferson had long been exultant about the prospect of building a new Virginian order. He longed to be in the thick of shaping the government once led by Peyton Randolph and mastered by Wythe.

Torn between the joys and demands of family and the demands and excitements of statecraft, he quickly found that his thoughts and emotions changed with the hour: **I must go home; I must engage; I must go home; I must engage,** and back and forth, and back and forth. His wife was still in precarious health, her frequent pregnancies exacerbating matters.

In Williamsburg, meanwhile, there was the remaking of Virginia; in Philadelphia, the making of a nation; and everywhere there was war.

His contemporaries believed Jefferson essential. The Virginia lawyer Edmund Pendleton looked forward to having Jefferson back in Williamsburg as the work of the new government began. "I hope you'll get cured of your wish to retire so early in life from the memory of man, and exercise your talents for the nurture of our new constitution, which will require all the attention of its friends to prune exuberances and cherish the plant," Pendleton wrote. Virginia needed him.

Jefferson decided he could serve in Williamsburg and still be attentive to his family. He and Patty accepted an offer from George and Elizabeth Wythe to use the Wythe house on the green in Williamsburg. This meant that Jefferson could take his family with him to Williamsburg, an arrangement that was not possible in far-off Philadelphia. The young family settled into the handsome brick house, giving Jefferson a rare hour of balance between his public and private lives. He spent his nonworking hours with Patty and Patsy. They slept upstairs, entertained on the first floor, and enjoyed the symmetrical gardens.

It was perfect.

But only for a moment.

PART III
REFORMER AND GOVERNOR

LATE 1776 to 1782

Those who expect to reap the blessings of freedom, must, like men, undergo the fatigues of supporting it.

—THOMAS PAINE, September 11, 1777

In Virginia, the Battle of Yorktown marked the end of the Revolutionary War, but only after a difficult period of British invasion that Jefferson failed to combat effectively in his years as governor.

ELEVEN

An Agenda for Liberty

> It is error alone that needs the support of government. Truth can stand by itself.
>
> —THOMAS JEFFERSON,
> on freedom of religion

IN WILLIAMSBURG, Jefferson soon faced a new decision. The Congress needed reliable men to represent America's interests in France and elected a delegation to go to Paris to make an alliance between the French and the Americans. On the floor of the Pennsylvania State House, the representatives chose to entrust the mission to Benjamin Franklin of Pennsylvania, to Silas Deane of Connecticut—and to Thomas Jefferson of Virginia.

Without a successful alliance with France, the outmatched Americans were likely to lose the war. Britain was simply too strong. There were worries, moreover, that Russia might dispatch troops to aid the British, overwhelming the patriots. Writing as president of the Congress, John Hancock assumed Jefferson's acceptance of the mission to

France, asking him "to acquaint me, by the return of the express . . . at what time and place it will be most convenient for you to embark." The express reached Jefferson in Williamsburg, where he was with his family and at work on the new government of Virginia.

He asked the messenger to await his reply.

Thus began three days of agony. One of the benefits of being in Williamsburg was that Patty could be with him. Given her health, she could not go to France. If he went to Paris, he would be making a decision that would separate them once more. How could he sail the Atlantic, and possibly never see her again?

Yet how could Jefferson say no to one of the great assignments—one of the great honors—of the age? Power, drama, glamour were at hand; all could be savored while he was engaged in serious, essential public service. He had long traveled the world in his imagination. Here was the opportunity to do it not only in dreams but in fact.

The messenger waited. It was temptation on a sweeping scale. Jefferson loved the esteem the selection implied. "It would argue great insensibility in me could I receive with indifference so confidential an appointment from your body," he would write Hancock. "My thanks are a poor return for the partiality they have been pleased to entertain for me." He veered back and forth, talking himself first into one decision, then into another. He could not leave his family; might he bring them with him after all?

Not, he thought, with Patty's health. As excruciating as it was, he made his choice.

Jefferson loved his family; he loved Virginia; he loved his nascent nation. Raised in a tight-knit universe of kith and kin, accustomed to spending his hours reading in his father's first-floor library, singing on the banks of the Rivanna with his sister Jane, and learning to supervise his lands at his mother's side, he cherished his domestic worlds while being simultaneously drawn to politics.

In the fall of 1776, he could not have both in France; he could in Virginia.

He called the messenger. "No cares for my own person, nor yet for my private affairs would have induced one moment's hesitation to accept the charge," he wrote in a note to Hancock. "But circumstances very peculiar in the situation of my family, such as neither permit me to leave nor to carry it, compel me to ask leave to decline a service so honorable and at the same time so important to the American cause."

Jefferson spent the period after the writing of the Declaration of Independence learning how to translate ideas about human nature into political action. Like the Day of Fasting and Prayer resolution during the Stamp Act crisis, the declaration had taught him the power of language in the art of leadership. To project a vision of what might be and to inspire people to share that vision was, and is, an essential element of statesmanship. So, too, was the capacity to exert one's will in the legislative arena, convincing other politicians to enlist in a cause.

October 1776 marked the beginning of Jefferson's pursuit of a remarkable legislative agenda for liberty in Virginia. With Patty in Williamsburg with him, he fought to transform the promise of the Declaration of Independence into reality in a series of bills in the new General Assembly.

For him politics was informed by philosophy, but one could achieve the good only by putting philosophy into action. To do so required the acquisition of power. He moved carefully in Williamsburg, first introducing bills in order to test "the strength of the general pulse of reformation." Satisfied that the lawmakers were, in fact, interested in a new order, Jefferson pressed on—but only after becoming sure of his ground.

As a delegate to the General Assembly in Williamsburg and through his consistent work among his fellow Virginians, cajoling and seeking to convince, Jefferson put himself in a position to effect genuine change—to make the world into something it had not been before.

Jefferson's first significant initiative in Williamsburg in the fall of 1776 was a strike against entail and primogeniture, ancient conventions under which large landowners were compelled to pass their property to a single heir, creating, in Jefferson's words, "a distinct set of families, who, being privileged by law in the perpetuation of their wealth were thus formed into a patrician order, distinguished by the splendor and luxury of their establishments." Jefferson had benefited from just this system but believed the greater good demanded reform.

No part of the legal code governing life in Virginia went unexamined. There were bills altering criminal justice by ending the harshest of punishments (including limiting the death penalty to murder and treason); for creating a system of general public education to broaden opportunities for many white Virginians; for speeding the naturalization of the foreign-born into citizens (Jefferson favored a two-year residence requirement).

As he worked, Jefferson took note of a newcomer on the political scene, a young, diminutive man who had grown up near Orange, Virginia, about thirty miles northeast of Charlottesville. He was twenty-five; Jefferson was thirty-three. He was small; Jefferson was tall. He was assiduously understated; Jefferson was given to making grand pronouncements.

The newcomer, James Madison, was to become Thomas Jefferson's most trusted and invaluable counselor. Born in 1751 to tobacco-growing gentry, Madison had gone north to be educated at the College of New Jersey (later Princeton University). Quiet, intense, and tireless, Madison "acquired a habit of self-possession, which placed at ready command the rich resources of his luminous and discriminating mind, and of his extensive information, and rendered him the first of every assembly afterwards, of which he became a member," Jefferson recalled.

When Madison became Jefferson's successor as president of the United States three and a half decades later, the writer Washington Irving would describe him as "but a withered little apple-John." In Madison's case appearances were misleading. Despite his small stature, Madison possessed a powerful political personality. As Jefferson once observed: "Never wandering from his subject into vain declamation, but pursuing it closely, in language pure, classical, and copious, soothing always the feelings of his adversaries by civilities and softness of expression," Madison rose to national greatness—and through loyal and wise counsel, Madison was an invaluable architect of Jefferson's own career.

Their first battle together was waged in Virginia over freedom of religion. As a student of William Small's at William and Mary, Jefferson had become a reader of several Enlightenment-era skeptics about traditional Christianity. (Madison shared Jefferson's convictions about the necessity of freedom of conscience.) Jefferson had come to believe the apostolic faith was superstitious and therefore unreasonable—one of the most damning of Jeffersonian indictments.

In his **Notes on the State of Virginia,** a book written a few years after his service revising the laws in the General Assembly, Jefferson was honest about his state's abysmal record on liberty of conscience. It was a crime in Virginia not to baptize infants in the Anglican church; dissenters were denied office, civil or military; children could be taken from their parents if the parents failed to profess the prescribed creeds. It was said that James Madison heard Baptist ministers preaching from prison in these years. The church was all too evidently an institution as susceptible to corruption as any other. In 1767, Jefferson was involved in a case in which the parishioners of St. Anne's in Albemarle—the Monticello parish—sought to remove the Reverend John Ramsay for drunkenness and the attempted seduction of a woman not his wife. One allegation: that Ramsay "got drunk with the sacrament wine."

Though Jefferson had long cultivated a skeptical religious worldview, he undertook his work in the General Assembly because of freedom, not because of a lack of faith. In political terms, Jefferson believed it unjust (and unwise) to use public funds to support an established church and to link civil rights to religious observance. He said such a system led to "spiritual tyranny." In theological terms, according to notes he made on John Locke, Jefferson concurred with a Christian tradition that held the church should not depend on state-enforced compulsion. Summarizing Locke, Jefferson wrote that "our Savior chose not to propagate his religion by temporal punishments or civil incapacitation"; had Jesus chosen to do so, "it was in his almighty power" to force belief. Instead, "he chose to . . . extend it by its influence on reason, thereby showing to others how [they] should proceed." Or as Jefferson's notes on the issue say:

Obj[ection]. Religion will decline if not supported
Ans[wer]. Gates of Hell shall not prevail

It did not speak well of the power of God, in other words, if He needed a human government to prop him up.

Dissenters across Virginia petitioned the assembly for relief from legislated fealty to the Anglican Church in the autumn of 1776. The cries for religious liberty, Jefferson recalled, "brought on the severest contests in which I have ever been engaged." Edmund Pendleton and Robert Carter Nicholas—"honest men, but zealous churchmen," as Jefferson called them—supported the established church. It took incremental legislation and several years, but in the end, in 1786, a statute for religious liberty from Jefferson's pen became law. The bill, Jefferson said, was "meant to comprehend, within the mantle of its protection, the Jew and the Gentile, the Christian and Mahometan, the Hindoo, and infidel of every denomination."

———————

Slavery was perhaps the only issue as emotionally and politically charged in Virginia as religion. Jefferson's experience with the question of emancipation in the General Assembly affirmed the tragic view that he had come to when he had earlier failed to make progress against slavery in the House of Burgesses—a view further validated when the delegates to the Continental Congress had cut his attack on the slave trade from the Declaration of Independence.

At the General Assembly, as part of the revisal of the laws, Jefferson and his allies prepared an amendment stipulating "the freedom of all [slaves] born after a certain day, and deportation at a proper age"—deportation because it was inconceivable to Jefferson that free whites and free blacks could live together peaceably.

Recalling the episode in his retirement at Monticello after he served as president, Jefferson wrote, "It was found that the public mind would not yet bear the proposition [of emancipation and deportation], nor will it bear it even at this day." Jefferson took a bleak view. "Yet the day is not distant when it must bear and adopt it, or worse will follow," he wrote in retirement, reflecting on the General Assembly days. "Nothing is more certainly written in the book of fate, than that these people are to be free; nor is it less certain that the two races, equally free, cannot live in the same government. Nature, habit, opinion have drawn indelible lines of distinction between them."

Jefferson was never able to move public opinion on slavery. His powers failed him—and they failed America.

Whether there would be an independent America to stand "among the powers of the earth" (as Jefferson had put it in the Declaration of Independence) at all was an open question as 1776 ended. The year closed much as it had begun: in uncertainty and danger. "The enemy," a correspondent told Jefferson from the American camp on the Delaware River, were "like locusts."

George Washington's army did what it could, but the military situation was dire. "No man . . . ever had a greater choice of difficulties and less means of extricating himself than I have," Washington said at the end of the year. The American enterprise seemed unlikely to survive the winter.

Worries about destruction from British forces within were constant. Richard Henry Lee told Jefferson of reports that Germany was attempting to supply Tories in Connecticut, New York, and New Jersey. The plan, Lee told Jefferson, was for the British officer John Burgoyne, with "10,000 men chiefly Germans," to attack Virginia and Maryland. "The Southern and Middle colonies [were then] to be put under **military government**."

His work in Williamsburg at the General Assembly done for the season, Jefferson moved his family—Patty was again pregnant—back to Monticello, where, on Wednesday, May 28, 1777, Patty gave birth to a son.

The little boy lived only seventeen days. If the Jeffersons gave him a name it does not survive. In their grief they sought consolation in each other, for Patty was soon pregnant again. At home on the first of August 1778, at one-thirty in the morning, Patty gave birth to a little girl who was baptized Mary and called Polly. She was to become the only child of Mr. and Mrs. Thomas Jefferson other than her older sister Patsy to survive into adulthood.

Despite her illnesses and pregnancies, Patty Jefferson remained resilient, recording the domestic details of life at Monticello in an account book. Her handwriting was strong and clear. There are doodles, too, suggesting a dreaminess and an active imagination. Like her husband, she had a perfectionist streak. According to a granddaughter, a book of music that Patty Jefferson copied down was "free from blot and blemish"—which, taken together with her notes on the household, "told of neatness, order, good housewifery and womanly accomplishment." The description went on: "She was not only an excellent housekeeper and notable mistress of a family, but a graceful, ladylike and accomplished woman, with considerable powers of conversation, some skill in music, all the habits of good society, and the art of welcoming her husband's friends to perfection."

Patty engaged with the war effort. Replying to a request from Martha Washington to sew clothes and supply the army, Patty enlisted James Madison's mother, Eleanor Conway Madison, to help as well. "Mrs. Washington has done me the honor of communicating the enclosed proposition of our sisters of Pennsylvania and of informing me that the same grateful sentiments are displaying themselves in Maryland," Patty wrote. "Justified by the sanction of her letter in handing forward the scheme I undertake with cheerfulness the duty of furnishing to my countrywomen an opportunity of proving that they also participate of those virtuous feelings which gave birth to it."

The soldiers needed what they could get, for the Revolutionary War was about to come south with ferocity. In Baltimore, Thomas Nelson unsuccessfully tried to take a cheerier view. "Could we but get a good regular army we should soon clear the continent of these damned invaders," Nelson had written Jefferson in January 1777. "They play the very Devil with the girls and even old women to satisfy their libidinous appetites. There is scarcely a virgin to be found in the part of the country that they have passed through."

The sense of threat was constant. "We have pretty certain intelligence that a considerable reinforcement (the N. York papers of the 1st of May say 8000 men) will be sent over immediately," a correspondent wrote Jefferson in May 1779, "and if so there will, no doubt, be an active campaign, which it is generally supposed will be chiefly confined to the southern states, where we are the most vulnerable—and from thence the enemy can more easily withdraw their troops to the West Indies, if occasion should require it."

Amid rising concerns over British designs to invade and subjugate Virginia as a critical element in London's bid to defeat the American rebellion and restore order in the empire, Thomas Jefferson was elected governor of Virginia, succeeding Patrick Henry as chief executive.

In accepting the post Jefferson was explicit about the significance he saw in the good opinion of the public. "In a virtuous and free state, no rewards can be so pleasing to sensible minds, as those which include the approbation of our fellow citizens," Jefferson wrote. His "great pain," he said, was the fear that "my poor endeavors should fall short of the kind expectations of my country."

The balloting had pitted John Page against Jefferson. In the first round, Jefferson led 55–38, and Thomas Nelson had 32. In a runoff between Jefferson and Page, Jefferson won 67–61.

After two decades of friendship, Jefferson and John Page were compelled to explain themselves to each other, pledging that neither harbored any of

what Page called "low dirty feelings" over the gubernatorial election. Page had been unable to see
Jefferson since the balloting and, scheduled to be
away from Williamsburg for a brief time, he wanted
the new governor to understand he was not avoiding such a meeting. "I can assure you . . . that were
it not for the world who may put a wrong construction on my conduct I should scarcely trouble you
with this apology," Page told Jefferson on Wednesday, June 2, 1779.

Jefferson replied that "it had given me much pain
that the zeal of our respective friends should ever
have placed you and me in the situation of competi-
tors. I was comforted however with the reflection
that it was their competition, not ours, and that the
difference of the numbers which decided between
us, was too insignificant to give you a pain or me a
pleasure [had] our dispositions towards each other
been such as to have admitted those sensations."

By pointing out the narrowness of the margin between the two, Jefferson was trying to soothe his
friend's feelings, but he knew that no one likes to
come up short in any contest. Picking up on Page's
allusion to the opinion of others, Jefferson sought
to create a sense of unbreakable camaraderie with
his friend: "I know you too well to need an apology for anything you do, and hope you will be forever assured of this; and as to the constructions of
the world, they would only have added one to [the
many sig]ns for which they [are] to go to the devil."

However kind the two men were to each other, though, the contest had still been a contest, with one winner and one loser. Jefferson, who knew how he would have felt had the results been reversed and who hated such tensions, moved to assuage Page. "As this is the first, so I hope it will be the last instance of ceremony between us," he wrote, adding that Mrs. Page's company in Williamsburg would be one of the only consolations for Patty when she came to the capital.

Jefferson wanted familiar faces around him, people he could trust, as he assumed his post. Isaac Granger Jefferson recalled riding down to Williamsburg in a wagon; James Hemings, Robert Hemings, and Martin Hemings came, too.

Governor Jefferson was to serve for two years, from June 1779 until June 1781. He was to preside over the destiny of his beloved Virginia at a time when the future of everything he cared about was at risk.

TWELVE

A Troublesome Office

They certainly mean another campaign, a last effort; as Georgia and South Carolina, with the frontiers and sea coasts appear to be their objects at present.

> —RICHARD HENRY LEE,
> on British military plans, 1779

I am thoroughly satisfied that the attachment of the people to the cause in which we are engaged and their hatred to Great Britain remain unshaken.

> —THOMAS JEFFERSON, amid rising
> military pressures from the British

They formed in line and marched up to the palace with drums beating; it was an awful sight—seemed like the Day of Judgment was come.

> —ISAAC GRANGER JEFFERSON,
> describing the British attack on Richmond,
> January 1781

IN WILLIAMSBURG, the royal Governor's Palace of Thomas Jefferson's youth—that enormous residence on the green, with its elaborate gardens—was to be his. Hardly twenty years had passed since Jefferson had been a fortunate guest of Francis Fauquier's, dining and talking and listening and playing music, a student in the presence of greater, more learned, and more powerful men. Now Jefferson was thirty-six, a husband, a father, the governor of Virginia, and a statesman of the United States of America.

Jefferson's two-year tenure as governor would be consumed with the threat and then the reality of British invasion. Up until this point, military concerns in Virginia had centered on threats by proxy (Indians, slaves), not direct danger from the full force of British troops. The war in Virginia had been real but still somehow abstract—more theoretical than tangible—from the time of Dunmore to 1779–81.

That had changed not long before Jefferson took office. Georgia had collapsed after the British attacked Savannah. South Carolina was next for the British troops.

For a man who loved control and appreciated order and harmony, Jefferson found himself facing the most disorderly and chaotic of crises: a two-front war. The regular British were a force to the east; to the west Jefferson had to contend with British soldiers and their Indian allies based in Detroit.

As he walked the halls and surveyed the grounds of the palace, listening to the conversation of his wife and the voices of his children, he could not have helped but hear the echoes of his education in these rooms and at these tables. By any standard, Jefferson's rise had been rapid, and the man who took over the governorship of Virginia in the early summer of 1779 was ambitious but not blindly so. Power meant much to him, but he cloaked his driven nature with a mien of intellectual curiosity and aristocratic confidence.

Like many legislators, Jefferson was ambivalent about executive power—until he bore executive responsibility. He emerged from his wartime governorship with a different view of authority than the one he had held on first accepting the office, and with a deeper appreciation of the perils and possibilities of command. His sense of the price of public service was also to become keener than it had been. Jefferson foresaw years of "intense labor and great private loss" ahead, and by "loss" he meant more than money. The approval and esteem that led to election rarely endured, and Jefferson knew that few men left office with the standing they enjoyed on entering it.

From Philadelphia, a correspondent sent qualified salutations. "I will not congratulate you, but my country on their choice of a chief magistrate," the writer told Jefferson. "It will break in on your domestic plan and you'll find it a troublesome office during the war." Jefferson would indeed.

From captives to defense to frontier security to suppressing Tory dissent, Governor Jefferson proved himself capable of making difficult, even harsh, decisions.

The capture of Henry Hamilton, the Irish-born British commander of Fort Detroit, offered one such case. Reputed to have given bounties to Indians for white scalps—hence his nickname "the Hair Buyer General"—Hamilton was kept in irons at Jefferson's direction and over British objections.

Jefferson's willingness to do whatever it took for the sake of security was already on record. In May 1778 he had drafted a bill of attainder—an automatic conviction of an individual by legislative fiat—for a man named Josiah Philips for "committing murders, burning houses, wasting farms and doing other acts of hostility." Philips was given a certain amount of time to surrender himself for trial; if he failed to turn himself in, he would be declared guilty.

Jefferson's bill was an extraordinary expression of power and the work of a pragmatic politician. Essentially it denied Philips the rights the Americans said they were fighting for. For Jefferson, the practical need to end the Philips insurrection outweighed the ideal application of the principles of the Declaration of Independence.

Noting the failure to recruit sufficient infantry volunteers in June 1778, he suggested that the Congress "commute a good part of the infantry required from us for an equivalent force in horse. This service opens to us a new fund of young men, who have not yet stepped forth; I mean those whose indolence or education has unfitted them for foot-service." As governor he also lamented the state of Virginia's navy, noting that a shipbuilding effort had been "unsuccessful beyond all my fears. But it is my opinion we should still persevere in spite of disappointment, for this plain reason that we can never be otherwise defended." He had made a point of touring Virginia's gunnery east of Fredericksburg.

And he insisted on attempting to secure the West. He and George Rogers Clark planned an expedition against Britain's Fort Detroit. A decade younger than Jefferson, Clark was a tall, adventurous Virginian who had studied surveying in his youth. Clark was a pioneering figure in Kentucky and played a critical role in defending the western lands from British-supported Indian attack. He captured Kaskaskia on the Mississippi River and Vincennes (a point roughly halfway between St. Louis and Louisville) under pressure from "Hair Buyer" Hamilton. Clark's exploits in the Northwest in the icy winter of 1778–79 secured American influence over the Illinois country. He was a tough man. Years later, after severely burning his leg in an accident, Clark watched a parade of Kentucky militia out the window of the doctor's office where he was undergoing an amputation. Listening to the martial music, he endured the brutal operation, reportedly turning to the doctor only afterward, asking, "Well, is it off?" Clark was the kind of man Jefferson needed: a bold commander who could execute the vision Jefferson formulated and fought for in the political world.

Ultimately, though, the George Rogers Clark expedition to Detroit was deemed too dangerous. Jefferson told Washington that "the want of men, want of money, and difficulty of procuring provisions" made the mission impossible for now. He reported the decision with regret. (Nearly a quarter of a century later, Jefferson was to entrust a journey to the Pacific to George Rogers Clark's brother William Clark and Meriwether Lewis.)

Jefferson soon needed Clark for another project: putting down Loyalists. "There is reason to apprehend insurrection among some discontented inhabitants (Tories) on our South-Western frontier," he wrote Clark in March 1780. "I would have you give assistance on the shortest warning to that quarter. . . . Nothing can produce so dangerous a diversion of our force, as a circumstance of that kind if not crushed in its infancy." Jefferson was in no humor to be merciful.

As with Josiah Philips and with Henry Hamilton, Jefferson took the fight straight to the enemy. Diplomacy, grace, and mercy had their place. So did steel, vengeance, and strength. Thomas Jefferson was quite capable of deploying whatever weapon he thought best to defend those entrusted to his care.

It had been the coldest winter anyone could remember. The rivers were frozen so solid as 1779 became 1780 that horses and wagons could cross the James and the Potomac.

In the thaw of spring, Jefferson and his colleagues made a historic move, shifting the capital of Virginia from Williamsburg to Richmond. They believed they would be safer farther inland. As Jefferson settled his family in a house on Richmond's Shockoe Hill, borrowed from an uncle by marriage, he had every reason to believe he was acting in a climate of extreme emergency.

Charleston fell to the British on Wednesday, May 10, 1780. Jefferson was surrounded, and he knew it. "While we are threatened with a formidable attack from the northward on our Ohio settlements and from the southern Indians on our frontiers convenient to them," Jefferson said in June 1780, "our eastern country is exposed to invasion from the British army in Carolina."

There was another Tory uprising on the New River in Montgomery County in southwestern Virginia over the summer as well as more Indian violence. Elected to a second yearlong term as governor on Friday, June 2, 1780, Jefferson had no relief from bad news.

In the closing weeks of August, Lord Cornwallis

routed the American general Horatio Gates and the Virginia, Maryland, Delaware, and North Carolina militias at Camden, South Carolina.

Jefferson was despondent. Citing the "disaster which has lately befallen our Army," he summoned the council to help him formulate "an immediate and great exertion to stop the progress of the enemy." He knew his options were limited: "The measures most likely to effect this are difficult both in choice and execution."

At last, the most serious blow came. Beginning on Friday, December 29, 1780, Benedict Arnold, the American general who had become a traitor, selling himself to the British, led an invasion of Virginia. Word of the British attack off the Virginia capes reached Richmond on New Year's morning, 1781.

Living as long as he had in an era of exaggeration and of flawed reports, Jefferson was slow to credit the intelligence. A series of invasion rumors since 1777 had led to popular discontent and ambivalence about a summons to arms. To call out the militia, Jefferson said in December 1779, created "disgust" when the militiamen "find no enemy in place."

For two days in 1781, then, he declined to summon the militia. A messenger found him at the house on the hill in Richmond, calm and collected—too calm and collected.

As the days passed, it became clear that the invading forces were quite real. By then Jefferson had issued the proper orders, but it was too late to field a serious opposition.

With the British troops moving toward Richmond on Friday, January 5, 1781, Robert Hemings and James Hemings drove Patty and the rest of the Jefferson family to safety at a piece of property Jefferson owned on Fine Creek, west of the capital.

At about one o'clock on the afternoon of January 5, the British arrived at Richmond, formed a line, and launched cannon fire into the city. One shot took off the top of a butcher's house near Jefferson's Shockoe Hill quarters. According to Isaac Granger Jefferson, "In ten minutes not a white man was to be seen in Richmond; they ran hard as they could" to a camp of American soldiers on Bacon's Quarter Branch in northern Richmond.

It was chaos. "The British was dressed in red," Isaac Granger Jefferson recalled; he "saw them marching." Thomas Jefferson had left the governor's residence to avoid capture and spent the hours of the invasion circling Richmond in efforts to secure supplies and to rendezvous with American officers.

He was right to leave the center of the action. The British had brought along handcuffs in expectation of arresting the author of the Declaration of Independence.

Reaching the house on Shockoe Hill, a British officer asked where Jefferson was. "He's gone to the mountains," said George Granger, Isaac's father, protecting the master.

"Where is the keys to the house?" the officer asked, in Isaac's recollection. Isaac's father handed over the keys.

"Where is the silver?" the officer asked.

"It was all sent up to the mountains," George Granger said. It was a lie: As Isaac recalled it, his father had "put all the silver about the house in a bed tick and hid it under a bed in the kitchen and saved it too."

Benedict Arnold soon removed himself back to the coast. The British, meanwhile, seized a large number of Jefferson's slaves, including Isaac Granger Jefferson. As they were marched out of Richmond, they heard the sounds of war—one blast, Isaac Granger Jefferson recalled, was "like an earthquake."

Would it have made a difference to the defense of Richmond if the call for militia had gone out earlier? Writing from Richmond a month after the invasion, Jefferson himself believed that "men of enterprise and firmness" would have been able to capture Arnold "on his march to and from this place." Presumably, then, an activated militia would have been of military value. Jefferson had plenty of strength in his soul, but on this occasion he misjudged the moment.

By waiting, Jefferson had made a common political mistake. He had followed the people rather than led them. Many of the Virginians who did the actual fighting in militias were unhappy and skeptical about the elite that Jefferson embodied and represented. The culture of Virginia was not conducive to rapid military deployment in the best of times; now, in wartime, militias were even more difficult to muster. "Mild laws, a people not used to war and prompt obedience, a want of the provisions of war and means of procuring them render our orders often ineffectual, oblige us to temporize and when we cannot accomplish an object in one way to attempt it in another," Jefferson told a French newcomer in March 1781—the Marquis de Lafayette, who had reached Virginia to take command of Continental troops.

It may not have been fear of the British that kept Jefferson in check for those two days. It is possible that he feared mobilizing a public when he could not be sure the threat was real, thus risking the wrath of the people. By hesitating, he failed to bring his constituents along to the place they needed to be.

The lessons Jefferson was learning—painfully—in Virginia would help him immensely in later years when his responsibilities were even larger. Boldness and decisiveness were sometimes virtues in a leader. Having failed to be either bold or decisive during the invasions of Virginia, he gained valuable experience about the price of waiting. At the time, however, he could not have known that one day he would owe something of his presidential success to his failures of 1781.

THIRTEEN

Redcoats at Monticello

Such terror and confusion you have no idea of.
Governor, Council, everybody scampering.

—BETSY AMBLER,
daughter of Rebecca Burwell

JEFFERSON'S VIRGINIA WAS TEETERING in the face of British force. Lord Cornwallis and Lieutenant Colonel Banastre Tarleton, who was noted for his ferocious tactics, turned their attention toward the state in the late spring of 1781. Fearing the conquering redcoats, Governor Jefferson and the Virginia General Assembly retreated from Richmond to Charlottesville, but even there the legislature could barely muster a quorum.

In this difficult period the Jeffersons endured a by-now all-too-familiar tragedy: the death of yet another child—three of their children had now died. This one, Lucy Elizabeth, not quite six months old, died at about ten o'clock on an April morning in 1781. Jefferson chose to stay with Patty the next day, declining to attend a meeting of the state council.

The weather was bad in any event, Jefferson wrote his colleagues, "and there being nothing that I know of very pressing, and Mrs. Jefferson in a situation in which I would not wish to leave her, I shall not attend today."

His day with Patty as they grieved together was a rare moment of domestic communion, for there were now few respites from the press of business. By Monday, May 28, 1781, Jefferson knew a reckoning was at hand. British troops were advancing inland, toward Charlottesville. There were riots over a draft for militiamen across Virginia. Jefferson was reduced to asking George Washington for the general's personal assistance.

As things stood, Jefferson wrote to Washington, with an inadequate militia facing British regulars, "the minds of the people" could conceive of "no human power . . . to ward off" the inevitable victory of British forces. Only Washington's "appearance among them, I say, would restore full confidence of salvation, and would render them equal to whatever is not impossible."

Jefferson wrote these words on the twenty-eighth, and he intended to stand down as governor at the expiration of his term a few days hence. As he told Washington, his "long declared resolution of relinquishing [the governorship] to abler hands has prepared my way for retirement to a private station."

To speak of private stations and the end of one's burdens (what he called "the labors of my office") in such an emergency does not put Jefferson in a flattering light. With the assembly on the run and the state in jeopardy, one wishes Jefferson had transformed himself into a heroic savior on horseback, rallying Virginians to the field to stop the British.

He was not, however, a savior on horseback. The tragedy of the British invasion of Virginia in the spring of 1781 was that no patriot leader rose to the occasion to repel Arnold, Cornwallis, or Tarleton. The war was too diffuse, the circumstances too fluid to be in anyone's control—even Jefferson's, and he had devoted the previous two years to working on the military defense of Virginia's borders.

He spent Saturday, June 2, 1781, at Monticello with his family and houseguests, including the speakers of the Virginia House and Senate. The lawmakers were availing themselves of Jefferson's hospitality as they waited for the legislative session scheduled to take place in Charlottesville on Monday, June 4. Jefferson's successor was to be elected at this meeting.

Jefferson's considered counsel to his colleagues in the government was that they elect Thomas Nelson, Jr., a man with political and military experience. It was time, Jefferson said, for a "union of the civil and military power in the same hands"—a move that the previous two years had taught him "would greatly facilitate military measures."

Unbeknownst to the party at Monticello, Cornwallis had ordered Tarleton to pursue the government to Charlottesville. Riding fast, the British dragoons passed the Cuckoo Tavern in Louisa on Sunday, June 3, 1781. It was late—somewhere between nine and ten p.m.—when the British rode by. A giant of a Virginia militiaman named Jack Jouett (said to be six foot four and 220 pounds) was in Louisa. Realizing that the enemy was en route to capture Jefferson, Jouett broke away for a daring nighttime ride of forty miles.

Mounted on a horse said to be "the best and fleetest of foot of any nag in seven counties," Jouett crashed through the wilderness. Careering through woodlands and along ridges, Jouett avoided well-known roads in order to stay clear of the enemy. According to one account, his face was "cruelly lashed by tree-branches as he rode forward, and scars which are said to have remained the rest of his life were the result of lacerations sustained from these low-hanging limbs." The British broke their march at a plantation around eleven p.m. There they rested for about three hours, thus giving Jouett a bit of time. Tarleton stopped again deep in the night to set fire to a wagon train of supplies en route to confronting the rebel troops.

Jouett arrived at Monticello just before dawn and told Jefferson of the impending strike. Coolly, Jefferson ordered breakfast served to the household, summoned a carriage for his family, and bade farewell to the legislators, who descended the mountain back to Charlottesville. Patty and the two children and two slaves set out in search of safety at a nearby plantation.

At Monticello, Jefferson was largely alone. At least two slaves were still there—one was Martin Hemings—and were hiding silver in anticipation of the raid. Jefferson tried to rescue his documents: "In preparing for flight, I shoved in papers where I could."

He then did something in character. He decided to see things for himself. His instincts for control and for action drove him from Monticello to a neighboring peak known both as Montalto and as Carters Mountain. He took his spyglass with him. Looking out at Charlottesville he did not note anything extraordinary. He turned to go, but realized that his sword cane had slipped to the ground. As he retrieved it, his curiosity got the better of him. He peered through his glass again.

That was when he saw the British.

Back at Monticello, Jefferson mounted his best horse, Caractacus, and took off after his family. The redcoats arrived five minutes after he left. One cocked a pistol, aimed it at Martin Hemings's chest, and demanded to be told where Jefferson was or he would fire. "Fire away, then," Hemings said.

There would be no gunfire at Monticello during its brief occupation by the British, nor would there be any looting. (One exception: The redcoats drank some of Jefferson's wine; legend has it that they used it to toast George III's birthday.) Cornwallis was far less circumspect about Jefferson's other plantations, especially Elk Hill, where the British burned his barns and crops and scattered his slaves. Twenty-three of Jefferson's slaves ran away from his plantations amid the Tarleton-Cornwallis invasion; at least fifteen of these died of disease in British camps at Yorktown or Portsmouth.

Riding away from Monticello, Jefferson caught up with Patty and the children, and they ultimately sought refuge at Poplar Forest, the family's Bedford County estate. His family was safe, and he was safe.

His reputation was not.

On Tuesday, June 12, 1781, the legislature, now meeting at Trinity Church in Staunton, Virginia, expressed its gratitude to Jack Jouett with a brace of pistols and a sword—tokens to honor his brave journey through the darkness. It also passed a resolution that cut Jefferson to the core:

> **Resolved,** That at the next session of the Assembly an inquiry be made into the conduct of the Executive of this State for the last twelve months.

Jefferson could imagine nothing worse. His courage and his competence were both in the dock. It was bad enough that such calamities had struck while he was in office. Though he might not have admitted it even to himself as he played and replayed recent history in his mind, he must have known that two invasions and the chasing of the state government from Charlottesville to Staunton were debacles to be charged to his political account. Those he could probably handle. George Washington's standing had survived defeats. What he needed was time—time to decide in tranquillity how best to serve the cause in which he so believed.

Instead he was now forced into a fight over his own past. He did not bother to conceal his anger. In a tart note, Jefferson wrote that since the motion "could not be intended just to stab a reputation by a general suggestion under a bare expectation that facts might be afterwards hunted up to bolster it, I hope you will not think me improper in asking the favor of you to specify to me the unfortunate passages in my conduct which you mean to adduce against me."

In the same Trinity Church session in which the lawmakers voted to investigate Jefferson, they debated a motion that implicitly suggested the fault for the chaos of the invasions lay not with the office-holder but with the office itself. It was argued that the time had come for a "dictator . . . who should have the power of disposing of the lives and fortunes of the citizens thereof without being subject to account."

Patrick Henry spoke in favor of the "dictator" measure, saying that executive, whatever he was called, needed to be "armed with such powers . . . necessary to restrain the unbridled fury of a licentious enemy." The motion and the debate tend to exculpate Jefferson, suggesting as they do that those closest to the events believed the problems of authority were structural. The problem had been the governorship, not the governor. (The motion failed, narrowly.)

Accounts of Jefferson's terrible time as governor often fail to try to reconcile the two votes. The first, the vote for an inquiry, amounted to an indictment of Jefferson's conduct. Yet the second, the vote for new powers for Jefferson's successors, amounted to a tacit admission that Jefferson had not possessed authority commensurate with the challenges of the time. To blame Jefferson for failure in an executive office while simultaneously attempting to reform that office logically shifts responsibility from the individual to the institution.

Logic, however, is rarely a big part of politics. Jefferson's foes saw an opportunity to embarrass him. Though the house inquiry was short-lived—the assembly ended up commending, not condemning, Jefferson—the episode lived on in the mind of Jefferson and in the memories of his political opponents. His bitterness at the charge that he had been derelict in his duty was palpable. There was, Jefferson said, "no foundation" for any official aspersion.

Another opportunity for Jefferson to serve as an envoy in France came in September—a further sign that Jefferson's performance as governor, while no one's finest hour (with the possible exceptions of Jouett and of Martin Hemings), was not politically fatal. Yet Jefferson declined the diplomatic appointment. He had, he said, "taken my final leave of everything of that nature, have retired to my farm, my family and books from which I think nothing will evermore separate me."

With this disinterested assertion of bucolic retirement, though, came a determination to stay in Virginia politics long enough to clear his name. "A desire to leave public office with a reputation not more blotted than it has deserved will oblige me to emerge at the next session of our assembly and perhaps to accept of a seat in it, but as I go with a single object, I shall withdraw when that shall be accomplished," he said in September 1781. He was to stay out of office for about a year and a half—a period in which he suffered much from the pain of the rumors about his governorship. Yet he could never totally withdraw from the world—and the world's opinion still mattered to him.

In October 1781, the Americans triumphed at Yorktown, effectively ending the war. Still captive, as were several other Jefferson slaves, Isaac Granger Jefferson witnessed the battle. "There was tremendous firing and smoke—seemed like heaven and earth was come together," he recalled. He remembered hearing the cries of the wounded. "When the smoke blow off, you see the dead men laying on the ground."

The war was won, and to most appearances, Thomas Jefferson had triumphed, his cause vindicated and victorious. A French visitor to Monticello in 1782, the Marquis de Chastellux, came away dazzled by its master.

> Let me describe to you a man, not yet forty, tall, and with a mild and pleasing countenance, but whose mind and understanding are ample substitutes for every exterior grace. An American, who without ever having quitted his own country, is at once a musician, skilled in drawing, a geometrician, an astronomer, a natural philosopher, legislator, and statesman. A senator of America, who sat for two years in that famous Congress which brought about the revolution . . . a governor of Virginia, who filled this difficult station during the invasions of Arnold, of Phillips, and of Cornwallis; a philosopher, in voluntary retirement from the world and public business because he loves the world, inasmuch only as he can flatter himself with being useful to mankind. . . . For no object had escaped Mr. Jefferson; and it seemed as if from his youth he had placed his mind, as he has done his house,

on an elevated situation, from which he might contemplate the universe.

This was how Jefferson wanted to be seen. The reality, he felt, was rather different. He believed himself a failure. Even the American victory could not take Jefferson's mind completely off his controversial final hours as governor. He told James Monroe that one of the worst aspects of the legislative inquiry was the possibility that the public would believe that he "stood arraigned for treasons of the heart and not mere weakness of the head." Attacks on his service, he said, "had inflicted a wound on my spirit which will only be cured by the all-healing grave."

He added a final note: "Mrs. Jefferson has added another daughter to our family." The child was named Lucy Elizabeth, after the sister who had died not long before her own birth. Patty had no more strength. There were no reserves to draw on, no means by which to rally. "She has been ever since," Jefferson said, "and still continues, very dangerously ill."

FOURTEEN

To Burn on Through Death

Mrs. Jefferson has at last shaken off her tormenting pains, by yielding to them, and has left our friend inconsolable.

—Jefferson friend EDMUND RANDOLPH
to James Madison

HIS WIFE WAS DYING. The latest child, the second Lucy Elizabeth, was Patty Jefferson's sixth in ten years. Patty was only thirty-three, but her body was exhausted. The tensions and exertions of the war, culminating in the family's evacuation of Monticello, exacerbated the state of her health. She may have suffered from tuberculosis. By the early summer of 1782 she was confined to her bed.

Her husband refused to leave her side. Day after day, week after week, month after month, Jefferson "was never out of calling," his daughter Patsy recalled long afterward. He spared himself few details of his wife's care, helping her take medicines and guiding cups to her lips.

Either at her bed or in a small room nearby that opened onto hers, he kept vigil. Patty, too, craved Jefferson's company. "Her eyes ever rested on him, ever followed him," according to family tradition. "When he spoke, no other sound could reach her ear or attract her attention. When she waked from slumber, she looked momentarily alarmed and distressed, and even appeared to be frightened, if the customary form was not bending over her, the customary look upon her." Monticello and each other became their only reality.

She had strength enough to begin writing some lines from Sterne—they were from **Tristram Shandy**—on a small piece of paper.

> **Time wastes too fast: every letter**
> **I trace tells me with what rapidity**
> **Life follows my pen. The days and hours**
> **Of it are flying over our heads like**
> **Clouds of windy day never to return—**
> **More every thing presses on—**

She faded at this point. Jefferson finished the passage for her:

> **And every**
> **Time I kiss thy hand to bid adieu, every absence**
> **which**
> **Follows it, are preludes to that eternal separation**
> **Which we are shortly to make!**

Sterne's message here is tragic, unrelentingly so, for even moments of human communion and love are seen not as fulfilling in themselves but ephemeral: a stark yet realistic vision of life.

James Monroe sensed the scope of the crisis and the depth of his patron's sadness. "I have been much distressed upon the subject of Mrs. Jefferson and have feared . . . that the report of each succeeding day would inform me she was no more." Monroe called on God for her recovery. "It may please heaven to restore our amiable friend to health and thereby to you a friend whose loss you would always lament, and to your children a parent which no change of circumstances would ever compensate for."

The prayer was futile. It was nearly noon on Friday, September 6, 1782, when the end came. According to Monticello tradition, "the house servants," including Elizabeth Hemings, were among those with Patty Jefferson as she lay dying. Edmund Bacon, who managed the plantation in later decades, said that the Monticello slaves "have often told my wife that when Mrs. Jefferson died they stood around the bed. Mr. Jefferson sat by her, and she gave him directions about a good many things that she wanted done."

Like her late mother-in-law, Patty was commanding to the last. "When she came to the children, she wept and could not speak for some time. Finally she held up her hand, and . . . told him she could not die happy if she thought her . . . children were ever to have a stepmother brought in over them." To extract a promise of eternal faithfulness from a man like Jefferson—vital, sexually energetic, only thirty-nine—could be seen as a selfish deathbed request. Patty, however, was most likely thinking of her children and their happiness. She may have believed that the combined maternal influences of the girls' aunts and perhaps of Elizabeth Hemings—whom Patty had known so long and so intimately—were sufficient without risking the introduction of an unknown woman as mistress of the house. Patsy was nearly ten, Polly four, Lucy an infant. Jefferson was rich, celebrated, and charming. But he gave his promise. He would, he assured his dying wife, never marry again.

Among the reported witnesses to that pledge was Sally Hemings, Patty's half sister, who was not quite ten years old.

At a quarter to twelve on that Friday, Patty Jefferson died. In the final moments, Jefferson's sister Martha Carr had to help the grieving husband from his wife's bedside. He was, his daughter recalled, "in a state of insensibility" when Mrs. Carr "with great difficulty, got him into the library, where he fainted"—and not for a brief moment. Jefferson "remained so long insensible that they feared he would never revive."

When he did come to, he was incoherent with grief, and perhaps surrendered to rage. There is a hint that he lost all control in the calamity of Patty's death. According to his daughter Patsy, "The scene that followed I did not witness"—presumably "the scene" unfolded in the library when he revived—"but the violence of his emotion, when, almost by stealth, I entered his room by night, to this day I dare not describe to myself." (Patsy was writing half a century later.)

A pallet to lie on was brought to give him some comfort in the little library. Yet his grief drove him out of doors in a kind of frenzy. Patsy attached herself to her father, as if clinging to the one remaining constant in her life. For her, siblings had come and gone, and now her mother was dead. Given the demands of his wartime leadership, Jefferson would have seemed a loving if somewhat distant figure to her. Yet he adored his family, idealizing it in many ways, and he would have seen in Patsy—with her strength and evident maturity in dealing with a father in the grip of grief—images of his mother, of his sister Jane, and, of course, of Patty. He held her close; she held him close. The pattern of warmth and intimacy between father and daughter that set in during this dark spell of despair persisted for the rest of their lives.

"He kept his room [for] three weeks, and I was never a moment from his side," Patsy said. "He walked almost incessantly night and day, only lying down occasionally, when nature was completely exhausted, on a pallet that had been brought in during his long fainting fit. My aunts remained constantly with him for some weeks—I do not remember how many."

He could not remain still. "When at last he left his room, he rode out, and from that time he was incessantly on horseback, rambling about the mountain, in the least frequented roads, and just as often through the woods. In those melancholy rambles I was his constant companion—a solitary witness to many a burst of grief, the remembrance of which has consecrated particular scenes of that lost home beyond the power of time to obliterate." He drove himself as though sheer movement could alleviate his loss. In one of the first letters he wrote after the disaster of September 6, 1782, he said, "I had had some thoughts of abstracting myself awhile from this state by a journey to Philadelphia or somewhere else Northwardly."

Rumor had Jefferson nearing madness. "I ever thought him to rank domestic happiness in the first class of the chief good," Edmund Randolph told James Madison, "but scarcely supposed that his grief would be so violent as to justify the circulating report of his swooning away whenever he sees his children."

His epitaph for Patty came from Homer, from the

heart of the **Iliad**. He had the words inscribed in Greek—only the educated would be able to share in his memorial to his wife. Alexander Pope had translated the lines Jefferson selected this way:

If in the melancholy shades below,
The flames of friends and lovers cease to glow,
Yet mine shall sacred last; mine undecay'd
Burn on through death and animate my shade.

In his mind the connection with Patty was eternal, able even to overcome the customs of Hades. For now, though, a phrase on the tombstone captured the unavoidable truth: "Martha Jefferson . . . Intermarried with Thomas Jefferson January 1st, 1772; Torn from him by death September 6th, 1782."

A month later he was alluding to the possibility of suicide. "This miserable kind of existence is really too burdensome to be borne," he wrote, "and were it not for the infidelity of deserting the sacred charge left me, I could not wish its continuance a moment." His world seemed to have died with Patty. "All my plans of comfort and happiness reversed by a single event and nothing answering in prospect before me but a gloom unbrightened with one cheerful expectation," he wrote his sister-in-law Elizabeth Eppes.

He would endure for Patsy, Polly, and Lucy. He knew his duty to his children and to his neighbors. "I will endeavor to . . . keep what I feel to myself that I may not dispirit you from a communication with us," he told Mrs. Eppes. "I say nothing of coming to Eppington because I promised you this should not be till I could support such a countenance as might not cast a damp on the cheerfulness of others."

He was a long way from that point. His wanderings in the woods and his rides with Patsy were all he could manage.

PART IV
THE FRUSTRATED CONGRESSMAN

LATE 1782 to MID-1784

I know no danger so dreadful and so probable as that of internal contests. And I know no remedy so likely to prevent it as the strengthening of the band which connects us.

—THOMAS JEFFERSON, on America under the Articles of Confederation

A Monsieur de Faujac de S

ond, de Plusieurs Accadémies.

Fascinated by the new possibilities—and the dangers—of flight, Jefferson carefully followed the progress of manned balloon exhibitions like this one in the Tuileries in the mid-1780s.

FIFTEEN

Return to the Arena

> The states will go to war with each other in
> defiance of Congress; one will call in France
> to her assistance; another Great Britain, and so
> we shall have all the wars of Europe brought
> to our own doors.
>
> —THOMAS JEFFERSON, on his fears
> about a weak national government

H E WAS NEARLY FORTY years old, and, until recently, he had never really failed at anything. A favored son, a brilliant student, a legislator of his state at age twenty-five, author of the **Summary View** at thirty-one and of the Declaration of Independence at thirty-three, governor of Virginia at thirty-six: Thomas Jefferson was accustomed to public success and popular praise, to moving from strength to strength and from glory to glory.

No more. His beloved wife had died. His administration of Virginia in the face of the attacks of Benedict Arnold and Charles Cornwallis was widely seen as little less than disastrous. The details did not much matter. The fact was that people thought Jefferson's leadership had been found wanting. It was a fact Jefferson hated, but it was a fact nonetheless.

Like the poet Dante, who found himself wandering "in a dark wood" at about the same age, Jefferson was forced to make his peace with the bitterness of his recent experience. He had to come to terms with the reality that he was no longer an immaculately golden public figure. Unless he convinced himself that no great life was without its mishaps and its mistakes, he would not be able to return to the arena.

Musing on the perils of fame as he prepared to put himself before the world again, he wrote George Rogers Clark, who had won celebrated victories during the war and faced criticism: "That you have enemies you must not doubt, when you reflect that you have made yourself eminent."

It is impossible to read these lines without thinking of how they applied to their author as they did to his correspondent. "If you meant to escape malice you should have confined yourself within the sleepy line of regular duty," Jefferson wrote Clark. "When you transgressed this and enterprised deeds which will hand down your name with honor to future times, you made yourself a mark for malice and envy to shoot at. Of these there is enough both in and out of office."

Anguish was the price a public man paid for adulation. Since his governorship, Jefferson understood that in a way he never had before. He also knew that pressing ahead was the only way to leave the past behind. There was no other way to do it, unless one chose to retire forever, which could make things worse, for then there was no opportunity to leave marks large enough to overshadow the marks of failure. Given that adversity itself was an intrinsic element of the political life Jefferson had chosen, the test of such a life came when one had to choose which path to take in adversity's wake.

The personal and political miseries of 1781 and 1782—the invasions by the British, the aspersions on his character, and the death of his wife—might well have sent lesser men back to their plantations in bitterness and in anger at the injustice of it all.

Not Jefferson. He chose advance over retreat.

When news of Patty Jefferson's death reached Philadelphia, Jefferson's allies in the Congress asked him to serve on the Paris peace commission in France tasked with crafting the postwar order.

Jefferson accepted with alacrity. "I had two months before that lost the cherished companion of my life, in whose affections, unabated on both sides, I had lived the last ten years in unchequered happiness," Jefferson recalled. "With the public interests, the state of my mind concurred in recommending the change of scene proposed."

Tuesday, November 26, 1782, proved something

of a turning point in Jefferson's life. Visiting Amp-thill, the plantation on the James River near Falling Creek that belonged to Archibald Cary, a revolutionary colleague, Jefferson was overseeing family inoculations for smallpox when he fully reengaged with his correspondence, and with the world beyond the one delineated by his grief of the previous three months.

In a draft message accepting his appointment as an envoy to France, Jefferson said that he intended to "pursue the object of my mission with integrity and impartial regard to the good of the whole states." His emphasis on his broader vision and global portfolio served, he may have hoped, to turn the page on the last unhappy chapter in his political career. He was, in any event, eager to get started. "I shall lose no moment," Jefferson said, "in preparing for my departure."

In a letter to the Marquis de Chastellux he returned to the grim events of that autumn. He had not replied to earlier correspondence, Jefferson said, for he was only now "a little emerging from that stupor of mind which had rendered me as dead to the world as she was whose loss occasioned it."

He left his two younger children, Polly and Lucy, with Francis and Elizabeth Eppes, married relatives of his late wife. The eldest, Patsy, was to travel with her father to his new assignment in Paris. From Monticello on Sunday, December 15, 1782, Jefferson published a notice in **The Virginia Gazette** announcing that he had "confided the care of his affairs" to his brother-in-law Francis Eppes of Chesterfield and to his friend Nicholas Lewis of Albemarle County. Jefferson and Patsy left home four days later. He did not know when they would return.

Jefferson was eager to get away—the farther the better—but neither the British nor the weather was cooperating. He and Patsy expected to sail from Baltimore with the French minister on the frigate **Romulus**. The ship was frozen in a few miles below Baltimore, so Jefferson remained in Philadelphia reacquainting himself with the national political scene he had left six years before. He and his daughter took rooms at Mary House's establishment at Fifth and Market.

Mrs. House's boardinghouse offered charming political company (including Madison) and provided the grieving Jefferson with what he had always needed (and, since his friendship with his sister Jane, had always had): a connection with a sympathetic woman—in this case, Eliza House Trist, the daughter of his landlady. Eliza Trist came to play a sustaining role in Jefferson's life as a longtime admiring friend.

At Mrs. House's lodgings, Jefferson played a supporting role in the domestic drama of the thirty-two-year-old Madison's wooing of fifteen-year-old Catherine "Kitty" Floyd. The beautiful daughter of the New York congressman William Floyd, Kitty won the solemn Madison's heart. Jefferson joined what he called the household's "raillery" as it charted the romance.

In addition to spending time among colleagues old and new, Jefferson took detailed notes on a "Secret Journal of Foreign Affairs" kept by Charles Thomson, the secretary of the Continental Congress. Jefferson studied the diplomatic correspondence between the Congress and Benjamin Franklin in France, John Jay in Spain, and John Adams in Holland. He reviewed instructions to commissioners to foreign states and the appointments of envoys to Vienna, Russia, Prussia, and Tuscany. He read Madison's paper **Observations Relating to the Influence of Vermont and the Territorial Claims on the Politics of Congress** and considered documents related to Spanish-American disputes over the lands east of the Mississippi.

Attuned to how others saw the world—and understanding that most of them saw it with themselves at the center—Jefferson reached out to his future colleague John Jay, then an American diplomat in Europe: "Had I joined you at a more early period I am sure I should not have added to the strength of the commission and, coming in at the eleventh hour, I can propose no more than to avoid doing mischief." It was a disarming note, designed to allay any jealousies or annoyances at the late arrival of a new diplomat. Jefferson was taking care to cultivate those around him.

And those above him, too: He wrote George

Washington an ingratiating letter. Washington's preeminence in the life of the nation was clear. In war Jefferson had maintained the most cordial of relations with him. At the possible approach of peace, he wanted to make himself pleasant to Washington, and perhaps useful. He offered Washington "my individual tribute to your Excellency for all you have suffered and all you have effected for us."

Then came news that concluded Jefferson's mission before it had begun: Jay and the incumbent American representatives in France had completed a draft of the Treaty of Paris with Great Britain, the document officially ending the Revolutionary War. The text of the pact was en route to the United States, where the Congress would have to ratify it.

Jefferson returned to Virginia, a reluctant private citizen once more, yet made his ambitions clear to James Madison. He wanted to be in the action again. "Should the call be made on me, which was sometimes the subject of our conversation," Jefferson wrote, he would enthusiastically return to the national stage.

It did not take long. On Friday, June 6, 1783, Jefferson was elected to the Congress. Edmund Randolph's report of the news to Madison was succinct: "Mr. Jefferson was placed at the head of the delegation not without his approbation."

Jefferson had been without a public position for less than a month.

———

The Congress to which Jefferson was elected was the only institution of national government. Created by the Articles of Confederation, it was an inherently weak body. There was neither a separate executive nor a judicial branch—only the Congress. A state could not be represented without two members. A majority of nine of the thirteen states had to agree on most large questions, limiting the government's effectiveness. Even if there were a quorum present and in agreement about major issues, the Congress had little power: It could not tax, regulate national trade, or create a military (though it was authorized to declare war). There was no means of enforcement; the states were essentially sovereign nations, which left the national government ill-equipped to create coherent foreign and commercial policies that might strengthen the young country.

The year 1783 had much in common with 1774: It was a time of twilight, an hour when the answers to great questions were unclear. In 1774 the issue was war. In 1783 it was peace—or, more precisely, whether Americans could emerge from the conflict and govern themselves as a sovereign power.

Beginning with Benjamin Franklin's 1775 proposal for an "Articles of Confederation," Jefferson had been thinking about the practicalities of governing at the national level. He served on the committee to consider Franklin's paper and was appointed to another panel in 1783 to devise a "visible head of the government during vacations of Congress." The result was a Committee of the States, and Jefferson was a persistent advocate of more, rather than less, central control.

The committee failed. "This was then imputed to the temper of two or three individuals," Jefferson recalled, "but the wise ascribed it to the nature of man." Later in his career Jefferson was able to draw on the experience of wartime Virginia and the collapse of the mid-1780s national structure to become a disciple of a unitary (but accountable) executive. History offered no contrary examples. "Our plan best, I believe, combines wisdom and practicability, by providing a plurality of counselors, but a single arbiter for ultimate decision," he said of the American presidency.

Contemplating the situation in the Confederation Congress of 1783, Jefferson worried about nothing less than anarchy. Now that the Revolutionary War was won, what was to keep state from turning on state, or region on region?

A power of central, national, and binding force was the only answer. The task was clear: Jefferson and his contemporaries had to lay their "shoulders to the strengthening of the band of our confederacy and averting those cruel evils to which its present weakness will expose us."

The problems would persist for much of the 1780s.

"I have long thought and become daily more convinced that the construction of our federal government is fundamentally wrong," John Jay wrote to Jefferson in 1786. "To vest legislative, judicial and executive powers in one and the same body of men, and that too in a body daily changing its members, can never be wise." The same year Jefferson told James Monroe, "There never will be money in the treasury till the confederacy shows its teeth. The states must see the rod; perhaps it must be felt by some one of them."

Without a powerful union, he expected the worst.

The question was not only of political science or of law but of character. The prospects for the survival of the new nation lay with the people themselves. In 1782 the issue had been framed pithily and well. "What, then, is the American, this new man?" asked J. Hector St. John de Crèvecoeur in his **Letters from an American Farmer.**

Jefferson had been trying to answer that query for several years, albeit with a provincial, not a national, focus. In 1780, the Marquis de Barbé-Marbois, secretary of the French legation in America, had sent Jefferson a series of questions about Virginia. The result was Jefferson's most sustained literary effort, a book—not published until a few years later, in Paris—entitled **Notes on the State of Virginia.** Organized as answers to the specific questions posed by

Marbois—from "An exact description of the limits and boundaries of the state of Virginia?" to "The **particular** customs and manners that may happen to be received in that state?"—the work is precise but eclectic, formal yet conversational.

His pride in his native land is evident; the text is full of rhapsodic descriptions of the natural beauties of Virginia. He was also realistic about the difficulties of governing in a time of revolution. The government of his state was an unusual combination of elements. "It is a composition of the freest principles of the English constitution, with others derived from natural right and natural reason. To these nothing can be more opposed than the maxims of absolute monarchies."

What was true in Virginia, Jefferson was to find, was also true in America more broadly. The search for the point of temperate power between competing elements of life—the national government and the states, the states and the people—was far from over.

In an evening's conversation on a rainy journey home to Orange, James Madison sounded fellow Virginian George Mason out on the questions of the day, discovering only one real example of "heterodoxy": Mason, Madison told Jefferson, was "too little impressed with either the necessity or the proper means of preserving the confederacy."

In two largely neglected pieces published anonymously in **The Pennsylvania Journal, or, Weekly Advertiser** in this period, Madison made an impassioned case for a strong national government—a case that, as Mason's views indicated, was failing to resonate broadly.

Madison was having problems of a personal nature, too. Kitty Floyd broke off their engagement, crushing him. Concerned about his friend, Jefferson rapidly replied with warmth and empathy: "I sincerely lament the misadventure which has happened from whatever cause it may have happened. . . . No event has been more contrary to my expectations, and these were founded on what I thought a good knowledge of the ground. But of all machines ours is the most complicated and inexplicable."

Jefferson's words of consolation came from a good friend, one who knew sadness and who tried to take—as of old—a philosophical view of life's disappointments. He had experienced heartbreak and desolation, and he had—painfully and arduously—kept his own emotional machinery working well enough to propel him forward despite all. He believed Madison would, too.

Jefferson, meanwhile, could never know too much. Ten days after his election to the national Congress, he asked a delegate to the Virginia General Assembly at Richmond to keep him minutely informed about state politics. "Parliamentary news is interesting and I hear little or nothing of it," he wrote the delegate on Tuesday, June 17, 1783. "What have you done? What are you doing? What are the maneuvers of your leaders? Who are they? What the dispositions of the two houses? etc."

Information, as ever, was power.

SIXTEEN

A Struggle for Respect

Foreign civil arrangement, and foreign treaties. Domestic civil arrangement. Domestic peace establishment of arsenals and posts. Western territory. Indian affairs. Money.

—THOMAS JEFFERSON, listing the issues facing postwar America

THE CONGRESS WAS HOMELESS as well as largely powerless. Seated in Philadelphia, slated to move to Annapolis later in 1783, the lawmakers were driven out of Pennsylvania in the third week of June when three hundred Continental soldiers mutinied, storming the Congress to demand pay. Pennsylvania officials, who had jurisdiction over the city, refused to intercede, prompting the Congress to evacuate Philadelphia for Princeton, in New Jersey.

The national government, in other words, was on the run from its own people.

Appearances mattered much at this delicate hour. James Madison reported a strong inclination among the national lawmakers to leave Princeton and return to Philadelphia even at the risk of physical danger in order to "prevent any inferences abroad of disaffection in the mass of so important a state to the revolution or the federal Government."

The Congress nevertheless remained at Princeton until it moved to Annapolis in November 1783. Though uncertain where the Congress would be sitting by the time his term began in the autumn, Jefferson had asked Madison to secure him a room—of any size—with Mrs. House if in Philadelphia, and he sought Mrs. Trist's counsel on schooling for Patsy, who was to stay in that city no matter where the legislature held its sessions.

Jefferson left Monticello on Thursday, October 16, 1783. Traveling through Philadelphia, he arrived in Princeton to take his seat on November 4. It was the briefest of stays. On the evening of Jefferson's arrival there, the Congress adjourned to Annapolis. Princeton had offered "scanty accommodations." Madison dismissed it as a "village where the public business can neither be conveniently done, the members of Congress decently provided for, nor those connected with Congress provided for at all."

To achieve order required authority, which the states wanted but the Congress needed. Neither a reflexive nationalist nor a states'-rights purist—categories that were already taking form—Jefferson was grappling with the distribution of power in a country of diverse interests.

His view of the role of the Confederation Congress in 1783–84 was in keeping with his thinking in the wake of his governorship. Whoever was in charge needed to be clearly and certainly in command. As "the United States in Congress assembled represent the sovereignty of the whole Union," he wrote, "their body collectively and their President individually should on all occasions have precedence [over] all other bodies and persons." Even if he were referring only to ceremonial occasions, the point was clear. To be effective, the Congress had to be granted pride of place.

Annapolis was quiet—too quiet, Jefferson believed, for the seat of the Congress of a victorious nation. "It is now above a fortnight since we should have met, and six states only appear," he wrote Madison in December 1783. They needed nine to form a quorum and proceed. "We have some hopes of Rhode Island coming in today, but when two more will be added seems as insusceptible of calculation as when the next earthquake will happen." Franklin, Adams, and Jay—the commissioners abroad—wrote that "the riot of Philadelphia and departure of Congress thence made the most serious impressions in Europe, and have excited great doubts of the stability of our confederacy, and in what we shall end," Jefferson said.

The business at hand was momentous: The Congress had only a limited amount of time to ratify the

William Randolph I of Turkey Island was perhaps Virginia's greatest patriarch; Thomas Jefferson's mother, Jane Randolph Jefferson, was a descendant, firmly establishing Thomas as a member of the Virginia elite.

As the wife of William Randolph I of Turkey Island, Mary Isham Randolph had nine children. One son, Isham Randolph of Dungeness, was a merchant, sea captain, and the father of Jane Randolph, who married Peter Jefferson in 1739.

P. RANDOLPH.

Known as "the Speaker," Peyton Randolph was a crucial influence on Thomas Jefferson. As Speaker of the House of Burgesses and various Virginia assemblies in the early Revolutionary era, Randolph played a key role in governing the colony as it moved toward a break with Great Britain. He died in Philadelphia in 1775 after being elected president of the Continental Congress.

WILLIAM & MARY COLLEGE, WILLIAMSBURG, VA.

Wren Hall, the College of William and Mary. Jefferson thought the college, where he studied from 1762 to 1764, the "finest school of manners and morals in America." His years there were a delight for the young scholar.

The American colonists long held out hopes that George III of Britain would manage to effect some kind of reconciliation, but to no avail. "Blows must decide whether they are to be subject to this country or independent," said George.

Worldly and well read, Francis Fauquier was royal governor of Virginia during Jefferson's student days, including the young man in intimate dinners and encouraging him in his cultivation of the violin.

William Small, a Scottish-born professor who taught briefly at William and Mary, changed Jefferson's life by introducing him to the writers, scientists, and thinkers of the Enlightenment.

Brilliant and hawk-nosed, George Wythe was Jefferson's law teacher, friend, and Revolutionary colleague. The two men shared a love of learning, the law, and fine things. Wythe was murdered in Richmond in 1806, midway through Jefferson's second presidential term.

Jefferson's political education began when he listened to Patrick Henry, a burgess from Louisa County, Virginia, protest the Stamp Act in 1765. "He appeared to me to speak as Homer wrote," Jefferson, himself a poor public speaker, recalled admiringly.

The last royal governor of Virginia, John Murray, 4th Earl of Dunmore, issued an inflammatory proclamation in 1775 offering freedom to slaves and indentured servants who chose to fight on the side of the British against the American rebels. The announcement galvanized much of white Virginia to the Revolutionary cause.

Martha Jefferson Randolph, known as "Patsy," was the last surviving child of Patty and Thomas Jefferson. As a child she traveled to Paris with her father; she married a cousin, Thomas Mann Randolph, Jr., shortly after the Jeffersons' return to the United States in 1789–90.

Husband of Jefferson's daughter Patsy, member of Congress, and governor of Virginia, Thomas Mann Randolph, Jr., was long close to his father-in-law and lived in the President's House while serving as a congressman during Jefferson's presidency. Randolph grew erratic and quarrelsome in later years.

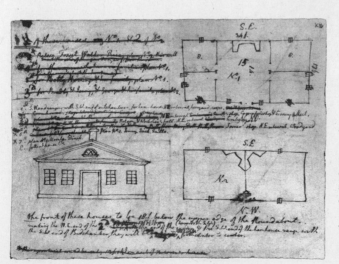

In 1770, the year he began work clearing the top of Monticello to build his house and plantation, Jefferson also drew these plans for projected slave quarters. Ultimately the center of plantation life—Mulberry Row—would look very different.

John Adams of Massachusetts and Thomas Jefferson of Virginia first met as fellow delegates to the Continental Congress in Philadelphia in 1775; they were to be alternately friend and foe for the next half century.

Written at Monticello in the summer of 1774, *A Summary View* was an early expression of Jefferson's creed—and of America's. Published on both sides of the Atlantic, the pamphlet, first composed as instructions to the Virginia delegates to the Continental Congress, gave Jefferson what a contemporary called "the reputation of a masterly pen."

A
SUMMARY VIEW
OF THE
RIGHTS
OF
BRITISH AMERICA.
Set forth in some
RESOLUTIONS
INTENDED FOR THE
INSPECTION
OF THE PRESENT
DELEGATES
OF THE
PEOPLE OF VIRGINIA.
NOW IN
CONVENTION.

BY A NATIVE, AND MEMBER OF THE
HOUSE OF BURGESSES.

WILLIAMSBURG: PRINTED;
PHILADELPHIA: Re-Printed by JOHN DUNLAP.
M,DCC,LXXIV.

Assigned the task of drafting a Declaration of Independence in June 1776, Jefferson worked away in his small suite of rooms at the house of the bricklayer Jacob Graff, Jr., in Philadelphia, seeking to create a document, he later said, that would capture the essence of "the American mind."

The "Original Rough Draft" of the Declaration of Independence, in Jefferson's hand.

Benjamin Franklin, John Adams, Roger Sherman, Robert Livingston, and Jefferson were assigned to the committee to produce a Declaration. The writing fell to Jefferson, Adams recalled, partly because the politics of the moment dictated that a Virginian be seen "at the head of this business."

The British invasion of Virginia in 1780–81 began badly but ended well, with the American triumph at Yorktown. Along the way, however, Jefferson, then governor of Virginia, presided over a chaotic period with the Americans under attack from Banastre Tarleton and Lord Cornwallis. Suggestions that Jefferson had failed as a wartime leader persisted for the rest of his life.

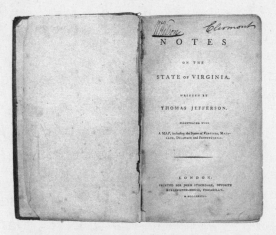

Drafted in reply to a series of queries about his native state, *Notes on the State of Virginia* was Jefferson's only book.

Treaty of Paris, the pact ending the Revolutionary War and granting America recognition as an independent nation. On Saturday, December 13, 1783, Jefferson was appointed to a committee to consider the treaty.

There were ten major provisions, among them a generous grant of territory and a promise by the British to return confiscated property (including slaves). Critical, too, was article 10, concerning process: The treaty had to be ratified within six months of its signing, which had occurred in Paris on Wednesday, September 3, 1783.

Though Jefferson's committee moved the ratification of the treaty, there was still no quorum in the Congress. No quorum, no action. Jefferson hated the feeling of powerlessness.

It was a troubling Christmas Eve. He was not feeling well, and he was worried. "I cannot help expressing my extreme anxiety at our present critical situation," Jefferson wrote a Virginia correspondent on Wednesday, December 24, 1783. There was now only "a little over two months" to ratify the treaty and return it to Paris. "All that can be said is that it is yet possible," Jefferson wrote, hoping for action before Britain attempted to force new changes should the ratification not come in time.

On New Year's Day 1784 Jefferson was gloomy and sick. "I have had very ill health since I have been here and am getting rather lower than otherwise," he told Madison.

If the Congress did not act quickly, the United States would humiliate itself abroad by failing to ratify and deliver the treaty in time. If it acted without the nine states, though, the national government risked the appearance of usurpation.

Jefferson sought a compromise, some means of preserving—establishing, actually—the nation's international reputation without exposing the Congress to charges of overreaching. With lawyerly precision, Jefferson drafted a motion that took advantage of an earlier vote and extended its authority to the finished treaty. The means of saving the day were secured. (In the end, Connecticut and New Jersey at length arrived, and the treaty was ratified by nine states.)

For the moment, the system had succeeded in ratifying the treaty that, in turn, ratified the Revolution. Jefferson drafted a proclamation to announce the news. In it he called on "all the good citizens of these states" to draw on "that good faith which is every man's surest guide" to respect, and to fulfill the articles of peace "entered into on their behalf under the authority of that federal bond by which their existence as an independent people is bound up together, and is known and acknowledged by the nations of the world."

There was much work to be done. Jefferson thought "that were it certain we could be brought to act as one united nation" on trade policy, then

Britain "would make extensive concessions." As it was, however, "she is not afraid of retaliation."

Still, the resolution of months of tension and uncertainty lifted Jefferson's spirits and may have improved his health. "I have been just able to attend my duty in the state house, but not to go out on any other occasion," he told Patsy. The day after ratification, however, he said he was "considerably better." The author of the Declaration of Independence had declared the peace, affirming anew the national—not sectional—identity of the country.

With its attention to the occupation of forts, the treaty raised issues about the future of the American West, a longtime interest of Jefferson's. His was an obsession romantic, scientific, and practical. He loved the image of endless forests—in this vision he was like a Saxon of old, dwelling in primordial liberty—and he was fascinated by what he called "the different species of bones, teeth, and tusks of the Mammoth" and other natural specimens. The French naturalist the Comte de Buffon, who argued that animal and plant life in the New World was inferior, was always on Jefferson's mind. In Philadelphia in 1784 Jefferson would buy an "uncommonly large panther skin" to show Buffon.

He was also a patriot and a politician, and he worried, as he had during the years of the war, about the threat of a frontier beyond American control. "I find they have subscribed a very large sum of money in England for exploring the country from the Mississippi to California," Jefferson wrote George Rogers Clark from Annapolis in December 1783. "They pretend it is only to promote knowledge. I am afraid they have thoughts of colonizing into that quarter. Some of us have been talking here in a feeble way of making the attempt to search that country." He fretted, though, about finding the means to do it. "But I doubt whether we have enough of that kind of spirit to raise the money. How would you like to lead such a party?"

The man who saw America's story in terms of the march of "human events" was aware of the scale of the experiment in which he was participating. In the first week of December 1783, Jefferson made inquiries about purchasing a mechanical copying device through Samuel House, a brother of Eliza House Trist and a Philadelphia merchant. He wanted to ensure that his role was part of the saga of the age when the time came for the telling of tales and the weaving of history. Jefferson had been thinking in such terms since he began sending out his original version of the Declaration of Independence. Now he was taking steps to preserve the daily, even hourly, record of a life lived on the largest possible stage.

SEVENTEEN

Lost Cities and Life Counsel

The Governor is a most ingenuous naturalist
and philosopher, a truly scientific and learned
man, and every way excellent.

—EZRA STILES, the president of
Yale College, on Jefferson

IN PHILADELPHIA all the talk was of balloons. "Congress imagined that when they removed to Annapolis to pout we should all be in deep distress and for every **pout** return a **sigh**—but the event is far otherwise," Jefferson's friend Francis Hopkinson wrote him in March 1784. "The name of Congress is almost forgotten, and for one person that will mention that respectable body a hundred will talk of an air balloon."

It was a season of grand ballooning experiments in Paris; word of the flights, including a manned one in November 1783, spread rapidly. Jefferson sensed the revolutionary possibilities of human control of the air. "What think you of these balloons? They really begin to assume a serious face," he wrote. Reports had people flying six miles in twenty minutes at three thousand feet. He took a jocular tone, but his words were prescient. "This discovery seems to threaten the prostration of fortified works unless they can be closed above, the destruction of fleets and what not. The French may now run over their laces, wines etc. to England duty free. The whole system of British statutes made on the supposition of goods being brought into some port must be revised. Inland countries may now become **maritime** states unless you choose rather to call them **aerial** ones as their commerce is in [the] future to be carried on through that element. But jesting apart I think this discovery may lead to things useful." Ten years later, in Philadelphia, Jefferson saw the first successful manned balloon flight in America.

His friend Hopkinson, a lawyer, writer, and signer of the Declaration of Independence, saw a witty connection between the political and the scientific. "A high-flying politician," Hopkinson wrote, "is I think not unlike a balloon—he is full of inflammability, he is driven along by every current of wind, and those who will suffer themselves to be carried up by them run a great risk that the bubble may burst and let them fall from the height to which a principle of levity had raised them."

Jefferson's scientific curiosity never abated. One day James Madison wrote with extraordinary news from abroad: He had been told "a subterraneous city has been discovered in Siberia, which appears to have been once populous and magnificent. Among other curiosities it contains an equestrian statue around the neck of which was a golden chain 200 feet in length, so exquisitely wrought that Buffon inferred from a specimen of 6 feet sent him by the Empress of Russia that no artist in Paris could equal the workmanship."

The Reverend James Madison, the president of William and Mary and a cousin of Jefferson's political ally James Madison, wrote Jefferson about climate (he was annoyed that "the British robbed me of my thermometer and barometer"), about new scientific books, and about a comet. "You have no doubt observed the comet which made its appearance here last Friday evening for the first time. . . . I shall endeavor to trace its progress and will send you the result."

J. Hector St. John de Crèvecoeur contacted Jefferson with a curious scientific inquiry: whether there was truth to a rumor in France that "in some of the remotest settlements of Virginia or Carolina, brandy has been distilled from potatoes." He was asking Jefferson, he said, because of the "respect with which I have heard your name mentioned as well as from your extensive knowledge and taste for the arts and sciences."

Jefferson believed in trial and error, exploring Buffon's theory of heat and seeking breakthroughs in botany. "I have always thought that if in the experiments to introduce or to communicate new plants, one species in a hundred is found useful and succeeds, the ninety-nine found otherwise are more than paid for," he remarked.

He wrote the Marquis de Barbé-Marbois to thank him for finding Patsy a French tutor in Philadelphia and for suggestions for her reading. Jefferson reported that he had given her a copy of **Gil Blas**, a French picaresque novel by Alain-René Lesage, and of Cervantes's **Don Quixote**—"which are among the best books of their class as far as I am acquainted with them." His selections suggested a love of intellectual adventure that he hoped his daughter would come to share.

He was a generous father, but could be a stern one, too. "The acquirements which I hope you will make under the tutors I have provided for you will render you more worthy of my love, and if they cannot increase it they will prevent its diminution," he wrote to his daughter. He had engaged Mrs. Thomas Hopkinson, Francis Hopkinson's mother, to watch over Patsy, and he invested Mrs. Hopkinson with the authority of his beloved late wife.

> Consider the good lady who has taken you
> under her roof, who has undertaken to see that
> you perform all your exercises, and to admonish
> you in all those wanderings from what is right or
> what is clever to which your inexperience would
> expose you, consider her I say as your mother, as

the only person to whom . . . you can now look
up; and that her displeasure or disapprobation
on any occasion will be an immense misfortune
which should you be so unhappy as to incur
by any unguarded act, think no concession too
much to regain her good will.

The love of the woman he was putting in her
mother's place, then, was to be contingent, not constant. Jefferson expected his daughter to apply herself to the work he prescribed with the same energy
and effort he gave everything he did.

With respect to the distribution of your time,
the following is what I should approve:

From 8 to 10 o'clock, practice music.
From 10 to 1, dance one day and draw another.
From 1 to 2, draw on the day you dance, and
    write a letter the next day.
From 3 to 4, read French.
From 4 to 5, exercise yourself in music.
From 5 till bed-time, read English, write, etc.

His tutelage was not limited to Patsy. "You are
now old enough to know how very important to
your future life will be the manner in which you
employ your present time," he wrote his nephew
Peter Carr, son of his sister Martha and Dabney, in
December 1783. "I hope therefore you will never

waste a moment of it." He entrusted Carr to James Maury, his old teacher.

Jefferson had large ambitions for Carr—ambitions that mirrored those he had for himself. Jefferson wished Carr to become "a man of learning and influence" and expected him to be preparing for "the public stage of life." (He also advised Carr to learn Spanish. "Our future connection with Spain renders that the most necessary of the modern languages, after the French," he told him. "When you become a public man you may have occasion for it, and the circumstance of your possessing that language may give you a preference over other candidates.")

Later, he told his nephew that religion required careful thought, not reflexive acceptance. "Fix reason firmly in her seat, and call to her tribunal every fact, every opinion. Question with boldness even the existence of a God; because, if there be one, he must more approve the homage of reason, than that of blindfolded fear."

Jefferson longed for order, control, affection. "Monroe is buying land almost adjoining me," Jefferson wrote to Madison from Annapolis in February 1784. "[William] Short will do the same. What would I not give [if] you could fall into the circle. . . . Think of it. To render it practicable only requires you to think it so. Life is of no value but as it brings us gratifications. Among the most valuable of these is rational society. It informs the mind, sweetens the temper, cheers our spirits, and promotes health."

Jefferson was an attentive and good friend through the years. "Though the different walks of life into which we have been led do not bring us together, yet I inquire of your health, with anxious concern, from everyone who comes from you," he once wrote George Wythe. "I shall forever cherish the remembrance of the many agreeable and useful days I have passed with you, and the infinite obligations I owe you for what good has fallen to me through life." Jefferson's friend Alexander Donald, of Richmond, was hosting Warner Lewis at home when a letter from Jefferson arrived in late 1787. The note, Donald told Jefferson, "was so friendly, and so very flattering to my pride, that I could not resist the vanity of showing it to him. He added to my pride by declaring . . . that of all the men he ever knew in his life, he believed you to be the most sincere in your profession of friendship. . . . Some people in your high character would be very apt to forget their old acquaintance, but you are not, and I must be allowed to do myself the justice to declare, I never entertained an idea that you would."

The Confederation Congress remained a mess seemingly beyond Jefferson's control; it was difficult even to gather a quorum. "Admonition after admonition has been sent to the states, to no effect," he told Madison in February 1784. "I fear that our chance is at this time desperate."

Reimbursement of the legislators' personal expenses was also a problem. "Among other legislative subjects our distresses ask notice," Jefferson said. "I had been from home four months and had expended 1200 dollars before I received one farthing." For a few of Jefferson's colleagues the money came too late. "In the meantime some of us had had the mortification to have our horses turned out of the livery stable for want of money. There is really no standing this."

On a graver note, chatter about kings or a reassertion of British influence was frequent enough to inform Jefferson's thinking about politics through the decades. In late January 1784, Jefferson drafted a reply to a letter from a correspondent in Boston, who had written to warn of "encroachments . . . made on the territories of the state of Massachusetts by the subjects of his Britannic majesty from the government of Nova Scotia."

After reading a report from Benjamin Franklin several weeks later, Jefferson warned George Washington that it

> gives a picture of the disposition of England towards us; he observes that though they have made peace with us, they are not reconciled to us nor to the loss of us. He calls to our attention

the numerous royal progeny to be provided for, the military education giving to some of them, the ideas in England of distraction among ourselves, that the people here are already fatigued with their new governments, the possibility of circumstances arising on the Continent of Europe which might countenance the wishes of Great Britain to recover us, and from thence inculcates a useful lesson to cement the friendships we possess in Europe.

As he fought "an attack of my periodical headache" in March 1784, he wrote Washington: "I suppose the crippled state of Congress is not new to you. . . . The consequence is that we are wasting our time and labor in vain efforts to do business."

The British were dunning the Americans for prewar debts, and at least two elements of the Treaty of Paris were open issues: the British promise to abandon their forts in the West and their pledge to return captured and escaped slaves. Both, naturally, were of concern to Virginians, and the questions kept the two countries in a state of agitation for years.

The West let him dream big, and he proposed a trade route connecting the Ohio and Potomac rivers. "This is the moment . . . for seizing it if ever we mean to have it," he said. "All the world is becoming commercial." Jefferson was pushing Virginia to approve a special tax for the river project, but, as he told George Washington, "a most powerful objection always arises to propositions of this kind. It is that public undertakings are carelessly managed and much money spent to little purpose."

Jefferson's plan for overcoming these obstacles: recruit Washington from retirement to head up the project. The idea had fascinated Washington for decades, but the general's reply was pragmatic. Though he agreed with Jefferson about the merits of the project, Washington said, "I have no expectation that the public will adopt the measure; for besides the jealousies which prevail, and the difficulty of proportioning such funds as may be allotted for the purposes you have mentioned, there are two others, which in my opinion, will be yet harder to surmount. These are (if I have not imbibed too unfavorable an opinion of my countrymen) the impracticability of bringing the great and truly wise policy of this measure to their view, and the difficulty of drawing money from them for such a purpose if you could do it." Nevertheless, Jefferson's letter renewed Washington's interest. Their hope was to clear navigation on the Potomac to a point where a portage road could link it to the Ohio. Washington supervised improvements to the Potomac as head of a private company, but it would take decades before the Chesapeake & Ohio Canal came into being.

In April, Washington implicitly complimented Jefferson by writing for his "opinion of the Institution of the Society of Cincinnati," an organization of Washington's officers that some feared was a nascent aristocratic order that could corrupt the republic.

Jefferson was happy that Washington had asked. The issue of the Cincinnati, he said, "is interesting, and, so far as you have stood connected with it, has been a matter of anxiety to me. . . . I have wished to see you stand on ground separated from it; and that the character which will be handed to future ages at the head of our revolution may in no instance be compromised in subordinate altercations."

Nothing could be better calculated to win Washington's attention than the suggestion that his own reputation was at risk. Jefferson said that he was certain that Washington meant no harm. The "moderation and virtue of a single character"— Washington—"has probably prevented this revolution from being closed as most others have been by a subversion of that liberty it was intended to establish," but even he "is not immortal, and his successor or some one of his successors at the head of this institution may adopt a more mistaken road to glory." Congress, Jefferson said, shared his views.

He argued against the Order on two grounds. First, that the political nature of man made it highly unlikely that a society designed to meet regularly would remain peaceable. "The way to make friends quarrel is to pit them in disputation under the public eye," Jefferson said. A second Jeffersonian objection was that a hereditary society was out of harmony with the spirit of a republic based on what Jefferson called the "natural equality of man."

Washington appears to have taken Jefferson's counsel seriously. The general pressed the Society to end the granting of honorary memberships, a category Jefferson had written "might draw into the order all the men of talents, of office and wealth; and in this case would probably procure an ingraftment into the government."

Jefferson thought broadly and boldly about the national government and national enterprises. "I see the best effects produced by sending our young statesmen here," he told Madison. "They see the affairs of the Confederacy from a high ground; they learn the importance of the Union and befriend federal measures when they return."

On Monday, March 1, 1784, Congress accepted the Virginia cession of territory northwest of the Ohio River, the culmination of several years of negotiations and clashing interests. The final cession transferred claims to the northwestern territory from Virginia to the United States. The lands ceded, the question was what would happen next.

Rarely without a thought in such a situation, Jefferson had already been at work on a plan to create new states. He even had names for them: Sylvania, Cherronesus, Assenisipia, Metropotamia, Illinoia, Michigania, Washington, Saratoga, Polypotamia, and Pelisipia. The Ordinance of 1784 is significant in that it left many of the details of organization to the future states themselves. They were, however, to "forever remain a part of this confederacy of the United States of America" and "their respective governments shall be republican."

Most significantly, the version of the Ordinance of 1784 that Jefferson supported banned the expansion of slavery into the new territories. The plan failed by a single vote in the Congress (a delegate from New Jersey was too ill to attend, dooming the bill). Reflecting on the closeness of the decision, Jefferson wrote: "Thus we see the fate of millions unborn hanging on the tongue of one man, and heaven was silent in that awful moment."

After an early legal and legislative life attempting to abolish slavery, Jefferson, now at midlife, made a calculated decision that he would no longer risk his "usefulness" in the arena by pressing the issue. (There was a partial victory later: The Northwest Ordinance of 1787 prohibited slavery north of the Ohio and east of the Mississippi rivers.) In all, though, for Jefferson public life was about compromise and an unending effort to balance competing interests. To have pursued abolition, even when coupled, as it was in Jefferson's mind, with deportation, was politically lethal. And Jefferson was not going to risk all for what he believed was a cause whose time had not yet come.

For Jefferson, Friday, May 7, 1784, was long and consequential. Through the morning and into the afternoon, he wrote more than a dozen letters and papers on subjects ranging from Continental bills of credit to western territory commercial resolutions to the Society of the Cincinnati to the lost Siberian city that Madison had spoken of to family matters with Polly and the Eppeses and the Carrs.

At five p.m., after the regular post had left Annapolis, the Confederation Congress added Jefferson to its mission to Europe. He was to join Franklin and Adams in establishing alliances for the new nation. Hurrying to write William Short, a young lawyer and kinsman by marriage who he hoped would come to Paris with him as his private secretary, Jefferson also sent for James Hemings, whom Jefferson wanted trained as a French cook.

"I am now to take my leave of the justlings of states and to repair to a field where the divisions will be fewer but on a larger scale," Jefferson wrote Madison on the day after the appointment was official. He would be guided, he said, by the broad principles that had brought him to this point in his public life: "I shall pursue there the line I have pursued here, convinced that it can never be the interest of any party to do what is unjust, or to ask what is unequal."

At the same time, he asked Madison to keep him in the know. "At the close of every session of assembly a state of the general measures and dispositions, as well as of the subordinate politics of parties or individuals will be entertaining and useful." He could not imagine life without such news. It was his daily bread.

His love for and trust in Madison had deepened, and he left what he called "a tender legacy" to his friend: the education of Peter Carr. Peter's father, the late Dabney Carr, remained as real to Jefferson in 1784 as he had in their youths. "I will not say it is the son of my sister, though her worth would justify my resting it on that ground; but it is the son of my friend, the dearest friend I knew, who, had fate reversed our lots, would have been a father to my children," Jefferson wrote Madison. At fourteen, Peter was "nearly master of the Latin, and has read some Greek. . . . I would wish him to be employed till 16 in completing himself in Latin, Greek, French, Italian and Anglo-Saxon. At that age I mean him to go to the college" at Williamsburg.

On Tuesday, May 11, 1784, Jefferson wrote a farewell to the Virginia House. In it he underscored anew his central political concern: the strength of the too-shaky confederation. He had, he said, "made the just rights of my country and the cement of that union in which her happiness and security is bound up, the leading objects of my conduct." With that he ended his six months of service as one of Virginia's delegates in the Congress—a time in which he had seen firsthand the price of loose affiliations and feeble national authority.

The prospect of Paris was both enticing and intimidating. In writing Jefferson about the politics of place, William Short noted that appearances and subtleties mattered enormously. The "foolish World in Paris . . . [is] a formidable Monster which must be obeyed," Short said.

As Jefferson awaited passage from Boston, he gathered intelligence on the commerce of the northern states, taking copious notes. His goal: to learn enough that "might in some degree enable me to answer the purposes of my mission."

On the evening of Sunday, July 4, 1784, Jefferson finished his congressional business. It had been eight years since he wrote the Declaration of Independence, and the nation defined in that summer of 1776 faced serious doubts about its viability.

At four o'clock on the Monday morning of July 5, 1784, Jefferson, with Patsy and James Hemings, left Boston harbor on the **Ceres,** a man of the New World bound for the Old.

PART V

A MAN OF THE WORLD

1785 to 1789

He is full of honor and sincerity and loves his country greatly, but [is] too philosophic and tranquil to hate or love any other nation unless it is for the interest of the United States to do so.

—THE CHEVALIER DE LA LUZERNE, on Thomas Jefferson as America's envoy to France

Jefferson loved the architectural innovation of the dome of the Halle aux Blés, the grain market in Paris. It was on a trip here that Jefferson first met Maria Cosway.

EIGHTEEN

The Vaunted Scene of Europe

A coward is much more exposed to quarrels
than a man of spirit.

—THOMAS JEFFERSON

THE VOYAGE ACROSS THE ATLANTIC was swift
and largely pleasant; Patsy always remembered the "good company, and . . . excellent
table" of the **Ceres**. "The winds were so favorable
through the whole passage that we never deviated
from the direct course more than was necessary to
avoid shoals, etc.," Jefferson recalled.

He was in love with France before he even
reached Paris. Jefferson's work in Europe offered
him a new battlefield in the war for American
union and national authority that he had begun
in the Congress. His sojourn in France is often
seen as a revolutionary swoon during which he
fell too hard for the foes of monarchy, growing
overly attached to—and unhealthily admiring of—
the French Revolution and its excesses. Some of
his most enduring radical quotations, usually con-

sidered on their own with less appreciation of the larger context of Jefferson's decades-long political, diplomatic, and philosophical careers, date from this era.

His relationship to France and to the French, however, should be seen for what it was: a political undertaking in which Jefferson put the interests of America first. He was determined to create a balance of global power in which France would help the United States resist commercial and possible military threats from the British. From the ancien régime of Louis XVI and Marie-Antoinette to the French Revolution to the Age of Napoleon, Jefferson viewed France in the context of how it could help America on the world stage.

Much of Jefferson's energy was spent striving to create international respect for the United States and to negotiate commercial treaties to build and expand American commerce and wealth. His mind wandered and roamed and soared, but in his main work—the advancement of America's security and economic interests—he was focused and clear-headed. Countries earned respect by appearing strong and unified. Jefferson wanted America to be respected. He, therefore, took care to project strength and a sense of unity. The cause of national power required it, and he was as devoted to the marshaling of American power in Paris as he had been in Annapolis.

En route across the Atlantic, Jefferson arranged for the captain of the **Ceres** to transport hares, rabbits, and partridges back to friends in Virginia "to raise and turn out breeders"; Jefferson also ordered Stilton cheeses and porter to be sent to his brothers-in-law.

After nineteen days, the **Ceres** encountered what he called "very thick weather" off the French coast. A fever struck Patsy in the last days at sea, and Jefferson stopped with her at the Isle of Wight for about a week before they crossed the English Channel to France. The Jeffersons arrived at Le Havre on Saturday, July 31, 1784, and the journey from the port to the capital was entrancing. They rode, Jefferson said, "through a country than which nothing can be more fertile, better cultivated or more elegantly improved." By the time he arrived in Paris on Friday, August 6, he was in the opening moments of what became a lifelong romance with a nation he thought "the most agreeable country on earth."

While in France, Jefferson negotiated treaties on whale oil and tobacco, fighting for American producers. He kept a wary eye on a French expedition to the South Seas, worrying that perhaps the voyage was really about establishing influence on the Pacific coast. When the French Revolution came in 1789, he hoped the upheaval would lead to the purchase of American exports, particularly foodstuffs, and to the opening of St. Domingue for American trade. Above all, he worked to maintain a relationship with Paris that would keep London in some kind of check. Amid the high fashion and the high-flown talk, Jefferson remembered his chief task was the protection and promotion of a republican United States in a world of competing imperial powers.

J. Hector St. John de Crèvecoeur advised Jefferson on the places to be. "I beg you'd put Mr. Franklin in mind of introducing you to the good duke of La Rochefoucauld. He is the pearl of all the dukes, a good man, and a most able chemist. His house is the center of . . . reunion where men of genius and abilities often meet." The Italian polymath Philip Mazzei added a chatty, detailed memorandum on a few of the key figures in France. (An example: "The Duke de la Vauguyon is entitled to the gratitude of the Americans; and it will be proper to make him sensible that it is well known in America.") One friend Jefferson was to make, the Marquis de Condorcet, believed the destinies of America and of France were bound up with each other. He wrote a pamphlet, **De l'influence de la révolution de l'Amérique sur l'Europe,** and held Paine-like visions of the possibilities of the hour. "Everything tells us that we are bordering the period of one of the greatest revolutions of the human race. The present state of enlightenment guarantees that it will be happy."

Jefferson took up residence first in lodgings in the rue de Richelieu, then in the Hôtel d'Orléans in the rue des Petits-Augustins. He saw that Patsy was appropriately and fashionably outfitted for the city and for her new school at the convent Abbaye Royale de Panthemont, where she boarded. In the middle of October Jefferson moved again, taking a house for 4,000 livres a year called the Hôtel Lândron in the Cul-de-Sac Taitbout. Wine, furniture, music, horses, and linen consumed Jefferson's resources. "For the articles of household furniture, clothes, and a carriage . . . I have been obliged to anticipate my salary from which however I shall never be able to repay it," Jefferson wrote to Monroe. "I will pray you to touch this string, which I know to be a tender one with Congress, with the utmost delicacy. I'd rather be ruined in my fortune, than in their esteem."

He joined fellow American commissioner John Adams in Paris, where Abigail Adams had come to live with her husband in a lovely house in Auteuil. Abigail found Jefferson charming. "Mr. Adams's colleague Mr. Jefferson is an excellent man," she wrote. The Adamses' daughter Nabby thought Jefferson "a most agreeable man," and Jefferson grew so close to the Adamses' son John Quincy that John Adams later remarked that the young man in those days had seemed "as much your boy as mine."

The Paris in which Jefferson lived and worked was in the midst of enormous growth; it was, he said, "every day enlarging and beautifying." There were houses, theaters, the wall of the farmers-general—a barrier to ensure the collection of taxes on goods coming into Paris—and nearly fifty neoclassical customs houses. The Palais Royal, a kind of urban shopping mall filled with cafés, gaming parlors, bookstalls, and (at night) more than a few prostitutes, opened in 1784, the year of Jefferson's arrival, and its festive chaos fascinated him. He considered it one of the "principal ornaments of the city" and said he thought Richmond could use such a marketplace.

Across the capital and later in the intoxicatingly beautiful south of France, Jefferson learned all he could about the architecture, the art, the theater, the music, the literature, the food, the wine, and the people of this "great and good" country. "So ask the travelled inhabitant of any nation," he wrote later in his autobiography, "in what country on earth would you rather live?" The first answer, he said, would be in one's own. But the second? France, of course, always France.

As Jefferson worked to make it clear that the United States was mature enough to hold its own against the European nations in terms of foreign and commercial policy, he faced a crisis in the Mediterranean in which he would advocate American action—up to and including war.

The Barbary States—Morocco, Algiers, Tunis, and Tripoli—threatened American commerce. They were seen as a collection of renegade Muslim states that demanded payments from Western nations in exchange for protection from pirates. (A book of the era entitled **Geography: Or, A Description of the World,** said: "These States are noted for their hostility to the Christian name, and for their piracies exercised chiefly in the Mediterranean sea, against all those Christian powers which do not purchase their forbearance by a disgraceful tribute.") The danger was real enough for many European countries to pay annual tribute to the Barbary States to keep ships safe from harm.

Jefferson had been subtly investigating how much the other countries gave "to purchase their peace." No one wanted to tell him, he wrote to James Monroe, "yet from some glimmerings it appears to be very considerable"—somewhere between $100,000 and $300,000 a year. "Surely our people will not give this," he continued. "Would it not be better to offer them an equal treaty? If they refuse, why not go to war with them? . . . We ought to begin a naval power, if we mean to carry on our own commerce. Can we begin it on a more honorable occasion or with a weaker foe?"

In the wake of the capture of an American ship by the emperor of Morocco, Jefferson pressed again for a warlike response. "Be assured that the present disrespect of the nations of Europe for us will inevitably bring on insults which must involve us in war," he told Monroe. He also saw English intrigue at work in reports of the Barbary States' hostility toward America: "These are framed in London to justify their demands of high insurance on our vessels."

Jefferson was known to believe Britain a perpetual threat. "He has a principle that it is for the happiness and welfare of the United States to hold itself aloof from England," wrote Luzerne, and "that as a consequence of this system it becomes them to attach themselves particularly to France."

Worried about how adept the British were at using newspapers to undermine America in the theater of European public opinion, Jefferson took matters into his own hands. In a series of articles for a Dutch publication, he invented a fictitious French officer in whose mouth Jefferson put a pro-American argument designed to counter the British propaganda. "I have fought and bled for [America] because I thought its cause just," Jefferson wrote in the officer's voice. Once home, however, "the Frenchman" found his friends offering "condolences . . . on the bitter fruits of so prosperous a war." How could such good people, Jefferson's officer wondered, be so misinformed?

Because, he wrote, answering his own rhetorical question, they have been reading the English newspapers. "Nothing is known in Europe of the situation of the U.S. since the acknowledgement of their independence but through the channel of these papers," he said. "But these papers have been under the influence of two ruling motives 1. Deep-rooted hatred, springing from an unsuccessful attempt to injure; 2. A fear that their island will be depopulated by the emigration of its inhabitants to America."

The article was published in two installments in December 1784 in the **Leyden Gazette**. Jefferson understood the mechanics of the media of his age, and his 1784 letter was calculated to change public opinion by engaging the enemy on his terms.

Jefferson told Francis Eppes he was dispatching barrels of brandy—for Eppes and for another brother-in-law, Henry Skipwith, who had married a sister of his late wife—and planned to order claret for Eppes from Bordeaux. He had his own cravings, too: "Send me a dozen or two hams from Monticello if any vessel [travels] from James River to Havre."

In January 1785, distressing news arrived from Eppington. Jefferson's daughter Lucy, age two, was dead, a victim of the whooping cough. The affliction was described as a "convulsive strangulating cough . . . returning by fits that are usually terminated by a vomiting, and being contagious." The Eppeses had lost a daughter of their own, too. "It's impossible to paint the anguish of my heart on this melancholy occasion," Elizabeth Eppes wrote. "A most unfortunate whooping cough has deprived you, and us of two sweet Lucys, within a week. Ours was the first. . . . She was thrown into violent convulsions, lingered a week and then expired. Your dear angel was confined a week to her bed, her sufferings were great though nothing like a fit. She retained her senses perfectly, called me a few moments before she died, and asked distinctly for water. . . . Life is scarcely supportable under such severe afflictions."

Her husband, Francis Eppes, gave Jefferson the brutal truth. The two Lucys, he said, "both suffered as much pain, indeed more than ever I saw two of their ages experience. . . . They were beyond the reach of medicine." Jefferson's depth of feeling was evident in his valedictory to his middle daughter, Polly: "Present me affectionately to Mrs. Eppes, who will kiss my dear, dear Polly for me. Oh! Could I do it myself!"

Lucy's death made a difficult season even worse. "Mr. J. is a man of great sensibility, and parental affection," Abigail and John Adams's daughter Nabby Adams wrote in her journal. "His wife died when this child [Lucy] was born, and he was in a confirmed state of melancholy; confined himself from the world, and even from his friends, for a long time; and this news has greatly affected him."

Now it was winter. He hated the damp of Paris. "Behold me at length on the vaunted scene of Europe!" Jefferson wrote in 1785. "I find the general fate of humanity here most deplorable. The truth of Voltaire's observation offers itself perpetually, that every man here must be either the hammer or the anvil." As much as Jefferson loved France, residence abroad gave him a greater appreciation for his own nation. "My God! How little do my countrymen know what precious blessings they are in possession of, and which no other people on earth enjoy," Jefferson wrote Monroe. "I confess I had no idea of it myself." This was the voice of the republican Jefferson, the political philosopher who recoiled at the idea that the United States might one day meet the same fate that led so many nations of the Old World into monarchy, priestly authority, and corruption.

It was only when spring came that he began to recover. By early May he had made a significant personal decision: He wanted to bring his family together. He was now walking up to six or eight miles a day as he tried to keep the demons of his latest loss at bay. With Lucy gone, he was eager to have Polly join him and Patsy in France. "I must have Polly," Jefferson wrote Francis Eppes in May 1785. "As would not have her at sea but between 1st of April and September this will allow time for decision—is there any woman in Virginia [who] could be hired to come?"

Relations between America and Britain were poor and growing poorer still. John and Abigail Adams moved from Paris to London, where John became minister to Great Britain. In London, Abigail missed Jefferson. "I think I have somewhere met with the observation that nobody ever leaves Paris but with a degree of tristeness," she wrote to Jefferson in June 1785. "I own I was loath to leave my garden because I did not expect to find its place supplied. I was still more loath on account of the increasing pleasure and intimacy which a longer acquaintance with a respected friend promised, [and] to leave behind me the only person with whom my companion could associate with perfect freedom and unreserve: and whose place he had no reason to expect supplied in the land to which he is destined."

Jefferson had been appointed America's sole minister to France. "Our country is getting into a ferment against yours, or rather have caught it from yours," Jefferson wrote to an English correspondent. "God knows how this will end: but assuredly in one extreme or the other. There can be no medium between those who have loved so much."

Jefferson sensed that, as with lovers and intimate friends, there can often be no middle ground between engagement and estrangement. In the presence of passion, or of former passions, acquaintance is impossible. It is all or nothing, for once affections have cooled it is very difficult to bring them back to a middling temperature. In such cases human nature tends to rekindle the flames to their old force, or consign them to perpetual chill. America and Britain would one day have to choose between permanent enmity or permanent affection.

There were constant fears about foreign designs in America. "We have intelligence (which though not entirely authentic is believed by many) that the British are enticing our people to settle lands within our lines under their government and protection by gratuitous supplies of provisions, implements of husbandry etc.," John Jay wrote Jefferson in July 1785.

From South Carolina, Ralph Izard, a former diplomat who had also served in the Continental Congress, affirmed Jefferson's own anxieties about America. "It is said that Great Britain has encouraged the piratical states to attack our vessels. If this could be proved, I should prefer a war against her, rather than against Algiers," wrote Izard. "But it is a melancholy fact that we are not in a condition to go to war with anybody. . . . The revenues of America, under the present management, do not appear to be adequate to the discharge of the public debt. Where then shall we find resources to carry on war?"

Izard took a comprehensive view, including the failure of American politicians to master the craft of governing. "Our governments tend too much to democracy. A handicraftsman thinks an apprenticeship necessary to make him acquainted with his business. But our back countrymen are of [the] opinion that a politician may be born such as well as a poet."

Like poetry, politics was partly inspiration, but it was, as Izard said and Jefferson knew, a craft that required relentless practice. It was a lesson Jefferson had learned in Williamsburg, and which now served him well an ocean away.

NINETEEN

The Philosophical World

Will you take the trouble to procure for me
the largest pair of bucks horns you can?
—THOMAS JEFFERSON to Archibald Cary

J EFFERSON FOUND THE SHOPPING in France wonderful. He bought silver and china and wine. Intrigued by a new innovation—"phosphoretic" matches—he purchased three dozen to send to friends in America. There were opera tickets and Italian comedy tickets and tickets to the occasional **concert spirituel,** musical performances in the Salle des Machines of the Palais des Tuileries. (Jefferson's first included a song of Handel's.) He acquired more than sixty paintings in his five years in Paris, many of them portraits or images of religious subjects or scenes. Particular purchases: a **Prodigal Son,** a **Democritus and Heraclitus,** a **St. Peter Weeping,** a **Magdalen Penitent,** and a **Herodias Bearing the Head of St. John the Baptist.**

Twice he attended masquerade balls at the Opéra—parties that began at eleven p.m. and ran until six in the morning. (Once he and William S. Smith, John Adams's son-in-law, were the targets of a forward baroness: "When Mr. Jefferson had made his escape," Smith wrote, "she had fastened her talons on me.") On Tuesdays he made his way to Versailles for Ambassadors' Day. He also visited Patsy at her convent school, the Abbaye Royale de Panthemont, which was run by Bernardine nuns—"a house of education altogether the best in France, and at which the best masters attend," Jefferson wrote to one of his sisters in Virginia.

He tried to play chess with Parisians but found that they were too accomplished for him. When he arrived in Paris, he had accepted an invitation to join an elite chess club at the Palais Royal, the Salon des Échecs. "I have heard him say that when, on his arrival in Paris, he was introduced into a chess club, he was beaten at once, and that so rapidly and signally that he gave up all competition," one of his granddaughters recalled. He was not a man who liked to lose.

He devoted his energies to the delights of the city's intellectual society. In June 1785, Jefferson called on the Comtesse d'Houdetot at Sannois, hoping that the trip "has opened a door of admission for me to the circle of literati with which she is environed." There the party heard a nightingale's song, Jefferson said, "in all its perfection: and I do not hesitate to pronounce that in America it would be deemed a bird of the third rank only, our mocking-bird and fox-colored thrush being unquestionably superior to it."

Jefferson remained ambivalent about the tension he found between the virtues and vices of European culture and politics. He was a tireless advocate for things American while abroad, and a promoter of things European while at home. Moving between the two worlds, translating the best of the old to the new and explaining the benefits of the new to the old, he created a role for himself as both intermediary and arbiter. From ideas of political power to Lombardy poplars, from architectural style to pasta, Jefferson put himself at the heart of the transatlantic conversation—always in the service of his nation.

He scouted the finest artists. Officials in Virginia had asked Jefferson and Franklin to execute a sacred charge: the commissioning of a statue of Washington for the new state capitol in Richmond. Jefferson found the perfect artist, Jean-Antoine Houdon, the man Jefferson considered the finest sculptor of the age. Writing Washington, Jefferson said that Houdon would like to come to America "for the purpose of forming your bust from the life."

Whatever Jefferson learned, he acted upon. "An improvement is made here in the construction of the musket which it may be interesting to Congress to know," Jefferson wrote John Jay in August 1785. "It consists in the making [of] every part of them so exactly alike that what belongs to any one, may be used for every other musket in the magazine." Jefferson also asked George Washington "to communicate to me what you can recollect of Bushnell's experiments in submarine navigation during the late war, and whether you think his method capable of being used successfully for the destruction of vessels of war." Jefferson sent John Jay documents about French marines on the chance that establishing a marine corps "may become interesting to us."

He took particular pains to convince the Comte de Buffon that American animals were not, as the count believed, inferior. Jefferson asked Archibald Cary to secure him the horns of a buck: He planned to demonstrate his point with a native example. Jefferson traveled to a school for the blind to learn what he could about its methods of teaching (he also owned a book on instructing deaf-mutes). With Malesherbes, a great French politician and botanist, he exchanged American nuts and berries for French grapevines. He also supported the plans of the American explorer John Ledyard, who was in Paris and called Jefferson "a brother to me." Ledyard was planning a journey from Siberia to Kamchatka and thence to North America to the Atlantic.

Jefferson held a unique position. "It is certainly of great importance to us to know what is done in the philosophical world; but our means of information are confined almost entirely to you," the Reverend James Madison wrote him from Williamsburg in April 1785. His home country's hunger for news was palpable. In a postscript, Madison wrote: "Has the Abbé Rochon published any thing upon his new discovery in optics? How is the effect produced? What is the specific gravity of the crystal? In what way does it differ from other rock crystals?" Jefferson was thrilled to be able to answer.

He also enjoyed shopping for John and Abigail Adams. He purchased a porcelain Mars to complete a set of Minerva, Diana, and Apollo for Abigail. "This will do, thinks I, for the table of the American Minister in London, where those whom it may concern may look and learn that though Wisdom is our guide, and Song and Chase our supreme delight, yet we offer adoration to that tutelar god also who rocked the cradle of our birth, who has accepted our infant offerings, and has shown himself the patron of our rights and avenger of our wrongs." (The figurines were accidentally destroyed en route to London.) He once sent corsets—by request—to the Adamses' daughter Abigail Smith. "He wishes they may be suitable," Jefferson wrote in the third person, "as Mrs. Smith omitted to send her measure. . . . Should they be too small however, she will be so good as to lay them by a while. There are ebbs as well as flows in this world." In return, John and Abigail Adams supervised Jefferson's English tailoring and shoemaking needs.

"I have at length procured a house in a situation much more pleasing to me than my present," he told

Abigail Adams in September 1785. It was the Hôtel de Langeac, at the corner of the Champs-Élysées and the rue de Berri. "I cultivate in my own garden here Indian corn for the use of my own table, to eat green in our manner," he wrote Nicholas Lewis in 1787.

Gardening kept him emotionally connected to home. "I am now of an age which does not easily accommodate itself to new manners and new modes of living: and I am savage enough to prefer the woods, the wilds, and the independence of Monticello, to all the brilliant pleasures of this gay capital."

He was not exactly a barbarous savage. "I observed that although Mr. Jefferson was the plainest man in the room, and the most destitute of ribbons, crosses and other insignia of rank that he was the most courted and most attended to (even by the courtiers themselves) of the whole diplomatic corps," wrote Thomas Shippen, a young American studying law in London who visited Jefferson in Paris, in 1788.

His public life was going well. "He is everything that is good, upright, enlightened, and clever," Lafayette wrote the Maryland physician and politician James McHenry from Paris in 1785, "and is respected and beloved by everyone that knows him." In a sketch published two years later, Luigi Castiglioni, an Italian count, wrote: "Mr. Jefferson is a man of about 50 years of age, lean, of a serious and modest appearance. His uncommon talents are not readily visible at a first encounter, but as one talks with him about the various subjects in which he believes himself to be informed, he very quickly gives evident proof of his judgment and application."

Jefferson's ability to absorb and assess the world around him, whether political, scientific, or social, was evident in a description of Parisian life he gave an American friend in his French years. Imaginatively offering a portrait of the daily routine amid the "empty bustle of Paris," he wrote:

> At eleven o'clock it is day chez Madame. The curtains are drawn. Propped on bolsters and pillows, and her head scratched into a little order, the bulletins of the sick are read, and the billets of the well. She writes to some of her acquaintance and receives the visits of others. If the morning is not very thronged, she is able to get out and hobble round the cage of the Palais royal: but she must hobble quickly, for the coiffeur's turn is come; and a tremendous turn it is! Happy, if he does not make her arrive when dinner is half over! The torpitude of digestion a little passed, she flutters half an hour through the streets by way of paying visits, and then to the Spectacles. These finished, another half hour is devoted to dodging in and out of the doors of her very sincere friends, and away to supper. After supper cards; and after cards bed, to rise at noon the next day, and to tread, like a mill-horse, the same trodden circle over again.

Thus the days of life are consumed, one by one, without an object beyond the present moment: ever flying from the ennui . . . eternally in pursuit of happiness which keeps eternally before us. If death or a bankruptcy happen to trip us out of the circle, it is matter for the buzz of the evening, and is completely forgotten by the next morning.

This was Jefferson's cultural view of the French; politically, he worried, too, about how the French viewed America. "The politics of Europe render it indispensably necessary that with respect to everything external we be one nation only, firmly hooped together," he wrote Madison in February 1786. "And it should ever be held in mind that insult and war are the consequences of a want of respectability in the national character." (He also asked Madison for a "hundred or two nuts of the pecan. They would enable me to oblige some characters here whom I should be much gratified to oblige.")

Madison was making some progress at home on his and Jefferson's mutual worry over the power of the central government. A convention to deal with issues of commerce was being assembled in Annapolis and ended by calling for the Constitutional Convention of 1787 in Philadelphia. Progress was slow, but real. First the states had to agree to send delegations; the delegations then had to settle on a plan; and finally the plan would face ratification in the states. "I almost despair of success," Madison said.

While in France, Jefferson mused about the relationship of the individual to the state. He had a stimulating companion with whom to discuss such questions: At midsummer 1787, Thomas Paine visited Jefferson in Paris.

The son of a corset maker, Paine was born in Thetford, a town in Norfolk, England, in 1737. He was raised in an unconventional climate of dissent. His father was a Quaker; his mother was the daughter of an Anglican lawyer. Young Paine was baptized in the Church of England but sometimes went to Quaker meetings.

His **Common Sense** had galvanized America in 1776, selling more than half a million copies. A powerful writer, Paine followed **Common Sense** with **The Rights of Man,** an assault on monarchy, in 1791, and, in 1794–95, with **The Age of Reason,** an equally epic assault on organized religion. Paine and Jefferson became friends and longtime correspondents; they shared a vision of a new, enlightened world—though Jefferson never forgot that it was foolhardy to sacrifice real progress, however compromised, to the dreams of the ideal.

John Adams wanted Jefferson to come to London. After a series of meetings with the ambassador from Tripoli—sessions that included large pipes of tobacco, turbans, and hot coffee—Adams believed there was an opening to come to an arrangement with the Mediterranean power. Without such a resolution, Adams feared, the American experiment itself might be at risk. "What has been already done and expended will be absolutely thrown away," he told Jefferson, arguing that there could be a war in the region "which will continue for many years, unless more is done immediately." In a letter dated Tuesday, February 21, 1786, he asked Jefferson to travel to England.

Jefferson accepted, telling Patsy that he would be back before a letter from her might reach him. "I shall defer engaging your drawing master till I return," he told her. "I hope then to find you much advanced in your music. I need not tell you what pleasure it gives me to see you improve in everything agreeable and useful."

At a London dinner hosted by Sir John Sinclair with members of the ministerial party, Jefferson was seated next to a General Clarke, a Scotsman. "He introduced the subject of American affairs, and in the course of the conversation told me that were America to petition Parliament to be again received on their former footing, the petition would be very generally rejected."

Jefferson could not believe what he was hearing. "He was serious in this, and I think it was the sentiment of the company, and is the sentiment perhaps of the nation." As Jefferson saw it, "the object of the present ministry [in London] is to buoy up the nation with flattering calculations of their present prosperity, and to make them believe they are better without us than with us. This they seriously believe; for what is it men cannot be made to believe!"

He showed neither anger nor puzzlement, which is often anger in disguise. Honed through long years in company in Virginia and beyond, it was a gift, this capacity to maintain a placid exterior no matter how much turmoil lurked beneath. He was usually a master of his emotions. "I know of no gentleman better qualified to pass over the disagreeables of life than Mr. Jefferson, as he makes his calculations for a certain quantity of imposition which must be admitted in his intercourse with the world," said a friend of Jefferson's. "When it shows itself in high colors, he has only to count ten and he is prepared for the subject."

In London he and Adams had called at court, only to find that it would have been "impossible for anything to be more ungracious" than George III and Queen Charlotte's "notice of Mr. Adams and myself." Many things can be (and are) said of Jefferson, but he was not a rude man, and the monarchs' unwelcoming disposition, however understandable given that the callers had humiliated the realm over which the Hanoverians presided, confirmed everything Jefferson already believed about hereditary power.

Jefferson was struck by the vitriol about America

that he read in the London press. "They teem with every horror of which human nature is capable," Jefferson remarked to Abigail Adams. "Assassinations, suicides, thefts, robberies, and, what is worse than assassination, theft, suicide, or robbery, the blackest slanders!" Jefferson shared a self-aware confidence with Abigail: "It would have illy suited me. I do not love difficulties. I am fond of quiet, willing to do my duty, but irritable by slander and apt to be forced by it to abandon my post. These are weaknesses from which reason and your counsels will preserve Mr. Adams."

Before Jefferson returned to France, he and Adams decided to spend a few days surveying English gardens, traveling together and passing many warm and intimate hours absorbing the cultivated beauty of a landscape shaped by the creative imaginations of men who had set themselves the task of subtly mastering the natural world.

In Paris, Jefferson was nervous and garrulous about arrangements to bring Polly to him from Virginia. "My anxieties on this subject could induce me to endless details, but your discretion and that of Mrs. Eppes saves me the necessity," he wrote Francis Eppes. "I commit to Mrs. Eppes my kisses for dear Poll, who hangs on my mind night and day."

Then a simple letter arrived. "Dear Papa," read the one-sentence missive, "I want to see you and sister Patsy, but you must come to Uncle Eppes's house."

Jefferson found himself in debate with a seven-year-old: "I wish so much to see you that I have desired your uncle and aunt to send you to me," he wrote Polly. "I know, my dear Polly, how sorry you will be, and ought to be, to leave them and your cousins but your sister and myself cannot live without you. . . . In the meantime you shall be taught here to play on the harpsichord, to draw, to dance, to read and talk French and such other things as will make you more worthy of the love of your friends. But above all things, by our care and love of you, we will teach you to love us more than you will do if you stay so far from us."

He could console himself in dark moments with the optimism evident in a recent letter from Charles Thomson: "I will venture to assert, that there is not upon the face of the earth a body of people more happy or rising into consequence with more rapid stride, than the inhabitants of the United States of America. Population is increasing, new houses building, new lands clearing, new settlements forming and new manufactures establishing with a rapidity beyond conception."

Jefferson was counting on it.

TWENTY

His Head and His Heart

> We are not immortal ourselves, my friend;
> how can we expect our enjoyments to be so?
> We have no rose without its thorn; no pleasure
> without alloy.
>
> —THOMAS JEFFERSON

SHE WAS, A CONTEMPORARY WROTE, "a golden-haired, languishing Anglo-Italian, graceful . . . and highly accomplished, especially in music." Born near Florence in 1759—she was sixteen years younger than Jefferson—Maria Louisa Catherine Cecilia Hadfield was the daughter of an expatriate English merchant who ran an inn popular in Italy. According to Helen Duprey Bullock, a historian who richly detailed Maria Cosway's life, the young girl grew up in a world suffused with money, art, and religious fervor, and was barely rescued from the ministrations of a murderous nurse who had killed four of Maria's siblings from the conviction that she was mercifully returning the children to the arms of God. "Dear little thing," the nurse was overheard saying to Maria, "I have sent four to Heaven before you and shall send you also." Educated in convents, Maria simultaneously pursued the visual arts (she was elected to the Academy of Fine Arts at Florence in 1778) and the life of the church (she was organist for the Monastery of the Visitation).

As a young woman in London, the beautiful Maria found herself in the glamorous circles inhabited by the writer James Boswell, the painters Sir Joshua Reynolds and Angelica Kauffmann, and the collector Charles Townley. She met and married Richard Cosway, an eccentric, charming, and successful miniaturist. He was, one observer wrote, "a well-made little man" who was nevertheless "very like a monkey in the face." Flamboyant and ambitious, Cosway won the patronage of the Prince of Wales and held court in elegance in Pall Mall. "His new house Cosway fitted up in so picturesque, and indeed so princely, a style that I regret drawings were not made of each apartment, for many of the rooms were more like scenes of enchantment penciled by a poet's fancy than anything perhaps before displayed in a domestic habitation," wrote the antiquarian John Thomas Smith. Furniture was ornately carved, gilded, and covered in "the most costly Genoa velvets"; there were ivory cabinets and mosaic tables with the feet of lions and eagles. Huge musical clocks made of tortoiseshell and ormolu ticked away, and screens of "old . . . Japan" sat atop Persian carpets.

The scholar William Howard Adams detailed contemporary assessments of the Cosway milieu, finding that the English man of letters William Hazlitt had written that the couple "kept house in style, in a sort of co-partnership, of so novel a character as to surprise their new neighbors . . . and furnish wonderment for the table-talk of the town." Horace Walpole, the writer and politician, meanwhile, once saw Mademoiselle la Chevalière d'Éon, known in her day as a transvestite-diplomat-spy, teaching fencing to the Cosways' guests in the midst of a party. One Cosway friend whom Jefferson got to know, Pierre-François Hugues, was the illustrator of the erotically explicit **Monuments de la vie privée des douze Césars** and **Monuments du culte secret des dames romaines**.

In Paris in the late summer of 1786, Hugues and the Cosways met the artist John Trumbull—and, through Trumbull, they were to make the acquaintance of the American minister to France.

Jefferson was in a marvelous mood. He was doing what he loved to do: moving through Paris on a relaxed, high-minded yet practical mission to explore the art of architecture with an eye toward adapting the most brilliant innovations of Europe for America.

With Trumbull, Jefferson called on the men who had designed the dome of the Halle aux Blés, the grain market in Paris. The architects Jacques-Guillaume

Legrand and Jacques Molinos had built a wood-ribbed dome punctuated with glass. The effect was wondrous, allowing light to pour through the glass sections. Jefferson, who thought it "the most superb thing on earth," was eager to learn more. Hence the call on Legrand and Molinos at No. 6 rue St.-Florentin, where Jefferson and Trumbull met the Cosways.

Maria, twenty-seven, enchanted Jefferson, then forty-three, from the first. She had voluptuous lips, startling violet-blue eyes, and fashionably coiffed golden hair. His infatuation with her appears to have been instantaneous. In a way, he disappeared into those eyes and did not emerge for air for nearly a month.

Hungry for her company, he put the rest of the world at bay. Engaged to dine that day at the Duchess de la Rochefoucauld's, Jefferson lied—not very inventively—and sent word to the duchess that diplomatic dispatches had arrived that "required immediate attention." Everyone else in the party joined in the conspiracy: "Every soul of you had an engagement for that day," Jefferson wrote. "Yet all these were to be sacrificed, that you might dine together."

The day was nearly perfect. Maria spoke many languages, but her English was not particularly fluent, which may have made Jefferson's conversations with her all the more exotic and charming. Jefferson, the Cosways, and Trumbull had dinner together in St.-Cloud, took in a fireworks display, and called on Johann Baptist Krumpholtz, the composer and harpist.

At last came the hour for parting. For Jefferson and Maria, however, this was only the opening act in a very brief but intense drama in which Jefferson showed every sign of having fallen in love. Richard Cosway may or may not have noticed, and if he did it is difficult to say whether he would have cared. Flirtation, if not more, was part of the world in which the Cosways lived, and it was not unknown in Jefferson's. The pursuit of the seemingly unavailable was something he knew from his experience with Betsy Walker. He had done this kind of thing before.

The early autumn of 1786, however, was the first time he was able to undertake a romantic adventure with so little risk of censure from the world around him. The most perilous element for Jefferson: that Maria, if James Boswell was to be believed, treated "men like dogs."

He was willing to risk it. Day after day as August gave way to September, the two made Paris their own. From St.-Germain to the Pont de Neuilly, from the hills along the banks of the Seine to a number of elaborate, secluded gardens, for Jefferson "every moment was filled with something agreeable." They had a fondness for getaway spots. Bagatelle was a neoclassical domed folly built by the Comte d'Artois, brother of the king. The Désert de Retz was an expansive garden that included a forested apartment built in a fanciful ancient column by François Racine de Monville. ("How grand the idea excited by the remains of such a column!" Jefferson said. "The spiral staircase too was beautiful.") Jefferson and Maria were in a private world. "The wheels of time moved on with a rapidity of which those of our carriage gave but a faint idea," he said. "And yet in the evening, when one took a retrospect of the day, what a mass of happiness had we travelled over!"

Jefferson dislocated his right wrist in this period; he was mysterious about exactly how he had come to be injured. ("It was by one of those follies from which good cannot come, but ill may," he told William Smith in October 1786.) The episode—perhaps a faux-heroic leap over a fence—occurred sometime on or shortly before September 18, days after the delegates gathered back home for the September 11, 1786, opening of the Annapolis Convention.

Writing him as he tried to recover, Maria said, "I only mention my wish. . . . I would serve you and help you at dinner, and divert your pain after dinner with good music."

He was honest about how much his hand hurt. "I have passed the night in so much pain that I have not closed my eyes," Jefferson wrote Maria. "It is with infinite regret therefore that I must relinquish your charming company for that of the surgeon whom I have sent for to examine into the cause of this change. I am in hopes it is only the having rattled a little too freely over the pavement yesterday. If you do not go today I shall still have the pleasure of seeing you again. If you do, God bless you wherever you go. . . . Let me know if you do not go today."

Maria, who was due to leave Paris, replied quickly.

I am very, very sorry indeed . . . for having been the cause of your pains in the [night]. . . . You repeatedly insisted it would do you no harm, I felt interested and did not insist. . . . I shall write to you from England, it is impossible to be wanting to a person who has been so excessively obliging. I don't attempt to make compliments, they can be none for you, but I beg you will think us sensible to your kindness, and that it will be with infinite pleasure I shall remember the charming days we have passed together, and shall long for next spring.

On October 9, 1786, came a note from John Trumbull in Antwerp: "Mr. and Mrs. Cosway arrived this morning at 3 o'clock having rode all night in the rain."

Saying good-bye had been, he told her later, his "last sad office." The result was a long, revealing letter dated October 12, 1786. "Seated by my fireside, solitary and sad, the following dialogue took place between my Head and my Heart," began the more than four-thousand-word essay (for it was more an essay than a conventional letter). In it Jefferson, writing with his left hand, shows himself to be a shrewd student of the human character in general and of his own in particular.

Head. Well, friend, you seem to be in a pretty trim.

Heart. I am indeed the most wretched of all earthly beings. Overwhelmed with grief, every fiber of my frame distended beyond its natural powers to bear, I would willingly meet whatever catastrophe should leave me no more to feel or to fear.

Head. These are the eternal consequences of your warmth and precipitation. This is one of the scrapes into which you are ever leading us. You confess your follies indeed: but still you hug and cherish them; and no reformation can be hoped, where there is no repentance.

Heart. Oh my friend! This is no moment to upbraid my foibles. I am rent into fragments by the force of my grief! If you have any balm, pour it into my wounds: if none, do not harrow them by new torments. Spare me in this awful moment! At any other I will attend with patience to your admonitions.

Head. On the contrary I never found that the moment of triumph with you was the moment of attention to my admonitions. While suffering under your follies you may perhaps be made sensible of them, but, the paroxysm over, you fancy it can never return. Harsh therefore as the medicine may be, it is my office to administer it. . . .

Heart. May heaven abandon me if I do! . . .

Head. I wished to make you sensible how imprudent it is to place your affections, without reserve, on objects you must so soon lose, and whose loss when it comes must cost you such severe pangs. Remember the last night. You knew your friends were to leave Paris today. This was enough to throw you into agonies. All night you tossed us from one side of the bed to the other. No sleep, no rest. . . . To avoid these eternal distresses, to which you are forever exposing us, you must learn to look forward before you take a step which may interest our peace. Everything in this world [is] a matter of calculation. Advance then with caution, the balance in your hand. Put into one scale the pleasures which any object may offer; but put fairly into the other the pains which are to follow, and see which preponderates. The making [of] an acquaintance is not a matter of indifference. When a new one is proposed to you, view it all round. Consider what advantages it presents, and to what inconveniences it may expose you. Do not bite at the bait of pleasure till you know there is no hook beneath it. The art of life is the art of avoiding pain: and he is the best pilot who steers clearest of the rocks and shoals with which he is beset. Pleasure is always before us; but misfortune is at our side: while running after that, this arrests us. The most effectual means of being secure against pain is to retire within ourselves, and to suffice for our own happiness. . . . A friend dies or leaves us: we feel as if a limb was cut off. He is sick: we must watch over him, and participate of his pains. His fortune is shipwrecked: ours must be laid under contribution. He loses a child, a parent, or a partner: we must mourn the loss as if it was our own.

Heart. And what more sublime delight than to mingle tears with one whom the hand of heaven hath smitten! To watch over the bed of sickness, and to beguile its tedious and its painful moments! To share our bread with one to whom misfortune has left none! This world abounds indeed with misery: to lighten its burdens we must divide it with one another. . . . When nature assigned us the same habitation, she gave us over it a divided empire. To you she allotted the field of science, to me that of morals. When the circle is to be squared, or the orbit of a comet to be traced; when the arch of greatest strength, or the solid of least resistance is to be investigated, take you the problem: it is yours: nature has given me no cognizance of it. In like manner in denying to you the feelings of sympathy, of benevolence, of gratitude, of justice, of love, of friendship, she has excluded you from their control. To these she has adapted the mechanism of the heart. Morals were too essential to the happiness of man to be risked on the uncertain combinations of the head. She laid their foundation therefore in sentiment, not in science. That she gave to all, as necessary to all: this to a few only, as sufficing with a few. I know indeed that you pretend authority to the sovereign control of our conduct in all its parts: and a respect for your grave saws and maxims, a desire to do what is right, has sometimes induced me to conform to your counsels. . . . If our country, when pressed with wrongs at the point of the bayonet, had been governed by its heads instead of its hearts, where should we have been now? Hanging on a gallows as high as Haman's. You began to calculate and to compare wealth and numbers: we threw up a few pulsations of our warmest blood: we supplied enthusiasm against wealth and numbers: we put our existence to the hazard, when the hazard seemed against us, and we saved our country: justifying at the same time the ways of Providence, whose precept is to do always what is right, and leave the issue to him. In short, my friend, as far as my recollection serves me, I do not know that I ever did a good thing on your suggestion, or a dirty one without it. I do forever then disclaim your interference in my province. Fill paper as you please with triangles and squares: try how many ways you can hang and combine them together. . . .

We are not immortal ourselves, my friend; how can we expect our enjoyments to be so? We have no rose without its thorn; no pleasure without alloy. It is the law of our existence; and we must acquiesce.

So which won, the Head or the Heart? Jefferson gave the Heart both the last word and the highest accolade he could bestow when he credited it with victory in the American Revolution.

The immediate recipient of the letter was not sure how to react. "Your letter could employ me for some time, an hour to consider every word, to every sentence I could write a volume," Maria wrote Jefferson, before lapsing into nonsensical English. They conducted a friendly, if sporadic, correspondence for the rest of their lives.

Jefferson's letter represents his most extensive literary attempt to reconcile competing human impulses. His categories of reason versus emotion here are useful but too tidy. The heart, for instance, can be driven by affection, appetite, or some combination of the two. Were his feelings for Maria rooted in his soul, or in his glands, or—most likely—both? The truth appears to have been murky even to Jefferson.

What is clear is that he was self-aware and prepared to live with unresolved contradictions, approaching the crises of life with a sense of hope tempered by a recognition that he, at least, was not fated to live to see the end of heartbreak, failure, disappointment, and death. "We have no rose without its thorn; no pleasure without alloy," he had written—as the Heart, not the Head. "It is the law of our existence; and we must acquiesce." Jefferson believed that the future could be better than the past. He knew, though, that life was best lived among friends in the pursuit of large causes, understanding that pain was the price for anything worth having.

TWENTY-ONE

Do You Like Our New Constitution?

> Cherish therefore the spirit of our people, and keep alive their attention. Do not be too severe upon their errors, but reclaim them by enlightening them.
>
> —THOMAS JEFFERSON

D EBT-RIDDEN, FRANCE FACED A supreme test. In the mid-1780s, partly because of its spending on the American Revolution, the Bourbon government of Louis XVI was in a long-term financial crisis, exacerbated by widespread hunger and by anger over the concentration of wealth in the hands of a few. Jefferson was shocked by the poverty he saw among ordinary Frenchmen; Patsy always remembered the beggars who surrounded their carriage as they first traveled to Paris.

The financial and political difficulties facing the monarchy and the French nation were immense. Taxes were unequal and haphazardly collected; the heaviest burden of the cost of the Crown and its expensive ways and wars fell less on nobles or clergy, who were largely exempt, and more on commoners, creating understandable tension and popular hostility. "It is impossible to increase taxes, disastrous to keep on borrowing, and inadequate merely to cut expenses," Charles-Alexandre de Calonne, Louis's finance minister, told the king in an August 1786 memorandum. At Calonne's urging, the king summoned an Assembly of Notables—the first in more than a century and a half—to consider a plan of reform. "Of course it calls up all the attention of the people," Jefferson wrote to John Jay in January 1787. Still, Jefferson was no hothead, arguing that dealing with such large problems required a deft hand.

"Should they attempt more than the established habits of the people are ripe for, they may lose all, and retard infinitely the ultimate object of their aim," Jefferson wrote a friend in March 1787.

The Assembly of Notables failed, leading to calls— including one from the Marquis de Lafayette—for an Estates-General, an institution of nobles, clergy, and commoners created in the Middle Ages to advise the monarchy. Its last meeting had been held in 1614.

Hope for large-scale reform began to quicken. One member of a liberally minded club captured the spirit of the hour as the Estates-General approached, writing: "We talked about the establishment of a new constitution for the state, as [if it were] an easy job, a natural event." He continued, "In the ecstasy of those days of hopes and celebration, we scarcely cast a glance at the obstacles to be overcome, before laying the first bases of freedom, before establishing the principles rejected by the spirit of the court, the privileged orders, the great corporations, and the old customs."

While the French were dealing with an authoritarian state, the Americans had the opposite problem. "The inefficacy of our government becomes daily more and more apparent," John Jay had written Jefferson in October 1786. "Our credit and our treasury are in a sad situation, and it is probable that either the wisdom or the passions of the people will produce changes."

Which of the two—the wisdom or the passions—was the question. In New England, a group led by Daniel Shays, a Revolutionary veteran, rose up to protest a lack of debt relief. "A spirit of licentiousness has infected Massachusetts," Jay wrote Jefferson.

John Adams sought to reassure Jefferson about Shays in November 1786. "Don't be alarmed at the late turbulence in New England," Adams wrote. "The Massachusetts assembly had, in its zeal to get the better of their debt, laid on a tax, rather heavier than the people could bear; but all will be well, and this commotion will terminate in additional strength to government."

Jefferson was relieved. "I can never fear that things

will go far wrong where common sense has fair play," he told Adams.

Then the inevitable issue: Would Britain use the moment to cause trouble for the United States? Jay wrote Jefferson that there might be Canadian designs on America through an "understanding between the insurgents in Massachusetts and some leading persons in Canada." Jay also fretted that Britain could capitalize on an "idea that may do mischief": the notion that "the interests of the Atlantic and Western parts of the United States are distinct" and "the growth of the latter tend[s] to diminish that of the former."

Writing to a correspondent in America with the expectation that his views would be shared at home, the powerless congressman of 1783 to 1784 was now taking a softer, more sanguine tone about authority and order. There is no question that Jefferson's experience in France gave his politics a more democratic cast than they had had when he left America for Paris. Jefferson wrote:

> The basis of our governments being the opinion of the people, the very first object should be to keep that right; and were it left to me to decide whether we should have a government without newspapers, or newspapers without a government, I should not hesitate a moment to prefer the latter. But I should mean that every man

should receive those papers and be capable of reading them. . . . Do not be too severe upon [the people's] errors, but reclaim them by enlightening them. If once they become inattentive to the public affairs, you and I, and Congress, and Assemblies, judges and governors shall all become wolves. It seems to be the law of our general nature, in spite of individual exceptions; and experience declares that man is the only animal which devours his own kind.

Jefferson showed his grasp of politics and his understanding of the nature of both governor and governed in a letter to Madison on Tuesday, January 30, 1787.

There were, he said, three kinds of societies: those without government ("as among our Indians"); those "wherein the will of everyone has a just influence"; and those "of force: as is the case in all other monarchies and in most of the other republics." It was fine to think of the first as ideal, Jefferson said, but it was impractical where there was "any great degree of population"; he thus dispensed with an Edenic vision of free men dwelling together "without government." The second was where men should focus their attention and their care. "The mass of mankind under that enjoys a precious degree of liberty and happiness. It has its evils too: the principal of which is the turbulence to which it is subject. But weigh this against the oppressions of monarchy, and it becomes nothing."

Liberty, he was saying, requires patience, forbearance, and fortitude. Republics were not for the fainthearted. "I hold it that a little rebellion now and then is a good thing," he told Madison, "and as necessary in the political world as storms in the physical."

Leaving Paris in late February 1787, Jefferson set out alone on a journey through the south of France and the north of Italy. "Architecture, painting, sculpture, antiquities, agriculture, the condition of the laboring poor fill all my moments," he wrote William Short. At Aix-en-Provence he swooned at the beauty of the countryside, the excellence of the food, the joy of the wine. "I am now in the land of corn, wine, oil, and sunshine," he wrote Short. "What more can man ask of heaven? If I should happen to die at Paris I will beg of you to send me here, and have me exposed to the sun. I am sure it will bring me to life again." He loved the Roman ruins, the old bridges, the aqueducts, and the Maison Carrée at Nîmes, the first-century Roman temple, which inspired his design of the state capitol in Richmond. He was back in Paris on Sunday, June 10, 1787.

The world to which he returned seemed bright. In America, the Constitutional Convention had begun in May. Following the action in Philadelphia as closely as he could, Jefferson was skeptical of a proposal to give the federal Congress the authority to veto any individual act of a state legislature that concerned national affairs. Knowing human nature—and knowing the Congress, which was human nature writ large—he understood that the Congress would not be able to keep themselves from abusing their power by deciding that **everything** concerned the national interest.

On Tuesday, June 26, 1787, Polly Jefferson, age eight, arrived in London. Handed over to the care of Abigail Adams, Polly did not want to part with the man who had commanded the ship on which she had traveled, a man named Ramsey, and Captain Ramsey did not want to part with Sally Hemings. "The old nurse whom you expected to have attended her was sick and unable to come," Abigail Adams wrote Jefferson. "She has a girl about 15 or 16 with her, the sister of the servant you have with you."

There are no known images of Sally Hemings. From what little evidence we have, the fourteen-year-old Sally who accompanied Polly Jefferson into the Adamses's London house appeared nearly white and was "very handsome, [with] long straight hair down her back." There may have been some resemblance, more and less pronounced as the years went on, to the Wayles side of the family—which is to say Sally could well have shared some characteristics with her late half sister, Mrs. Thomas Jefferson. It is also possible that at around fourteen Sally Hemings was well developed: Abigail Adams guessed she was a year or two older than she was.

We know, too, that Captain Ramsey was hoping to take an unchaperoned Hemings back across the Atlantic with him, and it seems safe to assume he was not chiefly interested in her conversation. It is a reasonable surmise that the Sally Hemings who arrived in Europe in the summer of 1787 was physically desirable.

Polly, it emerged, was a bright child capable of uncomfortable candor. In London she sobbed when taken from Ramsey, who had become a familiar and probably fond figure during the voyage. Mrs. Adams tried to calm her by invoking the girl's sister, Patsy. "I tell her that I did not see her sister cry once," Mrs. Adams wrote Jefferson. "She replies that her sister was older and ought to do better, besides she had her pappa with her." Mrs. Adams then told Jefferson: "I show her your picture. She says she cannot know it, how should she when she should not know you."

Jefferson, Mrs. Adams said, should come fetch his younger daughter and perhaps bring Patsy along, for that might "reconcile her little sister to the thoughts of taking a journey." At the end of the day, Abigail reported: "Miss Polly . . . has wiped her eyes and laid down to sleep."

A night of rest did wonders for the little girl. On Wednesday the twenty-seventh, she was, Abigail said, "as contented . . . as she was miserable yesterday. She is indeed a fine child."

Mrs. Adams was less sure about Sally, who seems to have flummoxed her. "The girl who is with [Polly] is quite a child, and Captain Ramsey is of [the] opinion will be of so little service that he had better carry her back with him. But of this you will be a judge. She seems fond of the child and appears good natured."

Jefferson thanked Abigail profusely on Sunday, July 1, 1787, dispatching his French maître d'hôtel, Adrien Petit, to fetch Polly and Sally. He claimed that the crush of work—the "arrearages of 3 or 4 months all crowded on me at once," as he put it—kept him from coming personally.

In London, Polly was beside herself when she realized her father had delegated the duty of collecting her. Crying and "thrown into all her former distresses," Polly clung to Abigail, who wrote Jefferson: "She told me this morning that as she had left all her friends in Virginia to come over the ocean to see you, she did think you would have taken the pains to have come here for her, and not have sent a man whom she cannot understand." Lest Jefferson think Abigail was being too rough on him, she added: "I express her own words."

Polly Jefferson and Sally Hemings arrived in Paris on Sunday, July 15, 1787. "She had totally forgotten her sister," Jefferson wrote, "but thought, on seeing me, that she recollected something of me"—reversing the impression she had given Abigail Adams in London.

With Polly safely in hand, Jefferson sat down to thank his sister-in-law for all she and her husband had done for his little girl. "Her reading, her writing, her manners in general show what everlasting obligations we are all under to you," Jefferson wrote Elizabeth Eppes. "As far as her affections can be a requital, she renders you the debt, for it is impossible for a child to prove a more sincere affection to an absent person than she does to you."

Thinking of the Constitutional Convention in Philadelphia, Jefferson warmly wrote John Adams, "It is really an assembly of demigods."

One of the demigods, James Madison, was fretful. "Nothing can exceed the universal anxiety for the event of the meeting here," Madison wrote Jefferson. Virginia was particularly unsettled. "The people . . . are said to be generally discontented." Things had not yet gone as far as they did in Massachusetts, but a drought had wrecked the corn crop and "taxes are another source of discontent." Several prisons, courthouses, and clerk's offices had been "willfully burnt."

A fear of Jefferson's—one made all the stronger the more time he spent in proximity to the court of Louis XVI—was that the United States might tack toward hereditary power, up to and including the installation of a monarch.

Such rumors were in the air. "The report of an intention on the part of America to apply for a sovereign of the house of Hanover has circulated here; and should an application of that nature be made, it will require a very nice consideration in what manner so important a subject should be treated," Lord Sydney wrote Lord Dorchester from London on Friday, September 14, 1787. Alexander Hamilton was said to believe the "most plausible shape" of a reunion with Great Britain would be "the establishment of a son of the present monarch . . . with a family compact."

Dorchester reported the failure of all such enterprises, sending London a report in 1788 saying that an alleged plan of Hamilton's "that had in view the establishment of a monarchy, and placing the crown upon the head of a foreign prince . . . was overruled, although supported by some of the ablest members of the convention."

In the year of the Constitutional Convention, a British agent, probably George Beckwith, sent word of nascent American royalism to the British foreign secretary in London. "At this moment there is not a gentleman in the states between New Hampshire and Georgia, who does not view the present government with contempt, who is not convinced of its inefficacy, and who is not desirous of changing it for a monarchy." The letter continued:

They are divided into three classes.

The first class proposes a federal government somewhat resembling the Constitution of the State of New York, with an annual Executive, Senate, and House of Assembly.

The second wish to have a sovereign for life with two triennial Houses of Parliament.

The third are desirous of establishing an hereditary monarchy with a form of government as nearly resembling Great Britain as possible.

Of the first class many look up to General Washington; those of the second and third classes cast their eyes to the House of Hanover for a Sovereign, they wish for one of the king's sons.

The third class is the most powerful, and is composed of some of the most ablest men in the States. . . .

From other sources of information it is understood that men of ability in the states are in general strongly impressed with the necessity of establishing a monarchy; they find their present government neither efficient nor respectable; they are greatly divided in opinion on this subject, whether they shall raise an American to this dignity, or procure a Sovereign from Great Britain or from France.

Fearful of royal control, Jefferson nevertheless remained interested in strength, without which there could be no liberty. In 1787 he watched a crisis in the United Netherlands that he believed instructive for the United States. In a conflict between the stadtholder (backed by England) and a patriot party (backed by France), the stadtholder prevailed when Frederick William II of Prussia intervened against the patriots, and France failed to honor its commitments. "It conveys to us the important lesson that no circumstances of morality, honor, interest, or engagement are sufficient to authorize a secure reliance on any nation, at all times and in all positions," Jefferson wrote Jay in November 1787.

To Jefferson, a nation that was to stand among the powers of the earth had to do so on its own. Alliances were always chancy. "We are, therefore, never safe till our magazines are filled with arms," he wrote Jay.

On the day after the Constitutional Convention ended in Philadelphia, George Washington dispatched a copy of the draft Constitution to Jefferson in Paris. Benjamin Franklin sent one along, too, and letters about the Constitution flowed into Jefferson's Hôtel de Langeac. After reading a copy of the draft, John Adams told Jefferson that he thought it "seems to be admirably calculated to preserve the Union, to increase affection, and to bring us all to the same mode of thinking."

Adams asked Jefferson: "What think you of a Declaration of Rights? Should not such a thing have preceded the model?"

Jefferson believed so. On first reading the document, he reacted badly. "How do you like our new constitution?" he wrote Adams. "I confess there are things in it which stagger all my dispositions to subscribe to what such an assembly has proposed."

The details of the presidency troubled him. "He may be reelected from 4 years to 4 years for life," Jefferson said. "Reason and experience prove to us that a chief magistrate, so continuable, is an officer for life. When one or two generations shall have proved that this is an office for life, it becomes on every succession worthy of intrigue, of bribery, of force, and even of foreign interference."

He blamed the British for features he did not like, arguing that the British press had exaggerated American instability for so long that "the world has at length believed them, the English nation has believed them, the ministers themselves have come to believe them, and what is more wonderful, we have believed them ourselves." Jefferson continued:

We have had 13 states independent 11 years. There has been one rebellion [in Massachusetts]. That comes to one rebellion in a century and a half for each state. What country before ever existed a century and a half without a rebellion? And what country can preserve its liberties if their rulers are not warned from time to time that their people preserve the spirit of resistance? Let them take arms. The remedy is to set them right as to facts, pardon and pacify them. What signify a few lives lost in a century or two? The tree of liberty must be refreshed from time to time with the blood of patriots and tyrants. It is its natural manure. Our Convention has been too much impressed by the insurrection in Massachusetts.

Jefferson acknowledged he was being hyperbolic. "The want of facts worth communicating to you has occasioned me to give a little loose to dissertation. We must be contented to amuse, when we cannot inform."

To Madison, on Thursday, December 20, 1787, he reacted to the Constitution in specific terms. Jefferson liked the division of powers into executive, legislative, and judicial branches, and he was impressed that the federal government would have sufficient autonomy and power to be effective "without needing continual recurrence to the state legislatures." He was pleased, too, by "the power given to the Legislature to levy taxes; and for that reason solely approve of the greater house being chosen by the people directly."

Jefferson did not like the omission of a declaration (or bill) of rights to guarantee "freedom of religion, freedom of the press, protection against standing armies, restriction against monopolies, the eternal and unremitting force of the habeas corpus laws, and trials by jury."

He allowed that such matters could be addressed

by future amendment or by the calling of a new convention. In the end, he was prepared to accept the verdict of the ratifying process. "After all, it is my principle that the will of the majority should always prevail," he told Madison. "If they approve the proposed Convention in all its parts, I shall concur in it cheerfully, in hopes that they will amend it whenever they shall find it work wrong."

Yet the more he thought about it, the more he hoped that the rights issue could be resolved before the new government was formed. Jefferson suggested that the first nine states ratify the Constitution but the remaining four states reject it until a declaration of individual rights could be added.

Jefferson decided to make his peace with the Constitution as drafted. "There are indeed some faults which revolted me a good deal in the first moment: but we must be contented to travel on towards perfection, step by step," he wrote in May 1788.

This was a key element of Jefferson's vision: He wrote beautifully of the pursuit of the perfect, but he knew good when he saw it. He would not make the two enemies.

Jefferson followed the politics of ratification with precision and passion. Seeking news from each state convention, he kept careful records of vote tallies. In May 1788 he believed the outcome certain. "It is very possible that the President and new Congress may be sitting at New York in the month of September," he said on May 15.

The significance of the presidency was clear to Jefferson from the beginning. Writing of George Washington, James Monroe told Jefferson: "Having . . . commenced again on the public theatre the course which [Washington] takes becomes not only highly interesting to him but likewise so to us: the human character is not perfect; and if he partakes of those qualities which we have too much reason to believe are almost inseparable from the frail nature of our being, the people of America will perhaps be lost."

So much depended on a single man.

Arriving home in Paris after a European journey in April 1788, Jefferson glimpsed Maria Cosway's handwriting in his pile of letters. He opened her note before any other and replied to her before reading his other mail.

He had, he said, dreamed of her on his trip. "At Heidelberg I wished for you. . . . In fact I led you by the hand through the whole garden," he wrote. "You must . . . now write me a letter teeming with affection; such as I feel for you." He shared a joke with her about the connection between noses and phalluses from Laurence Sterne's **Tristram Shandy,** a fairly standard flirtatious allusion.

One suspects, though, that on the road Sally Hemings may have also figured in his imagination. In Düsseldorf, Jefferson was fascinated by a 1699 painting of Abraham taking the young servant Hagar to his bed, an image by the Dutch artist

Adriaen van der Werff. The picture, Jefferson said, was "delicious. I would have agreed to have been Abraham though the consequence would have been that I should have been dead five or six thousand years."

In May 1788, back at the Hôtel de Langeac, he wrote a friend: "Paris is now become a furnace of politics. All the world is run politically mad. Men, women, children talk nothing else."

TWENTY-TWO

A Treaty in Paris

> He desired to bring my mother back to Virginia with him, but she demurred.
>
> —MADISON HEMINGS

THE YEARS 1788 AND 1789 were a time of cascading events in Jefferson's public and private lives. In Holland there were difficult financial negotiations. In France there was the rush of revolution. And within the walls of the Hôtel de Langeac there was Sally Hemings.

The French impulse for liberty—both in its laws against slavery and in the revolution against Louis XVI—tested Jefferson personally and politically in 1788 and 1789, threatening him in the most intimate of spheres and forcing him to confront the full implications of his philosophical creed.

In this tempestuous time, Jefferson apparently began a sexual relationship with his late wife's enslaved half sister. Since her arrival with Polly in the summer of 1787, Hemings had been paid some small wages—twelve livres a month for ten months.

Jefferson had bought clothing for her and had her inoculated against smallpox. Her brother James was trained as a chef. Sally's day-to-day routine is less clear, though she may have served the Jefferson daughters as a maid at the convent school during part of her time in Paris.

Jefferson could hardly have been leading a more complicated life. His work was urgent, his life in Parisian intellectual and social circles busy and dizzying. He was trying to raise his two daughters. He feared for his young, vulnerable republic, and he had been engaged in a flirtation with a married woman, slipping in and out of hired carriages in the shaded suburbs of Paris and strolling through the romantic forests of the city. From Versailles to the city's theaters and opera, he was living vibrantly and fretting constantly. Any hour could bring devastating news about America—about her security, her stability, her standing.

There, in the midst of the swirl and the storms, was a beautiful young woman at his command—a woman who may have reminded him of her half sister, his wife. The emotional content of the Jefferson-Hemings relationship is a mystery. He may have loved her, and she him. It could have been, as some have argued, coercive, institutionalized rape. She might have just been doing what she had to do to survive an evil system, accepting sexual duty as an element of her enslavement and using what leverage she had to improve the lot of her children. Or each of these things may have been true at different times.

Sex, Jefferson himself once remarked, was "the strongest of the human passions," and he was not a man to deny himself what he wanted. Sally Hemings, for her part, was "light colored and decidedly good-looking," Jefferson grandson Thomas Jefferson Randolph recalled. In following years Jefferson was always at Monticello at the times she was likely to have conceived the children she is known to have borne.

What little evidence we have strongly suggests that Sally Hemings was an intelligent, brave woman who did as much as she could with what little the world had given her. She began this phase of her life as she apparently intended to carry on: with strength and an instinct for survival.

For in this opening hour, geography and culture—those things that had conspired to enslave her—were on her side. In France, enslaved persons could apply for their liberty and be granted it—and there was nothing their masters could do about it.

Jefferson knew this well. As the American minister he had once advised a fellow slave owner on the system. And Sally Hemings was no lonely slave girl in Europe: Her big brother James was there with her, at the Hôtel de Langeac, and could have helped her win her freedom.

According to their son Madison Hemings's later account, Sally, who had become "Mr. Jefferson's concubine," was pregnant when Jefferson was preparing to return to the United States. "He desired to bring my mother back to Virginia with him but she demurred," Madison Hemings said.

To demur was to refuse, and Jefferson was unaccustomed to encountering resistance to his absolute will at all, much less from a slave. His whole life was about controlling as many of the world's variables as he could. Yet here was a girl basically the same age as his own eldest daughter refusing to take her docile part in the long-running drama of the sexual domination of enslaved women by their white masters.

"She was just beginning to understand the French language well, and in France she was free, while if she returned to Virginia she would be re-enslaved," said Madison Hemings. "So she refused to return with him."

It was an extraordinary moment. Fresh from arranging terms with the bankers of Europe over a debt that was threatening the foundation of the French nation, Thomas Jefferson found himself in negotiations with a pregnant enslaved teenager who, in a reversal of fortune hardly likely to be repeated, had the means at hand to free herself.

She, not he, was in control. It must have seemed surreal, unthinkable, even absurd. For the first time in his life, perhaps, Jefferson was truly in a position of weakness at a moment that mattered to him. So he began making concessions to convince Sally

Hemings to come home to Virginia. "To induce her to do so he promised her extraordinary privileges, and made a solemn pledge that her children should be freed at the age of twenty-one years," Madison Hemings said.

Sally Hemings agreed. "In consequence of his promise, on which she implicitly relied, she returned with him to Virginia," said Madison Hemings. "Soon after their arrival, she gave birth to a child, of whom Thomas Jefferson was the father. It lived but a short time. She gave birth to four others, and Jefferson was the father of all of them. Their names were Beverly, Harriet, Madison (myself), and Eston—three sons and one daughter."

Their father kept the promise he had made to Sally in Paris. "We all became free agreeably to the treaty entered into by our parents before we were born," Madison Hemings said. It was one of the most important pacts of Jefferson's life.

In Paris, the Assembly of Notables had given way to the calling of the Estates-General for May 1789. "I imagine you have heard terrible stories of the internal confusions of this country," Jefferson wrote a correspondent in July 1788. "These things swell as they go on. . . . As yet the tumults have not cost a single life according to the most sober testimony I have been able to collect." He would not be able to say this much longer.

On the diplomatic front, the American failure to

pay its European debts—chiefly its debt to France, which was one of the many reasons the royal treasury was in such trouble—was problematic for Jefferson and Adams. In early 1788 the two men met in Amsterdam for sessions with Dutch bankers. Among Jefferson's concerns was finding capital enough to repay French officers for their services to America during the Revolution and to ensure that there was money to support the American diplomatic establishments in Europe. He and Adams accomplished both ends in 1788.

As confidence in American stability grew, so did America's credit in European markets. Jefferson, a man with large personal debts, deplored the weakness that came with weighty borrowing. "I am anxious about everything which may affect our credit," he wrote Washington in May 1788. "My wish would be to possess it in the highest degree, but to use it little."

With deftness, Jefferson also negotiated the first treaty to be ratified under the new Constitution: a consular convention with France that defined diplomatic relations between the two nations. The initial version of this convention, negotiated by Franklin in 1784, was rejected by the Congress for being too accommodating to the French. Jefferson reentered the fray, saying that he took as his guide the principle that "instead . . . of declining every article which will be useless to us, we accede to every one which will not be inconvenient."

It was a practical way of executing a delicate duty. Under the convention as ratified, the United States was seen and treated as a stronger, more sophisticated, more respected force in the world. Jefferson had done his work well.

American politics under the Constitution fascinated him. Washington was to be president, Madison told him. John Hancock and John Adams were "talked of principally" for vice president. "Mr. Jay or General Knox would I believe be preferred to either, but both of them will probably choose to remain where they are," said Madison. "It is impossible to say which of the former would be preferred, or what other candidates may be brought forward."

The speculation was irresistible. "It is . . . doubtful who will be Vice President," Jefferson wrote a correspondent in August 1788. "The age of Dr. Franklin, and the doubt whether he would accept it, are the only circumstances that admit a question but that he would be the man. . . . J. Adams, Hancock, Jay, Madison, Rutledge will be all voted for."

The maneuvering became more pronounced as the October days passed. Given Washington's Virginia roots, the choice for vice president, Madison reported, lay between Hancock and Adams. For Madison, the two-man field left much to be desired. "Hancock is weak, ambitious, a courtier of popularity given to low intrigue. . . . J. Adams has made himself obnoxious to many, particularly in the

Southern states, by the political principles avowed in his book."

Jefferson watched it avidly. There was, he said in November 1788, an "ill understanding between Mr. Adams and Mr. Hancock. Both proposed as vice presidents."

Always there were whispers about monarchy. Supporters of a strong national government, "who had been utterly averse to royalty, began to imagine that hardly anything but a king could cure the evil," Washington aide David Humphreys told Jefferson. "It was truly astonishing to have been witness to some conversations, which I have heard."

Jefferson wanted to come home, at least for a while, and he was especially interested in establishing personal contact with Washington. To be on the scene in America had its political uses, for he hated the thought that things were said of him behind his back, a subject of annoyance his friend Francis Hopkinson touched on in a letter from Philadelphia in December 1788: "By the bye, you have been often dished up to me as a strong Antifederalist, which is almost equivalent to what **a Tory** was in the days of the war."

Jefferson took the occasion to attack the spirit of faction. "I am not a Federalist, because I never submitted the whole system of my opinions to the creed of any party of men whatever in religion, in philosophy, in politics, or in anything else where I was capable of thinking for myself," Jefferson replied to

Hopkinson in March 1789. "Such an addiction is the last degradation of a free and moral agent. If I could not go to heaven but with a party, I would not go there at all. Therefore I protest to you I am not of the party of federalists. But I am much farther from that of the Antifederalists."

Reiterating his positions, he said: "My great wish is to go on in a strict but silent performance of my duty: to avoid attracting notice and to keep my name out of newspapers, because I find the pain of a little censure, even when it is unfounded, is more acute than the pleasure of much praise."

From America, Madison archly reported John Adams's failed attempt to coin a grand title for the president. "J. Adams espoused the cause of titles with great earnestness. . . . The projected title was—His Highness the President of the United States and protector of their liberties. Had the project succeeded it would have subjected the President to a severe dilemma and given a deep wound to our infant government."

Jefferson called Adams's proposal "the most superlatively ridiculous thing I ever heard of. It is a proof the more of the justice of the character given by Dr. Franklin of my friend: 'Always an honest man, often a great one, but sometimes absolutely mad.'"

It was a brutally cold winter in France, but Jefferson was cheerful. "Our new constitution . . . has succeeded beyond what I apprehended it would have done," he wrote in January 1789.

Whether something similar might one day be said of the French was a live, explosive question. The cold winter of 1788–89, a scarcity of bread, and general political unease made for a potent mix. As the Estates-General met in May 1789 riots in Paris killed about one hundred people. Beginning a pattern that persisted, Jefferson interpreted the violence in the most benign light possible, arguing that the episode was unconnected to the larger national questions.

In the first week of June, Jefferson had sketched a charter of rights for the French and sent it to the Marquis de Lafayette. Jefferson's draft was minutely practical. There was no rhetoric about human liberty, no rigorous listing of rights to free speech and the like. It was, rather, a document about process and the workings of power. ("Laws shall be made by the [Estates-General] only, with the consent of the king," for example, and "The military shall be subordinate to the civil authority.") He wrote it in a hurry, caught up in the drama of the hour and engaged by its possibilities.

On Wednesday, June 17, 1789, the frustrated Third Estate of commoners successfully designated itself the National Assembly, effectively igniting what history calls the French Revolution. Reacting to centuries of royal absolutism and popular powerlessness, embarking on an odyssey that would lead to successive attempts at republican government, the murders of the king and queen, the institution of a Reign of Terror, and finally the establishment of a dictatorial empire under Napoleon Bonaparte, the French would spend the next quarter century struggling to find their way into modernity. It was a struggle with concrete implications not only for France but for the world, not least for the United States, the nation it had helped bring into being, and for its leaders, including the American minister living at the Hôtel de Langeac, Thomas Jefferson.

The unrest in Paris struck home for Jefferson. His house was robbed three times. He monitored a street battle between mobs of Parisians and German cavalry at the Place Louis XV that began with the people hurling stones and ended with "considerable firing" from the mercenary troops.

On the night of Tuesday, July 14, 1789, he was at his friend Madame de Corny's when he learned of the storming of the Bastille. As he reported two days later: "The tumults in Paris which took place on the change of the ministry, the slaughter of the people in the assault of the Bastille, the beheading [of] the Governor and Lieutenant Governor of it, and the Prevost de Marchands, excited in the king so much concern" that he went to the Estates-General promising to disperse the troops and pledging reform "to restore peace and happiness to his people."

The next act remained uncertain. "The heat of this

city is as yet too great to give entire credit to this, and they continue to arm and organize the Bourgeoisie." By the following day, the seventeenth, Jefferson was telling Thomas Paine that "a more dangerous scene of war I never saw in America, than what Paris has presented for 5 days past."

He confronted the prevailing terror with grace. Writing Maria Cosway, he said that "here in the midst of tumult and violence," the "cutting off heads is become so much a la mode, that one is apt to feel of a morning whether their own is on their shoulders."

On Tuesday, August 25, 1789, Lafayette asked Jefferson to "break every engagement to give us a dinner tomorrow, Wednesday. We shall be some members of the National Assembly—eight of us whom I want to [coalesce] as being the only means to prevent a total dissolution and a civil war." The next day the National Assembly adopted the Declaration of the Rights of Man and of the Citizen, written by Lafayette. This central document of the French Revolution had been influenced by the Declaration of Independence, and Jefferson had counseled Lafayette during its drafting.

That Wednesday evening, dinner began at four at the Hôtel de Langeac, and conversation continued until ten. For six hours, he was, Jefferson recalled, "a silent witness to a coolness and candor of argument unusual in the conflicts of political opinion; to a logical reasoning, and chaste eloquence, disfigured by no gaudy tinsel of rhetoric or declamation, and truly worthy of being placed in parallel with the finest dialogue of antiquity, as handed to us by Xenophon, by Plato, and Cicero." At Jefferson's table, the group had agreed to a structure for the new republic and "decided the fate of the [French] Constitution."

Expectations for revolutionary success ran high. Lafayette, who had sent George Washington the key to the Bastille, was in charge of the security of Louis XVI and Marie-Antoinette, hoping to preserve order as the revolution moved forward. Patsy Jefferson recalled standing at the window with some friends looking out into the streets of Paris as the king and queen rode by under the protection of her father's colleague and friend. First came the royal coach, and a chamberlain bowed to her. Next the young women heard cries that resembled "the bellowings of thousands of bulls." They were cheers for Lafayette. "Lafayette! Lafayette!" cried the crowds, and the young Frenchman, noticing Patsy watching from the window, bowed to her—a mark of respect she never forgot. All her life she kept a tricolored cockade, the symbol of the early days of the Revolution, as a memento.

Jefferson himself was to remain cheerful despite violence and threats of violence. "So far it seemed that your revolution had got along with a steady pace: meeting indeed with occasional difficulties and dangers, but we are not to expect to be translated from despotism to liberty in a feather-bed," Jefferson would tell Lafayette.

In early September 1789, fighting illness, Jefferson wrote a long letter to James Madison. He composed it in the fevered context of the French Revolution, and by his own account his thinking sprang from particular events in Europe. "I set out on this ground, which I suppose to be self evident, 'that the earth belongs in usufruct to the living': that the dead have neither powers nor rights over it." A little later, he added: "The earth belongs always to the living generation. They may manage it then, and what proceeds from it, as they please, during their usufruct. They are masters too of their own persons, and consequently may govern them as they please. . . . Every constitution, then, and every law, naturally expires at the end of 19 years [the Jeffersonian definition of a generation]."

Taken literally, these musings are a prescription for chaos. If there were no authority from precedent, no laws governing property or examples to guide us, then society would be reduced to a state of nature in which the strong could thrive most effectively, taking advantage of the disorder to consolidate power.

A key question is whether Jefferson meant posterity to follow his thoughts to the letter, or whether, as he so often did, he was sharing the churnings of an eager mind in a time of change. The latter possibility is most likely, for while he long held to the idea of the exaltation of the present rather than the re-flexive preservation of the past, he did not seriously press for the expiration of all laws at generational intervals. In 1789 in particular, he was thinking of the world in which he had lived for the past five years: the French nation in which individual and institutional destinies were determined largely by hereditary station. "This principle that the earth belongs to the living, and not to the dead, is of very extensive application and consequences, in every country, and **most especially in France** [emphasis added]."

Writing to the Reverend Charles Clay in 1790, within months of returning to the United States, Jefferson was decidedly earthbound. Clay was seeking a congressional seat at the time. Jefferson wrote that "you are too well informed a politician, too good a judge of men, not to know that the ground of liberty is to be gained by inches, that we must be contented to secure what we can get from time to time, and eternally press forward for what is yet to get."

So which was the real Jefferson—the philosopher advocating the end of binding laws, or the politician who believed "that we must be contented to secure what we can get from time to time"?

The likely truth is that these competing Jeffersons were both real. He thought one way in one era and another way in other eras—and sometimes he thought differently more or less simultaneously, a common human trait, particularly among the curious and the intellectually active.

As a political man he was able to operate on these sundry levels yet always returned to the arena from the mountaintop to take up governing an imperfect world—in his phrase, eternally pressing forward for what is yet to be had. (In France, he was soon back on the issue of rifle manufacturing—a sign he remained tethered to reality.)

Madison took care with his reply to Jefferson's rhapsodic letter. It often fell to him to absorb raw Jefferson thoughts. One of Madison's many services to the republic was the mediating role he played in Jefferson's life, often protecting Jefferson from himself.

This was such an occasion, and Madison was gently but frankly skeptical. "The spirit of philosophical legislation has never reached some parts of the Union, and is by no means the fashion here, either within or without Congress," he wrote Jefferson. "Besides this . . . our hemisphere must be still more enlightened before many of the sublime truths which are seen through the medium of philosophy, become visible to the naked eye of the ordinary politician."

The medium of philosophy: Madison is saying that Jefferson's enthusiasm for the revolutionary nature of the rights of man in Europe was an enthusiasm divorced from the realities of governing in

America. It was a fair point, and the exchange offers an example of Madison's utility to Jefferson as an affectionate, respectful, discreet check on his episodic flights of philosophy. Madison would always be there for Jefferson, reminding him—deftly—of his own core convictions about the limits of politics, the imperfections of government, and the realities of human nature.

On the last Sunday in September 1789, Thomas Jefferson left Paris with his daughters and Sally and James Hemings to return to America. At Le Havre and Cowes, he showed others how to measure the width of a river and tutored Polly in Spanish. He also set out "roving through the neighborhood of this place to try to get a pair of shepherd's dogs," he wrote. "We walked 10 miles, clambering the cliffs in quest of the shepherds, during the most furious tempest of wind and rain I was ever in." No dogs, but on the walk he encountered a disturbing scene. "On our return," he wrote, "we came on the body of a man who had that moment shot himself. His pistol had dropped at his feet, and himself fallen backward without ever moving. The shot had completely separated his whole face from the forehead to the chin and so torn it to atoms that it could not be known. The center of the head was entirely laid bare." The day after the storm and the discovery of the suicide, Jefferson found a dog to buy, purchasing "a chienne bergere big with pup." He thought sheepdogs "the most careful intelligent dogs in the world."

He soon set sail. Aboard the ship, Sally Hemings was among those in service to Jefferson and his family, as she would remain until the day he died, thirty-seven summers later.

PART VI

THE FIRST SECRETARY OF STATE

1789 to 1792

We have been fellow-laborers and fellow-sufferers, and heaven has rewarded us with a happy issue from our struggles. It rests now with ourselves alone to enjoy in peace and concord the blessings of self-government, so long denied to mankind: to show by example the sufficiency of human reason for the care of human affairs and that the will of the majority, the natural law of every society, is the only sure guardian of the rights of man.

—THOMAS JEFFERSON, in reply to the Address of the People of Albemarle County, Virginia, on the eve of his becoming secretary of state

George Washington took the oath as the first president of the United States in the spring of 1789 in New York City. Jefferson was soon to arrive to serve as Washington's secretary of state.

TWENTY-THREE

A New Post in New York

> In general, I think it necessary to give as well
> as take in a government like ours.
> —THOMAS JEFFERSON

J EFFERSON WAS AT EPPINGTON, the Eppes estate on the Appomattox River in Chesterfield
County, southwest of Richmond, when the
official request arrived. With his daughters Polly
and Patsy and with Sally and James Hemings, he
had crossed aboard the **Clermont** in "fine autumn
weather," reaching Norfolk, Virginia, on Monday,
November 23, 1789, at a quarter to one in the afternoon. Slowly making their way to Monticello, they
had stopped at the Eppeses', not least to give Polly the
chance to reunite with the aunt and uncle she loved.

Friday, December 11, 1789, brought an offer from
the president—one that had been mentioned in the
newspapers in circulation when Jefferson arrived in
Virginia from Paris. Would Jefferson become secretary of state?

Jefferson sent Washington an inconclusive reply.

Believing the State Department was to be responsible for many domestic as well as all foreign affairs, Jefferson was daunted, and said so, admitting that he feared the "criticisms and censures of a public just indeed in their intentions, but sometimes misinformed and misled, and always too respectable to be neglected."

He was trapped in a familiar paradox. Devoted to the stage and anxious for applause, Jefferson feared failure and disapproval. In times of trial and hours of public attack, he could eloquently articulate his longing for retirement from politics. Yet what repelled him about public life was of a piece with what drew him to it. He longed to be great, and felt greatly. His will to serve and sacrifice was as ferocious as the anguish he experienced when those whom he was serving and for whom he was sacrificing found him wanting.

One might think that a man who so hated "criticisms and censures" would indeed withdraw from the scene of affairs and live out his days relatively safe from conversational and political condemnation. Such a withdrawal, however, would have been unnatural for Jefferson—a denial of his essential character, a character at once human and heroic. He was both an unflinching political warrior and an easily wounded soul. He always would be.

Washington left the tactical work of bringing Jefferson aboard to James Madison, who came to Monticello at the end of 1789 to talk things over and correct Jefferson's mistaken view of the duties of the office. The secretary of state was not to be in charge of all domestic affairs; he was, rather, to serve as the president's chief foreign-policy adviser. "All whom I have heard speak on the subject are remarkably solicitous for [Jefferson's] acceptance," Madison wrote to Washington, "and I flatter myself that they will not in the final event be disappointed."

The prospect of broad approval resonated with Jefferson and reassured Washington that Jefferson was worth the back-and-forth over the post. After conferring with Madison in New York in mid-January, Washington wrote Jefferson, making a strong case for the cabinet over returning to France to resume his work there.

Washington told Jefferson that "in order that you may be the better prepared to make your ultimate decision on good grounds, I think it necessary to add" that "your late appointment has given very extensive and very great satisfaction to the public."

Washington wanted an answer. Jefferson could come to New York or return to France—but he needed to decide.

What to do? He loved Paris, and a diplomatic appointment gave him an unusual degree of autonomy and insulation from constant criticism. Yet he had devoted his life to the success of the American Revolution and now had to determine where—

in the cabinet or in France—he could render the most valuable service to that larger cause.

He accepted Washington's offer. Explaining his thinking to a friend, Jefferson spoke in practical political terms. Washington's communications "left me at liberty to accept it or return to France, but I saw plainly he preferred the former, and learnt from several quarters"—chiefly from Madison—"it would be more agreeable. Consequently to have gone back would have exposed me to the danger of giving disgust, and I value no office enough for that."

Jefferson's years as secretary of state were both tumultuous and thrilling. Out of them came the convictions and tactical sense that Jefferson took to the vice presidency and to the presidency itself. The drama of the country's first cabinet shaped Thomas Jefferson—and the nation—far beyond the life of Washington's administration.

On the Jeffersons' return to Virginia, Patsy, now seventeen, soon decided to marry her third cousin Thomas Mann Randolph, Jr., the twenty-one-year-old son of Jefferson's childhood housemate. They had met when Patsy was a child during two Jefferson family visits to Tuckahoe, once in 1781 during the British invasion and again in 1783. Ambitious, well educated, and black-haired, young Randolph had moved quickly once the family had landed at Norfolk in 1789. "Though his talents, dispositions, connections and fortune were such

as would have made him my own first choice . . .
I scrupulously suppressed my wishes, that my
daughter might indulge her own sentiments freely,"
Jefferson wrote a friend in France. He delayed his departure to arrange Patsy's marriage settlement with
the Randolphs. He wanted to make sure everything
was done correctly. The wedding took place in February 1790.

That Patsy married so soon upon arrival in the
United States to a man she did not know well is
something of a curiosity. Historians have speculated
that she was perhaps reacting to her father's liaison
with Sally Hemings. The daughter may have felt
displaced in her father's affections in some way.

It is also possible that things were just as they appeared to be. Patsy was of marriageable age, young
Randolph was a fitting suitor, and he appeared to
be a man not unlike her beloved father. Randolph
was interested in farming, science, law, and politics.
Patsy did not hesitate when offered the opportunity
to begin the next natural chapter with a man whom
her father liked and who shared her father's interests.

Sally Hemings was to remain at Monticello when
Jefferson moved to New York. Her main work
through the years was the care and tending of Jefferson's private rooms and his wardrobe. He trusted
her with the things he valued most. The precise
location of her living quarters at this time is unknown, but she may have lived in one of the new

log servants' houses constructed in the mid-1790s along Mulberry Row, the nearby principal plantation street which Monticello historians note was lined with about twenty dwellings, workshops, and sheds where dozens of slaves and free white workers lived and worked. During and after Jefferson's presidential years, Sally Hemings is thought to have had quarters in the South Terrace wing, constructed between 1802 and 1809.

Jefferson's journey north to New York was slow and at times snowy, yet it seemed a kind of political springtime. From London, Richard Price, an elderly radical English philosopher who had long supported the American Revolution, articulated the hopes of many. "The Congress under the new constitution is, I suppose, now met in America; and I am longing to hear that they go on prosperously," Price had written to Jefferson at the time of George Washington's inauguration. "Being now advanced into the evening of life, it is with particular gratitude I look back and reflect that I have been spared to see the human species improved, religious intolerance almost extinguished, the eyes of the lower ranks of men opened to see their rights; and nations panting for liberty that seemed to have lost the idea of it."

In New York, Jefferson could not find quarters on what he called "the Broadway," instead leasing a house at 57 Maiden Lane in lower Manhattan. (The house, he told Patsy, was "an indifferent one.") Old friends such as the Adamses were happy to see him. "Mr. Jefferson is here, and adds much to the social circle," Abigail Adams wrote in April 1790. The vice president and Mrs. Adams had taken a house called Richmond Hill in a then relatively remote neighborhood that became Greenwich Village.

The world was never quiet. At home and abroad—and the two spheres were connected, with foreign wars and confrontations shaping domestic life and politics—the 1790s were to prove complex. In the late summer of 1791, Leopold II, the Holy Roman Emperor (and brother of Marie-Antoinette), in company with Frederick William II of Prussia, issued the Declaration of Pillnitz in defense of the French royal family. In turn, in the spring of 1792, the French revolutionaries declared war on Austria, thus opening a thirteen-year series of wars between revolutionary (and later Napoleonic) France and monarchical Europe. The violence of the French Revolution, including the executions of Louis XVI and Marie-Antoinette (in 1793) and the institution of the Terror (in 1794), drew Britain and Spain into war with France.

The conflicts of the Old World created complications for the New. Before the decade was out, the United States would face possible wars against Britain because of Britain's war with France and with France because of France's war with Britain. Through these trials and their domestic manifestations, including a hard-line limitation of civil liberties amid fears of war with France in the last years of the 1790s, Jefferson was variously secretary of state; a leader of the opposition to the policies of George Washington and then of John Adams; and vice president of the United States.

Jefferson's conduct in the maelstroms of the decade was driven in large measure by his twin devotions to liberty and to power. He could be overly generous to France, but much of his sympathy for the French Revolution was connected to his antipathy for, and fear of, the royalism of the British.

For all the crises, Jefferson would end the decade of the 1790s as he began it: as a protector of the American experiment and defender of American interests.

On Sunday, March 21, 1790, the first secretary of state paid his first official call on the first president of the United States. It marked the beginning of four years of what Jefferson described as a "daily, confidential and cordial" relationship between the two men. There was so much to cover that the initial conversation could not be confined to a single meeting; the two men met again on Monday (after Washington sat for a portrait by the painter John Trumbull) and on Tuesday.

Washington and Jefferson had known each other for nearly a quarter of a century, since the days when both were Burgesses in Williamsburg, moving around the old colonial capital between the assembly room and the Raleigh Tavern.

Washington had reason to think well of the man sitting before him in the March light; many had testified to Jefferson's strengths. "Nothing can excel Mr. Jefferson's abilities, virtues, pleasing temper, and everything in him that constitutes the great statesman, zealous citizen, and amiable friend," Lafayette had told Washington in 1788. After spending time with Jefferson in France, the American merchant Nathaniel Cutting wrote: "I have found Mr. Jefferson a man of infinite information and sound judgment. Becoming gravity and engaging affability mark his deportment. His general abilities are such as would do honor to any age or country." From Paris a few years before, John Adams had told Secretary of War Henry Knox, "You can scarcely have heard a character too high of my friend and colleague Mr. Jefferson, either in point of power or virtues."

To Jefferson, Washington had been a grand, often distant figure whose grace and aloofness made him a living figure of myth. "He was incapable of fear, meeting personal dangers with the calmest unconcern," Jefferson wrote long afterward. "Perhaps the strongest feature in his character was prudence, never acting until every circumstance, every consideration was maturely weighed; refraining if he saw a doubt, but, when once decided, going through with his purpose, whatever obstacles opposed."

Jefferson was less impressed with Washington's intellectual gifts. "His mind was great and powerful, without being of the very first order; his penetration strong, though not so acute as that of a Newton, Bacon, or Locke; and as far as he saw, no judgment was ever sounder. It was slow in operation, being little aided by invention or imagination, but sure in conclusion."

There were hidden depths. "His temper was naturally irritable and high toned; but reflection and resolution had obtained a firm and habitual ascendency over it," Jefferson continued. "If ever, however, it broke its bonds, he was most tremendous in his wrath." Washington was a man, in other words, around whom one was careful.

Shortly after arriving in New York, Jefferson was struck by one of his episodic headaches, suggesting that he was perhaps uneasy about the duties—and the scrutiny—that awaited him.

For five years he had been largely removed from the daily, even hourly, cut and thrust of American politics. As a diplomat in a foreign land he had been more of an observer than an actor. As the senior cabinet officer in the new government, he was exposed to the voracious attention of the New York political class.

It took time for him to acclimate himself, and his dependence on Madison was explicit and rather touching. Seeking Madison's opinion on a question of form—how the states should communicate with the federal House and Senate—Jefferson acknowledged his debt. "Be so good as to say what you think," Jefferson wrote. "I must be troublesome to you till I know better the ground on which I am placed."

He was clear on one thing: He held an executive office of responsibility and of authority. "The transaction of business with foreign nations is Executive altogether," he wrote in April 1790. "It belongs then to the head of that department, **except** as to such portions of it as are specially submitted to the Senate. **Exceptions** are to be construed strictly."

Jefferson marked his forty-seventh birthday in his first weeks in New York. One of the most celebrated Americans in the world, he was an unfamiliar figure to many of those who had come to the national stage during the five years he spent in Paris. William Maclay, a senator from Pennsylvania who was hostile to the administration, found Jefferson's demeanor surprising and rather disappointing. "He had a rambling, vacant look, and nothing of that firm, collected deportment which I expected would dignify the presence of a secretary or minister," said Maclay. "I looked for gravity, but a laxity of manner seemed shed about him. He spoke almost without ceasing. But even his discourse partook of his personal demeanor. It was loose and rambling, and yet he scattered information wherever he went, and some even brilliant sentiments sparkled from him."

Others saw him differently through the years. To the newspaper publisher Samuel Harrison Smith, he was "lofty and erect; his motions flexible and easy; neither remarkable for, nor deficient in grace; and such were his strength and agility."

"His information was equally polite and profound, and his conversational powers capable of discussing moral questions of deepest seriousness, or the lighter themes of humor and fancy," wrote an English traveler named John Bernard. "Nothing could be more simpler than his reasonings, nothing more picturesque and pointed than his descriptions. On all abstract subjects he was plainness—a veritable Quaker; but when conveying his views of human nature through [that] most attractive medium—anecdote—he displayed the grace and brilliance of a courtier."

Jefferson believed in the politics of the personal relationship. "When the hour of dinner is approaching, sometimes it rains, sometimes it is too hot for a long walk, sometimes your business would make you wish to remain longer at your office or return there after dinner, and make it more eligible to take any sort of a dinner in town," Jefferson wrote Henry Knox in July 1791. "Any day and every day that this would be the case you would make me supremely happy by messing with me, without ceremony or other question than whether I dine at home. The hour is from one quarter to three quarters after three, and, taking your chance as to fare, you will be sure to meet a sincere welcome."

He saw himself as a political creature. Replying to a correspondent who questioned his anti-British tone in the **Notes on the State of Virginia**, Jefferson noted that those words dated from the war, but that Britain had done little to build constructive relations with her former colonies. "Perhaps their conduct and dispositions towards us since the war have not been as well calculated as they might have been to excite more favorable dispositions on our part," Jefferson said in November 1790. "Still as a political man they shall never find any passion in me either for or against them. Whenever their avarice of commerce will let them meet us fairly halfway, I should meet them with satisfaction, because it would be for our benefit: but I mistake their character if they do this under present circumstances."

Though he tried to make himself pleasant, Jefferson found New York politically uncomfortable. He suffered, he recalled, from "wonder and mortification" at the prevailing Federalist climate in governing circles.

On evenings out he believed himself "for the most part, the only advocate on the republican side of the question." The quasi-regal air around the president—the levees and the bows, the enormous carriage with numerous horses—bothered Jefferson, who believed substance could follow style. A tilt toward the monarchical in form might, he feared, precede a move toward the autocratic in fact.

Further evidence for such conclusions could be found in the **Gazette of the United States,** published in New York by John Fenno. In a series of essays entitled **Discourses on Davila,** John Adams, writing pseudonymously, made the case that pure democracy was unnatural. "One question only shall be respectfully insinuated: whether equal laws, the result only of a balanced government, can ever be obtained and preferred without some signs or other of distinction and degree?" Adams continued: "We are told that our friends, the National Assembly of France, have abolished all distinctions. But be not deceived, my dear countrymen. Impossibilities cannot be performed. Have they leveled all fortunes, and equally divided all property? Have they made all men and women equally wise, elegant and beautiful?"

Worried about the implications of Adams's argument—that distinctions, possibly hereditary, were intrinsic and might prevail in the New World as well as the Old—Jefferson arranged for Fenno to publish a translation of a National Assembly address to the people: "The **Nation,** The **Law,** The **King.** The **Nation** is yourselves, the **Law** is still yourselves, it is your will: The **King** is the guardian of the **Law.**"

By urging Fenno to print translated excerpts from the **Gazette de Leide,** a reliably republican Dutch paper published in French, Jefferson was putting his own views in the pages that promulgated the Federalist line. By early August 1790 Fenno became entirely a creature of the Federalist faction, but for a brief time Jefferson was able to avail himself of the paper.

He was not fighting solely tactical battles. He was also thinking grandly. "I have but one system of ethics for men and for nations," he wrote a French friend in April 1790. "To be grateful, to be faithful to all engagements and under all circumstances, to be open and generous, promotes in the long run even the interests of both: and I am sure it promotes their happiness."

There was a late snow in New York in the last week of April 1790. Not long afterward, President Washington became so ill that he was thought to be dying. By early June, however, the president was well enough to take Jefferson along on a fishing trip off Sandy Hook. Jefferson, ever practical and optimistic, hoped any seasickness would "carry off the remains of my headache."

After he had returned from the fishing excursion, Jefferson ran into Alexander Hamilton near Washington's house one evening.

Born in 1755 on the British West Indian island of Nevis, Hamilton spent much of his early life on St. Croix. An illegitimate child, he was the son of a French Huguenot mother and a Scottish laird. His mother died when he was thirteen; he became a self-taught man, driven by ambition to overcome the obscurity of his origins. He clerked for a time and then, with the financial support of locals who sensed his potential, went to New York for schooling, ultimately enrolling at King's College (present-day Columbia University). Quick with his pen—he was a prolific essayist—he became a top aide to General Washington during the Revolution. He married into a powerful New York family, the Schuylers, and served as a delegate to the Constitutional Convention. His father-in-law, Senator Philip Schuyler, was said to be "amazingly fond of the old leaven" of monarchism.

Hamilton favored a strong national government and to a degree sought to emulate the basic British financial and commercial systems. His was a rational and coherent vision of public life, and he believed his vision the best course for the United States. Skeptical about the durability of republican institutions based on broad suffrage and regular elections—as any student of history and human nature would be; there was nothing like America in the world—Hamilton was more open than Jefferson was to the adaptation of old-world features to American government. And Hamilton was willing to entertain the possibilities of a hereditary (or at least lifelong) presidency or Senate.

In a speech to the Constitutional Convention, Hamilton had spoken of a possible American monarch who would be "capable of resisting the popular current." More immediately, Hamilton advocated a strong relationship with Britain, which, given the realities of the day, meant the United States would be a subordinate power to London.

Many (though not all) of Hamilton's views set him apart from Jefferson—and some of those views were so strongly expressed that Jefferson began to define himself in opposition to the Treasury secretary. Jefferson, for example, had long believed in, and fought for, a respected and effective national government. After his experience of the ancien régime in France, though, and given his anxiety about British designs on America, Jefferson found the discovery of a quasi-monarchical culture growing up around President Washington unsettling. Jefferson believed in a powerful **republican** government.

As the Washington administration unfolded, Jefferson came to see Hamilton as the embodiment of the deepest of republican fears: as a man who might be willing to sacrifice the American undertaking in liberty to the expediency of arbitrary authority. And Hamilton came to see Jefferson as a man who might be willing to throw everything the Americans had built to the revolutionary winds blowing from France. It was an extreme, overheated view of Hamilton (as of Jefferson), but it was a time of extreme and overheated views. Such was the political reality of the day, and Hamilton and Jefferson were politicians.

In later years, when passions had cooled, Jefferson acquired a bust of Hamilton and placed it opposite one of himself in the entrance hall at Monticello. According to the biographer Henry Randall, "The eye settled with a deeper interest on busts of Jefferson and Hamilton, by Ceracchi, placed on massive pedestals on each side of the main entrance—'opposed in death as in life,' as the surviving original sometimes remarked, with a pensive smile, as he observed the notice they attracted."

On this particular night in New York City in 1790, Jefferson found the Treasury secretary "somber, haggard, and dejected beyond description," Jefferson wrote. "Even his dress was uncouth and neglected."

Hamilton had reason to be out of sorts. In his **Report on the Public Credit** in early 1790 (another followed at the end of the year), Hamilton had argued for a national financial system in which the central government would fund the national debt, assume responsibility for all state debts, and establish a national bank. Money for the federal government would be raised by tariffs on imports and excise taxes on distilled spirits.

Funding the debt—which basically meant the federal government would pay holders of federal securities their nominal (or face) value, which was higher than their original value—was controversial, for speculators had been purchasing those securities from the securities' initial holders for less than Hamilton was proposing to pay the current holders. A political and emotional complication was that many of the initial holders were Revolutionary veterans unaware that the paper they owned was about to be worth more. (They had often been paid for their services in Continental paper.) Shrewder speculators, Madison told Jefferson, were "exploring the interior and distant parts of the Union in order to take advantage of the ignorance of the holders."

Despite these concerns, Hamilton carried the day on the federal purchase of the securities, successfully beginning to put the federal government in the center of the nation's financial system.

The second element of Hamilton's plan—the assumption of all the state debts by the federal government—would further secure the federal establishment's standing. The consolidation of debts at the federal level would create the need for federal taxes to pay down the debts, and the power to tax was, as ever, the most fundamental and far-reaching of all the powers of government, with the possible exception of the war-making power (which is actually also partly about taxes, since wars are so costly).

The assumption proposal, however, instantly divided the nation. Four states (Virginia, North Carolina, Georgia, and Maryland) had already been fiscally responsible and paid off much of their Revolutionary debts. Others (chiefly Massachusetts, South Carolina, and Connecticut) had not, and were therefore quite happy to send their bills to Hamilton in New York. The more fiscally responsible states believed that they would inevitably end up paying federal taxes to bail out their lagging neighbors.

On Monday, April 12, 1790, about three weeks after Jefferson's arrival in New York, the Madison-led forces in the House voted down federal assumption of state debts by three votes. It was a devastating defeat for the Treasury secretary.

The unkempt Hamilton that Jefferson met near the president's house needed allies. He asked for a word with his cabinet colleague, and the two men spoke in the street near Washington's door. Would Jefferson help Hamilton with the assumption issue? Without a solution, Hamilton believed the "continuance of the Union" was at risk.

Jefferson knew matters were dire. The Congress seemed paralyzed. "It was a real fact," he said, "that the Eastern and Southern members . . . had got into the most extreme ill humor with one another," leading to an atmosphere marked by "the most alarming heat [and] the bitterest animosities."

Jefferson appreciated the need for unified action. Unlike many of his fellow Virginians, the secretary of state was not reflexively opposed to assumption. Those who were, though, wanted something in return for seeming to invest the northern part of the nation with even more financial power.

The location of the national capital offered some hope for a deal. New York was already the financial center of the nation, and the middle and southern states were eager to see the political seat of government elsewhere. Philadelphia, Baltimore, and Georgetown on the Potomac were candidates. There was also talk of Trenton, New Jersey, or a site along the Susquehanna River. "The Potomac stands a bad chance, and yet it is not impossible that in the vicissitudes of the business it may turn up in some form or other," Madison wrote Monroe in June 1790.

As Jefferson listened to Hamilton, as he read correspondence from the South, and as he thought through the sundry issues at hand, he realized that perhaps, just perhaps, there was room for a compromise.

The beginning of wisdom, Jefferson thought, might lie in a meeting of the principals out of the public eye. So he convened a dinner. Jefferson believed things could be worked out, he said, for "men of sound heads and honest views needed nothing more than explanation and mutual understanding to enable them to unite in some measures which might enable us to get along."

No deal meant disaster. It was clear, Jefferson wrote, "that if everyone retains inflexibly his present opinion, there will be no bill passed at all for funding the public debts, and . . . without funding there is an end of the government."

At dinner Madison agreed to ease his opposition to assumption and "leave it to its fate" in the Congress—a victory for Hamilton. In Jefferson's account, either Madison or Hamilton then said that "as the pill would be a bitter one to the Southern states, something should be done to soothe them": The capital ought be sited along the Potomac.

The final result, Jefferson believed, was "the least bad of all the turns the thing can take." It was true that he hated the financial speculation that would result from the Hamiltonian vision of commerce. "It is much to be wished that every discouragement should be thrown in the way of men who undertake to trade without capital," Jefferson said. "The consumers pay for it in the end, and the debts contracted, and bankruptcies occasioned by such commercial adventurers, bring burden and disgrace on our country."

Yet Jefferson also believed in compromise. He advised his daughter Patsy to approach all people and all things with forbearance. "Every human being, my dear, must thus be viewed according to what it is good for, for none of us, no not one, is perfect; and were we to love none who had imperfections this world would be a desert for our love," Jefferson wrote in July 1790. "All we can do is to make the best of our friends: love and cherish what is good in them, and keep out of the way of what is bad: but no more think of rejecting them for it than of throwing away a piece of music for a flat passage or two." It was sound counsel for life at Monticello—and at New York.

In December 1790, a Virginian wrote Jefferson

about the state General Assembly's official protest over the debt assumption. "One party charges the Congress with an **unconstitutional** act; and both parties charge it with an act of injustice."

So be it. Jefferson had struck the deal he could strike, and, for the moment, America was the stronger for it.

TWENTY-FOUR

Mr. Jefferson Is Greatly Too Democratic

> I own it is my own opinion . . . that the present government is not that which will answer the ends of society . . . and that it will probably be found expedient to go into the British form.
>
> —ALEXANDER HAMILTON, according to an account of Jefferson's

JEFFERSON HAD BECOME SECRETARY of state on Monday, March 22, 1790. His first opinion on the possibility of an American war was written for President Washington 112 days later—hardly an epoch of peace. Little wonder his headache plagued him so much in these months.

A world war seemed at hand. In July 1789, Spain, long the dominant power in the Pacific Northwest, had seized two English ships at Nootka Sound, a distant inlet on the western coast of Vancouver Island. With its lucrative fur trade and importance to any significant system of commerce with Asia, the region was of interest to Spain as well as to Russia and Great Britain.

In 1778, Captain James Cook, the English explorer, had landed at Nootka and renamed it King George's Sound. The Spanish, who dated their claims to the area to a decree of Pope Alexander VI in the fifteenth century, were determined to fend off the encroachments of other nations. A Spanish explorer, Esteban José Martínez, arrived in the spring of 1789 and took control of the British vessels **Princess Royal** and **Argonaut** and of their captains and crews.

News of the Spanish attack stunned Britain, inciting talk of war with Spain. Writing from London after dining with members of Parliament late one night in early May 1790, the South Carolina lawyer and politician John Rutledge told Jefferson that he had never "been amongst such insolent bullies" as these British lawmakers. "They were all for war, talked much of **Old England** and the **British Lion,** laughed at the idea of drubbing the Dons, [and] began to calculate the millions of dollars [Spain] would be obliged to pay for having insulted **the first power on Earth**."

Merriment in England meant anxiety in America. Jefferson fretted about a sprawling war. Britain would be likely to dispatch its troops in Canada to seize Louisiana and the Floridas, both Spanish territories. France, an ally of Spain's, would be pulled into the fight. There would be combat on oceans the world over. And the United States—with just over a year's experience under its new Constitution—would be in the middle of it all. War, Jefferson said, was "very possible."

His worst fear, perhaps, was the prospect of encirclement by the British. Vice President Adams agreed with Jefferson, and Secretary of War Knox believed English control of the Floridas and of the Mississippi would lead to "great and permanent evils."

As a nation in the middle of an emerging conflict, America had to decide whether to allow foreign troops to march through U.S. territory. Jefferson favored what he called "a middle course," which meant delaying any answer in the event of a request from Britain. If an answer had to be given, however, he supported allowing the British troops passage since a refusal was likely to start a U.S.-British war. While willing to fight, Jefferson also said "war is full of chances," suggesting it was wisest to keep as many options open as possible. It was the practical position.

The Nootka Sound episode coincided with a planned American campaign against the Shawnee and Miami Indians to be led by Arthur St. Clair, the governor of the Northwest Territory. An important issue arose: Should the Americans tell the British about the operation at the risk of having the British pass along advance word to the Indians, their allies in harassing Americans along the frontier?

Jefferson told Washington that the Americans

should keep the Indian mission a secret. What neither the president nor the secretary of state knew was that Alexander Hamilton had already informed England through a British envoy named George Beckwith, who had played a role in turning Benedict Arnold away from the American cause.

Hamilton's relationship with Beckwith sheds light on the Treasury secretary's basic sympathies and operating style. In 1789, Hamilton had privately asked Beckwith to tell the British authorities that Washington's government was open for business with London. "I have always preferred a connection with you, to that of any other country," Hamilton said to Beckwith, continuing: "**we think in English,** and have a similarity of prejudices and of predilections." It was a clear effort to become part of Britain's sphere rather than France's—the opposite of the course Jefferson favored.

In the event of war between France and Britain, America's "naval exertions," Hamilton told Beckwith, "may in your scale be greatly important, and decisive." Such views, Hamilton said, "may be depended upon as the sentiments of the most enlightened men in this country."

But they were not Jefferson's sentiments, which the Hamiltonians knew. "Mr. Jefferson . . . is greatly too democratic for us at present," William Samuel Johnson, a senator from Connecticut, told Beckwith.

The pro-British interest in America embarked on a campaign to paint Jefferson as a dreamer, not a man of affairs. "Mr. Jefferson . . . is a man of some acquirements . . . but his opinions upon government are the result of fine spun theoretic systems, drawn from the ingenious writings of Locke, Sydney and others of their cast, which can never be realized," Senator William Paterson of New Jersey told George Beckwith.

In the end, Spain backed down. (The expedition against the Indians failed for reasons unrelated to Hamilton's disclosure.) For Jefferson and his contemporaries, the Nootka episode's possible enormousness, its suddenness, and its coming at such an early hour in the life of the government helped create a habit of mind that persisted through the years. The world was rife with danger, any particular event could produce universal calamity, and the Old World—especially Britain, France, and Spain—remained threats to American serenity and security.

The national capital moved from New York to Philadelphia in 1790, its temporary home until the District of Columbia could be made ready at the beginning of the next decade. En route to Philadelphia in early November, Jefferson and Madison stopped at Mount Vernon to spend the night with Washington. Jefferson was impressed by the president's skills as a planter and accepted the gift of some wheat to send to Patsy's husband, Thomas Mann Randolph, Jr., to plant at Monticello. Jefferson offered specific directions for his son-in-law: "The richest ground in the garden will be best," he said, and the seed should be planted "in distinct holes at proper distances."

Leasing a four-story brick house from Thomas Leiper at 274 High Street in Philadelphia, Jefferson ordered shipments of wine for himself and for Washington, and then immersed himself in the passion and action of the season.

On three separate but related issues, Jefferson fought to create an America that could, so far as possible, become respected, prosperous, and peaceable without being overly dependent on any one ally. From decisions about commercial and diplomatic relations with Britain and France to the struggle over the British impressment of an American seaman named Hugh Purdie to the projection of force against pirates in the Mediterranean, Jefferson sought free trade, mutual regard, and justice.

Yet on the establishment of a national bank and the imposition of an excise tax on what Jefferson called "ardent spirits," Hamilton's financial program took precedence.

The tax passed without much drama. With the funding of the debt and assumption now settled, the government needed revenue to operate under its new obligations.

The proposal for a national bank, however, precipitated a significant debate about the role of the federal government and the relative influence of

Hamilton and Jefferson in Washington's orbit. Hamilton wanted the bank to be funded by federal deposits but run, in part, for the benefit of private investors.

Jefferson and Madison objected. They feared that the Hamiltonian program would enable financial speculators to benefit from commercial transactions made possible by government funds.

Washington privately asked Jefferson for his view on the bank bill's constitutionality. Jefferson replied with an argument for strict construction—that any power not specifically mentioned in the Constitution was reserved for the states, not the federal government. "To take a single step beyond the boundaries thus specially drawn around the powers of Congress, is to take possession of a boundless field of power, no longer susceptible of any definition," Jefferson wrote in February 1791.

An improviser and a nationalist, Jefferson would not prove dogmatic on such issues. Only when viewed in the light of the moment (as the only means available to register a protest against the triumph of Hamilton's vision) and when considered with an appreciation for Jefferson's interpretation of that vision (that it tended to create a climate more congenial to absolutism than to republican democracy) does the opinion fit into the whole of Jeffersonian thinking. Even in 1791 Jefferson was not doctrinaire about his opinion, closing his letter to Washington with pragmatic counsel: "If the pro and con hang so even as to balance [the president's] judgment, a just respect for the wisdom of the legislature would naturally decide the balance in favor of their opinion."

Hamilton replied brilliantly, arguing that "an adherence to the letter of [the Constitution's] powers would at once arrest the motions of government." Hamilton won, but only barely. Washington had Madison draft a veto message, which was never issued, and took the maximum time allowed by the Constitution to sign the bill. Yet, in a victory for Hamilton, the president did sign it.

"Congress may go home," wrote William Maclay. "Mr. Hamilton is all-powerful, and fails in nothing he attempts."

It was springtime in Philadelphia. Writing Polly, Jefferson recorded the burst of colors:

April 5. Apricots in blossom.
Cherry leafing.
9: Peach in blossom.
Apple leafing.
April 11. Cherry in blossom.

Still, Hamilton was not far from Jefferson's mind. Jefferson wrote to James Monroe, "We are ruined, Sir, if we do not over-rule the principles that 'the more we owe, the more prosperous we shall be,' 'that a public debt furnishes the means of enterprise,' . . . etc. etc." That same day he wrote Patsy about bonnets and a new style of hat in Philadelphia: "Mrs. Trist has observed that there is a kind of veil lately introduced here, and much approved. It fastens over the brim of the hat and then draws round the neck as close or open as you please."

Just over a week later, Jefferson set off a new storm with a brief letter. The note he wrote was not long—only four sentences, two of which were formulaic—but few communications of Jefferson's life produced equal effects. Madison had passed on to Jefferson a borrowed copy of the first part of Thomas Paine's **Rights of Man,** just published in England. The pamphlet's owner (John Beckley, clerk of the House of Representatives) asked Jefferson to send it on to Jonathan B. Smith, a Philadelphia merchant whose brother, Samuel Harrison Smith, planned to publish it in America. In his accompanying note of April 26, 1791, Jefferson mused, briefly, in the third person.

Jefferson said that he was "extremely pleased to find [Paine's work] will be re-printed here, and that something is at length to be publicly said against the political heresies which have sprung up among us. He has no doubt our citizens will rally a second time round the standard of Common sense"—by which, of course, he meant Paine's **Common Sense** of 1776.

In a matter of days Jefferson opened a copy of the newly republished text to find that his words in the covering note had been reprinted as well. The implication was clear: Jefferson not only appeared to be Paine's sponsor but also believed there were "heresies" in circulation "among us." So it was that the secretary of state appeared to be declaring war on the vice president of the United States and the secretary of the Treasury.

"That I had in my view the **Discourses on Davila,** which have filled Fenno's papers for a twelve-month, without contradiction, is certain," Jefferson told the president in the wake of the publication. "But nothing was ever further from my thoughts than to become myself the contradictor before the public." He had written it, he told Madison, "to take off a little of the dryness of the note."

Hamilton, Jefferson believed, was seizing on the **Rights of Man** note to Jonathan Smith as evidence of Jefferson's "opposition to the government." Jefferson disagreed strongly, telling Madison that his remarks had been "meant for the enemies of the government, to wit those who want to change it into a monarchy." He added that he believed Hamilton was attacking him with vigor: "I have reason to think [Hamilton] has been unreserved in uttering these sentiments." And there was little Jefferson hated more than the thought that people were disparaging him in the shadows.

There is much truth in the tendency to encapsulate the competing traditions of the early American republic as a contest between Jefferson and Hamilton. For partisans of each man, it was then—and has been ever since—convenient to caricature the other, with Hamilton as the scheming proto-Brit bent on monarchy and Jefferson as the naïve proto-Frenchman intoxicated by visions of excessive democracy. Inevitably, though, such shorthand is incomplete.

In the first hours of the decade and sporadically throughout, Jefferson sometimes found himself in agreement with Hamilton (and with Washington and Adams as well), for Jefferson was a working politician and diplomat who believed in an effective central government—his experience in the Virginia governorship and during the Confederation years had convinced him of that—and often asserted the need to project power.

There was, however, a foundational point on which Jefferson never compromised, a conviction that drove much of his political life from 1790 until his death. He feared monarchy or dictatorship, which is different from fearing a strong national government, though Jefferson is often thought to have believed them the same thing. One of the terms he used to describe his opponents—"Monocrats"—is telling, for the word means government by the one.

Jefferson fretted over the prospect of the return of a king in some form, either as an immensely powerful president unchecked by the Constitution of 1787 or in a more explicitly monarchical or dictatorial role. He did not oppose the wielding of power. He was a good-hearted, fair-minded student of how best to accumulate it and use it. In romantic moments, he dreamed of a future of virtuous yeomen living in harmony. In realistic ones, he suspected the America of which he was an architect could be yet another short-lived chapter in the story of the tyranny of the few over the many. "We were educated in royalism: no wonder if some of us retain that idolatry still," Jefferson had once written to Madison.

Eternal vigilance was critical. "Courts love the people always, as wolves do the sheep," Jefferson once remarked. Even John Adams was susceptible to such worries. He wrote Jefferson in October 1787:

If the Duke of Angouleme, or Burgundy, or especially the Dauphin should demand one of your beautiful and most amiable daughters in marriage, all America from Georgia to New Hampshire would find their vanity and pride so agreeably flattered by it that all their sage maxims would give way; and even our sober New England Republicans would keep a day of thanksgiving for it, in their hearts. If General Washington had a daughter, I firmly believe, she would be demanded in marriage by one of the royal families of France or England, perhaps by both, or if he had a son he would be invited to come a courting to Europe.

Intermarriage with noble families in America and Europe, Adams believed, would lead to trouble, and to the United States repeating the mistakes and miming the bad habits of the Old World. "In short, my dear friend, you and I have been indefatigable laborers through our whole lives for a cause which be thrown away in the next generation, upon the vanity and foppery of persons of whom we do not now know the names perhaps."

Talk of threats came from the American West ("The politics of the western country are verging fast to a crisis, and must speedily eventuate in an appeal to the patronage of Spain or Britain," wrote "a Gentleman of Kentucky"—James Wilkinson—in 1789) and the palaces of London ("There is such a rooted aversion to us grown up in the court that if we could be smitten without the hazard of a general war, or a risk of shaking the present ministry from their places, hostilities would be recommenced against the United States, if it were only to gratify the irascible feelings of the monarch," the American lawyer John Brown Cutting had written Jefferson from London in August 1788).

In a report of a conversation with John Graves Simcoe, a British army officer and lieutenant governor of Upper Canada, at Niagara in June 1793, Peirce Duffy, an American military aide, recalled that Simcoe had asked "if the wishes of the people were as much in favor of General Washington as they formerly were or if I thought they would incline to have a British Government."

The Jefferson of the cabinet, of the vice presidency, and of the presidency can be best understood by recalling that his passion for the people and his regard for republicanism belonged to a man who believed that there were forces afoot—forces visible and invisible, domestic and foreign—that sought to undermine the rights of man by reestablishing the rule of priests and nobles and kings. His opposition to John Adams and to Alexander Hamilton, to the British and to financial speculators, grew out of this fundamental concern.

Like significant politicians before and after him, Jefferson was devoted to an overarching vision, but governed according to circumstance. Committed to the broad republican creed, supported by allies in politics and in the public who believed him to be an unshakable advocate of liberty under the law, Jefferson felt himself free to maneuver in matters of detail.

Where some saw hypocrisy, others saw political agility. As long as a political leader has some core strategic belief—and Jefferson did, in his defense of republicanism—then tactical flexibility can be a virtue. Even Alexander Hamilton recognized Jefferson's commitment to the nation, no matter how deeply the two disagreed about means. "To my mind a true estimate of Mr. J's character warrants the expectation of a temporizing rather than a violent system," Hamilton said in 1801.

Such mature reflections came toward the end, not at the beginning, of their conflicts. The battle between Jefferson and the men he saw as "Monocrats" (and the "Monocrats" believed Jefferson an American Jacobin who would not have minded the erection of a Parisian guillotine in Philadelphia) was interesting not least because they were implacable foes who could—and did—agree and cooperate from time to time, and who, even in their hours of starkest hostility, served in the same cabinet, dined at the same tables, and moved through the same intimate American world. Wars are often fought between brothers. As Jefferson's decade or so of struggle with the Federalists shows, there can be no more brutal or more bewildering battles than those that divide a family against itself.

In 1790 and in 1791, on the island of St. Domingue (now Haiti), slaves and their free allies rose in rebellion against their French imperial masters. In bloody warfare that was to last well over a decade, the blacks of the island, deeply affected by the promises of the French Revolution, fought to win the liberties proclaimed in the Declaration of the Rights of Man.

For slaveholding Americans, the war on St. Domingue seemed a glimpse of what could come to the United States should the slaves rise en masse.

Many of the whites of the island fled, and Jefferson noted their flight with interest. "The situation of the Saint-Domingue fugitives (aristocrats as they are) calls aloud for pity and charity," he wrote. "Never was so deep a tragedy presented to the feelings of man. . . . I become daily more and more convinced that all the West India islands will remain in the hands of the people of color, and a total expulsion of the whites [will] sooner or later take place." For Jefferson, the only way to make the best of the rebellion was to treat it as a warning. "It is high time we should foresee the bloody scenes which our children certainly, and possibly ourselves (South of Potomac) [will] have to wade through, and try to avert them," Jefferson said. Throughout the 1790s slaveholding Americans feared that the example of St. Domingue would lead to the long-dreaded slave war, possibly with the explicit help of refugees from the island. These anxieties would grow to the point that "every account of the success of the negro chiefs has been accompanied by an increased audacity in the people of the same color here," the British diplomat Edward Thornton reported to London in 1802.

As the years went by, Jefferson wondered whether St. Domingue might become the asylum he sought for America's slaves. (It did not.) And as he watched the St. Domingue rebellion from his vantage point as secretary of state, Jefferson could not know that the triumph of the blacks, under the leadership of Toussaint-Louverture, would so fatally weaken

France in the New World that Paris would one day reassess its ambitions along the American borders.

Washington spent part of 1791 touring southern states. "I write today indeed merely as the watchman cries, to prove himself awake, and that all is well, for the last week has scarcely furnished anything foreign or domestic worthy of your notice," Jefferson wrote Washington on the first day of May 1791.

Jefferson and Madison decided to take a trip of their own—to New York State and to part of New England. It was Federalist country, and their opponents were watching. Jefferson and Madison claimed they were traveling on a botany excursion; Jefferson was also interested in studying the Hessian fly.

The trip was political as well as scientific. In their brief time together in New York City—Jefferson stayed on Beekman Street—the two Virginians met with New York chancellor Robert R. Livingston and Aaron Burr and with Philip Freneau, a writer they hoped to recruit to start a newspaper to compete with the pro-Hamilton **Gazette of the United States**. Freneau, whom Madison had known at Princeton, initially declined, but finally accepted and published his first edition of the **National Gazette** on October 31, 1791. He was to be subsidized by the Department of State, where Jefferson employed him as a translator.

The Freneau appointment was a critical step for

the emerging Republican Party. By creating a newspaper, Jefferson was playing the part of leader of the opposition. As the years went on, John Beckley, the clerk of the U.S. House, became the Republicans' most effective tactician in the battles against the Federalists, helping to orchestrate the disparate mechanics of organized political action. Those "destined for commands," Jefferson once said, had to bring "the floating ardor of our countrymen" to "a point of union and effect." That was precisely the work of popular leadership.

Madison remained behind after Jefferson returned southward in the middle of June. Writing from New York, Madison captured the feel of the city. "Nothing new is talked of here," he told Jefferson in July 1791. "In fact stockjobbing drowns every other subject. The Coffee House is in an eternal buzz with the gamblers."

In Philadelphia, Jefferson was still settling in. It was not easy: His belongings were scattered between shipments from France to Philadelphia and to Monticello. "You mentioned formerly that the two commodes were arrived at Monticello," he wrote Polly. "Were my two sets of ivory chessmen in the drawers? They have not been found in any of the packages which came here."

On Saturday, August 13, 1791, Jefferson and Hamilton spoke privately about Adams and the political storm over **Davila.** According to Jefferson,

Hamilton said that while he believed a British form of government would be a stronger one, "since we have undertaken the experiment, I am for giving it a fair course, whatever my expectations may be."

Jefferson's opposition was political. "Whether these measures be right or wrong abstractly," Jefferson said of the Hamiltonian program, "more attention ought to be paid to the general opinion." He asked Livingston in New York whether "the people in your quarter are as well contented with the proceedings of our government as their representatives say they are?" Jefferson also noted that "there is a vast mass of discontent gathered in the South, and how and when it will break God knows. I look forward to it with some anxiety."

He worried, too, about the corruption of the legislature—that lawmakers were becoming financially enmeshed with the Hamiltonian system of securities and bank shares. Such economic ties were not bribes in the overt sense, Jefferson believed, but they did create a pernicious climate of cooperation between the Congress and the Treasury. This subtle form of "corruption" troubled Jefferson, who saw it as the means by which Hamilton and his allies could control the general direction of government. And control was something Jefferson never liked seeing in other men's hands.

Born at Shadwell, his family's plantation on the Rivanna River, on April 13, 1743, Thomas Jefferson was an eldest son who grew up expecting to play a central and commanding role in the lives of others. This portrait was painted in 1776 during Jefferson's service in the Continental Congress.

In his Paris years, by Mather Brown, circa 1786. Jefferson loved France and relished his life in the Hôtel de Langeac. "He is full of honor and sincerity and loves his country greatly," said the Chevalier de la Luzerne, the French foreign minister.

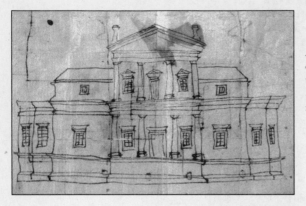

A 1770 sketch by Jefferson of Monticello (Italian for "little mountain"), the house he began building near Shadwell, his family home in Albemarle County.

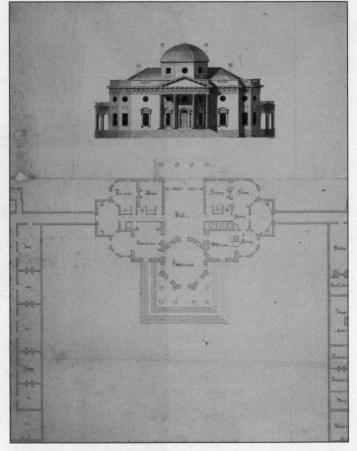

A circa 1803 plan for Monticello by the architect Robert Mills. Jefferson essentially rebuilt the entire house beginning at the time of his retirement from Washington's administration. Work continued throughout Jefferson's own presidency from 1801 to 1809; the result bore little resemblance to Mills's sketch.

The Hôtel de Salm under construction on the banks of the Seine in Paris. Jefferson knew the building when he was in Paris in the 1780s, and its design influenced both the second Monticello and the President's House. "While at Paris, I was violently smitten with the hotel de Salm, and used to go . . . almost daily to look at it," Jefferson wrote.

JEFFERSON'S INFLUENCES

While in Paris, Jefferson ordered copies made of several critical figures in America's story. This image of Christopher Columbus was painted from an anonymous portrait in the Gioviana Collection of the Uffizi in Florence.

Americus Vespucius, also copied from an anonymous image in the Gioviana Collection.

Jefferson admired Sir Walter Raleigh's exploration of the New World, and wanted a copy "to add . . . to those of other principal American characters which I have or shall have."

Sir Francis Bacon was one of Jefferson's most exalted heroes; Bacon's *Essays* and *The Advancement of Learning* informed Jefferson's thinking and understanding of the Enlightenment ethos.

Sir Isaac Newton's scientific thought—and its philosophical implications—made him another Jefferson icon.

John Locke's writings on liberty and on government earned him the third place in Jefferson's trinity of the "greatest men the world had ever produced," along with Bacon and Newton.

The surrender of
Cornwallis at York-
town, the victory that
marked the military
end of the Revolution
for the Americans.

FOUNDERS

George Washington, whom Jefferson respected, admired, and feared—but did not love.

Benjamin Franklin, whose Renaissance interests reflected Jefferson's own.

Gilbert Stuart's portrait of James Monroe, a longtime protégé and Virginia ally of Jefferson's. When Jefferson needed a man he could trust totally to go to France about the Louisiana Territory, he turned to Monroe.

John Adams by Mather Brown, in a portrait painted while Jefferson and Adams were in Europe in the 1780s.

Abigail Adams thought Jefferson "one of the choice ones of the earth," but the two friends grew distant as the political battles of the late 1790s put the Adamses and Jefferson on different sides of many questions.

James Madison, Jefferson's closest political confidant, often found himself in the position of protecting Jefferson from going public with extravagant statements expressed in the heat of given moments. "Take care of me when dead," Jefferson asked Madison, a sacred charge.

Dolley Payne Madison was one of the few women to be close to Jefferson in his presidential years; she served occasionally as his hostess while her husband held the office of secretary of state.

JEFFERSON AND FRANCE

Marie-Joseph Paul Yves Roch Gilbert du Motier, Marquis de Lafayette, the embodiment of the French alliance that made the success of the American Revolution possible. Lafayette and Jefferson grew extremely close while Jefferson was in France in the early days of the French Revolution.

Napoleon Crossing the Alps, by Jacques-Louis David. The Corsican-born soldier-turned-emperor's decision to sell Louisiana gave Jefferson the opportunity to transform America forever, and the rivalry between Britain and Napoleon's France fundamentally shaped America's foreign and domestic policies throughout the years of the early republic.

Beautiful and beguiling, Maria Cosway, the Italian-born daughter of English parents and wife of the artist Richard Cosway, provoked perhaps Jefferson's most intimate letter, one in which his head and his heart entered into open debate.

Before the 1793 executions of Louis XVI and Marie Antoinette, prevailing opinion in America supported the French Revolution; afterward, the question came to define and divide the new country more sharply.

Descent from the Cross, by Frans Floris (c. 1516–1570), from Jefferson's personal collection.

Herodias Bearing the Head of John the Baptist, by unknown copyist, after circa 1631 original by Guido Reni (1575–1642), from Jefferson's personal collection.

Jesus in the Praetorium, copy after original by Jan Gossaert ("Malbodius") (c. 1478–1532), from Jefferson's personal collection.

Sarah Presents Hagar to Abraham, by Adriaen van der Werff (1659–1722). Jefferson saw this painting at about the time he is said to have begun his sexual relationship with Sally Hemings, and he may well have identified with the image of a patriarch taking a slave as a concubine.

Young Chief of Sack Nation, unknown artist, circa 1805, from Jefferson's personal collection.

An engraving of Virginia's Natural Bridge, which Jefferson wrote was "so beautiful" that it was "really indescribable!"

Lewis and Clark on the Lower Columbia River, Charles Marion Russell (1864–1926). The Corps of Discovery's journey to the Pacific was a crowning achievement of the Jefferson presidency.

An 1804 political attack entitled "A Philosophic Cock" portrayed Jefferson as a sexually predatory slave owner after James Thomson Callender's allegations about Sally Hemings were published in a Richmond newspaper.

Jefferson long feared that his rival Alexander Hamilton's vision of government could lead the United States back into monarchy, or at least into a quasi-British model that would end the American experiment. As fellow Cabinet members, Jefferson said, he and Hamilton were like "two cocks" in a pit, fighting for dominion.

The enigmatic Aaron Burr, grandson and son of presidents of what became Princeton University, was a daunting and elusive political force. Critical to the rise of the Republican interest in the politics of the 1790s, Burr tied Jefferson in the presidential balloting in 1801. Jefferson never trusted him afterward and removed him from the 1804 ticket. Burr's alleged designs on the American West led to a celebrated treason trial in the latter years of Jefferson's presidency.

A ferocious Federalist, Timothy Pickering never trusted Jefferson, and fomented secessionist sentiment in New England. He was secretary of state under both Washington and Adams and served as senator from Massachusetts from 1803 to 1811.

America was engaged in a seemingly perennial war against the Barbary pirates in the Mediterranean; from his service in France to his years as secretary of state to his two terms as president, Jefferson dealt with the issue for decades.

Jefferson's eldest grandson, Thomas Jefferson Randolph, by Charles Willson Peale.

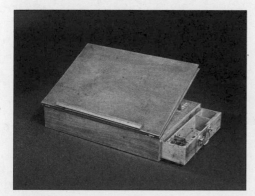

The portable writing desk on which Jefferson wrote the Declaration of Independence. "Politics as well as religion has its superstitions," Jefferson wrote. "These, gaining strength with time, may, one day, give imaginary value to this relic, for its association with the birth of the Great Charter of our Independence." Designed by Jefferson, it was made by Benjamin Randolph of Philadelphia.

A rendering of the house and grounds at Poplar Forest, Jefferson's retreat in Bedford County, Virginia, where he went to escape the constant stream of visitors and callers at Monticello.

The joy and consuming interest of Jefferson's retirement years, the University of Virginia was designed to give educational expression to Jefferson's devotion to the life of the mind and to the pursuit of reason.

TWENTY-FIVE

Two Cocks in the Pit

> How unfortunate . . . that whilst we are en-
> compassed on all sides with avowed enemies
> and insidious friends, that internal dissensions
> should be harrowing and tearing our vitals.
>
> —GEORGE WASHINGTON

DINNER WAS OVER, and the senior officers of the American government were sitting together, drinking wine. President Washington was out of town, at Mount Vernon, and had asked Jefferson to summon Vice President Adams and the cabinet to handle some pending business.

The matter was dispatched, and the talk drifted to more general topics. Jefferson's guests were an impressive lot—John Adams, Alexander Hamilton, Secretary of War Henry Knox, Attorney General Edmund Randolph—and the after-dinner conversation at the secretary of state's quarters was dominated by a "collision of opinion" between Adams and Hamilton.

The subject: the British system of government. In

the candlelight, Adams said that in his view "if some of its defects and abuses were corrected, it would be the most perfect constitution of government ever devised by man."

Jefferson sat in a kind of predictable horror, listening to this paean to a nation that perpetuated the role of hereditary power.

Then Hamilton went a step further than Adams, saying that "it was the most perfect model of government that could be formed; and that the correction of its vices would render it an impracticable government." To Jefferson's ears, this meant that Hamilton (and, to a lesser extent, Adams) might well believe more strongly in the British way than in the American way.

This impression was underscored by a passing remark of Hamilton's at dinner. Jefferson had decorated the walls of his quarters with a collection of portraits that included Sir Francis Bacon, John Locke, and Sir Isaac Newton, all men of the Enlightenment. Hamilton asked Jefferson who they were. "I told him they were my trinity of the three greatest men the world had ever produced, naming them," Jefferson recalled.

Taking this in, Hamilton paused, thinking. After a moment, he broke his silence.

"The greatest man that ever lived," Hamilton said, "was Julius Caesar."

As the evening ended, Jefferson reflected on the distinctions between Adams and Hamilton. "Mr.

Adams was honest as a politician, as well as a man; Hamilton honest as a man, but, as a politician, believing in the necessity of either force or corruption to govern men."

Neither man was Jefferson's ally in the wars of President Washington's years. Both represented forces and tendencies that Jefferson found unsettling, disturbing—and dangerous.

Early on the afternoon of Tuesday, February 28, 1792, Jefferson was running late. He had hoped to come see Washington well before three o'clock, the time when the president received public callers. The meeting was important to Jefferson—he was arguing for improvements to the postal service by "doubling the velocity of the post-riders" from fifty to one hundred miles a day—but various other matters delayed him.

Arriving at last, Jefferson hurried through his proposals, explaining that the post office should fall under his own State Department, not Hamilton's Treasury Department, for "the Treasury possessed already such an influence as to swallow up the whole Executive powers."

The matter was not one of "personal interest," Jefferson said, for he intended to serve in office only as long as Washington himself were to serve. Jefferson's only purpose, he told the president, was to seek "to place things on a safe footing" for the public good.

Before he could reply, Washington was summoned

to greet the afternoon callers. Would Jefferson come to breakfast the next morning?

He would, and did. After the meal the two men reviewed the postal question. The president then brought the talk back to the broader topics Jefferson had raised the day before. Washington said he intended to leave the presidency after four years both because of his age ("he really felt himself growing old") and for fear of appearing greedy for place ("were he to continue longer, it might [give] room to say that having tasted the sweets of office he could not do without them"). Yet the president was anxious to prevent the cabinet from following suit, worrying, he said, that "this might produce a shock in the public mind of dangerous consequence."

Jefferson replied with his own implicit evocations of Cincinnatus, casting his political career as an accident of the age. "I told him that no man had ever had less desire of entering into public offices than myself: that the circumstance of a perilous war, which brought everything into danger, and called for all the services which every citizen could render, had induced me to undertake the administration of the government of Virginia" and that he had twice refused diplomatic appointments before "a domestic loss . . . made me fancy that absence, and a change of scene for a time, might be expedient for me," which led him to accept the assignment in France.

In Washington's company on this late winter morning, engaged by but perhaps tired from struggling against Federalist interests, Jefferson may have felt a quiet comradeship with the president who was flatteringly urging that he stay at his exalted post.

The two Virginians, linked by common heritage and shaped by the same forces of Revolution, were, however briefly, comfortable with each other, pausing at the pinnacle to review the paths they had traveled to the summit. The stories they told to each other about ambition and obligation and power were the stories they told themselves about ambition and obligation and power. They wished to be seen as above party and removed from the hurly-burly of politics.

In the warmth of the moment Washington confided a fear to Jefferson, and Jefferson repaid the confidence with candor. The government, Washington said, "had set out with a pretty general good will of the public, yet . . . symptoms of dissatisfaction had lately shown themselves far beyond what he could have expected, and to what height these might arise in case of too great a change in the administration could not be foreseen."

Jefferson did not miss his chance. Speaking bluntly and at some length, he said that there was, in his opinion, "only a single source of these discontents": Hamilton's Treasury.

Hamilton, Jefferson said, was "deluging the states with paper-money instead of gold and silver" to encourage speculation, rather than "other branches of useful industry." Jefferson told Washington of his conviction that Hamiltonian lawmakers had "feathered their nests with paper."

That was not all. Jefferson said that his foes "had now brought forward a proposition, far beyond every one ever yet advanced, and to which the eyes of many were turned, as the decision which was to let us know whether we live under a limited or an unlimited government."

Jefferson soon took his leave.

Jefferson and Hamilton were now "daily pitted in the Cabinet like two cocks," as Jefferson recalled. A savvy politician, Jefferson recognized— and grudgingly appreciated—Hamilton's political craft. Hamilton, for instance, carefully managed relations with George Hammond, the official British envoy. Jefferson noticed that Hamilton always seemed to know precisely what Hammond was thinking, which Jefferson said "proved the intimacy of their communications: insomuch that I believe he communicated to Hammond all our views and knew from him in return the views of the British court."

Even Washington himself was not exempt from Jefferson's dark thoughts about the possibility of a breach of faith with the republican promise. Once, in a conversation about whether the House would vote to provide money stipulated by treaty, Washington grew impatient. "He said that he did not like throwing too much into democratic hands, that if [the members of the House] would not do what the Constitution called on them to do, the government would be at an end, and must **then assume another form**," Jefferson wrote in April 1792.

For Jefferson, the images of monarchy swirled. The rhetoric of the American Revolution—**Jefferson's** rhetoric, the product of his own pen—seemed fainter in the clatter of a capital that he believed was beginning to feel more like a king's court than the seat of a republic.

The public debt, paper money, excise taxes, the alleged corruption of the Congress: Jefferson believed it all could lead to the consummate betrayal as 1792 wore on. The "ultimate object of all this is to prepare the way for a change from the present republican form of government to that of a monarchy, of which the English constitution is to be the model," Jefferson told Washington. Jefferson unmistakably alluded to Hamilton's 1787 advocacy of a more monarchical system. "That this was contemplated in the Convention is no secret, because its partisans have made none of it," Jefferson said. "To effect it then was impracticable; but they are still eager after their object, and are predisposing everything for its ultimate attainment."

Jefferson believed that members of Congress had a vested interest in the Hamiltonian financial system. It "will be the instrument for producing in future a king, lords and commons, or whatever else those who direct it may choose," he told Washington. The aim of the "Monarchial Federalists" was to use "the new government merely as a stepping stone to monarchy."

He was thinking of the calamitous possibility of southern secession to protest Federalist dominance. "I can scarcely contemplate a more incalculable evil than the breaking of the union into two or more parts," Jefferson said, yet if northern interests were to predominate, it would become impossible to say what might happen.

This was where Jefferson believed Washington came in. "The confidence of the whole union is centered in you. . . . North and South will hang together, if they have you to hang on."

Give us a few years, Jefferson said, and perhaps all would be well. "One or two sessions will determine the crisis: and I cannot but hope that you can resolve to add one or two more to the many years you have already sacrificed to the good of mankind."

Jefferson dined at Washington's on Thursday, June 7, 1792. At the table with John Jay, Jefferson recalled that he and Jay "got, towards the close of the afternoon, into a little contest whether hereditary descent or election was most likely to bring **wise** and **honest** men into public councils." Jefferson argued for democracy; Jay for aristocracy.

Washington was listening to the exchange. "I was not displeased to find the P. attended to the conversation as it will be a corroboration of the design imputed to that party in my letter."

Jefferson confided his fears to Lafayette. "Too many of these stock jobbers and King-jobbers have come into our legislature, or rather too many of our legislature have become stock jobbers and king-jobbers."

Washington gently tried to calm Jefferson's rising anxieties about a monarchical threat. "There might be **desires,** but he did not believe there were **designs** to change the form of government into a monarchy," Jefferson recalled Washington telling him in July 1792. It was hardly a full-throated reassurance.

In August, Washington returned to the divide between Jefferson and Hamilton, writing Jefferson:

How unfortunate, and how much is it to be regretted then, that whilst we are encompassed on all sides with avowed enemies and insidious friends, that internal dissensions should be harrowing and tearing our vitals. . . . I believe it will be difficult, if not impracticable, to manage the reins of government or to keep the parts of it together: for if, instead of laying our shoulders to the machine after measures are decided on, one pulls this way and another that, before the utility of the thing is fairly tried, it must inevitably be torn asunder—And, in my opinion the fairest prospect of happiness and prosperity that ever was presented to man, will be lost—perhaps for ever!

Jefferson replied with passion and at length, mounting his case with a new level of intensity. The sharper tone he took with Washington—still diplomatic, but nonetheless more confrontational than usual—was in reaction to the implicit criticism in the president's August letter. Jefferson hated to be told he was wrong, and he defended himself with ferocity. "That I have utterly, in my private conversations, disapproved of the system of the Secretary of the Treasury, I acknowledge and avow: and this was not merely a speculative difference."

He was challenging Washington directly, answering the president's assertion that differences of opinion should be worked out in the forge of experience. No, Jefferson was saying, something deeper and more fundamental was at stake between him and Hamilton. Hamilton's system, Jefferson said, "flowed from principles adverse to liberty, and was calculated to undermine and demolish the republic, by creating an influence of his department over the members of the legislature."

Bureaucratic struggles assumed epic dimensions, with Jefferson casting himself as a loyal lieutenant victimized by an ambitious, bullying Treasury secretary. "He undertook, of his own authority, the conferences with the ministers of [France and Britain], and . . . on every consultation [he] provided . . . some report of a conversation with the one or the other of them, adapted to his views."

Finally, Jefferson told Washington that, once in private life, he reserved the right to take his stand in "newspaper contests" if events required it: "I will not suffer my retirement to be clouded by the slanders of a man whose history, from the moment at which history can stoop to notice him, is a tissue of machinations against the liberty of the country which has not only received and given him bread, but heaped its honors on his head."

Early on the morning of the first day of October 1792, Jefferson spoke again with the president, this time at Mount Vernon on the banks above the Potomac. Washington still hoped Jefferson would not leave the government. According to Jefferson, the president "thought it important to preserve the check of my opinions in the administration in order to keep things in their proper channel and prevent them from going too far."

The president and the secretary of state disagreed anew on the scope of the threat of monarchy. Washington said that he "did not believe there were ten men in the U.S. whose opinions were worth attention who entertained such a thought." Jefferson replied that "there were many more than he imagined. . . . I told him that though the people were sound, there was a numerous sect who had monarchy in contemplation. That the Secretary of the Treasury was one of these. That I had heard him say that this constitution was a shilly shally thing of mere milk and water which could not last, and was only good as a step to something better." Soon breakfast ended the conversation.

Washington took a sensible view of the conflict between his top two lieutenants. "For I will frankly and solemnly declare that I believe the views of both of you are pure, and well-meant; and that experience alone will decide with respect to the salubrity of the measures which are the subjects of dispute," he wrote Jefferson on Thursday, October 18, 1792. It was an understandable way for a president, who saw the whole picture, to frame the issue.

"Why, then," Washington continued, "when some of the best citizens in the United States—men of discernment—uniform and tried patriots, who have no sinister views to promote, but are chaste in their ways of thinking and acting are to be found, some on one side, and some on the other of the questions which have caused these agitations, should either of you be so tenacious of your opinions as to make no allowances for those of the other?"

At the same time he was dealing with Jefferson and Hamilton, Washington worried about rebellion in western Pennsylvania over the excise tax. Opposition in the region, he told Jefferson, was now "too open, violent and serious to be longer winked at by the government without prostrating its authority and involving the executive in censurable inattention to the outrages which are threatened." Particularly anxious about the resistance to this tax on distilled spirits, Hamilton drafted a harsh proclamation to be issued by the president. Washington took care to include Jefferson in the consultations and won the secretary of state's signature on the document. The president wanted the appearance of a unified administration, even if it were, in fact, an administration at war with itself.

Jefferson may have been exaggerating the threat of monarchy, but he was not inventing it. "Should Congress adopt a Prince of the House of Brunswick for their future President or King, the happiness of the two nations would be interwoven and united—all jealousies removed and the most durable affections cemented that perhaps ever were formed between two independent nations," the lieutenant governor of Upper Canada, John Graves Simcoe, wrote in August 1792—the same season in which Washington was securing Jefferson's endorsement of the excise-tax proclamation. "This is an object worthy [of] the attention of Great Britain and which many of the most temperate men of the United States have in contemplation. And which many events, if once systematically begun, may hasten and bring to maturity." Jefferson's friends fed such fears. One reported an after-dinner conversation with Hamilton in which the Treasury secretary said, "there was no stability, no security, in any kind of government but a monarchy."

Hamilton had other worries as well. In late 1792 there were revelations of an affair between Hamilton and a married woman, Maria Reynolds, whose husband, James, colluded in the seduction of the Treasury secretary—a seduction which, by Hamilton's own account, was not difficult. The couple blackmailed Hamilton, and word of the affair, embellished by rumors of financial impropriety, led a delegation of lawmakers to investigate. They found Hamilton guilty of adultery but nothing else.

In early 1793, Congressman William Branch Giles of Virginia introduced resolutions designed to force Hamilton to explain something other than his private life. Giles wanted to hear more about the Treasury's fiscal policies.

Viewed by Federalists as a partisan attack on Hamilton allegedly orchestrated by the Virginian Republican interest—including Jefferson—the resolutions burned intensely but quickly as a political issue. One draft attributed to Jefferson concluded dramatically: "**Resolved,** That the Secretary of the Treasury has been guilty of maladministration in the duties of his office, and should, in the opinion of Congress, be removed from his office by the President of the United States." The final submission to the House by Giles did not include a call for Hamilton's dismissal, and even the somewhat milder resolutions failed to pass.

Jefferson let his frustration show only in private. In March 1793, in a note about Giles's resolutions, he wrote that Giles "and one or two others were sanguine enough to believe that the palpableness of these resolutions rendered it impossible the House could reject them." It was not a surprise, Jefferson said, to those, like him, who were more familiar with a House he believed was composed of "1 . . . bank directors. 2. Holders of bank stock. 3. Stock jobbers. 4. Blind devotees. 5. ignorant persons who did not comprehend [the resolutions]. 6. Lazy and good humored persons, who comprehended and acknowledged them, yet were too lazy to examine, or unwilling to pronounce censure."

Despite the legislative defeat, Jefferson thought perhaps the episode would play well for the Republican interest. "The public will see from this the extent of their danger," he said. Or so Jefferson hoped.

In the end, Washington had consented to reelection to the presidency, and Jefferson agreed to stay on in office for a time. Under assault in the papers, Jefferson hated to think that people might believe he was driven from office. His pride was too great for that. He would remain at his post until "those who troubled the waters before" withdrew. "When they suffer them to get calm," Jefferson said, "I will go into port."

Reports of rising violence in France grew in the autumn of 1792, reaching a historic height with the September 1793 declaration of the Reign of Terror by revolutionaries determined to slaughter those they viewed as enemies of the cause. The seemingly endless bloodshed gave fresh strength to the pro-British forces in America.

Support for the French Revolution had once been a unifying factor in American politics. "We were all strongly attached to France—scarcely any man more strongly than myself," recalled John Marshall. "I sincerely believed human liberty to depend in a great measure on the success of the French Revolution." Despite some Federalist misgivings from the start, common wisdom held that the French struggle for liberty was of a piece with the American Revolution. From the autumn of 1792 forward, though, as the French Revolution became ever bloodier, American opinion came to be divided—especially after extremists fomented ever-deadlier riots and purges, forced Lafayette abroad, and took Louis XVI to the scaffold in January 1793.

Jefferson's reaction to the events in Paris was complicated. He lost friends to the guillotine. After being driven from his homeland, Lafayette spent five years in captivity in Europe, the prisoner of Austrian and Prussian powers. Yet Jefferson saw the disturbances in France in the context of the larger contest between republicanism and absolutism he believed defined the age. "In the struggle which was necessary, many guilty persons fell without the forms of trial, and with them some innocent," he wrote William Short on Thursday, January 3, 1793. Jefferson continued:

> These I deplore as much as anybody, and shall deplore some of them to the day of my death. But I deplore them as I should have done had they fallen in battle. . . . The liberty of the whole earth was depending on the issue of the contest, and was ever such a prize won with so little innocent blood? My own affections have been deeply wounded by some of the martyrs to this cause, but rather than it should have failed, I would have seen half the earth desolated. Were there but an Adam and an Eve left in every country, and left free, it would be better than as it now is. I have expressed to you my sentiments, because they are really those of 99 of a hundred of our citizens.

The passage's hyperbole is partly rooted in the symbolic role France continued to play in American politics. To Jefferson, to be for the French Revolution was to be a republican and friend to liberty; to be against it, or to have reservations about it, was to be a monarchist and a traitor to freedom.

This was not a radical interpretation of current political sentiment. As late as Tuesday, January 29, 1793, pro-French organizers in Boston announced plans for a rally in support of the revolutionaries, noting that "a number of citizens anxious to celebrate the success of our Allies, the French, in their present glorious struggles for liberty and equality . . . have agreed to provide an ox, with suitable liquors."

In February 1793, Washington approached Jefferson with a new thought. Would he consider returning to Paris for a year or two to represent American interests there? Jefferson refused.

Washington's reply was pointed. The president said that Jefferson "had pressed" Washington "to a continuance in public service and [now] refused to do the same" in his own case.

Jefferson struck back with a determination masked, if thinly, by flattery and modesty. "I said the case was very different: he united the confidence of all America, and was the only person who did so: his services were therefore of the last importance: but for myself my going out would not be noted or known, a thousand others could supply my place to equal advantage. Therefore I felt myself free."

In retreat, Washington coolly asked Jefferson "to consider maturely what arrangement should be made." There the matter closed.

Jefferson had secured the fulfillment of his own wishes over those of the most popular and powerful man in the nation. He had done so with a mixture of politeness and pragmatism, praising Washington while noting that he could manage the affairs of the hour better in America than in France—a compelling argument.

It was not an easy thing to do, to defy George Washington, but Jefferson's subtlety enabled him to assert his own will against that of the president in such a seemingly gracious way that Washington was unable to counterattack. The moment illuminates the political Jefferson—a man who got his way quietly but unmistakably, without bluster or bombast, his words congenial but his will unwavering.

TWENTY-SIX

The End of a Stormy Tour

> I feel for your situation but you must bear it.
> Every consideration private as well as public
> requires a further sacrifice of your longings for
> the repose of Monticello.
> —JAMES MADISON to Thomas Jefferson

THE PLANTATION WAS CALLED Bizarre. Home to Richard Randolph—a distant Jefferson cousin, inevitably—the estate on the Appomattox River in Cumberland County, Virginia, was the center of intense speculation and scandal in 1792–93 after a brutal and disturbing episode that tested even Jefferson's outward equanimity.

The unmarried Ann Cary Randolph, a sister of Thomas Mann Randolph, Jr. (and thus Jefferson's daughter Patsy's sister-in-law), was apparently impregnated by her brother-in-law, Richard Randolph. Ann, called Nancy, delivered the baby (though she may have suffered a miscarriage), while on a visit to a neighboring plantation with her brother-in-law and her sister. The dead infant was taken outdoors;

no corpse was ever found. The story was so mysterious and tantalizing that it rapidly spread, leading to a trial at which Richard Randolph was defended by lawyers that included John Marshall and Patrick Henry.

For Jefferson, the violence in Virginia was an occasion to think about the harmony so little in evidence in the capital. Urging Patsy to be generous of spirit with their besieged kin, he wrote: "Never throw off the best affections of nature in the moment when they become most precious to their object; nor fear to extend your hand to save another, lest you should sink yourself." He believed in the virtues of civility, understanding that they were the most required when they were the least convenient. Jefferson faced such tests of harmony every hour in Philadelphia.

As Washington's second inauguration approached, the national experiment still felt provisional. In a small session to discuss the ceremonies for the president's swearing-in, Henry Knox's anxiety led to an outburst. "In the course of our conversation Knox, stickling for parade, got into great warmth and swore that our government must either be entirely new modeled or it would be knocked to pieces in less than 10 years," Jefferson wrote, "and that as it is at present he would not give a copper for it, that it is the President's character, and not the written constitution, which keeps it together."

In a letter he never sent, Robert R. Livingston of New York wrote that he hoped Jefferson would not resign amid the attacks of 1792–93. Jefferson, Livingston said, should not "suffer yourself in appearance to be drummed out of the regiment and that too when there is every reasonable ground to hope that upon the first vacancy you will be promoted to the command of the troops." He referred, too, to Jefferson's position in Washington's cabinet as a "post in an enemies' country."

The war between Hamilton and Jefferson was unending. In September 1792, in the **Gazette of the United States**, Hamilton wrote: "Mr. Jefferson [is] . . . distinguished as the quiet, modest, retiring philosopher—as the plain, simple, unambitious republican. He shall not now for the first time be regarded as the intriguing incendiary—the aspiring turbulent competitor."

In late 1792, Jefferson moved out of the city of Philadelphia to a house on the Schuylkill River. He was hungry for news of home. "From Monticello you have everything to write about which I have any care," he told his family. "How do my young chestnut trees? How comes on your garden? How fare the fruit blossoms etc."

Thoughts of Monticello were a relief from the strain of a life in which Jefferson was often out of sync with Washington, Adams, and Hamilton. A small instance: Jefferson had used the phrase "our republic" in letters drafted for Washington's signature (as in, "your Min. plen. to our republic").

According to Jefferson, Washington told him that "certainly ours was a republican government, but yet we had not used that style in this way: that if anybody wanted to change its form into a monarchy he was sure it was only a few individuals, and that no man in the U.S. would set his face against it more than himself: but that this was not what he was afraid of: his fears were from another quarter, that there was more danger of anarchy being introduced."

Washington was out of sorts in any event. "Knox told some little stories to aggravate the Pr[esident]," Jefferson recalled. "To wit, that Mr. King had told him, that a lady had told him, that she had heard a gentleman say that the Pr. was as great a tyrant as any of them and that it would soon be time to chase him out of the city."

Jefferson believed the Hamiltonians were drafting excessively critical articles about Washington in the voice of Republicans in order to alienate the president and "make him believe it was that party who were his enemies, and so throw him entirely into the scale of the monocrats."

With Jefferson, Washington also alluded to a Freneau newspaper piece he disliked. "He was evidently sore and warm," Jefferson wrote, "and I took his intention to be that I should interpose in some way with Freneau, perhaps withdraw his appointment of translating clerk to my office, but I will not do it: his paper has saved our constitution which was galloping fast into monarchy."

Jefferson would not submit. In this battle of wills, the secretary of state, as usual, refused to give way.

The wars of the Old World were once again a subject of concern in the first half of 1793. On February 1, eleven days after the execution of Louis XVI, the French Republic declared war on Britain. Washington was determined to declare the United States' neutrality in the conflict. Jefferson disliked the draft of the proclamation, which he found Hamiltonian and pro-British.

The Neutrality Proclamation also raised some Republican questions about an overreaching executive. "It has been asked also," Madison wrote Jefferson, "whether the authority of the Executive extended by any part of the Constitution to a declaration of the disposition of the U.S. on the subject of war and peace? . . . The right to decide the question . . . [of] war or peace . . . [is] vested in the Legislature."

Was Washington acting too kingly? James Monroe thought the proclamation "unconstitutional and improper."

The president was sensitive about the questions over neutrality, noting at a November cabinet meeting that he had used it in a draft of a document and "we had not objected to the term." After dinner

Washington remained sour. "Other questions and answers were put and answered in a quicker altercation than I ever before saw the President use," Jefferson recalled.

Washington was tired of the strife of governing. In November 1793, the cabinet debated whether the president should propose the creation of a military academy. No, Washington decided, for "though it would be a good thing, he did not wish to bring on anything which might generate heat and ill humor."

Both heat and ill humor were at hand in the prospect of a visit from an envoy from France, Edmond-Charles Genet. Hamilton questioned whether the Frenchman should be officially received, raising what Jefferson called "lengthy considerations of doubt and difficulty."

Jefferson hoped an enthusiastic public reception would demonstrate broad support for France. Instead, Genet was a disaster, insulting Washington and making himself generally obnoxious. It was, however, more than a question of personality: The envoy was organizing privateers in violation of Washington's Neutrality Proclamation. Genet was, Jefferson said, "Hotheaded, all imagination, no judgment, passionate, disrespectful and even indecent towards the P. in his written as well as verbal communications. . . . He renders my position immensely difficult." Indeed Genet did, confiding in Jefferson about the possibility of fomenting rebellions against British and Spanish holdings—

confidences Jefferson chose to keep, noting that Genet had spoken to him "not as secretary of state but as Mr. Jeff."

At Hamilton's urging, the cabinet decided to ask the French government to recall Genet in August 1793. Jefferson saw the result was inevitable: Hamilton had won this battle. "He will sink the republican interest if they do not abandon him," Jefferson wrote Madison.

Madison sensed Jefferson's dwindling patience with service in the administration but advised him to stay the course. Jefferson could not bring himself to agree with his old friend. "To my fellow-citizens the debt of service has been fully and faithfully paid," Jefferson wrote in June 1793. After a quarter century of public service, in revolution, in war, and in a fraught, fragile peace, Jefferson was tired. "The motion of my blood," he said, "no longer keeps time with the tumult of the world."

Then, in a cry of frustration, he cataloged the irritations he felt and the sense of futility that sometimes seized him. "Worn down with labors from morning till night, and day to day; knowing them as fruitless to others as they are vexatious to myself, committed singly in desperate and eternal contest against a host who are systematically undermining the public liberty and prosperity," he was, he said, "giving everything I love, in exchange for everything I hate, and all this without a single gratification in possession or prospect, in present enjoyment or future wish."

The battles seemed endless, victory elusive. James Monroe fed Jefferson's worries, saying he was concerned that America was being "torn to pieces as we are, by a malignant monarchy faction."

A rumor reached Jefferson that Alexander Hamilton and the Federalists Rufus King and William Smith "**had secured** an asylum to themselves in England" should the Jefferson faction prevail in the government. The source of the report "could not understand whether they had secured it themselves, or whether they were only notified that it was secured to them. So that they understand that they may go on boldly, in their machinations to change the government, and if they should be overset and choose to withdraw, they will be secure of a pension in England as Arnold . . . had."

A sign of public dissatisfaction with the Federalist leadership in New York came with the organization and popularity of what were called Democratic-Republican societies, which were led by the working and middle classes and which had a strong immigrant presence. The groups' rhetoric about republicanism and the threat of aristocracy enraged Washington, who lost his temper at a cabinet meeting after Henry Knox alluded to popular abuse of the president. As Jefferson recalled it, "The President was much inflamed, got into one of those passions when he cannot command himself. . . .

Defied any man on earth to produce one single act of his since he had been in the government which was not done on the purest motives. . . . That **by God** he had rather be in his grave than in his present situation. That he had rather be on his farm than to be made **emperor of the world** and yet that they were charging him with wanting to be a king."

The meeting was effectively over.

Jefferson wanted out. It was time for a tactical retreat to see whether the larger war could be won. Washington did not want Jefferson to go, and he paid a call at Jefferson's Schuylkill house in August.

The president was unhappy. Hamilton also wanted to resign, and Washington felt he was losing control. Would Jefferson stay on until the end of the next congressional session? Jefferson declined, alluding to the "particular uneasiness of my situation in this place where the laws of society oblige me to move always exactly in the circle which I know to bear me peculiar hatred, that is to say the wealthy aristocrats, the merchants closely connected with England, [and] the new created paper fortunes."

Washington replied that "the constitution we have is an excellent one if we can keep it where it is, that it was indeed supposed there was a party disposed to change it into a monarchial form, but that he could conscientiously declare there was not a man in the U.S. who would set his face more decidedly against it than himself."

Jefferson told Washington that "no rational man in the U.S. suspects you of any other disposition, but there does not pass a week in which we cannot prove declarations dropping from the monarchial party that our government is good for nothing, it is a milk and water thing which cannot support itself, we must knock it down and set up something of more energy."

When Jefferson suggested naming a temporary secretary of state who would then move to the Treasury, Washington demurred, observing that "men never chose to descend: that being once in a higher department he would not like to go into a lower one."

Yellow fever struck Philadelphia in late summer 1793. "It has now got into most parts of the city and is considerably infectious," Jefferson wrote. "At first 3 out of 4 died. Now about 1 out of 3. It comes on with a pain in the head, sick stomach, then a little chill, fever, black vomiting and stools, and death from the 2nd to the 8th day." (One job seeker tried to find some personal gain in the epidemic: "Viewing with sorrow the large number of victims in all ranks and professions felled by the late distressing disease, I suppose that some vacancies have taken place amongst the persons employed in public offices. In this conception I take the liberty of addressing your Honor with the offer of my best services in that line.")

Jefferson was unkind about Hamilton. "Hamilton is ill of the fever, it is said," Jefferson wrote Madison. "He had two physicians out at his house the night before last. His family thinks him in danger, and he puts himself so by his excessive alarm. . . . A man as timid as he is on the water, as timid on horseback, as timid in sickness, would be a phenomenon if the courage of which he has the reputation in military occasions were genuine."

Jefferson was so much concerned about public opinion that he was willing to risk illness. "I would really go away, because I think there is rational danger, but . . . I do not like to exhibit the appearance of panic."

On New Year's Eve, 1793, Jefferson extended his official resignation to Washington, who accepted it on the first day of 1794.

The president did so, he said, "with sincere regret." He reassured Jefferson about his tenure in terms both men valued: those of reputation. Washington could not "suffer you to leave your station without assuring you that the opinion which I had formed of your integrity and talents . . . has been confirmed by the fullest experience; and that both have been eminently displayed in the discharge of your duties."

Washington's benediction was warm: "Let a conviction of my most earnest prayers for your happiness accompany you in your retirement."

Preparing to leave Philadelphia, Jefferson advised friends and correspondents "that Richmond is my nearest port and that to which both letters and things had best be addressed to me in future."

How long he was to stay in seclusion was a subject of no little speculation. Few believed he was withdrawing forever. Hearing the news, a Revolutionary hero thought Jefferson's retirement was likely to be short-lived. Writing from Rose Hill in New York, Horatio Gates told Jefferson that he was leaving office "covered with glory; the public gratitude may one day force you from that retreat, so make no rash promises, lest like other great men you should be tempted to break them." John Adams was more succinct, noting the marvel of how well political plants grow in the shade. The friendship that had begun between Adams and Jefferson nearly twenty years before was a victim of the acrimony of the age. "Jefferson went off yesterday, and a good riddance of bad ware," Adams wrote Abigail on Monday, January 6, 1794. "He has talents I know, and integrity I believe; but his mind is now poisoned with passion, prejudice, and faction."

Jefferson spoke as though his retirement was to be permanent. "My private business can never call me elsewhere, and certainly politics will not, which I have ever hated both in theory and practice," Jefferson wrote Horatio Gates on Monday, February 3,

1794. "I thought myself conscientiously called from those studies which were my delight by the political crisis of my country and by those events **quorum pars magna fuisti**"—the last an allusion to Virgil, meaning "in which we played great parts." Returning to his nautical imagery, Jefferson went on: "In storms like those all hands must be aloft. But calm is now restored, and I leave the bark with joy to those who love the sea. I am but a landsman, forced from my element by accident, regaining it with transport, and wishing to recollect nothing of what I have seen, but my friendships."

A man who ascribes his engagement in the world in terms of the elements, though, cannot rule out a return to that world should the storms come again—which storms tend to do.

PART VII

THE LEADER OF
THE OPPOSITION

1793 to 1800

To preserve the freedom of the human mind then and freedom of the press, every spirit should be ready to devote itself to martyrdom; for as long as we may think as we will, and speak as we think, the condition of man will proceed in improvement.

—THOMAS JEFFERSON, during what he called "the reign of witches" of the Adams administration

An emblem from the chaotic contest of 1800.

TWENTY-SEVEN

In Wait at Monticello

I live on my horse from an early breakfast to a
late dinner, and very often after that till dark.
—THOMAS JEFFERSON

"I THINK IT IS MONTAIGNE who has said that ignorance is the softest pillow on which a man
can rest his head," Jefferson wrote a friend from
Monticello in February 1794. "I am sure it is true
as to everything political, and shall endeavor to
estrange myself to everything of that character."
Within weeks of being home from Philadelphia Jefferson was struck by how distant the politics of the
capital could seem to many Americans. "I could not
have supposed, when at Philadelphia, that so little
of what was passing there could be known . . . as
is the case here," he told James Madison. "Judging
from this . . . it is evident to me that the people are
not in a condition either to approve or disapprove of
their government, nor consequently to influence it."

Jefferson's stay at Monticello between his resignation from Washington's cabinet and his return to

national politics as a candidate for president against John Adams in 1796 lasted only about two years. This period was entirely characteristic, for in these years he practiced a kind of quiet politics at a distance, allowing himself to serve as an emblem of Republican hope as events in Britain, Philadelphia, western Pennsylvania, and among Democratic-Republican societies around the country cast the Federalists in a harsher monarchical light. Jefferson knew that heroes are often summoned from afar—after all, Washington himself had been, not so long ago. Americans had turned to a tall, retired Virginian for rescue before. They might do so again.

John Adams, serving still as vice president, sent a friendly note along with a book to Monticello in April 1794. "I congratulate you on the charming opening of the spring and heartily wish I was enjoying of it as you are upon a plantation, out of the hearing of the din of politics and the rumors of war." Thanking Adams, Jefferson wrote, "Instead of writing 10 or 12 letters a day, which I have been in the habit of doing as a thing of course, I put off answering my letters now, farmer-like, till a rainy day, and then find it sometimes postponed by other necessary occupations." Yet he could not forbear a comment on foreign policy. "My countrymen are groaning under the insults of Gr. Britain. I hope some means will turn up of reconciling our faith and honor with peace: for I confess to you I have seen enough of one war never to wish to see another."

This was an interesting point, for in New York and in Philadelphia Jefferson had rarely mentioned the military side of the Revolution. In Albemarle County, though, he may not have been able to keep his mind from the scenes of terror and the depredations of the British. Confronted with renewed reminders about the horrors of war, he had a perspective on events he might not have had in the hurry of a diplomatic struggle. Arnold, Cornwallis, and Tarleton were not forgotten.

Adams, too, abhorred the prospect of war and echoed Jefferson's hopes for peace with Britain. He closed with his own wish that he, like Jefferson, might soon "get out of the **Fumum et Opes Strepitumque Romae**"—"the smoke, wealth, and din of Rome."

The latest threat to the peace both men wanted came from a series of British naval outrages on American shipping with the French West Indies. Now that Britain and France were at war, London had issued a secret Order in Council aimed essentially at closing down the lucrative (for the French) trade out of the islands—a trade largely carried on by American vessels. Americans also worried about unfair British trade policies, encouragement of the Barbary pirates in the Mediterranean, and support for hostile Indian tribes on the American frontier. "We must adopt such a mode of retaliation as will stake their kingdom to the centre," a Republican newspaper declared.

Resisting pressure for war, George Washington dispatched John Jay to London. The former Confederation foreign affairs secretary who was now serving as the nation's first chief justice, Jay was on a diplomatic mission that Jefferson hoped "may extricate us from the event of a war, if this can be done saving our faith and our rights." It would not be easy. "The spirit of war has grown much stronger in this part of the country," Jefferson told Monroe in April 1794.

Back on his mountain, Jefferson wanted to construct as self-sufficient a world as possible. In the mid-1790s he decided to pull down much of his house in order to build even more grandly; the first Monticello thus gave way to the Monticello familiar to ensuing generations. The estate was undergoing constant construction and renovation. "We are now living in a brick-kiln, for my house, in its present state, is nothing better," Jefferson had written George Wythe during the building of the first house, and now, years later, it had all started again.

The house he wanted would not be finished until after he left the presidency in 1809, but he seems to have rarely been happier than when he was in the midst of construction. "He is a very long time maturing his projects," a visitor once remarked, not particularly insightfully, given that Jefferson began work on the mountaintop in 1768 and was still at it four decades later. Jefferson himself admitted, "Architecture is my delight, and putting up and pulling down one of my favorite amusements."

While construction at Monticello progressed through the years, Mulberry Row, which ran along the southeastern edge of the main house, expanded to meet his needs. According to Monticello historians, he added new slave quarters, a smokehouse, dairy, blacksmith's shop, carpenter's shop, wash house, sawpit, and, in April 1794, he launched a new manufacturing enterprise there: a nailery, where enslaved boys produced as many as 10,000 nails a day.

Visiting in 1796, a French caller was impressed by Jefferson's easy sense of command and grasp of detail on the estate. "As he cannot expect any assistance from the two small neighboring towns, every article is made on his farm; his negroes are cabinet-makers, carpenters, masons, bricklayers, smiths, etc.," the visitor wrote. "The children he employs in a nail factory. . . . The young and old negresses spin for the clothing of the rest." Completed in 1809, the renovations doubled the size of the main house, and the two L-shaped terraces, which he first envisioned in the early 1770s, largely concealed the work and living spaces below. The dairy, smokehouse, and wash house were moved here, alongside the kitchen, ice cellar, store rooms, carriage bays, and a few slave quarters.

As he built and farmed, he fought bouts with

rheumatism (which kept him "in incessant torment") yet found joy in his family. Writing of grandson Thomas Jefferson Randolph, Patsy's son, in early 1795, he said: "Jefferson is very robust. His hands are constantly like lumps of ice, yet he will not warm them. He has not worn his shoes an hour this winter. If put on him, he takes them off immediately and uses one to carry his nuts etc. in. Within these two days we have put both him and Anne into moccasins, which being made of soft leather, fitting well and lacing up, they have never been able to take them off."

He loved his guns and his horses; he loved to hunt and to fish. His mounts tended to have noble names, from Allycroker, Jefferson's first known horse, to Gustavus to Cucullin to The General to Alfred, Caractacus, Ethelinda, Silvertail, Orra Moor, Peggy Waffington, Zanga, Polly Peachum, and the carriage horses Romulus and Remus. There was also a Raleigh, a Tarquin, a Castor, a Diomede, a Bremo, a Wellington, a Tecumseh, a Peacemaker, and The Eagle, Jefferson's last horse, which was purchased in 1820.

Jefferson liked to fish at home and while away. He had a favorite spot "below the old dam" on the Rivanna, he enjoyed outings on the Schuylkill River when he was in Philadelphia, and he relished a day at Lake George in the Adirondacks on his trip through the north with James Madison in 1791. "An abundance of speckled trout, salmon trout, bass and other fish with which it is stored, have added to our other amusements the sport of taking them," Jefferson had written Patsy. He had been as unhappy with Lake Champlain as he had been happy with Lake George, noting that the larger Champlain was "a far less pleasant water. It is muddy, turbulent, and yields little game"—all things Jefferson disliked in fishing as in life.

He kept guns and traveled armed (he once left behind a gun locked in a box at the inn at Orange Courthouse, and had to write the innkeeper to track it down). To Jefferson hunting was the best form of exercise. He often recommended it, though riding was the great solace and activity of his later years. Jefferson hunted "squirrels and partridges," recalled Isaac Granger Jefferson. "Old Master wouldn't shoot partridges settin'." A fair-minded sportsman, Jefferson would "scare . . . up" partridges or rabbits before firing. He would also drive hunters away from Monticello's deer park.

Jefferson's gun collection included a "two shot-double barrel" and a set of Turkish pistols with "20 inch barrels so well made that I never missed a squirrel at 30 yards with them." He was a man of his time on the question of guns, writing in 1822 that "every American who wishes to protect his farm from the ravages of quadrupeds and his country from those of biped invaders" should be a "gun-man," adding: "I am a great friend to the manly and healthy exercises of the gun."

Led by James Madison, correspondents kept Jefferson current on politics and foreign affairs. Animosity between Federalists and Republicans was a constant theme. "Personalities, which lessen the pleasures of society, or prevent their being sought, have occurred in private and at tables," Tench Coxe, an American economist who served as Hamilton's assistant secretary of the Treasury, wrote from Philadelphia. The next week James Monroe detailed the fight over resolutions connected to Jefferson's commerce report; the Senate's vote to expel Albert Gallatin, a Pennsylvania Republican, on the grounds that when elected he had not been a citizen of the United States for the requisite nine years; a battle over a congressional call to see Gouverneur Morris's correspondence; an Indian treaty; and, of course, the disastrous mission of Edmond-Charles Genet. Jefferson was living in relative isolation, but details of the world were in constant supply.

In March 1794, Federalist congressman Theodore Sedgwick of Massachusetts had introduced legislation to create a new army of fifteen thousand men and give the president extraordinary powers to control sea traffic. The argument, Monroe told Jefferson, was "founded upon the idea of providing for our defense against invasion, and the probability of such an event, considering the unfriendly conduct of G.B. towards us for sometime past." However concerned the Republicans were about Great Britain, they were also skeptical of the Federalist plan, fearing that this was but a first step toward creating an army that might be raised to defend America but could end up being used to undermine the Constitution in a time of crisis. Republics tended to fall to military dictatorships, and military dictators needed a military. "A change so extraordinary must have a serious object in view," Monroe wrote Jefferson. "They are to be raised in no given quarter, and although they may be deemed a kind of minute men in respect to their situation except in time of war, yet in every other respect they will be regulars. . . . The order of Cincinnati will be placed in the command of it."

The Republicans struck where they could. As part of a naturalization bill, William Branch Giles proposed requiring new American citizens to renounce any hereditary titles they held in other countries— thus, the Jeffersonians hoped, reducing the chance of emigrant aristocrats creating an old-world ethos in America.

In reaction, the Federalist congressman Samuel Dexter of Massachusetts suggested that slaveholding immigrants disclose their human property. "You want to hold us up to the public as aristocrats," said Dexter. "I, as a retaliation, will hold you up to the same public as dealers in slaves." Giles's amendment passed; Dexter's failed. Both efforts illuminated the emotional issues shaping American politics— Republican fear of the prospect of hereditary power and the Federalist anxiety about the strength of slaveholders.

The accumulation of power in the hands of Federalists was a running source of worry to Jefferson and his comrades. As Congress gathered in the late autumn of 1794, lawmakers who attended Washington's delivery of his annual message heard the president's account of the Whiskey Rebellion—and an unapologetic attack on the Democratic-Republican societies.

The Whiskey Rebellion in the West was rooted in farmers' fury over Hamilton's excise taxes. Episode built upon episode until there were attacks on Bower Hill, the home of General John Neville, a federal tax inspector. A leader of the protesters, James McFarlane, was shot and killed. A large government force under both Hamilton and "Light-Horse Harry" Lee was mustered and dispatched to western Pennsylvania; Washington himself rode out with the troops for a time. Though the rebellion collapsed, the violence was connected in Washington's mind with the political agitation of the Democratic-Republican societies, and he attacked both the Whiskey Rebellion and the societies in 1794.

Jefferson took a sage tone with William Branch Giles in mid-December. "The attempt which has been made to restrain the liberty of our citizens meeting together, interchanging sentiments on what subjects they please, and stating these sentiments in the public papers, has come upon us, a full century earlier than I expected."

Taking the view that the administration was trying not only to quell the Pennsylvania uprising but to curtail peaceable freedom of assembly, Jefferson made himself plain to Madison. "The denunciation of the democratic societies is one of the extraordinary acts of boldness of which we have seen so many from the faction of Monocrats." And what did the Whiskey Rebellion amount to, really? To Jefferson it was hardly worth noting. "There was indeed a meeting to consult about a separation," he wrote Madison in December 1794. "But to consult on a question does not amount to a determination of that question in the affirmative, still less to the acting on such a determination."

Drama, Jefferson knew, was one of the prices one paid for democracy.

Jefferson's love of control was evident when he was at home. He was precise and demanding about his horses. When he was younger and his mount was brought to him, he would use a white cambric handkerchief to brush the horse's shoulders. If there were dust, the horse was returned to the stables. Only the perfect would suffice.

His horses were sources of immense pleasure, but he also disliked animals with wills of their own, and his mask of equanimity could slip occasionally when it came to his horses. "The only impatience of temper he ever exhibited was with his horse, which he subdued to his will by a fearless application of the whip on the slightest manifestation of restiveness," said a grandson.

His family preserved two other stories about significant displays of anger. Both outbursts were the result of being contradicted. The first came when Jefferson ordered a slave to fetch a carriage horse for an errand. Jupiter, the slave who was in charge of those horses, refused not once but twice. "Tell Jupiter to come to me at once," Jefferson said, furious that his orders had been thwarted. The rebuke that Jupiter endured, according to the family story, was no ordinary one. It was epic, delivered by Jefferson "in tones and with a look which neither he nor the terrified bystanders ever forgot." Jefferson's commands were not to be challenged or questioned—ever.

A second hour of fury that lived on in the family's history unfolded on a river crossing. Two ferrymen had been fighting between themselves when they took Jefferson and his daughter Patsy aboard for the passage. The peace did not last long, and soon the two men were about to become violent. According to the story, Jefferson, "his eyes flashing," then "snatched up an oar, and, in a voice which rung out above the angry tones of the men, flourished it over their heads." Weapon in hand, Jefferson issued an unmistakable command. "Row for your lives, or I will knock you both overboard!"

There, in the midst of the waters, his safety and

that of his daughter in danger from the quarrels of other men, Jefferson seized control and forced his will on others. "And they did row for their lives; nor, I imagine, did they soon forget the fiery looks and excited appearance of that tall weird-like-looking figure brandishing the heavy oar over their offending heads," his granddaughter wrote. He let his true emotions show when something he loved—in this case, his daughter—was in danger.

He loved his country, too, and was growing ever more convinced that it, too, was in peril.

"If you visit me as a farmer, it must be as a condisciple: for I am but a learner; an eager one indeed but yet desperate, being too old now to learn a new art," Jefferson wrote William Branch Giles. He liked being with old friends. "Come then . . . and let us take our soup and wine together every day, and talk over the stories of our youth, and the tales of other times," he wrote one.

Madison struck at this idyll. "You ought to be preparing yourself . . . to hear truths which no inflexibility will be able to withstand," Madison wrote to Jefferson in March 1795. For Madison the central truth was this: Thomas Jefferson was destined to seek the presidency of the United States.

Jefferson admitted that the subject had been on his mind. Compelled, he said, by his enemies' "continual insinuations in the public papers" that he was contending to succeed Washington, Jefferson told

Madison that he had felt "my own quiet required that I should face it and examine it." His decision, he wrote in April 1795, was no. He would not stand for the office. "The little spice of ambition, which I had in my younger days, has long since evaporated, and I set still less store by a posthumous than present name." That was not strictly true, but Jefferson liked to tell himself it was. Public men were not to be seen as anxious for office or place, and Jefferson frequently denied his self-evident drive to shape the era in which he lived.

In this springtime of 1795, though, there may have been more conviction behind his rote protestations than usual. He had been sick with rheumatism, consumed with farming and financial matters long overlooked, delighted by grandchildren, and presumably enjoying, for the first extended period of time in four years, his liaison with Sally Hemings.

He was not lying when he wrote Madison and other friends of his permanent retirement. He was finding rest and refuge at Monticello. What he himself may not have fully realized was how intimately—how naturally and unthinkingly—he remained connected to politics. By now—nearly a quarter century since his first election to the House of Burgesses—the life of the nation was as much an element of his own life as science or music or Monticello. He could no more unwind himself from the affairs of the republic than he could have chosen to cease being interested in science or books.

He needed the world of politics and of consequence. It was crucial to his health, and to his sense of self and well-being. "I am convinced our own happiness requires that we should continue to mix with the world, and to keep pace with it as it goes; and that every person who retires from free communication with it is severely punished afterwards by the state of mind into which they get, and which can only be prevented by feeding our sociable principles," Jefferson wrote to Polly after he became president. "I can speak from experience on this subject. From 1793 to 1797 I remained closely at home, saw none but those who came there, and at length became very sensible of the ill effect it had upon my own mind, and of its direct and irresistible tendency to render me unfit for society, and uneasy when necessarily engaged in it. I felt enough of the effect of withdrawing from the world then, to see that it led to an antisocial and misanthropic state of mind, which severely punishes him who gives into it: and it will be a lesson I shall never forget as to myself."

The articulation of his beliefs, the holding of office, the championing of things republican against things monarchical: Politics was not only what Thomas Jefferson practiced. It was part of who he was, even if he himself sometimes failed to see it.

In June 1795, he asked the Philadelphia editor Benjamin Franklin Bache to "make me up a set of your papers for the year 1794." Madison sent along what he called "a fugitive publication" of his own: a pamphlet entitled **Political Observations**. William Branch Giles announced he was going to see Jefferson "before I go to winter quarters"—the Congress. In the fall, Aaron Burr of New York called at Monticello, leading to Federalist charges that the two men had "planned and approved" the Republican agenda in the ensuing Congress.

It had been a brief visit on Jefferson's mountaintop, only a single day. However few the hours they spent together this autumn, though, Jefferson and Burr were to be intimately linked for the next dozen years—first as allies, then as foes.

Born in Newark, New Jersey, in 1756, Aaron Burr was the grandson of Jonathan Edwards, the theologian, preacher, and president of the College of New Jersey (later Princeton). Burr's father, the Reverend Aaron Burr, Sr., married Edwards's daughter Elizabeth and himself became president of the college, where his son was educated.

Handsome, charming, adventurous, and ambitious, the younger Aaron Burr was a Revolutionary officer, a lawyer, and one of the most fascinating politicians of the age. He married the widow of a British officer, Theodosia Prevost, and they had a beautiful daughter, also named Theodosia.

Burr was an architect of Republican politics in New York, rising through the ranks from the state assembly to become the state attorney general and, in 1791, U.S. senator. Mastering the mechanics of election, Burr was to prove invaluable to the Jeffersonian cause—until, in Jefferson's view, the two men's causes came into conflict in the presidential election of 1800.

But that still lay in the future. For now, the issue confronting politicians of every sort, and indeed the country, was the possibility of war with Britain.

John Jay's mission to London had not produced the result Jefferson had hoped. Far from it: The treaty, which President Washington received on Saturday, March 7, 1795, appeared to concede too much to London, essentially codifying the economic ties between the two nations that Hamilton had been nurturing for years.

The political reaction was swift and, for Washington, brutal. Angry crowds burned Jay in effigy; there was even talk of impeaching Washington. Jefferson despised the treaty as a Hamiltonian document, and much of the country joined him. "From North to South this monument of folly or venality is universally execrated," Jefferson told Thomas Mann Randolph in August 1795.

Even mid-August floods could not replace the Jay Treaty as the overriding topic of the day. "So general a burst of dissatisfaction never before appeared against any transaction," said Jefferson.

Worried that Hamilton—"really a colossus to the

antirepublican party," Jefferson called him—might somehow win the war for public opinion, Jefferson urged Madison to write against the treaty, fretting about "the quietism into which the people naturally fall, after first sensations are over."

As Jefferson read the treaty, he saw that Hamilton had successfully managed to legislate through Jay's diplomacy. "A bolder party-stroke was never struck," Jefferson told Madison. "For it certainly is an attempt of a party, which finds they have lost their majority in one branch of the legislature, to make a law by the aid of the other branch and the executive, under color of a treaty, which shall bind up the hands of the adverse branch from ever restraining the commerce of their patron-nation."

The treaty was nevertheless narrowly ratified. Washington believed, as did a bare two-thirds majority of the Senate, that the pact was preferable to going to war.

The agreement with London faced an unusual additional obstacle: The House needed to approve funding for some elements of the treaty. Washington, under attack as "a supercilious tyrant" and a "ruler who tramples on the laws and Constitution," went to the House chamber in December 1795 to deliver his annual message.

He had enjoyed more hospitable greetings. "Never, till a few months preceding this session, had the tongue of the most factious slander dared to make a public attack on his character," wrote William Cobbett, the pamphleteer who wrote under the name Peter Porcupine. "This was the first time he had ever entered the walls of Congress without a full assurance of meeting a welcome from every heart." Now he was looking out over a crowd of members who "were ready to thwart his measures, and present him the cup of humiliation filled to the brim."

Yet the House joined the Senate in grudgingly voting to support the treaty. Finally, on Friday, May 6, 1796, Washington signed the Jay Treaty. "The N. England States have been ready to rise in mass against the H. of Reps.," Madison wrote Jefferson three days after Washington signed the documents. "Such have been the exertions and influence of Aristocracy, Anglicism, and mercantilism in that quarter, that Republicanism is perfectly overwhelmed." The day belonged to the Federalists.

The price of this diplomatic and political victory, however, was high, for the approval of the Jay Treaty by the Federalists gave the nascent Republicans a palpable and energizing sense of purpose.

They knew where to turn, and to whom.

Jefferson was already thinking about the politics of the hour in practical terms, turning a scientific eye to the world around him. In notes he drafted sometime after mid-October 1795, he sketched out his sense of the state of play. Jefferson wrote:

Two parties then do exist within the US. They embrace respectively the following descriptions of persons.

The Anti-republicans consist of

1. The old refugees and tories.
2. British merchants residing among us, and composing the main body of our merchants
3. American merchants trading on British capital. Another great portion.
4. Speculators and Holders in the banks and public funds.
5. Officers of the federal government with some exceptions.
6. Office-hunters, willing to give up principles for places. A numerous and noisy tribe.
7. Nervous persons, whose languid fibres have more analogy with a passive than active state of things.

The Republican part of our Union comprehends

1. The entire body of landholders throughout the United States
2. The body of laborers, not being landholders, whether in husbandry or the arts

The latter is to the aggregate of the former probably as 500 to one; but their wealth is not as disproportionate, though it is also greatly superior, and is in truth the foundation of that of their antagonists. Trifling as are the numbers of the Anti-republican party, there are circumstances which give them an appearance of strength and numbers. They all live in cities, together, and can act in a body readily and at all times; they give chief employment to the newspapers, and therefore have most of them under their command. The agricultural interest is dispersed over a great extent of country, have little means of intercommunication with each other, and feeling their own strength and will, are conscious that a single exertion of these will at any time crush the machinations against their government.

Jefferson's assessment of the foe mixed fear and pride. He worried about the Federalists but believed the Republicans capable of victory whenever they chose to bestir themselves. The anxiety produced by the enemy fueled the politician's sense of urgency; the faith in the virtues of his own cause gave him the power to endure the most hopeless and despairing of moments.

On the day after Christmas, 1795, Jefferson wrote Bache to subscribe to his newspaper, the **Aurora,** as well as to other editors in Philadelphia and Richmond to begin receiving their papers. Though he had hardly left the arena, he was now unmistakably back in it.

Jefferson had never doubted the power of the presidency. From his first reading of the draft Constitution while in France, he sensed that the office could become the center of action for the whole government. Experience had proved his instincts right. Reflecting on Washington's Jay Treaty victory, Jefferson wrote Monroe: "You will have seen . . . that one man outweighs them all in influence over the people who have supported his judgment against their own and that of their representatives. Republicanism must lie on its oars, resign the vessel to its pilot, and themselves to the course he thinks best for them."

Given the season of these remarks—the middle of June 1796, almost six months to the day before the electoral college was to meet to choose a successor to Washington—Jefferson was thinking about how different America's prospects would be if the pilot of the vessel were a Republican. And, more to the point, whether he himself should be that pilot. Decorous silence on the explicit question of a candidacy for the office was to be maintained, but Jefferson was about to face the most momentous decision of his public life since he chose country over king in the hurly-burly of the Revolution: Would he allow his name to go forward as a candidate for president of the United States after all?

First, he wanted to clear up some worrisome business with Washington himself. Always sensitive about the opinions of others and particularly anxious for Washington to think well of him, Jefferson had read a report in the June 9, 1796, **Aurora** that drew on a confidential document Washington had given to members of his cabinet during the neutrality debates. Jefferson was determined to convince Washington that he, at least, had not betrayed the president's trust. Swearing on "everything sacred and honorable," Jefferson promised Washington on June 19 that the document had "never been from under my own lock and key."

Jefferson was concerned about what Washington thought of him in these early summer weeks of 1796, for he knew that the president was hearing rumors that Jefferson had been privately critical of—even condescending toward—his old chief. Worried about such impressions, Jefferson wrote Washington warning that some people may "try to sow tares between you and me" by presenting Jefferson as "still engaged in the bustle of politics, and in turbulence and intrigue against the government."

When Washington replied in July 1796, he absolved Jefferson of responsibility for the **Aurora** matter but used the occasion to address Jefferson's views of the administration. "As you have mentioned the subject yourself," said Washington, "it would not be frank, candid, or friendly to conceal that your conduct has been represented as derogating from that opinion I had conceived you entertained of me."

The Federalists were busy maneuvering for the

approaching presidential election. Their tactics included overtures to Jefferson nemesis Patrick Henry to stand for president. Henry was uninterested, but the latter suggestion, which, if adopted, would have divided Virginia, underscored the Federalists' conviction that Jefferson was likely to be their main foe.

From the West, the legislator William Cocke, a native Virginian now among the leading men of Tennessee, made himself plain to Jefferson in August 1796. It was Cocke's happy duty, he wrote, "to inform you that the people of this State, of every description, express a wish that you should be the next President of the United States, and Mr. Burr, Vice President."

Jefferson's reply was at once clear and equivocal. "I have not the arrogance to say I would refuse the honorable office you mention to me; but I can say with truth that I would rather be thought worthy of it than to be appointed to it," he wrote Cocke. For "well I know that no man will ever bring out of that office the reputation which carries him into it."

TWENTY-EIGHT

To the Vice Presidency

> There is a debt of service due from every man
> to his country, proportioned to the bounties
> which nature and fortune have measured to
> him.
>
> —THOMAS JEFFERSON

> You and I have formerly seen warm debates
> and high political passions. But gentlemen
> of different politics would then speak to each
> other. . . . It is not so now. Men who have
> been intimate all their lives cross the streets to
> avoid meeting, and turn their heads another
> way, lest they should be obliged to touch their
> hat.
>
> —THOMAS JEFFERSON to
> Edward Rutledge

THE PUBLICATION OF WASHINGTON'S farewell
address on Monday, September 19, 1796,
set off America's first contested presidential
election. The Washington announcement was, Mas-

sachusetts congressman Fisher Ames said, "a signal, like dropping a hat, for the party racers to start."

Presidential elections in the first decades of the republic were odd affairs. Candidates did not campaign. They allowed, obliquely or through friends and allies, that they were available to be elected. Networks of the like-minded put together a ticket for president and vice president. In most states individual electors let it be known that a vote for them would be a vote for their favorites for both offices. Until the ratification of the Twelfth Amendment in 1804 there was no distinction between the two offices in the electoral college. The second place finisher became vice president.

However different in form presidential contests were, one feature has been constant from the beginning: They have been rife with attacks and counterattacks.

It took just ten days from the publication of Washington's farewell for Jefferson's enemies to strike against him, and strike hard. On Thursday, September 29, 1796, **The Columbian Mirror and Alexandria Gazette** published a statement from Charles Simms, a Federalist lawyer close to President Washington. Simms was campaigning to become a presidential elector for John Adams from Prince William, Stafford, and Fairfax counties in Virginia. He took Jefferson on directly in his late September broadside. Jefferson, Simms charged, was not fit for high office, for he had fled the wartime governorship "at the moment of an invasion of the enemy, by which great confusion, loss, and distress accrued to the State in the destruction of public records." Such a man was too weak to be president, Simms said, "for no one can know how soon or from whence a storm may come." Jefferson was, in other words, a coward driven by vanity. Adams, on the other hand, was a statesman who could be counted on to stay the course set by George Washington.

The Jeffersonians reacted with force. John Taylor of Caroline, a pro-Jefferson Virginian, drafted a reply for publication. It made the case that Governor Jefferson had **not** failed in his duty, telling again the story of the invasion of 1781. Most important, in what was to become a perennially useful political theme, the Republicans argued that the contest of the hour was about the present, not the past. It was, they said, about the conflict between republican and monarchical visions of American government.

Taylor illustrated his point by describing a 1794 conversation with Vice President Adams and New Hampshire senator John Langdon in which Adams allegedly said that "no government could long exist, or that no people could be happy, without an hereditary first magistrate, and an hereditary senate, or a senate for life." Campaign literature read: "Thomas Jefferson is a firm REPUBLICAN—John Adams is an avowed MONARCHIST."

After the Jay Treaty, the next president faced the rising prospect of war with France—a possibility that imbued the election with an even greater sense of urgency than it already had.

Enduring a late-autumn cold spell at Monticello—the temperature had dropped to 12 degrees, freezing the ink in its well on his desk—Jefferson awaited news of the 1796 election results. Given the tasks facing the next president, he said the vice presidency might be preferable to winning the presidency itself. "Few will believe the true dispositions of my mind on that subject," Jefferson wrote. "It is not the less true however that I do sincerely wish to be the second on that vote rather than the first."

Hamilton, who opposed both Adams and Jefferson, was a complicating factor. He devised a fascinating strategy to deny his two rivals the presidency by urging Federalist electors in South Carolina to cast ballots for Adams's choice for vice president, native son Thomas Pinckney, for president rather than vice president. Hamilton's motive? Madison wrote to Jefferson that Hamilton believed Adams "too headstrong to be a fit puppet for the intriguers behind the screen."

One sign that Jefferson was more invested in a personal victory than his formulaic protestations to the contrary lies in a note Madison wrote him on Saturday, December 10, 1796. "You **must** reconcile yourself to the secondary as well as the primary station, if that should be your lot," Madison told Jefferson. The emphasis on "must" is Madison's—suggesting that Jefferson's closest political friend and counselor knew the presidential candidate to be anxious for the top post. Madison was also preparing his friend for the possibility that the Hamiltonian maneuvering could throw the election into the House of Representatives if Adams and Jefferson ended up in a tie in the vote.

Jefferson knew that a subsequent numerical deadlock in the House was also possible—"a difficulty from which the constitution has provided no issue," he wrote Madison. Should he and Adams find themselves in such a situation, Jefferson authorized Madison "fully to solicit on my behalf that Mr. Adams may be preferred. He has always been my senior from the commencement of our public life, and the expression of the public will being equal, this circumstance ought to give him the preference."

As the returns reached Philadelphia, Pinckney faded to third, and Madison worried that Jefferson had been so set on becoming president that he might refuse the second spot. Appealing first to Jefferson's concern for reputation, Madison wrote that "it is expected that as you had made up your mind to obey the call of your country, you will let it decide on the particular place where your services are to be rendered." Moreover, having a Republican influence in close proximity to the president could be important, even critical. "There is reason to believe also that your neighborhood to Adams may have a valuable effect on his councils particularly in relation to our external system," Madison wrote.

On Wednesday, February 8, 1797, the electoral votes were tallied. Adams won, barely, by a margin of 71 to Jefferson's 68. Pinckney carried 59. The Federalists fretted about Jefferson's winning the vice presidency. One anti-Jeffersonian clergyman was reported to have prayed: "O Lord! Wilt Thou bestow upon the Vice President a double portion of Thy grace, **for Thou knowest he needs it.**"

Adams was thrilled to become president. As he had written Abigail, he believed deeply in "the sense, spirit, and resources of this country, which few other men in the world know so well [or] have so long tried and found solid." Despite the second-place finish, Jefferson found the results flattering. "I value the late vote highly," he said, "but it is only as the index of the place I hold in the esteem of my fellow-citizens."

Jefferson spent the cold weeks after the election ruminating on politics. "I knew it was impossible Mr. Adams should lose a vote North of the Delaware, and that the free and moral agency of the South would furnish him an abundant supplement," he wrote. "On principles of public respect I should not have refused [the presidency]: but I protest before my God that I shall, from the bottom of my heart, rejoice at escaping."

He took a wry, knowing tone: "The honeymoon

would be as short in that case as in any other, and its moments of ecstasy would be ransomed by years of torment and hatred." The vice presidency was the better place at this hour. "This is certainly not a moment to covet the helm," Jefferson said.

Whispers of possible secession to form a confederacy of northern states appeared in **The Connecticut Courant** in November and December 1796—whispers that hinted at a larger source of tension. At issue was the advantage Jefferson and his fellow Southerners had in national elections because of the three-fifths clause, the constitutional provision that counted a slave as three-fifths of a person to establish the number of congressmen and presidential electors allocated to each state. When Jefferson went on to win the presidency four years later, his Federalist critics would disparage him as the "Negro President" because of his dependence on the three-fifths clause. The battles over slavery were thus rooted not only in the debate over the morality of abolition but in the practical political reality that every additional slave state (ironically and tragically) increased the power of white office seekers from those states.

Jefferson found it preferable—and more comfortable—to strike grand notes on secession rather than engage his adversaries on the stark realities of the mathematics of power. "We shall never give up our union, the last anchor of our hope, and that alone which is to prevent this heavenly country from becoming an arena of gladiators," he told El-bridge Gerry.

In the last days of the 1796 election, Jefferson had drafted a kind letter to Adams. After the usual disclaimers ("I have no ambition to govern men"), Jefferson wrote that the presidency was "a pain-ful and thankless office." Should Adams be able to "shun for us this war by which our agriculture, com-merce and credit will be destroyed," then "the glory will be all your own; and that your administration may be filled with glory and happiness to yourself and advantage to us is the sincere wish of one who though, in the course of our voyage through life, various little incidents have happened or been con-trived to separate us, retains still for you the solid esteem of the moments when we were working for our independence."

On New Year's Day 1797, Jefferson sent Madison a draft of the letter to Adams. "I can particularly have no feelings which would revolt at a secondary position to Mr. Adams," Jefferson wrote. "I am his junior in life, was his junior in Congress, his ju-nior in the diplomatic line, his junior lately in our civil government." Nevertheless, he asked Madison whether he should send Adams the letter.

Madison replied with a six-point case against it. The key ones: Since things were currently cordial between the two men, "it deserves to be considered whether the idea of bettering it is not outweighed by the possibility of changing it for the worse." Another: "May not what is said of 'the sublime delights of riding the storm etc.' be misconstrued into a reflection on those who have no distaste to the helm at the present crisis? You know the temper of Mr. A. better than I do: but I have always conceived it to be a rather ticklish one." Another: "The tenderness due to the zealous and active promoters of your election, makes it doubtful whether their anxieties and exertions ought to be depreciated by any thing implying the unreasonableness of them. I know that some individuals who have deeply committed themselves, and probably incurred the political enmity at least of the P. elect, are already sore on this head." And finally: "Considering the probability that Mr. A.'s course of administration may force an opposition to it from the Republican quarter . . . there may be real embarrassments from giving written possession to him of the degree of compliment and confidence which your personal delicacy and friendship have suggested."

Jefferson was grateful for the counsel. He would not mail the letter.

Jefferson reached Philadelphia on Thursday, March 2, 1797. Without delay he called on the president-elect. Adams, who lodged at Francis's on Fourth Street, repaid the courtesy the next morning, visiting Jefferson in his temporary quarters. Closing the door behind him, the president-elect said he was glad Jefferson was alone. The two had much to talk about.

Adams spoke of France, telling Jefferson that he had considered asking the new vice president to undertake a mission to Paris, "but that he supposed it was out of the question, as it did not seem justifiable for him to send away the person destined to take his place in case of accident to himself, nor decent to remove from competition one who was a rival in the public favor." What did Jefferson think of dispatching Madison to join a diplomatic mission in Paris?

Jefferson agreed that he should not leave the country and thought Madison would refuse such a post. Adams, however, seemed determined. "He said that if Mr. Madison should refuse, he would still appoint him and leave the responsibility on him."

The ceremonial proceedings in Congress Hall on Saturday, March 4, 1797, were brief but memorable. Congress gathered for a short session; the business was the inauguration of the president and the vice president and the swearing-in of new senators and representatives. The president pro tempore of the Senate, William Bingham of Pennsylvania, administered the oath of office to Jefferson in the second-floor Senate chamber.

The first American secretary of state was now the second vice president of the United States. Jefferson, in turn, swore in the eight new senators and delivered a short speech. He alluded to his broad political convictions and, graciously but unmistakably, to the mortality of the president: "No one more sincerely prays that no accident may call me to the higher and more important functions which the constitution eventually devolves on this office."

In a sign of the virulence of the time, some Jefferson supporters found his speech too conciliatory. "His first act in the Senate was to make a **damned time-serving, trimming speech** in which he declared that it was a great pleasure to him to have an opportunity of serving his country under such a tried patriot as John Adams, which was saying to his friends—I am in; kiss my—and go to H-ll," one New York Republican was said to have remarked.

After Jefferson was done, they reconvened in the House chamber on the ground floor of Congress Hall for the presidential inauguration of John Adams. As Adams recalled it, George Washington seemed cheerful—even relieved: "Methinks I heard him think 'Ay, I am fairly out and you fairly in! See which of us will be happiest.'" Jefferson thought Washington a lucky man. "The President is fortunate to get off just as the bubble is bursting, leaving others to hold the bag," he wrote Madison. Privately, Jefferson repeated his claims of satisfaction at the results of the election. "The second office of this government is honorable and easy," Jefferson said. "The first is but a splendid misery."

Two days after the inauguration, Adams and Jefferson dined with Washington. The new president and vice president left the table together. On the street, Jefferson told Adams that Madison would decline the appointment to France.

It was just as well. The new president had spent time with his cabinet that day and found opposition among the Federalists to his thought of sending Madison. "He immediately said that on consultation some objections to that nomination had been raised which he had not contemplated," Jefferson recalled, "and was going on with excuses which evidently embarrassed him, when we came to 5th Street where our road separated, his being down Market street, mine off along 5th and we took leave: and he never after that said one word to me on the subject, or ever consulted me as to any measures of the government."

John Adams governed amid stress and strain. As president he fought to keep the peace, or at least a semblance of it, during what became known as the Quasi-War with France, a sustained series of expensive naval engagements. (Adams referred to it as "the half war with France.") To see him through his years in office, he retained Washington's cabinet, including the Federalist secretary of state, Timothy Pickering. This proved problematic, for the cabinet officers tended to see themselves as autonomous, complicating Adams's administration by undercutting the president. And as vice president, Jefferson spent most of his time presiding over the Senate and tending—quietly—to the construction and nurture of the Republican opposition to Adams's Federalist government.

Reflecting on the evening conversation with Adams and on the events of Monday, March 6, 1797, Jefferson wrote: "The opinion I formed at the time on this transaction was that Mr. A. in the first moments of the enthusiasm of the occasion (his inauguration) forgot party sentiments, and as he never acted on any system, but was always governed by the feeling of the moment, he thought for a moment to steer impartially between the parties; that Monday the 6th of March being the first time he had met his cabinet, on expressing ideas of this kind he had been at once diverted from them, and returned to his former party views."

The Adams presidential years were busy personal ones in Jefferson's domestic sphere. Patsy Randolph had three children between 1796 and 1801. In 1796 the Duc de la Rochefoucauld called at Monticello and found that Patsy's younger, beautiful sister Polly "constantly resides with her father; but as she is seventeen years old, and is remarkably handsome, she will doubtless soon find that there are duties which it is sweeter to perform than those of a daughter." The next year Polly married John Wayles Eppes, a cousin. They would have two children. And Jefferson himself arrived at Monticello for a visit on Tuesday, July 11, 1797. Eight months and three weeks later, Sally Hemings gave birth to a son. The baby was named William Beverly, called Beverly.

During the vice presidential years Jefferson became more philosophical about criticism, seeing it as an inevitable feature of political life, something to be endured—like storm or fire—if one wished to prevail in the public arena. "I have been for some time used as the property of the newspapers, a fair mark for every man's dirt," he wrote. "Some too have indulged themselves in this exercise who would not have done it, had they known me otherwise than thro' these impure and injurious channels. It is hard treatment, and for a singular kind of offense, that of having obtained by the labors of a life the indulgent opinions of a part of one's fellow citizens. However these moral evils must be submitted to, like the physical scourges of tempest, fire etc." It was a more mature and measured view than he had held even while in France or at the beginning of his term as secretary of state—a sign that Jefferson had the capacity to grow and to learn. He did not have to like it, but he knew he had to put up with it.

He was thinking along the same lines in terms of partisanship. By the end of the 1790s he could even be contemptuous of politicians who held themselves above party. "A few individuals of no fixed system at all, governed by the panic or the prowess of the moment, flap as the breeze blows against the republican or the aristocratic bodies, and give to the one or the other a preponderance entirely accidental," he wrote Burr in June 1797.

The Jefferson political style, though, remained smooth rather than rough, polite rather than confrontational. He was a warrior for the causes in which he believed, but he conducted his battles at a remove, tending to use friends and allies to write and publish and promulgate the messages he thought crucial to the public debate. Part of the reason for his largely genial mien lay in the Virginia culture of grace and hospitality; another factor was a calculated decision, based on his experience of men and of politics, that direct conflict was unproductive and ineffective.

Jefferson articulated this understanding of politics and the management of conflicting interests in a long, thoughtful letter to a grandson. "A determination never to do what is wrong, prudence, and good humor, will go far towards securing to you the estimation of the world," he wrote to Patsy's son Thomas Jefferson Randolph. Good humor, Jefferson added, "is the practice of sacrificing to those whom we meet in society all the little conveniences and preferences which will gratify them, and deprive us of nothing worth a moment's consideration; it is the giving a pleasing and flattering turn to our expressions which will conciliate others and make them pleased with us as well as themselves. How cheap a price for the good will of another!" Jefferson went on:

When this is in return for a rude thing said by another, it brings him to his senses, it mortifies and corrects him in the most salutary way, and places him at the feet of your good nature in the eyes of the company. But in stating prudential rules for our government in society I must not omit the important one of never entering into dispute or argument with another. I never yet saw an instance of one of two disputants convincing the other by argument. I have seen many, on their getting warm, becoming rude, and shooting one another. Conviction is the effect of our own dispassionate reasoning, either in solitude, or weighing within ourselves dispassionately what we hear from others standing uncommitted in argument ourselves. It was one of the rules which above all others made Doctr. Franklin the most amiable of men in society, "never to contradict anybody."

The pro-English Jay Treaty had produced a cataclysmic reaction in France. The efforts to keep peace with Britain in part because of France now led to fears of war with France because of Britain. Such were the politics of the 1790s.

French ships began seizing American craft. "I anticipate the burning of our seaports, havoc of our frontiers, household insurgency, with a long train of etceteras which it is enough for a man to have met once in his life," Jefferson wrote.

The perpetual threat of conflict—first with one European power, then with another—infused American politics with a sense of constant crisis. Both Federalists and Republicans believed the fate of the United States could turn on the confrontation of the hour. In the broad public discourse, driven by partisan editors publishing partisan newspapers, there seemed no middle ground, only extremes of opinion or of outcome.

Into this culture of entrenched division came the publication of a 1796 letter of Jefferson's that appeared to attack President Washington as a tool of the British interest.

It was May 1797 when Philip Mazzei publicized the Washington letter Jefferson had written him the year before. "It would give you a fever were I to name to you the apostates who have gone over to these heresies, men who were Samsons in the field and Solomons in the council, but who have had their heads shorn by the harlot England," Jefferson had written of the Jay Treaty controversy. "In short, we are likely to preserve the liberty we have obtained only by unremitting labors and perils." The letter was taken as a Jeffersonian assault on Washington and the president's allegedly pro-British tendencies, which made it perfect fodder for the Federalist press. "The passions are too high at present to be cooled in our day," Jefferson wrote an old friend.

About that, at least, both Republicans and Federalists might have agreed, for anecdotes suggesting the other side's extremism and unreasonableness were in substantial supply.

The Federalists had Jefferson's Mazzei letter, and Republicans heard plenty about their enemies, too. On Christmas Day, 1797, Madison repeated worries that Adams was using a new yellow fever epidemic to seize additional power by possibly postponing the meeting of Congress.

And word reached Jefferson that Adams, upset at Republican George Clinton's respectable showing in the 1792 balloting for vice president, had said: "Damn 'em, Damn 'em, you see that an elective government will not do," and that Adams had reportedly recently remarked that "Republicanism must be disgraced, sir."

Jefferson was intrigued by similar tales about Hamilton. In late 1797, Tench Coxe alleged that Hamilton had said " 'For my part . . . I avow myself a monarchist; I have no objection to a trial being made of this thing of a republic, but' etc." Such stories did little to calm Jefferson's fears about his Federalist colleagues.

TWENTY-NINE

The Reign of Witches

> No, I think a party is necessary in a free state
> to preserve its freedom—the truly virtuous
> should firmly unite and form a party capable
> at all times of frustrating the wicked designs of
> the enemies of the doctrine of equality and the
> rights of man.
>
> —Jefferson friend JOHN PAGE

IN THE NEW YEAR, two of Jefferson's housemates at Francis's tavern—Congressmen Abraham Baldwin of Georgia and Thomson J. Skinner of Massachusetts—told Jefferson a disturbing story about 1787. As they described it, "a very extensive combination had taken place in N. York and the Eastern states among . . . people who were partly monarchical in principle or frightened with Shays's rebellion and the impotence of the old Congress." Representatives, Jefferson was informed, "had actually had consultations on the subject of seizing on the powers of a government and establishing them by force, had corresponded with one another, and had sent a deputy to Genl. Washington to solicit his cooperation."

Washington did not join the plot, and the Constitutional Convention proposed by Virginia had been called in the meantime. Still, the monarchists (in this account) had been—and **were**—counting on the failure of the new government. Monarchy would then step into the breach.

Jefferson's vice presidency, which ran from 1797 to 1801, unfolded in a fevered climate. One congressman, the Republican Matthew Lyon of Vermont, spat in the face of another, the Federalist Roger Griswold of Connecticut, after Griswold insulted Lyon's courage. An effort to expel Lyon, a ferociously partisan editor, failed. Frustrated, Griswold attacked Lyon with a cane. Fighting back, Lyon seized some fireplace tongs and the two brawled on the House floor.

The driving source of national fear was a potential war with France after the Jay Treaty. Then, in March 1798, Adams revealed that a diplomatic mission to France had failed when three French officials— known as X, Y, and Z in state papers—demanded bribes, a huge loan, and an American apology as the price of doing business in the wake of the treaty debacle. The political effect of the episode in the United States was electric. Americans felt insulted by the French, and talk of war intensified. The news of the attempted extortion, Jefferson said, "produced such a shock on the republican mind as has never been seen since our independence."

John Adams issued a message calling on Americans to prepare for war. He ordered the country to "adopt with promptitude, decision, and unanimity" measures to protect "our seafaring and commercial citizens, for the defense of any exposed portions of our territory, for replenishing our arsenals, establishing foundries and military manufactures, and to provide such efficient revenue as will be necessary to defray extraordinary expenses and supply the deficiencies which may be occasioned by depredations on our commerce." Such was the "Quasi-War," a series of naval attacks that pitted the United States against its first and most important ally in a brutal if undeclared war.

The sulfurous events of the period cast Jefferson in a role for which he was well suited: that of the eloquent champion of individual rights against a John Adams–led campaign to quell dissent in America amid anxieties about French power and French agents. It was not the last time Americans would curb civil liberties for the sake of national security.

The main occasion for the tumult of the Adams administration was the four pieces of legislation popularly known as the Alien and Sedition Acts. Passed in reaction to the war climate, the bills invested the president with extraordinary powers at the expense, Republicans argued, of the liberties of a free people. The alien laws collectively invested the president the authority to deport resident aliens he considered dangerous. The sedition bill criminalized free speech, forbidding anyone to "write, print, utter or publish . . . any false, scandalous, and malicious writing or writings against the government of the United States, or either House of the Congress of the United States, with intent to defame . . . or to bring them . . . into contempt or disrepute, or to excite against them, or either or any of them, the hatred of the good people of the United States."

So began a furiously divisive time of intensity and vitriol. Jefferson and the Republicans believed they were no longer expecting but were instead experiencing the end of American liberty. "Everyone has a right to explain himself," John Taylor wrote, adding that the government was now "manufacturing a law which may even make it criminal to pray to God for better times."

Some Republicans detected monarchical autocracy at work. John Dickinson, Jefferson's former colleague from the Continental Congress, drew on the history of the English Civil War to illustrate how far he believed President Adams had strayed: "How incredible was it once, and how astonishing is it now, that every measure and every pretense of the stupid and selfish Stuarts should be adopted by the posterity of those who fled from their madness and tyranny to the distant and dangerous wilds of America?"

Once sedition legislation passed and was signed by Adams, the speaking of one's mind—a foundational freedom—could result in fines up to $2,000 and up to two years in prison. "For my own part I consider these laws as merely an experiment on the American mind to see how far it will bear an avowed violation of the Constitution," Jefferson said. "If this goes down, we shall immediately see attempted another act of Congress declaring that the President shall continue in office during life, reserving to another occasion the transfer of the succession to his heirs, and the establishment of the Senate for life." It would, in other words, be the death of what Jefferson's generation had fought for.

Adams and the Federalists believed they were limiting liberty's excesses in order to preserve liberty itself. The danger of war was real, and war called for extraordinary measures. (And the Sedition Act was set to expire in 1801.) To Adams and his allies, the combination of foreign aliens within the United States and a brutal press calling into question the legitimacy of the administration was a possibly lethal one.

Madison described the state of play well in May 1798: "The management of foreign relations appears to be the most susceptible of abuse of all the trusts committed to a Government, because they can be concealed or disclosed, or disclosed in such parts and at such times as will best suit particular views.... Perhaps it is a universal truth that the loss of liberty at home is to be charged to provisions against danger real or pretended from abroad." Extreme measures seemed suited to extreme times.

On Thursday, February 15, 1798, Jefferson dined with Adams. The "company was large," Jefferson wrote, but the two men found a moment afterward to talk. They spoke of rising prices (blaming Hamilton's "bank paper," of course). "We then got on the Constitution and . . . he said that no republic could ever last which had not a Senate and a Senate deeply and strongly rooted, strong enough to bear up against all popular storms and passions. . . . That as to trusting to a popular assembly for the preservation of our liberties . . . it was the merest chimera imaginable."

In Philadelphia, Adams took the long view while addressing a crowd of demonstrators. "Without wishing to damp the ardor of curiosity, or influence the freedom of inquiry, I will hazard a prediction that after the most industrious and impartial researches, the longest liver of you all, will find no principles, institutions, or systems of education more fit, in general, to be transmitted to your posterity, than those you have received from your ancestors." This backward-looking point of Adams's was so anathema to Jefferson that it agitated his mind long afterward.

To Jefferson, the imperfections of life and the limits of politics were realities. So were the wonders and the possibilities of the human mind. "I am among those who think well of the human character generally," he wrote twenty-one months before becoming president. "It is impossible for a man who takes a survey of what is already known, not to see what an immensity in every branch of science yet remains to be discovered."

Astronomy, botany, chemistry, natural history, anatomy: These were "branches of science . . . worth the attention of every man," Jefferson said, adding that "great fields are yet to be explored to which our faculties are equal, and that to an extent of which we cannot fix the limits." It was "cowardly" to think "the human mind is incapable of further advances."

Jefferson's vision for the United States was expansive. The work was never done, of course, however strong the performance of a particular era. "The generation which is going off the stage has deserved well of mankind for the struggles it has made, and for having arrested that course of despotism which had overwhelmed the world for thousands and thousands of years," Jefferson said. A course arrested, though, was not the same thing as a course extinguished.

In Philadelphia in May 1798, a parade of about 1,200 supporters of the alien bill presented Adams with a statement in favor of the administration's measures against France. Adams had proclaimed

May 9 a fast day—as Jefferson knew from Virginia during the Revolution, such maneuvers had their uses—and violence broke out between pro-Adams Federalists and the Republicans. (In his diary, Nathaniel Ames, a New England Republican, drily noted that "Adams' Fast" had been designed "to engage Powers above against the French.") According to Jefferson, "a fray ensued and the light horse was called in. I write in the morning and therefore do not yet know the details. But it seems designed to drive the people into violence. This is becoming fast a scene of tumult and confusion." Such scenes evoked the worst aspects of his time in Paris.

Jefferson was in a conspiratorial frame of mind. "I know that all my motions at Philadelphia, here, and everywhere, are watched and recorded." He feared his mail was being intercepted and read. It was a chaotic time. In July 1798, Virginia senator Henry Tazewell said he feared the sedition law would be "executed with unrelenting fury." At the same time Jefferson anticipated the new arrival of an old foe: Alexander Hamilton was to become a senator from New York. (Hamilton ultimately declined to seek the Senate seat.)

The madness of the scene reminded Jefferson of an elemental force: heat. "Politics and party hatreds destroy the happiness of every being here," he wrote Patsy. "They seem, like salamanders, to consider fire as their element."

———

Jefferson was pressed for cash, which left him with a feeling of powerlessness. "I have not at this moment more than 50 dollars in the world at my command, and these are my only resource for a considerable time to come," he wrote in April 1798. He was learning, too, of the tragic nature of one of his sister's marriages. His sister Mary's husband, John Bolling, was apparently alcoholic and abusive. "Mr. B.'s habitual intoxication will destroy himself, his fortune and family," he wrote to Polly. "Of all calamities this is the greatest." Jefferson was practical, even cold, about the matter. "I wish my sister could bear his misconduct with more patience. It might lessen his attachment to the bottle, and at any rate would make her own time more tolerable. When we see ourselves in a situation which must be endured and gone through, it is best to make up our minds to it, meet it with firmness, and accommodate everything to it in the best way practicable."

In a letter dated January 22, 1798, Patsy announced the death of Harriet Hemings, the two-year-old daughter of Jefferson and Sally Hemings; Patsy made no allusion to the little girl's parentage.

Later, in August 1799, Dolley Madison visited Monticello. Jefferson composed a letter for her to take to her husband. It spoke of many things—an order of nails from the Monticello factory, the art of plastering, the Virginia and Kentucky resolutions. Jefferson did not mention a significant piece of domestic news, for secrecy forbade it: Sally Hemings was pregnant with another child. The unnamed daughter, who was not to live long, was born in early December 1799.

Politics remained raw. "The X. Y. Z. fever has considerably abated through the country, as I am informed, and the Alien and Sedition laws are working hard," he said in October 1798. "I fancy that some of the state legislatures will take strong ground on this occasion. . . . At least this may be the aim of the Oliverians, while Monck and the Cavaliers (who are perhaps the strongest) may be playing their game for the restoration of his most gracious majesty George the Third."

In a contentious crisis, here again was the language of the English Civil War and its royalist outcome. The allusions were directly drawn from the seventeenth-century drama. Oliverians were republicans and Monck was a nobleman who backed the restoration of Charles II, as did the Cavaliers. Jefferson's point is explicitly made: He feared there were modern-day monarchists seeking to return an English king to power, in this case George III.

The prosecutions under the new laws were egregious. Republican editors were arrested, indicted, and tried for publishing pieces the Adams administration deemed seditious. Among the most notable cases were those of Benjamin Franklin Bache of the **Aurora** in Philadelphia and James Thomson Callender of the **Examiner** in Richmond.

Editors were not the only targets. Vermont congressman Matthew Lyon—that rare creature, a Republican from Federalist New England—was charged with sedition for a letter he had written to the **Vermont Journal** protesting the sedition law weeks before it was even signed. In strong but hardly traitorous terms, Lyon had denounced President Adams for the president's alleged "continual grasp for power . . . unbounded thirst for ridiculous pomp, foolish adulation, and selfish avarice." Of Irish descent, Lyon was attacked by Federalists as "**a seditious foreigner**" who "may endanger us more than **a thousand Frenchmen** in the field." Driven by Republican zeal, Lyon was indicted, tried, and convicted in a trial presided over by the Washington-appointed Federalist U.S. Supreme Court justice William Paterson, who sentenced Lyon to four months in jail and fined him $1,000 with these words: "Matthew Lyon, as a member of the federal legislature, you must be well acquainted with the mischiefs which flow from an unlicensed abuse of government."

Jefferson was distraught. "I know not which mortifies me most, that I should fear to write what I think or my country bear such a state of things," Jefferson wrote. "Yet Lyon's judges . . . are objects of national fear." Lyon himself found strength and vindication in the conviction. He reported to jail, sought reelection to the House from prison, and won.

For Jefferson, the Alien and Sedition Acts were a cause of both near-despair and wonderment. "What person who remembers the times and tempers we have seen could have believed that within so short a period, not only the jealous spirit of liberty which shaped every operation of our revolution, but even the common principles of English whiggism would be scouted, and the tory principles of passive obedience under the new fangled names of **confidence** and **responsibility,** become entirely triumphant?" he wrote New York chancellor Robert R. Livingston.

Never one to stay out of the fray, Jefferson privately lobbied Republican candidates to run for office. In early 1799 he pleaded with John Page to seek a congressional seat. "Pray, my dear Sir, leave nothing undone to effect it. . . . For even a single vote may decide the majority" in the makeup of the House.

More dramatically, Jefferson secretly drafted resolutions for the state legislature in Kentucky protesting the Alien and Sedition Acts. (Madison did the same for Virginia.) The vice president of the United States was thus at work on an official rebuke for one of the American states to send to the president of the United States. The Kentucky draft was a purely Republican document, though Jefferson went far down the path to endangering the Union he loved so. In the resolution he endorsed the idea of nullification—the right of a state to refuse to comply with federal laws that it deemed unconstitutional. Here was the great advocate of a stronger, more effective national government proposing a mechanism for chaos and almost certain disunion.

Viewed in terms of philosophy, the contradictions between Jefferson the nationalist and Jefferson the nullifier seem irreconcilable. Viewed in terms of personality and of politics, though, Jefferson was acting in character. He was always in favor of whatever means would improve the chances of his cause of the hour. When he was a member of the Confederation Congress, he wanted the Confederation Congress to be respected. When he was a governor, he wanted strong gubernatorial powers. Now that he disagreed with the federal government (though an officer of that government), he wanted the states to have the ability to exert control and bring about the end he favored. He was not intellectually consistent, but a consistent theme did run through his politics and statecraft: He would do what it took, within reason, to arrange the world as he wanted it to be.

John Breckinridge, a Kentucky Republican and speaker of the State House, reported that the Kentucky Senate had balked at the nullification language. "In the Senate," wrote Breckinridge, "there was a considerable division, particularly on that sentence which declares, 'a Nullification of those acts by the States, to be the rightful remedy.' " On reflection, Jefferson confided his faith in a middle course to Madison. "I think we should . . . leave the matter in such a train as that we may not be committed absolutely to push the matter to extremities, and yet may be free to push as far as events will render prudent."

If Jefferson had overreacted with his talk of nullification, he was coming to a more settled view of the nature of faction. "In every free and deliberating society, there must from the nature of man be opposite parties, and violent dissensions and discords; and one of these for the most part must prevail over the other for a longer or shorter time," he wrote John Taylor in June 1798. "Perhaps this party division is necessary to induce each to watch and debate to the people the proceedings of the other. . . . A little patience and we shall see the reign of witches pass over, their spells dissolve, and the people recovering their true sight."

The last years of the eighteenth century were unhappy ones for Jefferson, but he never despaired. He knew politics was an intimate enterprise, and he took care to assuage his foes where he could. "No one can know Mr. Jefferson and be his **personal** enemy," said Supreme Court justice William Paterson, who had presided over the Lyon sedition trial. "Few, if any, are more opposed to him as a politician than I am, and until recently I utterly disliked him as a man as well as a politician." Then the two men had occasion to travel together, talking and getting a sense of each other. "I was highly pleased with his remarks," Paterson said, "for though we differed on

many points, he displayed an impartiality, a freedom from prejudice."

To Elbridge Gerry, Jefferson made a testament of
political faith in January 1799, writing:

> I am for freedom of religion, and against all
> maneuvers to bring about a legal ascendancy
> of one sect over another: for freedom of the
> press, and against all violations of the Constitu-
> tion to silence by force and not by reason the
> complaints or criticisms, just or unjust, of our
> citizens against the conduct of their agents.
> And I am for encouraging the progress of sci-
> ence in all its branches; and not for raising a
> hue and cry against the sacred name of philoso-
> phy . . . [and not] to go backwards instead of
> forwards to look for improvement, to believe
> that government, religion, morality, and every
> other science were in the highest perfection in
> ages of the darkest ignorance, and that noth-
> ing can ever be devised more perfect than what
> was established by our forefathers. . . . The first
> object of my heart is my own country. In that is
> embarked my family, my fortune, and my own
> existence. I have not one farthing of interest, nor
> one fiber of attachment out of it, nor a single
> motive of preference of any one nation to an-
> other but in proportion as they are more or less
> friendly to us.

Still, Jefferson was not overly dreamy. He solicited friends to author attacks on the alien and sedition laws, among other measures, and discussed public-opinion strategies with Madison. The public mind was open to the Republican case, Jefferson said, which made him "sensible that this summer is the season for systematic energies and sacrifices. The engine is the press." He sent Republican pamphlets to Monroe to promulgate. "I wish you to give these to the most influential characters among our country-men. . . . Do not let my name be connected with the business." On another occasion he asked the chairman of the Virginia Republican committee to distribute some tracts. "I trust yourself only with the secret that these pamphlets go from me," he wrote.

Jefferson could only do so much as vice president. "A decided character at the head of our government is of immense importance by the influence it will have upon public opinion," John Taylor wrote Jefferson in February 1799. Taylor was talking about the governorship, but the point applied, as he and Jefferson knew, to the presidency as well.

THIRTY

Adams vs. Jefferson Redux

> I should be unfaithful to my own feelings were
> I not to say that it has been the greatest of all
> human consolations to me to be considered by
> the republican portion of my fellow citizens, as
> the safe depository of their rights.
>
> —THOMAS JEFFERSON

I T WAS NOT the most sophisticated of strategies, but it worked. On Monday, February 25, 1799, the Republicans in the House planned to take up petitions against the alien and sedition laws. The Federalists, with a bare but sufficient majority, caucused beforehand and decided, Jefferson told Madison, "that not a word should be spoken on their side in answer to anything which should be said on the other."

On the floor, when Albert Gallatin, the Swiss-born Pennsylvania Republican House leader, addressed the Alien Act and Virginia congressman John Nicholas the Sedition, the majority sabotaged the proceedings in the most elemental of ways: by drowning out the speakers. The Federalists "began to enter into loud conversations, laugh, cough etc."

The din of the House was disorienting and dispiriting. The Republicans felt powerless. "It was impossible to proceed," Jefferson said.

At Monticello in the Albemarle spring, Jefferson worried that Adams was going to raise a "Presidential army, or Presidential militia," the formation of which would "leave me without a doubt that force on the Constitution is intended." He believed, too, that Hamilton would be the real power behind the new regiments. "Can such an army under Hamilton be disbanded?" Jefferson wrote in April 1799. The debate turned violent. In the House, John Randolph of Roanoke, a Jefferson cousin and lawmaker, attacked the idea of a standing military establishment, referring to regular soldiers as "mercenary forces" and "ragamuffins." The next evening two marines accosted Randolph at the New Theatre; he was, Jefferson said, "jostled and [had] his coat pulled."

As the eighteenth century ended, the presidential contest was the supreme battle in the war of ideas and personalities in American politics. Jefferson was determined to seek the top office again. He had seen enough of what he had called a "reign of witches" to underscore his conviction that republicanism was in danger.

So much seemed at stake. A correspondent reported that Hamilton had led a louder cheer and toast to George III than to John Adams at a dinner of the St. Andrews Club of New York. "No mortal can foresee in favor of which party the election will go," Jefferson said in March 1800.

Hyperbole was the order of the day. For Republicans, Adams was an aspiring monarch. Americans, one Republican wrote, "will never permit the chief magistrate of the union to become a **King** instead of a president." For Federalists, Jefferson was a dangerous infidel. The **Gazette of the United States** told voters to choose "GOD—AND A RELIGIOUS PRESIDENT" or impiously declare for "JEFFERSON—AND NO GOD."

Jefferson's views on religious liberty, however, appealed to many more moderate voters. New Jersey Republicans charged that Jefferson's enemies used religion as a means of assault "because he is not a fanatic, nor willing that the Quaker, the Baptist, the Methodist, or any other denominations of Christians, should pay the pastors of other sects; because he does not think that a Catholic should be banished for believing in transubstantiation, or a Jew, for believing in the God of Abraham, Isaac, and Jacob."

Still, the religious refrain about Jefferson's unconventional faith was a frequent one. From the federal bench, Supreme Court justice Samuel Chase, a devoted Federalist, had "harangued" a grand jury with what Monroe reported were "allusions which supported by Eastern calumnies" about Jefferson. "He declared solemnly that he would not allow an atheist to give testimony in court"—an implied reference to Jefferson.

Chase also moved to indict and try the Scottish-born newspaperman James Thomson Callender, a virulent Republican—whom Jefferson had supported financially—for sedition. The immediate cause of the charges was a little book with a high-minded title—**The Prospect Before Us**—but a slashing style. "The reign of Mr. Adams has, hitherto, been one continued tempest of **malignant** passions," Callender wrote. "As president, he has never opened his lips, or lifted his pen, without threatening and scolding. The grand object of his administration has been to exasperate the rage of contending parties, to calumniate and destroy every man who differs from his opinions. Mr. Adams has labored, and with melancholy success, to break up the bonds of social affection, and, under the ruins of confidence and friendship, to extinguish the only beam of happiness that glimmers through the dark and despicable farce of life."

Jefferson told Callender that the tract "cannot fail to produce the best effect."

Reading it, Abigail and John Adams seethed.

George Washington died in December 1799 at Mount Vernon. As solicitous as Jefferson had been to his old president in private, the two men were so far apart politically that Jefferson believed it the wisest course to remain at Monticello rather than to attend any of the many ceremonies commemorating Washington's life. Jefferson admired Washington's gifts in the art of leadership but could not help but see the first president as what he had become: a Federalist icon whose party, Jefferson thought, was moving the United States in the wrong direction.

Theirs had always been a complicated relationship. Jefferson had been dishonest about his support of Philip Freneau and the **National Gazette,** preferring to mislead Washington rather than force a confrontation over the Republican attacks on the first president. It was Hamilton, not Jefferson, who had emerged as Washington's political son. "Perhaps no man in this community has equal cause with myself to deplore the loss," Hamilton said after Washington's death. "I have been much indebted to the kindness of the General, and he was an **Aegis very essential to me.**"

Reacting to the flood of tributes to Washington, Freneau wrote some verses to check the popular tide:

> No tongue can tell, no pen describe
> The frenzy of a numerous tribe,
> Who, by distemper'd fancy led,
> Insult the memory of the dead.
>
> He was no god, ye flattering knaves,
> He own'd no world, he ruled no waves;

> But—and exalt it, if you can,
> He was the upright, Honest Man.
>
> This was his glory, this outshone
> Those attributes you doat upon:
> On this strong ground he took his stand,
> Such virtue saved a sinking land.

James Madison was also striking somber notes about the Federalists. "The horrors which they evidently feel at the approach of the electoral epoch are a sufficient warning of the desperate game by which they will be apt to characterize the interval," he wrote Jefferson in April 1800. To his sister Martha Carr, Jefferson connected the sedition laws to the 1800 race. "The batteries of slander are fully opened for the campaign which is to decide the Presidential election. The other party have begun it by a furious onset on the printers, that they may have the field to themselves, and allow no means to return their fire." To Patsy he said: "Our opponents perceive the decay of their power. Still they are pressing it, and trying to pass laws to keep themselves in power."

Jefferson harbored a real hope in the good sense of the people. His belief in democracy was not a pose, but a conviction: Educate the public, he believed, and by and large a majority would find its way to the right place.

Now, in 1800, Jefferson was sure the "madness and extravagance" of the Federalists was too profound and evident to fool the voters. "The people through all the states," Jefferson said, "are for republican forms, republican principles, simplicity, economy, religious and civil freedom."

In early May, Adams made some cabinet changes, nominating John Marshall to replace Timothy Pickering as secretary of state and naming Samuel Dexter to take the place of Secretary of War James McHenry. Adams was belatedly trying to make up the ground he had lost by keeping Washington's cabinet intact, a decision that had given him less control over the government than he would have liked for much of his tenure. Adams also disbanded what Jefferson had called "the Presidential militia." To his son-in-law Thomas Mann Randolph, Jr., Jefferson noted that the Federalists "are, on the approach of an election, trying to court a little popularity, that they may be afterwards allowed to go on 4 years longer in defiance of it."

On the eve of Fourth of July celebrations in 1800, the Baltimore **American** published rumors that Jefferson had died at Monticello after "an indisposition of 48 hours"—a detail that, in its specificity, lent credence to the report. Several papers followed suit, and the **Gazette of the United States** said that the report "appears to be entitled to some credit." By July 6 the truth—that Jefferson was alive and well—was known, prompting a letter from the French economist Pierre-Samuel du Pont de Nemours in New York. "I thought I had lost the greatest man of this continent, the one whose enlightened reason can be the most useful to both worlds," he wrote. "I spent several days in unutterable despair."

In Sharon, Connecticut, a Federalist enclave, the Reverend Cotton Mather Smith dined in a small gathering that included Uriah McGregory, a Jefferson supporter. "I found him an **engaged Federal** politician," McGregory said. Smith had asked McGregory if he truly wanted to see "Mr. Jefferson [in] the Presidential Chair?"

McGregory had answered yes, he did, prompting, "with much other malicious invective," a diatribe about alleged financial and legal misconduct on Jefferson's part. The claim from Smith: that Jefferson "had obtained . . . property by fraud and robbery—and that in one instance you had defrauded and robbed a widow and fatherless children of an estate, to which you [were] executor, of ten thousand pounds sterling; by keeping the property and paying them in money at the nominal amount that was worth no more than forty for one." McGregory refused to believe it, and said so. Smith was adamant, replying that "it was true and that 'it could be proved.' "

Writing Jefferson in July 1800, McGregory noted the uniqueness of the dinnertime attack. "I know, Sir, that you suffered much abuse in this state— and from faithful inquiry believe it to be unmerited and malicious—but never, until the above instance, knew that the vilest of your traducers had ventured to impeach your honesty in pecuniary concerns." He thought Jefferson should know of the charges, and he hoped to be armed with a reply. "I wish to have it in my power, Sir, to publish a clear and full refutation, together with the vile assertion."

Jefferson denied it all—there was no basis for the assertions—and lamented such rumors. On the whole, Jefferson had to count on the coming of "a day when the false witness will meet a judge who has not slept over his slanders."

In the fall of 1800 a conspiracy organized by a slave named Gabriel in Henrico County, Virginia, unraveled on the night of its execution. A sprawling effort, the insurrection would have used recruits to take over part of Richmond, Norfolk, and Petersburg. The white authorities struck back mercilessly, hanging twenty-six conspirators.

From jail in Richmond, James Callender told Jefferson, "Their plan was to massacre all the whites, of all ages, and sexes; and all the blacks who would not join them; and then march off to the mountains, with the plunder of the city. Those wives who should refuse to accompany their husbands were to have been butchered along with the rest, an idea truly worthy of an African heart!"

Like the warfare on St. Domingue, Gabriel's conspiracy underscored Jefferson's view that there was no sustainable future in a society in which blacks and whites lived freely in proximity to one another. In the wake of the Gabriel episode and a panic over slave violence in Virginia, the state's House of Delegates asked Jefferson to explore whether a foreign land might be open to receiving American blacks. An approach was made to the Sierra Leone Company, but negotiations lapsed for various reasons.

Politically, in New York, Alexander Hamilton was unhappy that Republicans were doing well in his home state under the leadership of Aaron Burr. In the spring of 1800, New York election results had effectively given the Republicans, who had won what Jefferson called "a great majority in their legislature," the votes they needed to carry the presidential ballot in the winter. (Legislatures chose presidential electors in New York and ten other states; in only five of the sixteen states in the Union were the electors popularly chosen.) In New York, Edward Livingston reported, there was "a most auspicious gloom on the countenances of every Tory."

Hamilton and his father-in-law, Philip Schuyler, appealed to John Jay, now governor of New York, to change the state's election laws before the new Republican majority took office, effectively overturning the verdict of the vote. It was a classic Hamilton maneuver: "In times like this in which we live," he entreated Jay, "it will not do to be overscrupulous."

The overriding goal, Hamilton said, was to "prevent an **atheist** in religion and a **fanatic** in politics from getting possession of the helm of State."

Governor Jay was unmoved. On Hamilton's letter he wrote "Proposing a measure for party purposes, which I think it would not become me to adopt." The Republican win in New York would stand, opening a path to the presidency for Hamilton's nemesis.

On the day of the news of the New York results, Jefferson met with Adams on other business in Philadelphia. The president, Jefferson said, was "very sensibly affected" by the Jeffersonian victory in New York and "accosted" the vice president.

"Well, I understand that you are to beat me in this contest," Adams told Jefferson, "and I will only say that I will be as faithful a subject as any you will have."

"Mr. Adams, this is no personal contest between you and me," Jefferson recalled himself saying. To Adams, he continued:

> Two systems of principles on the subject of government divide our fellow-citizens into two parties. With one of these you concur, and I with the other. As we have been longer on the public stage than most of those now living, our names happen to be more generally known. One

of these parties therefore has put your name at its head, the other mine. Were we both to die today, tomorrow two other names would be in the place of ours, without any change in the motion of the machine. Its motion is from its principle, not from you or myself.

"I believe you are right that we are but passive instruments," said Adams, "and should not suffer this matter to affect our personal dispositions."

From Jefferson's perspective, however, Adams "did not long retain this just view of the subject. I have always believed that the thousand calumnies which the Federalists, in bitterness of heart, and mortification at their ejection, daily invented against me, were carried to him by their busy intriguers, and made some impression."

Jefferson was right that the Federalists were not going quietly. There was talk of fielding another potentially disruptive Pinckney of South Carolina. In 1796 it had been Thomas; in 1800 it was to be his brother Charles Cotesworth Pinckney who would stand as a Federalist candidate along with Adams. It was the 1796 play all over again. The letter of the law said that each elector voted for two candidates but could not designate which was for president and which for vice president. Anti-Adams Federalists such as Hamilton hoped that South Carolina's electors would choose Jefferson and their native son Pinckney, thus propelling Pinckney (who, combining the votes he won in Adams states with South Carolina's vote, stood a good chance of winning the whole election) to the presidency.

"To support **Adams** and **Pinckney** equally is the only thing that can possibly save us from the fangs of **Jefferson**," Hamilton wrote a fellow Federalist in May 1800. Although Jefferson referred to the Federalists' tactics as "hocus-pocus maneuvers," he could be vulnerable if everything broke Hamilton's way.

Adams was under assault from all directions. In October 1800, Hamilton published an attack on the second president. Entitled **Letter from Alexander Hamilton, Concerning the Public Conduct and Character of John Adams, Esq., President of the United States,** it argued that Adams did "not possess the talents adapted to the administration of **government**," and that "there are great intrinsic defects in his character which unfit him for the office of chief magistrate." Writing to the diplomat Rufus King in Great Britain, the New York Federalist Robert Troup said he thought the Hamilton-Adams division fatal to Federalist hopes: "Our enemies are universally in triumph."

Hamilton, however, believed there was little to lose. "If we must have an **enemy** at the head of the Government," Hamilton said, "let it be one whom we can oppose and for whom we are not responsible, who will not involve our party in the disgrace of his foolish and bad measures."

————

The fall of 1800 was the most momentous of autumns for Jefferson, a time of dizzying anxiety and exultant hopes. He was on the cusp of consummate command, of national approval, of glorious victory. The emotions of the hour were stormy.

At Monticello, he fell into existential worry. "I have sometimes asked myself whether my country is the better for my having lived at all," Jefferson wrote in a private memorandum. "I do not know that it is. I have been the instrument of doing the following things; but they would have been done by others; some of them perhaps a little later." He listed the navigational improvements he made to the Rivanna River in his burgess days, the Declaration of Independence, his work on the revision of the laws of Virginia—and the introduction of olive trees to the United States.

Slowly but steadily results from the states reached Monticello. Republicans were winning where they needed to win, holding the South and doing well in Pennsylvania and New York. "Democratic principles seem to be evidently increasing," said former secretary of state Timothy Pickering, unhappily.

On hearing that the South Carolina ploy to elect Pinckney had failed and that Jefferson was likely to become president, a New England clergyman wrote, "I have never heard bad tidings on anything which gave me such a shock."

On Friday, December 12, 1800, Jefferson felt

confident enough of the results to declare privately that he was likely to be the next president of the United States. "I believe we may consider the election as now decided," he wrote Thomas Mann Randolph, Jr. Delaware Republican Caesar A. Rodney rejoiced; he was convinced that Jefferson's election signaled the end of the "tempests and tornadoes" of the Adams years.

Still, Jefferson's sense of fragility kept him in mind of Federalist traps. Several "highflying Federalists," Jefferson wrote Aaron Burr, "have expressed their hope that the two republican tickets may be equal, and their determination in that case to prevent a choice by the H. of R. (which they are strong enough to do) and let the government devolve on a President of the Senate."

The possibility of a tie, Jefferson told Madison in December, "has produced great dismay and gloom on the republican gentlemen here, and equal exultation in the federalists, who openly declare they will prevent an election, and will name a President of the Senate pro tem by what they say would only be a **stretch** of the Constitution. . . . The month of February therefore will present us storms of a new character."

There was much uncertainty. "Some of the Jacobins are afraid Mr. J. will not administer the Govt. according to their wishes," Massachusetts Federalist George Cabot wrote Rufus King on Sunday, December 28, 1800. "Others of them think it was easy and pleasant to rail and find fault but difficult to govern and vindicate; they are unwilling to take responsibility upon themselves or friends: others are afraid Burr will be Chief."

The drama was seen by some in light of the larger struggle between monarchy and republicanism. "Our Tories begin to give themselves air[s] already in expectation of a **tie**," John Randolph of Roanoke wrote Representative Joseph Nicholson of Maryland on Tuesday, December 16, 1800. "I fear that, in this event, they will give us some trouble; at the same time I know that it will be damnatory of their party with [those] who are not devoted to the monarchy."

Though some Federalists spoke of throwing support to Burr in exchange for political and policy concessions, the New Yorker showed no outward signs of working against Jefferson. "I do not . . . apprehend any embarrassment even in case the votes should come out alike for us—My personal friends are perfectly informed of my wishes on the subject and can never think of diverting a single vote from you," Burr told Jefferson. "On the contrary, they will be found among your most zealous adherents." There is no evidence that Burr considered betraying Jefferson, but Jefferson soon came to believe that his running mate was an unreliable and undesirable ally. The eventual outcome of the election of 1800,

Jefferson told his son-in-law John Wayles Eppes, passed all understanding.

"The President, I am told, is in a state of deep dejection; his feelings are not to be envied," wrote Timothy Pickering on Monday, January 5, 1801. "To his UNADVISED (to use a mild term) measures are traced the evils with which the whole of our country is now perplexed and depressed. And many discerning Federalists at least doubted which was to be most deprecated—his reelection, or Mr. Jefferson's elevation to the Presidency."

Republicans worried about a Federalist defeat of the popular will. "The dread now," a correspondent wrote the Republican John Breckinridge in late December 1800, "is that Jefferson and Burr are equal as the vote of the electors, and that Burr will be preferred by the Eastern states, not because they think him really the most capable, but because Jefferson is the choice of the people . . . and their will **shall not prevail;** this certainly would be a wicked and contrary disposition in them. But what will they not do or attempt?"

The year ended in fog and mystery. "The Feds appear determined to prevent an election, and pass a bill giving the government to Mr. Jay, appointed Chief Justice, or to Marshall as Secy. of State," Jefferson wrote Madison on the day after Christmas. "Yet I am rather of the opinion that Maryland and Jersey will join the 7 republican majorities." By the last Sunday in December 1800, the votes were all in. They came to Jefferson as president of the Senate.

It was a tie.

James McHenry put the key question to Rufus King on the second day of 1801.

"Where," McHenry asked, "is all this to end?"

THIRTY-ONE

A Desperate State of Affairs

Rumors are various, and intrigues great.

—GOUVERNEUR MORRIS

It is extremely uncertain on whom the choice will fall.

—JOHN MARSHALL

THE WASHINGTON, D.C., OF 1800–1801 was a makeshift affair. Six or seven boarding-houses were in competition with Conrad and McMunn's, where Jefferson lodged. A Philadelphia boot maker had recently set up shop near the Capitol, as had a bookstore. Benjamin W. Morris and Co. Groceries stocked Madeira wine, brandy, and spirits, along with soap, lamp oil, and hair powder. The sides of Capitol Hill itself were still wild, wooded, and filled with game.

Moving between the Senate, where he remained the presiding officer, and his quarters at Conrad and McMunn's, Jefferson tried to keep his equilibrium.

It was not easy. No one knew what each day would bring. "The election," Jefferson wrote a son-in-law, "is still problematical."

Once an ally, Aaron Burr now seemed a possible threat. On Monday, January 5, 1801, the **Philadelphia Gazette** wrote that Burr "was heard to insinuate that he felt as competent to the exercise of the Presidential functions as Mr. Jefferson." On the same day, Benjamin Hichborn, a Jeffersonian, reported, "Some of our friends, as they call themselves, are willing to join the other party in case they should unite in favor of Col. Burr."

Jefferson's enemies were indeed at work, open to considering any scenario that would keep Jefferson out of power. "There would be really cause to fear that the government would not survive the course of moral and political experiments to which it would be subjected in the hands of Mr. Jefferson," said Delaware congressman James Bayard, a Federalist.

Albert Gallatin, writing to his wife, said, "What will be the plans of the Federalists? Will they usurp the Presidential powers? . . . I see some danger in the fate of the election."

Roger Griswold lamented the sorry pass things had come to. "Jefferson as a politician I believe to be the weakest of all men—he may be honest but it is a point which is much doubted by those acquainted with his private life," Griswold said.

On Sunday, January 11, 1801, Jefferson attended morning services in the Capitol. The Right Reverend

Thomas Claggett, the Episcopal bishop of Maryland and chaplain of the Senate, was presiding. Roger Griswold was there, too, and could watch Jefferson as the sermon unfolded. Claggett—with, Griswold said, "more learning perhaps than wisdom"—was trying to link some biblical prophecy to the events of the French Revolution. In doing so, Griswold wrote, the bishop "was obliged to dwell at some length upon the mischief which had grown out of the visionary plans of the French philosophers. . . . Then [their] infidelity was described, and [the] pernicious tendency of their schemes, both as they related to politics and morals, was painted in glowing colors."

To Griswold's eye, Jefferson "took every word to himself, and thought the Bishop was delivering a Philippic upon his theories, and visions." Jefferson "blushed like a young girl of fifteen, and I make no doubt wished the Bishop and his prophecies at the devil."

Along the mid-Atlantic, Jefferson partisans considered arming themselves to march on the capital. The denial of the popular will, Jefferson said privately, "opens upon us an abyss at which every sincere patriot must shudder." Elbridge Gerry was told by "high authority" that Jefferson's election "would put the constitution to the test."

Rumors grew as days passed. "Some strange reports are circulating here of the views of the Federal party in the present desperate state of its affairs," Monroe wrote Jefferson from Richmond on Tuesday, January 6, 1801. "It is said they are resolved to prevent the designation by the H. of Reps. of the person to be president, and that they mean to commit the power by a legislative act to John Marshall, Samuel A. Otis or some other person till another election."

Lawmakers in Richmond were debating whether to remain in session, Monroe said, "to be on the ground to take such steps as might be deemed proper to defeat" any measure that denied Jefferson the presidency.

Everyone was to be watched. "Unfriendly foreign ministers should be observed," wrote Tench Coxe on Saturday, January 10, 1801. "The professions of Federalists should not be too hastily credited. . . . It is a case wherein we cannot fear too far, if we preserve our firmness, and temper."

With the outcome uncertain, the Federalists struck while they could, passing the Judiciary Act of 1801 in February. If Jefferson or Burr prevailed, who knew when the Federalist interest might again have the power to act?

Taking advantage of the hour, then, the Congress approved, and President Adams signed, a bill that increased the number of federal judicial officers, strengthened and expanded the circuit courts, and reduced the number of Supreme Court justices from six to five, thus depriving any Republican president of at least one appointment. "The Judiciary bill has been crammed down our throats without a word or letter being suffered to be altered," wrote Senator Stevens Thomson Mason of Virginia, a Republican.

Jefferson believed the law, coming so late in Adams's term, was a "parasitical plant engrafted at the last session on the judiciary body" and that the Federalist appointees to the new positions had "retired into the judiciary as a stronghold . . . and from that battery all the works of republicanism are to be beaten down and erased." Such appointees became colloquially known as Adams's "midnight judges," and there were "midnight appointments" to lesser offices as well.

The most significant decision Adams made in these months was to name John Marshall, his secretary of state, as chief justice of the United States, giving a Jefferson foe lifetime tenure as head of one of the three branches of the federal government. The Federalists believed Jefferson's Republicans to be every bit as dangerous as Jefferson's Republicans believed the Federalists to be.

Adams and Marshall met in January 1801, while Marshall was still secretary of state, to discuss possible successors to Chief Justice Oliver Ellsworth, who was retiring. Though Adams had sought to reenlist John Jay, the first chief justice, to return to the bench, Jay chose to remain in the New York governorship.

"Who shall I nominate now?" Adams asked Marshall.

As Marshall recalled the conversation, he told the president that he had no counsel to give.

"I believe I must nominate you," Adams said.

Marshall recalled being "pleased as well as surprised, and bowed in silence."

The U.S. Senate confirmed the president's nomination in the last week of January 1801.

In the weeks after Marshall's confirmation, Republicans took care to encourage one another about the presidential election. "Mr. Jefferson is undoubtedly the rock of our political salvation from which no concurrence of circumstances . . . should compel us to depart," Caesar A. Rodney of Delaware wrote Joseph Nicholson on Tuesday, February 17, 1801. "We should consider ourselves as indissolubly bound to him, by a Gordian knot which no intrigue should untie and no force cut asunder."

Jefferson himself was worried enough about talk of installing the president pro tempore of the Senate in the President's House that he paid a call on Adams with one subject in view: "to have this desperate measure prevented by his [veto]."

Hearing Jefferson's business, Adams flew into a temper. "He grew warm in an instant," Jefferson recalled, and replied "with a vehemence he had not used towards me before."

"Sir," Adams said to Jefferson, "the event of the

election is within your own power," arguing that Jefferson need only commit to certain Federalist policies to end the suspense and become president: The government, Adams said, would "instantly be put in your hands."

"Mr. Adams," Jefferson replied, "I know not what part of my conduct, in either public or private life, can have authorized a doubt of my fidelity to the public engagements. I say however I will not come into the government by capitulation. I will not enter on it but in perfect freedom to follow the dictates of my own judgment."

"Then things must take their course," Adams said, and the conversation ended.

It was a bitter, uncomfortable moment—"the first time in our lives we had ever parted with anything like dissatisfaction," Jefferson recalled. Such was the season; such were the stakes.

From Pennsylvania, Governor Thomas McKean saw every possibility. "Interest, character, duty, love of country all conspire to insure [Jefferson's election]; but I have been told that envy, malice, despair and a delight in doing mischief will prompt the Anglo-Federalists to set all other considerations at nought, and that it is intended to so manage as to keep the states equally divided, in order that Congress may in the form of a law appoint a President for us until a new election shall take place." Though he said he could not believe such a thing could happen, he also believed in preparing for the worst.

"But should it be possible that gentlemen will act the desperate part that has been suggested by the partisans of anarchy and civil war," McKean asked, by what authority would they be acting? To install anyone other than Jefferson or Burr would be unconstitutional, an act of usurpation.

McKean was clear about his intentions. "If bad men will dare traitorously to destroy or embarrass our general government and the union of the states, I shall conceive it my duty to oppose them at every hazard of life and fortune; for I should deem it less inglorious to submit to foreign than domestic tyranny." The Pennsylvania militia was to be readied, McKean said, and arms prepared for "upwards of twenty thousand," including "brass field-pieces etc. etc." The governor was also ready to issue an order "for the arresting and bringing to justice every member of Congress, or other person found in Pennsylvania, who should have been concerned in the treason."

A few fires at official buildings in Washington raised suspicions. "The burning of the war-office last month and now the treasury have probably been accidental, but as these events were predicted in Philadelphia and subjects of conversation in July last, suspicions of design will be entertained by many," McKean said. Reporting the fires at the Treasury and War offices, Roger Griswold observed, "It seems heaven has pointed its curses against our national establishments in this city of the wilderness."

The tension of the time exhausted Jefferson. "I long to be in the midst of the children, and have more pleasure in their little follies than in the wisdom of the wise," he wrote Patsy. "Here too there is such a mixture of the bad passions of the heart that one feels themselves in an enemy's country."

The House planned to meet on Wednesday, February 11, 1801, to choose a president. From Albemarle County, Thomas Mann Randolph, Jr., wrote: "The approach of the 11th Feb. makes the people here **breathe long** with suspense, their anxiety is so great."

As the lawmakers gathered, the mysteries only deepened. According to notes Jefferson made on Thursday, February 12, of a conversation with Edward Livingston, there was shadowy talk of deal making. "Edward Livingston tells me that [Federalist James] Bayard applied today or last night to Gen. Samuel Smith and represented to him the expediency of his coming over to the states who vote for Burr, that there was nothing in the way of appointment which he might not command, and particularly mentioned the Secretaryship of the navy. Smith asked him if he was authorized to make the offer. He said he was authorized. . . . Bayard in like manner tempted Livingston. . . . To Dr. Linn of New Jersey they have offered the government of New Jersey."

Bayard soon shifted tack and went to Maryland

Republican congressman Samuel Smith with a proposition for Jefferson. Bayard later claimed that he explained to Smith what could be done to resolve the impasse and give Jefferson the presidency. If Jefferson would pledge not to dismiss all Federalist officeholders and to preserve the navy and the public debt, all would be well. According to Bayard, Smith went to Jefferson, received Jefferson's acquiescence, and then returned to Bayard with those answers.

"This is absolutely false," Jefferson wrote later. "No proposition of any kind was ever made to me on that occasion by Genl. Smith, nor any answer authorized by me." Smith supported Jefferson's version of events, saying that he had discussed broad policy questions with Jefferson but had not told Jefferson why he was asking. Smith's assurances to Bayard, then, were Smith's interpretations of Jefferson's intentions, not a proffer.

Did Jefferson strike a deal to win the presidency? His denials are firm, but the election was unfolding in a charged atmosphere in which no one spoke of anything else. It seems likely that Bayard **believed** he had sufficient assurance that Jefferson was not going to tear down the whole works of the previous dozen years. With Smith's representations—however specific or explicit they were—in mind, Bayard moved to end the drama and deliver the presidency to Jefferson.

By his own account the Federalist terms were well known to Jefferson, who had been invited at least twice—once by President Adams himself—to calm the worst of the opposition's fears. New York senator Gouverneur Morris encountered Jefferson one day outside the Senate chamber. "He stopped me and began a conversation on the strange and portentous state of things then existing, and went on to observe that the reasons why the minority of states were so opposed to my being elected, was that they apprehended that 1. I should turn all Federalists out of office, 2. put down the Navy 3. wipe off the public debt and 4. that I need only to declare, or authorize my friends to declare, that I would not take these steps, and instantly the event of the election would be fixed."

Standing on the steps, absorbing Morris's words, Jefferson replied: "I told him that I should leave the world to judge of the course I meant to pursue by that which I had pursued hitherto; believing it to be my duty to be passive and silent during the present scene; that I should certainly make no terms, should never go into the office of President by capitulation, nor with my hands tied by any conditions which should hinder me from pursuing the measures which I should deem for the public good."

Jefferson knew what he was passing up. "It was understood that Gouverneur Morris" could have swayed "another vote and decided the election," Jefferson recalled.

Jefferson had similar exchanges with Adams in their meeting on Pennsylvania Avenue and again with the Federalist Dwight Foster, who called on Jefferson at Conrad and McMunn's to seek assurances. Yet Jefferson had already said what he had to say, and that was as far as he was willing to go. "I do not recollect that I ever had any particular conversation with General Samuel Smith on this subject," Jefferson wrote. "Very possibly I had, as the general subject and all its parts were the constant themes of conversation in the private **tete a tetes** with our friends. But certain I am that neither he, nor any other Republican ever uttered the most distant hint to me about submitting to any conditions or giving any assurances to anybody; and still more certainly was neither he nor any other person ever authorized by me to say what I would or would not do."

Hamilton understood this. "Jefferson is to be preferred" over Burr, he said. "He is by far not so dangerous a man; and he has pretensions to character." Jefferson, Hamilton noted, "is as likely as any man I know to temporize—to calculate what will be likely to promote his own reputation and advantage; and the probable result of such a temper is the preservation of systems, though originally opposed, which being once established, could not be overturned without danger to the person who did it." Other Federalists agreed. "Mr. Jefferson is a man of too much virtue and good sense to attempt any material change in a system which was adopted by our late beloved Washington, and has been since steadily pursued by Mr. Adams, and which has preserved our country in peace and prosperity for 12 years, during which period almost the whole civilized world has been deluged in blood," William Fitzhugh, a Virginia Federalist who had been close to George Washington, wrote in January 1801.

The voting was slow. Ballot after ballot came and went inside the Capitol. Lawmakers slept on pallets. The weather was terrible. An ailing representative, Joseph Nicholson of Maryland, was carried through the snow on a stretcher and set up in a room next to the House; his wife helped guide his hand to fill in his choice.

Finally, at one p.m. on Tuesday, February 17, 1801, on the thirty-sixth ballot, Jefferson prevailed.

Republicans thought of the Federalists as "the Conspirators," and Margaret Bayard Smith, the wife of the Jeffersonian editor Samuel Harrison Smith, noted how quickly the Federalists "hurried to their lodgings under strong apprehensions of suffering from the just indignation of their fellow citizens" for attempting to subvert the election.

Afterward James Bayard claimed New England was prepared "to go without a constitution and take the risk of a Civil War." Jefferson told McKean that "in the event of a usurpation I was decidedly with those who were determined not to permit it. Because that precedent once set, would be artificially reproduced, and end soon in a dictator."

Jefferson's public serenity and strength had been essential to inspiring Republicans to stay the course. "When I look back I cannot but shudder at the prospect which presented itself during the late contest," wrote the lawyer Archibald Stuart from Staunton, Virginia. "The minds of men from extreme anxiety seemed to settle down into a firm resolution to resist every attempt to give us a President who had not been the choice of the people. . . . I was pleased to discover this temper as it proves our liberties cannot be lost without a **struggle**."

The roar of cannons announced the news. In Alexandria, thirty-two rounds were fired (sixteen on the courthouse square, another sixteen over the Potomac); in Richmond, there were fireworks; and in Pennsylvania, Republicans rang bells from before noon to sundown. "Our people in this county are running perfectly mad with enthusiasm about the man of the people, the savior of his country (as they term him)," said a New York Federalist. "Drunken frolics are the order of the day, and more bullocks and rams are sacrificed to this newfangled deity than were formerly by the Israelitish priests." An evangelical minister, William Scales, took a more optimistic view: "Many declare you an atheist," Scales wrote to Jefferson, "but be it so, I much rather a liberal atheist should govern the people, than a bigoted saint, who knows not God."

John Marshall, serving concurrently as secretary

of state and as chief justice until Jefferson took office, looked on with wonder and anxiety. He declined to speculate on the causes of what he thought "the strange revolution which has taken place in public opinion" in replacing Adams with Jefferson. "The course to be pursued . . . is of more importance and is not easily to be determined by those who have no place in the confidence of the President-elect," Marshall wrote Rufus King. On foreign policy, Marshall shared the old Federalist fear that Jefferson would "excite the resentment and hate of the people against England" but "without designing to proceed to actual hostilities."

For all the strife of recent years, Jefferson and the Adamses had managed to maintain quietly civil relations. In early January 1801 the president and the First Lady asked the vice president to dinner. "Mr. Jefferson dines with us and in a card reply to the President's invitation, he begs him to be assured of his homage and high consideration," Abigail wrote one of their sons on Saturday, January 3, 1801. She was to leave Washington on Friday, February 13; before she departed, she received Jefferson for tea. As Abigail told it, Jefferson "made me a visit . . . in order to take leave and wish me a good journey. It was more than I expected."

Such small human moments speak well of both the Adamses and of Jefferson. They had been through so much together; few others alive could have understood as well or as thoroughly what their lives had been like in the previous quarter century or so. Politics had brought them together, and politics had now driven them apart. And yet they still found it in themselves to treat one another with outward grace.

Jefferson quietly exulted at the outcome of the election. "I cannot regret entirely the disappointment of [not] meeting [Polly] and yourself at Monticello, because of the cause, which must be a subject of pleasure to us all," he wrote Patsy of his new need to be in Washington.

He liked that his victory was seen in global terms. "As to the future, thou art to be the principal Actor," wrote his Revolutionary colleague John Dickinson. "Perhaps we are the selected people upon Earth, from whom large portions of Mankind are to learn, that Liberty is really a transcendent blessing, as capable by its enlightened energies of calmly dissipating its internal enemies, as of triumphantly repelling its foreign foes." Another admirer wrote Jefferson: "To you, Sir, doth the groaning republicans over the world look up to for relief."

Jefferson did not let such talk inflate his expectations. "If we spend any in hypothetical discussions," he said, "we shall want time for real business." He knew what he needed do. The "duty of the chief magistrate," Jefferson once said, was "to unite in himself the confidence of the whole people" to "produce a union of the powers of the whole, and point them in a single direction, as if all constituted but one body and one mind." And he knew how hard all of that was. "I sincerely thank you for your congratulations on my election, but this is only the first verse of the chapter," he wrote his friend John Page. "What the last may be nobody can tell."

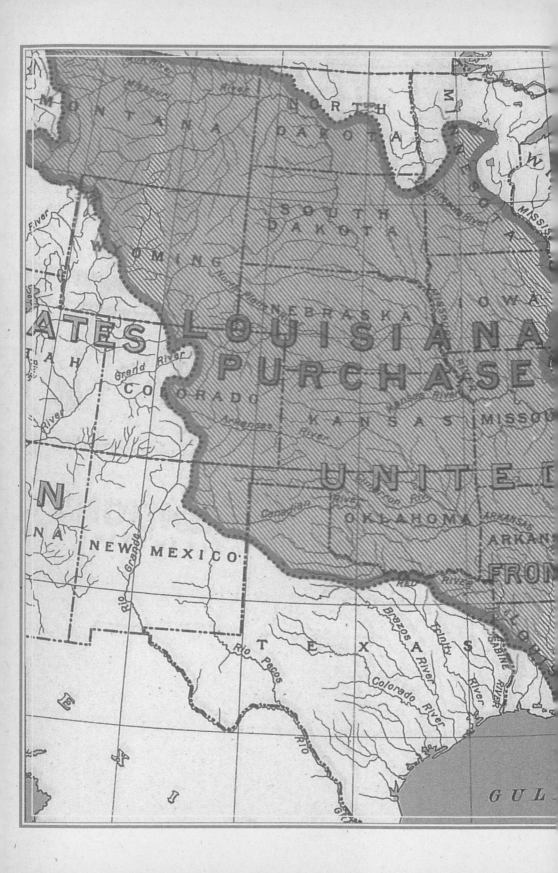

PART VIII

THE PRESIDENT OF THE UNITED STATES

1801 to 1809

All . . . will bear in mind this sacred principle, that though the will of the majority is in all cases to prevail, that will to be rightful must be reasonable; that the minority possess their equal rights, which equal law must protect, and to violate would be oppression. Let us, then, fellow-citizens, unite with one heart and one mind.

—THOMAS JEFFERSON, in his first inaugural address, March 4, 1801

THE PRESIDENT
OF THE UNITED
STATES

1801–1809

In the words of a Jefferson friend, the
Louisiana Purchase, the greatest acquisition
of land in American history, had nothing less
than an "air of enchantment" about it.

THIRTY-TWO

The New Order of Things Begins

You always had the people and now have the government on your side, so that the prospect is as favorable as could be wished. At the same time it must be admitted you have much trouble and difficulty to encounter.

—JAMES MONROE

I know indeed there are monarchists among us.

—THOMAS JEFFERSON

IT WAS NOT the warmest of exchanges. To make arrangements for the inaugural, Jefferson had to write to his cousin John Marshall—the Federalist whom John Adams had named chief justice and who only days before had been a possible rival of Jefferson's for the presidency. "As the two houses have notice of the hour, I presume a precise punctuality to it will be expected from me," Jefferson wrote. Marshall replied that he would "make a point of being punctual."

Both men were on time. As noon approached on

Wednesday, March 4, 1801, President-elect Thomas Jefferson prepared to make the short walk from Conrad and McMunn's to the Capitol. John Adams was not present. The second president had made plans to leave Washington on the four a.m. stage, heading north toward home (he went through New York, it was said, "like a shot"). "Sensible, moderate men of both parties would have been pleased had he tarried until after the installation of his successor," wrote the **Massachusetts Spy**. "It certainly would have had good effect." Yet Adams was still grieving over the death, in November 1800, of his son Charles, and, with Abigail awaiting him at home in Massachusetts, he was more than ready to leave the capital. Though he was to live another quarter of a century, Adams never returned to Washington.

On Capitol Hill cannon fire sounded outside Jefferson's boardinghouse; it was a salute from the District of Columbia's artillery corps. At one point in the morning hours Samuel Harrison Smith called on Jefferson to pick up a package: a copy of the inaugural address, written in Jefferson's small, neat hand, to be set in type and published in the **National Intelligencer**.

At ten o'clock, a company of riflemen from Alexandria, Virginia, had arrived to form a small parade. Shortly before noon, Jefferson stepped outside to meet a detachment of militia officers that escorted him to the inaugural ceremonies. A delegation of congressmen joined him, and the politicians followed a group of officers to the Capitol. Their swords drawn, the militiamen parted to allow Jefferson through, and stood, saluting, as he passed by. After another blast of cannon rang out, echoing across the hilltop village, Jefferson went inside the Capitol building.

About a thousand people awaited him in the Senate chamber, a room one lawmaker described in a letter home to his wife as "magnificent in height, and decorated in a grand style." The room was 86 by 48 feet, the ceiling 41 feet high. Each senator had a desk and a red leather chair. Margaret Bayard Smith wrote that it was "so crowded that I believe not another creature could enter." Members of the House and the Senate rose in deference to Jefferson as he made his way to the well of the room.

After Marshall administered the oath of office, Thomas Jefferson delivered his inaugural address. In his weak voice—few in the crowded room could hear him distinctly—he read one of the most significant state papers in American history, a brief for freedom and forbearance.

> All . . . will bear in mind this sacred principle, that though the will of the majority is in all cases to prevail, that will to be rightful must be reasonable; that the minority possess their equal rights, which equal law must protect, and to violate would be oppression. Let us, then, fellow-citizens, unite with one heart and one

mind. Let us restore to social intercourse that harmony and affection without which liberty and even life itself are but dreary things. . . . Every difference of opinion is not a difference of principle. We have called by different names brethren of the same principle. We are all Republicans, we are all Federalists. If there be any among us who would wish to dissolve this Union or to change its republican form, let them stand undisturbed as monuments of the safety with which error of opinion may be tolerated where reason is left free to combat it. I know, indeed, that some honest men fear that a republican government cannot be strong, that this government is not strong enough; but would the honest patriot, in the full tide of successful experiment, abandon a government which has so far kept us free and firm on the theoretic and visionary fear that this government, the world's best hope, may by possibility want energy to preserve itself? I trust not. I believe this, on the contrary, the strongest government on earth. I believe it the only one where every man, at the call of the law, would fly to the standard of the law, and would meet invasions of the public order as his own personal concern. Sometimes it is said that man cannot be trusted with the government of himself. Can he, then, be trusted with the government of others? Or have we found angels in the forms of kings to govern him? Let history answer this question. . . .

I repair, then, fellow-citizens, to the post you have assigned me. With experience enough in subordinate offices to have seen the difficulties of this the greatest of all, I have learnt to expect that it will rarely fall to the lot of imperfect man to retire from this station with the reputation and the favor which bring him into it. . . . I shall often go wrong through defect of judgment. When right, I shall often be thought wrong by those whose positions will not command a view of the whole ground. I ask your indulgence for my own errors, which will never be intentional, and your support against the errors of others, who may condemn what they would not if seen in all its parts.

The address was a political masterpiece. "Today the new political year commences—The new order of things begins," John Marshall wrote Charles Cotesworth Pinckney in the moments before the inauguration, adding: "The democrats are divided into speculative theorists and absolute terrorists: With the latter I am not disposed to class Mr. Jefferson." Still, "If he arranges himself with them it is not difficult to foresee that much calamity is in store for our country—if he does not they will soon become his enemies and calumniators." Returning to his letter writing at four p.m., Marshall was slightly cheerier. "You will before this reaches you see his inauguration speech," Marshall wrote. "It is in the general well judged and conciliatory."

James Bayard thought it "in political substance better than **we** expected; and not answerable to the expectations of the partisans of the other side." Hamilton admitted that it was "virtually a candid retraction of past misapprehensions, and a pledge to the community, that the new president will not lend himself to dangerous innovations, but in essential points will tread in the steps of his predecessors." To Benjamin Rush, the physician and Jefferson admirer, it was an occasion for thanksgiving. "Old friends who had been separated by party names, and a supposed difference of **principle** in politics for many years, shook hands with each other, immediately after reading it, and discovered, for the first time, that they had differed in **opinion** only, about the best means of promoting the interests of their common country."

In his personal grief, John Adams wrote Jefferson from Quincy, Massachusetts, about his dead son. "It is not possible that anything of the kind should happen to you, and I sincerely wish you may never experience any thing in any degree resembling it." Then Adams added a gracious political note: "This part of the Union is in a state of perfect tranquility and I see nothing to obscure your prospect of a quiet and prosperous administration, which I heartily wish you."

Jefferson was eager to wield the power he had long sought. "We reflect . . . that it is according to nature for the strongest to bear the burden," Thomas Mann Randolph, Jr., wrote to Jefferson, "and we know well that your mind does from nature exult in grand scenes, in ample fields for exertion, in extraordinary toils."

He was to spend his presidential years, he said, "pursuing steadily my object of proving that a people, easy in their circumstances as ours are, are capable of conducting themselves under a government founded not in the fears and follies of man, but on his reason. . . . This is the object now nearest to my heart."

Jefferson privately acknowledged the burdens he faced. "I feel a great load of public favor and of public expectation," he wrote the day after the inauguration. "More confidence is placed in me than my qualifications merit, and I dread the disappointment of my friends."

Whether seeking the approval of his father, his mother, his teachers, his contemporaries, or his countrymen, Jefferson had moved through life at once exhilarated and exhausted by the role of patriarch. Raised to be responsible for the lives and welfare of others, he knew nothing else. He had thought much about human nature and human government, and he believed it his duty to bring what in his inaugural he had called "harmony and affection" to the life of the American nation.

From war making to economic life to territorial acquisition to federal spending to subpoenas and the sharing of information with Congress and the courts, Jefferson maintained or expanded the authority of the presidential office. He was fortunate to preside over Republican congressional majorities; the Senate margin grew from a narrow 17 Republicans to 15 Federalists in 1801–1803 to 28–6 by Jefferson's last year in office. The Republican rhetoric of limited and minimal government was heartfelt but hardly controlling. Jefferson had reached the pinnacle by articulating the ideal but acting pragmatically. He could have resigned the vice presidency to protest the Alien and Sedition Acts, for instance; he had, instead, preserved his position in the existing political order, awaiting the hour when he might ascend to the summit. As president he fully intended to rule in the way he had risen.

The story of his two terms in the President's House is one of a lifelong student of control and power bringing all of his virtues and vices to the largest possible stage. Federalists who expected him to begin the world over again by seeking to minimize the executive office misjudged him.

Critics of Jefferson have argued that his vision of an agrarian nation with a weak central government puts him on the wrong side of history. It was Hamilton, they say, who correctly anticipated a future that would require a system of capital and large-scale action to create the means of national greatness.

This critique of Jefferson, while familiar, is incomplete. Jefferson sent a reassuring signal to the manufacturing and financial interests who had learned to fear him as a champion of the agrarian over the commercial. "One imputation in particular has been repeated till it seems as if some at least believed it: that I am an enemy to commerce," Jefferson wrote a correspondent on Wednesday, February 18, 1801. "They admit me a friend to agriculture, and suppose me an enemy to the only means of disposing of its produce."

The presidency Jefferson left in 1809 was rich in precedent for vigorous, decisive, and often unilateral action. It is not too much to say that Jefferson used Hamiltonian means to pursue Jeffersonian ends. He embraced ultimate power subtly but surely.

Open political warfare was not for him; he preferred to impress himself on the course of events without bombast or drama, leading so quietly that popular history tends to make too little of his achievements as president.

He understood the country was open to—even eager for—a government that seemed less intrusive and overbearing than the one Washington and Adams had created. In his eight years in office Jefferson brought the national debt down from $83 million to $57 million. He cut taxes and spending. In a new time of peace—the Quasi-War ended six months before his inauguration—Jefferson reduced military spending to prewar levels and downsized the Navy to thirteen frigates. For the moment, he believed, it was impossible for the United States to attempt to rival the naval powers of Europe. His maritime strategy was one of defense, except in regard to the Barbary pirates, whom he continued to pursue and combat.

Jefferson had long cared about two things: American liberty and American strength. For eight years he summoned all the power he believed he required to make America more like what he thought it should be. In the partisan wars of the 1790s, many of his foes had misinterpreted his disposition toward individual freedom rather than toward Hamiltonian authority as dreaminess and weakness. They would learn—quickly and unmistakably—that they were wrong.

The outward reformation of Federalist America began on the morning of the inauguration, when Jefferson declined to wear a ceremonial sword to the swearing-in, breaking tradition with Washington and Adams. After the solemnities, Jefferson took his dinner as usual at Conrad and McMunn's. He soon sold President Adams's coaches and silver harnesses, another symbolic strike against Federalist trappings.

The Adamses had moved into the President's

House on the first day of November 1800. Abigail Adams hung laundry in the East Room, which Mrs. Adams had called the "great unfinished audience-room." Jefferson now installed his secretary, Meriwether Lewis, there. For his own office the president took a room in the southwest corner of the first floor looking out toward the Potomac. There was a table with drawers for Jefferson's tools and knickknacks; he kept geraniums in the window and mockingbirds at hand.

He liked quiet but could not stand silence. He was usually humming or singing softly to himself, and from the early 1770s forward Jefferson kept pet mockingbirds. He cherished the birds for their music, and in hours of contemplative leisure he sometimes opened their cage to allow them to flit about his private suite at Monticello or his President's House office.

Jefferson bought his first bird from a slave of his father-in-law John Wayles in Charles City County in November 1772. It took another twenty years for mockingbirds to reach Monticello naturally. "Learn all the children to venerate it as a superior being in the form of a bird, or as a being which will haunt them if any harm is done to itself or its eggs," Jefferson wrote home, when he learned of the mockingbirds' arrival on the mountaintop.

As president, Jefferson kept a bird he named Dick, hanging its cage in the window in his office amid geraniums and roses. According to Margaret Bayard Smith, Dick "was the constant companion of his solitary and studious hours," sometimes settling on Jefferson's shoulder or accepting "food from his lips. Often when he retired to his chamber it would hop up the stairs after him and while he took his siesta, would sit on his couch and pour forth its melodious strains."

As Jefferson took over the presidential mansion, he ordered the demolition of an existing wooden privy on the lawn and had the parts for "water closets . . . of superior construction" sent from Philadelphia. Accustomed to mastery at Monticello, Jefferson sought to establish the same dynamic at the President's House. He decided which pieces of furniture should stay and which should go. The room Adams had used for levees (the modern State Dining Room) was the one he had chosen for his working office, and an oval room on the first floor (the modern Blue Room) was made into a drawing room. He ordered the hanging of household bells in the mansion so that he could summon servants at will—a convenience contemplated by the Adamses but completed by Jefferson in his first months. His chief domestic, Rapin, kept Jefferson informed about the progress of renovations and construction. (Etienne Lemaire soon became Jefferson's majordomo in Washington.)

The members of his cabinet represented the major regions of the country. James Madison of Virginia

The Paris of Thomas Jefferson's ministerial years. He lived in the Hôtel de Langeac.

The storming of the Bastille on July 14, 1789.

Writ of manumission for James Hemings, who served Jefferson as a chef. James Hemings was a son of Elizabeth Hemings and a brother of Sally Hemings.

The arguments between Jefferson and Hamilton, shown here conferring with President Washington, had implications that stretched far beyond the life of Washington's first administration. Though both Jefferson and Hamilton opposed each other mightily, they were both patriots, fighting for the good of the country, as they defined that good.

John Jay was a critical Founder, an architect of American foreign policy, chief justice of the United States, and, as governor of New York, the man who refused a request of Alexander Hamilton's that might have denied Jefferson the presidency in 1800.

A diplomat and statesman, Rufus King of Massachusetts was the Federalist candidate for vice president in 1804, the year Jefferson won reelection, and in 1808, when James Madison succeeded Jefferson.

A banner commemorating Jefferson's 1800 presidential victory.

The President's House, circa 1814, the era of the James Madison administration.

Jefferson's design for the President's House, submitted for consideration in 1792.

Described dismissively as a "virago" by Jefferson, Elizabeth Merry was the wife of British minister Anthony Merry. A social skirmish over diplomatic and dinner-party precedence created political tension during Jefferson's years in the President's House.

Margaret Bayard Smith, Washington chronicler, Jefferson friend, and wife of Republican editor Samuel Harrison Smith. Her papers provide an intimate glimpse of life in the capital and of Jefferson in retirement at Monticello.

The treaty ceding Louisiana to Jefferson's United States from Napoleonic France.

Erratic and cutting, John Randolph of Roanoke led a small breakaway faction of Republicans from the Jefferson administration.

Appointed to the bench just before Jefferson took office as president, Chief Justice John Marshall was a shrewd defender of the Federalist interest and architect of the principle of judicial review. He and his cousin Jefferson were longtime rivals; Marshall married the daughter of Jefferson's first love.

George Clinton of New York was a decided Republican from the early 1790s forward. He succeeded Aaron Burr as vice president for Jefferson's second presidential term and remained in office as Madison's vice president.

The patriot-physician Benjamin Rush of Pennsylvania was a longtime friend and colleague of Jefferson's; they shared passions for politics, science, and philosophy. It was Rush who brokered the epistolary reconciliation between Jefferson and John Adams in 1812.

Isaac Granger Jefferson, a Monticello slave who left posterity a valuable oral history of life in Jefferson's universe.

Overwhelmed by the patriarch's debts, Jefferson's heirs could not save Monticello in the wake of Jefferson's death in 1826.

A Moment on Mulberry Row, by Nathaniel Gibbs, attempts to depict the life of enslaved people on Jefferson's estate.

From her deathbed, Jefferson's wife, Patty, was said to have given this servant bell to Sally Hemings.

Ellen Randolph Coolidge, a Jefferson granddaughter, visited Monticello after her grandfather's death and could not help but feel his presence in the house he loved so.

Ann Cary Randolph Bankhead was a favorite Jefferson granddaughter; her husband, Charles Bankhead, was a troubled alcoholic who nearly killed his wife's brother, Thomas Jefferson Randolph.

Jefferson's memorandum on his grave and epitaph—one that underscored his Enlightenment achievements over those of his long political career: author of the Declaration of Independence, of the Virginia bill for religious liberty, and founder of the University of Virginia. Unmentioned were the offices he held through a tumultuous and consequential public life from his election to the House of Burgesses in 1769 until he left the presidency in 1809.

was appointed secretary of state; Albert Gallatin of Pennsylvania accepted the Treasury Department; Henry Dearborn from Massachusetts became secretary of war; Levi Lincoln of Massachusetts was to be attorney general; Robert Smith of Maryland became secretary of the navy.

The appointment of Gallatin was one of the shrewdest. Born in Geneva in 1761, Gallatin came to the United States in 1780, served in the Revolution, taught French at Harvard, mastered finance, and held a variety of elective posts (including, briefly, the Senate seat from which he was ejected in 1794 for failing to meet the citizenship requirement). He was a key Republican leader in the House of Representatives during the years of the Alien and Sedition Acts and the Quasi-War with France from 1798 to 1800. Gallatin and his second wife, Hannah, got along well with Jefferson, who trusted Gallatin's financial and political counsel. He would serve as secretary of the Treasury from 1801 until 1814.

Listing the Republican gains in Congress and in the states, the French diplomat Louis-André Pichon told Paris that Jefferson stood at a remarkable pinnacle. The fall of the Federalists from their seeming invincibility during the fever of the Quasi-War was striking—"one cannot help," Pichon said, "but be astonished by its rapidity." Even New England was not immune to the rise of the Republicans. "Henceforth, we can predict that Mr. Jefferson will have only a weak opposition," Pichon wrote, noting that the expansion of western populations would only add to Jefferson's power since such people would be "invariably opposed to the cities on the coast."

In Jefferson's enthusiasm, the new president fell back on his favored nautical imagery. "The storm through which we have passed has been tremendous indeed," Jefferson wrote John Dickinson two days after the inauguration. "The tough sides of our Argosy have been thoroughly tried. Her strength has stood the waves into which she was steered with a view to sink her. We shall put her on her republican tack, and she will now show by the beauty of her motion the skill of her builders."

To the English scientist and theologian Joseph Priestley he allowed his historical imagination to take flight. "We can no longer say there is nothing new under the sun. For this whole chapter in the history of man is new. The great extent of our republic is new. Its sparse habitation is new. The mighty wave of public opinion which has rolled over it is new."

Such was the idealistic Jefferson. But he was also realistic. "I am sensible how far I should fall short of effecting all the reformation which reason would suggest and experience approve, were I free to do whatever I thought best," he wrote. "But when we reflect how difficult it is to move or inflect the great machine of society, how impossible to advance the notions of a whole people suddenly to ideal right, we see the wisdom of Solon's remark that no more good must be attempted than the nation can bear, and that will be chiefly to reform the waste of public money, and thus drive away the vultures who prey on it, and improve some little on old routines."

Even more bluntly and vividly, Jefferson referred to the Federalists as madmen: "Their leaders are a hospital of incurables, and as such entitled to be protected and taken care of as other insane persons are." Still, there was hope—for to Jefferson, where there was freedom, there was always hope. "The times have been awful," he said, "but they have proved a useful truth that the good citizen must never despair of the commonwealth."

Priestley hoped, too, that "**Politics** will not make you forget what is due to **science**." Jefferson, in fact, saw them as connected. A politics of personal liberty created a sense of free inquiry. A man liberated from monarchical or hereditary limitations stood a greater chance of possessing a mind free to roam and to grow and to create and to innovate in a climate in which citizens lived together in essential harmony and affection. This was Jefferson's ideal republic—and he was committed to making it real.

He did not lack for advice on how to govern in the wake of the narrow decision in the House. "Many friends may grow cool from disappointment," wrote James Monroe, "the violent who have their passions too much excited will experience mortification in not finding them fully gratified: in addition . . . . the discomfited Tory party, profiting of past divisions and follies which have contributed much to overwhelm them, will reunite their scattered force against us. . . It will intrigue with foreign powers and therefore ought to be watched." Tench Coxe issued a warning: "**The dangers to our form of government, at home and abroad, yet exist,**" he wrote Jefferson.

According to Virginia's William Branch Giles, "The ejected party is now almost universally considered as having been employed in conjunction with G.B. in a scheme for the total destruction of the liberties of the people."

On any given day Jefferson dealt with a range of issues and problems from his office on the first floor of the presidential mansion. Appointments to office, politics in New England, the Barbary Coast, agricultural policy, the West Indies, French and English diplomacy: Paper flowed in and out of Jefferson's hands.

Neither Patsy nor Polly came to live with him in Washington, nor is there any record that Sally Hemings ever left Albemarle County to visit the President's House. A social creature, Jefferson nevertheless lived in relative domestic isolation in Washington. Only Meriwether Lewis kept house with him in the unfinished mansion. Jefferson said that they lived like "two mice in a church."

He felt lonely early in his tenure. His colleagues were slow to assemble. "I am still at a great loss," he said as he settled in. Neither the James Madisons nor the Albert Gallatins were yet in residence in the capital. When the Gallatins arrived, they received a blanket invitation from Jefferson, who asked them to dine every day. It would, he said, be "a real favor." But he was disappointed when the Gallatins decided to move farther away from the President's House. "The city is rather sickly, my family has their share, and they are extremely anxious on that account to move on Capitol hill," Gallatin wrote Jefferson in August. The Treasury secretary was quick to reassure the president that he would remain nearby: "It is substituting precisely 20 minutes ride to ten."

Unlike many of his fellow officials and lawmakers, Jefferson liked the new capital city. "We find this a very agreeable country residence," he wrote. "Good society, and enough of it, and free from the noise, the heat, the stench, and the bustle of a close built town."

Building a new American future required redeeming the excesses of the Federalist past, and Jefferson issued presidential pardons for some of the printers convicted under the Sedition Act. The case of his old ally James Thomson Callender, who had been convicted, fined, and imprisoned, was the most personal for him; Callender's pardon was dated Monday, March 16, 1801.

Callender had three children to support and wanted his $200 fine to the government refunded. It was not forthcoming, and by Sunday, April 12,

1801, Callender was "hurt" by the "disappoint-ment" of not having his fine repaid. "I now begin to know what ingratitude is," he said.

Jefferson wanted to keep the Republican version of reality alive in the minds of the people. On Fri-day, March 20, 1801, he asked Albert Gallatin to reply to a circular letter by the Federalist Robert Goodloe Harper that extolled the virtues of the Washington-Adams years. It was, Jefferson said, a "false and frivolous" account, and "the other side of the medal requires to be shown." In a sign of good care, Jefferson did not put his name to the request.

Orchestrating Republican writings from behind the scenes was nothing new for Jefferson, and it is revealing that he turned to Gallatin now that the administration had commenced. Callender, whom Jefferson had patronized in years gone by, had been out of favor since 1800.

Why did Jefferson turn on Callender? Part of the reason may lie in a recurring feature of American politics: a successful president's discomfort with the less respectable men and means that got him to vic-tory. There is usually a moment in the life of a new president when he begins to see himself not as an as-pirant desperate to win but as a statesman above the squalor and the sweat of actual vote getting. Rising men do not like to be reminded of the smell of the stables; dignitaries dislike recollections of the dust through which they have come. The polemicist had been useful on the journey, but there was apparently no place for his acidic attacks now that the popular votes were cast and his machinations had been put on display at trial. In Callender, in the pursuit of power, Jefferson made a devil's bargain: He supported and consorted with a man skilled in the dark arts of partisan warfare, but he seems not to have considered that the same man might one day turn on him.

When repayment for the fine was not forthcoming, Callender told Madison, "Mr. Jefferson has not returned one shilling of my fine. . . . I am not a man who is either to be oppressed or plundered with impunity." Callender decided that the fine was important, but perhaps a sinecure as postmaster of Richmond would be even better. Traveling to Washington, he met with Madison. "The money was refused with cold disdain, which is quite as provoking as direct insolence," Callender wrote. "Little Madison . . . exerted a great deal of eloquence to show that it would be improper to repay the money at Washington."

There were many factors at work. "Do you know that besides his other passions he is under the tyranny of that of love?" Madison asked Monroe. "The object of his flame is in Richmond. I did not ask her name; but presume her to be young and beautiful, in his eyes at least, and in a sphere above him. He has flattered himself into a persuasion that the emoluments and reputation of a post-office would obtain her in marriage. Of these recommendations, however, he is sent back in despair."

Madison also briefed the president, who dispatched Meriwether Lewis to give Callender fifty dollars to tide him over until the fine could be repaid in full. Callender's attitude toward Lewis suggested that Jefferson might well have a larger problem on his hands than he realized. "His language to Capt. Lewis was very high toned," Jefferson wrote Monroe. "He intimated that he was in possession of things which he could and would use of a certain case: that he received the 50 D not as charity but as a due, in fact as hush money; that I knew what he expected, viz, a certain office, and more to this effect."

Angry and hurt, Callender awaited the hour of vengeance.

In the President's House, Jefferson craved control. In November 1801, he sent a note to his cabinet about how his government was to work—and as usual with questions of process, it was a document about power.

Jefferson wanted to be in on every detail, and he framed his approach to the public business in terms of following President Washington's precedent. Nearly all letters of business had passed through Washington's hands. "By this means," Jefferson told his own cabinet, President Washington "was always in accurate possession of all facts and proceedings in every part of the Union, and to whatsoever department they related," Jefferson said.

This was how Jefferson wanted things, too. He felt, he said, "a sense of obligation imposed on me by the public will to meet personally the duties to which they have appointed me." And so it would be. He looked forward to intelligence of any kind, telling Gallatin that papers "conveying information of **what is passing** or of **the state of things,** are . . . desirable."

He wanted to know everything. He **had** to know everything.

THIRTY-THREE

A Confident President

The measures recommended by the President
are all popular in all parts of the nation.
—JOHN QUINCY ADAMS

Here are so many wants, so many affections
and passions engaged, so varying in their interests and objects, that no one can be concili-
ated without revolting others.
—THOMAS JEFFERSON, on the political
culture of Washington, D.C.

BY MID-NOVEMBER 1801, the presidency settled
into what Jefferson called "a steady and uniform course." He worked from ten to thirteen
hours a day at his writing table, doing paperwork and
receiving callers from early morning until midday;
that gave him, he figured, "an interval of 4 hours
for riding, dining and a little unbending." At noon
he tried to leave the President's House for a ride or a
walk before returning to be "engaged with company
till candle-light." It was only at night—and it was

the rare night—that he spent time on the "mechanics, mathematics, philosophy etc." that he loved.

Jefferson was keen about his privacy. He was glad to see one particular servant at the President's House go. "I had good reason to believe he read the papers which happened to be on my table whenever I went out of my cabinet; and it was impossible for me to lock them up every time I stepped out of the room."

Jefferson's hours were vulnerable. On one occasion he had to move quickly to quell some tension with a supporter. "Some enemy, whom we know not, is sowing tares among us," Jefferson wrote Nathaniel Macon, the Republican Speaker of the House from North Carolina. There was nothing to it, Jefferson said, but they should talk things over. "This evening my company may perhaps stay late: but tomorrow evening or the next I can be alone," he told Macon.

On the eve of each congressional session, he held engagements with friends whom he knew he would not see again until the lawmakers left Washington. "As Congress will meet this day week, we begin now to be in the bustle of preparation. I am this week getting through the dining all my friends of this place, to be ready for the Congressional campaign," he wrote his granddaughter Ellen Wayles Randolph Coolidge. "When that begins, between the occupations of business and of entertainment, I shall become an unpunctual correspondent."

One such friend was Margaret Bayard Smith, who, with her husband, Samuel Harrison Smith, grew close to Jefferson and to Dolley and James Madison in these years. The Madisons stayed briefly with Jefferson in the President's House before setting up their own home, first on Pennsylvania Avenue four blocks toward Georgetown, and then settling at 1333 F Street. There Dolley established a hospitable salon within their three-story brick house; her dining room and parlors were full of politics and what she called "fashionable talk" (and the occasional game of cards; she was fond of gambling).

In May 1801, with the gathering of the cabinet, Mrs. Smith said the capital was "as gay as in the winter; the arrival of all the secretaries seems to give new animation to business, and the settlements of their families affords employment to some of our tradesmen." At a small dinner in the President's House with the Madisons, Mrs. Smith sat next to Jefferson and was entranced anew by his "easy, candid and gentle manners." Watching the president and James Madison in the drawing room later, Mrs. Smith thought the two "were so easy and familiar that they produced no restraint."

The Gallatins were also familiar faces in the president's circle. They decided to live on M Street near Thirty-second, and Mrs. Gallatin was a congenial, if less than beautiful, woman. "Her person is far less attractive than either her mind or her heart, and yet I do not wish her to have any other than that which she has got," Albert Gallatin had candidly written of his wife at the time of their marriage. "Her understanding is good; she is as well informed as most young ladies; she is perfectly simple and unaffected; she loves me and she is a pretty good democrat."

Jefferson governed personally. He knew no other way. He had watched Peyton Randolph lead the House of Burgesses, sometimes in meetings in Randolph's deep-red clapboard house at Nicholson and North England streets in Williamsburg. From his time spent in the Confederation Congress and presiding over the Senate for four years as vice president, Jefferson appreciated how to handle lawmakers, for he had long been one. Even then a president's attentions meant the world to politicians and ordinary people alike. For all his low-key republican symbolism, Jefferson understood that access to the president himself could make all the difference in statecraft—hence his dinners with lawmakers and his willingness to receive callers.

The strategy worked. In the Jefferson years Republicans were heard to acknowledge that "the President's dinners had silenced them" at moments when they were inclined to vote against the administration.

He believed in constant conversation between the president and lawmakers, for Jefferson thought that "if the members are to know nothing but what is important enough to be put into a public message . . . it becomes a government of chance and not of design." The president had to be able to trust lawmakers with insights and opinions that he might not offer a broader audience, creating a sense of intimacy and common purpose. Making speeches at other politicians—or appearing to be only making speeches at them—was not the best way to enlist their allegiance or their aid, nor to govern well.

Jefferson preferred to project power without being showy about it. "What sort of government is that of the U.S.?" Napoleon once asked a French traveler who had just returned from spending time with President Jefferson. "One, Sire," the traveler said, "that is neither seen or felt." That was precisely what Jefferson wanted the world to think.

Another caller in the President's House, the European naturalist Alexander von Humboldt, visited Jefferson in the cabinet room. Observing that a ferociously negative Federalist newspaper was lying about here at the center of Republican power, Baron Humboldt asked Jefferson, "Why are these libels allowed? Why is not this libelous journal suppressed, or its editor at least, fined and imprisoned?"

The question gave Jefferson a perfect opening. "Put that paper in your pocket, Baron, and should you hear the reality of our liberty, the freedom of our press, questioned, show this paper, and tell where you found it."

President Washington had consciously cut a formal figure; President Jefferson received morning and midafternoon callers as though he had just—as he sometimes had—come in from a ride. "Mr. Jefferson has put aside all showing off; he greets guests in slovenly clothes and without the least formality," Louis-André Pichon wrote Paris in 1802. "He leaves every day on foot or on horseback, the most often on horseback, and without even being accompanied by a servant."

Jefferson knew who he was, and he knew his place in the world, so he had nothing to prove by constantly appearing perfectly turned out. Quite the opposite: Often only the well born or the socially serene can forgo badges of status—the neglect or absence of which is in itself a badge of status. Jefferson wore different combinations of old frock coats, velveteen breeches, yarn stockings, and ancient slippers.

When the British diplomat Augustus J. Foster was presented to Jefferson, Foster found that the president "behaved very civilly in general." In the President's House, "the door opened suddenly" and there was Jefferson. "He thrust out his hand to me as he does to everybody, and desired me to sit down," Foster wrote his mother. "Luckily for me I have been in Turkey, and am quite at home in this primeval simplicity of manners."

Foster was surprised at Jefferson's appearance. "He is dressed and looks extremely like a very plain farmer, and wears his slippers down at his heels," Foster wrote home. Unlike Foster, Joseph Story of Massachusetts, a lawyer and legislator who went on the Supreme Court in 1811, understood what Jefferson was doing. The man who obsessed over Europe's view of the taste and culture of America was not a provincial slob. He was, rather, who he was. "You know Virginians have some pride in appearing in simple habiliments," wrote Story, "and are willing to rest their claim to attention upon their force of mind and suavity of manners."

Edward Thornton, another British diplomat, shared Story's sense of things. Jefferson may have been attracted by the "leveling spirit" of republicanism, Thornton wrote in a dispatch home, but none of it was evident in the President's House, which was "far better arranged than in the time of Mr. Adams, or in the economy of his household and in the style of his living, which are upon a more expensive scale than during [the administrations] of either of the former Presidents, but with less of form and ostentation than was observed by General Washington."

Jefferson's confidence in himself and his leadership was unmistakable. He believed the results of the 1800 election were a mandate for change, and while he usually exercised his power quietly, he did exercise it, keeping himself in command of the executive branch and making his wishes known to his allies in Congress. John Quincy Adams believed Jefferson's "whole system of administration seems founded upon this principle of carrying through the legislature measures by his personal or official influence." Jefferson tended to get his way as he had for so long: by smoothly but definitively bending the world to his will as much as he could.

He was more of a chess player than a traditional warrior, thinking out his moves and executing them subtly rather than reacting to events viscerally and showily. In Washington, in fact, he found himself in need of a book he had left at Monticello: a work of strategy by the chess master François-André Danican Philidor. It was important enough to him that he recalled its place precisely: "You will find [it] in the book room, 2nd press on the left from the door of the entrance," he wrote Thomas Mann Randolph, Jr.

At a cabinet meeting in the middle of May 1801, Jefferson and his advisers debated the Barbary States. At issue was whether the United States ought to dispatch a squadron under Commodore Richard Dale to the Mediterranean in a display of power to discourage further piracy against American shipping. "All concur in the expediency of [the] cruise," Jefferson noted.

He wanted to make sure they concurred in something else, too: that the naval forces were authorized—by executive, not legislative, authority—to "search for and destroy the enemy's vessels wherever they can find them." Should Dale find that any of the Barbary States had declared war on the United States, he was to "place [his] ships in a situation to chastise them." Should he find that all of them had declared war, he was told to distribute his force in such a manner "so as best to protect our commerce and chastise their insolence—by sinking, burning, or destroying their ships and vessels wherever you shall find them."

On Saturday, August 1, 1801, Andrew Sterett of the **Enterprize,** who was serving under Dale, defeated the Tripolitan vessel **Tripoli** near Malta. "Too long . . . have those barbarians been suffered to trample on the sacred faith of treaties, on the rights and laws of human nature," Jefferson told Sterett. "You have shown to your countrymen that that enemy cannot meet bravery and skill united." Sterett hobbled the Barbary ship and let it loose, continuing on his way. In the wake of the episode, Jefferson described the American victory and asked Congress to authorize offensive actions against aggressors in the Mediterranean.

Yet he had clearly already provided such authority without Congress back in the spring. Sterett had been acting under those orders. Here Jefferson was effectively exerting control over military and foreign policy while appearing to defer to the legislature. It was typical Jefferson: having his way without precipitating confrontation or a distracting crisis.

Congress fell into Jefferson's hands, essentially retroactively approving the orders to Dale and granting the president even wider authority in the wake of the Sterett action. The executive, Congress declared, was "to cause to be done all such other acts of precaution or hostility as the state of war will justify, and may, in his opinion, require."

Under this provision, Jefferson attempted an elaborate operation to replace the pasha of Tripoli, who had assassinated his own father and a brother, with a more compliant brother, Hamet, who had escaped to Tunis. Over the next several years the Americans unsuccessfully attempted to effect a military overthrow of the regime in Tripoli in Hamet's favor—an undertaking that had grown out of Jefferson's initial unilateral projection of power in the region. The man who had, as secretary of state, argued against broad construction in the case of the establishment of the Bank of the United States, found that his own powers as president benefited from the broadest kind of construction.

Meriwether Lewis rode up Capitol Hill from the President's House. It was Tuesday, December 8, 1801, and Lewis, as the president's private secretary, was slated to carry Jefferson's first annual message to Congress.

The world was largely at peace, Jefferson said, save for the Barbary States. He was reserved but steely, noting that he trusted the news of Sterett's victory would be "a testimony to the world that it is not a want of [bravery] which makes us seek their peace; but a conscientious desire to direct the energies of our nation to the multiplication of the human race, and not to its destruction."

Jefferson's campaign to reduce federal taxes and spending, to suppress the new courts, and to allow the states to take the lead in determining the course of domestic affairs marked a significant turn from the basic direction of the country under Washington and Adams.

The reaction to the president's message was warm. "Nothing can exceed our exultation on account of the president's message," said John Taylor of Caroline, "and . . . nothing can exceed the depression of the monarchists."

The Federalists were less enamored with the course of things. "Virginia literally dominates," Robert Troup wrote Rufus King in April 1802. "Jefferson is the supreme director of measures—he has no levee days—observes no ceremony—often sees company in an undress, sometimes with his slippers on—always accessible to, and very familiar with, the sovereign people."

Connecticut congressman Roger Griswold grasped the substance behind the Jeffersonian symbolism. After the annual message came to the Capitol, Griswold wrote:

Under this administration nothing is to remain as it was. Every minutia is to be changed. When Mr. Adams was President, the door of the president's House opened to the East. Mr. Jefferson has closed that door and opened a new door to the West. General Washington and Mr. Adams opened every session of Congress with a speech. Mr. Jefferson delivers no speech, but makes his communication by a written message. I fear

that you Aristocrats of New England will think
these important changes unnecessary and be apt
to say that they are made with a view only to
change, but you ought to recollect that you are
neither Philosophers or skilled in the mysteries
of Democratic policy.

In the **New-York Evening Post,** Alexander Hamilton wrote that Jefferson's message should "alarm all who are anxious for the safety of our government, for the responsibility and welfare of our nation." His portrait of Jefferson was venomous and laced with envy and anger. "Mine is an odd destiny," Hamilton wrote Gouverneur Morris in these months. "Perhaps no man in the United States has sacrificed and done more for the present Constitution than myself; and . . . I am still laboring to prop the frail and worthless fabric. . . . What can I do better than withdraw from the scene? Every day proves to me more and more that this American world was not meant for me."

The world did feel more Jeffersonian than Hamiltonian in the closing days of 1801. "Every day we see vanish the phantoms that the enemies of Mr. Jefferson had built up to discredit him," Pichon wrote his superiors in Paris.

One day a vast cheese arrived for the president from the people of Cheshire, Massachusetts. It was a curiosity that became an emblem of republican tribute in the popular culture. "It is not the last stone in the Bastille, nor is it of any great consequence as an article of worth; but as a free-will offering, we hope it will be received," said the citizens of Cheshire.

God and politics were on Jefferson's mind on New Year's Day 1802. In Colebrook, Connecticut, in October 1801, the Danbury Baptist Association had assembled to applaud Jefferson's views on religious liberty.

In reply, he offered a testament to freedom of conscience that unsettled his Federalist foes. "Believing with you that religion is a matter which lies solely between Man and his God, that he owes account to none other for his faith or his worship, that the legitimate powers of government reach actions only, and not opinions, I contemplate with sovereign reverence that act of the whole American people which declared that their legislature should 'make no law respecting an establishment of religion, or prohibiting the free exercise thereof,' thus building a wall of separation between Church and State."

Benjamin Rush had helped inform Jefferson's views on church and state in 1800. "I agree with you likewise in your wishes to keep religion and government independent of each other," Rush had told Jefferson. "Were it possible for St. Paul to rise from his grave at the present juncture, he would say to the clergy who are now so active in settling the political affairs of the world: 'Cease from your political labors your kingdom is not of **this** world. Read my epistles. In no part of them will you perceive me aiming to depose a pagan emperor, or to place a Christian upon a throne. Christianity disdains to receive support from human governments.' "

Among Federalists, the contempt for Jefferson ran high. George Cabot of Massachusetts feared what he called "the terrible evils of democracy," but believed Jefferson was unstoppable. The evidence of the winter and the spring of 1801–02 suggested Cabot's assessment of Jefferson's power was right.

In these months Jefferson convinced Congress to abolish all internal taxes, authorize military force against Tripoli, found the U.S. Military Academy at West Point, ease naturalization rules, and, perhaps most significantly, repeal the Judiciary Act of 1801, the law that had expanded federal jurisdiction and created additional courts and judgeships filled by Federalists before Adams left office.

Told that the president was redesigning a set of medals intended as gifts for Indian tribes, former secretary of war James McHenry took a wry tone. "Would to God that he had confined his revolutionary genius to things of no greater importance, we should have had less today to apprehend for the fate of the Constitution and our country."

Beginning with the struggle in the House for the presidency, Aaron Burr had become a seemingly uncontrollable political actor in Jefferson's Republican Party. Partly because of the Republicans' belief that Burr had not energetically shut down Federalist efforts to use Burr to deny Jefferson victory in 1800–1801, and partly because of the complications of New York state politics—Burr represented just one faction—Jefferson chose to thwart Burr's ambitions once the presidential contest was settled. One Burrite, Matthew L. Davis, called on the president to plead his own case for a federal post. Hearing Davis out, Jefferson noticed a buzzing fly and deftly reached out and snatched it out of the air. The gesture was hardly reassuring to the visitor: a president quick enough and wily enough to snag a fly was unlikely to be moved in any direction he did not wish to move. Davis did not get the job, and the snub, Gallatin remarked, was seen as a snub of Burr. "There is hardly a man who meddles with politics in New York," Gallatin told Jefferson, "who does not believe that Davis's rejection is owing to Burr's recommendation."

Hamilton shrewdly assessed the political tension between President Jefferson and Vice President Burr. "There is certainly a most serious schism between the Chief and his heir apparent; a schism absolutely incurable, because founded in the breasts of both is the rivalship of an insatiable and unprincipled ambition," Hamilton wrote King in June 1802. "Mr. Burr will surely arrive at the Presidency," wrote Louis-André Pichon. "Nobody conducts better than him a political intrigue."

At a celebratory Federalist dinner in honor of

George Washington's birthday in the capital in 1802, Burr arrived unexpectedly and cleverly "asked whether he was an intruder—he was answered in the negative—and treated with becoming civility," Troup reported to King. Burr bided his time a bit and then asked whether he might propose a toast. Given the floor, Burr raised a glass and said: "**To the union of all honest men.**" The implication was clear to the gathering. "This was generally received by the Federalists as an offer on his part to coalesce," Troup said.

On Thursday, July 1, 1802, Republicans celebrated Jefferson's repeal of internal taxes. On the Fourth of July in Charleston, South Carolina, the Reverend Richard Furman linked the American Revolution to Jefferson's administration, arguing that the two events were divinely ordained. "The special feasts and rejoicings on the 1st of July, and the toasts of the 4th of July, as they have been received from different quarters prove that all republicans are pleased with them."

Pichon was privately critical of Jefferson's administration. "The principles which direct it are evident: the party spirit has passion, an ambition which wants to conserve the power in pleasing the greatest number, a singular propensity to new ideas, and a childish vanity concealed under an exterior of simplicity." Pichon complained, too, of Jefferson's excluding him and his wife from an invitation extended to houseguests of the French envoy.

"That would scarcely happen in a capital city," said Pichon. "It's a pointed rudeness in this desert."

The Federalists, though, realized the political facts. "Jefferson is the idol to whom all devotion is paid; and Burr will doubtless be dropped at another election, if they can do it without endangering Jefferson," Troup wrote King in April 1802.

Though he never went beyond Hot Springs, Virginia, Jefferson loved the West. Twenty years before, he had proposed an expedition to be led by George Rogers Clark. A decade later, in 1793, Jefferson took the lead for the American Philosophical Society in planning an exploratory journey by the French botanist André Michaux. Neither the Clark mission nor the Michaux effort came to pass, and it finally took a threat from the British to press Jefferson (and the United States) into action. The anxiety was by now ancient: that the British (as well as the Spanish and the French and various Indian tribes) would establish or, depending on the circumstances, extend holdings in the New World to hem the United States in, thus limiting American growth and creating the constant possibility of invasion.

The new occasion was the publication of the fur trader Alexander Mackenzie's book **Voyages from Montreal**. Reading it in the summer of 1802, Jefferson was struck by Mackenzie's account of traveling through Canada and reaching the Pacific in 1793.

Mackenzie wrote enthusiastically of the prospects for Britain in the farther reaches of North America, arguing "it requires only the countenance and support of the British government" to "secure the trade of that country to its subjects." There was more: "Many political reasons"—presumably including the possible restoration of the power of the British Empire over its lost colonies—"must present themselves to the mind of every [man] acquainted with the enlarged system and capacities of British commerce," Mackenzie had suggested. It was all connected to an old Jefferson fear, one he had articulated to George Rogers Clark in 1783: "I am afraid," Jefferson had written of the British and the West, that they "have some thoughts of colonizing into that quarter."

The time was right for the exploratory journey Jefferson had long pondered. He wanted to find a route to the Pacific and limn the contours of a West that might well become a theater of contention between the United States and imperial powers.

To lead the enterprise Jefferson did not look far, choosing Meriwether Lewis, his private secretary. Born in 1774 at Locust Hill, ten miles from Monticello, Lewis came from what Jefferson called his own "neighborhood." Bold and blue-eyed, young Lewis had been a lieutenant in the U.S. Army, serving under James Wilkinson, when Jefferson asked him to come to Washington to serve in the President's

House in 1801. Impressed with Lewis's "knowledge of the Western country, of the army and its situation," Jefferson apparently drew on Lewis's sense of the officer corps as the president evaluated the military he had inherited from John Adams.

Jefferson trusted Lewis and admired his hardiness, and, after Congress secretly agreed to fund an expedition to find the best route to the Pacific, asked him to lead it. (The president asked for, and received, $2,500; the final bill came in at about fifteen times that amount.) "Capt. Lewis is brave, prudent, habituated to the woods, and familiar with Indian manners and character," Jefferson told Benjamin Rush. Lewis asked William Clark, George Rogers Clark's brother, to join him in organizing what became known as the Corps of Volunteers for North West Discovery.

Jefferson thought of America as an "empire of liberty." Now he would have a keener, more detailed grasp of the continent that stretched far beyond the nation's existing borders—and a chance at claiming that sprawling West.

THIRTY-FOUR

Victories, Scandal, and a Secret Sickness

> By this wench Sally, our president has had sev-
> eral children. There is not an individual in the
> neighborhood of Charlottesville who does not
> believe the story; and not a few who know it.
>
> —JAMES CALLENDER, the Richmond
> **Recorder,** September 1802

THERE HAD BEEN a time, not so very long
ago, that Jefferson believed he could, if not
end, then transcend, partisanship. It was an
ideal of the age: the concept of "party" was viewed
with fear and suspicion. The great George Washington himself had warned against partisan spirit in his
farewell address.

The warning did no good, and Jefferson's hopes
of enduring political unity were never to be realized. In early 1801, even before Jefferson declared
that Americans were all Federalists and all Republicans in his inaugural address, Albert Gallatin reported the reality on the ground in the capital: "You

may suppose that being thrown together in a few boarding houses, without any other society than ourselves, we are not likely to be either very moderate politicians or to think of anything but politics." Federalist Simeon Baldwin shared the sentiment, writing, "The men of the different parties do not associate intimately." Yet another observer said, "No tavern or boarding house contains two members of opposite sentiments."

Jefferson did try. "Nothing shall be spared on my part to obliterate the traces of party and consolidate the nation, if it can be done without abandonment of principle," he said in March 1801. Thirty-four months later, after the partisan wars of his first term, he struck more practical notes, accepting the world as it was. "The attempt at reconciliation was honorably pursued by us for a year or two and spurned by them," he said.

As Jefferson well knew, in practice the best he could hope for was a truce between himself and his opponents, not a permanent peace. Political divisions were intrinsic; what mattered most was how a president managed those divisions.

Jefferson's strategy was sound. Believing in the promise of democratic republicanism and in his own capacity for transformative leadership, he took a broad view: "There is nothing to which a nation is not equal where it pours all its energies and zeal into the hands of those to whom they confide the direction of their force."

He proposed a covenant: Let us meet the political challenges of the country together and try to restrain the passions that led to the extremist, apocalyptic rhetoric of what Jefferson called the "gloomy days of terrorism" of the 1790s, and perhaps politics could become a means of progress, not simply a source of conflict.

The prevailing Federalist view was that such a covenant was lovely to talk about but impossible to bring into being. John Quincy Adams was right when he told his diary that political war was to be the rule, not the exception, in American life. "The country is so totally given up to the spirit of party, that not to follow blindfold the one or the other is an inexpiable offense," Adams wrote during Jefferson's first term.

The Founders' dream of a nation beyond partisanship was one that simply could not survive the very nature of a free politics in a culture of diverse interests.

Republican or Federalist, to anyone who bothered to pay attention, there was no mystery about Jefferson's agenda in the capital. "Mr. Jefferson doesn't at all hesitate to say that the previous administration conducted itself under anti-republican maxims," the French envoy Louis-André Pichon reported home to Paris, and the new president was determined to correct such "inequalities and errors."

Jefferson was relentless in pursuing and putting

down threats to his vision of a republican nation. Whether they were Federalist judges and other officeholders—including the chief justice of the United States—or hostile newspapermen, Jefferson's foes faced spirited challenges from the President's House. By virtue of the Republican successes in the 1800 presidential and congressional elections, Jefferson had the strength to do largely as he wished. He had made his essential views known; candidates for the House and the Senate had made their support for him and for those views clear as well. A majority of the voting population wanted to move on from the Federalism of the 1790s, and Jefferson was ready to lead the way. The Federalists had a lot to say, but their words were no match for what the president had: the votes.

The new Judiciary Act of 1802 was a monument to Jefferson's power. The 1801 act was a Federalist bid to protect the faction from popular reaction by giving lifetime tenure to the like-minded. The 1802 bill, written and passed by Jefferson's Republicans, sought to break the Federalist hold on the judiciary. On one side stood Federalists arguing that the courts—including courts created only months before—were sacrosanct. On the other stood Jefferson and his followers asserting that no branch of government could rightly lie beyond the reach of reform.

The principles at stake were self-evident. So were the political realities. Though Jefferson proceeded with caution—there were no declarations of war on the judiciary—he did proceed. In Jefferson's first annual message, in December 1801, he drily wrote that "the judicial system of the United States, and especially that portion of it recently erected, will of course present itself to the contemplation of Congress." Behind those seemingly benign words lay a presidential determination that the Republicans in Congress would strike against the new judgeships created by the 1801 act.

The repeal passed on Monday, March 8, 1802. The House vote reflected the Republican advantage in the lower chamber. In the Senate, the bill succeeded by a single vote, but it succeeded. Then, in April, the Congress approved a new Judiciary Act of 1802. Among other aspects, the bill, which Jefferson signed into law, eliminated the new circuit judgeships that had come into being in the last phase of the Adams administration. It was an enormous victory for Jefferson, and the Federalists were horrified.

Jefferson's hatred of his cousin John Marshall was cordial, but it was hatred nonetheless. ("The judge's inveteracy is profound, and his mind of that gloomy malignity which will never let him forego the opportunity of satiating it on a victim," Jefferson once wrote.) In February 1803, the chief justice issued the opinion of the Supreme Court in the case of **Marbury v. Madison,** a confrontation between one of John Adams's midnight appointees, William

Marbury, and the Jefferson administration. The decision, which held that Madison had been wrong to withhold Marbury's commission, went against the president, but Marshall wisely avoided a showdown while helping lay the foundations for the concept of judicial review.

U.S. judge John Pickering of New Hampshire, meanwhile, was the object of impeachment in the House in the winter of 1803, as was Supreme Court associate justice Samuel Chase. Pickering was unstable, a drinker who may have been insane; his impeachment and conviction were of less ultimate moment than the effort against Chase, who had given the Republicans an opening with a provocative charge to a grand jury in Baltimore and who had been openly hostile to Jefferson's party. "Where law is uncertain, partial, or arbitrary, where justice is not impartially administered to all; where property is insecure, and the person is liable to insult and violence without redress by law,—the people are **not free,** whatever may be their form of government," Chase said in May 1803. He attacked the repeal of the Judiciary Act of 1801, telling the Baltimore jury, "Our republican Constitution will sink into a mobocracy,—the worst of all possible governments."

Infuriated by Chase's diatribe—one issued from the sanctuary of the bench—Jefferson wrote Maryland congressman Joseph H. Nicholson, who had recently brought charges against Judge Pickering.

"Ought this seditious and official attack on the principles of our Constitution and on the proceedings of a State to go unpunished; and to whom so pointedly as yourself will the public look for the necessary measures?" In conclusion, Jefferson noted: "I ask these questions for your consideration; for myself, it is better that I should not interfere."

Except, of course, that he just had interfered. It was a characteristic Jeffersonian tactic, instigating a course of action from afar. Ultimately the Senate convicted John Pickering and the House impeached Samuel Chase, who won an acquittal from the Senate on the Friday before Jefferson's second inauguration in 1805. The failure to remove Chase from office has long been interpreted as a defeat for Jefferson, but the president's point was made. Judges who, in John Randolph's phrase, played the part of an "electioneering partisan" were not safe from censure of some kind. The Federalist judiciary was on notice.

Such successes drove Jefferson's enemies mad. One correspondent wrote to the president of hopes "that your Excellency might be beheaded within one year." An anonymous letter from New York told Jefferson that the writer—who signed himself "A Federalist Democrat"—had been asked "to go to Washington and then assassinate you." Twelve days later came another letter from New York, this one signed "A—X," saying: "You are in danger a dreadful plot is forming against you. . . . Julius Caesar was cautioned for the Ides of March—I caution you for the last of April."

In victory, Jefferson moved carefully on the politically treacherous issue of federal appointments. The composition of the government was among the key questions to challenge the newly inaugurated president—and the newly inaugurated president's hope to lead a less divided nation. How many Federalist officeholders should be removed and replaced with Republicans? Jefferson's Republican allies were pushing for aggressive action. "An energetic tone towards the leaders of the royalist party will keep the republicans and new converts together and gain strength daily to your administration," Monroe had written Jefferson eight days after the inaugural in 1801.

Jefferson replied that he hoped the spell of the late 1790s had broken and that the Federalist manipulation of the XYZ affair and other supposed threats to the nation had come to be seen as manufactured. "At length the poor arts of tub plots etc were repeated till the designs of the party became suspected." The "tub plots" reference was from the English Civil War, when forged evidence of a 1679 conspiracy to keep James, the Catholic Duke of York, from the throne was found in a tub of meal. Jefferson's evocation of the episode in the context of the 1790s shows that he continued to view history partly through the prism of the wars and conflicts of the seventeenth century—a time of conspiracy, intrigue, and perpetual tension between monarchists and republicans.

Believing the American people essentially sound and aware of the Federalist excesses, Jefferson favored a moderate tone ("We must be easy with them," he said of the Federalists), but he did not fail to take decisive action.

Scholarly estimates put Jefferson's removal rate quite high: He displaced about 46 percent of incumbent officeholders in 1801, the strong majority of whom were Federalists. Such a rate places Jefferson in the historical company of Andrew Jackson, whose removals three decades later shocked establishment sensibilities. Jefferson was especially hard on Adams's last-minute decisions. One of Adams's midnight appointments was that of Elizur Goodrich to the collectorship of the port at New Haven. The post had fallen open only in February 1801. Responding to Republican sentiment in Connecticut, Jefferson removed Goodrich and appointed Samuel Bishop, the mayor of New Haven, to his place.

A group of merchants in New Haven issued a remonstrance against Goodrich's removal, prompting Jefferson to lay out his thinking on federal appointments. "Declarations by myself in favor of **political tolerance**, exhortations to **harmony** and affection in social intercourse, and to respect for the **equal rights** of the minority, have, on certain occasions, been quoted and misconstrued into assurances that the tenure of offices was to be undisturbed." But,

Jefferson went on, "Is it **political intolerance** to claim a proportionate share in the direction of the public affairs? Can they not **harmonize** in society unless they have everything in their own hands?"

He was pragmatic. He could see the whole. He understood that removals like the one in New Haven would produce political discord, but that was the nature of the enterprise.

As were scathing newspaper attacks. Thomas McKean of Pennsylvania, the governor who had been so forthright in his support for Jefferson in the 1800 election, felt that the partisan papers in his state were abusing their freedom of expression, and he was weighing whether to take legal action. "The infamous and seditious libels, published almost daily in our newspapers, are become intolerable," McKean wrote Jefferson in February 1803. "If they cannot be altogether prevented . . . they may be greatly checked by a few prosecutions."

Jefferson replied carefully but clearly. "On the subject of prosecutions, what I say must be entirely confidential, for you know the passion for torturing every sentiment and word which comes from me," Jefferson wrote McKean on Saturday, February 19, 1803. "I have . . . long thought that a few prosecutions of the most eminent offenders would have a wholesome effect in restoring the integrity of the presses. Not a general prosecution, for that would look like persecution: but a selected one."

Most newspapers, however, were out of reach, including James Callender's. On Wednesday, September 1, 1802, in the Richmond **Recorder,** Callender had his revenge on Jefferson, publishing an account of the Jefferson-Sally Hemings relationship.

> It is well known that the man, **whom it delighteth the people to honor,** keeps, and for many years past has kept, as his concubine, one of his own slaves. Her name is SALLY. The name of her eldest son is TOM. His features are said to bear a striking although sable resemblance to those of the president himself. The boy is ten or twelve years of age. His mother went to France in the same vessel with Mr. Jefferson and his two daughters. The delicacy of this arrangement must strike every person of common sensibility. What a sublime pattern for an American ambassador to place before the eyes of two young ladies! . . .
>
> By this wench Sally, our president has had several children. There is not an individual in the neighborhood of Charlottesville who does not believe the story; and not a few who know it. . . .
>
> Behold the favorite, the first born of republicanism! The pinnacle of all that is good and great! In the open consummation of an act which tends to subvert the policy, the happiness, and even the existence of this country!
>
> 'Tis supposed that, at the time when Mr. Jefferson wrote so smartly concerning negroes, when

he endeavored so much to **belittle** the African race, he had no expectation that the chief magistrate of the United States was to be the ringleader in showing that his opinion was erroneous; or, that he should choose an African stock whereupon he was to engraft his own descendants. . . .

We give it to the world under the firmest belief that such a refutation **never can be made**. The AFRICAN VENUS is said to officiate, as housekeeper at Monticello. When Mr. Jefferson has read this article, he will find leisure to estimate how much has been lost or gained by so many unprovoked attacks upon J. T. CALLENDER.

Callender had many of his facts right, and he corrected those he missed. (He later noted, for instance, that Hemings had traveled with Polly, alone, and not with Jefferson and Patsy.) "The license that has been indulged against the President has exhausted its violence in revealing some very old so-called liaisons between him and one of his slaves," Pichon reported to Paris.

Jefferson never directly responded to the charge. Historians have long taken an 1805 letter as an implicit denial. In that note, he said that the allegations about his courtship of the married Betsy Walker was the "only" allegation against him that was true. It is possible, though, that Jefferson was not addressing the Hemings allegations at all in that letter, which included a now-lost enclosure, presumably a clipping or copy of Federalist attacks on Jefferson's character. Without the enclosure, we cannot know for certain that he was denying the Hemings story—only that the enclosure mentioned the Walker affair and some other alleged transgressions. In any event, the charges remained in wide circulation during his lifetime and afterward. "Callender and Sally will be remembered as long as Jefferson as blots on his character," John Adams wrote privately. "The story of the latter is a natural and almost unavoidable consequence of that foul contagion in the human character, Negro slavery." Soon Callender was found drowned in three feet of water in the James River on a day when he had been observed wandering drunkenly through Richmond. The inquest discovered no evidence of foul play; it was a pathetic end to a tragic life.

In 1806 Thomas Moore, an Irish poet, published verses mentioning the rumors about Jefferson and Sally Hemings.

The weary statesman for repose hath fled
From halls of council to his negro's shed,
Where blest he woos some black Aspasia's grace,
And dreams of freedom in his slave's embrace!

Patsy and a former Jefferson secretary, William A. Burwell, showed the "obnoxious passages" to Jefferson, who laughed them off, effectively ending a discussion before one could begin.

So far as we know, no one else in Jefferson's family or official circle ever raised the Sally Hemings question with him except to denounce any discussion of it in the public press as reprehensible. For Jefferson, the code of silence on the issue of sex across the color line appears to have been total.

In December 1801, Jefferson had obliquely confided in Benjamin Rush about something else entirely: his physical well-being. "My health has always been so uniformly firm, that I have for some years dreaded nothing so much as . . . living too long," Jefferson wrote. "I think however that a flaw has appeared which ensures me against that."

He went into no detail, adding only that secrecy about any such question was essential. "I have said as much to no mortal breathing," Jefferson added, "and my florid health is calculated to keep my friends as well as foes quiet as they should be."

After Rush pressed his friend for specifics, Jefferson provided them. The complaint was diarrhea, a serious illness of the day. In his **Medical Lexicon: A Dictionary of Medical Science**, Dr. Robley Dunglison, who was to attend Jefferson at the time of his death a quarter century later, described diarrhea as a "disease characterized by frequent liquid . . . evacuations and generally owing to inflammation or irritation of the mucous membrane of the intestines." It could be "acute or chronic," and in some cases fatal "because like hectic fever it seems to obtain habitual possession of the constitution to operate upon it with scarcely any perceptible intermission, and, in general, to defy the most powerful remedies." The affliction would trouble Jefferson for the rest of his life.

His family came to Washington for Christmas 1802. Patsy and Polly were together; Margaret Bayard Smith spent a good deal of time with them both. "Mrs. Eppes is beautiful, simplicity and timidity personified when in company, but when alone with you of communicative and winning manners," Mrs. Smith wrote. "Mrs. R[andolph] is rather homely, a delicate likeness of her father, but still more interesting than Mrs. E. She is really one of the most lovely women I have ever met with, her countenance beaming with intelligence, benevolence and sensibility, and her conversation fulfills all her countenance promises. Her manners, so frank and affectionate, that you know her at once, and feel perfectly at your ease with her."

Patsy, Mrs. Smith continued, "gave me an account of all her children, of the character of her husband and many family anecdotes. She has that rare but charming egotism which can interest the listener in all one's concerns."

It was a busy season. "I have only time to write a line to you My dearest husband, the incessant round of company we are in scarcely allowing time to dress to receive them," Polly wrote her husband

John Wayles Eppes. "I am at this moment writing whilst waiting for a gown to be smoothed, though the drawing room is full of ladies."

The visitors from Virginia were struck by Jefferson's lonely accommodations. "Adieu once more," Polly wrote to Jefferson in January 1803. "How much I think of you at the hours which we have been accustomed to be with you alone, my dear Papa, and how much pain it gives me to think of the unsafe and solitary manner in which you sleep upstairs." (Jefferson set about acquiring the proper furniture to provide fitting bedrooms for his large family on future visits.)

He loved it when everyone was there. A caller once observed the president sitting on the drawing room floor in the midst of grandchildren, "so eagerly and noisily engaged in a game of romps" that the visitor went unnoticed for a moment. "I will catch you in bed on Sunday or Monday morning," Jefferson jovially wrote to a granddaughter before a visit.

From Monticello, Patsy wrote about her control over the house with a firmness that must have pleased her father. "I have wrought an entire reformation on the . . . household," she told Jefferson. "Nothing comes in or goes out without my knowledge and I believe there is as little waste as possible. I visit the kitchen smoke house and fowls when the weather permits and according to your desire saw the meat cut out."

There was still some hope of Jefferson's having a

small family with him in Washington: Both John Wayles Eppes and Thomas Mann Randolph, Jr., were seeking congressional seats. If either or both won, they would come to live with Jefferson in the President's House. (In the event, they were both elected.)

Despite all—the attacks from Callender, the toll of governing, the loneliness in the mansion— Jefferson liked being president. He was driven by a need to secure the Republic from all enemies, foreign and domestic. Most leaders can only hope to shape their nation for a brief time. In the middle of 1803, a report from Paris would give Jefferson the power to transform his for all time.

THIRTY-FIVE

The Air of Enchantment!

The news of the cession of Louisiana. . . .
forms an era in our history, and of itself
must render the administration of Jefferson
immortal.

—SAMUEL HARRISON SMITH

The fame of your political wisdom is now so
permanently established, that it is past the
power of a disappointed faction ever to diminish it.

—HORATIO GATES, on learning
of the Louisiana Purchase

BEFORE HIS FIRST MONTH as president was
done, Jefferson received reports of rumors in
London that Spain had signed a treaty giving France more than half of her North American
colonies. Known as the Third Treaty of San Ildefonso, the agreement had been reached in a glorious
eighteenth-century palace north of Madrid used as
a summertime retreat by Spanish monarchs. The

arrangement, negotiated in late 1800, gave France ownership of the Spanish territory of Louisiana in the New World. The cession, as it was called, "works most sorely on the U.S.," Jefferson wrote in April 1802. "It completely reverses all the political relations of the U.S. and will form a new epoch in our political course."

Napoleon now had a vast interest in (and on) the American continent. "I am willing to hope, as long as anybody will hope with me" that the reports were wrong, Jefferson said.

They were not wrong. Jefferson understood he needed to act, but act subtly. "I believe that the destinies of great countries depend on it," he wrote the French economist Pierre-Samuel du Pont de Nemours.

To Jefferson it was an existential matter. "There is on the globe one single spot, the possessor of which is our natural and habitual enemy. It is New Orleans, through which the produce of three eighths of our territory must pass to market, and from its fertility it will ere long yield more than half of our whole produce and contain more than half our inhabitants." In a conversation "of some length" with the British diplomat Edward Thornton in Washington, Jefferson said that "the occupation of this country by France gave an entirely new character to all . . . American relations with her." Jefferson was not sanguine: "The inevitable consequences of such a neighborhood," Thornton recorded Jefferson saying, "must be jealousy, irritation, and finally hostilities."

As frightening as the moment was, Jefferson approached it with confidence: The success of his first year in office buoyed him for the struggle with Napoleon. The story of the Louisiana Purchase is one of strength, of Jefferson's adaptability and, most important, his determination to secure the territory from France, doubling the size of the country and transforming the United States into a continental power. A slower or less courageous politician might have bungled the acquisition; an overly idealistic one might have lost it by insisting on strict constitutional scruples. Jefferson, however, was neither slow nor weak nor overly idealistic.

He drew on a lifetime of political experience, of victories and defeats, to manage the Louisiana crisis. He knew he needed to control the mechanics of decision as best he could (in this case by sending his own envoy, James Monroe, to Paris), a lesson learned in Williamsburg during the Stamp Act debates. He knew he needed to communicate in a way to rally the public, a lesson learned in 1774 when writing the Day of Fasting and Prayer resolution and again in 1776 with the Declaration of Independence. Most important, he knew he needed to seize the initiative when he could, a lesson learned in his days as governor during the Revolution.

Now that Napoleon was in the picture, Jefferson understood what had to be done. "The day that

France takes possession of New Orleans . . . we must marry ourselves to the British fleet and nation." With national interests at stake, Jefferson was willing to shift his sympathies from Paris to London—or at least be seen that way to improve America's negotiating power.

Jefferson was clear-eyed. The fading Spanish empire had been one thing; Napoleonic France was quite another. "France placing herself in that door assumes to us the attitude of defiance," Jefferson said. "Spain might have retained it quietly for years. . . . Not so can it ever be in the hands of France. The impetuosity of her temper, the energy and restlessness of her character, placed in a point of eternal friction with us . . . render it impossible that France and the U.S. can continue long friends when they meet in so irritable a position." (The cession was rumored but not confirmed until February 1802, when a copy of a subsequent treaty, of Aranjuez, reached Washington, sent by Rufus King, the American minister to Britain.)

In a letter written just before he left the United States for France, Pierre S. du Pont gave Jefferson a tutorial on the practicalities of power. Most important, America should not offend or threaten Napoleon. Among the issues for Europe was the fear that the United States had designs on Spanish-held Mexico. The question came to this: "How then do you intend to acquire Louisiana and persuade France to surrender its ownership in an amicable way? Alas, Mister President, contractual freedom and a natural taste for wealth in all nations and all individuals (poverty strikes all great powers and only second-rate powers escape it) leave you with only one alternative, since you have no land to trade: it is financed purchase."

Jefferson could not go to France himself, and so he reached out to a trusted friend. The president and James Madison weighed the possibilities and, in what Dolley Madison called "a most important piece of political business," decided to ask their fellow Virginian James Monroe to travel to France as a presidential envoy. "In this situation we are obliged to call on you for a temporary sacrifice of yourself, to prevent this greatest of evils in the present prosperous tide of our affairs," Jefferson wrote Monroe, who agreed to the assignment.

A snowstorm and unfavorable winds delayed Monroe's departure, and he took advantage of the unexpected time on his hands to write Jefferson about the politics of his mission: "I hope the French govt. will have wisdom enough to see that we will never suffer France or any other power to tamper with our interior; if that is not the object there can be no reason for declining an accommodation to the whole of our demands."

The incumbent minister to France, Robert R. Livingston, had meanwhile learned much in a drawing room gathering in Paris hosted by Joséphine Bonaparte. According to custom, Madame Bonaparte entered first, and Napoleon followed her, making conversation first with the ladies on hand and then with the men. "When the First Consul has gone the round of one room, he turned to me and made some of those common questions usual on such occasions," Livingston told Jefferson. A moment later Napoleon moved toward Lord Whitworth, the British envoy, and, Livingston said, "accosted Lord Whitworth with some warmth, told him that there would probably be a storm." It was a public declaration of what Lord Whitmore had been told in private two days earlier: "if you do not evacuate Malta there will be war."

Napoleon then suddenly withdrew altogether after roiling European diplomacy in a drawing room. "You may easily surmise the sensation that this excited," Livingston said. "Two expresses were dispatched to England that very night and I daresay to every court in Europe in the course of the next day."

Livingston interpreted the incident in the same way everyone else did: as a sign of Napoleon's intention to go to war with England. And that possibility increased the chances that France might want to simplify its North American problems by putting Louisiana in the hands of the United States.

For France, holding and defending lands so far from Europe was growing too expensive and troublesome. The defeat at the hands of slave forces in St. Domingue was especially galling to Napoleon, who believed he needed to husband his resources for campaigns closer to home.

Napoleon was in his bath, soaking in cologne-scented water, when his brothers came in to protest the decision to sell Louisiana. "You will have no need to lead the opposition," Napoleon told his brothers, "for I repeat there will be no debate, for the reason that the project . . .conceived by me, negotiated by me, shall be ratified and executed by me, alone. Do you comprehend me?"

"I renounce Louisiana," Napoleon announced to finance minister Barbé-Marbois, early on the morning of Monday, April 11, 1803. Within hours, foreign minister Charles Maurice de Talleyrand was enquiring whether the United States would be interested in the entire territory. "It is not only New Orleans that I will cede, it is the whole colony without any reservation. I know the price of what I abandon. . . . I renounce it with the greatest regret. But to attempt obstinately to retain it would be folly."

Livingston knew what he had to do. "The field open to us is infinitely larger than our instructions contemplated," Livingston told Madison, and the chance "must not be missed." He and Monroe, who had arrived in Paris, negotiated a treaty giving the United States the Louisiana Territory—a landmass so vast the borders were unclear even to the buyers and the sellers—for about $15 million, or three cents an acre.

Word reached Jefferson on Sunday evening, July 3,

1803. Rufus King had arrived in New York and dispatched a packet to Washington. The key document was a letter from Livingston and Monroe announcing that they had signed a treaty with France on April 30 "ceding to us the island of N. Orleans and all Louisiana as it had been held by Spain," Jefferson wrote Thomas Mann Randolph, Jr., from Washington on Tuesday, July 5. "The price is not mentioned."

Jefferson was stunned—happily stunned, but stunned nonetheless. Reading the correspondence in the President's House he slowly grasped the scope of the news. "It is something larger than the whole U.S., probably containing 500 millions of acres, the U.S. containing 434 millions," he wrote, seemingly thinking aloud as his mind took in what had happened. "This removes from us the greatest source of danger to our peace."

It was wondrous. "It must . . . strike the mind of every true friend to freedom in the United States, as the greatest and most beneficial event that has taken place since the Declaration of Independence," wrote Horatio Gates on Thursday, July 7. "I am astonished when I see so great a business finished, which but a few months since we whispered to one another about; it has the air of enchantment!"

"Every face wears a smile, and every heart leaps with Joy," Andrew Jackson wrote Jefferson from the West. "The thing is new in the annals of the world," wrote another correspondent. "The great matter now is to make the wonderful event a blessing to the human race."

As Jefferson absorbed the news, he wrote Meriwether Lewis, who left Washington on that Tuesday, July 5, 1803, to begin the expedition Jefferson described as "the journey which you are about to undertake for the discovery of the course and source of the Mississippi, and of the most convenient water communication from thence to the Pacific."

It was the letter of a president at once optimistic and realistic. He hoped Lewis would reach the Pacific and armed the party with the means necessary to return home, come what may, authorizing Lewis to draw on the credit of the United States if necessary.

Jefferson had now done all he could to control the largely uncontrollable nature of the mission that was to take Lewis, Clark, and their party of forty or so up the Missouri River, into the winter of present-day North Dakota, then along the Columbia River to the Pacific. Jefferson had written detailed instructions, offered counsel, and worried over details. At last it was in the hands of the explorers, and Jefferson waited, eagerly, for word from the fields he had long traveled in his mind.

The Fourth of July fell on Monday. The President's House was filled with festive callers. Samuel Harrison Smith thought there were more visitors than usual. The party was abuzz with the

Louisiana news and "enlivened too by the presence of between 40 and 50 ladies clothed in their best attire, cakes, punch, wine, etc. in profusion," Smith wrote.

In the flush of success, Jefferson was sanguine about everything—even the fate of the Union. "The future inhabitants of the Atlantic and Mississippi states will be our sons," Jefferson wrote John Breckinridge. "We leave them in distinct but bordering establishments. We think we see their happiness in their union, and we wish it. Events may prove it otherwise; and if they see their interest in separation, why should we take side with our Atlantic rather than our Mississippi descendants? It is the elder and the younger son differing. God bless them both, and keep them in union if it be for their good, but separate them if it be better."

To Joseph Priestley he boasted of his diplomatic subtlety. "I very early saw that Louisiana was indeed a speck in our horizon which was to burst in a tornado; and the public are unapprised how near this catastrophe was. Nothing but a frank and friendly development of causes and effects on our part, and good sense enough in Bonaparte to see that the train was unavoidable, and would change the face of the world, saved us from that storm." He closed the letter with a scholarly query: "Have you seen the new work of Malthus on population? It is one of the ablest I have ever seen."

How like Jefferson—amid the greatest of possible

events affecting every aspect of American life and beyond, he was reading Malthus.

The treaty had to be ratified by Sunday, October 30, 1803. Jefferson consulted with the cabinet and called for Congress to meet on Monday, October 17, 1803, to consider what he called "great and weighty matters."

Jefferson's initial view was that purchasing Louisiana and then governing it required a constitutional amendment. To John Breckinridge, he wrote: "This treaty must of course be laid before both houses because both have important functions to exercise respecting it. They I presume will see their duty to their country in ratifying and paying for it so as to secure a good which would otherwise probably be never again in their person. But I suppose they must then appeal to **the nation** for an additional article to the Constitution, approving and confirming an act which the nation had not previously authorized."

What he had done thus far by allowing his representatives to negotiate and sign the treaty with France was, in his current view, beyond the scope of his powers. "The Executive in seizing the fugitive occurrence which so much advanced the good of their country, have done an act beyond the Constitution. The legislature in casting behind them metaphysical subtleties, and risking themselves like faithful servants, must ratify and pay for it, and throw themselves on their country for doing for them unauthorized what we know they would have done for themselves had they been in a situation to do it." He used a lawyerly analogy to underscore his point. "It is the case of a guardian investing the money of his ward in purchasing an important adjacent territory; and saying to him when of age, I did this for your good; I pretend to no right to bind you. You may disavow me, and I must get out of the scrape as I can. I thought it my duty to risk myself for you."

Jefferson's opinion in the second week of August 1803, then, was that the laborious machinery of amendment was crucial to ratify the purchase. Six days after writing Breckinridge, though, Jefferson hurriedly wrote him again, essentially calling back the point. "I wrote you on the 12th. inst. on the subject of Louisiana, and the constitutional provision which might be necessary for it," he wrote on Thursday, August 18. "A letter received yesterday shows that nothing must be said on that subject which may give a pretext for retracting but that we should do **sub silentio** what shall be found necessary. Be so good therefore as to consider that part of my letter as confidential. It strengthens the reasons for desiring the presence of every friend to the treaty on the first day of the session."

The unwelcome letter received on Wednesday, August 17, had come from Paris. Reporting from the French capital, Livingston and Monroe warned that France was growing uncomfortable with the deal. Fearing trouble, Jefferson moved decisively, pressing for a fast congressional vote in October and changing his mind about the need for a constitutional amendment. "You will find that the French government, dissatisfied perhaps with their late bargain with us, will be glad of a pretext to declare it void," Jefferson wrote Gallatin on Tuesday, August 23, 1803. "It will be necessary therefore that we execute it with punctuality and without delay."

Speed was essential. "Whatever Congress shall think it necessary to do should be done with as little debate as possible; and particularly so far as respects the constitutional difficulty," Jefferson wrote Senator Wilson Cary Nicholas of Virginia from Monticello on Wednesday, September 7.

Attorney General Levi Lincoln worried that there could be opposition to an acquisition, which was all the more reason for Jefferson to move quickly and unilaterally. "Is there not danger that the Eastern States, including even Rhode Island and Vermont, if not New York, and other States further South, would object to the ratification of a treaty directly introducing a state of things, involving the idea of adding to the weight of the southern States in one branch of the Govt. of which there is already too great a jealousy and dread . . . ? No plea of necessity, of commercial utility, or national security, will have weight with a violent party, or be any security against their hostile efforts and opposition clamor."

Thomas Paine suggested an extraordinary scenario to Jefferson on Friday, September 23, 1803. What if Napoleon successfully defeated and subjugated England? "The English Government is but in a tottering condition, and if Bonaparte succeeds the Government will break up," Paine wrote Jefferson. "In that case it is not improbable we may obtain Canada, and I think that Bermuda ought to belong to the United States."

Paine mused about Bonaparte's war plans for England, too. The First Consul, Paine said, had only to choose "a dark night and a calm" to land along the North Sea coast. Paine's implied point: With such momentous things afoot, it was foolish to worry over constitutional niceties.

Alexander Hamilton could not have put it better.

The philosophical Jefferson had believed an amendment necessary. The political Jefferson, however, was not going to allow theory to get in the way of reality. "I confess . . . I think it important in the present case to set an example against broad construction by appealing for new power to the people," he wrote Wilson Cary Nicholas. "If however our friends shall think differently, certainly I shall acquiesce with satisfaction, confiding that the good sense of our country will correct the evil of construction when it shall produce ill effects."

So he left himself room to maneuver. It was the same kind of political craft he had practiced in the debate over the Bank of the United States, when he made the case against Hamilton's broad construction only to (wisely) leave open the possibility that Washington could sign the bill.

Jefferson's decision to acquire Louisiana without seeking a constitutional amendment expanded the powers of the executive in ways that would likely have driven Jefferson to distraction had another man been president. Much of his political life, though, had been devoted to the study and the wise exercise of power. He did what had to be done to preserve the possibility of republicanism and progress. Things were neat only in theory. And despite his love of ideas and image of himself, Thomas Jefferson was as much a man of action as he was of theory.

Indian tribes knew this well. Though he would not live to see the Trail of Tears of the 1830s, Jefferson was among the architects of Indian removal. He eagerly acquired lands from the tribes throughout the American interior—up to two hundred thousand square miles—and, as in the case of the Louisiana Purchase, did all he could to encourage white settlement ever farther west and south. In 1803, writing to William Henry Harrison, then governor of the Indiana Territory, Jefferson said that he believed the Indians "will in time either incorporate with us as citizens of the United States or remove beyond the Mississippi." He threatened to retaliate against any attacking tribes by "seizing . . . the whole country of that tribe, and driving them across the Mississippi, as the only condition of peace."

Jefferson was triumphant on every front. "Our business is to march straight forward to the object which has occupied us for eight and twenty years, without either turning to the right or left," Jefferson wrote former New York governor George Clinton on New Year's Eve 1803. "In the hour of death we shall have the consolation to see established in the land of our fathers the most wonderful work of wisdom and disinterested patriotism that has ever yet appeared on the globe."

To his opponents, Jefferson's success seemed insurmountable and unendurable. "The [Republicans] have, as I expected, done more to strengthen the executive than Federalists dared think of even in Washington's day," Gouverneur Morris wrote to Roger Griswold in November 1803.

In January 1804, the Federalist Timothy Pickering, now a senator from Massachusetts, suggested secession and the formation of a northern confederacy. "If, I say, Federalism is crumbling away in New England, there is no time to be lost, lest it should be overwhelmed and become unable to attempt its own relief," he said. New York would be essential if the project—what Griswold euphemistically called "a reunion of the Northern states"—were to succeed. "The people of the East cannot reconcile their habits, views, and interests with those of the South and West," said Pickering. "The latter are beginning to rule with a rod of iron." The opposition was more than a little desperate. "Many persons are at this moment prepared to declare Jefferson President for life," Griswold wrote on Tuesday, January 10, 1804.

Which was what the Federalists feared most.

THIRTY-SIX

The People Were Never More Happy

If we can keep the vessel of state as steadily in her course for another four years, my earthly purposes will be accomplished.

—THOMAS JEFFERSON

I think you ought to get a damn kicking, you red-headed son of a bitch. You are a pretty fellow to be President of the United States of America, you dirty scoundrel.

—ANONYMOUS

O N MOST AFTERNOONS when he was in Washington, Jefferson received his dinner guests at the President's House around three thirty or four o'clock. He entertained constantly, handsomely, and with a purpose. His instinct to open his house and table was natural, something he had learned growing up as a son of the world of Virginia hospitality.

Jefferson believed, too, that sociability was essential to republicanism. Men who liked and respected and enjoyed one another were more likely to cultivate the virtuous habits that would enable the country's citizens to engage in "the pursuit of happiness." An affectionate man living in harmony with his neighbors was more likely to understand the mutual sacrifice of opinion of which Jefferson had spoken, and to make those sacrifices.

There was, of course, a more immediate point to frequent gatherings of lawmakers, diplomats, and cabinet officers at the president's table. It tends to be more difficult to oppose—or at least to vilify—someone with whom you have broken bread and drunk wine. Caricatures crack as courses are served; imagined demonic plots fade with dessert.

Jefferson understood this, but he was ruthless about the use of his limited time in power. To create an ethos of supra-partisan civility would have required bringing politicians of opposing views together under his aegis. Jefferson disliked confrontation so much, however, that he forewent inviting Republicans and Federalists to dine together with him. He had only four or eight years to impress himself on the country and was unwilling to waste any of those hours presiding over arguments, even polite ones, between differing factions at his table. The possibilities of conflict in a setting designed to promote comity were too great.

Jefferson chose, then, to use dinner at the President's House partly as a means of weaving attach-

ments to **him**. It was his stage and his production.
He ended the more formal arrangements common
to Presidents Washington and Adams, forbidding
seating by precedence—he preferred "pell-mell," or
the more democratic practice of having guests sit
where they chose—and the drinking of toasts to
one's health, a tedious custom he replaced with more
free-flowing, eclectic conversation. Like his aristocratic habit of dressing as though he were at Monticello rather than the capital—with his old slippers,
which made such an impression on so many—the
gentle creation of disorder at dinner magnified his
own strengths as a conversationalist.

The architect Benjamin H. Latrobe reveled in
his first dinner at the President's House. The food,
Latrobe wrote his wife, "was excellent, cooked
rather in the French style (larded venison), the dessert was profuse and extremely elegant, and the
knickknacks, after withdrawing the cloths, profuse
and numberless. Wine in great variety, from sherry
to champagne, and a few decanters of rare Spanish wine. " At first Jefferson hung back, playing the
host, then joined the stream of talk brilliantly.

Latrobe loved it all. "It is a long time since I have
been present at so elegant a mental treat," he said.
"Literature, wit, and a little business, with a great
deal of miscellaneous remarks on agriculture and
building, filled every minute. There is a degree of
ease in Mr. Jefferson's company that everyone seems
to feel and to enjoy."

Jefferson had a conservationist's turn of mind and once mused on the subject of the rapidly depleting number of trees along the sides of Capitol Hill and on the banks of the Potomac and the Anacostia rivers. "Such as grew on the public grounds ought to have been preserved, but in a government such as ours, where the people are sovereign, this could not be done," Margaret Bayard Smith recalled. "The **people**, the poorer inhabitants, cut down these noble and beautiful trees for fuel"; others felled trees for profit.

"How I wish that I possessed the power of a despot," Jefferson said one day, surprising his guests. "Yes," he went on, "I wish I was a despot that I might save the noble, the beautiful trees that are daily falling sacrifices to the cupidity of their owners, or the necessity of the poor."

A guest asked, "And have you not authority to save those on the public grounds?"

"No," said Jefferson, "only an armed guard could save them. The unnecessary felling of a tree, perhaps the growth of centuries, seems to me a crime little short of murder, [and] it pains me to an unspeakable degree."

Jefferson's social civility softened the more strident hours of partisanship. The Federalist senator William Plumer of New Hampshire had begun his Washington career with a predictably harsh view of

Jefferson. Early in the decade of the 1800s, Plumer dismissed the president as the leader of a "feeble, nerveless administration," later adding: "I did think he had great talents, wisdom and a portion of those virtues that render a man amiable and useful; but craft and cunning are as distant from wisdom as meanness is from economy, or his views from true greatness."

As the years passed, Plumer's opinion of Jefferson, formed at close quarters as a guest in the President's House, evolved from hostility to one of partial respect. "The more critically and impartially I examine the character and conduct of Mr. Jefferson the more favorably I think of his integrity," Plumer wrote in 1806. The senator still disagreed strongly with the president on policy, but Jefferson's grace and hospitality did its work. "I have a curiosity, which is gratified, by seeing and conversing" with Jefferson, Plumer wrote. "I gain a more thorough knowledge of his character, and of his views, and those of his party—for he is naturally communicative."

At the President's House, Jefferson gave Plumer some pecans to cultivate, and the two men engaged in the most chivalrous of exchanges. "After twenty years they will bear," Jefferson said.

"I shall, then, despair of eating of them," Plumer said.

"Your children will eat with pleasure the fruit of your industry," said Jefferson.

"I will teach them to bear in remembrance to whose politeness they are indebted for the nuts that produced these trees of fruit," replied Plumer.

Jefferson left no guest behind. Struggling to make small talk with the president, the wife of the mayor of Georgetown could remember only that she had heard of Carters Mountain—the redoubt where Jefferson was alleged to have run away from the British in 1781. Unaware of the trauma and embarrassment evoked by even the mention of the place, she asked Jefferson if he lived near Carters Mountain.

"Very close," he said, "it is the adjoining mountain to Monticello."

"I suppose it's a very convenient, pleasant place," the wife said, plunging on unknowingly as her husband sat awkwardly, powerless to stop her.

Jefferson maintained his poise, replying simply, "Why, yes, I certainly found it so, in the war time." There the subject was dropped.

At dinner late on another afternoon, the table talk was dominated by a few men whom Mrs. Smith, who was also there, described as "distinguished persons." The conversation was "earnest and animated," but one guest, who had lived in Europe for a time, sat "silent and unnoticed," apparently feeling overwhelmed by the high-powered company. He began thinking himself "a stranger in his own country [who] was totally unknown to the present company."

Then the president of the United States fixed his attention on the returning American. "To you, Mr. C., we are indebted . . . [and] no one more deserves the gratitude of his country."

The chatter stopped. The capital crowd at the table was startled by this presidential praise, and suddenly attention warmed the long-ignored guest. "Yes, sir," Jefferson went on, "the upland rice which you sent from Algiers, and which thus far succeeds, will, when generally adopted by the planters, prove an inestimable blessing to our Southern states."

With a stroke of grace, Jefferson had transformed an unnoticed guest into what Mrs. Smith called "a person of importance," and the president fulfilled the most fundamental duty of a host: He showed respect to those under his roof, making them feel comfortable and cared for.

To Jefferson, each guest who came into his orbit was significant, and he had little patience—**no** patience, in fact—with the trappings of rank. His blend of politics, republican simplicity, and haute cuisine was not universally popular. Anthony Merry, the new minister from Britain, found that his and Jefferson's ideas of the deference due a representative of George III were difficult to reconcile. The president's reception of the new envoy passed without incident. Not so the dinner to which Merry and his wife were invited at the President's House. Mrs. Madison was the hostess for the evening, and Jefferson took her into dinner. The Merrys ended up in what they believed to be inferior seats at the table.

Thus began a small but pitched social and diplomatic battle in the drawing and dining rooms of Washington. The Merry faction included the family of the Spanish minister, who also favored more ceremony and nicety. Mrs. Merry, Jefferson said, was "a virago, and in the short course of a few weeks has established a degree of dislike among all classes which one would have thought impossible in so short a time."

It was the Old World versus the New, and on Jefferson's watch the New was to win. "We say to them, no; the principle of society with us, as well as of our political constitution, is the equal rights of all: and if there be an occasion where this equality ought to prevail preeminently, it is in social circles collected for conviviality," Jefferson wrote in January 1804.

There was a specific political element to the tempest. The British representatives, Jefferson said, thought that "we are not as friendly now to Great Britain as before our acquisition of Louisiana." Jefferson denied it: "This is totally without foundation. Our friendship to that nation is cordial and sincere: so is that with France. . . . We consider each as a necessary instrument to hold in check the disposition of the other to tyrannize over other nations."

Anthony Merry never warmed to Jefferson, and

the British diplomat followed any whisper of American discontent. Jefferson's popularity was such—he was renominated by the Republican congressional caucus in February 1804 for a second term as president—that Federalist concern was turning into desperation.

On Saturday, February 11, 1804, Senator Timothy Pickering sat down in Washington to lament the sorry state of things in the age of Jefferson. Federal judges and other officeholders were under assault. The Jefferson-led mob ruled. "And must we submit to these evils?" Pickering wrote the Massachusetts Federalist Theodore Lyman. "Is there no remedy?"

Secession, Pickering believed, could be the one way "to resist the torrent" of Jefferson's government. Massachusetts was thought to be the most likely leader. If she went, then Connecticut would, followed by New Hampshire, Rhode Island, and Vermont. If New York were convinced it would be the center of the new nation, she would surely join, he said, which could, in turn, bring along New Jersey and Pennsylvania east of the Susquehanna.

And Britain—Britain would probably agree to let parts of its North America holdings join forces with a northern union. In theory, it all seemed so reasonable. "It is not unusual for two friends when disagreeing about the mode of conducting a common concern, to separate, and manage each in his own way his separate interest; and thereby preserve a useful friendship which without such separation would infallibly be destroyed," Pickering said.

Pickering's vision probably meant civil war. Why would Jefferson's party let the North go? Another Pickering correspondent, Massachusetts Federalist George Cabot, thought the hour for separation was not yet at hand—but was open to finding the right one. "We are democratic altogether, and I hold democracy in its natural operation to be the government of the worst," Cabot wrote Pickering.

Pickering was adamant. "I am disgusted with the men who now rule us and with their measures," he wrote on the third anniversary of Jefferson's inauguration. Pickering was putting much faith in reports that Burr might try to become governor of New York, which would, he hoped, provide a counterweight to Virginia. "Jefferson would then be forced to observe some caution and forbearance in his measures," Pickering said.

The Federalist view, according to a correspondent of Rufus King's, was "that the shortest and beaten road of Tyranny is that which leads through Democracy."

King was no disunionist, but he said that Pickering's letter "ought to fix the attention of the real friends of liberty in this quarter of the Union, and the more so as things seem to be fast advancing to a crisis." Rumors of disunion persisted for several years. Anthony Merry heard them and reported them to London; the British diplomat Augustus J.

Foster wrote about them to his mother. "The possibility of a division is even openly talked of in the public papers and recriminations are exchanged between the Eastern and Southern states," he wrote in June 1805.

Then there was Aaron Burr, an elusive and daunting political force. On Thursday, January 26, 1804, Burr called on Jefferson at the President's House. After the electoral college tie of 1800–1801, the two men had had little contact in the first term, and Jefferson was determined to keep him off the ballot in 1804.

As Burr told his story, he cast himself in the warmest and best of lights. He was, he was saying, the humblest and most honest of men.

Burr knew he was under attack publicly and privately. Jefferson reported that Burr had said "many little stories had been carried to him, and he supposed to me also, which, he despised, but that attachments must be reciprocal or cease to exist, and therefore he asked if any change had taken place in mine towards him: that he had chosen to have this conversation with myself directly and not through any intermediate agent." Burr was willing to stand down, he said, but to do so he needed Jefferson's help: an appointment of some kind.

Jefferson's reply was maddening. The president disclaimed any role in electioneering. He said he could do nothing for Burr.

Meanwhile, the proposed Twelfth Amendment was making its way through the states. The amendment was designed to prevent any future electoral crisis by separating the ballots for president and vice president, meaning that there could be no more ties between candidates who were putatively running as a ticket. "That great opposition is and will be made by Federalists to this amendment is certain," Jefferson wrote Thomas McKean in January 1804. "They know that if it prevails, neither a President or Vice President can ever be made but by the fair vote of the majority of the nation, of which they are not."

A fire had devastated Norfolk, Virginia (Jefferson sent $200 "for the relief of the poor sufferers," but asked to remain anonymous). At Edgehill, Polly gave birth to a daughter on Wednesday, February 15. "A thousand joys to you, my dear Maria, on the happy accession to your family," Jefferson wrote on Sunday, February 26, 1804, using the name Polly had taken for herself in November 1789.

But all was not well. Polly was not recovering. Her husband, John Wayles Eppes, left Washington for home. It was a difficult journey complicated by high winds and ice. "I feel dreadfully apprehensive that the great debility under which she labors may terminate in some serious complaint," Eppes wrote Jefferson.

———

In the Mediterranean, on the last day of October 1803, the U.S. frigate **Philadelphia** had been captured by Tripolitan forces. Three and a half months later, in the middle of February 1804, Commodore Stephen Decatur led a courageous expedition to destroy the **Philadelphia** in order to keep it from being turned against the United States. In British vice admiral Horatio Nelson's view, Decatur's mission was "the most bold and daring act of the age," and Jefferson struck the same notes in his remarks on the episode. "In general I am mortified at the consternation which most of our public agents abroad have manifested at the loss of the **Philadelphia**," Jefferson wrote Madison in April 1804. "It seems as if they thought on the loss of one frigate, that everything was lost. This must humble us in the eyes of Europe, and renders it the more indispensable to inflict on Tripoli the same chastisement of which the two most powerful nations of Europe have given the world repeated examples."

Jefferson left Washington on Sunday, April 1, 1804, for Monticello. When he arrived three days later, he discovered Polly in much worse condition than he had anticipated. He immediately took charge of her care.

In a rare instance of understatement, Jefferson told Madison that things were not all they could be. "Our spring is remarkably uncheery," Jefferson wrote Madison on Friday, April 13—Jefferson's sixty-first birthday. As Polly grew worse, Jefferson wrote to Dearborn, Gallatin, and Madison, trying to turn his mind, if only for the briefest of moments, to business. It did not work. On a question about Spanish duties at Mobile, Jefferson told Dearborn that Polly's "distressing situation . . . disable[s] me from forming any opinion on the subject." On Tuesday, April 17, 1804, Polly died. "How the President will get over this blow I cannot pronounce," Thomas Mann Randolph, Jr., wrote Caesar A. Rodney. "He passed all last evening with his handkerchief in his hand. Adieu. I begin to feel the want of mine."

Dolley Madison learned the news directly from Jefferson. "A letter from the President announced the death of poor [Polly] and the consequent misery it has occasioned them all—this is among the many proofs . . . of the uncertainty of life!" Mrs. Madison wrote her sister. "A girl so young, so lovely—all the efforts of her father, doctors and friends availed nothing."

Exhausted and grieving, Jefferson returned to Washington. "I arrived here last night after the most fatiguing journey I have experienced for a great many years," Jefferson wrote Patsy, now his last surviving child with his late wife, from Washington on May 14.

On Saturday, June 2, an unexpected letter arrived

at the President's House from Quincy, Massachusetts. "It has been some time since that I conceived of any event in this life, which could call forth feelings of mutual sympathy," wrote Abigail Adams. "But I know how closely entwined around a parent's heart, are those cords which bind the filial to the parental bosom, and when snapped asunder, how agonizing the pangs of separation."

Jefferson replied, politely, and the brief correspondence touched on the things that had come to divide Jefferson and the Adamses—Callender's vicious **Prospect Before Us** and the midnight appointments.

Abigail Adams wrote him again on Sunday, July 1, explaining the source of her deepest anger toward Jefferson:

> I have never felt any enmity towards you, Sir,
> for being elected president of the United States.
> But the instruments made use of, and the means
> which were practiced to effect a change, have my
> utter abhorrence and detestation, for they were
> the blackest calumny, and foulest falsehoods. I
> had witnessed enough of the anxiety, and solicitude, the envy, jealousy and reproach attendant
> upon the office, as well as the high responsibility of the station, to be perfectly willing to see a
> transfer of it. . . .
> [N]ow, Sir, I will freely disclose to you what
> has severed the bonds of former friendship, and

placed you in a light very different from what I once viewed you in—

One of the first acts of your administration was to liberate a wretch who was suffering the just punishment of the law due to his crimes for writing and publishing the basest libel, the lowest and vilest slander, which malice could invent, or calumny exhibit against the character and reputation of your predecessor, of him for whom you professed the highest esteem and friendship, and whom you certainly knew incapable of such complicated baseness. The remission of Callender's fine was a public approbation of his conduct. Is not the last restraint of vice, a sense of shame, rendered abortive, if abandoned characters do not excite abhorrence? . . . The serpent you cherished and warmed, bit the hand that nourished him, and gave you sufficient specimens of his talents, his gratitude, his justice, and his truth.

This letter is written in confidence—no eye but my own has seen what has passed. Faithful are the wounds of a friend. Often have I wished to have seen a different course pursued by you. I bear no malice; I cherish no enmity. I would not retaliate if I could—nay more in the true spirit of Christian charity, I would forgive, as I hope to be forgiven.

————

Jefferson replied on Sunday, July 22, claiming that his support of Callender had been based on opposition to the sedition laws and his agreement with the writer's politics at the time. "My charities to him were no more meant as encouragements to his scurrilities than those I give to the beggar at my door are meant as rewards for the vices of his life."

Jefferson and Abigail held such starkly different views of the events of the last decade or so that, despite the exchange of a total of seven letters from May to October 1804, it became clear further conversation was pointless. The exchange ended as suddenly as it had begun. John Adams learned of it only after it came to a close in the autumn of 1804.

On Wednesday, July 11, 1804, in Weehawken, New Jersey, high above the Hudson River, the vice president of the United States shot the first secretary of the Treasury dead in a duel fought over allegedly disparaging remarks Alexander Hamilton had made about Aaron Burr.

Jefferson left only the most cursory allusions to Hamilton's death. There was no testimonial, no letter of tribute to a friend that Jefferson expected to reach the newspapers. His silence at the time—the middle of 1804—seems odd, even ungracious. The politics of the moment may help explain why Jefferson held his tongue and his pen on the subject. The public reaction to Hamilton's death was intense and emotional. He was eulogized as "the greatest and most virtuous of men" by the newspaper he founded, the **New-York Evening Post**. His huge New York funeral, concluding with his burial at Trinity Church at Broadway and Wall Street in lower Manhattan, was a spectacular occasion.

With the presidential election coming in the autumn, Jefferson likely believed a dignified silence—or at least silence he hoped would be seen as dignified rather than callous—was the best course. In the heat of the summer of 1804, praise of Hamilton was interpreted not as the elegant reaction to a shocking and untimely death but as an endorsement of his program and a condemnation of his opponents. John Adams saw this, later writing Jefferson that Hamilton's partisans had "seized the moment of public feeling to come forward with funeral orations and printed panegyrics. . . . And why? Merely to disgrace the old Whigs, and keep the funds and banks in countenance."

To Jefferson, Hamilton had represented the most dangerous of tendencies. As president, however, Jefferson did little to destroy the system Hamilton had built. "We had indeed no personal dissensions," Jefferson later said of Hamilton. "Each of us, perhaps, thought well of the other as a man, but as politicians it was impossible for two men to be of more opposite principles."

The more pressing issue was Burr, who was indicted for murder both by a coroner's jury in New

York and by a grand jury in New Jersey. The vice president escaped both states in late July. For Jefferson, the problem of Aaron Burr was just beginning, for on Monday, August 6, 1804—not quite a month after Hamilton's death—Anthony Merry told London that Burr wanted to "effect a separation of the western part of the United States from that which lies between the Atlantic and the mountains, in its whole extent."

As president Jefferson found it useful to be aware of what the opposition was saying and doing: Behind the scenes, he was a shrewd consumer of newspapers and political intelligence. Reading the enemy journals, Jefferson found inspiration for, and detected perils to, a possible second term. "I sincerely regret that the unbounded calumnies of the Federal party have obliged me to throw myself on the verdict of my country for trial, my great desire having been to retire at the end of the present term to a life of tranquility, and it was my decided purpose when I entered into office," he wrote Elbridge Gerry in 1804. "They force my continuance."

George Clinton replaced Burr as the Republican candidate for vice president in the 1804 election. A New Yorker, Clinton was the child of Irish immigrants, and his rise to power presaged much of the story of American politics. "Clinton's family and connections do not entitle him to so distinguished a pre-eminence," John Jay had once written of him.

That was a strongly Federalist view. The Jeffersonian view was different, allowing for social and political mobility among whites.

The Federalists fielded Charles Cotesworth Pinckney, who had been John Adams's vice-presidential candidate four years before. Any challenge to the incumbent was an honorable but hopeless cause: Jefferson's popularity, based on lower taxes, significant prosperity, and the Louisiana Purchase, was secure. The president was reelected decisively, carrying 162 electoral votes to Pinckney's 14. Once so dominant, the Federalist enterprise was failing.

Writing from Philadelphia in December 1804, a correspondent signing himself "A Friend of the Constitution" told Jefferson that "there is a plot formed to murder you. . . . A band of hardy fellows have joined to do it. They are to have ten thousand dollars if they succeed in the attempt. They are to carry daggers and pistols. I have been invited to join them but would rather suffer death. I advise you to take care and be cautious how you walk about as some of the assassins are already in Washington."

The virulence of such threats belied the larger reality in the country. "The power of the Administration rests upon the support of a much stronger majority of the people throughout the Union than the former Administrations ever possessed since the first establishment of the Constitution," John Quincy Adams said in the wake of Jefferson's victory. The political faith of Adams's own father was doomed.

What lived and ruled was quintessentially Jeffersonian. The vibrant, breathing, prevailing politics of the hour reflected the complicated character of the triumphant president. The America of Jefferson was neither wholly Federal nor wholly Republican. It was, rather, a marbled blend of the two, confected by a practical man of affairs. The significance of the case of Louisiana in shaping the destinies of the country and in illuminating Jefferson's political leadership cannot be overstated. He believed, for instance, in a limited government, except when he thought the nation was best served by a more expansive one. It was a moment to savor success.

The capital was quiet. "We have but few strangers in town," Jefferson wrote Patsy on Monday, January 7, 1805.

His second inaugural at hand, Jefferson's thoughts drifted back over the trials he and his compatriots had faced in the past forty years. "We entered young into the first revolution and saw it terminate happily," Jefferson wrote the New Hampshire statesman John Langdon. "We had to engage when old in a second more perilous, because our people were divided. But we have weathered this too and seen all come round and to rights."

Yet even in victory Jefferson felt the weight of expectation. He knew political serenity never lasted. In December 1804, the Federalist senator William Plumer had been invited to dine with Jefferson. The president was dressed well ("A new suit of black— silk hose—shoes—clean linen, and his hair highly powdered") and the company ate well ("His dinner was elegant and rich"). To Plumer, though, Jefferson did not seem a man at the height of his political fortunes. "He was today reserved—appeared rather low spirited—conversed little," Plumer wrote in his diary.

The president had much on his mind. It was the age of Napoleon and Nelson, of contending powers who seemed never truly at peace, and America remained a target for the designs of enemies determined to dominate all or part of it. His final four years in public office were like the previous decades: Jefferson still struggled to secure the nation.

It began—but hardly ended—with Britain, which still harbored doubts about the wherewithal of the United States. "We drove them into being a nation when they were no more fit for it than the convicts of Botany Bay," the British diplomat Augustus Foster wrote his mother in 1805.

On Saturday, March 2, 1805, Vice President Burr took his leave of the capital with a paean to the Senate, which he called "a sanctuary; a citadel of law, of order, and of liberty; and it is here—it is here, in this exalted refuge; here, if anywhere, will resistance be made to the storms of popular frenzy and the silent arts of corruption; and if the Constitution be destined ever to perish by the sacrilegious hands of a demagogue or the usurper, which God avert, its expiring agonies will be witnessed on this floor."

William Plumer thought Burr was finished in political life—then thought again. "He can never, I think, rise again," Plumer wrote in his diary. "But surely he is a very extraordinary man, and is an exception to all rules." Plumer could not yet know how close to the mark he was.

"All is now business, hurry, interruption," Jefferson said on the eve of his second inauguration.

His political dominance over the nation was a given. In a private letter, Augustus Foster referred to him sarcastically as "the successor of Montezuma"—an allusion to the sixteenth-century Aztec god-king—but the irony was a tribute to Jefferson's power.

Jefferson's second inauguration fell on a Monday. He dressed in black and left the grounds of the President's House on horseback. In the Senate chamber, again speaking too softly to be widely heard, Jefferson gave his second inaugural address. "During this course of administration, and in order to disturb it, the artillery of the press has been leveled against us, charged with whatsoever its licentiousness could devise or dare," he said. "These abuses of an institution, so important to freedom and science, are deeply to be regretted, inasmuch as they tend to lessen its usefulness and to sap its safety." The marketplace, however, should decide. Censorship should be in the hands of the people.

Afterward Jefferson opened the President's House to callers. It, too, was run according to "pell-mell," and Foster, who made his way down Pennsylvania Avenue to the celebration, reported that "all who chose attended and even towards the close blacks and dirty boys, who drunk his wine and lolled upon his couches before us all." Some music capped the day, Foster noted—"a few pipes and drums"—and the festivities, such as they were, came to a close.

Jefferson was now the second two-term president of the United States. As he returned to greet the public—even the "blacks and dirty boys" of Foster's formulation—he had every intention of following Washington's example and retiring in four years' time. Only one contingency could tempt him to a third election—a contingency he mentioned to John Taylor of Caroline in early 1805. "My opinion originally was that the President of the U.S. should have been elected for 7 years, and forever ineligible afterwards." Now he was not so sure:

I have since become sensible that 7 years is too long to be unremovable, and that there should be a peaceable way of withdrawing a man in midway who is doing wrong. The service for 8 years with a power to remove at the end of the first four, comes nearly to my principle as corrected by experience. And it is in adherence to that that I determine to withdraw at the end of my second term. The danger is that the indulgence and attachments of the people will keep a man in the chair after he becomes a dotard, that reelection through life shall become habitual, and election for life follow that. Genl. Washington set the example of voluntary retirement after 8 years. I shall follow it and a few more precedents will oppose the obstacle of habit to anyone after a while who shall endeavor to extend his term. Perhaps it may beget a disposition to establish it by an amendment of the Constitution. . . . There is however but one circumstance which could engage my acquiescence in another election, to wit, such a division about a successor as might bring in a monarchist. But this circumstance is impossible.

Visions of a crown worried him still.

In the spring of 1805, the first fruits of the Lewis and Clark expedition started coming east. "It being the wish of Captain Lewis, I take the liberty to send you, for your own perusal, the notes which I have taken in the form of a journal in their original state," William Clark wrote Jefferson in April. Briefing Jefferson, Meriwether Lewis wrote: "I can foresee no material or probable obstruction to our progress, and entertain therefore the most sanguine hopes of complete success."

From Fort Mandan, the expedition's winter encampment on the Missouri River in North Dakota, the two leaders sent Jefferson a collection of artifacts. There was a box with the skins and skeletons of antelope and weasels and wolves. There were elk horns. There were scores of plants, and four living magpies. For Jefferson, it was a joyous delivery.

Accounts of Lewis and Clark fascinated the public. "The voyage of discovery of Capt. Lewis has engaged the attention of the curious and attracted the notice of many who were prejudiced against that country," wrote William Eustis from Massachusetts in August 1805. "This nation was never more respected abroad. The people were never more happy at home."

In late 1805, on a tree overlooking the Pacific, after a journey of more than three thousand miles, Clark staked the claim Jefferson had long dreamt of:

Capt. William Clark
December 3rd, 1805.
By Land.
U States in 1804 & 1805

A mission conceived on the Potomac had culminated on the Pacific. It was a staggering achievement, a Jeffersonian projection of power to find a path through the wilderness—and to master a continent.

Jefferson delighted in receiving things from the

West and the East. From London he ordered an eight-volume edition of Baxter's **History of England;** copies of essays on brewing, geometry, and astronomy; and maps of Europe, Asia, Africa, and South America. He wanted a telescope, too, and a pair of British globes "with the new discoveries to 1800."

It all fit. In his years in office he turned the presidency—and the President's House—into something it had not been before: a center of curiosity and inquiry, a vibrant institution that played informal but important roles in the broader life of the nation, from science to literature.

Jefferson set aside a room in the mansion for fossils. There were pieces of skulls, jawbones and teeth, tusks and a foreleg, "one horn of a colossal animal," and two hundred small bones collected by William Clark. "The bones are spread in a large room where you can work at your leisure, undisturbed by any mortal, from morning to night, taking your breakfast and dinner with us," he wrote Caspar Wistar, Jr., the Philadelphia physician who later published **A System of Anatomy.**

The explorer Zebulon Pike purchased two bear cubs for Jefferson from an Indian along the Rio Grande. His men nursed them with milk, and they arrived safely at the President's House in 1808. "I would recommend if practicable that they should be confined together in a cell (without chains) and regularly supplied with food and water, when I am nearly convinced that they will harmonize and become much more docile than if chained and confined asunder," Pike told the president.

Jefferson took Pike's advice. "I put them together while here in a place 10.f. square," Jefferson wrote the naturalist and painter Charles Willson Peale. "For the first day they worried one another very much with play, but after that they played at times, but were extremely happy together." Unsurprisingly, it proved impracticable to keep bears at the President's House, and Jefferson sent them to Peale's zoo in Philadelphia.

Considering a request from a man seeking counsel on determining whether a stone had been a meteor, Jefferson said: "We certainly are not to deny whatever we cannot account for." He was not always as skeptical as he ought to have been. He could be hopelessly wrong about scientific matters. Alluding to the maneuvering between Madison and Monroe for the presidential succession, Timothy Pickering said that while the Republicans fought for 1808, "the actual President is exploring the wilds of Louisiana—its salt plains—its rock or mineral salt—its immense prairies—in which he has discovered the earthly **paradise**—its numerous tribes and remnants of tribes of Indians and how many languages they speak—the hot springs and the warm mud-puddles in their vicinity—and the wonderful phenomena in one of a small or 'very minute shell fish' in shape resembling a mussel, but having four legs; and in another 'a vermes about half an inch long, moving with a serpentine or vermicular motion'!"

Jefferson could be prideful about his passions. "A jealous sense of praise and censure [are] among the most striking features of Mr. Jefferson's character, and his gratitude for the former [is] in exact proportion to his implacable resentment against the latter," wrote the British diplomat Edward Thornton. Jefferson, Thornton said, "is well-placed to be considered as an able statesman; but he is still more proud of being thought to combine a capacity for public affairs with the abstraction necessary for scientific pursuit."

The British even attributed some of Jefferson's long-standing hostility toward London to the French cultivation of his love of science and letters. "I really believe that the little account made in England of his literary talents at an early period added considerably to the bitterness which other causes had excited in his mind against her," Thornton wrote. "The French, under the monarchy at least, seem to have understood better this part of his character, and they gained his heart by associating him in their literary societies."

Still, his curiosity was perennial. "Will you come and take an Indian dinner with us tomorrow?" Jefferson wrote John Breckinridge in March 1806. "There is one of the chiefs who is really a curiosity, as possessing the art of speaking by signs, of which we have often heard, but never before seen an example.

The hour, as usual, half after three." With William Dunlap, the playwright and painter, Jefferson shared notes on the croaking of frogs in Washington, "the early approach of spring, of gardening French and English, preferring the latter and praising their great taste in laying out their ground." With Samuel and Margaret Bayard Smith, over tea in the President's House, Jefferson spoke of "agriculture, gardening, the differences of both in different countries and of the produce of different climates." He sent Mrs. Smith home with winter melon seed from Malta.

The subject did not matter; he was forever working over political and philosophical problems. "What would you think of raising a force for the defense of New Orleans in this manner?" Jefferson wrote to Madison, Gallatin, and Dearborn in February 1806. "Give a bounty of 50 acres of land, to be delivered immediately, to every able bodied man who will immediately settle on it, and hold himself in readiness to perform 2 years military service (on the usual pay) if called on within the first seven years of his residence."

He was always ready with suggestions for the young. "I would . . . advise him to read Livy, Tacitus, and Horace this summer," he wrote a friend with a son. "The two former will give him a good knowledge of the Roman history, while they instruct him in the language. He may at the same time read Anacharsis in French, which will strengthen his knowledge of that language and possess him of the Grecian history. I would advise him to read too Baxter's history of England as a corrective of Hume, which he has read. Indeed it is Hume republicanized."

Much of the nation's political energy in 1805 was devoted to dealing with tensions with Spain over the exact boundaries of the Louisiana territory, the fate of the Floridas, which Madrid declined to hand over, and financial claims. Spain remained a presence in North America, and it was allied with France. A mission of Monroe's to the Spanish capital failed, giving rise to a debate within the Jefferson administration about the use of force against Spanish posts and holdings.

Should the United States risk a broader war against Spain and France by taking a strong stand? In such a case, would it make sense for America to make common cause with England, which wanted allies against Napoleon, thus turning London, a potential enemy, into a friend, at least for the time being?

Jefferson's ultimate answer was no. Despite exploring the possibilities of a provisional treaty with Britain that would have created an alliance in the event of an American war with Spain or France, Jefferson decided that neutrality was still the country's best course. "Our Constitution is a peace establishment—it is not calculated for war," Jefferson said. "War would endanger its existence." In Jefferson's reading of history, war was about armies and navies and debt and honors, all of which had played their part in the fall of republics and the rise of empires.

Yet occasionally one had to fight to preserve liberty. Jefferson knew this, and he recognized that combat, though a last resort, was still a resort. The man who had been hunted by Tarleton would use every other weapon he could think of before projecting American military force. Measures short of traditional warfare—the fortification of harbors with cannons, the building of gunboats for coastal defense, and the preparation of the militia for possible deployment—were to be aggressively pursued, and Jefferson called for all of these in his annual message to Congress at the end of 1805.

As the year drew to a close, Jefferson saw foes wherever he looked. The British and, to a lesser extent, the French were harassing American ships. Napoleon won a glorious victory at Austerlitz. Nelson had died a hero's death in his triumph at Trafalgar. Closest to home, Burr, the old vice president, was allegedly plotting against the United States.

Thinking of France and England, Jefferson tried to make the best of a troubling hour. "What an awful spectacle does the world exhibit at this instant," Jefferson wrote in January 1806. "Our wish ought to be that he who has armies may not have the dominion of the sea, and that he who has dominion of the sea may be one who has no armies. In this way we may be quiet, at home at least." Jefferson had to face the inevitable question: How long would the quiet last—how long **could** it last?

THIRTY-SEVEN

A Deep, Dark, and Widespread Conspiracy

The designs of our Cataline are as real as they are romantic.

—THOMAS JEFFERSON,
on Aaron Burr's western maneuvers

JEFFERSON'S WINTER WAS BRIGHTENED by Patsy's family's long stay in the President's House, where his only surviving daughter from his marriage gave birth to a grandson, James Madison Randolph, named in honor of the grandfather's secretary of state. Dolley Madison had helped Patsy prepare for the season, acquiring a "fashionable wig . . . a set of combs for dressing the hair, a bonnet, shawl and white lace veil" from Baltimore, as well as two lace half handkerchiefs.

The president also took a moment to tend to his cellar in Washington, checking to make sure he had sufficient Bordeaux (he did) but sending for some additional sparkling wines. He thought his current holdings "dry without any softness."

On Capitol Hill, though, a cousin brought whatever serenity Jefferson was enjoying to an end. Once an ally, always an eccentric, John Randolph of Roanoke broke with Jefferson in March 1806. The year before, Randolph had stopped a Jefferson-sponsored compromise settlement of a long-standing dispute involving the Yazoo land companies (a corrupt Georgia legislature had sold lands rightly belonging to the Creeks, creating a speculative market). That episode was a prelude to Randolph's more decisive move into opposition.

The new occasion was debate over resolutions to limit or even ban British imports in retaliation for British depredations against American shipping. On the floor of the House, Randolph declared war on the administration.

William Plumer left the Senate chamber that day to go to the House to hear him. "He considered Great Britain as now contending for her existence—as fighting the battles of the civilized world against Bonaparte who is usurping the dominion of the world," Plumer wrote of Randolph's speech. Randolph singled out Jefferson and Madison for particular assault. "It was the most bitter, severe and eloquent philippic I ever heard," wrote Plumer. Randolph struck again the next day and was, Plumer said, "uncommonly severe on the President. . . . Mr. Randolph has passed the Rubicon, neither the President or Secretary of State can after this be on terms with him. He has set them and their measures at defiance."

Cutting and sarcastic, Randolph seemed to spare no one. A colleague who rose to speak was waved away. "**Sit down,** Sir, I say **sit down,** Sir, **learn to keep your proper level,**" Randolph said. On the subject of the president himself, Randolph "astonished all his hearers by the boldness of his animadversions on executive conduct," wrote Senator Samuel Smith of Maryland.

Eventually known as either the "Quids" (after "**tertium quid,**" which in Latin means "a third something") or the "Old Republicans," Randolph's faction was a manifestation of purer, simpler Republican principles. Randolph's followers held that Jefferson had moved too far in a Federalist direction and that they, not the president or his men, were the true believers.

The break was in some ways a sign that Jefferson had transcended the simpler rhetorical categories of the post-1798 period. It was easy to speak theoretically and idealistically about politics when one is seeking power. The demands of exercising it once it is won, however, are so complex and fluid that ideological certitude is often among the first casualties of actual governing. Jefferson had achieved something that his Federalist foes would not have thought possible: He was, to some, no longer Republican enough. Jefferson was, in other words, a man who had displeased the extremes of his day—a sign that he had been guided not by dogma but by principled pragmatism.

The president was indeed considering projections of power that would have broadened the role of the public sector beyond the strict confines favored by some believers in limited government. Jefferson was the first president to advocate a broad program of public works, calling for a constitutional amendment to authorize the financing of "education, roads, rivers, canals," and other projects.

"By these operations," he said in his Sixth Annual Message, "new channels of communication will be opened between the States; the lines of separation will disappear, their interests will be identified, and their union cemented by new and indissoluble ties." Later, in the spring of 1808, Secretary of the Treasury Albert Gallatin delivered a landmark report proposing $20 million in infrastucture improvements to roads and canals. Due to the fiscal strains during the Embargo and rising tensions with England, and believing himself without the constitutional authority, Jefferson was unable to realize this ambitious program, but nearly every project that Gallatin outlined was eventually completed. The first of these was the federally sponsored Cumberland or National Road, running west from Maryland and in time reaching Illinois.

As Randolph saw it, Jefferson's largely moderate politics was a path to disaster. "Never, in my opinion, had the cause of free government more to fear than now," Randolph wrote in 1806. Republicans loyal to the president had become "secret enemies, or lukewarm advocates" of the cause of republicanism, " 'damning with faint praise' the principles they had sworn to support." Melodramatically, Randolph asked: "Is the present executive perfect? Amidst the various agents of that department has there been, or can there be, no wrong committed?"

To Randolph the answer was self-evident. Jefferson had proved too much of a compromiser. Moderation, Randolph said, was "the mask which ambition has worn" through the ages. By the last year of the president's term, Randolph would tell James Monroe, "The **old** republican party is already ruined, past redemption."

Jefferson affected an air of calm about the events of the current session, but the telltale headache was back, suggesting the Republican split and the complications of the European situation—which included the possibility of an American war—weighed heavily.

In late April 1806 in New York, the HMS **Leander** was screening American ships in search of British seamen. Firing a warning shot, the **Leander** mistakenly killed an American sailor. Two other British ships—the **Driver** and the **Cambrian**—were nearby. Ordering the three ships out of U.S. waters, Jefferson called for the arrest of the **Leander** captain for murder.

His headache was debilitating. "My present malady keeps me through the whole day incapable of business or conversation," Jefferson wrote the Pennsylvania senator George Logan; Jefferson could stand face-to-face meetings only in the evenings, when the pain seems to have ebbed. He was suffering pain in his leg, too (he called it "a lameness in the knee"). And he was worried about money. "I have gotten so into arrears at Washington, as to render it necessary for me not only to avoid new engagements, but to suspend every expense which is not indispensable: otherwise I shall leave that place with burdens contracted there, which if they should fall on my private fortune, will doom me to a comfortless old age," Jefferson wrote John Wayles Eppes in May 1806.

He lost his oldest mentor in early summer. George Wythe had risen as usual on Sunday, May 25, 1806, and eaten breakfast at home. At around nine o'clock that morning, he was sick to his stomach; the rest of his household was stricken, too. One member, a mixed-race teenager named Michael Brown, died a few days later. William Duval, a magistrate, was suspicious and ordered an autopsy. Four physicians attended, and Duval told Jefferson "from the inflammation on the stomach and bowels they said that it was the kind of inflammation produced by poison." The culprit was presumably George Sweeney, a Wythe grandnephew whose motives, if he did it, may have included jealousy and money.

"I am murdered," Wythe said on May 25, 1806, but Duval reported that Wythe "mentioned no name." As he faded, he said, "Let me die righteous."

It was a sensational story, one that raised interesting questions about George Wythe's private life. Married twice and now widowed, Wythe lived in Williamsburg with young Michael Brown and with his housekeeper Lydia Broadnax, a free woman of color. In Wythe's will, Broadnax was to inherit the Wythe house, among other property, and Wythe had included provisions asking Jefferson to oversee the education of Michael Brown in the event of Wythe's death.

The implications of these arrangements—that Brown was the son of Broadnax and Wythe—are clear but unproven. "Whether Brown, who was described as 'yellow' skinned, was his biological son or not, Wythe treated him as if he were, taking pains with his education," wrote the historian Annette Gordon-Reed. "Certainly asking his own favorite and most famous pupil, the current president of the United States, to become Michael's guardian shows the depth of his affection for the boy."

Wythe left Jefferson, whom he had loved, his books, silver cups, and a gold-headed cane. The crime disturbed and distressed the president, who told Duval that he would have happily taken on the education of Michael Brown. The task, he said, would have "gratified me unceasingly with the constant recollection and execution of the wishes of my friend." Did Jefferson believe Michael Brown to be the son of his old teacher? If so, what emotions would news of the alleged murder of his mentor by a disgruntled member of Wythe's white family have stirred up in Jefferson, who knew much about the living of such a life? We do not know, but it is interesting that Jefferson sought to understand the story as a severe aberration, not as something that could happen in the ordinary course of life. "Such an instance of depravity has been hitherto known to us only in the fables of the poets," Jefferson wrote Duval in June 1806. The more imaginative distance Jefferson could put between himself and Wythe's fate, the better.

In the summer there was something new—a debilitating drought in Virginia—and in the autumn something by now familiar: reports that Aaron Burr was making trouble.

Since the duel with Hamilton, Burr had set out on a Wanderjahr. He traveled west, and rumors had him variously plotting to convince some states to secede and form a western empire or planning an independent strike into Mexico.

The most fevered speculation carried matters even further by suggesting that Burr was contemplating raising troops to march on Washington and take over the United States. "Burr is unquestionably very actively engaged in the Westward in preparations to sever that from this part of the Union," Jefferson wrote in November 1806. The former vice president was allegedly recruiting men, stocking arms, and building boats.

Jefferson heard nothing to alleviate his concerns. "This is indeed a deep, dark and widespread conspiracy," the American general James Wilkinson wrote Jefferson in November, "embracing the young and the old, the democrat and the Federalist, the native and the foreigner, the patriot of 76 and the exotic of yesterday, the opulent and the needy, the Ins and the Outs, and I fear it will receive strong support in New Orleans."

Wilkinson himself was trouble. An officer long in the pay of the Spanish, he was a scoundrel of the first order and had been in conversations with Burr about possible plots. At some point Wilkinson decided it was in his interest to inform Jefferson of Burr's alleged treachery, thus saving himself for another day.

By November 27, 1806, Jefferson was worried enough to issue a proclamation warning that "sundry persons," including "citizens of the United States," were "conspiring and confederating together" to take over Spanish holdings.

What was Burr doing? It is not certain even now, more than two centuries later. At first he seemed interested in a military venture to seize control of Texas and other parts of Spanish America. Such an operation was known as a filibuster—an independent strike. Burr and his sundry compatriots seemed to be preparing for an expedition of some kind. The goal was unclear, except that Jefferson believed it involved Burr assuming power and land in the West, possibly as far south as Mexico, and perhaps forming an empire of his own.

On Saturday, December 27, 1806, New Hampshire senator William Plumer dined with Jefferson, who, over coffee, said he believed all would be well. Jefferson, Plumer said, "had no doubt the conspiracy would be crushed, extensive as it was, with little trouble and expense to the United States." Incriminating papers soon emerged, and Jefferson forwarded them to Congress in January 1807.

In the meantime, Jefferson was seeking sufficient power to deal with any domestic crisis. Eight days before his chat with Plumer, Jefferson had drafted a bill "authorizing the employment of the land or naval forces of the U.S. in cases of insurrection." He sent the proposed legislation to Virginia congressman John Dawson with this revealing note: "Th:Jefferson presents his compliments to Mr. Dawson, and his request that he will be so good as to copy the within and burn this original, as he is very unwilling to meddle personally with the details of the proceedings of the legislature."

This was the pure political Jefferson, fighting to defend the nation by asking for a grant of power while disguising his own role in the acquisition of that authority. His adversaries might see such maneuvers as hypocritical or underhanded, but in Jefferson's mind he was doing the right thing the right way. To seize power grandly would threaten the democratic ethos of the country—an ethos he thought essential. Better to work through allies in Congress, he thought, than to risk appearing monarchical—even if the control he sought was the kind a Federalist president might want, too. It was the method of a practical man.

Jefferson pursued Burr unapologetically. He did so less out of personal ambition or jealousy—since the killing of Hamilton, Burr could pose no threat within the traditional political system—than out of his concern for the security and sanctity of the nation. As in the case of Louisiana, the cause of preserving the Union was more important than what Jefferson called the "strict line of the law." In his report on Burr to Congress on Thursday, January 22, 1807, Jefferson took the extraordinary step of declaring that his former vice president's "guilt is placed beyond question"—a decision not unlike the ones he had made long ago in the Josiah Philips case and in the arrest of the "Hair Buyer General." If the liberties of the suspects, including Burr, were violated, then so be it.

By late March 1807, Burr was under arrest. Jefferson paid careful attention to the proceedings. "No man's history proves better the value of honesty," Jefferson wrote. "With that, what might he not have been!" Unfortunately his headache, he said, "leaves me but an hour and a half each morning capable of any business at all."

Burr was brought to Richmond for trial, where John Marshall presided over a courtroom set up in the Eagle Tavern. Jefferson took an obsessive interest in the case, gathering information and advising the prosecution counsel. He believed serious issues were at stake and characteristically threw himself into the matter in detail—but at a distance.

Though Burr was indicted for treason, the weaknesses of the case against him grew evident as the trial progressed. Coconspirator-turned-prosecution-witness James Wilkinson had charged that Burr intended to capture New Orleans—an allegation that had led Jefferson to declare martial law there to defend against any treachery—and to lead an attack on Spanish holdings. (A problematic allegation, since filibusters were not illegal.)

The messenger from Richmond rode up Jefferson's mountain in darkness. The vacationing president was still awake, and he perused the communication—and its enclosure—with care. It was no ordinary delivery: U.S. attorney George Hay, the prosecutor in the Burr case, was subpoenaing the president to testify at the trial in person. After consulting with Madison, a houseguest at Monticello, Jefferson refused to submit himself and his office to the control of others. Writing Hay the next day, he said: "As I do not believe that the district courts have a power of **commanding** the Executive government to abandon superior duties and attend on them, at whatever distance, I am unwilling by any notice of the subpoena to set a precedent which might sanction a proceeding so preposterous."

Jefferson's decision to reserve unto himself the authority to decide whether to obey a summons to testify set a significant precedent in executive power: The president, Jefferson was saying, had higher obligations to the common good than to answer the importunings of the legal system. He would, instead, send Hay relevant documents—a wise compromise that prevented a president from holding himself above the law but preserved his ability to do his job without being forced to travel at the command of distant courts. He enclosed the subpoena to Hay and dispatched it whence it had come.

Marshall's decisions and demeanor as the trial judge exacerbated matters for Jefferson, who tended to ascribe any setback for the prosecution to the chief justice's politics. The proceedings in Virginia joined the repeal of the Judiciary Act of 1801, the reaction to **Marbury,** and the impeachment of Samuel Chase as a front in Jefferson's long struggle against a judicial system that he disliked and distrusted more and more as the years passed.

Burr's eventual acquittal enraged the president. In truth, the evidence on the treason charge against the defendant was weak. Jefferson nevertheless hoped that the country would join him in seeing the hand of Marshall as the decisive force in thwarting the prosecution. "The nation will judge both the offender, and judges for themselves," Jefferson wrote William Branch Giles. "If a member of the Executive or Legislature does wrong, the day is never far distant when the people will remove him." Perhaps, Jefferson thought, outrage over the Burr verdict could be channeled into a constitutional amendment making judges more accountable to the public.

He had been miserable for a week. "I am now in the 7th day of a periodical head-ache, and I write this in the morning before the fit has come on," he wrote Patsy in March 1807. "The fits are by no means as severe as I have felt in former times, but they hold me very long, from 9 or 10 in the morning till dark. Neither Calomel nor bark has as yet made the least impression on them."

There were also the usual complaints and stresses. "I am tired of an office where I can do no more good than many others who would be glad to be employed in it," he wrote his old Revolutionary colleague John Dickinson in early 1807. "To myself personally it brings nothing but unceasing drudgery and daily loss of friends."

In this period a proposed treaty with Britain arrived in Washington. It did little for American interests. "The British commissioners appear to have screwed every article as far as it would bear, to have taken everything, and yielded nothing," Jefferson wrote of the treaty in March 1807. Diplomacy, in short, had not resolved conflict with Britain, particularly in terms of stopping the humiliating impressment of American seamen. Jefferson refused to send it to the Senate.

In February 1807, in a passing conversation with his sons-in-law, Jefferson invited John Wayles Eppes to join him on some occasion (the details are unknown) but did not include Thomas Mann Randolph, Jr. The slight, however unintentional, at once enraged and depressed Randolph, who wrote Jefferson an emotional letter complaining that the president favored Eppes, whom Randolph envied and saw as an all-too-successful rival for the affections and attentions of their father-in-law.

Jefferson was taken aback by the complaints. He had, he said, detected some tension between the two congressmen who had married daughters of his, but—typically for Jefferson—he had chosen not to inquire about the unease; avoiding overt conflict was a Jeffersonian specialty. "What acts of mine can have induced you to suppose that I felt or manifested a preference for [Eppes], I cannot conceive," Jefferson soothingly wrote Randolph.

In his apparent anger and anguish, Randolph had moved out of the President's House. "Your return to the house would indeed be a consolation to me," wrote Jefferson, who could not take his mind off the question. "Really loving you as I would a son (for I protest I know no difference) I took it too much for granted you were as sensible of it as myself," he said in a second note on February 19, 1807.

Randolph, who had decided not to stand for re-election to Congress, fell ill in his new lodgings, and Jefferson dispatched a retainer to keep watch over his condition.

Jefferson's paternal feelings toward Randolph were genuine. "I certainly would not urge anything that would be strongly repugnant to your feelings, but I wish, my dear Sir, you could consent to return to your former room here," Jefferson wrote Randolph on February 28.

Randolph did come back, but he was very sick and very depressed. He mused about suicide. Jefferson kept track of the number of paces the recuperating Randolph was able to walk in the circular room on the second floor of the President's House (500 or 600 steps the first day he tried; 1,200 the next) and wrote Patsy frequent optimistic reports. Domestic harmony mattered as much to him as political harmony did.

THIRTY-EIGHT

This Damned Embargo

> Never since the battle of Lexington have I seen this country in such a state of exasperation as at present, and even that did not produce such unanimity.
>
> —THOMAS JEFFERSON, on the British attack on the USS **Chesapeake**

IN WASHINGTON, Jefferson was on war footing. "Something now occurs almost every day on which it is desirable to have the opinions of the heads of departments," Jefferson wrote Treasury secretary Albert Gallatin in July 1807. The members of the cabinet were to feel free, Jefferson said, "to call on me at any moment of the day which suits their separate convenience."

The precipitating crisis was a Monday, June 22, 1807, attack on the USS **Chesapeake** by the HMS **Leopard** in the waters off Cape Henry on the Virginia coast. The British ship had ordered the American one to allow it to search the **Chesapeake** for deserters. The commanding officer of the **Chesapeake**, James Barron, refused, at which point the

Leopard opened fire on the American frigate. Twenty-two shots struck the **Chesapeake** before the Americans managed to get off a single rejoinder. Barron and seventeen others were wounded. Three men were killed.

It was an act of war—an insult to, and an attack on, the United States of America. The public reaction was swift. "After I had read the information of the outrageous attack on the **Chesapeake,** I felt as every true American should feel—indignation and resentment at the British," a correspondent wrote Jefferson from Philadelphia on Monday, June 29.

Jefferson instantly summoned the cabinet. Gallatin was away in Maryland. "I am sorry to be obliged to hasten your return," Jefferson wrote him, "and pray it may be without a moment's avoidable delay." Gallatin was sick but would be along quickly. "I am so much fatigued that I cannot ride all night by the mail; but I will be with you on Wednesday about two or three o'clock in the afternoon." Not a moment was to be wasted.

On the Fourth of July, Federalists made a point of appearing at Jefferson's annual levee; a newspaper reported that the president's foes "mingled with perfect cordiality with their republican brethren." At a dinner at Stelle's, there were patriotic toasts. "The American People—Ready at a moment's warning to vindicate the rights, and avenge the wrongs of their country," was one; another guest rose and said, "The President of the United States—The hand that drafted the Declaration of Independence will maintain, inviolate, the principles it recognizes."

Jefferson grasped the import of the moment, issuing a proclamation banning armed British ships from U.S. waters. At a cabinet meeting he decided to call on the governors of the states to have their quotas of one hundred thousand militiamen ready, and he ordered the purchase of arms, ammunition, and supplies. The president gave the order unilaterally, without congressional approval.

He believed he was the best judge of what was needed in the present crisis. "The moment our peace was threatened, I deemed it indispensable to secure a greater provision of those articles of military stores with which our magazines were not sufficiently furnished," Jefferson told Congress after the fact. "I trust that the legislature, feeling the same anxiety for the safety of our country, so materially advanced by this precaution, will approve, when done, what they would have seen so important to be done, if then assembled."

Congress agreed. The presidency was further strengthened, and Jefferson's view of power affirmed. "A strict observance of the written laws is doubtless **one** of the high duties of a good citizen, but it is not **the highest**," he wrote after he left office. "The laws of necessity, of self-preservation, of saving our country when in danger, are of higher obligation. To lose our country by a scrupulous adherence to written law, would be to lose the law itself, with life, liberty, property and all those who are enjoying them with us; thus absurdly sacrificing the end to the means."

A ship—the USS **Revenge**—was dispatched to England to receive an answer from the British government about the **Leopard**'s attack. Outrage came upon outrage: A revenue cutter was also fired upon; its most prominent passenger, Vice President George Clinton, later told Jefferson that the emotion generated by the British depredations was unsettling even the most extreme of Federalists. "To the Tories or British Federalists," Clinton said, "this is a mortifying circumstance as they cannot but perceive that in case of war they will be deserted by their electioneering allies and left to shift for themselves."

Anti-British feeling was certainly acute. "The spirit and enterprise of the American character are peculiarly fit for offensive enterprises," the journalist William Duane wrote Jefferson on Wednesday, July 8. He proposed a four-point attack on the British as an offensive move in the wake of the **Chesapeake**. Duane's suggestions: Strike Canada, capture Halifax, and invade Newfoundland and Jamaica.

Jefferson planned to call Congress for October 1807. "Reason and the usage of civilized nations require that we should give them an opportunity of disavowal and reparation," Jefferson wrote to John Wayles Eppes on Sunday, July 12. "Our own interest, too, the very means of making war, requires that we should give time to our merchants to gather in their vessels and property and our seamen now afloat."

Jefferson's openness to war was evident from the beginning of the crisis. " 'Reparation for the past and security for the future' is our motto; but whether the English will yield it freely, or will require resort to non-intercourse, or to war, is yet to be seen," he said. "We prepare for the last."

On the final day of July 1807, he called for the October special session of Congress. Worried about remaining fully informed during a visit to Monticello, he increased the mail service from Washington to Monticello, where he was to spend the latter part of the summer.

Despite the war fever in the first hours of the **Chesapeake** crisis, Jefferson had guessed that lawmakers would be more inclined to impose an embargo than to go immediately to war. He was not lost in a philosophic experiment in pacifism—he was willing to fight. But he believed Congress would prefer an embargo first.

Differing Jeffersonian impulses were in conflict. His fear of the threat large military establishments posed to republics was predominant at the moment. Yet he was also being practical. He knew America could not build a navy to compete with Britain's soon enough to make a difference in the struggle at hand. His experience of the past two decades in foreign policy had also taught him that time often resolved the issues of the hour.

From Nootka Sound to St. Domingue, shifting strategic concerns abroad—the fall of a government in London, the decision of an emperor in Paris, the outcome of a battle in a far-off place—could settle (or complicate) the problems facing the United States.

At dinner one day in November 1807 at the President's House, David Montagu Erskine, the new British minister, was sitting with Jefferson, Augustus Foster, the poet-diplomat Joel Barlow, and Louisa Catherine and John Quincy Adams. There were reports that London might transfer the negotiations over the maritime issues to Washington. If true, Jefferson said to Erskine, "I suppose [this] will take us all winter, and in the meantime your nation will make peace, and leave us nothing to dispute about—**that is all my hope**." Recording the incident in his diary, John Quincy Adams wrote: "If there was any sincerity in these words, **procrastination** includes the whole compass of Mr. Jefferson's policy, which I believe to be really the case."

The question of the moment, Jefferson told Thomas Mann Randolph, Jr., on Monday, November 30, was "whether War, Embargo or Nothing shall be the course. The middle proposition is most likely." But that was not to be the only American response. "In the meantime," Jefferson said, "there is a disposition 1. To vote a sufficient number of gunboats. 2. A sufficient sum (750,000 D.) for defensive works. 3. To classify the militia. 4. To establish a Naval militia. 5. To give a bounty in lands in Orleans on the West side of the river for a strong settlement of Americans as a Militia."

An embargo was a means, not an end. "The members, as far as I can judge are extremely disposed for peace: and as there is no doubt Gr. Br. will disavow the act of the **Leopard,** I am inclined to believe they will be more disposed to combat her practice of impressment by a non-importation law than by arms," he had written Thomas Mann Randolph, Jr., on Monday, October 26.

In December 1807, news from Paris and London roiled the already unsettled American capital. Napoleon announced he was extending the Berlin Decree banning British imports to all nations, including the United States. George III, far from making concessions on the impressment question, ordered British vessels to seize British subjects from merchant and warships.

Informing Congress that two of the world's great powers were increasing the pressure on American interests, Jefferson proposed that the United States order its own ships to remain in port in the United States while "making every preparation for whatever events may grow out of the present crisis."

What came next? Politically, war seemed impossible at the moment. The emotional intensity that had grown out of the **Chesapeake** affair in summer had faded. "The war fever is past," Jefferson wrote Patsy in November.

For now, the answer was embargo. It was far from ideal, and Albert Gallatin articulated its inherent flaws best. "In every point of view, privations, sufferings, revenue, effect on the enemy, politics at home, etc., I prefer war to a permanent embargo," Gallatin told Jefferson on Friday, December 18. Moreover, "Governmental prohibitions do always more mischief than had been calculated; and it is not without much hesitation that a statesman should hazard to regulate the concerns of individuals as if he could do it better than themselves."

In principle, Jefferson agreed. In practice, he was torn. "What is **good** in this case cannot be effected," he wrote Gallatin; "we have, therefore, only to find out what will be **least bad**."

Jefferson was guided in part by republican ideology: The end of war and the reign of reason was a dream of the age. War led to monarchy and aristocracy and evils that tended to destroy the liberty of the many while empowering the few. Yet Jefferson was no pacific purist. He had waged war in the Mediterranean, and he was willing to wage it against Britain and possibly against France.

But not yet. His calculation—one ratified by Congress—was that time was America's ally. "The embargo keeping at home our vessels, cargoes and seamen, saves us the necessity of making their capture the cause of immediate war, for if going to England, France had determined to take them; if to any other place, England was to take them," Jefferson wrote John Taylor. "This gives time. Time may produce peace in Europe. Peace in Europe removes all causes of differences till another European war, and by that time our debt may be paid, our revenues clear, and our strength increased."

The legislation had passed quickly, and Jefferson signed the embargo on Tuesday, December 22, 1807. It was a breathtaking bill, a projection of governmental power that surpassed even the hated Alien and Sedition Acts. After signing it, Jefferson was struck by "a tooth-ache . . . which brought on a very large and hard swelling of the face, and that produced a fever which left me last night," he wrote Patsy on Tuesday, December 29. He felt the burdens of office as never before.

The pain in his jaw compounded the stress he was feeling. For all intents and purposes, he was expanding federal power into every part of the economic life of every American. Trade with foreign nations was forbidden. Nothing could come into the country; nothing could go out. A subsequent enforcement act gave Jefferson himself power over shipping.

He was accustomed to wielding the weapons of economic war. Nonimportation with targeted countries, for instance, had been part of his life since Williamsburg. He believed in, and had long practiced, commercial diplomacy. The republican dream of a war-free world of open markets had proved unrealizable, which led Jefferson to adapt his principles to the realities that confronted the United States. Economic coercion was a widely accepted means of foreign policy.

The totality of an embargo was related but different: It was viewed as a limited means of securing time to prepare for war or to let the threat of war pass. As the American experience would show, embargoes were impractical over the long term. Jefferson understood that the nation was commercial as well as agrarian and that his duty extended to the whole country. "Our people have a decided taste for navigation and commerce," he said. "They take this from their mother country: and their servants are in duty bound to calculate all their measures on this datum."

In the beginning the country was willing to trust Jefferson's course. "Confidence now seems to be in Mr. Jefferson's hands, as effectual in producing a compliance with his recommendations as soldiers in the hands of Bonaparte in procuring submission to his commands," Timothy Pickering wrote on Monday, January 18, 1808. Passage of the embargo, he said, was the result of the public's "implicit, blind confidence" in the president.

"Our embargo, which has been a very trying measure, has produced one very happy, and permanent effect," Jefferson wrote Lafayette. "It has set us all on domestic manufacture, and will I verily believe reduce our future demands on England fully one half."

That was an overstatement, but the yearlong embargo did have an effect in Britain. There were protests from merchants and manufacturers against the anti-American policy that had led to Jefferson's reprisal. In April 1808, Britain, feeling the lack of an American market, essentially invited ships to break the embargo. Smuggling was an enormous problem, particularly to the north, where illicit trade with the British in the Canadian region flourished. Jefferson warned those "combining and confederating together on Lake Champlain and the country thereto adjacent for the purposes of forming insurrections against the authority of the laws of the United States." The executive branch was given extraordinary authority to enforce the embargo.

The embargo turned American politics upside down. Jefferson became the explicit advocate of strong central power. Republicans who favored less government became the most meddlesome of regulators. Connecticut became a bastion of states' rights, asserting that "in such a crisis of affairs, it is right, and has become the duty of the legislative and executive authorities in the State, to withhold their aid and cooperation from the execution of the act passed to enforce more effectually the embargo system."

The embargo succeeded in the sense that it postponed war with Britain, though neither it nor any other policy finally prevented what became known as the War of 1812. The diplomat William Pinkney probably had it right when he told Madison in 1809: "Any other measure than the embargo would have been madness or cowardice. For no others were in our choice but war with both aggressors, or submission to both; with the certainty, too, that that submission would in its progress either lead to war, or to a state of abject degradation."

The embargo was not out of character for Jefferson. In the broadest sense, it put him in control, but somewhat at a remove, and it avoided immediate conflict with the European powers. Like the Louisiana Purchase—which was, to say the very least, vastly more successful—the embargo illustrated Jefferson's flexibility and capacity to adapt his professed ideology to present realities. "The embargo is salutary," Jefferson wrote Benjamin Rush in January 1808. "It postpones war, gives time, and the benefit of events which that may produce, particularly that of peace in Europe, which will postpone the causes of difference to the next war."

History has not been kind to Jefferson's embargo; it is commonly seen as bad policy that delayed but did not prevent war and left America weaker. There is much to this criticism, but the options Jefferson had were such that the embargo, as he himself put it, may not have been a good idea, but it was the least bad. The country was not ready for war with Britain (or with France) either politically or militarily, and the politics of the moment worked against attempts to strengthen the army and the navy.

Prevailing opinion held that standing armies were bad and that naval establishments were invitations to—rather than defenses against—war, as well as incredibly expensive. These were Jefferson's opinions, too, in the abstract, but he had proved adept at adapting his convictions. He did ask Congress for measures that would have strengthened the nation's defenses at least somewhat. Congress resisted, or moved slowly, and that was that. Neither Jefferson nor the national leadership of the first decade or so of the nineteenth century comes off well in terms of military preparedness. The American failure to provide sufficiently for defense until war was actually upon her was a phenomenon the country would see again.

Jefferson tried to convince himself the embargo was working. "I have been happy in my journey through the country to this place to find the people unanimous in their preference of the embargo to war, and the great sacrifice they make rendered a cheerful one from a sense of its necessity," Jefferson wrote from Monticello in May 1808.

His own mail suggested otherwise. "You infernal villain," wrote a John Lane Jones from Boston in August. "How much longer are you going to keep this damned Embargo on to starve us poor people. One of my children has already starved to death of which I am ashamed and declared that it died of an apoplexy. I have three more children which I expect will starve soon if I don't get something for them to eat which cannot be had."

"You are the damdest fool that God put life into," an anonymous letter writer told Jefferson in the middle of 1808. "God dam you."

Another anonymous writer with a unique sense of capitalization wrote in June: "THY DESTRUCtion is NEAr At HAND THOMAS. THE, REtriBUTive, sword is SUSPENDED OVEr THY HEAD, BY A SlENDER THREAD.—BEWARE."

In some quarters in New England—especially in Boston—the reaction to the attack on the **Chesapeake** had been muted. John Quincy Adams, who was sympathetic to Jefferson in the crisis, had to convince Federalists in Boston to hold a town meeting "in an open, free-hearted manner, setting aside all party feeling . . . to support the government of their country." He succeeded but at a price: He was told that he "should have his head taken off for his apostasy to the Federalists."

Talk of disunion was revived. Timothy Pickering wrote a public letter attacking the embargo and the president; in New York, villagers burned Jefferson in effigy on the Fourth of July, 1808.

From Boston, the Republican governor of Massachusetts, James Sullivan, was convinced that the embargo was strengthening the hands of the pro-British forces. "The attempt is to . . . divide the nation, and establish in this part of this hemisphere a different form of government, under the protection of Great Britain," Sullivan wrote to Jefferson in April 1808. "You will laugh at this, and so would Southern members of Congress, but their destruction will come upon them as a whirlwind. . . . The walls of Monticello are not impregnable to the arm of civil contest, or the rapacious hand of tyranny."

The Federalists had more conventional means at their disposal to show that they, not the Jeffersonians, represented the American mainstream: the presidential election of 1808.

Early that year, James Madison was nominated for president by congressional caucus. Jefferson had long hoped that Madison would succeed him, but he worried about competition between Madison and James Monroe, who had also won votes in the caucus.

"I see with infinite grief a contest arising between yourself and another who have been very dear to each other, and equally so to me," Jefferson wrote Monroe from Washington in February 1808. "I sincerely pray that these dispositions may not be affected between you. . . . I know too well from experience the progress of political controversy, and the exacerbation of spirit into which it degenerates, not to fear for the continuance of your mutual esteem. One piquing thing said, draws on another, that a third, and always with increasing acrimony, until all restraint is thrown off, and it becomes difficult for yourselves to keep clear of the toils in which your friends will endeavor to interlace you, and to avoid the participation in their passions which they will endeavor to produce."

His delineation of the environment and the emotions of the politician was born of a lifetime of experience. The tension between social harmony and the demands of politics was not one that Jefferson—or anyone else—could ever resolve. It could only be managed.

The election of 1808 was a referendum on Jefferson. With Madison, his closest ally, as the Republican candidate, it could be no other. The Federalists put Charles Cotesworth Pinckney forward again. The arguments against Madison were echoes of old refrains against Jefferson—that Madison favored the French and disliked the British; that Virginia had held too much power for too long; that the Republican creed inevitably led to mob rule.

Nothing worked. Madison won a substantial victory, with 122 electoral votes to Pinckney's 47.

Jefferson's presidency was ending as his public life had begun: amid fears of monarchy. In Congress in early January 1809, there was a movement toward ending the embargo and, in the event of ongoing European hostilities, issuing letters of marque and reprisal, meaning private ships could act as vessels of war, attacking and capturing enemy craft. To Jefferson, writing in January, "the monarchists of the North (who have been for some time fostering the hope of separation) have . . . federalized the 5 Eastern states and . . . endanger[ed] N. York. . . . The Massachusetts legislature, which is to meet the middle of this month, it is believed will call a convention to consider the question of a separation of the Union, and to propose it to the whole country East of the North river, and they are assured of the protection of Gr. Br."

The enveloping fear was of British encroachment. "A line seems now to be drawing," Jefferson said, "between the really republican Federalists and the English party who are devoted, soul and body, to England and monarchy." Some things in Jefferson's world never changed.

THIRTY-NINE

A Farewell to Ultimate Power

> Considering the extraordinary character of the
> times in which we live, our attention should
> unremittingly be fixed on the safety of our
> country.
>
> —THOMAS JEFFERSON,
> in his final message to Congress

IT WAS ALMOST TIME to go. "The diseased jaw bone having exfoliated, the piece was extracted about a week ago, the place is healed, the swelling nearly subsided, and I wait only for moderate weather to resume my rides," Jefferson wrote Patsy in his last Washington winter.

"I am already sensible of decay in the power of walking, and find my memory not so faithful as it used to be," he wrote his old colleague Charles Thomson on Christmas Day 1808. "This may be partly owing to the incessant current of new matter flowing constantly through it; but I ascribe to years their share in it also."

He had been at this for so long. As he inventoried the furniture in the President's House and thought about how to pay his bills (he estimated he was eight to ten thousand dollars more in debt from his years as president), he knew an epoch was coming to a close—an age that had lasted more than forty years, through war and peace, at home and abroad, all over the Atlantic world from Williamsburg and Richmond to Philadelphia and New York and Annapolis to Paris and London and Amsterdam and finally to this nascent capital on the Potomac. He came to think of these decades in mythic terms: he and his colleagues—Madison, Adams, Washington, Rush, Page, and so many others now gone—as Argonauts of old.

He had, he believed, done his duty. "Nature intended me for the tranquil pursuits of science by rendering them my supreme delight," he wrote Pierre S. du Pont on Thursday, March 2, 1809. "But the enormities of the times in which I have lived have forced me to take a part in resisting them, and to commit myself on the boisterous ocean of political passions. . . . I leave everything in the hands of men so able to take care of them, that if we are destined to meet misfortunes, it will be because no human wisdom could avert them."

He inspired as much division in his exit as he had in his election eight years before. "A few fleeting years will scarce have passed away before the men even of the present day, casting a retrospective eye upon these times, will be seized with wonder and astonishment at the strange contrarity of opinions, the strange bickerings we have fallen into, and the unaccountable distrust that seems to exist," the Allegany County, Maryland, citizens wrote him on Monday, February 20, 1809.

The distrust was real, though, and sentiment could not blunt the parting attacks of his foes. "Thou strange inconsistent man!" a New Yorker wrote in February 1809.

"You have brought the government to the jaws of destruction," wrote "Cassandra" from Philadelphia on Tuesday, February 28. "I do not undertake to say whether by supineness, timidity, or enthusiasm. The effect is certain. On the cause I cannot pronounce."

Jefferson himself was reflective and candid. In reply to a request for recommendations for which books of history to read, Jefferson suggested a long list that included Edward Gibbon, and spoke of what it felt like to make, not just read, history. "I suppose indeed that in public life a man whose political principles have any decided character, and who has energy enough to give them effect, must always expect to encounter political hostility from those of adverse principles," Jefferson wrote. "But I came to the government under circumstances calculated to generate peculiar acrimony. I found all its offices in the possession of a political sect who wished to transform it ultimately into the shape of their darling model the English government."

The Republican victory of 1800, Jefferson said,

"had blown all their designs, and they found themselves and their fortresses of power and profit put in a moment into the hands of other trustees. Lamentations and invective were all that remained to them."

The target? Jefferson himself. "I became of course the butt of everything which reason, ridicule, malice and falsehood could supply," he said.

Still, accolades and tributes arrived regularly. From France, the U.S. consul at Paris sent Jefferson a book about Marcus Aurelius. "In the character of Marcus Aurelius I perceive only one error: he employed no sure means to perpetuate the blessings of his reign," the consul wrote. "He seemed constantly impressed with the idea that, at the moment of his extinction, the noble fabric which he [sewed], must infallibly sink in ruins. For this, as in every other respect, the citizens of the United States are more fortunate than the Romans, as there is every reason to believe that the benefits of the present enlightened administration will extend to other generations."

The challenges endured. Jefferson constantly weighed the question of war versus embargo. "We are all politics here," he wrote Charles L. Bankhead, who had married his granddaughter Ann Cary Randolph in September 1808. "The Congressional campaign is just opening," Jefferson had written Levi Lincoln in November 1808. "Three alternatives alone are to be chosen from. 1. Embargo. 2. War. 3. Submission and tribute. And, wonderful to tell, the last will not want advocates."

There were no good choices. "Here, everything is uncertain," Jefferson wrote Thomas Mann Randolph, Jr., from Washington in December.

James Madison's inauguration fell on a Saturday. The day before—March 3, 1809—Samuel Harrison Smith paid tribute to the departing Jefferson in the **National Intelligencer**. "Never will it be forgotten as long as liberty is dear to man," the paper said, "that it was on this day that Thomas Jefferson retired from the supreme magistracy amidst the blessings and regrets of millions."

On the morning of the inaugural, Jefferson left the President's House and rode up to the Capitol to watch his beloved friend and secretary of state take the oath as the fourth president of the United States. (He and a grandson departed the mansion by themselves; Madison was being escorted along Pennsylvania Avenue in military pomp.) No one on earth was closer to him politically, and Madison's success was a vindication for Jefferson—a tangible sign that the country approved of his basic vision and stewardship.

After the ceremonies in the House chamber—John Quincy Adams thought the setting "very magnificent"—the now-former president called on the new president at the Madisons' on F Street; Jefferson would not move out of the President's House until a week later. Mrs. Madison looked "extremely beautiful . . . dressed in a plain cambric dress with a very long train . . . all dignity, grace, and affability," said Margaret Bayard Smith.

As the Madisons stood at the drawing room door greeting the overflowing crowd of callers—the streets were crowded with carriages, and there was a half hour's wait to get inside—Jefferson saw Margaret Bayard Smith and reached for her hand.

"Remember the promise you have made me, to come to see us next summer, do not forget it," he said to Mrs. Smith, "for we shall certainly expect you."

Mrs. Smith, of course, reassured him that she and her husband would come to Monticello. She then alluded to the drama of the day.

"You have now resigned a heavy burden," she said to Jefferson.

"Yes indeed," he said, "and am much happier at this moment than my friend."

In the swirl of the celebration, Jefferson was soon told that "the ladies" hoped to follow him to the President's House. Twinkling, he said: "That is right, since I am too old to follow them. I remember in France, when his friends were taking leave of Dr. Franklin, the ladies smothered him with embraces, and on his introducing me as his successor, I told him I wished he would transfer these privileges to me, but he answered, 'You are too young a man.' "

That evening he joined celebrating Republicans

at an inaugural ball. John Quincy Adams was un-impressed. "The crowd was excessive—the heat op-pressive, and the entertainment bad."

At Monticello he planned to return to farming and gardening with passionate zeal. "I am full of plans of employment when I get there," he wrote Charles Thomson, and "they chiefly respect the ac-tive functions of the body. To the mind I shall ad-minister amusement chiefly. An only daughter and numerous family of grandchildren will furnish me great resources of happiness."

He had suggested that perhaps his sister Anne Scott Marks could act as mistress of Monticello. Patsy hated the thought. She—no one else—was to form the core of his world. "As to Aunt Marks it would not be desirable to have her," Patsy wrote on Thursday, March 2, 1809. "I had full proof of her being totally incom[petent] to the business the last summer. The servants have no sort of respect for her and take just what they please before her face. She is an excellent creature and a neat manager in a little way, but she has neither head nor a sufficient weight of character to manage so large an establishment as yours will be. I shall devote myself to it and with feeling, which I never could have in my own affairs, and with what tenderness of affection we will wait upon and cherish you My Dearest Father."

As he ended his Washington days, he ordered an

abridgment of John Bell's book **Principles of Surgery,** sent a geranium he had cultivated and kept in the President's House to Margaret Bayard Smith, and arranged payment for three dozen Windsor chairs he had ordered from Richmond for Poplar Forest, his retreat in Bedford County.

Edmund Bacon had come to Washington to help pack up and move Jefferson home. The Monticello overseer was struck by the unceasing demands the capital made on his employer. "He had a very long dining room, and his table was chock-full every one of the sixteen days I was there," Bacon wrote. Bacon supervised the loading of three wagons with boxes and shrubbery.

Bacon and this entourage set out from Washington on Thursday, March 9, 1809; Jefferson left the capital on Saturday, March 11, in a phaeton. There was a terrible snowstorm along the way, and Bacon prepared Jefferson's accommodations at Benjamin Shackelford's Culpeper Courthouse tavern by ordering a large fire to be built and by fending off a drunken well-wisher eager to see the man he called "Old Tom." Bacon tried to keep the crowds away from Jefferson when he arrived, but failed, and Jefferson delivered a short speech to the gathering. He was still a public man.

On Wednesday, March 15, 1809, Thomas Jefferson reached Monticello. He brought the great world with him. His chef Julien came to set up the Monticello kitchen to prepare the French dishes Jefferson loved. His correspondence and reading were varied and voluminous. Home to stay, he was never again to stray very far from his mountaintop. His mind was another matter. It never came to rest.

PART IX
THE MASTER OF MONTICELLO

1809 to the End

I steer my bark with hope in the head, leaving fear astern. My hopes, indeed, sometimes fail; but not oftener than the forebodings of the gloomy.

—Thomas Jefferson to John Adams

View of the University of Virginia, Charlottesville, and Monticello from Lewis Mountain, mid-nineteenth century.

FORTY

My Body, Mind, and Affairs

Amidst the din of war and the wreck of
nations his wisdom has hitherto secured
our peace; his eminent public services are
engraved on the hearts of his children.
　　　　—Toast to Thomas Jefferson at Tammany
　　　　Society of Washington on May 12, 1809

IN HIS ROOMS at Monticello, Jefferson slept facing east on a bed built into an alcove between
his working study (which was often called his
"cabinet") and a chamber anchored by a fireplace.
Red bed curtains hung on each side of the bed.
Though the rooms were peaceful, Jefferson was reminded of the passing of time by both sight and
sound whenever he rested his head on his pillow. A
1790 clock mounted between two obelisks rested
on a wooden shelf inside his sleeping alcove; with a
delicate ting, it chimed the hour and the half hour.
Below the clock hung a sword—the gift, it was said,
of "a long forgotten Arabian prince." And there were
the sounds of Jefferson's ubiquitous mockingbirds.

Overnight the silence of the chamber was also broken second by second by a tall-case clock placed along the western wall of the study. The tick-tick-tick of the tall clock was constant, growing louder as the house grew quieter through the hours of darkness. When the three doors connecting Jefferson's rooms to the rest of the house were closed, they formed a surprisingly effective barrier between the master and the household. Four tall windows flanked the sleeping Jefferson in the study to his right; a single window lit the bedroom with the fireplace to his left, a room where he kept his wife's walnut dressing table.

Jefferson had his own privy just steps away from his bed alcove, one of three in the house proper. He used pieces of scrap paper for hygiene purposes. (Examples were collected from his privy by a family member on the day of Jefferson's death and now survive in the Library of Congress.)

He generally got five to eight hours of sleep a night, always reading for half an hour or an hour before bedtime, using eyeglasses. As he grew older he had difficulty hearing different voices speaking at the same time. He enjoyed good health, suffering from extremely rare fevers. The headaches that had plagued him in times of stress seemed "now to have left me" once he was free of the clamor of office.

His chambers were in the sun's direct path. Much of his first sense of light each morning would have come from his right, from the first easterly window in the cabinet. If he awoke, as he said he did, at early sunrise, when the hands of the obelisk clock grew visible, then there would have been a steadily rising tide of light that began as a trickle but soon came to fill the room.

Jefferson would have sat up in his alcove and turned to his left to plunge his feet into his morning basin of cold water. There he would stay for a time, looking at the fireplace and intuitively tracking the rise of the sun by the amount of light coming through the bedroom skylight.

He and his Monticello were a little like the sun itself: at the center of the universe.

The eleven-thousand-square-foot, thirty-three-room house (there are ten other rooms in the pavilions and under the South Terrace) in which he woke up every morning was his joy, and it was only in the years after he retired from the presidency that it was exactly as he wished it to be.

Walking into the entrance hall by the glass front door on the East Front of Monticello, Jefferson, his family, and his guests were immediately immersed in the work of his life. Artifacts and emblems of America's natural and political worlds hung in the great hall; the floor was green (at the suggestion of Gilbert Stuart), the walls whitewashed with a yellow-orange dado below the chair rail. There were the antlers of moose and elk, the upper jawbone of a mastodon, and forty Indian objects, including carved stone sculptures, tools, a Mandan buffalo robe, and a small portrait of a young Sack chief. There were maps, including the Fry-Jefferson map of Virginia, drawn by his father so long before, and later ones of North America, Europe, Africa, and Asia. There was a scale model of the Pyramid of Cheops.

There was a sculpture, **Ariadne**, which Jefferson long mistook for one of Cleopatra before realizing the work was a depiction of the tragic mythological heroine. There were the paintings **St. Jerome in Meditation** and **Jesus in the Praetorium**, which Jefferson described in detail: "Jesus . . . stripped of the purple, as yet naked, and with the crown of thorns on his head. He is sitting. . . . The persons present seem to be one of his revilers, one of his followers, and the superintendent of the execution. The subject from Mark 15:16–20." There were portraits of Americus Vespucius, John Adams, and of Jefferson himself (by Gilbert Stuart), two engravings of the Declaration of Independence—one of John Trumbull's depiction of the signing, the other of the document itself—and busts of Hamilton, Voltaire, and Turgot, the French politician and economist.

There was method to the decoration of Monticello. For Jefferson, the portraits, busts, statues, and artifacts in the house were not a random collection but rather "memorials of those worthies whose remembrance I feel a pride and comfort in consecrating there." Anything—or anyone—represented within Monticello was meaningful to Jefferson in some way and to some degree.

Only steps into the house, then, the range of Jefferson's mind and heart, the universal nature of his interests and his sense of the sweep of history, were manifest to every eye. The fossils and antlers, the Indian artifacts, and the maps represented the primeval American world and the white man's first attempts to project power over the land. The pyramid and Ariadne were refugees from the ancient world. The paintings of St. Jerome and of Jesus in the moments before the crucifixion commemorated the vast and inarguable role of religion in the history of western civilization. Vespucius—and Columbus, whose portrait hung in the next room, the parlor—carried the story across the Atlantic to the New World. Voltaire and Turgot represented the work of the philosophes of the Enlightenment. Adams, Hamilton, Jefferson himself, and the Continental Congress in declaring independence from Britain brought the tale forward into the recent past, into the work of the master of the house's lifetime.

And so it goes, room after room, object after object, engraving after engraving, painting after painting, medallion after medallion throughout Monticello.

To reach the parlor, guests moved beneath the tall ceiling decorated with a plaster relief of an eagle surrounded by stars, across the floor, and under a brass Argand-style lamp and a balcony to cross onto a beautiful floor of cherry and beech—a parquet pattern Jefferson personally designed.

Like the hall, the parlor is eighteen feet, two inches high, and decorated with a Corinthian frieze from the Temple of Jupiter the Thunderer. Here Jefferson crafted a room of tiered artwork surrounding card tables, chairs, sofas, a chess set, a harpsichord, and a pianoforte—a room in which the present life of the house and of the family unfolded in the midst of emblems of the past that had made its owner, and its owner's nation, possible. "Portraits—24; Paintings—17; Medals—10; Busts—2; Miscellaneous—4," Jefferson wrote, cataloging the parlor's decorations.

Here hung paintings and here sat sculptures of the makers of the age—and of the ages: George Washington, Benjamin Franklin, Magellan, Napoleon, Lafayette, Columbus, Vespucius, Alexander I, David Rittenhouse, Sir Walter Raleigh, James Madison, Thomas Paine, James Monroe, Louis XVI, John Locke, Sir Isaac Newton, Francis Bacon, Adams, and Jefferson himself both by Trumbull and by Mather Brown. There was an elegant Charles Willson Peale portrait of Jefferson's grandson Thomas Jefferson Randolph and a medallion of Edward Preble, who triumphed at Tripoli in 1804. As in the hall, there were religious images, too: **The Penitent Magdalen, Descent from the Cross,** and **Herodias Bearing the Head of St. John the Bap-**

tist. Two small Sèvres figures—**Venus with Cupid** and **Hope with Cupid**—evoked the ancient world.

The brilliantly yellow dining room sits to the right. Through it, separated by double pocket doors on rollers, is the small octagonal tea room. There, Jefferson and his family would eat and converse in what he called his "most honorable suite," glancing up at busts of Washington, Franklin, Lafayette, and John Paul Jones, all plaster copies of works by Jean-Antoine Houdon.

Patsy had a blue sitting room near her father's private rooms, called the South Square Room, and there was a North Octagonal Room with an alcove bed often used by Dolley and James Madison when they visited.

The upstairs—including the beautiful Dome Room atop the house—was a series of small bedrooms. The center of the house, and the center of life, was downstairs, where Jefferson presided.

"If it had not been called Monticello," a visitor wrote in 1816, "I would call it Olympus, and Jove its occupant." Jefferson's family agreed. His "cheerfulness and affection," a granddaughter recalled, "were the warm sun in which his family all basked and were invigorated."

He was like a "patriarch of old," as he put it in a letter to Maria Cosway. "Our mother educated all her children to look up to her father, as she looked up to him herself—literally looked up, as to one standing on an eminence of greatness and goodness," wrote a granddaughter, Ellen Coolidge. "And it is no small proof of his real elevation that, as we grew older and better able to judge for ourselves, we were more and more confirmed in the opinions we had formed of it."

His grandchildren loved him and revered him. They followed him on garden walks (never, though, putting a foot on a garden bed, for that "would violate one of his rules"). He never had to raise his voice: Their sense of his authority was so complete that it was unnecessary for him to "utter a harsh word to one of us, or speak in a raised tone of voice, or use a threat," a granddaughter recalled. "He simply said, 'do,' or 'do not.' " And that was that.

He picked fruit for them—usually figs and cherries—with a long stick topped with a hook and net bag, and he organized and presided over races on the grounds. The course was the terrace or around the lawn. Jefferson gave head starts according to ages, and the contestants took off when he dropped his white handkerchief from his outstretched right hand. Awards were three figs, prunes, or dates for the winner; two for second place; and one for third. On some summer nights he had a chess table of his own design—it had been made by John Hemings—set up outside for matches with a granddaughter.

In the wintertime, when the days were short, Jefferson would sit with his family before a fire in the late afternoon. This was the hour, a granddaughter said, "when it grew too dark to read," and so "in the half hour before candles came in, as we all sat round the fire, he taught us several childish games, and would play them with us." There was "Cross Questions and Crooked Answers" and "I Love My Love with A," a pastime in which successive players had to come up with attributes throughout the alphabet.

The arrival of candles signaled an end to games and a resumption of reading. Everything fell quiet as Jefferson "took up his book to read, and we would not speak out of a whisper lest we should disturb him, and generally we followed his example and took a book—and I have seen him raise his eyes from his own book and look round on the little circle of readers, and smile and make some remark to mamma about it."

To preserve the privacy of his rooms, he had constructed Venetian porches, or "porticles," with blinds that shielded the visibility of his quarters from outside the main house. Still, he did not like being alone for any great length of time. Once, when he was snowed in at Poplar Forest, he wrote Patsy: "I am like a state prisoner. My keepers set before me at fixed hours something to eat and withdraw."

His command was total, his love enveloping. On journeys to Bedford he took care to wrap his family in capes, and, if needed, furs. He sang and conversed the whole way and served picnic lunches of cold meat and wine mixed with water.

He once overheard a young granddaughter lament that she had never had a silk dress. One arrived for her from Charlottesville the next day. On another occasion a granddaughter tore a beloved muslin dress on the glass door connecting the hall to the portico. "Grand-papa was standing by and saw the disaster," the granddaughter recalled. Several days later the former president of the United States came into Patsy's sitting room adjacent to his own apartment, "a bundle in his hand." To his granddaughter he said, "I have been mending your dress for you." It was a new frock.

He might hear a child express a wish for a watch, or for a saddle and bridle, or for a guitar, and would quietly provide them (doing so with borrowed money). He made sure his grandchildren were given Bibles and Shakespeare and writing tables. "Our grandfather seemed to read our hearts, to see our invisible wishes, to be our good genius, to wave the fairy wand, to brighten our young lives by his goodness and his gifts."

His sense of the needs of others was part of his nature—a nature, one granddaughter said, "so eminently sympathetic, that with those he loved, he could enter into their feelings, anticipate their wishes, gratify their tastes, and surround them with an atmosphere of affection." A patriarch's love is rather like a politician's skill. Both are about perceiving what others want, and trying, within reason, to provide it. That had been the work of Jefferson's public life and now, in retirement, it was that of his personal life, too.

The good cheer Margaret Bayard Smith had noted in Jefferson at Madison's inauguration remained evident in the first months of his return to Virginia. "Mr. Jefferson called last week, and dined here yesterday," Elizabeth Trist wrote a friend from Farmington in April 1809. "I never saw him look better nor appear so happy."

On her own promised visit to Monticello in the middle of 1809, Margaret Bayard Smith thought Jefferson in a perfect place and frame of mind. "The sun never sees him in bed, and his mind designs more than the day can fulfill, even his long day," she wrote. "There is a tranquility about him, which an inward peace could alone bestow."

As he began his retirement, Jefferson enjoyed reading of the public's confidence in him and the course he had set. "We have been permitted to hear the thunder of war at a distance, and peaceably tread the arduous path of intellectual improvement, unmolested by the awful din of battle, or the more dreadful scenes of devastation that now desolate the nations of the world," a group of college students wrote on Inauguration Day 1809. An anonymous writer praised him as the greatest of men: "You have, in your public capacity, been to me a father, a protector, a preserver. For these services I will forever render you the tribute of a grateful heart." An old friend from France offered him the highest flattery: "Though I am convinced that Mr. Madison, your friend and your student, will govern according to the same principles as you have, I cannot help regretting that you did not want to retain the presidency for four more years," Pierre-Samuel du Pont de Nemours wrote Jefferson in June 1809.

The world still looked to him, and to America, as emblems of hope. "No one knows better than you how difficult it is to do good: men are very evil; their heads are filled with nonsense, and it is so contagious, so tenacious, that not even the great, philosophical chemist Jefferson is able to reduce it to gas so that it evaporates from human judgment," wrote a Spanish diplomat at Philadelphia.

"What would become of mankind if republican government did not survive in your country?" asked a French correspondent. "I shudder to think of the consequences!"

In his cabinet he wrote with his legs stretched out along a red-leather bench beneath a plantation writing table. A fully engaged farmer, he grudgingly spent hours at his table, reading and keeping up with his correspondence. "My present course of life admits less reading than I wish," Jefferson wrote Benjamin Rush from Monticello. "From breakfast, or noon at latest, to dinner, I am mostly on horseback, attending to my farms or other concerns, which I find healthful to my body, mind, and affairs." He ordered samplings of the English mulberry and peach-apricot, as well as wild geese and a ram for the farm. "I am now on horseback among my farms from an early breakfast to a late dinner, with little regard to weather," he told Lafayette in January 1811. "I find it gives health to body, mind and affairs."

He had a ready refrain on the subject of politics. "I feel a much greater interest in knowing what has passed two or three thousand years ago, than in what is now passing," he wrote in 1819. "I read nothing, therefore, but of the heroes of Troy . . . of Pompey and Caesar, and of Augustus too."

Yet Jefferson could never fully remove himself from the life of the present. To Lafayette he expressed the hope that the tumults of Europe would work themselves out. "If there be a God, and he is just, his day will come. He will never abandon the whole race of man to be eaten up by the leviathans and mammoths of a day." He subscribed to the papers, telling Madison that he was "reading the newspapers but little and that little but as the romance of the day, a word of truth now and then comes like a drop of water on the tongue of Dives." One thing was very clear as he settled back into life on the mountain: He loved, he said, the "ineffable luxury of being owner of my own time."

With those hours he stayed in close touch with the scientific, educational, and philosophical worlds. William Clark continued to dispatch specimens to the President's House, and Madison sent the skin of a bighorn sheep from the Rocky Mountains to

Monticello on July 4, 1809. ("The bundle being too large for the mail, I shall forward it by some other opportunity.") Jefferson oversaw the English translation of a French commentary on Montesquieu's **Spirit of the Laws,** debated the origins of the potato with a correspondent, wrote for vine cuttings to cultivate wine, and mused on the role of libraries. "I have often thought that nothing would do more extensive good at small expense than the establishment of a small circulating library in every county to consist of a few well-chosen books, to be lent to the people of the county under such regulations as would secure their safe return in due time," he said.

In the fall, John Walker, his onetime friend whose wife Jefferson had tried to woo, was sick, and said that he would like to see his old friend. James Monroe wrote Jefferson to tell him "a visit by you to Col. Walker would at this time be considered by him an act of great kindness, and be received with much sensibility." Betsy Walker was ill, too. Apparently unwilling to risk a scene, Jefferson decided not to pay the call at Belvoir, declining to make the short journey he had so often made in that distant summer during his bachelor days. He sent a gift of a basket of ripe figs, prompting Hugh Nelson, a Walker son-in-law, to thank him and report the sad news that both Walkers were "still very feeble and low."

He was also forever prepared to refight the years of his governorship. Writing a historian seeking information on the Revolutionary period, he argued that Virginia had always contributed "above par" to the national efforts. Indeed, he said, "our whole occupation was in straining the resources of the state to their utmost, to furnish men, money, provisions and other necessaries to the common cause."

Word arrived of the brutal death of his old secretary Meriwether Lewis while traveling through Tennessee. As Jefferson heard the story, the sleeping wife of the man who kept the inn where Lewis was staying had heard two pistol shots. Lewis, who had been thought "deranged," was found "weltering in his blood" with a wound to his head and a fatal shot to the heart; the first had apparently failed to kill him, and he tried to finish the job with the second. This, too, seemed to have been insufficient, and the poor man was left to stab himself with his dirk.

Elijah Fletcher, a visitor from Vermont, left an unsparing account of Jefferson. "Mr. Jefferson is tall, spare, straight in body," Fletcher wrote in 1811. "His face not handsome but savage—I learnt he was but little esteemed by his neighbors. . . . The story of Black Sal is no farce—That he cohabits with her and has a number of children by her is a sacred truth—and the worst of it is, he keeps the same children slaves—an unnatural crime which is very common in these parts—This conduct may receive a little palliation when we consider that such proceedings are so common that they cease here to be disgraceful."

Jefferson coolly recorded the births of Hemings's children in his farm book along with other details of the lives of his slaves and of the fates of his crops. He was apparently able to consign his children with Sally Hemings to a separate sphere of life in his mind even as they grew up in his midst. "He was not in the habit of showing partiality or fatherly affection to us children," said Madison Hemings, who added that Jefferson was, however, "affectionate toward his white grandchildren."

It was, to say the least, an odd way to live, but Jefferson was a creature of his culture. "The enjoyment of a negro or mulatto woman is spoken of as quite a common thing: no reluctance, delicacy or shame is made about the matter," Josiah Quincy, Jr., of Massachusetts wrote after a visit to the Carolinas. "It is far from being uncommon to see a gentleman at dinner, and his reputed offspring a slave to the master of the table."

This was daily reality at Monticello. In a letter to fellow biographer James Parton, Henry Randall reported some observations of Thomas Jefferson Randolph's from the mountain. Discussing the physical similarities between Jefferson and the children of Sally Hemings, Randolph "said in one case that the resemblance was so close, that at some distance or in the dusk the slave, dressed in the same way, might be mistaken for Mr. Jefferson." On one occasion, Randolph reported, "a gentleman dining with Mr. Jefferson looked so startled as he raised his eyes from the latter to the servant behind him, that his discovery of the resemblance was perfectly obvious to all." (Randolph offered these reminiscences to support the theory that Jefferson's nephew Peter Carr was the father of Sally Hemings's children—a theory ultimately disproved by DNA research.)

For Jefferson such ambiguities and unacknowledged truths were part of life. "I asked Col. R[andolph] why on earth Mr. Jefferson did not put these slaves who looked like him out of the public sight by sending them to his Bedford estate or elsewhere," Randall wrote Parton. "He said Mr. Jefferson never betrayed the least consciousness of the resemblance—and although he (Col. R[andolph]) had no doubt his mother would have been very glad to have them removed, that both and all venerated Mr. Jefferson too deeply to broach such a topic to him. What suited him, satisfied them."

What suited Jefferson was the code of denial that defined life in the slave-owning states. It was his plantation, his world, and he would live as he wished. "The secrets of an old Virginia manor house," wrote Henry Randall, "were like the secrets of an Old Norman Castle." And such secrets were to be spoken of as little as possible.

———

Jefferson sometimes felt his age. "I am little able to walk about," he wrote Philip Mazzei in July 1811. "Most of my exercise is on horseback, and the powers of life are very sensibly decayed." Jefferson was acutely aware of his own capacities. "It is wonderful to me that old men should not be sensible that their minds keep pace with their bodies in the progress of decay," he wrote Benjamin Rush in August 1811. He was proud of his own insights on this score, mildly but unmistakably congratulating himself for recognizing human limitations: "Had not a conviction of the danger to which an unlimited occupation of the executive chair would expose the republican constitution of our government made it conscientiously a duty to retire when I did, the fear of becoming a dotard and of being insensible of it, would of itself have resisted all solicitations to remain."

His curiosity endured. "How do you do?" he wrote his friend and former attorney general Levi Lincoln in Massachusetts. "What are you doing? Does the farm or the study occupy your time, or each by turns? Do you read law or divinity? And which affords the most curious and cunning learning? Which is most disinterested? And which was it that crucified its Savior?"

On the second day of 1811, Benjamin Rush opened a quiet campaign to bring Jefferson and Adams back into correspondence. "Such an intercourse will be honorable to talents, and patriotism, and highly useful to the cause of republicanism not only in the United States but all over the world," Rush wrote Jefferson. "Posterity will revere the friendship of two ex-presidents that were once opposed to each other. Human nature will be a gainer by it." If Jefferson would make the first move, Rush said, all would be well. Adams was ready, and time was likely short. "Tottering over the grave," Rush said, Adams "now leans wholly upon the shoulders of his old revolutionary friends."

The Adams-Jefferson friendship had been a victim of the passions of the 1790s. "You remember the machinery which the Federalists played off, about that time," Jefferson wrote Rush. He recalled the Alien and Sedition Acts, which to Jefferson's mind were meant "to beat down the friends to the real principles of our Constitution, to silence by terror every expression in their favor, to bring us into war with France and alliance with England, and finally to homologise our Constitution with that of England."

Rush pressed ahead with his cause, if gently. "Many are the evils of a political life, but none so great as the dissolution of friendships, and the implacable hatreds which too often take their place," Rush replied.

The second president spent two days at home in Quincy with two visiting neighbors of Jefferson's. The conversation ranged widely. "Mr. Adams talked very freely of men and of things, and detailed many highly interesting facts in the history of our country, and particularly of his own administration, and of incidents connected with the presidential election of 1800," wrote Edward Coles, one of the callers. Adams "complained," too, about Jefferson. "I told him I could not reconcile what he had heard of Mr. Jefferson's language and conduct to him, with what I had heard [Jefferson] repeatedly say, and that too to friends who were political opponents of Mr. Adams," Coles wrote. "Upon repeating some of the complimentary remarks thus made by Mr. Jefferson, Mr. Adams not only seemed but expressed himself highly pleased."

Reassured and surprised by the warm report from the Virginians, Adams changed his tone about Jefferson, displaying, Coles said, "an exalted admiration of his character, and appreciation of his services to his country, as well during the Revolution as subsequently." Adams then criticized the press for its harshness toward Jefferson, adding: "I always loved Jefferson, and still love him."

These eight words were all it took for Jefferson. "This is enough for me," he wrote Rush. "I only needed this knowledge to revive towards him all the affections of the most cordial moments of our lives." Rush sent word of Jefferson's sentiments to Adams, who, in turn, wrote Jefferson on New Year's Day 1812, sending him a copy of John Quincy Adams's inaugural lectures at Harvard on rhetoric and oratory.

Replying, Jefferson struck the right notes. "A letter from you calls up recollections very dear to my mind," he wrote from Monticello on Tuesday, January 21, 1812. "It carries me back to the times when, beset with difficulties and dangers, we were fellow laborers in the same cause, struggling for what is most valuable to man, his right of self-government. Laboring always at the same oar, with some wave ever ahead threatening to overwhelm us and yet passing harmless under our bark we knew not how, we rode through the storm with heart and hand, and made a happy port."

Thus an ancient friendship, shattered by politics, was restored. When Adams answered from Quincy on Monday, February 10, 1812, he was already writing as though the intervening years had been nothing. He asked Jefferson about a pamphlet published in Virginia that predicted the apocalypse was set for June 1812. To Adams it was a wonder that such prophets endured despite the "continual refutation of all their prognostications by time and experience."

The aging revolutionaries exchanged thoughts and memories on questions both spiritual and temporal. "On the subject of the history of the American revolution, you ask who shall write it?" Jefferson wrote Adams in 1815. "Who can write it? And who ever will be able to write it? Nobody; except merely its external facts. All its councils, designs and discussions, having been conducted by Congress with closed doors, and no member, as far as I know, having even made notes of them. These, which are the life and soul of history, must forever be unknown."

Adams proved the more prolific correspondent. "So many subjects crowd upon me that I know not with which to begin," he wrote Jefferson. The second president saw the renewed connection in grand terms. "You and I ought not to die before we have explained ourselves to each other."

Jefferson loved the letters. "Mr. Adams and myself are in habitual correspondence," Jefferson wrote Benjamin Rush in March 1813. "I owe him a letter at this time, and shall pay the debt as soon as I have something to write about. For with the commonplace topic of politics, we do not meddle. When there are so many others on which we agree why should we introduce the only one on which we differ?"

Of the vagaries of politics, Adams wrote: "My reputation has been so much the sport of the public for fifty years, and will be with posterity, that I hold it a bubble, a gossamer, that idles in the wanton summer's air." Jefferson took the same tone, musing: "The summum bonum with me is now truly Epicurean, ease of body and tranquility of mind; and to these I wish to consign my remaining days," he wrote Adams in June 1813.

Men have differed in opinion, and been divided into parties by these opinions, from the first origin of societies; and in all governments where they have been permitted freely to think and to speak. The same political parties which now agitate the U.S. have existed through all time. Whether the power of the people, or that of the [best men; nobles] should prevail, were questions which kept the states of Greece and Rome in eternal convulsions. . . . As we had been longer than most others on the public theatre, and our names therefore were more familiar to our countrymen, the party which considered you as thinking with them, placed your name at their head; the other, for the same reason, selected mine.

It was past time, Jefferson said, for the political wars of the first decades of the republic to end. "And shall you and I, my dear Sir, like Priam of old, gird on the 'arma, diu desueta, trementibus aevo humeris'? Shall we, at our age, become the Athletae of party, and exhibit ourselves, as gladiators, in the arena of the newspapers? Nothing in the universe could induce me to it. My mind has been long fixed to bow to the judgment of the world, who will judge me by my acts, and will never take counsel from me as to what that judgment should be."

Adams was gracious but unyielding about their differences of opinion. "I believe in the integrity of both, at least as undoubtingly as in that of Washington," Adams wrote of Jefferson and Madison. "In the measures of administration I have neither agreed with you or Mr. Madison. Whether you or I were right posterity must judge." Adams acknowledged that the "nation was with you. But neither your authority nor that of the nation has convinced me. Nor, I am bold to pronounce, will convince posterity."

Their debates about the nature of democracy and the future of the country were fascinating, and the correspondence forced both men to clarity of thought and a kind of reasonableness. Gone were the pejorative exclamations of partisan days. "The natural aristocracy I consider as the most precious gift of nature, for the instruction, the trusts, and government of society," wrote Jefferson. "And indeed it would have been inconsistent in creation to have formed man for the social state, and not to have provided virtue and wisdom enough to manage the concerns of the society. May we not even say that that form of government is the best which provides the most effectually for a pure selection of these natural aristoi into the offices of government?" He added:

> I have thus stated my opinion on a point on
> which we differ, not with a view to controversy,
> for we are both too old to change opinions,
> which are the result of a long life of inquiry and
> reflection; but on the suggestion of a former let-
> ter of yours that we ought not to die before we
> have explained ourselves to each other. We acted
> in perfect harmony through a long and peril-
> ous contest for our liberty and independence. A

constitution has been acquired which, though neither of us think perfect, yet both consider as competent to render our fellow-citizens the happiest and the securest on whom the sun has ever shone. If we do not think exactly alike as to its imperfections, it matters little to our country which, after devoting to it long lives of disinterested labor, we have delivered over to our successors in life, who will be able to take care of it, and of themselves.

By the time they died in 1826, Jefferson and Adams had exchanged a total of 329 letters in their lifetime, with a substantial number—158—coming from 1812 until the end.

"We have had a wretched winter for the farmer," Jefferson had written Madison in March 1811. It had not been much better for statesmen. "The rancor of party was revived with all its bitterness during the last session of Congress," his son-in-law John Wayles Eppes wrote Jefferson the same month. "United by no fixed principles or objects and destitute of everything like American feeling, so detestable a minority never existed in any country—Their whole political creed is contained in a single word 'opposition'—They pursue it without regard to principle, to personal reputation or the best interests of their country."

From Monticello Jefferson watched as his anxieties of the decades—the fear of British power over America—were realized. Beginning in 1812, the scenario Jefferson had so often warned against came to pass as the United States once more went to war against England. Jefferson had begun his post–President's House life still believing that Britain could be dealt with short of armed conflict. Yet he advised Madison to rule nothing out. "War however may become a less losing business than unresisted depredation."

In September 1811, Jefferson wrote John Wayles Eppes that the President and Mrs. Madison as well as the secretaries of war and of the navy were expected at Monticello with their families. News of a British frigate and sloop of war "stationing themselves in the Delaware and refusing to withdraw" might, however, keep the cabinet officers away.

Benjamin Rush saw the whole. "Our country has twice declared itself independent of Great Britain—once in 1776, and again 1800. . . . Are we upon the eve of a declaration . . . being repeated a **third** time, not by the pen, or by a general suffrage but by the mouths of our cannon?"

As war approached Jefferson returned home from Poplar Forest. Rain and hail were damaging the wheat crops—ten inches of rain fell in ten days in May—as Virginians awaited word from Washington. In Jefferson's mind the conflict with Britain was also with Americans sympathetic to London. "Your declaration of war is expected with perfect calmness; and if those in the North mean systematically to govern the majority it is as good a time for trying them as we can expect," Jefferson wrote Madison in May 1812.

President Madison sent a war-preparation message to Congress on Tuesday, November 5, 1811. He argued that the depredations along the borders and on the oceans were too much to bear. The time had come to put the question of America's permanent independence to the test.

"We are to have war then? I believe so and that it is necessary," Jefferson wrote Charles Cotesworth Pinckney. "Every hope from time, patience and the love of peace is exhausted, and war or abject submission are the only alternatives left us."

On the last day of 1811, Jefferson offered warm words to Madison. "Your message had all the qualities it should possess, firm, rational, and dignified. . . . Heaven help you through all your difficulties."

FORTY-ONE

To Form Statesmen, Legislators and Judges

> In a republican nation whose citizens are to be led by reason and persuasion and not by force, the art of reasoning becomes of first importance.
>
> —THOMAS JEFFERSON

JEFFERSON HAD BEEN HERE before: the king's armies on the move, the American cause in jeopardy. For Jefferson and his generation, the conflict that had begun long ago in the wake of the French and Indian War had reached a climactic hour. For half a century, from the Stamp Act to impressments at sea, the British had never wholly accepted the idea that America was truly a sovereign power, and America knew it. As late as 1810, an American congressman still felt the need to say, "The people will not submit to be colonized and give up their independence." For the second time in Jefferson's life, then, war came between Britain and America.

For a long time, the War of 1812 was disastrous for the Americans. In August 1814 the British burned Washington; the salvation of documents and a portrait of George Washington was left to Dolley Madison, who fled the President's House just ahead of the enemy. Jefferson reacted fiercely to reports that some Americans were welcoming the British. "No government can be maintained without the principle of fear as well as duty," Jefferson wrote John Wayles Eppes in 1814. "Good men will obey the last, but bad ones the former only."

After victories at Baltimore and at Plattsburgh, America found its footing. Peace with Britain came with the Treaty of Ghent, a document that brought the half a century of hostilities with the mother country to an end. Another battle was done, too: that between Jeffersonian Republicans and unrepentant Federalists in New England. At a meeting in Connecticut—it was known as the Hartford Convention of 1814–15—the Federalists issued aggrieved resolutions amid some renewed talk of secession. News of the gathering, though, came as word of the peace with Britain spread, thus casting the Federalists in an extreme and unpopular light. "The cement of the Union is in the heartblood of every American," said Jefferson. "I do not believe there is on earth a government established on so immovable a basis."

By the middle of 1815, then, the America Jefferson had long envisioned and fought for was at last largely secure from external enemies.

In 1814 the Episcopal bishop of South Carolina arrived unannounced, yet found Monticello and its master welcoming and impressive. The bishop, Theodore Dehon, was forcibly struck by Jefferson's physical presence. "Mr. Jefferson's large person seemed the appropriate tenement of his capacious and largely stored mind," wrote the bishop's biographer. "He moved with great ease and more rapidity, than one unaccustomed to it could have done, over his well-waxed, tessellated mahogany floor."

Jefferson dazzled in conversation: "He spoke, almost constantly, on various topics seasonably introduced, very sensibly, and seemed never to hesitate for a thought or a word. The impression was unavoidable that he was a master mind." After spending the night and breakfasting with Jefferson, the bishop's party departed for Montpelier.

At home Jefferson was under constant siege from the public. Patsy guessed she had at least once been asked to find beds for fifty overnight guests.

The smashing of glass alerted the household to one visitor: A lady caller once jabbed her parasol through a window to clear her field of vision as she strained to see the great man. Strangers hoping for a glimpse of him were known to fill the hall between his study and the main part of the house, "consulting their watches, and waiting for him to pass from one to the other to his dinner, so that they could momentarily stare at him." Other groups would gather near the porticoes in the gathering evening, "approach within a dozen yards, and gaze at him point-blank until they had looked their fill, as they would have gazed on a lion in a menagerie."

After Jefferson's death, the nineteenth-century biographer Henry Randall once walked over Monticello with Wormley Hughes, a former slave of Jefferson's. Pointing to the three carriage bays under the North Terrace (each could accommodate a four-horse coach), Randall asked, "Wormley, how often were these filled, in Mr. Jefferson's time?"

"Every night, sir, in summer, and we commonly had two or three carriages under that tree," Hughes said, gesturing to another spot.

"It took all hands to take care of your visitors?" Randall asked.

"Yes, sir, and the whole farm to feed them."

A Virginia gentleman who had fallen out with Jefferson years before was visiting Montpelier, and Madison encouraged him to join another friend who was en route to Monticello. He decided to go. When the gentleman appeared at the house on the mountain, he was worried about his unannounced call.

On seeing him, Jefferson looked surprised for "about a second," but then "advanced instantly and saluted his guest with as prompt cordiality as if he had been looking for him." Jefferson seated the unexpected guest next to him at dinner and called for

Madeira, which Jefferson had somehow remembered was a favorite. The guest demurred, saying he would drink Jefferson's wine.

Afterward, when Jefferson excused himself, the guest asked his Montpelier companion, "Do you suppose I could get a glass of good brandy here? I have been so amused by Jefferson that here I have been sipping his . . . acid, cold French wine, until I am sure I shall die in the night . . . unless I take an antidote." But Jefferson was not to know: The guest would give no offense.

The next day the guest returned to Madison's, "lauding Jefferson to the skies." Yet he could not see " 'why a man of so much taste should drink cold, sour French wine!' He insisted to Mr. Madison that it would injure Jefferson's health. He talked himself warm on the topic. He declared it would kill him—that some night he would be carried off by it! Finally, he insisted that Madison write and urge him to change his wine. His altered tone towards Jefferson, and his warm solicitude in the particular just named, afforded great amusement to Madison and Jefferson. The trio thenceforth remained fast friends."

His hearing was failing a bit, and he needed eyeglasses more often. Ill in early 1818, he recovered, but his contemporaries continued to fall.

Late in the year he learned that Abigail Adams had died. He wrote warmly to John Adams, noting that words could do little in such an hour of grief, a lesson Jefferson had learned, he said, "in the school of affliction." Still, "mingling sincerely my tears with yours," Jefferson said, "it is of some comfort to us both that the term is not very distant, at which we are to deposit in the same cerement, our sorrows and suffering bodies, and to ascend in essence to an ecstatic meeting with the friends we have loved and lost, and whom we shall still love and never lose again."

Jefferson took pleasure in his family, but his kith and kin were also sources of anxiety. Thomas Mann Randolph, Jr., was in chronic financial trouble, appears to have drunk too much, and is said to have been jealous of Jefferson's centrality in the life of the family. He served three terms as governor of Virginia, but as he grew older Randolph never really found peace. He and his father fell out over the fate of Edgehill, the heavily indebted Randolph plantation. He could be violent; his own son, Thomas Jefferson Randolph, said he was "more ferocious than the wolf and more fell than the hyena"—hardly a warm familial characterization. (Randolph died in 1828.)

Another concern was Charles L. Bankhead, the husband of Ann Cary Randolph, Jefferson's beloved granddaughter. He was a drinker whose alcoholism and tendency to violence—including violence toward his wife—grew worse as the years passed.

Bankhead tried the law and tried farming, never making much of himself. Jefferson once sent Ann a copy of the novel **The Modern Griselda: A Tale,** by Maria Edgeworth, about a failing marriage.

Though son-in-law Thomas Mann Randolph, Jr., could be unstable, it was Bankhead who posed the most persistent threat to Jefferson's sense of order and harmony. "He was a fine-looking man, but a terrible drunkard," said the overseer Edmund Bacon. Bankhead made a dangerous spectacle of himself in Charlottesville and at Monticello. "I have seen him ride his horse into the barroom at Charlottesville and get a drink of liquor," said Bacon. "I have seen his wife run from him when he was drunk and hide in a potato hole to get out of danger."

Early in his retirement, Jefferson took Bankhead to Poplar Forest in a bid to encourage a move to Bedford County (one reason may have been to put more distance between Bankhead and the barroom). In the end, though, the Bankheads settled at Carlton, a plantation adjacent to Monticello.

By 1815, Jefferson felt compelled to ask Charles's father, a medical doctor, to treat his own son before it was too late. Promises of reform had been broken; Bankhead would come back from Charlottesville so drunk that Jefferson thought him "in a state approaching insanity."

Bankhead could be vicious toward Ann. Jefferson described "an assault on his wife of great violence" after which Bankhead "ordered her out of the room, forbidding her to enter it again and she was obliged to take refuge for the night in her mother's room. Nor was this a new thing."

One night Bankhead was berating Jefferson's butler Burwell Colbert at Monticello for refusing to hand over the keys to the liquor cabinet. Colbert "would not give him any more brandy," according to Bacon. Patsy tried to calm Bankhead down but failed, and called for Bacon. ("She would never call on Mr. Randolph at such a time, he was so excitable," Bacon said.) Nevertheless, Randolph heard the fight. "He entered the room just as I did, and Bankhead, thinking he was Burwell, began to curse him," Bacon wrote. Randolph seized a hot poker from a hearth and struck his son-in-law in the head, burning off a chunk of flesh and nearly killing him.

On Monday, February 1, 1819, outside the courthouse in Charlottesville, Bankhead got into a fight with his brother-in-law Thomas Jefferson Randolph, the former president's favorite grandson. The causes of the clash are unclear, but the result was not. Randolph horsewhipped Bankhead, leaving wounds on his head, and Bankhead gravely wounded Randolph by stabbing him twice.

Jefferson had just arrived back at Monticello from his daily ride when news of the attack reached him. He immediately set off for Charlottesville, riding furiously. Finding his grandson lying in Leitch's store on the square, Jefferson knelt and wept. Young Randolph survived, but the bloody episode only worsened Jefferson's fears for Ann.

"With respect to Bankhead," Jefferson wrote, "there is much room to fear, and mostly for his wife. I have for some time taken for granted that she would fall by his hands." Ann died in childbirth in 1826.

Despite all, Jefferson struggled to be optimistic. "I think, with you, that it is a good world on the whole; that it has been framed on a principle of benevolence, and more pleasure than pain dealt out to us," Jefferson wrote Adams in 1816. Jefferson took the broadest of views: "I steer my bark with hope in the head, leaving fear astern. My hopes, indeed, sometimes fail; but not oftener than the forebodings of the gloomy."

Adams was always less sanguine. "I dare not look beyond my nose into futurity," he wrote Jefferson. "Our money, our commerce, our religion, our national and state constitutions, even our arts and sciences, are so many seedplots of division, faction, sedition and rebellion. Everything is transmuted into an instrument of electioneering."

Jefferson believed in the future, and why not? His own lifetime was testament to the possibility of political and intellectual progress. The past, he thought, should hold no magical, unexamined claim over the present. "Some men look at Constitutions with sanctimonious reverence, and deem them, like the ark of the covenant, too sacred to be touched," he wrote in 1816.

> They ascribe to the men of the preceding age a wisdom more than human, and suppose what they did to be beyond amendment. I knew that age well: I belonged to it, and labored with it. It deserved well of its country. It was very like the present, but without the experience of the present: and 40 years of experience in government is worth a century of book-reading: and this they would say themselves, were they to rise from the dead. I am certainly not an advocate for frequent and untried changes in laws and constitutions . . . but I know also that laws and institutions must go hand in hand with the progress of the human mind. . . . We might as well require a man to wear still the coat which fitted him when a boy, as civilized society to remain ever under the regimen of their barbarous ancestors.

He loved the spirit of innovation. "The fact is that one new idea leads to another, that to a third and so on through a course of time, until someone, with whom no one of these ideas was original, combines all together, and produces what is justly called a new invention." The future was full of infinite possibilities. "When I contemplate the immense advances in science, and discoveries in the arts which have been made within the period of my life, I look forward with confidence to equal advances by the present generation; and have no doubt they will consequently be as much wiser than we have been, as we than our fathers were, and they than the burners of witches," he wrote in retirement.

There was now world enough and time to build as well as defend. In the wake of the British army's burning of the roughly 3,000 books belonging to Congress at Washington, Jefferson offered to sell the nation his own collection. There were 6,487 volumes in Jefferson's hands; in the words of the **National Intelligencer**, the library "for its selection, rarity and intrinsic value, is beyond all price." They formed the core of the new Library of Congress.

And as the years passed, he turned more and more of his attention to a project in Charlottesville that he believed would create the conditions in which succeeding generations could surpass those that came before.

It was a university—a university so thoroughly the work of his hands that it was to become known simply as "Mr. Jefferson's." In 1818, he left his mountain for a twenty-five-mile journey to the Mountain Top Tavern in Rockfish Gap between Nelson and Augusta counties in the Blue Ridge. There Jefferson and others approved a plan for a university to be built in Charlottesville. It was a formidable gathering. Jefferson, Madison, and Marshall were on hand, as were other notable Virginia politicians. Jefferson was clearly in charge and relished the role.

The mission, in Jefferson's words, was to "form the statesmen, legislators and judges, on whom public prosperity, and individual happiness are so much to depend." He invested the enterprise with the highest of stakes, writing: "I know of no safe depository of the ultimate powers of the society, but the people themselves: and if we think them not enlightened enough to exercise their control with a wholesome discretion, the remedy is, not to take it from them, but to inform their discretion by education. This is the true corrective of abuses of constitutional power."

The making of the University of Virginia was Jefferson's last great effort of will and leadership. It called on his political, intellectual, and architectural gifts. As with so much in his life, there were compromises and problems (he spent too much money), but also as with so much else, Jefferson created something that endured. The Declaration of Independence's words lived on past him. The nation built from the addition of Louisiana lived on past him. His conception of the possibilities of a strong presidency lived on past him. The university did, too.

Education had been a perennial interest. "I think by far the most important bill in our whole code is that for the diffusion of knowledge among the people," Jefferson had written George Wythe in the

1780s. "No other sure foundation can be devised for the preservation of freedom and happiness."

Jefferson conceived the work of the university as a critical element of the kind of American world he had long worked to bring about. "This institution will be based on the illimitable freedom of the human mind," he said. Echoing his first inaugural address, he added: "For here we are not afraid to follow truth wherever it may lead, nor to tolerate any error so long as reason is left free to combat it."

There was also a provincial element in his enthusiasm. "If our legislature does not heartily push our University we must send our children for education to Kentucky or Cambridge," Jefferson said in 1820, alluding to Transylvania College in Kentucky and to Harvard College. "The latter will return them to us fanatics and tories, the former will keep them to add to their population."

He envisioned a great new institution, and nothing could keep him away when he wanted to be on hand. In 1819, Eliza House Trist noted that Jefferson rode through "a perfect hurricane . . . to visit the college." He was said to have installed a telescope on a terrace at Monticello to watch the construction.

His first university appointment fell victim to the kind of sectarian religious strife that drove him to distraction. In 1820, Thomas Cooper, a Unitarian, was asked to come to the university as a professor. The state's religious world reacted badly, mounting what Jefferson called a "Holy Inquisition," and the zealots won. Jefferson was forced to back down.

The old man never lost his capacity to learn from his mistakes, however, and two years later, amid enduring criticism that the state university was hostile to religion, he offered a brilliant plan to assuage concerns that the institution was failing to nurture religious belief among its pupils. The immediate cause of worry for sectarian observers was Jefferson's refusal to include a professor of divinity on the faculty. In his 1822 annual report as rector, Jefferson gently but unmistakably shifted the burden back to the individual faiths themselves, offering any sect the opportunity to build and fund its own school on the grounds of the university. The library would be open to all, and officials would allow students the ability to attend classes of a sectarian nature as well as ordinary university courses—"but always understanding," Jefferson wrote, "that these schools shall be independent of the University and of each other."

Jefferson was once again exercising power passively and achieving his own ends under the guise of being reasonable and open. And he was being reasonable and open: The proposed compromise had much to recommend it as a sensible accommodation of interests. Faced with the prospect of having to build their own institutions, though, the different denominations declined. There would still be no professor of divinity, and there would be no separate seminaries. Jefferson may have lost Cooper, but he won the larger war.

The same year his belief in the power of reason led him into the regions of hyperbole. "I rejoice that in this blessed country of free enquiry and belief, which has surrendered its creed and conscience to neither kings nor priests," he said in 1822, "the genuine doctrine of only one God is reviving, and I trust that there is not a **young man** now living in the U.S. who will not die a Unitarian." (On the other side of the prediction ledger, Jefferson correctly foresaw the rise of coffee. The coffee bean, he wrote, "is become the favorite beverage of the civilized world.")

He was also closer to the mark—though, given the perennial popularity of traditional Christianity and Judaism, still wide of it—when he mused about the spread of less conventional spiritual beliefs. "Were I to be the founder of a new sect, I would call them Apiarians, and, after the example of the bee, advise them to extract the honey of every sect," he said. "My fundamental principle would be . . . that we are to be saved by our good works which are within our power, and not by our faith which is not within our power."

Jefferson believed in the existence of a creator God and in an afterlife. Most significantly, he defended the moral lessons of the life and teachings of Jesus, whose divinity Jefferson rejected but whose words and example he embraced. In his presidential years he had completed a forty-six-page work entitled **The Philosophy of Jesus of Nazareth extracted from the account of his life and doctrines as given by Matthew, Mark, Luke and John**. In retirement he returned to the project, privately creating a more ambitious work he called **The Life and Morals of Jesus of Nazareth Extracted Textually from the Gospels in Greek, Latin, French & English**. "The religion of Jesus is founded in the Unity of God, and this principle chiefly gave it triumph over the rabble of heathen gods then acknowledged," Jefferson wrote the Unitarian Jared Sparks in 1820. "Thinking men of all nations rallied readily to the doctrine of one only God [**sic**], and embraced it with the pure-morals which Jesus inculcated."

A churchgoer who carried his well-worn Book of Common Prayer to services, served as a vestryman, and invoked the divine in his public statements, Jefferson was, as he once put it, "of a sect by myself, as far as I know." Though he fought against the establishment of religion, he understood and appreciated the cultural role faith played in the United States. As a politician and a devotee of republicanism, Jefferson hoped that subjecting religious sensibilities to free inquiry would transform faith from a source of contention into a force for good, for he knew that religion in one form or another was a perpetual factor in the world. The wisest course, then, was not to rail against it but to encourage the application of reason to questions of faith. The more rational that men became about religion, Jefferson believed, the better lives they would lead; in turn the life of the nation would become more stable and virtuous.

It was not going to be a quick or easy war to win, especially given the power of traditional Christianity. To John Adams, Jefferson wrote: "The truth is that the greatest enemies to the doctrines of Jesus are those calling themselves the expositors of them, who have perverted them for the structure of a system of fancy absolutely incomprehensible, and without any foundation in his genuine words. And the day will come when the mystical generation of Jesus, by the supreme being as his father in the womb of a virgin, will be classed with the fable of the generation of Minerva in the brain of Jupiter. But we may hope that the dawn of reason and freedom of thought in these United States will do away [with] all this artificial scaffolding, and restore to us the primitive and genuine doctrines of this the most venerated reformer of human errors."

Jefferson had a fairly detailed vision of the afterlife, seeking comfort from the present pain of the loss of loved ones in the expectation that they would meet again beyond time and space. Of Heaven, he wrote Adams: "May we meet there again, in Congress, with our ancient colleagues, and receive with them the seal of approbation."

At heart, he believed "the doctrines of Jesus are simple, and tend all to the happiness of man," writing:

1. That there is only one God, and he all perfect.
2. That there is a future state of rewards and punishments.
3. That to love God with all thy heart and thy neighbor as thyself is the sum of religion.

His own faith, he told Adams, "is known to my God and myself alone. Its evidence before the world is to be sought in my life; if that has been honest and dutiful to society, the religion which has regulated it cannot be a bad one." As a young man, Jefferson recalled with pride, he had been "bold in the pursuit of knowledge, never fearing to follow truth and reason to whatever results they led, and bearding every authority which stood in their way."

He remained bold to the end. "It is too late in the day for men of sincerity to pretend they believe in the Platonic mysticisms that three are one, and one is three. . . . But this constitutes the craft, the power, and the profit of the priests. Sweep away their gossamer fabrics of factitious religion, and they would catch no more flies. We should all then, like the Quakers, live without an order of priests, moralize for ourselves, follow the oracle of conscience, and say nothing about what no man can understand, nor therefore believe; for I suppose belief to be the assent of the mind to an intelligible proposition." Still, he donated money to the American Bible Society, agreeing that "there never was a more pure and sublime system of morality delivered to man than is to be found in the four evangelists."

In October 1819, he was felled with a stricture of the ileum, an intestinal crisis that his doctors believed possibly fatal. He rallied, as he always had, but his convalescence gave way to a period of intense worry over the Union in 1820 and beyond. "The boisterous sea of liberty is never without a wave," he wrote a correspondent that year. A powerful one from the West was coming fast.

FORTY-TWO

The Knell of the Union

From the Battle of Bunker's Hill to the Treaty
of Paris we never had so ominous a question.
—THOMAS JEFFERSON, on the admission
of Missouri to the Union

J EFFERSON LIKED TO THINK WELL of the future.
It suited the prevailing nature of his tempera-
ment. He knew, too, that the public preferred
a promise of progress rather than reversal, of light
rather than dark. "I have much confidence that
we shall proceed successfully for ages to come," he
wrote the Marquis de Barbé-Marbois in 1817. "My
hope of its duration is built much on the enlargement of the resources of life going hand in hand
with the enlargement of territory."

On Friday, December 10, 1819, Jefferson took note
of a debate in Congress with vast implications: the
conditions under which Missouri would be added
to the Union. The House voted for admission only
if antislavery provisions were part of the agreement;

the Senate, where slave states held more sway, refused to go along.

From the Constitutional Convention through the Louisiana Purchase, the Northeast had feared that an expanding slaveholding South and West would give the slave interests permanent control over the country. At the same time, the South and West feared for the future of slavery.

To Jefferson it was the worst of hours. He knew slavery was a moral wrong and believed it would ultimately be abolished. He could not, however, bring himself to work for emancipation. As a politician he understood that sectional tensions represented the greatest threat to the union. In his own public career, they already had threatened it in the secessionist movements in the Northeast over the Louisiana Purchase and, later, over the embargo.

Now slavery was the explicit issue—and slavery was the highest order of problem. Missouri, Jefferson said, was "like a fire bell in the night . . . the knell of the Union." He added: "A geographical line, coinciding with a marked principle, moral and political, once conceived and held up to the angry passions of men, will never be obliterated; and every new irritation will mark it deeper and deeper."

By his own admission, Jefferson's solution for the problem of slavery was too complex to be executed. "The cession of that kind of property, for so it is misnamed, is a bagatelle which would not cost me a second thought, if, in that way, a general emancipation and **expatriation** could be effected: and, gradually, and with due sacrifices, I think it might be," he wrote. "But, as it is, we have the wolf by the ear, and we can neither hold him, nor safely let him go. Justice is in one scale, and self-preservation in the other."

To John Adams, Jefferson was candid about his anxieties. "The banks, bankrupt law, manufactures, Spanish treaty, are nothing," he wrote in December. "These are occurrences which, like waves in a storm, will pass under the ship. But the Missouri question is a breaker on which we lose the Missouri country by revolt, and what more, God only knows."

The resolution was a compromise. Slavery was to be allowed below the 36th parallel but other than in Missouri itself it was forbidden any farther north. Fugitive slaves were to be returned to their owners in the event of escape into the free regions.

Jefferson saw the issue in terms of power. If the federal government began regulating slavery within the states, then a precedent would be established, for regulation could finally lead to abolition.

He believed, too, the North was trying to create new free states that would strengthen the national hand of the antislavery interest, possibly giving free states a lock on the electoral college. "It is not a moral question, but one merely of power," he wrote Lafayette. "Its object is to raise a geographical principle for the choice of a president, and the noise will be kept up till that is effected."

The terms in which he thought and spoke of the Missouri matter suggest the depth of his feeling about it. Jefferson linked the question to one that had driven him for a lifetime: that of the threat of monarchy. "The leaders of Federalism, defeated in their schemes of obtaining power by rallying partisans to the principle of monarchism . . . have changed their tack," he said, and were now attempting to build political support by appealing to antislavery sentiment.

In the end Jefferson could see slavery only as tragedy. He may have believed it to be "a hideous blot," as he wrote in September 1823, but it was not a blot he felt capable of erasing. The man who believed in the acquisition and wielding of power—political power, intellectual power, domestic power, and mastering life from the fundamental definition of human liberty in the modern world down to the smallest details of the wine he served and the flowers he planted—chose to consider himself powerless over the central economic and social fact of his life.

Writing to a correspondent who asked him to devise a way to free the slaves of Virginia, Jefferson demurred. "This, my dear sir," Jefferson said, "is like bidding old Priam to buckle the armor of Hector. . . . This enterprise is for the young. . . . It shall have all my prayers, and these are the only weapons of an old man."

Slavery was the rare subject where Jefferson's sense of realism kept him from marshaling his sense of hope in the service of the cause of reform. "There is nothing I would not sacrifice to a practicable plan of abolishing every vestige of this moral and political depravity," he wrote in 1814, but that was not true. He was not willing to sacrifice his own way of life, though he characteristically left himself a rhetorical escape by introducing the subjective standard of practicability.

By his lights nothing other than a removal of blacks from the established United States would work—a removal that would have dwarfed even the removal of Indians from what was understood by Jefferson and so many of his contemporaries to be white America. Indians were to be unjustly driven across the Mississippi. Blacks would have to be dispatched not across a river but an ocean. "Nothing is more certainly written in the book of fate than that these people are to be free. Nor is it less certain that the two races, equally free, cannot live in the same government."

A multiracial society was beyond his imagination, except it was not beyond his experience, since he had created just such a society at Monticello. Mixed-race children such as those he had with Sally Hemings—children whom he saw every day, in his house, alongside his white family—suffered, in his general view, from an intrinsic "degradation" produced by the "amalgamation" of white and black.

How is it possible to explain the disorienting contradiction between his harsh views of "amalgamation" and his own paternity of such children? Perhaps Jefferson felt, as he often did, that if he were in control—which he was, in his eclectic domestic sphere—then he would be able to keep matters in hand. He felt this way about his debts, and he had felt this way about the country writ large when he was seeking and held the presidency. The human products of "amalgamation," to use his term, were thought to be sources of chaos in the world beyond his own mountain. In his domain, though, he could have convinced himself that his centrality made Monticello the exception to what he supposed to be the rule in other realms.

Rendering moral judgments in retrospect can be hazardous. It is unfair to judge the past by the standards of the present. Yet we can assess a man's views on a moral issue—which slavery unquestionably was—by what others in the same age and facing the same realities thought and did. Beginning with Robert Carter, the planter who freed his slaves in 1791, some Virginians of Jefferson's class recognized that the blight of slavery had to go and did what was within their power by emancipating their slaves.

More broadly, the politicians of the North were steadily creating a climate in which antislavery rhetoric and sentiment could take root and thrive. The very fact of the debate over Missouri suggested that the antislavery forces were gathering strength—and were willing to use it. As important for a sophisticate such as Jefferson was the French view of the institution. He had lived in that world, and had presumably feared that the Hemingses, and particularly Sally Hemings, might have successfully sought their freedom while in France.

So it is not as though Jefferson lived in a time or in places where abolition was the remotest or most fanciful of prospects. It had not only been thought of but had been brought into being in his lifetime in lands he knew intimately. Jefferson was wrong about slavery, his attempts at reform at the beginning of his public life notwithstanding.

Here again, though, and in dramatic relief, we see that Jefferson the practical politician was a more powerful persona than Jefferson the moral theorist. He was driven by what he had once called, in a 1795 letter to Madison, "the Southern interest," for the South was his personal home and his political base. He could not see a pragmatic way out of the conundrum, so he did what politicians often do: He suggested that the problem would be handled in the fullness of time—just not now. He did not believe full-scale colonization was feasible. "I do not say this to induce an inference that the getting rid of them is forever impossible," he wrote in 1824. "For that is neither my opinion nor my hope. But only that it cannot be done in this way."

Could it be done in any way? Jefferson did not know. "Where the disease is most deeply seated, there it will be slowest in eradication," he wrote in 1815, a point that reflects the sensibility of—as well as the sensitivities of—a vote counter accustomed to seeking popular approval for proposed courses of action.

"The march of events has not been such as to render its completion practicable within the limits of time allotted to me; and I leave its accomplishment as the work of another generation," Jefferson wrote the reformer Frances Wright in 1825. "And I am cheered when I see that. . . . The abolition of the evil is not impossible: it ought never therefore to be despaired of. Every plan should be adopted, every experiment tried, which may do something towards the ultimate object."

They just were not to be experiments he could undertake—an extremely rare case of the innovative, ever curious, inventive Jefferson refusing to engage in work he knew to be essential. And so he did what he almost never did: He gave up.

Personal debt was another enduring irony of Jefferson's life. Planters of his time and place were often land rich and cash poor, borrowing heavily against their farms, their slaves, and their prospective crops. The need for ready money drove Jefferson, his father, and many of their contemporaries into the growing of tobacco, a cash crop that exhausted the soil but tended to command a greater price at market than wheat or other grains. As such, when tobacco was high, the Virginians made money; when tobacco was low, Virginians muddled along or lost money, depleting their land no matter how much cash came in. Thomas Jefferson shifted away from tobacco at Monticello when he returned to Virginia in 1794, but he always grew the crop on his more distant plantations.

A confluence of factors kept Jefferson in debt. There was the gentry culture of his time. There were promissory notes to be signed for friends and family members. Most of all, there was the inherited debt. In an effort to pay it down, he sold inherited property worth £4,000, but skyrocketing inflation during the Revolutionary War made what was owed him under the land agreements worth "but a shadow"—while the debt remained, with the spiraling effect of accumulating interest.

Why would Jefferson, a man who sought power over men and events, concede his power to creditors and continue to incur debts when he was already so burdened? Part of the explanation may lie in his tendency, as he put it, to take things "by the smooth handle" and avoid difficult personal choices. It was always easier, it seemed, to sign another note and defer payment to another day, than it was to face a stark financial reckoning. Oddly, too, his innate sense of control and place may have enabled him to see debt as an abstract problem rather than a concrete one. He was part of a family and class in which borrowing money and mortgaging lands was as much a part of the culture as hospitality or hunting. The prospect of ruin was real but in Jefferson's mind remote—or at least remote enough for him to allow his essential sense of security about his standing in society to trump fiscal discipline. Ironically, then, Jefferson's feeling of power in general led him to sacrifice his power—and his family's future—in particular. As with slavery, Jefferson's capacity to live with contradiction was nothing less than epic.

The Missouri question made Jefferson even more eager to get on with the building of the University of Virginia, for he believed the rising generation of leaders should be trained at home, in climes hospitable to his view of the world, rather than sent north.

His had been a largely comfortable old age, particularly given the circumstances of the time. In his late seventies he was thought by a friend to look "as well as he did 10 years ago."

That began to change in the 1820s. His wrist, injured in Paris in 1786, grew worse, and he became ever more elegiac as the first years of the 1820s passed. Worried about Missouri, his wrist aching, he wrote to Adams on the first day of June 1822: "The papers tell us General Stark is off at the age of 93. Charles Thomson still lives at about the same age, cheerful, slender as a grasshopper, and so much without memory that he scarcely recognizes the members of his household. An intimate friend of his called on him not long since; it was difficult to make him recollect who he was, and, sitting one hour, he told him the same story four times over. Is this life? . . . It is at most but the life of a cabbage; surely not worth a wish."

One day toward the end of 1822 he put a foot wrong at Monticello. A step down from a terrace gave way under his weight. He collapsed, struck the ground, and broke his left arm. It healed fairly well, but now both his right and left hands had been significantly injured. "During summer I enjoy its temperature," Jefferson said, "but I shudder at the approach of winter, and wish I could sleep through it with the dormouse, and only wake with him in spring, if ever."

Jefferson had few doubts about his generation's place in history. In a letter to John Adams introducing his grandson Thomas Jefferson Randolph, Jefferson said: "Like other young people he wishes to be able, in the winter nights of old age, to recount to those around him what he has heard and learnt of the Heroic age preceding his birth, and which of the Argonauts particularly he was in time to have seen."

But he did worry about how history would treat the times in which he had lived and led. "We have been too careless of our future reputation, while our Tories will omit nothing to place us in the wrong," he wrote Supreme Court justice William Johnson of South Carolina in 1823. Jefferson was contemptuous of John Marshall's five-volume biography of George Washington, which he believed Federalist propaganda, and as the years went by he worried about works on Alexander Hamilton and on John Adams.

> Besides the five-volumed libel which represents us as struggling for office, and not at all to prevent our government from being administered into a monarchy, the life of Hamilton is in the hands of a man who, to the bitterness of the priest, adds the rancor of the fiercest Federalism. Mr. Adams' papers, too, and his biography, will descend of course to his son, whose pen, you know, is pointed, and his prejudices not in our favor. And doubtless other things are in preparation, unknown to us. On our part we are depending on truth to make itself known, while history is taking a contrary set which may become too inveterate for correction.

As he continued to grow older, he refused to surrender his independence. In May 1823, Jefferson was on his solitary daily ride. Crossing the Rivanna, his horse became "mired in the river," a granddaughter wrote, and Jefferson, his legs tangled, fell into the current. His family was horrified, worrying that "he would inevitably have been drowned had not the rapidity of the current carried him down to a much shallower place, where by reaching the bottom of the river with his hand he was enabled to rise on his feet and get out." He got soaked and his arm wound up in a sling, but he refused to accede to family demands that he give up his solitary rides. He had just turned eighty.

In October 1823 he answered a letter of President Monroe's seeking counsel on whether the United States should join with England to oppose Spanish efforts to retain Madrid's South American colonies, which were in revolt. The real issue, Jefferson replied, was more general than particular: How should the United States think of European adventurism in its hemisphere?

"The question presented by the letters you have sent me is the most momentous which has ever been offered to my contemplation since that of Independence," Jefferson wrote Monroe. "Our first and fundamental maxim should be, never to entangle ourselves in the broils of Europe. Our second—never to suffer Europe to intermeddle with [cross]-Atlantic affairs. America, North and South, has a set of interests distinct from those of Europe, and peculiarly her own."

The doctrine that bears Monroe's name—that the United States opposes all European intervention in the Western Hemisphere—owes much to the work of Monroe's secretary of state, John Quincy Adams, who was instrumental in the formulation of the policy. But it was also at least partly of Jeffersonian inspiration. In Jefferson's case, it was fitting that a man who had spent his life in pursuit of control would extend it as far as he could in the service of his nation, leaving a kind of last declaration of independence. This time it was a matter of policy, not of revolution. It was a declaration all the same.

In the 1824 presidential election, Jefferson saw anew that the Founders' dream of the end of party was still a dream, something that might come true in the future but surely not in the present. Writing Lafayette, Jefferson said, "You are not to believe that these two parties are amalgamated, that the lion and the lamb are lying down together. The Hartford Convention, the victory of Orleans, the peace of Ghent, prostrated the name of Federalism. Its votaries abandoned it through shame and mortification; and now call themselves Republicans. But the name alone is changed, the principles are the same."

The presidential field was unusually large in 1824. There was John Quincy Adams of Massachusetts; Henry Clay of Kentucky; John C. Calhoun of South Carolina; William Crawford of Georgia; and Andrew Jackson of Tennessee. The race in part represented a generational shift. Jackson had been born the year Jefferson began his law practice and had been a fourteen-year-old prisoner of war in 1781, the year Jefferson escaped from Tarleton at Monticello.

Jefferson favored Crawford, a veteran of Madison's and Monroe's cabinets. The Georgian suffered a stroke in late 1823, however, and the election was ultimately decided in the House of Representatives in February 1825. Though Jackson won the most popular votes, Adams was chosen in the House after Clay, who was to become Adams's secretary of state, gave his support to Adams. (Jackson's charges of a "corrupt bargain" would fuel his own ambitions to avenge his defeat in 1828, which he did.)

Arriving at Monticello in a procession of trumpets and banners, Lafayette stepped out of his carriage on a brilliant autumn day in November 1824 at the East Front of the house. Lafayette, now sixty-seven years old, had come to America for a triumphant farewell tour, a living monument (like Adams and Jefferson) to days that seemed ever more glorious and distant.

Finally stooped with age in his eighty-first year, Jefferson walked toward his guest. They embraced without embarrassment, two old revolutionaries who had seen the best and the worst of their times and of their countries.

"My dear Jefferson!" said the guest.

"My dear Lafayette!" replied the host.

They had not laid eyes on each other for more than thirty years, and Jefferson was graciously determined to honor Lafayette not only for the Frenchman's services to the Revolutionary cause but to the cause of the young nation during Jefferson's years in France.

At a banquet in Lafayette's honor in Charlottesville, Jefferson drafted a toast to be read:

His deeds in the war of independence you have heard and read. They are known to you and embalmed in your memories, and in the pages of faithful history. His deeds in the peace which followed that war are perhaps not known to you; but I can attest them. When I was stationed in his country . . . [h]e made our cause his own. . . . His influence and connections there were great. All doors of all departments were open to him at all times; to me, only formally and at appointed times. In truth, I only held the nail, he drove it. Honor him, then, as your benefactor in peace, as well as in war.

There was a benedictory quality to Jefferson's toast, a broader message to his countrymen there and far beyond, for he knew his words would be published and read everywhere.

Born and bred among your fathers, led by their partiality into the line of public life, I labored in fellowship with them through that arduous struggle which, freeing us from foreign bondage, established us in the rights of self-government; rights which have blessed ourselves, and will bless, in their sequence, all the nations of the earth.

In a particular place, a universal theme: In old age Jefferson was the Jefferson of youth, a man who honored the work of politics, the comradeship of service, and the ideas that drove flawed men to fight for causes larger than themselves.

As Jefferson aged he retained his conversational skill of speaking of topics of special interest to his companion of the moment. When those were exhausted, he would muse widely about the past and the future. He was always gracious. "In conversation, Mr. Jefferson is easy and natural, and apparently not ambitious; it is not loud, as challenging general attention, but usually addressed to the person next to him," Daniel Webster wrote of an 1824 stay at Monticello. Jefferson spoke of "science and letters, and especially the University of Virginia, which is coming into existence almost entirely from his exertions. . . . When we were with him, his favorite subjects were Greek and Anglo-Saxon, historical recollections of the times and events of the Revolution, and of his residence in France from 1783–4 to 1789."

A New Englander, Webster was unhappy about the rise of Andrew Jackson in the West. Jefferson apparently shared at least some of Webster's fears. "I feel much alarmed at the prospect of seeing General Jackson President," Jefferson said, according to Webster. "He is one of the most unfit men I know of for such a place. He has had very little respect for laws or constitutions, and is, in fact, an able military chief. His passions are terrible."

On reading Webster's account, the biographer

Henry Randall wondered about its accuracy, and put the question to a grandchild, who replied:

> I cannot pretend to know what my grandfather said to Mr. Webster, nor can I believe Mr. Webster capable of misstatement. Still I think the copy of the portrait incorrect, as throwing out all the lights and giving only the shadows. I have heard my grandfather speak with great admiration of General Jackson's military talent. If he called him a "dangerous man," "unfit for the place" to which the nation eventually called him, I think it must have been entirely with reference to his general idea that a military chieftain was no proper head for a peaceful republic as ours was in those days. . . . He did not like to see the people run away with ideas of military glory.

As always, Jefferson was in significant debt, yet he had, as a favor to a friend, cosigned a note for $20,000 for Virginia governor Wilson Cary Nicholas in 1819. It was the act of a gentleman and a kinsman: a Nicholas daughter had married a Jefferson grandson.

Nicholas was forced to default on the note, leaving the former president responsible for the debt. On the granddaughter-in-law's first call at Monticello since news of the disaster, Jefferson took care to seek her out. Abashed and horrified by the news, she was unsure how to conduct herself around Jefferson. When he emerged from his rooms, he immediately called for her. "She heard his voice and flew to meet him," Henry Randall wrote. "Instead of the usual hearty hand-shake and kiss, he folded her in his arms. His smile was radiant." At dinner he spoke with her with great grace; the shame the young woman had felt disappeared. "Neither then nor on any subsequent occasion," wrote Randall, "did he ever by a word or look make her aware that he was even conscious of the misfortune her father had brought upon him."

Governor Nicholas himself lived along the route Jefferson traveled to Poplar Forest, and Jefferson knew he could not fail to call on him. "I ought not to stop; I have not time; but it would be cruel to pass him," Jefferson said to a family member as they turned off the road toward Nicholas's place. Meeting his old friend, Jefferson behaved perfectly. "He showed no depression, and did not make an equal exposure of his feelings by feigning extraordinary cheerfulness," wrote Randall. For the rest of Nicholas's life, Jefferson treated him as though nothing had happened. A busybody lady once spoke meanly of Nicholas in Jefferson's presence at Monticello, and the former president cut her off politely but firmly. He had, he told her, "the highest opinion of Governor Nicholas, and felt the deepest sympathy for his misfortunes." Such was the private character of the man whose public enemies accused him of selfishness, duplicity, inordinate ambition, and cold-bloodedness.

The debilitating burden of debt facing Jefferson forced him to do what he liked least in the world: put himself in the hands of others. The market was bad, and so traditional routes of raising capital—finding buyers for his land—were out. Then inspiration struck. He had been, Patsy said, "lying awake one night from painful thoughts" when he conceived the notion of holding a lottery. In an appeal to the General Assembly of Virginia, he sought permission to sell tickets in exchange for chances at his lands, mills, and—to his horror—Monticello itself, if his debts were to be retired. However devastating to his pride this would be, he had no other choice. His grandson Thomas Jefferson Randolph was in charge of the arrangements.

The former president was in a valedictory frame of mind. Asked to send counsel to a young namesake, he composed a significantly longer letter than he tended to write at this point. The subject engaged him, however, and always had: How to live a virtuous life? "Adore God," he wrote. "Reverence and cherish your parents. Love your neighbor as yourself, and your country more than yourself. Be just. Be true. Murmur not at the ways of Providence. So shall the life into which you have entered be the portal to one of eternal and ineffable bliss."

There was more: a paraphrased version of Psalm 15.

THE PORTRAIT OF A GOOD MAN BY THE MOST SUBLIME OF POETS, FOR YOUR IMITATION.

Lord, who's the happy man that may to thy
    blest courts repair;
Not stranger-like to visit them, but to inhabit
    there?
'Tis he whose every thought and deed by rules
    of virtue moves;
Whose generous tongue disdains to speak the
    thing his heart disproves.
Who never did a slander forge, his neighbor's
    fame to wound;
Nor hearken to a false report, by malice whis-
    pered round.
Who vice in all its pomp and power, can treat
    with just neglect;
And piety, though clothed in rags, religiously
    respect.
Who to his plighted vows and trust has ever
    firmly stood;
And though he promise to his loss, he makes
    his promise good.
Whose soul in usury disdains his treasure to
    employ;

Whom no rewards can ever bribe the guiltless
   to destroy.
The man who by this steady course has happiness insur'd,
When earth's foundations shake, shall stand,
   by Providence secur'd.

And there was yet more.

A DECALOGUE OF CANONS FOR
OBSERVATION IN PRACTICAL LIFE.

1. Never put off till tomorrow what you can do today.
2. Never trouble another for what you can do yourself.
3. Never spend your money before you have it.
4. Never buy what you do not want, because it is cheap; it will be dear to you.
5. Pride costs us more than hunger, thirst, and cold.
6. We never repent of having eaten too little.
7. Nothing is troublesome that we do willingly.
8. How much pain have cost us the evils which have never happened.
9. Take things always by their smooth handle.
10. When angry, count ten, before you speak; if very angry, a hundred.

————

In a bizarre episode in his last years, history almost killed him. A New York artist arrived at Monticello to take a plaster cast of Jefferson's face—a life mask. Something went wrong, however, and the plaster almost suffocated him; only by banging a chair next to the sofa on which he lay did Jefferson manage to alert his butler Burwell Colbert to his plight. His life was saved, as his life had been shaped, by the act of a slave.

Musing about abolition—and presumably repatriation—in the fading spring, he wrote: "The revolution in public opinion which this cause requires, is not to be expected in a day, or perhaps in an age; but time, which outlives all things, will outlive this evil also."

His health had been deteriorating since the first day of 1826. "It is now three weeks since a re-ascerbation of my painful complaint [a severe attack of diarrhea] has confined me to the house and indeed my couch," Jefferson wrote a friend in Richmond on January 1, 1826. "Required to be constantly recumbent I write slowly and with difficulty. . . . Weakened in body by infirmities and in mind by age, now far gone into my 83rd year, reading one newspaper only and forgetting immediately what I read." Still, he refused to give up riding, even though he had to mount his horse Eagle by putting the horse on a terrace below and lowering himself into the saddle.

With the fiftieth anniversary of the Declaration of Independence coming in the summer of 1826, organizers of the Washington celebrations were eager to bring Jefferson back to the capital for the day. He was too ill to consider it, but in his sun-filled cabinet he drafted a letter to commemorate the occasion. "All eyes are opened, or opening, to the rights of man," he wrote. "The general spread of the light of science has already laid open to every view the palpable truth that the mass of mankind has not been born with saddles on their backs, nor a favored few booted and spurred, ready to ride them legitimately, by the grace of God. These are grounds of hope for others. For ourselves, let the annual return of this day forever refresh our recollections of these rights, and an undiminished devotion to them."

These were to be his last words to the nation he had helped found, and which he had led through so much. His farewell to Madison, his friend of half a century, was more personal but as heartfelt. "Take care of me when dead," Jefferson asked in a letter to his old friend in February.

Still, he was not expecting an imminent death. After dispatching his letter about liberty to the Fourth of July commemoration in Washington, Jefferson wrote another on a different passion: wine, making arrangements to pay the customs collector at Baltimore the tax on an incoming shipment.

He would not live to drink it. Soon Jefferson was confined to his bed. He continued to read, browsing through the Bible, Aeschylus, Sophocles, and Euripides, musing on the great tragedians as time and illness finally caught up with him in the last days of June.

The end was at hand.

FORTY-THREE

No, Doctor, Nothing More

> The loss of Mr. Jefferson is one over which the whole world will mourn. He was one of those ornaments and benefactors of the human race, whose death forms an epoch, and creates a sensation throughout the whole circle of civilized man.
>
> —Thomas Jefferson's nephew
> DABNEY CARR, JR.

O N SATURDAY, JUNE 24, 1826, Jefferson painfully put pen to paper to ask Dr. Robley Dunglison to call. Dunglison left Charlottesville as soon as he received the note. When he arrived, he found Jefferson had forced himself from his bedroom into the parlor, as though to greet him in the old ordinary way.

Dunglison put him back in bed. The doctor said he was "apprehensive that the attack would prove fatal. Nor did Mr. Jefferson himself indulge in any other opinion. From this time his strength gradually diminished and he had to remain in bed."

Jefferson now marshaled his will toward the realization of one last mission: He wanted to survive until the Fourth of July.

As he lay dying, his daughter sat with him during the day. Thomas Jefferson Randolph and Nicholas Trist kept watch in the nights. Thomas Mann Randolph, Jr., the man who had been his son-in-law since moments after the return from Paris more than thirty years before, stayed away. "His mind was always clear—it never wandered," his grandson Thomas Jefferson Randolph said. "He conversed freely, and gave directions as to his private affairs."

Jefferson told his grandson what he wanted done about his coffin and his burial. There was to be nothing showy or grand. He would take his leave of the world with a simple Episcopal service and be laid to rest in the cemetery on the western slope of Monticello where he had interred Dabney Carr so many decades before—and then his mother, and then his wife.

Henry Lee, son of Light-Horse Harry Lee, called on Jefferson in the last days of June. Lee was on a mission: He was editing a new edition of his father's **Memoirs of the War,** a book that treated Jefferson's wartime governorship in an unfavorable light. Even in extremis, Jefferson could not resist one more chance to revise the history of those days. He invited Lee into his sick chamber on Thursday, June 29, 1826.

At Monticello, Patsy stopped Lee in the main part of the house. Her father was simply too sick to see him, she said. Saddened, Lee reflected that he was "never more to behold the venerable man, who had entered all the walks of politics and philosophy, and in all was foremost—and to whom the past, and the present, and all future ages are, and will be, so much indebted."

Learning Lee was on hand, Jefferson, lying in his bed, sent for the visitor anyway. "My emotions at approaching **Jefferson's dying bed** I cannot describe," Lee wrote. "You remember the alcove in which he slept. There he was extended, feeble, prostrate; but the fine and clear expression of his countenance not all obscured." He recognized Lee and warmly offered his hand from the bed. "The energy of his grasp, and the spirit of his conversation, were such as to make me hope that he would yet rally—and that the superiority of mind over matter in his composition, would preserve him yet longer."

Jefferson could not help Lee as he had wished. He was too ill to locate the papers he had promised him that gave Jefferson's side of the Arnold-Tarleton-Cornwallis story. He spoke of death in philosophical, even colloquial, terms. "He alluded to the probability of his death—as a man would to the prospect of being caught in a shower—as an event not to be desired, but not to be feared."

Lee noticed an intriguing detail. Jefferson waved any buzzing flies away from the alcove himself, taking charge of the operation without help from the party gathered around him.

He wanted as much control as possible. "Mrs. Randolph afterwards told me this was his habit—that his plan was to fight old age off, by never admitting the approach of helplessness," Lee wrote. After he left the bedroom for the main part of the house, Lee never laid eyes on Jefferson again.

Jefferson's rooms, ordinarily so private, filled as his strength ebbed. He said good-bye to his family, addressing each in turn. Of an eight-year-old grandson, he smiled and said, "George does not understand what all this means." To a great-granddaughter he quoted the Gospel of Luke: "Lord, now lettest thou thy servant depart in peace."

Thomas Jefferson Randolph suggested he was looking better, but Jefferson would have none of it. "Do not imagine for a moment that I feel the smallest solicitude about the result," Jefferson said. "I am like an old watch, with a pinion worn out here, and a wheel there, until it can go no longer." He was nearing what he had once referred to as "that eternal sleep which, whether with or without dreams, awaits us hereafter."

He awoke to a noise and wondered whether he had heard the name of the Reverend Frederick Hatch, the rector of the parish. No, he was told. "I have no objection to see him, as a kind and good neighbor," Jefferson said, turning over.

He had composed a poem for Patsy, alluding to his imminent reunion with Patty and Polly, and enclosed the lines in a little casket she did not open until after he died.

Life's visions are vanished, its dreams are no
    more;
Dear friends of my bosom, why bathed in
    tears?
I go to my fathers, I welcome the shore
Which crowns all my hopes or which buries
    my cares.
Then farewell, my dear, my lov'd daughter,
    adieu!
The last pang of life is in parting from you!
Two seraphs await me long shrouded in death;
I will bear them your love on my last parting
    breath.

Lying in his alcove bed, Jefferson mused about
the Revolution, telling stories of the great drama.
The smallest details reminded him of the largest
of struggles. His bed curtains, he noted, had come
from the first postwar importations in 1782.

In the chambers of his mind Jefferson may have
been hurtling back into the past, hearing again the
voices of the House of Burgesses or of the Pennsylvania State House or of Versailles or of the President's
House, but part of him remained firmly rooted in
the present, somehow keeping track of time, willing
himself to live to see, however dimly, the fiftieth anniversary of the Declaration of Independence.

"A few hours more, Doctor, and it will be all over,"
he said at one point, only to rally.

At five forty-five p.m. on the second, he took laudanum in grog. He was given tea three hours later and brandy four hours after that. He slept fitfully as the clock tinged.

Then, on the evening of the third, at about seven p.m., he asked Dunglison, "Ah! Doctor, are you still there?" Jefferson's central concern, though, was time: "Is it the Fourth?"

"It soon will be," Dunglison replied.

Jefferson took what would be his last dose of laudanum, muttering "Oh God!"

Two hours later, at nine p.m., Dunglison woke him for more medicine.

"No, Doctor, nothing more," Jefferson said.

The remaining three hours passed with agonizing slowness. Jefferson woke late on the night of the third and said, in questioning voice, "This is the Fourth?" Nicholas Trist remained silent, for it was not. Jefferson spoke again. "This is the Fourth?" He would not be stymied. Trist could not bring himself to disappoint the old man, and lied by nodding that yes, it was indeed the Fourth. "Ah," said Jefferson. "Just as I wished."

Perhaps he knew, somehow, that it was not, in fact, the anniversary of his declaration, at least not quite yet, and so Jefferson fought on, breathing still.

At last the clock above Jefferson's bed tinged twelve times, ushering in the Fourth of July.

Drifting in and out of consciousness, Jefferson appeared to dream of ancient crises met and overcome, murmuring about the Revolutionary Committee of

Safety and gesturing as if he were writing. "Warn the Committee to be on the alert," he said. He was dwelling on danger. In his last hours he was still struggling to defend the American cause, if only in his flickering imagination.

At four o'clock in the morning, he gave the attending slaves some directions. The final words of a man whose first memory was of being handed up to a slave on a pillow were addressed to his slaves. For a man who had worked for, and witnessed, so much change, in the end some things were as they were in the beginning.

At ten he stirred and stared at a grandson, trying but failing to signal what he wanted. It was Burwell Colbert who interpreted the glance correctly. Jefferson wanted his head elevated; the butler arranged him as he wished. An hour later he was moving his parched lips but saying nothing. Much to his evident relief, a grandson lifted a wet sponge to Jefferson's mouth.

It was over. At ten minutes before one o'clock on Tuesday, July 4, 1826, Thomas Jefferson died in his bed, three miles from Shadwell, where he had been born a subject of the British Empire eight decades before.

He died with his eyes open, his gaze fixed on his beloved alcove, his shelter from the storms of a world in which he had long warred, often triumphed, and always loved.

Thomas Jefferson Randolph touched his grandfather's cooling skin, gently closing the great man's eyes. Nicholas Trist quietly clipped a few small locks of his still-sandy hair, relics for the family. The wooden coffin built by John Hemings was made ready. The body was transferred to it, and the coffin was taken to the parlor to rest in state.

"To me he has been more than a father, and I have ever loved and reverenced him with my whole heart," Dabney Carr, Jr., wrote Nicholas Trist a week later. A grieving James Madison wrote Trist: "He lives and will live in the memory and gratitude of the wise and the good, as a luminary of science, as a votary of liberty, as a model of patriotism, and as a benefactor of humankind." The professor of ancient languages at the University of Virginia said: "He ought to be revered by all who enjoy the advantage of being educated in his University, and ever remembered as one of the great men whom Virginia has produced. His great deeds are recorded in the epitaph which he wrote for his own tomb."

Wormley Hughes, the gardener, dug Jefferson's grave on the western side of the mountain. The weather had been wet when the funeral party gathered inside Monticello for Jefferson's final journey. The mourners were few. Jefferson had not wanted a large service, and a delegation from the university in Charlottesville got a late start, missing much of the final rites.

A small group of family, friends, and slaves escorted the wooden coffin down the hill from the house. The Reverend Hatch read the burial office over the grave.

The service was conducted from the Episcopal Book of Common Prayer. " 'I am the resurrection and the life,' saith the Lord," Hatch read, " 'he that believeth in me, though he were dead, yet shall he live: and whosoever liveth and believeth in me, shall never die.' "

The promise of Paris was honored. In his life and in his will Jefferson had kept his word to Sally Hemings. Of the four children of Jefferson and Sally's who survived to adulthood, Beverly and Harriet had been allowed to leave Monticello in the early 1820s, and both are said to have lived as whites. According to their son Madison Hemings, "Harriet married a white man in good standing in Washington City. . . . She raised a family of children, and so far as I know they were never suspected of being tainted with African blood in the community where she lived or lives." Madison was freed in Jefferson's will and ultimately moved to Ohio, as did Eston, who eventually settled in Wisconsin and changed his name to Eston Jefferson and declared himself to be white. In his will Jefferson also freed three other members of the Hemings family: Burwell Colbert, John Hemings, and Joe Fossett. Jefferson freed no other slaves—only Hemingses.

Sally Hemings herself, now fifty-three years old, soon moved to Charlottesville and lived without incident as a free woman. Jefferson did not name her in his will, yet there is evidence that his wishes may have been implicitly clear to Patsy and his heirs: Sally Hemings was to be treated with respect. In 1834, Patsy gave Sally Hemings "her time"—an unofficial emancipation, and Sally had been free in fact since Jefferson's death. In time—Sally died in 1835—she bequeathed some mementos of Jefferson to her children: a pair of his glasses, an inkwell, and a shoe buckle.

Jefferson's tenuous hold on life had been the only thing keeping his heavily indebted plantations from his creditors. The lottery he had hoped would rescue his affairs died with him. When Jefferson died, he owed creditors, in early twenty-first-century terms, between $1 million and $2 million—so much that Monticello and his slaves had to be sold. Jefferson's ideas and his public work endured. His personal world did not.

Six hundred miles away, John Adams, ninety years old, had died on the same day as Jefferson, also at home in bed, a coincidence the incumbent president, John Quincy Adams, called "visible and palpable marks of Divine Favor, for which I would humble myself in grateful and silent adoration before the Ruler of the Universe." Preparing a eulogy to deliver at Faneuil Hall in Boston, Daniel Webster wrote his remarks one morning before breakfast, later recalling that when he was done "my paper was wet with my tears." On a beautiful day in Boston, with President Adams in the hall, Webster painted an indelible portrait of Jefferson's and Adams's ascent to the American pantheon: "On our fiftieth anniversary, the great day of national jubilee, in the very hour of public rejoicing, in the midst of echoing and reechoing voices of thanksgiving, while their own names were on all tongues, they took their flight together to the world of spirits."

On his own deathbed some of John Adams's final words were said to be about his old rival and friend: "Thomas Jefferson survives."

And so he does.

All Honor to Jefferson

> Jefferson's principles are sources of light be-
> cause they are not made up of pure reason, but
> spring out of aspiration, impulse, vision, sym-
> pathy. They burn with the fervor of the heart.
> —WOODROW WILSON, 1912

HE SURVIVES AS HE LIVED—in many ways and in many different lights. In the imme-diate aftermath of his death he was, together with Adams, recognized chiefly for the Revolution of 1776, the virtues of which were beyond dispute in the American mind. "To have been the instrument of expressing, in one brief, decisive act, the concentrated will and resolution of a whole family of states," said Congressman Edward Everett of Massachusetts in an 1826 eulogy, "of unfolding, in one all-important manifesto, the causes, the motives, and the justifica-tion of the great movement in human affairs . . . this is the glory of Thomas Jefferson."

Jefferson's finished work was the creation of an imperfect but lasting democratic habit of mind and heart. "Mr. Jefferson meant that the American system should be a democracy, and he would rather have let the whole world perish than that this principle, which to him represented all that man was worth, should fail," wrote the historian Henry Adams. "Mr. Hamilton considered democracy a fatal curse, and meant to stop its progress."

Ellen Wayles Coolidge was en route from Boston to Charlottesville when the news of her grandfather's death reached her in New York. She arrived at Monticello long after the funeral was over. To her, the place that had been home was now a foreign land. "He was gone," she wrote Henry Randall many years later, recalling the pain of her return. "His place was empty. I visited his grave, but the whole house at Monticello, with its large apartments and lofty ceilings, appeared to me one vast monument."

Such was the power of Jefferson, though, that Ellen expected him to appear to her at any moment—to hear his voice, to look into his eyes, to feel his touch once more. "I wandered about the vacant rooms as if I were looking for him," she said.

> Had I not seen him there all the best years of
> my life? . . . I passed hours in his chamber. It
> was just as he had left it. There was the bed
> on which he had slept for so many years—the
> chair in which, when I entered the room, I al-

ways found him sitting—articles of dress still
in their places—his clock by which he had told
so many useful hours—In the cabinet adjoining
were his books, the beloved companions of his
leisure—his writing table from which I gathered some small relics, memoranda and scraps of
written paper which I still preserve. All seemed
as if he had just quitted the rooms and there
were moments when I felt as if I expected his
return.

She was in a curiously dreamlike state.

For days I started at what seemed the sound of
his step or his voice, and caught myself listening
for both. In the dining room where, in winter,
we passed a good deal of time, there was the
low arm chair which he always occupied by the
fireside, with his little round table still standing as when it held his book or his candle. . . .
In the tea-room was the sofa where, in summer,
I had so often sat by his side—In the large parlor, with its parquet floor, stood the Campeachy
chair . . . where, in the shady twilight, I was
used to see him resting. In the great Hall, with
its large glass doors, where, in bad weather, he
liked to walk, how much I liked to walk with
him!—Everything told of him. An invisible
presence seemed everywhere to preside!

Finally she left the house, and the estate, never to return. Her grandfather lived, for her, in her heart and mind.

And in her nation's. Like his grieving grand-daughter in the summer of 1826, Americans have never quite let Jefferson go. "If Jefferson was wrong," wrote the biographer James Parton in 1874, "America is wrong. If America is right, Jefferson was right."

That is a remarkable burden to put on any one man or any one vision of politics, but the observation resonates because in death Jefferson remains much as he was in life: a vivid, engaging, breathing figure, brilliant and eloquent, at once monumental and human. It is difficult to imagine having a glass of wine with George Washington at Mount Vernon and talking of many things; it seems the most natural thing in the world to imagine doing so with Thomas Jefferson at Monticello, surrounded by paintings from France and busts from Philadelphia and artifacts from the dazzling world of the expedition of Meriwether Lewis and William Clark.

Jefferson speaks to us now because he spoke so powerfully and evocatively to us then. His circumstances were particular, yet the general issues that consumed him are constant: liberty and power, rights and responsibilities, the keeping of peace and the waging of war. He was a politician, a public man, in a nation in which politics and public life became—and remain—central. As Jefferson wrote, "Man . . . feels that he is a participator in the government of affairs not merely at an election, one day in the year, but every day."

Had he been only a philosopher he would not have endured as he does. Had he been only a legislator, or only a diplomat, or only an inventor, or only an author, or only an educator, or even only a president he would not have endured as he does.

He endures because we can see in him all the varied and wondrous possibilities of the human experience—the thirst for knowledge, the capacity to create, the love of family and of friends, the hunger for accomplishment, the applause of the world, the marshaling of power, the bending of others to one's own vision. His genius lay in his versatility; his larger political legacy in his leadership of thought and of men.

With his brilliance and his accomplishment and his fame he is immortal. Yet because of his flaws and his failures he strikes us as mortal, too—a man of achievement who was nonetheless susceptible to the temptations and compromises that ensnare all of us. He was not all he could be. But no politician—no human being—ever is.

We sense his greatness because we know that perfection in politics is not possible but that Jefferson passed the fundamental test of leadership: Despite all his shortcomings and all the inevitable disappointments and mistakes and dreams deferred, he left America, and the world, in a better place than it had been when he first entered the arena of public life.

Jefferson is the founding president who charms us most. George Washington inspires awe; John Adams respect. With his grace and hospitality, his sense of taste and love of beautiful things—of silver and art and architecture and gardening and food and wine—Jefferson is more alive, more convivial.

Nineteenth-century secessionists and twentieth-century states'-rights purists have found him a hero; progressive leaders from Woodrow Wilson to FDR to Truman have believed him to embody the best impulses in the American tradition of popular government.

So who was he, really? In the most literal sense, the only real Jefferson is the man who lived and loved and led and was carried to his grave in a wooden coffin on a wet summer's day in 1826. The real Jefferson was like so many of us: a bundle of contradictions, competing passions, flaws, sins, and virtues that can never be neatly smoothed out into a tidy whole. The closest thing to a constant in his life was his need for power and for control. He tended to mask these drives so effectively, however, that even the most astute of observers of his life and work have had trouble detecting them. "The leadership he sought was one of sympathy and love, not of command," wrote Henry Adams, but that was not quite the case. For him sympathy and love among the members of his political circle were means to an end—and the end was command. If he had found that affection was insufficient to accumulate the power he wanted, he would have found other ways to govern.

All the other Jeffersons—the emblematic ones, the metaphorical ones, the ones different generations and differing partisans interpret and invent, seeking inspiration from his example and sanction from his name—all these Jeffersons tell us more about ourselves than they do about the man himself. He can be claimed by many, and always will be.

The greatest of men often are. They are spoken of and thought about because their ideas resonate and their battles recur. His most significant successors have defined him in terms of his vision of liberty and union. To do so, of course, requires choosing between the author of the Declaration of Independence and the author of the Kentucky Resolutions; of deciding to trumpet the voice of the man who believed secession fatal to America instead of the man who wrote about the primacy of states' rights.

The finest presidents working in Jefferson's wake have made those choices and taken those decisions, creating a Jefferson that represents the best of the American spirit and the possibilities of politics in an imperfect world.

In the early days of April 1859, from Springfield, Illinois, Abraham Lincoln wrote to a group in Boston declining its invitation to speak to a Jefferson birthday celebration. The moment gave Lincoln the chance, though, to link Jefferson to the cause of freedom in an hour of danger for the Union. "The principles of Jefferson are the definitions and axioms of free society," Lincoln wrote. "And yet they are denied, and evaded, with no small show of success. . . . Those who deny freedom to others, deserve it not for themselves; and, under a just God, cannot long retain it."

The slave owner was thus being drafted to serve as an emblem of liberty not only for white men but for blacks. Such, in Lincoln's view, was the core of the Jefferson vision, and he hailed the author of the Declaration of Independence for turning the ideal into the real amid the war and chaos of the Revolution. "All honor to Jefferson," said Lincoln, "to the man who, in the concrete pressure of a struggle for national independence by a single people, had the coolness, forecast, and capacity to introduce into a merely revolutionary document, an abstract truth, applicable to all men and all times, and so to embalm it there, that today, and in all coming days, it shall be a rebuke and a stumbling block to the very harbingers of reappearing tyranny and oppression."

Seventy years later, in St. Paul, Minnesota, in 1932, Franklin D. Roosevelt did what Lincoln had done in 1859: He sought the mantle of Jefferson. "It is not necessary for us in any way to discredit the great financial genius of Alexander Hamilton or the school of thought of the early Federalists to point out that they were frank in their belief that certain sections of the Nation and certain individuals within those sections were more fitted than others to conduct Government," Roosevelt told the Jefferson Day dinner in St. Paul. "It was the purpose of Jefferson to teach the country that the solidarity of Federalism was only a partial one, that it represented only a minority of the people, that to build a great Nation the interests of all groups in every part must be considered, and that only in a large, national unity could real security be found."

A master of politics himself, FDR appreciated a kindred spirit. Jefferson, he said, "has been called a politician because he devoted years to the building of a political party. But this labor was in itself a definite and practical act aimed at the unification of all parts of the country in support of common principles. When people carelessly or snobbishly deride political parties, they overlook the fact that the party system of Government is one of the greatest methods of unification and of teaching people to think in common terms of our civilization."

Jefferson's words were elemental parts of the language of America. In September 1948, at the Bonham High School football stadium in Bonham, Texas, hometown of House Speaker Sam Rayburn, Harry S. Truman invoked Jefferson:

I have a profound faith in the people of this country. I believe in their commonsense. They love freedom and that love for freedom and justice is not dead. Our people believe today, as Jefferson did, that men were not born with saddles on their backs to be ridden by the privileged few.

We believe, as Jefferson did, that [the] "God who gave us life gave us liberty." We protect our liberty against those who threaten it from abroad, and we do not propose to give it up to those who threaten it at home. We will not give up our democratic way to a dictatorship of the left; neither will we give it up to a despotism of special privilege.

In the waning days of his own presidency, in December 1988, Ronald Reagan traveled to the lawn of Mr. Jefferson's University of Virginia to speak to students. For Reagan, Jefferson's pure republicanism and quotations about a limited national government had long been sacred texts.

Saluting Jefferson's "transforming genius," Reagan said: "The pursuit of science, the study of the great works, the value of free inquiry, in short, the very idea of living the life of the mind—yes, these formative and abiding principles of higher education in America had their first and firmest advocate, and their greatest embodiment, in a tall, fair-headed, friendly man who watched this university take form from the mountainside where he lived, the university whose founding he called a crowning achievement to a long and well-spent life."

The men—and now the women—of the university were not alone in feeling the great man's living spirit. "Presidents know about this, too," Reagan said. Jefferson was a permanent guardian over his successors, for "directly down the lawn and across the Ellipse from the White House are those ordered, classic lines of the Jefferson Memorial and the eyes of the 19-foot statue that gaze directly into the White House, a reminder to any of us who might occupy that mansion of the quality of mind and generosity of heart that once abided there and has been so rarely seen there again."

Reagan—himself a visionary with a pragmatic streak, a deft communicator of political ideals, a transformative leader—intuitively understood the third president. "He knew how disorderly a place the world could be," Reagan said. "Indeed, as a leader of a rebellion, he was himself an architect, if you will, of disorder. But he also believed that man had received from God a precious gift of enlightenment—the gift of reason, a gift that could extract from the chaos of life meaning, truth, order." Jefferson would have been hard put to describe the matter more clearly.

From Roosevelt to Reagan, Jefferson provided inspiration for radically different understandings of government and culture. Yet it was not Jefferson who had changed. It was his nation, tacking this way and then that way. That Jefferson has been a lodestar from generation to generation, from agenda to agenda, from vision to vision, speaks as much to his own literary versatility as to anything the real Jefferson did when he stood at the helm, directing America through the storms of his own time.

One thing is unmistakably consistent, however, in his successors' understanding of Jefferson: Like him, they believed in the power of words in public life, in the molding of popular opinion—and in the centrality of presidential power to keep the nation safe and strong in the most difficult of hours.

The three achievements he ordered carved on his tombstone—as author of the American Declaration of Independence and of the Virginia Statute for Religious Liberty, and as founder of the University of Virginia—speak to his love of the liberty of the mind and of the heart, and to his faith in the future. They point toward the least disputable elements of his long, turbulent life, to the primacy of reason and the possibilities of freedom and the eternal quest for wisdom. They point, too, to the making of things, to leadership. He fought for each of these causes, convincing enough of the world of the rightness of his vision that he left behind living monuments. And there is no greater monument to Jefferson than the nation itself, dedicated to the realization, however gradual and however painful, of the ideal amid the realities of a political world driven by ambition and selfishness.

For Jefferson never gave up on America, a country

in many ways he brought into being and which he nurtured through tender, fragile hours. "And I have observed this march of civilization advancing from the sea coast, passing over us like a cloud of light, increasing our knowledge and improving our condition . . . and where this progress will stop no one can say," he wrote in 1824.

Jefferson arranged the world as he wanted it until the very end, and beyond. When he died in the midsummer of 1826, he was borne across the sprawling West Lawn, past willow trees and down the hill to the graveyard. The cemetery was, of course, of his own design. Here he had buried his mother, his wife, his children, his best friend. Here he was to be buried.

The little graveyard sits on the western side of the mountain. When dusk comes, darkness seems to fall slowly. To the east shadows lengthen over the Rivanna and over Shadwell. They fall over Monticello itself and over Mulberry Row. They fall over his pavilions and his gardens. Only then do the shadows fall over the remains of Thomas Jefferson, a man who always loved the light.

AUTHOR'S NOTE AND ACKNOWLEDGMENTS

IN LATE 1803, the French chargé d'affaires in Washington, Louis-André Pichon, drafted a special letter about President Jefferson to send back to the foreign ministry in Paris. "It is difficult, Citizen Minister," Pichon began, "to give a definitive judgment on the character of Mr. Jefferson, as well as on the effect that could be produced internally by his policy and his systems."

It is indeed. It is not, however, impossible. This book, I hope, neither lionizes nor indicts Jefferson, but instead restores him to his full and rich role as an American statesman who resists easy categorization.

Jefferson has not had an easy time of it in recent years. The 1998 DNA findings and subsequent scholarly reevaluation that established the high likelihood of his sexual relationship with his slave Sally Hemings—a liaison long denied by mainstream white historians—gave fresh energy to the image of Jefferson-as-hypocrite. Then came nearly two decades of highly acclaimed biographies of John Adams, Alexander Hamilton, and George Washington that understandably emphasized the virtues of their protagonists, often at Jefferson's expense. (My friend Joseph J. Ellis started this trend with **Passionate Sage: The Character and Legacy of John Adams,** published twenty years ago.) Even in his own day Jefferson faced the seemingly contradictory charges that he was at once an unrealistic philosopher and a scheming political creature.

The truth in Jefferson's case (as in so many lives) is complex. George Washington, Abraham Lincoln, and Theodore and Franklin Roosevelt were great men and impressive presidents, but only Thomas Jefferson ranged across so many different aspects of American life over such a long period of time. Cool and cerebral, Jefferson could not resist the heat of political combat, and he adapted his brilliantly expressed principles to the realities of elections and of governing with seeming effortlessness. Many Americans idolized him; others shared the views of an anonymous letter writer who told him, "You are the damdest fool that God put life into. God dam you."

My view is that at his core, from year to year and age to age, Thomas Jefferson was a politician who sought office and, once in office, tried to solve the problems of his day and set a course for the future within the constraints of his time and place. That he often did so with skill and effectiveness is a tribute to his life and is, I think, the heart of his legacy. For without a compelling political figure making the case for the principles and practices in which he believed against the Federalist interest of the time—and Jefferson was surely a compelling political figure—American life and politics could have turned out very differently. Jefferson the politician, then, was a man who stood on the ramparts of history, fighting for a particular habit of mind and of government that gave the many more of a role to play in the fullness of time than the few.

I did not set out to write a full life and times of Jefferson; too much happened to him and around him for a single volume to do justice to the immensity of scholarship about the late eighteenth and early nineteenth centuries. This book is a portrait, rather, of the man and of the world in which he lived and which he longed to bend to his purposes. The Jefferson I found in my reading and research was a public man of Renaissance interests but with an abiding, overarching concern: the fate of democratic republicanism in America.

The most remarkable stories are those of politicians who do the best they can given time and chance, and whose faults are at once personal and universal. The most accomplished presidents manage, however briefly, to transcend those constraints and overcome those faults in order to leave the nation a better, more just place than they found it. The test cannot be perfection or an American Valhalla, for no one can meet such a standard. Thomas Jefferson surely did not.

He did his best, though, and his best left the world a definition, if not a realization, of human liberty that has endured, and gave America the means to ascend to global power.

I do not believe we can make sense of Jefferson without a grasp of how seriously he took the possibility of the imminent end of the American experiment and the return of a monarchical government. Beginning with George Washington himself, contemporaries and later historians have treated Jefferson's fears of monarchy as fanciful, paranoid, or at best exaggerated to the point of unseriousness. Based on my reading of Jefferson's papers and archival explorations in the United States and in Britain, however, I contend that the threat of a revival of British authority in the United States was as fundamental to Jefferson's thought and actions as the cold war with the Soviet Union was to American presidents from Truman to George H. W. Bush. The analogy is imprecise, to be sure, for Britain and the United States alternated between friendship and enmity. Another imprecise analogy, but one worth considering, is that Jefferson was to Washington and Adams what Dwight Eisenhower was to Franklin D. Roosevelt and Harry Truman: a president who reformed but essentially ratified an existing course of government.

It is also impossible to understand the historical, human Jefferson without appreciating the perennial place the events and legacy of the English Civil War played in his imagination and in the imaginations of many of his contemporaries. The important role of the Whig tradition of individual liberty has been long noted. Less remarked upon is the frequency with which the battles and incidents of the struggle appear in Jefferson's correspondence—a sign that the war and the fate of the Commonwealth, which was a military dictatorship followed by restoration of monarchy, were never far from Jefferson's consciousness. As a rule, politicians tend to remember the things they wish to emulate or the things they hope to avoid. For America, Jefferson wanted neither a Cromwellian absolutism nor the restoration of Charles II in 1660 nor even the installation of William and Mary in 1688—two monarchs who had fewer prerogatives but who were still monarchs. Such outcomes, Jefferson believed, were all too plausible.

This project began with a delightful lunch in Princeton with Barbara Oberg, the editor of the Jefferson Papers, which is one of the most formidable and significant scholarly undertakings in American life. Barbara and her colleagues were welcoming and generous, providing me with digital files of correspondence for the volumes-in-progress covering Jefferson's presidency after early 1803. Anyone writing about Jefferson or early America is indebted to the illuminating annotations of the papers stretching back to the very first volume, which was published in 1950. Barbara and her team are brilliantly carrying on the tradition begun by Julian P. Boyd. I am especially indebted to Martha King and Elaine Pascu, both of whom assisted Barbara in a review of my manuscript.

Jefferson's papers from 1809 until his death in 1826, known as the Retirement Series, are being edited in Charlottesville. J. Jefferson Looney, the general editor, took time out to answer queries and spend a beautiful Saturday afternoon talking things Jeffersonian; Jeff was also kind about follow-up queries. I am deeply grateful to him and to his colleagues in Virginia.

Leslie Greene Bowman, the president of the Thomas Jefferson Foundation, has been an enthusiastic and tireless friend to me on this book. I am grateful to her for her grace, hospitality, and insights. Thanks, too, to her husband, Cortland Neuhoff, for putting up with itinerant biographers who turn up in his house and borrow his clothes. Among many other acts of generosity, Leslie agreed to take me on a horseback ride along the road Jefferson would have traveled up Monticello; to the best of my knowledge she managed not to laugh openly at my rather poor horsemanship.

I am indebted to many people at Monticello. Susan Stein was generous with her time and expertise, as were Andrew Jackson O'Shaughnessy and Melanie Bowyer. I am also grateful to Anna Berkes, Monticello's reference librarian, and to Fraser Neiman, director of archaeology.

One of the great pleasures of this project came in November 2011, when I was graciously granted extraordinary access to Monticello in the overnight and early-morning hours in order to observe as closely as possible the material culture in which Jefferson lived and worked. I am grateful to the board of trustees of the Thomas Jefferson Foundation, which was instrumental in the approval of the request to spend time in the house. The curatorial staff helped arrange the occasion and gave me invaluable guidance on the house as it would have been in Jefferson's day: my thanks to Susan Stein, Richard Gilder Senior Curator and vice president for museum programs; to Elizabeth V. Chew, curator; and to Jodi Frederickson, curatorial assistant. Thanks as well to Barry Claytor, safety and security administrator; and to Fred O'Brien, Bryan Glover, and Terrell Thompson.

Many archives and libraries were welcoming and helpful. In particular I am grateful to Del Moore, reference librarian, John D. Rockefeller, Jr., Library, Colonial Williamsburg, and to Katherine A. Ludwig at the David Library of the American Revolution. The New York Public Library and the Brooklyn Public Library were critical resources. At the New York Public Library, I am especially indebted to the Irma and Paul Milstein Division of United States History, Local History, and Genealogy. The general holdings of the Stephen A. Schwartzman Building, their microfilm collection, and other NYPL branches were also invaluable, as was the staff of the Jessie Ball duPont Library at the University of the South. Also thanks to the staffs of the David Library of the American Revolution; Library and

Archives Canada; Archives of Ontario; the Loyalist Collection, University of New Brunswick; and the Devon Record Office, Exeter, Devon, United Kingdom.

In France, Melissa Lo and Tom Stammers worked in the diplomatic archives and translated those manuscripts for me; Melissa also undertook archival work in England, along with Louisa Thomas. I am also grateful to Jamie Johnston, Stephanie Gorton, Kolby Yarnell, Matthew Price, Caitlin Watson, Baobao Zhang, and Jessica Gallagher for their work transcribing manuscript sources. In the Senate Historical Office, I am again grateful to historian Donald A. Ritchie and to his colleague Betty Koed.

Of the making of books about Jefferson there will be no end, and that's a very good thing. Readers seeking an intelligent, accessible, and thorough survey of the current state of Jefferson scholarship will find it in the essays collected by editor Francis D. Cogliano in **A Companion to Thomas Jefferson**, a new volume published as one of the Blackwell Companions to American History. Frank Cogliano has been welcoming and generous to me, and the book he edited is invaluable. Contributors include Annette Gordon-Reed, Michael A. McDonnell, Kristofer Ray, Robert G. Parkinson, Peter Thompson, John A. Ragosta, Johann N. Neem, Iain McLean, Todd Estes, Joanne B. Freeman, Robert M. S. McDonald, Jeremy D. Bailey, Leonard J. Sadosky, Andrew Burstein, Andrew Cayton, Lucia Stanton, Cassandra

Pybus, Catherine Kerrison, Billy L. Wayson, Richard Samuelson, Kevin J. Hayes, David Thomas Konig, Hannah Spahn, Caroline Winterer, Peter S. Onuf, R. B. Bernstein, Max M. Edling, Cameron Addis, Matthew E. Crow, Barbara B. Oberg and James P. McClure, Brian Steele, and Jack N. Rakove.

For their counsel and friendship, I am grateful to historians and biographers who kindly took the great trouble to advise me on different points. Evan Thomas and Michael Beschloss are eternally generous with me, as are Oscie Thomas and Affie Beschloss.

Annette Gordon-Reed, whose work on Jefferson and the Hemings family is a landmark contribution to American history, has been a wonderful friend and invaluable reader. Susan Kern, the author of a remarkable book on Jefferson's origins, **The Jeffersons at Shadwell,** graciously spent a morning with me on the Shadwell site and read parts of the manuscript. Lucia "Cinder" Stanton arranged that visit, and so much else. Gordon S. Wood, a longtime hero of mine, generously read the manuscript and offered valuable insights.

At Monticello, both Cinder Stanton and Susan Stein read and commented on the manuscript, improving it greatly. Peter Onuf, the Thomas Jefferson Foundation Professor of History at the University of Virginia and mentor to a generation or two of scholars of Jefferson and of American history, read my draft carefully and made helpful comments, rescuing me, as did my other readers, from mistakes.

Professor Onuf also offered this book a benediction when it was done, something for which I will be always grateful.

In 2012, I was fortunate to be invited to a conference hosted in Charlottesville by the National Society of the Sons of the American Revolution and the Robert H. Smith International Center for Jefferson Studies. Entitled "Thomas Jefferson's Lives: Biography as a Construction of History," the gathering was fittingly dedicated to Onuf. For their roles in organizing and directing the conference, I am grateful to Andrew O'Shaughnessy, the Saunders Director of the International Center and a longtime friend; to Robert McDonald of West Point; and to Joseph W. Dooley of the SAR. The papers presented were intriguing and illuminating, and I learned much from them, and from a roundtable discussion moderated by Barbara Oberg. Professor McDonald, who also presented a paper co-authored by Christine Coalwell McDonald, is preparing a volume of the papers. Contributors include Jefferson Looney, Andrew Burstein, Nancy Isenberg, Joanne B. Freeman, Jan Ellen Lewis, Richard A. Samuelson, Brian Steele, Herbert Sloan, Annette Gordon-Reed, Frank Cogliano, R. B. Bernstein, and Gordon S. Wood.

Walter Isaacson, Henry Wiencek, Pauline Maier, Ron Chernow, Joseph J. Ellis, Daniel Jordan, Sean Wilentz, David McCullough, Andrew Burstein, Nancy Isenberg, Stacy Schiff, Robert A. Caro, Doris Kearns Goodwin, Gary E. Moulton, Michael

Kranish, and the late Christopher Hitchens were selfless readers, advisers, interlocutors, and editors along the way. The responsibility for the book, of course, lies with me.

For kindnesses large and small, thanks to Richard and Lisa Plepler, Jonathan Karp, John Huey, Julia Reed, May Smythe, Mark Miller, Clara Bingham, Anna Quindlen, Tom Brokaw, Perri Peltz and Eric Ruttenberg, Graydon Carter, John Danforth, Gardiner and Nicholas Lapham, Mika Brzezinski, Joe Scarborough, Willie Geist, Mike Barnicle, Ann Edelberg, Alex Korson, Cate Cetta, Sally Quinn and Ben Bradlee, Linda and Mort Janklow, Alice Mayhew, Richard Stengel, Nancy Gibbs, Jane and Brian Williams, Jeffrey Leeds, Claire and John Reishman, Leslie and Dale Richardson, Hardwick Caldwell III, Tammy Haddad, Chloe Dupree, Barbara DiVittorio, Bill Owens, Jeffrey Fager, Rebecca Pratt, George Gilliam, Samuel R. Williamson, Jr., Kitty Boone, Betsy Fischer, David Gregory, Neal Shapiro, Alison Stewart, Wayne Fields, Lenora Fisher, Richard Cohen, Robley Hood, Ruby Walker, Shaima Ally, Madeline Magee, Roger Hertog, Nora Frances and Vaughan McRae, Charlie Rose, Jim Kelly, Dina and Rick Powell, Kevin Sheekey, Justin Reynolds, Teresa Smith, and Donna Pahmeyer and her colleagues at the University Book and Supply Store.

Once again I am indebted to my friend Mike Hill, who was as invaluable and gracious as ever. Louisa Thomas was indispensable, and I am looking forward to her book about Louisa Catherine Adams. (I am sure it will be quite kind about Jefferson.) Jack Bales once again worked his bibliographical magic. My thanks to Christine Mejia for her grace and hard work, and to Rob Crawford, who played a critical role in checking the manuscript. Lucy Shackelford also checked a final draft.

This is my fifth book with Random House, and I continue to be dazzled by, and grateful for, Gina Centrello. Gina is the best of publishers, and the most generous of friends. Her intelligence, friendship, and support are without peer. My editor, Kate Medina, is a master of the craft, and her impeccably high standards inspire those of us lucky enough to benefit from her wisdom. Thanks, too, to Anna Pitoniak and Lindsey Schwoeri for their steadfast grace and good work. Will Murphy was a generous reader. Susan Kamil and Tom Perry are terrific, and they lead a wonderful publication team. As ever, I am indebted to the erratic but charming Sally Marvin and to Barbara Fillon. Thanks also to Benjamin Steinberg, Jonathan Jao, Andy Ward, Allison Dobson, Bill Takes, Porscha Burke, Selby McRae, Sara Velazquez, Sanyu Dillon, Avideh Bashirrad, Erika Greber, Carole Lowenstein, Paolo Pepe, and Carol Poticny. Michelle Daniel was a superb copy editor. In my view, had the incomparable Benjamin Dreyer and Dennis Ambrose been in charge of Operation Overlord, the Allies would have braved the rain and stuck to schedule, attacking on June 5. As it is, I am grateful they do what they do, and do it so well. And as ever, I agree with Christopher Buckley's view that Amanda Urban will be my first call if I ever fall into the hands of the Taliban.

This book is dedicated to Herbert Wentz, my teacher and friend. I owe him and his wife, Sofia, debts I cannot possibly repay.

My wife, Keith, has long endured my journeys into the past, offering love, support, and (not always initially welcome) counsel. She makes all things possible, and our children—Mary, Maggie, and Sam—are, now and forever, the things that matter most.

NOTES

ABBREVIATIONS USED

Anas   The Complete Anas of Thomas Jefferson, ed. Frank B. Sawvel

APE, I   Gil Troy, Arthur M. Schlesinger, Jr., and Fred L. Israel, eds., History of American Presidential Elections, 1789–2008. 4th ed. Vol. 1, 1789–1868.

EOL   Gordon S. Wood, Empire of Liberty: A History of the Early Republic, 1789–1815

FB   Thomas Jefferson's Farm Book: With Commentary and Relevant Extracts from Other Writings, ed. Edwin Morris Betts

GB   Thomas Jefferson's Garden Book: 1766–1824, With Relevant Extracts from His Other Writings, ed. Edwin Morris Betts

Henry Adams, History   Henry Adams, History of the United States of America During the Administrations of Thomas Jefferson

Jefferson, Writings   Thomas Jefferson, Writings, ed.

Merrill D. Peterson (Library of America)

JHT, I-VI	Dumas Malone, **Jefferson and His Time**
LOC	Library of Congress
MB, I-II	**Jefferson's Memorandum Books: Accounts, with Legal Records and Miscellany, 1767–1826**, ed. James A. Bear, Jr., and Lucia C. Stanton
Parton, **Life**	James Parton, **Life of Thomas Jefferson**
PTJ, I-XXXIX	**The Papers of Thomas Jefferson**
PTJRS, I-VIII	**The Papers of Thomas Jefferson. Retirement Series**
Randall, **Jefferson**, I-III	Henry S. Randall, **The Life of Thomas Jefferson**
TDLTJ	Sarah N. Randolph, **The Domestic Life of Thomas Jefferson**
TJ	Thomas Jefferson
TJF	The Thomas Jefferson Foundation
VTM	Merrill D. Peterson, **Visitors to Monticello**

EPIGRAPHS

ix "A FEW BROAD STROKES" Henry Adams, **History**, 188.

ix "I THINK THIS IS THE MOST EXTRAORDINARY" John F. Kennedy, "Remarks at a Dinner Honoring Nobel Prize Winners of the Western Hemisphere," April 29, 1962. Online, by Gerhard

Peters and John T. Woolley, The American Presidency Project. http://www.presidency.ucsb.edu/ws/?pid=8623 (accessed 2012).

PROLOGUE · The World's Best Hope

xvii HE WOKE AT FIRST LIGHT TJ to Vine Utley, March 21, 1819. Extract published at Papers of Thomas Jefferson Retirement Series Digital Archive, http://www.monticello.org/familyletters (accessed 2011). "But whether I retire to bed early or late, I rise with the sun," he wrote Utley. (Ibid.) "He said in his last illness that the sun had not caught him in bed for fifty years," grandson Thomas Jefferson Randolph recalled to the biographer Henry S. Randall. (Randall, **Jefferson,** III, 675.) Visiting Monticello in December 1824, when Jefferson was eighty-one, Daniel Webster wrote: "Mr. Jefferson rises in the morning as soon as he can see the hands of his clock, which is directly opposite his bed, and examines his thermometer immediately, as he keeps a regular meteorological diary." (VTM, 98.)

xvii LEAN AND LOOSE-LIMBED Margaret Bayard Smith thought him "tall and slender." (**The First Forty Years of Washington Society in the Family Letters of Margaret Bayard Smith,** ed. Gaillard Hunt [New York, 1965], 80.) In 1760, Jefferson was, James Parton wrote, "tall, raw-boned, freckled, and sandy-haired. . . . With his large feet and hands, his thick wrists, and prominent cheek-bones and chin, he could not have been accounted handsome or graceful. He is described, however, as a fresh, bright, healthy-looking youth, as straight as a gun-barrel, sinewy and strong, with that alertness of movement which comes of early familiarity with saddle, gun, canoe, minuet, and contra-dance. . . . His teeth, too, were perfect. . . . His eyes, which were of hazel-gray, were beaming and expressive; and his demeanor gave assurance of a gentle heart, and a sympathetic, inquisitive mind." (Parton, **Life,** 1.) For a collection of contemporary accounts of Jefferson's physical appearance and demeanor, see TJF, "Physical Descriptions of Jefferson," http://www.monticello.org/site/research-and-collections/physical-descriptions-jefferson (accessed 2011). "This sandy face, with hazel eyes and sunny aspect; this loose, shackling person; this rambling and often brilliant conversation, belonged to the controlling influences of American history, more necessary to the story than three-fourths of the official papers, which only hid the truth," wrote Henry Adams, the unflinching but sometimes appreciative historian of the Jefferson presidency. "Jefferson's personality during these eight years appeared to be the government, and impressed itself, like that of Bonaparte, although by a different process, on the mind of the nation." (Henry Adams, **History,** 127.)

xvii CONRAD AND MCMUNN'S Allen C. Clark,

"Daniel Rapine, the Second Mayor," **Records of the Columbia Historical Society** 25 (1923), 198. See also **MB**, II, 1032.

xvii A BASIN OF COLD WATER **PTJRS**, VIII, 544. "I have for 50 years bathed my feet in cold water every morning . . . and having been remarkably exempt from colds (not having had one in every 7 years of my life on an average) I have supposed it might be ascribed to that practice," Jefferson wrote James Maury. "When we see two facts accompanying one another for a long time, we are apt to suppose them related as cause and effect." (Ibid.) See also Gordon Jones and James A. Bear, "Thomas Jefferson's Medical History," unpublished manuscript, Jefferson Library. Jones and Bear attributed Jefferson's habit to a reading of Sir John Floyer's popular book **Psychrolousia: Or, the History of Cold Bathing**; Jefferson owned a 1706 edition of the work. (Ibid.) For details on Floyer, see D. D. Gibbs, "Sir John Floyer, M.D. (1649–1734)," **British Medical Journal** 1, no. 5638 (1969): 242–45.

xvii WORE A GROOVE Susan R. Stein, "Notes on Jefferson's Bed Chamber," memorandum to author, November 10, 2011. Stein is Richard Gilder Senior Curator and Vice President of Museum Programs, Thomas Jefferson's Monticello. The groove is on the side of Jefferson's bed facing the fireplace. (Author observation.)

xvii SIX FOOT TWO AND A HALF James A. Bear, Jr., ed., **Jefferson at Monticello** (Charlottesville,

Va., 1967) 70. According to Edmund Bacon, a Monticello overseer, "Mr. Jefferson was six feet two and a half inches high, well proportioned, and straight as a gun barrel." (Ibid.)

xvii His sandy hair   Parton, **Life,** 1.

xvii freckled skin   Ibid.

xvii wrinkling a bit   **TDLTJ,** 337.

xvii alternately described as blue, hazel, or brown   TJF, http://www.monticello.org/site/re search-and-collections/eye-color (accessed 2012).

xvii He had great teeth   Parton, **Life,** 1. "His teeth, too, were perfect," reported Parton. Writing in 1824, Daniel Webster observed: "His mouth is well formed and still filled with teeth; it is strongly compressed, bearing an expression of contentment and benevolence." (**VTM,** 97.)

xvii muddy avenues and scattered buildings **Records of the Columbia Historical Society** 25, 198–99. Federalist lawmaker James A. Bayard of Delaware wrote this to Andrew Bayard on January 8, 1801: "We have the name of a city [Washington], but nothing else. The [North] wing of the Capitol which is finished is a beautiful building. The President's House is also extremely elegant. Besides these objects you have nothing to admire but the beauties of nature. There is a great want of Society, especially female." A week later, Albert Gallatin wrote to his wife, Hannah Gallatin: "Our local situation is far from being pleasant, or even convenient. Around the Capitol are 7 or 8 boarding houses, one tailor, one shoemaker, one printer, a washing woman, a grocery shop, a pamphlets and stationery shop, a small dry goods shop, and an oyster house. This makes the whole of the Federal City as connected with the Capitol." (Ibid.)

xviii SECLUDED INSIDE **PTJ**, XXXII, 513. In a note dated January 27, 1801, Jefferson, who, as vice president, served as the presiding officer of the Senate, wrote that he was "at home always when not in [the] Senate." (Ibid.)

xviii WITH STABLES FOR SIXTY HORSES Washington **National Intelligencer,** January 30, 1801. An advertisement for the boardinghouse read: "Have opened houses of entertainment in the range of buildings formerly occupied by Mr. Law, about two hundred paces from the Capitol, in New Jersey Avenue, leading from thence to the Eastern Branch. They are spacious and convenient, one of which is designed for stage passengers and travelers, the other for the accommodation of boarders. There is stableage sufficient for 60 horses. They hope to merit public patronage." (Ibid.)

xviii TWO HUNDRED PACES AWAY Ibid.

xviii A VICIOUS ELECTION See James Roger Sharp, **The Deadlocked Election of 1800: Jefferson, Burr, and the Union in the Balance** (Lawrence, Kan., 2010); Susan Dunn, **Jefferson's Second Revolution: The Election Crisis of 1800 and the Triumph of Republicanism** (Boston, 2004); John Ferling, **Adams vs. Jefferson: The Tumul-**

tuous Election of 1800 (New York, 2004); James Horn, Jan Ellen Lewis, and Peter S. Onuf, eds., **The Revolution of 1800: Democracy, Race, and the New Republic** (Charlottesville, Va., 2002); and **APE,** I, 49–78. Henry Adams, **The Life of Albert Gallatin** (LaVergne, Tenn., 2009), 232–66, tells the story from the perspective of a crucial Jefferson ally.

xviii HAD RECEIVED THE SAME NUMBER OF ELEC-TORAL VOTES The potential problem for a tie had been clear from the first presidential election, in 1789. The practice was for a few electors to "throw away" their votes for the vice presidential candidate to a candidate who had no chance of winning, thus giving the presidential candidate the most votes. "The votes were unanimous with respect to General Washington, as appears to have been the case in each of the States," James Madison had told Jefferson, who was then in France. "The secondary votes were given, among the Federal members, chiefly to Mr. J. Adams, one or two being thrown away in order to prevent a possible competition for the Presidency." (**PTJ,** XV, 5.) Things had not gone so smoothly this time, hence the crisis.

xviii "WORN DOWN HERE" **PTJ,** XXXII, 556–57. The letter, to his daughter Martha Jefferson Randolph, known as Patsy, was written from Washington on February 5, 1801.

xix "THE THEME OF ALL CONVERSATION" Ibid., 263.

xix "THE CRISIS IS MOMENTOUS" **Washington Federalist,** February 12, 1801. The paper also wrote: "We waited all yesterday in the hourly expectation of being able to announce to our anxious countrymen the result of the presidential election, but it remains to this moment undecided and the happiness of five millions of people awfully suspended in the balance!" (Ibid.)

xix "FUN AND HONOR AND PROFIT" **EOL,** 280.

xix BE MADE PRESIDENT Nancy Isenberg, **Fallen Founder: The Life of Aaron Burr** (New York, 2008), 196–220.

xx HAD "HEARD A MEMBER OF CONGRESS LAMENT" **Anas,** 206.

xx "A DESIRE TO PROMOTE . . . DIVISION" Ibid., 466.

xx A RUMOR THAT JOHN MARSHALL JHT, III, 495.

xx HAD JUST BEEN NAMED CHIEF JUSTICE Kathryn Turner, "The Appointment of Chief Justice Marshall," **William and Mary Quarterly,** 3d ser., 17 (1960): 143–63.

xx "IF THE UNION COULD BE BROKEN" **PTJ,** XXXII, 404. For McKean on the overall crisis, see ibid., 432–36.

xx WAS TOLD THAT TWENTY-TWO THOUSAND MEN James Roger Sharp, **American Politics in the Early Republic: The New Nation in Crisis** (New Haven, Conn., 1993), 269.

xx WERE "PREPARED TO TAKE UP ARMS" Ibid. Others worried that Hamilton would take advantage of the uncertainty. "An army . . . with Alexander Hamilton at their head could get possession of forts, arsenals, stores and arms in a short time," one Pennsylvania Republican told Jefferson. (**PTJ**, XXXII, 485.) Jefferson himself told James Madison that any "legislative usurpation would be resisted by arms." (Ibid., XXXIII, 16.)

xx AFTER A SNOWSTORM STRUCK WASHINGTON Diary of Gouverneur Morris, February 1801, LOC. It snowed on February 11 and again on the 13th; Jefferson was chosen on February 17. (Ibid.)

xx THE THIRTY-SIXTH BALLOT   **PTJ**, XXXII, 578.

xxi FOR THIRTY-SIX OF THE FORTY YEARS   As noted in the text, aside from Jefferson himself, James Madison, James Monroe, Andrew Jackson, and Martin Van Buren considered themselves part of the Jeffersonian tradition. John Quincy Adams, the sixth president, is the exception. For excellent overviews of the years between 1800 and 1840, see **EOL**; Daniel Walker Howe, **What Hath God Wrought: The Transformation of America, 1815–1848** (New York, 2007); and Sean Wilentz, **The Rise of American Democracy: Jefferson to Lincoln** (New York, 2005).

xxi JEFFERSON SOUGHT, ACQUIRED, AND WIELDED POWER   My contention is that Jefferson was at heart a politician—a politician with a wide-ranging philosophical mind and oft-expressed principles, to be sure, but still a politician. See, for instance, Bernard Bailyn, **To Begin the World Anew: The Genius and Ambiguities of the American Founders** (New York, 2003), 37–59. Bailyn concluded:

> So it was Jefferson—simultaneously a radical utopian idealist and a hardheaded, adroit, at times cunning politician; a rhetorician, whose elegant phrases had propulsive power, and a no-nonsense administrator—who, above all others, was fated to confront the ambiguities of the Enlightenment program. He had caught a vision, as a precocious leader of the American Revolution, of a comprehensive Enlightenment ideal, a glimpse of what a wholly enlightened world might be, and strove to make it real, discovering as he did so the intractable dilemmas. Repeatedly he saw a pure vision, conceptualized and verbalized it brilliantly, and then struggled to relate it to reality, shifting, twisting, maneuvering backward and forward as he did so. (Ibid., 47.)

xxiii "THE WORLD'S BEST HOPE" **PTJ**, XXXIII, 149.

xxiii "WHATEVER THEY CAN, THEY WILL" **PTJRS**, VIII, 32.

xxiii "MR. JEFFERSON WAS AS TALL" Bear, **Jefferson at Monticello**, 11.

xxiii JEFFERSON "WAS LIKE A FINE HORSE" Ibid., 71.

xxiv NOTING THE TEMPERATURE EACH DAY See,

for instance, **MB**, I, 771. "My method is to make two observations a day, the one as early as possible in the morning, the other from 3 to 4 o'clock, because I have found 4 o'clock the hottest and daylight the coldest point of the 24 hours," he wrote Thomas Mann Randolph, Jr., his son-in-law, on April 18, 1790. "I state them in an ivory pocket book . . . and copy them out once a week." (Ibid.)

xxiv A TINY, IVORY-LEAVED NOTEBOOK   Ibid., I, xvii. The typical contents of Jefferson's pockets are illustrated in William L. Beiswanger and others, eds., **Thomas Jefferson's Monticello** (Chapel Hill, N.C., 2001), 65. The book notes that the items included an English pocketknife, key ring and trunk key, gold toothpick, goose quill toothpick, ivory rule, watch fob, steel pocket scissors, and a red-leather pocketbook. (Ibid.)

xxiv HE DROVE HIS HORSES HARD AND FAST   James A. Bear, Jr., ed., **Jefferson at Monticello** (Charlottesville, Va., 1967), 5.

xxiv HIS "ALMIGHTY PHYSICIAN"   **PTJ**, VIII, 43.

xxiv DRANK NO HARD LIQUOR BUT LOVED WINE   Randall, **Jefferson**, III, 450. Isaac Jefferson "never heard of his being disguised in drink." (Bear, **Jefferson at Monticello**, 13.)

xxiv GIFTS OF HAVANA CIGARS   **PTJRS**, I, 466.

xxiv DUMBWAITERS AND HIDDEN MECHANISMS   Beiswanger and others, **Thomas Jefferson's Monticello**, 53.

xxiv HIS OWN VERSION OF THE GOSPELS   Thomas

Jefferson, **The Jefferson Bible: The Life and Morals of Jesus of Nazareth** (Boston, 1989). In the afterword to this edition, Jaroslav Pelikan wrote: "There has certainly never been a shortage of boldness in the history of biblical scholarship during the past two centuries, but for sheer audacity Thomas Jefferson's two redactions of the Gospels stand out even in that company." (Ibid., 149.)

xxiv PALLADIAN PLANS FOR MONTICELLO Beiswanger and others, **Thomas Jefferson's Monticello,** 2–33. A book of Palladio's that belonged to Jefferson emerged in the collections of Washington University in St. Louis in 2011, which I was generously allowed to see.

xxiv THE ROMAN-INSPIRED CAPITOL OF VIRGINIA Susan R. Stein, **The Worlds of Thomas Jefferson at Monticello** (New York, 1993), 19–20.

xxiv PATRON OF PASTA TJF, http://www.monticello. org/site/research-and-collections/macaroni (accessed 2012).

xxv RECIPE FOR ICE CREAM Marie Kimball, **Thomas Jefferson's Cook Book** (Charlottesville, Va., 1976), 2–3. See also TJF, http://www.monti cello.org/site/research-and-collections/ice-cream (accessed 2012).

xxv THE PERFECT DRESSING FOR HIS SALADS TJF, http://www.monticello.org/site/house-and -gardens/thomas-jeffersons-favorite-vegetables (accessed 2011). "Salad oil was a perennial obsession for Jefferson. He referred to the olive as 'the richest gift of heaven,' and 'the most interesting plant in existence.' When he found domestic olive oil imperfect and imported olive oil too expensive, Jefferson turned to the possibilities of oil extracted from sesame seed or benne (**Sesamum orientale**)." (Ibid.)

xxv HE KEPT SHEPHERD DOGS   MB, I, 745. See also **PTJ**, XXIX, 26–27.

xxv HE KNEW LATIN, GREEK, FRENCH TJF, http://www.monticello.org/site/research-and-collections/languages-jefferson-spoke-or-read (accessed 2012).

xxv ADMIRED THE LETTERS OF MADAME DE SÉVIGNÉ   TJ to Ellen Wayles Randolph, March 14, 1808, Coolidge Collection of Thomas Jefferson Manuscripts, Massachusetts Historical Society. "Among my books which are gone to Monticello, is a copy of Madame de Sevigné's letters, which being the finest models of easy letter writing you must read." (Ibid.)

xxv MADAME DE STAËL'S   **Corinne, or Italy**   Hannah Thornton to TJ, January 15, 1808, Coolidge Collection of Thomas Jefferson Manuscripts, Massachusetts Historical Society. "Mrs. Thornton's Compliments to the President of the U.S, and having heard that he possesses a copy of Made. Stäel's celebrated Novel 'Corinne' and not being able to procure it elsewhere at present, hopes he will excuse the liberty she takes in requesting the favor of a perusal of it, if disengaged," she wrote. (Ibid.)

xxv A COLLECTION OF WHAT A GUEST CALLED "REGAL SCANDAL" **PTJRS**, VIII, 240.

xxv A DIAMOND NECKLACE AND MARIE-ANTOINETTE Simon Schama, **Citizens: A Chronicle of the French Revolution** (New York, 1990), 203–10.

xxv AMID CHARGES THAT HE HAD ALLOWED HIS MISTRESS Philip Harling, "The Duke of York Affair (1809) and the Complexities of War-Time Patriotism," **The Historical Journal** 39, no. 4 (December 1996): 963–84.

xxv "WITH A SATISFACTION" **PTJRS**, VIII, 240.

xxv A GUEST AT A COUNTRY INN **TDLTJ**, 38.

xxvi "TO SEE THE STANDARD OF REASON" **PTJ**, X, 604.

xxviii "WHAT IS PRACTICABLE MUST OFTEN CONTROL" Jefferson, **Writings**, 1101.

xxviii "THE HABITS OF THE GOVERNED" Ibid.

xxviii THE DEBATE AND THE DIVISION Jefferson has tended to be depicted in what I believe to be an overly harsh light in recent years, often portrayed as, at best, a mystery and, at worst, a cynical politician. In an illuminating essay, Gordon S. Wood explored the distorting dynamic of excessive celebration and excessive condemnation. "We seriously err in canonizing and making symbols of historical figures who cannot and should not be ripped out of their own time and place," Wood wrote. "By turning Jefferson into the kind of transcendent moral hero that no authentic historically situated human being could ever be, we leave ourselves demoralized by the time-bound weaknesses of this eighteenth-century slaveholder." (Wood, "The Ghosts of Monticello" in **Sally Hemings and Thomas Jefferson: History, Memory, and Civic Culture**, ed. Jan Ellen Lewis and Peter S. Onuf [Charlottesville, Va., 1999], 29.) For influential recent portraits of Jefferson, see, for instance, Joseph J. Ellis, **American Sphinx: The Character of Thomas Jefferson** (New York, 1997); David McCullough, **John Adams** (New York, 2001); Ron Chernow, **Alexander Hamilton** (New York, 2004); and Chernow, **Washington: A Life** (New York, 2010).

xxix "IT IS A CHARMING THING" **PTJ**, XXXVII, 20. The letter was written to Ann Cary, Thomas Jefferson, and Ellen Wayles Randolph from Washington on March 2, 1802.

xxix LEADING SOME PEOPLE TO BELIEVE Joseph J. Ellis, **American Creation: Triumphs and Tragedies at the Founding of the Republic** (New York, 2007), 168. Ellis quotes John Adams's grandson Charles Francis Adams, who observed: "More ardent in his imagination than his affections, he did not always speak exactly as he felt towards friends and enemies. As a consequence, he has left hanging over a part of his public life a vapor of duplicity, or, to say the least, of indiscretion, the presence of which is generally felt more than it is seen." (Ibid.)

xxix CALLING ON SAMUEL HARRISON SMITH Margaret Bayard Smith, **First Forty Years,** 6.

xxix THE CHILD OF A FEDERALIST FAMILY   Ibid., vi. Margaret Bayard Smith was born in 1778; her father was Colonel John Bayard, a Pennsylvania statesman and member of the Continental Congress. Her family included James A. Bayard, a Federalist lawmaker and diplomat from Delaware, who was to play a noted role in Jefferson's election to the presidency in February 1801. (Ibid.)

xxix FOUND HERSELF "SOMEWHAT CHECKED"   Ibid., 6.

xxix THE STRANGER ASSUMED "A FREE AND EASY"   Ibid., 6–7.

xxx SHE DID NOT KNOW   Ibid., 7.

xxx AT THIS POINT THE DOOR TO THE PARLOR OPENED   Ibid.

xxxi "AND IS THIS THE VIOLENT DEMOCRAT"   Ibid., 5–6.

xxxi TAKING HIS LEAVE   Ibid., 8.

xxxi A GRIEF THAT LED HIM TO THOUGHTS OF SUICIDE   Randall, **Jefferson,** I, 382. See also Parton, **Life,** 265–66, and **JHT,** I, 396–97.

xxxi PROMISED HIS DYING WIFE   Parton, **Life,** 265.

xxxi A DECADES-LONG LIAISON WITH SALLY HEMINGS   Annette Gordon-Reed has done by far the finest work on this subject; my debt to her is incalculable. See **Thomas Jefferson and Sally Hemings: An American Controversy** (Charlottesville, Va., 1997) and the monumental work **The Hemingses of Monticello: An American Family** (New York, 2008). See also the findings in the "Report

of the Research Committee on Thomas Jefferson and Sally Hemings," TJF, January 2000,
http://www.monticello.org/site/plantation-and
-slavery/report-research-committee-thomas-jef
ferson-and-sally-hemings (accessed 2012); Lewis
and Onuf, **Sally Hemings and Thomas Jefferson**; and Catherine Kerrison, "Sally Hemings"
in Francis D. Cogliano, ed., **A Companion to
Thomas Jefferson** (Oxford, 2011), 284–300.
For a contrary view, see William G. Hyland,
Jr., **In Defense of Thomas Jefferson: The Sally
Hemings Sex Scandal** (New York, 2009), and
David Barton, **The Jefferson Lies: Exposing the
Myths You've Always Believed About Thomas
Jefferson** (Nashville, Tenn., 2012), 1–30.

The 1998 DNA finding that a male in the
Jefferson line had fathered at least one of Sally
Hemings's children led to a scholarly reevaluation of the entire question of the Jefferson-
Hemings connection. The then-president of the
Thomas Jefferson Foundation, Daniel P. Jordan,
charged a committee with the task of examining
the issue. "Although paternity cannot be established with absolute certainty, our evaluation of
the best evidence available suggests the strong
likelihood that Thomas Jefferson and Sally
Hemings had a relationship over time that led to
the birth of one, and perhaps all, of the known
children of Sally Hemings," Jordan wrote when
the committee's report was published in 2000.
"We recognize that honorable people can dis-

agree on this subject, as indeed they have for over two hundred years. Further, we know that the historical record has gaps that perhaps can never be filled and mysteries that can never be fully resolved."

I agree with Jordan and with the committee. [One member dissented and wrote a minority report, which is available at TJF, http://www.monticello.org/site/plantation-and-slavery/report-research-committee-thomas-jefferson-and-sally-hemings (accessed 2012).] In my view, there is convincing biographical evidence that Jefferson was a man of appetite who appreciated order, and that the ability to carry on a long-term liaison with his late wife's enslaved half sister under circumstances he could largely control would have suited him.

Dissenters have pointed to Jefferson's younger brother Randolph Jefferson as a candidate for paternity, a possibility that would fit with the DNA finding. Isaac Granger Jefferson, the Monticello slave who left his recollections, reported that Randolph Jefferson "used to come out among black people, play the fiddle and dance half the night." As the committee pointed out, however, Isaac Granger Jefferson left Monticello in 1797, which means "his reference probably predates that year, and most likely refers to the 1780s, the period that is the subject of the majority of his recollections."

To those who continue to argue that there

was no relationship between Sally Hemings and Thomas Jefferson, I am taking the liberty of quoting at length the "Assessment of Possible Paternity of Other Jeffersons" from the "Report of the Research Committee on Thomas Jefferson and Sally Hemings":

> One reaction to the DNA study of Jefferson and Hemings descendants has been the accurate observation that the test results only prove that a Jefferson fathered the last of Sally Hemings's children—not that Thomas Jefferson himself was the father. In order to investigate this possibility, Monticello researchers reviewed Thomas Jefferson's papers as well as Jefferson family genealogies to determine the identities and whereabouts of other male members of his family.
>
> Sally Hemings's confirmed times of conception extend from early December of 1794 through mid-September of 1807. During these eighteen years at least twenty-five adult male descendants of Jefferson's grandfather Thomas Jefferson (1677–1731) lived in Virginia: his younger brother Randolph and five of his sons, as well as one son and eighteen grandsons of his uncle Field Jefferson. Of this total, most were living in the Southside region—over a hundred miles from Monticello—and do not figure in Jefferson's correspondence or his memoranda.

There remained eight out of the twenty-five for whom age and proximity warranted further documentary investigation. These include Randolph Jefferson and his five sons (Isham, Thomas, Jr., Field, Robert, and Lilburne) as well as two grandsons of Field Jefferson (George and John Garland Jefferson). While each of these individuals had some interaction with Thomas Jefferson and spent some time at or in the vicinity of Monticello, most had no documented presence at Monticello during the times when Sally Hemings conceived her children. Several of them were at Monticello when Thomas Jefferson was absent (Sally Hemings is not known to have conceived in his absences). Randolph Jefferson's sons Thomas, in 1800, and Robert Lewis, in 1807, may well have been at Monticello during the conception periods of Harriet and Eston Hemings. Randolph Jefferson was invited to Monticello during the period of Eston Hemings's conception, but it is not known that he actually made the visit.

The committee concludes that convincing evidence does not exist for the hypothesis that another male Jefferson was the father of Sally Hemings's children. In almost two hundred years since the issue first became public, no other Jefferson has ever been referred to as the father; denials of Thomas Jefferson's paternity named the Carr nephews.

Furthermore, evidence of the sort of sustained presence necessary to have resulted in the creation of a family of six children is entirely lacking, and even those who denied a relationship never suggested Sally Hemings's children had more than one father. Finally, the historical evidence for Thomas Jefferson's paternity of Eston Hemings and his known siblings overwhelmingly outweighs that for any other Jefferson.

Readers who do wish to examine the issue in detail will find TJF, http://www.monticello.org/site/plantation-and-slavery/report-research-committee-thomas-jefferson-and-sally-hemings (accessed 2012) to be invaluable.

xxxiii ONE THAT OPENED IN 1764 PTJRS, IV, 599. Jefferson believed March 1764 marked the "dawn of the revolution."

xxxiii LIVED AND GOVERNED IN A FIFTY YEARS' WAR To Jefferson, the conflict ran from 1764 (ibid.) to the end of the War of 1812 in 1815. Louise Burnham Dunbar, **A Study of 'Monarchical' Tendencies in the United States from 1776 to 1801** (New York, 1970), details American attitudes toward monarchy and the handful of attempts that were made to move the young nation in the direction of hereditary or lifetime power. George C. Herring, **From Colony to Superpower: U.S. Foreign Relations Since 1776** (New York, 2008), 11–133, covers America's relations with the world generally, but the story of U.S.–British tensions is at center stage. Also illuminating are Robert Middlekauff, **The Glorious Cause: The American Revolution, 1763–1789** (New York, 2005); Alan Taylor, **The Civil War of 1812: American Citizens, British Subjects, Irish Rebels, and Indian Allies** (New York, 2010); and Edmund S. Morgan, **The Birth of the Republic, 1763–89** (Chicago, 1977). Bernard Bailyn, **The Ideological Origins of the American Revolution** (Cambridge, Mass., 1992), is a landmark work on the role of deeply held notions of liberty and of the pervasiveness of conspiracy.

Several related issues must be explored in order to describe and assess the idea of a Fifty Years' War. One question is the pervasive paranoia at the time, something that has been the subject of scholarly debate since Bernard Bailyn did his study of pamphlets in the revolutionary era and Richard Hofstadter laid out his vision of "the paranoid style." (Hofstadter, **The Paranoid Style in American Politics** [Cambridge, Mass., 1996].) A seminal paper is John R. Howe, Jr., "Republican Thought and Political Violence of the 1790s," **American Quarterly** 19 no. 2 (Summer, 1967): 147–65. Howe contends that the political climate in the 1790s was so emotional and overheated that "stereotypes stood in the place of reality." (Ibid., 150.) He attributes this climate to the intensity of the Founders' awareness of the fragility of republicanism and the failure of previous experiments, an awareness of the immensity of their historical moment followed by a profound anxiety about the decline of virtue, which was, of course, to be the glue of their free society. Under pressure, Howe argues, the Americans of the time could become deranged.

Gordon S. Wood, for one, disagrees. He has written that the paranoia and conspiracy theories were actually the rational thoughts of rational men, really reflected by the dominant currents of the era. Men of the Enlightenment assumed that history was a course of events in which men could cause effects—that they were agents in control of their fates. This meant that when something happened, someone was behind it. Wood gives Jefferson more credit than many scholars for his fears of a monarchical plot. In her 1922 study, Louise Burnham Dunbar held that there were indeed monarchical plots seriously considered, but that the American people by and large were antimonarchical.

A second key question is how one defines monarchism and republicanism. What the Federalists wanted was what John Adams described a little too openly as a "monarchical republic" (**EOL**, 82)—modeled on England's system but without the "corruption," that is, the blurring of branches, which occurred because crown ministers were members of Parliament. (Wood, **The Idea of America: Reflections on the Birth of the United States** [New York: 2011], 182.) They wanted a strong federal government where citizens owed fealty to the nation over the states, with a strong centralized economy and a powerful army that could challenge the European monarchies on their level. Certainly from the start George Washington and John Adams drew on the iconography of a monarchy, and the Federalists who defended the Constitution did so because of their disillusionment with the idea of a confederacy and fears of the excesses of democracy. They had a sense of themselves as working within an English tradition, hence Jefferson's Anglophobia. Wood points out that, being from the West Indies, Hamilton did not have loyalty to a state. (**EOL**, 90.) Hamilton very consciously modeled the American financial system on that of Britain. The monarchy debate also plays into Jefferson's role in the battles over the judiciary, since that was the branch most easily seen as a fortress against democracy and the source of permanent establishment.

xxxvi "PLANTING A NEW WORLD" TJ to John Page, March 18, 1803, American Antiquarian Society, Worcester, Mass.

xxxvi "IT WAS INCUMBENT" Ibid.

xxxvi "THE CIRCUMSTANCES OF OUR COUNTRY" Margaret Bayard Smith, **First Forty Years**, 81.

xxxvi "BOLD AND DOUBTFUL ELECTION" TJ to Roger C. Weightman, June 24, 1826. Extract published at Papers of Thomas Jefferson Retirement Series Digital Archive, http://www.monti

cello.org/familyletters (accessed 2011). This was very nearly the last letter of his life, a message sent to the Washington organizers of celebrations to mark the fiftieth anniversary of the Declaration of Independence on July 4, 1826. Jefferson, in fact, wrote two additional letters after this one, both about business matters, including arranging for the payment of duties on a shipment of wine. See J. Jefferson Looney, "Thomas Jefferson's Last Letter," **The Virginia Magazine of History and Biography** 112, no. 2 (2004): 178–84.

ONE · A Fortunate Son

xxxviii "THE POLITICAL OR PUBLIC CHARACTER" Gerald W. Mullin, **Flight and Rebellion: Slave Resistance in Eighteenth-Century Virginia** (New York, 1972), 8.

3 "IT IS THE STRONG IN BODY" TDLTJ, 20.

3 THE KIND OF MAN PEOPLE NOTICED I have drawn on several sources for my discussion of Peter Jefferson. See TDLTJ, 17–26; JHT, I, 9–33; Randall, **Jefferson,** I, 5–18; and Parton, **Life,** 9–10.

3 WHAT BECAME ALBEMARLE COUNTY The county was founded in 1744. For an overview, see John Hammond Moore, **Albemarle, Jefferson's County, 1727–1976** (Charlottesville, Va., 1976), 1–67, which covers the period from the second quarter of the eighteenth century through the Revolution. See also S. Edward Ayres, "Al-

bemarle County, Virginia, 1744–1770: An Economic, Political, and Social Analysis," **Magazine of Albemarle County History** 25 (1966–67): 37–72. **JHT**, I, 435–39, discusses Peter Jefferson's lands, slaves, and estate. For a sense of Virginia as a whole, see Michael A. McDonnell, "Jefferson's Virginia," in Cogliano, ed., **A Companion to Thomas Jefferson**, 16–31.

3 AFTER THE LONDON PARISH **TDLTJ**, 22.

4 THE WILDERNESS OF THE MID-ATLANTIC Alan Taylor, **American Colonies** (New York, 2002), 117–37, tells the story of Virginia from 1570 to 1650; 138–57 carry the account forward to 1750 in the "Chesapeake Colonies." For more background on the formation of the planter culture of Virginia and of the larger Chesapeake region, Daniel K. Richter, **Before the Revolution: America's Ancient Pasts** (Cambridge, Mass., 2011), is excellent, especially 187–211; 346–368 are illuminating on slavery. See also Norman K. Risjord, **Jefferson's America, 1760–1815**, 3d ed. (Lanham, Md., 2010), 1–33, for a portrait of America in 1760; April Lee Hatfield, **Atlantic Virginia: Intercolonial Relations in the Seventeenth Century** (Philadelphia, 2003); James Horn, **Adapting to a New World: English Society in the Seventeenth-Century Chesapeake** (Chapel Hill, N.C., 1994); and Edmund S. Morgan, **American Slavery, American Freedom: The Ordeal of Colonial Virginia** (New York, 1975). For a discussion of Anglican influences,

see Daniel J. Boorstin, "The Church of England in Colonial Virginia," in **The American Past in Perspective,** vol. I, **To 1877,** ed. Trevor Colbourn and James T. Patterson (Boston, 1970), 33–43. For details on Bacon's Rebellion, see Wilcomb E. Washburn, **The Governor and the Rebel: A History of Bacon's Rebellion in Virginia** (Chapel Hill, N.C., 1957), and Anthony S. Parent, Jr., **Foul Means: The Formation of a Slave Society in Virginia, 1660–1740** (Chapel Hill, N.C., 2003).

4 BORN ON APRIL 13, 1743 Randall, **Jefferson,** I, 11. The April 13 date is according to the New Style calendar.

4 ONCE SINGLEHANDEDLY PULLED DOWN Ibid., 13.

4 UPRIGHTED TWO HUGE HOGSHEADS Ibid.

4 A SUPERLATIVE AND SENTIMENTAL LIGHT Jefferson, **Writings,** 3–4.

4 "THE TRADITION IN MY FATHER'S FAMILY" Ibid. The recollections are in an autobiography Jefferson wrote between January 6, 1821, and July 29, 1821. (Ibid., 3, 101.) He ended his narrative with his arrival in New York to become secretary of state in 1790.

4 THE ANCIENT ROOTS I believe the best work on the pre-Monticello Jeffersons can be found in the scholarship of Susan Kern, who was enormously helpful to me and to whom I owe a great debt. In both her dissertation on the subject and in her resulting book **The Jeffersons at Shadwell**

(New Haven, Conn., 2010), Kern paints a remarkably detailed portrait of the lives of Thomas Jefferson's ancestors and particularly of his parents, Peter and Jane Jefferson. The results of her archaeological work and analysis of Shadwell, she wrote, "demands reinterpretation of historians' characterizations of Peter Jefferson, Jane Randolph Jefferson, and Thomas Jefferson's boyhood experience. The material provisions of the plantation suggest that Peter and Jane Jefferson fashioned a world wholly familiar to Virginia's elite." (Ibid., 5.)

5 At age ten, Thomas "Memoir of Thomas Jefferson Randolph," Edgehill-Randolph Papers, Collection 1397, Box 11, University of Virginia.

5 "Finding a wild turkey" Ibid.

6 The family had immigrated to Virginia **TDLTJ**, 20.

6 listed among the delegates Ibid.

6 The future president's great-grandfather Kern, **Jeffersons at Shadwell**, 292–93. See also **JHT**, I, 7.

6 the daughter of a justice Kern, **Jeffersons at Shadwell**, 293.

6 speculated in land at Yorktown Ibid.

6 He died about 1698 Ibid.

6 He kept a good house Ibid.

6 a dinner of roast beef and persico Ibid.

6 Born in Chesterfield County Ibid., xiii, 18.

6 With Joshua Fry Jefferson, **Writings**, 3.

7 "MY FATHER'S EDUCATION" Ibid.

7 PETER JEFFERSON BECAME A COLONEL Edgar C. Hickish, "Peter Jefferson, Gentleman," unpublished manuscript, Thomas Jefferson Foundation.

7 PROVED HIMSELF A HERO TDLTJ, 19–20. See also Randall, **Jefferson**, I, 13–14. Arthur T. McClinton and others, **The Fairfax Line: A Historic Landmark** (Edinburg, Va., 1990), includes an account by the surveyor Thomas Lewis of the September 10, 1746, to February 24, 1747, expedition to map "the southwest line of Thomas Lord Fairfax's princely domain in Virginia." Peter Jefferson was said to have been at one point "very indisposed." (Ibid., 44.)

7 FOUGHT OFF "THE ATTACKS" TDLTJ, 20.

8 "NEVER WEARIED OF DWELLING" Ibid., 19.

8 VIRGINIA'S LEADING FAMILY Randall, **Jefferson**, I, 7–10. See also Kern, **Jeffersons at Shadwell**, 17–19; Jonathan Daniels, **The Randolphs of Virginia** (Garden City, N.Y., 1972); Clifford Dowdey, **The Virginia Dynasties: The Emergence of "King" Carter and the Golden Age** (Boston, 1969); and H. J. Eckenrode, **The Randolphs: The Story of a Virginia Family** (Indianapolis, 1946).

8 IN 1739, HE WED JANE RANDOLPH TDLTJ, 18.

8 ISHAM RANDOLPH JHT, I, 13–17.

8 BORN IN LONDON IN 1721 Ibid., 13. See also Kern, **Jeffersons at Shadwell**, 44.

8 DUNGENESS IN GOOCHLAND COUNTY   Kern, **Jeffersons at Shadwell**, 19.

8 WALLED GARDENS   Ibid.

8 TRACED ITS COLONIAL ORIGINS   Daniels, **Randolphs of Virginia**, 17–18.

8 THRIVED IN VIRGINIA   Ibid.

8 HOME TO ENGLAND IN 1669   Ibid., 18.

8 PREVAILED ON A YOUNG NEPHEW, WILLIAM   Ibid., 17. Daniels wrote: "Almost certainly William came to Virginia at the behest—or with the encouragement—of his Uncle Henry Randolph." (Ibid.)

9 AT SOME POINT BETWEEN 1669 AND 1674   Ibid., 17. William Cabell Bruce, **John Randolph of Roanoke 1773–1833: A Biography Based Largely on New Material** (New York: G. P. Putnam's Sons, 1922), however, says that he specifically came over about 1673 at around age 24 (Ibid., I, 9.)

9 TAKING HIS UNCLE'S PLACE   Daniels, **Randolphs of Virginia**, 18.

9 AN ALLY OF SIR WILLIAM BERKELEY   Ibid., 24.

9 SHIPPING, RAISING TOBACCO, AND SLAVE TRADING   Ibid., 27.

9 FAMILY SEAT ON TURKEY ISLAND   Bruce, **John Randolph of Roanoke**, I, 10.

9 DESCRIBED AS "A SPLENDID MANSION"   Ibid.

9 MARY ISHAM RANDOLPH   Daniels, **Randolphs of Virginia**, 23.

9 "ARE SO NUMEROUS THAT THEY ARE OBLIGED"   Ibid., 32–33.

9 A CAPTAIN AND A MERCHANT Ibid., 40–42. See also Kern, **Jeffersons at Shadwell**, 44, and Virginia Scharff, **The Women Jefferson Loved** (New York, 2010), 3–4.

9 A "PRETTY SORT OF WOMAN" Scharff, **Women Jefferson Loved**, 3.

10 "A VERY GENTLE" Randall, **Jefferson**, I, 10. The merchant, Peter Collinson, also warned that such Virginians were liable to "look perhaps more at a man's outside than his inside," advising his correspondent, the botanist John Bartram, to "pray go very clean, neat and handsomely dressed to Virginia." (Ibid.)

10 "THE POWERFUL SCOTCH EARLS" Ibid., 7. Jefferson was always skeptical about the value of such claims to nobility. His mother's family, he wrote, "trace their pedigree far back in England and Scotland, to which let every one ascribe the faith and merit he chooses." (Jefferson, **Writings**, 3.) See also **PTJ**, I, 62.

10 "I ROSE AT 6 O'CLOCK" Diary of William Byrd II, February 27, 1711, Elliot J. Gorn, Randy Roberts, and Terry D. Bilhartz, eds., **Constructing the American Past**, I (New York, 2004), 71. An additional passage from the day describes the Byrds' treatment of a slave, Jenny: "In the evening my wife and little Jenny had a great quarrel in which my wife got the worst but at last by the help of the family Jenny was overcome and soundly whipped." (Ibid.)

11 VISITING VIRGINIA AND MARYLAND Ed-

mund S. Morgan, **Virginians at Home: Family Life in the Eighteenth Century** (Charlottesville, 1963), 7.

11 "THE YOUTH OF THESE MORE INDULGENT SETTLEMENTS" Ibid.

11 INSTRUCTED IN MUSIC Ibid., 18.

11 TAUGHT TO DANCE Ibid.

11 "WAS INDEED BEAUTIFUL" Ibid.

11 A PROSPEROUS, CULTURED, AND SOPHISTICATED FAMILY Kern, **Jeffersons at Shadwell,** 1–13. For a discussion of the political impact of Jefferson's social background, particularly on affairs in Virginia, see Ronald L. Hatzenbuehler, "Growing Weary in Well-Doing: Thomas Jefferson's Life Among the Virginia Gentry," **The Virginia Magazine of History and Biography** 101 (January 1993): 5–36. See also Jack P. Greene, **The Quest for Power: The Lower Houses of Assembly in the Southern Royal Colonies, 1689–1776** (New York, 1972), and Charles S. Sydnor, **Gentlemen Freeholders: Political Practices in Washington's Virginia** (Chapel Hill, N.C., 1952), for assessments of the politically, economically, and culturally privileged world in which Jefferson grew to maturity.

11 HIS STUDY ON THE FIRST FLOOR Kern, **Jeffersons at Shadwell,** 29.

11 A CHERRY DESK Ibid., 43.

11 PETER JEFFERSON'S LIBRARY Ibid., 33–38. Kevin J. Hayes, **The Road to Monticello: The**

Life and Mind of Thomas Jefferson (Oxford, 2008), 15–29, is also useful.

12 "WHEN YOUNG" Hayes, **Road to Monticello,** 27.

12 **VOYAGE ROUND THE WORLD** AND JOHN OGIL-BY'S **AMERICA** Ibid., 26–27.

12 "FROM THE TIME WHEN" **TDLTJ,** 37.

12 A WORLD OF LEISURE Ibid., 23–24.

12 "MY FATHER HAD A DEVOTED FRIEND" Ibid., 24.

12 BELIEVED HIS FIRST MEMORY Ibid., 23. His great-granddaughter reported that Jefferson "often declared that his earliest recollection in life was of being . . . handed up to a servant on horseback, by whom he was carried on a pillow for a long distance." (Ibid.)

12 BOUND FOR TUCKAHOE **JHT,** I, 18–20.

13 "HENRY WEATHERBOURNE'S BIGGEST BOWL" Randall, **Jefferson,** I, 7.

13 THE JEFFERSONS WOULD STAY Why not bring the Randolph children to Shadwell and remotely manage Tuckahoe, rather than moving his own family to Tuckahoe and remotely managing Shadwell? Was Peter Jefferson in an inferior position, essentially coming to work for Randolph? Some Randolph descendants thought so, and later enjoyed asserting that their more celebrated Jefferson cousins descended from a father who had taken wages from an ancestor of theirs.

Writing a century later, in 1871, however, Jefferson's great-granddaughter noted that the fact that Peter Jefferson "refused to receive any other compensation for his services as guardian is not only proved by the frequent assertion of his son in after years, but by his accounts as executor, which have ever remained unchallenged." In an arch footnote, the great-granddaughter added: "In spite of these facts, however, some of Randolph's descendants, with more arrogance than gratitude, speak of Colonel [Peter] Jefferson as being a paid agent of their ancestor." (**TDLTJ**, 22–23.)

13 THE ROOTS OF THE ADULT JEFFERSON'S DISLIKE Fawn M. Brodie, **Thomas Jefferson: An Intimate History** (New York, 1998), 48, speculates on the psychological impact of Jefferson's life at Tuckahoe, though she focuses on his affection for his own home, not his avoidance of conflict, which I think a likely legacy.

14 "THE WHOLE COMMERCE" Jefferson, **Writings,** 288.

14 ANOTHER SMALL CHILDHOOD MOMENT **TDLTJ**, 23.

15 "AT 14 YEARS OF AGE" Ibid., 26. Yet his mother was alive, and there were no fewer than four executors of his father's will. (**JHT**, I, 437–38.) Still, Jefferson apparently could not imagine any one of those men taking the place of his father as patriarch and counselor.

15 THOMAS'S MOTHER, JANE RANDOLPH JEFFERSON Jane Jefferson has long been depicted as a riddle, a mystery at the heart of the story of Thomas

Jefferson. There are several reasons for this. For one, Jefferson appears to have spoken more often and more fully about his father than about his mother, leaving more family stories that, combined with the extant public records available for leading colonial men (who held office and left more traces than women of the day), have given us a more detailed sense of Peter Jefferson than we have had for Jane Jefferson. Another reason is the Shadwell fire in 1770 destroyed family papers that may have shed light on the relationship between mother and son. And another reason lies in Jefferson's larger reticence about the women in his life. Evidence of Jefferson's musing about either his mother or his wife is sparse. The relatively thin traditions about Jane Jefferson have led some writers to speculate that mother and son were estranged. See, for instance, Brodie, **Thomas Jefferson,** 40–46.

Reflecting on Merrill Peterson's observation that "By his own reckoning she was a zero quantity in his life" (Peterson, **Thomas Jefferson and the New Nation: A Biography** [New York, 1970], 9), Brodie wrote: "No mother is a zero quantity in any son's life, and the fact that Jefferson, whether deliberately or not, managed to erase all traces of his opinion and feeling for her seems evidence rather of very great influence which he deeply resented, and from which he struggled to escape." (Brodie, **Thomas Jefferson,** 43.) More recent scholarship has attempted to revise the estrangement interpretation, most notably Kern, **Jeffersons at Shadwell,** and Scharff, **Women Jefferson Loved,** 3–57.

16 "A WOMAN OF A CLEAR" TDLTJ, 21–22.

16 A METICULOUS RECORD KEEPER Kern, **Jeffersons at Shadwell,** 230.

16 THOMAS'S SISTER ELIZABETH Brodie, **Thomas Jefferson,** 48.

16 "THE MOST FORTUNATE OF US ALL" PTJ, I, 10.

17 "SHE WAS AN AGREEABLE" Randall, **Jefferson,** I, 16–17. See also Kern, **Jeffersons at Shadwell,** 70. From the traditions we have of Jane Jefferson, bluster and threats were out of character. In contrast to her own mother, Mrs. Isham Randolph, Jane Jefferson was described by the family as "mild and peaceful by nature, a person of sweet temper and gentle manners." (Brodie, **Thomas Jefferson,** 41.) Even allowing for familial sentimentality, this description of Mrs. Jefferson of Shadwell differs from that of Mrs. Randolph of Dungeness, who was said to be "a stern, strict lady of the old school, much feared and little loved by her children." Her daughter Jane, however, was different. (Ibid., 681.) The source of these traditions is Ellen Wayles Randolph.

17 REBUILT SHADWELL AFTER IT BURNED Kern, **Jeffersons at Shadwell,** 64.

17 "HE WAS BORN" Jefferson, **Writings,** 3.

17 SURVEYING AND MAPMAKING Ibid., 3–4.

18 "HE DIED AUGUST 17TH, 1757" Ibid., 4.

18 A BRIEF MENTION IN A LETTER PTJ, I, 409.

"The death of my mother you have probably not heard of," Jefferson wrote William Randolph. "This happened on the last day of March after an illness of not more than an hour. We suppose it to have been apoplectic." (Ibid.)

18 PAYING A CLERGYMAN   **MB**, I, 444.

18 "MY MOTHER'S HOUSE"   **PTJ**, I, 34. The characterization was in a letter Jefferson wrote to John Page.

18 HE DID NOT MOVE   **MB**, I, 212.

19 HER YOUNGER BROTHER'S "CONSTANT COMPANION"   Randall, **Jefferson**, I, 40–41. See also **TDLTJ**, 38–39.

19 COMMON PASSIONS   Randall, **Jefferson**, I, 41.

19 JANE SANG HYMNS FOR HER BROTHER   **TDLTJ**, 34.

19 "HE EVER REGARDED HER"   Ibid.

19 SENT TO STUDY CLASSICS   **JHT**, I, 39–40. See also Randall, **Jefferson**, I, 17–18.

19 THE REVEREND WILLIAM DOUGLAS   **JHT**, I, 39–40.

19 JEFFERSON LATER THOUGHT DOUGLAS   Jefferson, **Writings**, 4.

19 THE REVEREND JAMES MAURY   Parton, **Life**, 17–18.

19 "A CORRECT CLASSICAL SCHOLAR"   Jefferson, **Writings**, 4.

19 MAURY DID SPLENDIDLY   **JHT**, I, 40–43.

20 "WOULD BEGUILE OUR LINGERING HOURS"   **PTJRS**, IV, 671. The letter was written on April 25, 1812.

20 Born in 1743   TJF, http://www.monticello
.org/site/research-and-collections/dabney-carr
-1743-1773 (accessed 2011). See also **TDLTJ,**
45–46.

20 from Louisa County   Ibid.

20 they took the books   Parton, **Life,** 44. My
portrait of the friends' time together is drawn
from this page of Parton and from **TDLTJ,**
45–46.

20 No man, Jefferson recalled later   TJ to
Dabney Carr, Jr., January 19, 1816, Thomas Jefferson Papers, LOC.

20 Whoever survived the other   **TDLTJ,** 45.
See also Parton, **Life,** 44.

21 **Dissertation on Education**   Helen D. Bul-
lock, ed., "A Dissertation on Education in the
Form of a Letter from James Maury to Robert
Jackson, July 17, 1762," **Papers of the Albemarle
County Historical Society** 2 (1941–42): 36–60.
See also Hayes, **Road to Monticello,** 30–42.

21 "An acquaintance with"   Hayes, **Road to
Monticello,** 36.

21 Greek and Latin   Ibid.

21 remarking that, given the choice   **TDLTJ,**
25.

21 1759–60 holidays   **PTJ,** I, 3. The letter describing the visit and his uncle's counsel is the
oldest extant written document of Jefferson's.
(Ibid.)

21 holidays at Chatsworth   Ibid. For details
about the estate itself, see Marc R. Matrana,

Lost Plantations of the South (Jackson, Miss., 2009), 26–27.

21 "BY GOING TO THE COLLEGE" Ibid.

22 THE TEST FOR POTENTIAL STUDENTS Hayes, **Road to Monticello,** 47.

TWO · What Fixed the Destinies of My Life

23 "ENLIGHTENMENT IS MAN'S EMERGENCE" Michael Allen Gillespie, **The Theological Origins of Modernity** (Chicago, 2008), 258.

23 "THE BEST NEWS I CAN TELL YOU" John J. Reardon, **Peyton Randolph, 1721–1775: One Who Presided** (Durham, N.C., 1982), 39.

24 GAMBLED ON HORSES Randall, **Jefferson,** I, 23. Jefferson discussed his extracurricular activities in a letter to his grandson Thomas Jefferson Randolph dated November 24, 1808. (Ibid., 22–23.)

24 WASHINGTON RECEIVED HIS SURVEYING CERTIFICATE William and Mary Alumni Association, http://www.wmalumni.com/general (accessed 2011). A writer for the **London Magazine** delivered a mixed verdict on the College of William and Mary before Jefferson arrived, writing that while "the masters were men of great knowledge and discretion," the college could not "yet vie with those excellent universities . . . of the **Massachusetts**," arguing that students were "pampered much more in softness and ease" in Virginia than they were in New England. (Susan H. Godson, **The College of William and**

Mary: A History, I, **1693–1888** [Williamsburg, Va., 1993], 84.)

24 A FRENCH TRAVELER IN WILLIAMSBURG "Journal of a French Traveller in the Colonies, 1765, I," **American Historical Review** 26 (July 1921): 745.

24 THE WREN BUILDING Colonial Williamsburg Foundation, http://www.history.org/almanack/places/hb/hbwren.cfm (accessed 2012).

24 THREE BLOCKS EAST I drew on several sources for this portrait of Williamsburg. In 1724, a professor at William and Mary described the basic scene Jefferson saw in the spring of 1760: "From the church runs a street northward called Palace Street; at the other end of which stands the Palace or Governor's House, a magnificent structure built at the public expense, finished and beautified with gates, fine gardens, offices, walks, a fine canal, orchards, etc. . . . This likewise has the ornamental addition of a good cupola or lanthorn, illuminated with most of the town, upon birth-nights, and other nights of occasional rejoicings." Hugh Jones, **The Present State of Virginia** (London, 1724), 31. See also Colonial Williamsburg Foundation, http://www.history.org/almanack/Tour The Town/index.cfm (accessed 2012).

25 NOT QUITE HALF A SQUARE MILE I am grateful to Del Moore of the John D. Rockefeller, Jr., Library in Williamsburg for guidance on these details. See John W. Reps, **Tidewater Towns: City Planning in Colonial Virginia and Maryland**

(Williamsburg, Va., 1972); and the Williamsburg Map, Colonial Williamsburg Foundation, http://research.history.org/ewilliamsburg2/ (accessed 2012).

25 "THE FINEST SCHOOL OF MANNERS AND MORALS" "Memoir of Thomas Jefferson Randolph," Edgehill-Randolph Papers, Collection 1397, Box 11, University of Virginia.

25 DR. WILLIAM SMALL, A SCOTTISH LAYMAN **JHT**, I, 51–55.

25 "IT WAS MY GREAT GOOD FORTUNE" Jefferson, **Writings**, 4. Jefferson added: "He, most happily for me, became soon attached to me, and made me his daily companion when not engaged in the school; and from his conversation I got my first views of the expansion of science, and of the system of things in which we are placed." (Ibid.)

26 BORN IN SCOTLAND IN 1734 TJF, http://www.monticello.org/site/jefferson/william-small (accessed 2011).

26 A "POLITE, WELL-BRED MAN" **Virginia Magazine of History and Biography** 16 (1908): 209. This letter, from Stephen Hawtrey to his brother Edward Hawtrey, was written from London on March 26, 1765, and reported a conversation with Small, who had since left America, about William and Mary.

26 LIVED IN TWO ROOMS Ibid., 210.

26 ETHICS, RHETORIC, AND BELLES LETTRES Hayes, **Road to Monticello,** 50–51.

26 NATURAL PHILOSOPHY TJF, http://www.mon

ticello.org/site/jefferson/william-small (accessed 2011).

26 LECTURING IN THE MORNINGS   Ibid.

26 SEMINAR-LIKE SESSIONS IN THE AFTERNOONS   Ibid.

26 BACON, LOCKE, NEWTON   Ibid. See also Hayes, **Road to Monticello,** 50–56.

26 KEY INSIGHT OF THE NEW INTELLECTUAL AGE   Henry F. May, **The Enlightenment in America** (New York, 1976), is useful.

27 "ENLIGHTENMENT IS MAN'S EMERGENCE"   Gillespie, **Theological Origins of Modernity,** 258.

27 "TO ME . . . A FATHER"   **PTJRS,** VIII, 200.

27 STUDIED FIFTEEN HOURS A DAY   My portrait of his student days at Williamsburg is drawn from **TDLTJ,** 31–32; Randall, **Jefferson,** I, 24–32; and **JHT,** I, 55–57.

27 "OF ALL THE CANKERS"   **PTJ,** XI, 250–51.

28 "KNOWLEDGE," JEFFERSON SAID   Ibid., X, 308.

28 A VIGOROUS BODY HELPED CREATE A VIGOROUS MIND   Ibid. "It is of little consequence to store the mind with science if the body be permitted to become debilitated," Jefferson said. (Ibid.) See also Ibid., VIII, 405–8.

28 "NOT LESS THAN TWO HOURS"   Ibid., X, 308.

28 THEIR MORNINGS TO THE LAW   Ibid., VIII, 408.

28 WITH "THE MECHANIC"   **TDLTJ,** 37–38.

28 A "WALKING ENCYCLOPEDIA"   Ibid., 37.

28 "A LITTLE TOO SHOWY"   Randall, **Jefferson,** I, 22.

29 LATER IN LIFE, JEFFERSON WROTE   Ibid., 22–23.

29 THE MOTTO AT WILLIAMSBURG'S POPULAR RALEIGH TAVERN Willard Sterne Randall, **Thomas Jefferson: A Life** (New York, 1993), 43. The motto in the tavern was in Latin.

29 HELD FREQUENT GATHERINGS **TDLTJ,** 27–28.

30 JEFFERSON CALLED FAUQUIER'S "FAMILIAR TABLE" Ibid., 28.

30 INVITED TO JOIN Randall, **Jefferson,** I, 30–31. In British America, the architects of revolution were delighted to learn the civilizing arts from their colonial masters. George Washington had a similar experience in northern Virginia, where his connection to the Fairfax family seat of Belvoir introduced him to more sophisticated and cultivated ways of life than he might have otherwise known. (Douglas Southall Freeman, John Alexander Carroll, and Mary Wells Ashworth, **George Washington: A Biography,** I [New York, 1948], 199–203.)

30 THE GOVERNOR LOVED SCIENCE Ibid., 30–32. "With some allowance he was everything that could have been wished for by Virginia under a royal government," the Virginia chronicler John Daly Burk wrote in a history published in 1804. "Generous, liberal, elegant in his manners and acquirements, his example left an impression of taste, refinement, and erudition on the character of the colony, which eminently contributed to its present high reputation in the arts." (Ibid., 30.)

30 THE STORY WAS TOLD Ibid., 31. According to

Burk, Fauquier "was but too successful in extending the influence of this pernicious and ruinous
practice." When not in residence at the Palace,
it was reported, Fauquier "visited the most distinguished landholders in the colonies, and the
rage for playing deep, reckless of time, health,
or money, spread like a contagion among a class
proverbial for their hospitality, their politeness,
and fondness of expense." (Ibid.)

30 FAUQUIER'S FATHER WAS A HUGUENOT PHYSI-
CIAN JHT, I, 76. I am indebted to Malone
for this short portrait of Fauquier. See also Parton, Life, 27–29; and "Francis Fauquier (bap.
1703–1768)," http://www.encyclopediavirginia
.org/fauquier_francis_bap_1703-1768 (accessed
2012).

30 BECAME A FELLOW OF THE ROYAL SOCIETY
JHT, I, 76.

31 AN UNUSUAL JULY HAILSTORM Ibid., 77.

31 A SCIENTIFIC PAPER "Francis Fauquier (bap.
1703–1768)."

31 THE LAWYER GEORGE WYTHE Imogene E.
Brown, American Aristides: A Biography of
George Wythe (Rutherford, N.J., 1981) was
helpful on Wythe, as was Bruce Chadwick's I
Am Murdered: George Wythe, Thomas Jefferson, and the Killing That Shocked a New Nation (Hoboken, N.J., 2009).

31 HAWK-NOSED Chadwick, I Am Murdered,
7–9, offers a fine descriptive section on Wythe.

31 "OF THE MIDDLE SIZE" TDLTJ, 30.

31 A HOUSE NEAR BRUTON PARISH Imogene E. Brown, **American Aristides**, 87.

31 "MR. WYTHE CONTINUED" TDLTJ, 28.

31 EXPENSIVE TASTES Imogene E. Brown, **American Aristides**, 81–82.

32 "MRS. WYTHE PUTS" Ibid., 82. See also **MB**, I, 328.

32 INTRODUCED JEFFERSON TO THE PRACTICE OF LAW Randall, **Jefferson**, I, 46.

32 "APART FROM THE INTELLECTUAL" Ibid., 31.

33 JEFFERSON ALSO INCLUDED HIS COUSIN Ibid., 22.

33 RANDOLPH WAS "OF AN AFFABLE" Ibid., 51.

33 HE ALSO "COMMANDS" Ibid.

33 "UNDER TEMPTATIONS AND DIFFICULTIES" Ibid., 22.

34 "VERY HIGH STANDING" Ibid.

34 MET PATRICK HENRY John P. Kaminski, **The Founders on the Founders: Word Portraits from the American Revolutionary Era** (Charlottesville, Va., 2008), 260–61.

34 CONCEIVED OF LIFE IN SOCIAL TERMS Gordon S. Wood, **The Creation of the American Republic** (Chapel Hill, N.C., 1998), ix, and **Revolutionary Characters: What Made the Founders Different** (New York, 2006), 104–7. See also Jack Rakove, **Revolutionaries: A New History of the Invention of America** (Boston, 2010), 299–302. With industry and skill, Jefferson studied much, but he was no cloistered

intellectual or lonely scholar. We often think of him as a grand, solitary figure, alone with his thoughts and his pen and his inventions, shut off in his chambers at Monticello or upstairs in the President's House. He was very rarely alone, however, and would have thought it odd if he had found himself long in isolation.

34 "I AM CONVINCED" TDLTJ, 284. The quotation, from a letter to his daughter Polly Jefferson Eppes, continues: "and that every person who retires from free communication with it is severely punished afterwards by the state of mind into which he gets, and which can only be prevented by feeding our sociable principles." (Ibid.)

35 A SECRET SOCIETY MB, I, 338.

35 LONGED FOR INTELLIGENCE PTJ, I, 5.

35 A YOUNG WOMAN NAMED REBECCA Ibid., 6.

35 THE EPISODE IS CHIEFLY INTERESTING For the basic details, see ibid.; for analysis, see JHT, I, 80–86.

35 RATS AND RAIN PTJ, I, 3–6.

36 COMPARED HIMSELF TO JOB Ibid., 3–5.

36 "ALL THINGS HERE" Ibid., 7.

36 "WE MUST FALL" Ibid., 15.

37 JEFFERSON DECIDED TO DECLARE Ibid., 11–12.

37 THE APOLLO ROOM OF THE RALEIGH TAVERN Lyon Gardiner Tyler, **Williamsburg: The Old Colonial Capital** (Richmond, Va., 1907), 232–35.

37 "I WAS PREPARED" PTJ, I, 11.

37 HE TRIED TO SPEAK Ibid.

37 A CONVERSATION Ibid., 13–14.

38 "I ASKED NO QUESTION" Ibid., 14.

38 "ABOMINABLY INDOLENT" Ibid., 16.

38 A LETTER TO A FRIEND Ibid., 15–17.

38 HIS "SCHEME" TO MARRY Ibid.

38 THE WEALTHY JACQUELIN AMBLER Alfred J. Beveridge, **The Life of John Marshall**, I (Boston, 1916), 149.

38 "MANY AND GREAT ARE THE COMFORTS" PTJ, I, 16. E. M. Halliday, **Understanding Thomas Jefferson** (New York, 2001), thinks it unlikely that Jefferson would have availed himself of the obvious means of satisfying his sexual desires (Ibid., 16–17), but his views are as speculative as those suggesting Jefferson might well have done so. Such activity in the elite of his time was hardly unknown.

Kathleen M. Brown, **Good Wives, Nasty Wenches, and Anxious Patriarchs: Gender, Race, and Power in Colonial Virginia** (Chapel Hill, N.C., 1996), 319–66, offers a compelling account of issues of sexuality and power in the world in which Jefferson grew up and ultimately lived. William Byrd II, the prominent planter, left a diary that included accounts of his sexual designs on women of inferior rank, both white and black. "On one of his first trips to Williamsburg as a councillor," Brown wrote, "Byrd 'sent for the wench to clean my room and when I came [to the room] I kissed her and felt her, for which God forgive me.' Several days later, Byrd kissed Mrs. Chiswell with excessive passion in front of his wife 'until she [Chiswell] was angry and my wife also was uneasy.' After that incident, Byrd confined his philandering to private encounters with women who were clearly his social inferiors: He tried unsuccessfully to entice a chambermaid to his room in Williamsburg, engaged in some group 'sport' with a drunken Indian woman along with members of his militia, and kissed various women he and his male companions met during their visits to Williamsburg." After Byrd's wife died, Brown wrote, "Byrd began to visit prostitutes and initiated several longer affairs with white women who were not of his social rank." Ultimately these women included enslaved women. (Ibid., 331–32.)

For his part, Halliday found it more likely that Jefferson resorted to masturbation. (Halliday, **Understanding Thomas Jefferson**, 20–21.) Andrew Burstein, **Jefferson's Secrets: Death and Desire at Monticello** (New York, 2005), explores the influence of contemporary medical thought about human sexuality on the mature Jefferson. In Burstein's interpretation, masturbation would have been seen as an exercise in depletion, whereas moderate sexual activity was essential to give "a healthy balance to the body's internal forces," Burstein wrote. "Sex was seen much as diet was, part of a regimen of self-control, and important to understand if one was to enjoy a productive life." (Ibid., 157; see especially 151–88.) In my view, it is likely that Jefferson, like William Byrd II, took advantage of available women—those in dependent stations such as service or slavery—to experiment sexually.

THREE · Roots of Revolution

40 "OUR MINDS WERE CIRCUMSCRIBED" Jefferson, **Writings**, 5.

40 "MAY WE OUTLIVE OUR ENEMIES" **MB**, I, 283.

40 HE HAD SENT TO LONDON Ibid., 16.

40 "NO LIBERTY, NO LIFE" Ibid.

40 THE DEFINITION OF LIBERTY I am indebted to many sources for my analysis of the intellectual, political, and cultural background to the American Revolution. In general, see Bailyn, **Origins of American Politics** (New York, 1968), and **Ideological Origins of the American Revolution**; Wood, **Creation of the American Republic, 1776–1787, The Radicalism of the American Revolution** (New York, 1993), **The American Revolution: A History** (New York, 2003), and **The Idea of America: Reflections on the Birth of the United States** (New York, 2011); Lawrence Henry Gipson, **The British Empire Before the American Revolution**: vol. XIII, **The Triumphant Empire: The Empire Beyond the Storm, 1770–1776** (New York, 1967), 171–224, which offers a valuable "Summary of the Series"; Gipson, "The American Revolution as an Aftermath of the Great War for the Empire" in Colbourn

and Patterson, **American Past in Perspective,**
I, 103–20; Clinton Rossiter, "Political Theory
in the Colonies," in ibid., 121–31; Page Smith,
"David Ramsay and the Causes of the American Revolution," in ibid., 132–60; T. H. Breen,
**American Insurgents, American Patriots: The
Revolution of the People** (New York, 2010);
Taylor, **American Colonies;** Esmond Wright,
ed. **Causes and Consequences of the American
Revolution** (Chicago, 1966); Edmund S. Mor-
gan and Helen M. Morgan, **The Stamp Act Cri-
sis: Prologue to Revolution** (Chapel Hill, N.C.,
1995), 6–7; John Ferling, **Independence: The
Struggle to Set America Free** (New York, 2011),
8–51; Morgan, **Birth of the Republic,** 15–60;
Charles M. Andrews, "The American Revolu-
tion: An Interpretation," **American Historical
Review** 31, no. 2 (January 1926): 219–32; and
Don Higginbotham, **War and Society in Revolutionary America: The Wider Dimensions of
Conflict** (Columbia, S.C., 1988).

Middlekauff, **Glorious Cause,** 7–97, covers
the origins of the conflict through the Stamp
Act Crisis, concluding: "By late August [1765]
two major colonies, Virginia and Massachusetts,
each in its own way, had vented their anger at
the Stamp Act. They in fact had started more
than they knew; they had started a fire. Its spread
seemed virtually inevitable." (Ibid., 97.) Taylor,
American Colonies, xiv, generally describes the
rise of scholarly attention to the Atlantic world.

"The Atlantic approach examines the complex and continuous interplay of Europe, Africa, and colonial America through the transatlantic flows of goods, people, plants, animals, capital, and ideas." (Ibid.) See also Eliga H. Gould and Peter S. Onuf, eds., **Empire and Nation: The American Revolution in the Atlantic World** (Baltimore, Md., 2005); Edmund S. Morgan, "The American Revolution Considered as an Intellectual Movement" in Wright, **Causes and Consequences of the American Revolution**, 172–92; and Risjord, **Jefferson's America, 1760–1815**, 47–69.

41 THE ALBANY PLAN OF UNION   Walter Isaacson, **Benjamin Franklin: An American Life** (New York, 2003), 158–62. See also Gipson, "American Revolution as an Aftermath," 100. Gipson suggested that the American Revolution might have been prevented had the 1754 proposal been accepted. For a critical view of Gipson's epic series in general and of his thoughts on 1754 in particular, see Patrick Griffin, "In Retrospect: Lawrence Henry Gipson's 'The British Empire Before the American Revolution,' " **Reviews in American History** 31, no. 2 (June 2003): 171–83. Griffin wrote: "Was the American Revolution inevitable? Gipson by and large does not fancy such counter-factuals, but he does point to one moment that seemed to offer an opportunity to construct a more enduring imperial scheme: the Albany Plan of Union. Under the

aborted plan drawn up in 1754, the American colonies, united together through friendship and common concerns, would be tied to Britain under the Crown but by little else. If Americans, [Gipson] suggests, had embraced this plan, they could have avoided the touchy constitutional issues that led to rebellion." (Ibid., 176.)

Late in life, Franklin himself saw the failure of the Albany Plan as a critical step on the road to revolution. "The colonies so united would have been sufficiently strong to have defended themselves," he said. "There would then have been no need of troops from England; of course the subsequent pretense for taxing America, and the bloody contest it occasioned, would have been avoided." (Isaacson, **Benjamin Franklin,** 161–62.) See also Middlekauff, **Glorious Cause,** 32.

41 ITS AUTHOR, BENJAMIN FRANKLIN Isaacson, **Benjamin Franklin,** 158–62. The proposal was the brainchild of Franklin, who wrote of it: "By this plan the general government was to be administered by a president-general appointed and supported by the crown, and a grand council was to be chosen by the representatives of the people of the several colonies, met in their respective assemblies. . . . Its fate was singular: the assemblies did not adopt it as they all thought there was too much prerogative in it, and in England it was judged to have too much of the democratic." (**A Benjamin Franklin Reader,** ed. Walter Isaacson [New York, 2003], 512–13.)

41 HE INHERITED HIS FATHER'S EDITION Francis D. Cogliano, **Thomas Jefferson: Reputation and Legacy** (Charlottesville, Va., 2006), 22.

41 INEXTRICABLY LINKED WITH THE STORY OF ENGLAND Ibid., 22–24.

42 A CONSTANT STRUGGLE TO PRESERVE INDIVIDUAL LIBERTY Trevor Colbourn, **The Lamp of Experience: Whig History and the Intellectual Origins of the American Revolution** (Indianapolis, 1998), 3–47. See also Cogliano, **Thomas Jefferson**, 21.

42 HISTORY WAS "PHILOSOPHY" Cogliano, **Thomas Jefferson**, 21. Bolingbroke attributed the aphorism to Dionysius of Halicarnassus.

42 HISTORY, THEN, MATTERED ENORMOUSLY In Query XIV of his **Notes on the State of Virginia**, Jefferson offered an expansive vision of the role history should play in the lives of nations and of peoples: Nothing was more important, he said, than "rendering the people safe, as they are the ultimate, guardians of their own liberty." The reading of history was essential for this enterprise.

> History by apprising them of the past will enable them to judge of the future; it will avail them of the experience of other times and other nations; it will qualify them as judges of the actions and designs of men; it will enable them to know ambition under every disguise it may assume; and knowing

it, to defeat its views. In every government on earth is some trace of human weakness, some germ of corruption and degeneracy, which cunning will discover, and wickedness insensibly open, cultivate, and improve. Every government degenerates when trusted to the rulers of the people alone. The people themselves are its only safe depositories. And to render even them safe their minds must be improved to a certain degree. (Jefferson, **Writings,** 274.)

Cogliano, **Thomas Jefferson,** 26, quotes this passage from the **Notes,** concluding: "In Jefferson's view knowledge of history was necessary for the people of Virginia if they were to protect their liberty. It was a political necessity in a republic." (Ibid.)

42 SOCIETIES WERE LIKELY TO BE DIVIDED   Cogliano, **Thomas Jefferson,** 22–26.

42 THE DRAMA OF THE ENGLISH CIVIL WAR   See Alfred F. Young, "English Plebeian Culture and Eighteenth-Century American Radicalism," in **The Origins of Anglo-American Radicalism,** ed. Margaret Jacob and James Jacob (London, 1984), 187–212, for an account of the cultural impact of the Cromwellian legacy in America.

43 LIVED IN AN ATMOSPHERE   Bailyn, **Origins of American Politics,** 131. Bailyn wrote: "Their intellectual world framed by the concept of the mixed constitution, the colonists found ready at

hand, in the terms of that powerful paradigm, a means of comprehending the disturbances around them. Some, reflecting on the socio-constitutional structure of colonial society, were struck by the discrepancies between the ideal and the real, the English model and the colonial duplicates, and attributed their ills to these discrepancies. It was often noted that the all-important middle order, the element of aristocracy—so vital, according to the standard constitutional theory, in keeping the extremes of power and liberty from tearing each other apart—was not properly represented in the colonies, in certain cases did not exist at all." (Ibid.)

43 SECURITY COULD BE FOUND ONLY Ibid., 151–52. Bailyn wrote: "England stood almost completely alone in the Old World, sustained in its distinctive role, so far successfully, by the skillful rebalancing of its constitution in the settlement that had followed the Glorious Revolution. But that settlement had not extended, fully, to America. The phalanx of strong guarantees against the authoritarian power of the state was missing here, and the situation here, consequently, was peculiarly dangerous, peculiarly delicate, peculiarly demanding of the powers of vigilance and resistance." (Ibid.)

43 THE HISTORY AMERICANS WANTED Ibid., 106. On the question of ideology and power, Bailyn wrote:

I have suggested that a paradox lay at the
heart of provincial politics in eighteenth-
century America: on the one hand an enlargement, beyond what was commonly
thought compatible with liberty, of the
legal authority possessed by the first branch
of government, the executive; and on the
other hand, a radical reduction of the actual
power in politics exercised by the executive, a reduction accounted for by the weakness of the so-called influence by which the
crown and its ministers in England actually managed politics in that country. At
once regressive and progressive—carrying
forward into the Augustan world powers associated with Stuart autocracy yet embody-
ing reforms that would remain beyond the
reach of reformers in England for another
century or more—American politics in the
mid-eighteenth century was a thoroughgoing anomaly. Conflict was inevitable: conflict
between a presumptuous prerogative and
an overgreat democracy, conflict that had
no easy resolution and that raised in minds
steeped in the political culture of eighteenth-
century Britain the specter of catastrophe.
(Ibid.)

Bailyn found the impetus for Revolution in the
degree to which the colonists believed America

was not fully sharing in the classic eighteenth-century balance of monarchy, aristocracy, and commons. It was not, in other words, a dislike of or objection to the English constitution but rather disappointment that the New World was not allowed to live wholly within the post-Glorious Revolution system. "What the colonial opposition at every stage saw in contemplating the role of government, of power, of the executive, in the colonies were evidences—scattered to be sure, fading in and out of focus, rising and falling in importance, but palpable evidences nevertheless—of . . . conspiracy against the constitutional guarantees of liberty." (Ibid., 136.)

43 RAPIN'S MULTIVOLUME HISTORY OF ENGLAND Colbourn, **Lamp of Experience**, 43–44.

43 PETER JEFFERSON WAS "A STAUNCH" Randall, **Jefferson**, I, 14.

44 FREEDOM-LOVING SAXONS Colbourn, **Lamp of Experience**, 237–43. For details about the long-standing Whig argument, see Joseph J. Ellis, **American Sphinx**, 32–34. The section is an excellent explanation of the theory, its origins, and how, in Ellis's words, "Jefferson clung to the theory with nearly obsessive tenacity throughout his life, though even he admitted that 'I had never been able to get any one to agree with me but Mr. Wythe.' " (Ellis, **American Sphinx**, 38.)

44 JEFFERSON AND LIKE-MINDED AMERICANS Bailyn, **Origins of American Politics**, 159–61.

Within two years of the Stamp Act repeal, in 1766, Bailyn noted:

> The train of events that manifestly led to Independence was clearly visible: Stamp Act, Townshend Duties, Massacre. But these enactments and the other famous events of the period are not self-evidently incendiary. The stamp tax was not a crushing tax; it was generally considered to be an innocuous and judicious form of taxation. The Townshend Duties, which were also far from crippling, were withdrawn. And the Massacre was the result of a kind of urban riot common both in England and America throughout the century. Yet these events were in fact incendiary; they did in fact lead to the overthrow of constituted authority and, ultimately, to the transformation of American life. For they were not in some pure sense simply objective events, and they were not perceived by immaculate minds aloft in a cosmic perch. To minds steeped in the literature of eighteenth-century history and political theory, these events, charged with ideology, were the final realization of tendencies and possibilities that had been seen and spoken of, with concern and foreboding, since the turn of the seventeenth century. There was no calm before the storm. The storm was

continuous, if intermittent, throughout the century. An inflamed, unstable politics, incapable of duplicating the integration and control that "influence" had created in England, had called forth the full range of advanced ideas, not as theories simply, not as warnings merely of some ultimate potentiality, but as explanations of present conflicts, bitter conflicts, conflicts between a legally overgreat executive and an irrepressible though shifting opposition.

The Seven Years' War was the catalyst.

For before 1763 there had been no relentless pressures within the system of Anglo-American politics, no sustained drive or inescapable discipline guided by central policy. When, after the conclusion of the Seven Years' War, that impetus and control appeared in the form of a revamped colonial system with more effective agencies of enforcement; when the system finally tightened and the pressure was maintained; and when, associated with this, evidence accumulated in the colonies that corruption was softening the vigilance that had heretofore preserved England's own mixed constitution—that an escalation of ministerial power initially stimulated by John Stuart, Earl of Bute, was taking place in England itself—when all of this happened, the latent tendencies of American politics moved swiftly to their ultimate fulfillment. (Ibid.)

45 AT THE CONCLUSION OF THE FRENCH AND IN-
DIAN WAR Fred Anderson, **Crucible of War:
The Seven Years' War and the Fate of Empire
in British North America, 1754–1766** (New
York, 2001), is a masterful account of the origins, course, and implications of the war. See
also Middlekauff, **Glorious Cause**, 17–73, and
Risjord, **Jefferson's America, 1760–1815**, 71–96.
Risjord wrote:

> At the close of the French and Indian War in
> 1763, Great Britain stood at the pinnacle of
> its power. The peace conference at Paris that
> year was a triumphant recognition of British
> conquests in seven bloody years of war. The
> French empire in North America had disappeared; from Canada to the Floridas, the territory east of the Mississippi River was under
> British dominion. Yet . . . it almost seemed
> as if the empire had been won too quickly
> and too easily. Unaccustomed to managing
> dominions flung in desultory fashion around
> the world, British politicians were slow to
> comprehend the meaning of their victory
> and even slower in developing a comprehensive worldview to match their world empire.
> They remained wedded to local politics, en-

cumbered by petty rivalries, stubborn, and unimaginative. As a result, the first British empire began to crumble almost as soon as it was fully formed. . . . The very size of the empire set loose centrifugal forces that had to be countered with more efficient administrative ties. (Ibid., 71.)

45 EMPIRES ARE EXPENSIVE Risjord, **Jefferson's America, 1760–1815**, 71–72. "Adding to the sense of urgency was the enormous debt Britain had incurred in fighting the war and financing allies, such as Frederick the Great of Prussia. Interest on the debt alone amounted to $5 million a year, while the government's annual income was little more than $8 million." (Ibid.) As Middlekauff pointed out, Britain had fought three wars since the Glorious Revolution, each with France and her allies "in three lengthy periods," leading to rising debt and military and administrative costs. (Middlekauff, **Glorious Cause**, 23–26.) The landowning interest in Parliament understandably pressed for taxes on imports. "Excises on a vast array of items—soap and salt, beer and spirits, cider, paper, and silk, among other things consumed by ordinary and mighty folk alike—replaced land as the largest source of revenue from taxes. . . . Customs, that is, duties on trade, also increased as commerce grew in the century." (Ibid., 23.)

45 SHOULD BEAR MORE OF THE COST Morgan and Morgan, **Stamp Act Crisis**, 6.

45 TROOPS WERE TO REMAIN IN NORTH AMERICA Ibid., 21–23.

45 GRANTS OF THE WESTERN LANDS Risjord, **Jefferson's America, 1760–1815**, 72–74. See also Thomas Perkins Abernethy, **Western Lands and the American Revolution** (New York, 1959); and Middlekauff, **Glorious Cause**, 58–60. To Middlekauff, "Among the white Americans no group was more aggressive or greedy than the Virginians." (Ibid., 58.) A commonly cited example of the colonists' holdings is that of the Ohio Company, whose investors included George Washington, which had received 200,000 acres whose value was now endangered. (Ibid.)

45 AN UPRISING OF OHIO VALLEY INDIAN TRIBES Middlekauff, **Glorious Cause**, 59–60. The campaign was led by Pontiac, chief of the Ottawa. See Gregory Evans Dowd, **War Under Heaven: Pontiac, the Indian Nations, and the British Empire** (Baltimore, Md., 2004).

46 SOUGHT TO GIVE THE KING THE POWER Ibid., 60. The Proclamation of 1763, issued on October 7, closed the West to white settlement and established Quebec, East Florida, and West Florida. (Ibid.) According to Risjord,

> Seeking to reserve all lands west of the Appalachian ridge for the tribes, the proclamation

prohibited any further land grants or sales in the West without royal license and ordered the removal of all white squatters. . . . The result, it was hoped, would prevent border warfare and reduce the expense of maintaining an army in America. The ministry intended to negotiate further land cessions from the Native Americans, thus permitting a gradual advance of the frontier; and the proclamation itself permitted land grants to veterans of the French war. Despite these loopholes, colonists—especially the Virginians, who had the best legal claims to the West, were outraged. . . . The proclamation was the first seed of imperial disunion. (Risjord, **Jefferson's America, 1760–1815**, 73–74.)

46 ENFORCEMENT OF NAVIGATION ACTS Risjord, **Jefferson's America, 1760–1815**, 74–75.

46 A CAMPAIGN TO USE "WRITS OF ASSISTANCE" Ibid. See also Middlekauff, **Glorious Cause,** 65, and Oliver M. Dickerson, **The Navigation Acts and the American Revolution** (Philadelphia, 1951), 172–89.

46 THE SUGAR ACT OF 1764 Morgan and Morgan, **Stamp Act Crisis,** 21–40. See also Middlekauff, **Glorious Cause,** 64–66.

46 LOWERED THE TAX ON MOLASSES Morgan and Morgan, **Stamp Act Crisis,** 24.

46 MADEIRA WINE, A FAVORITE OF THE YOUNG JEFFERSON Ibid., 25. We know about Jefferson's af-

fection for the wine from his remarks about Mrs. Wythe's entertaining (see above). See also TJF, http://www.monticello.org/site/research-and-col lections/wine (accessed 2011). He ultimately lost his preference for Madeira. (Ibid.)

46 ATTEMPT TO ESTABLISH A PRINCIPLE AND A PREC-EDENT   Ibid., 27.

46 HAD RISEN TO ANNOUNCE   Ibid., 54–55.

47 JAMES OTIS'S **RIGHTS OF THE BRITISH**   Morgan, **Birth of the Republic**, 18.

47 WYTHE DRAFTED A PETITION   **JHT**, I, 91–92. See also Morgan and Morgan, **Stamp Act Crisis**, 97.

47 "THAT THE PEOPLE"   Morgan and Morgan, **Stamp Act Crisis**, 39–40.

48 HAD LEFT WILLIAMSBURG FOR HOME   Henry Mayer, **A Son of Thunder: Patrick Henry and the American Republic** (New York, 2001), 81.

48 "YET A STUDENT"   Jefferson, **Writings**, 5.

48 A NUMBER OF ANTI-STAMP ACT RESOLUTIONS   Mayer, **Son of Thunder**, 82–85. See also Morgan and Morgan, **Stamp Act Crisis**, 95–97.

48 STOOD AT THE DOOR OF THE HOUSE   Jefferson, **Writings**, 5.

49 "GREAT INDEED"   Ibid., 6. Henry's talents as a "popular orator," Jefferson wrote, were "such as I have never heard from any other man." (Ibid.)

49 HENRY SAID TARQUIN AND CAESAR   "Journal of a French Traveller in the Colonies, 1765, I," 745.

49 ACCORDING TO THE SINGLE CONTEMPORANEOUS

ACCOUNT   Ibid. A grander account, oft-repeated, appeared in William Wirt, **Sketches of the Life and Character of Patrick Henry** (Philadelphia, 1878), 78–83. In 1921 the account of the French traveler emerged. (Morgan and Morgan, **Stamp Act Crisis**, 93–95.)

49 "HE APPEARED TO ME"   Jefferson, **Writings**, 6.

49 "SPOKE TREASON"   "Journal of a French Traveller in the Colonies, 1765, I," 745.

49 "HE WAS READY TO ASK PARDON"   Ibid.

49 "MOST BLOODY"   Mayer, **Son of Thunder**, 85.

49 THE "FIFTH RESOLUTION"   Morgan and Morgan, **Stamp Act Crisis**, 96–97.

50 MEN SUCH AS PEYTON RANDOLPH   Reardon, **Peyton Randolph**, 21–23.

50 "BY GOD"   Ibid., 22.

50 THE SENSE THAT THEY HAD LOST CONTROL   Morgan and Morgan, **Stamp Act Crisis**, 97–98, explains the dynamics well. "Why Randolph, Robinson, Robert Carter Nicholas, and even Richard Bland and George Wythe, all of whom are said to have opposed the resolutions, should have been so hostile to them is not apparent," wrote Morgan and Morgan.

George Wythe, who had drawn the petition to the House of Commons, told Jefferson that his first draft had required toning down because the other members of the committee thought it treasonable. And Richard Bland was soon to express in print a view of Par-

liament's authority which was at least as re-
stricted as that taken in the resolutions. The
argument of the opposition . . . was that the
petitions of the preceding year were a sufficient statement of the colonial position and
that no further step should be taken until
some answer was received to these. But this
argument was specious, for the Burgesses
knew that the petitions had not received a
hearing. In all probability, the opposition
is not to be explained so much by the measure itself as by the men who were backing
it. Henry and his friends were upstarts in
Virginia politics, and their introduction of
the resolves constituted a challenge to the
established leaders of the House of Burgesses.
(Ibid.)

50 HENRY LEFT THE CAPITAL Mayer, **Son of
Thunder,** 88. Mayer referred to Henry's early
exit as "unaccountab[le]." (Ibid.)

50 ARRIVED AT THE CHAMBER EARLY PTJRS, VII,
544–51. See also Morgan and Morgan, **Stamp
Act Crisis,** 97–98.

50 EXAMINING THE RECORDS OF THE HOUSE
PTJRS, VII, 544–51. "The cautious leaders
found themselves arguing for quiet submission
in the most angry terms," wrote Henry Mayer.
"This was no time for hot-headed, ill-considered,
and possibly treasonous assertion, they insisted."
(Mayer, **Son of Thunder,** 85.)

51 FAUQUIER WROTE THE BOARD OF TRADE   Morgan and Morgan, **Stamp Act Crisis**, 98.

52 THE ANNUAL BIRTH-NIGHT BALL   "Journal of a French Traveller in the Colonies, 1765, I," 746. See also Hayes, **Road to Monticello**, 81.

52 TO BEND THE NATURAL WORLD   JHT, I, 115–16. See also Parton, **Life**, 42.

53 "WILD AND ROMANTIC"   PTJRS, I, 386.

53 IN OCTOBER 1765   JHT, I, 115.

53 "LAUDABLE AND USEFUL"   Ibid.

53 "CLEARING THE GREAT FALLS"   PTJ, I, 88.

54 HELPED BRING A MARYLAND PUBLISHER   Hayes, **Road to Monticello**, 88. Hayes cites Isaiah Thomas, **The History of Printing in America: With a Biography of Printers and an Account of Newspapers** (New York, 1970), 556.

54 "UNTIL THE BEGINNING"   Jeffrey L. Pasley, **'The Tyranny of Printers': Newspaper Politics in the Early American Republic** (Charlottesville, Va., 2003), 37.

54 ONTASSETE, THE CHEROKEE CHIEF   Jefferson, **Writings**, 1263.

54 WHO CROSSED THE ATLANTIC IN 1762   JHT, I, 60–61.

54 "THE MOON WAS IN FULL SPLENDOR"   Jefferson, **Writings**, 1263.

55 "ONE OF THE CHOICE ONES"   PTJ, VIII, 181.

55 "HIS POWERS OF CONVERSATION WERE GREAT"   Randall, **Jefferson**, I, 45.

55 THE STORY OF A "MOST INTELLIGENT"   Ibid., 45–46.

56 MARTHA HAD MARRIED HIS FRIEND DABNEY CARR **MB**, I, 21.

56 HIS SISTER JANE DIED Randall, **Jefferson**, I, 41.

56 "THE LOSS OF SUCH A SISTER" **TDLTJ**, 38–39.

57 THE ENGLISH POET WILLIAM SHENSTONE **MB**, I, 247.

57 "AH, JOANNA" Ibid. See also Hayes, **Road to Monticello**, 87–88.

57 BEGAN HIS GARDEN BOOK **GB**, 1.

57 "PURPLE HYACINTH" Ibid.

57 "PUCKOON FLOWERS FALLEN" Ibid.

57 AN EXCURSION NORTH **PTJ**, I, 18–21. See also **JHT**, I, 98–101.

58 WITH ELBRIDGE GERRY **JHT**, I, 100.

58 BROKE AWAY FROM HIM **PTJ**, I, 19.

58 TERRIBLE RAINS Ibid.

58 FORDING A STREAM Ibid.

58 STOPPING IN ANNAPOLIS Ibid.

58 "I WAS SURPRISED" Ibid., 19–20.

59 "I WOULD GIVE YOU" Ibid., 20.

59 PARLIAMENT HAD STOOD DOWN Morgan and Morgan, **Stamp Act Crisis**, 279–92.

59 "IN ALL CASES WHATSOEVER" Ibid., 288.

59 CASES TOOK HIM Frank L. Dewey, **Thomas Jefferson, Lawyer** (Charlottesville, Va., 1987), covers this aspect of his life well.

59 HIS SISTER MARTHA WROTE HIM **GB**, 6.

59 HIS CARNATIONS WERE IN BLOOM Ibid.

59 CALCULATED HOW MUCH HAY Ibid., 7.

60 A BRIGHT, ENTHUSIASTIC "He pursued the law with an eager industry," said Edmund Ran-

dolph. "Reserved toward the world at large, to his intimate friends he showed a peculiar sweetness of temper and by them was admired and beloved. . . . He panted after the fine arts and discovered a taste in them not easily satisfied with such scanty means as existed in a colony. . . . It constituted a part of Mr. Jefferson's pride to run before the times in which he lived." (Willard Sterne Randall, **Thomas Jefferson**, 100.)

60 A BOTTLE OF WHISKEY AND A SHIRT **JHT**, I, 123.

60 "HE SAW [FRAME]" Ibid.

FOUR · Temptations and Trials

61 "YOU WILL PERCEIVE THAT" **JHT**, I, 448.

61 "ALL MEN ARE BORN FREE" Gordon-Reed, **Hemingses of Monticello**, 100.

62 PETER JEFFERSON HAD MADE WALKER'S FATHER **JHT**, I, 449. Malone devotes an appendix to this volume to what he called "The Walker Affair, 1768–1809." (Ibid., 447–51.) See also Jon Kukla, **Mr. Jefferson's Women** (New York, 2007), 41–63, for an extended discussion of the Walker-Jefferson story.

62 "WE HAD PREVIOUSLY" **JHT**, I, 449.

62 DAUGHTER OF BERNARD MOORE Robert A. Lancaster, Jr., **Historic Virginia Homes and Churches** (Philadelphia, 1915), 266–67.

62 "JACK WALKER IS ENGAGED" **PTJ**, I, 15.

62 THE ABSENCE OF HIS HORSES Ibid.

63 DATED FROM "DEVILSBURG" Ibid., 14.

63 "BUT I HEAR" Ibid., 15.

63 THE FIRST WEEK OF JUNE JHT, I, 449.

63 "THE FRIEND OF MY HEART" Ibid.

63 BY 1768 THE WALKERS WERE LIVING Ibid., 154.

63 BOUND FOR FORT STANWIX Ibid., 449.

63 APPOINTED "MR. JEFFERSON . . . MY NEIGHBOR" Ibid.

63 DEPARTED FOR NEW YORK Kukla, **Mr. Jefferson's Women**, 51.

63 ABOUT TWO YEARS YOUNGER Ibid., 44.

63 SEEMS TO HAVE FALLEN IN LOVE JHT, I, 449–50, details the Walkers' version of events. As noted below, Jefferson conceded his culpability though he is not known to have commented on the particulars of the Walkers' account.

64 JOHN WALKER RECALLED Ibid., 449.

64 "RENEWED HIS CARESSES" Ibid.

64 JOHN COLES, A NOTED HUNTER **The Virginia Magazine of History and Biography** 7 (1900): 101.

64 "HE PRETENDED TO BE SICK" JHT, I, 449.

65 CONFIRMED THE WALKER STORY Ibid., 448.

65 AFTER A POLITICAL BREAK Ibid., 447–48.

65 AN INCORRECT THING TO DO Ibid., 448.

65 A GLORIOUS AUTUMN MB, I, 73.

65 DAVIES, A PRESBYTERIAN CLERGYMAN Lyon Gardiner Tyler, **Williamsburg: The Old Colonial Capital** (Richmond, Va., 1907), 230.

65 OFFERINGS IN THE CAPITAL MB, I, 73.

65 BRINGING THE ITALIAN MUSICIAN FRANCIS AL-
BERTI   Ibid., 70.

66 FAUQUIER DIED AT THE GOVERNOR'S PALACE
Ibid., 97.

66 REGRET THAT HIS SLAVES WOULD HAVE TO BE
SOLD   Ibid.

66 HE "MAY BECOME MORE USEFUL"   William and
Mary College Quarterly Historical Magazine,
VII, ed. Lyon G. Tyler (Richmond, Va., 1900),
174.

66 FAUQUIER'S BURIAL FIVE DAYS LATER   The Official Papers of Francis Fauquier, I (Charlottesville, Va., 1980), xxxviii.

66 "THE ABLEST MAN"   Jefferson, Writings, 33.

66 DETERMINED TO MAKE HIMSELF PLEASANT
JHT, I, 139.

67 "CHARMING, CHARMING!"   Ibid.

67 HAPPILY JOINED THEM   Ibid.

67 ON THE SAME DAY   The Virginia Gazette,
March 10, 1768.

67 THE NINTH INSTALLMENT   Ibid.

67 "LET US THEN TAKE ANOTHER STEP"   Milton
E. Flower, John Dickinson: Conservative Revolutionary (Charlottesville, Va., 1983), 66–67.

67 "LEVEL 250 FT. SQUARE"   GB, 12–13.

68 REPORTED THOMAS JEFFERSON'S ELECTION
JHT, I, 129–31.

68 THE TOWNSHEND ACTS   Morgan, Birth of the
Republic, 34–35.

69 A SENSE OF URGENCY   JHT, I, 134–37.

69 SUMMONED THE BURGESSES   Ibid., 136.

69 WALKED TO THE APOLLO ROOM   Ibid., 137.

69 LEAD BUST OF SIR WALTER RALEIGH   Tyler, **Williamsburg: Old Colonial Capital**, 233.

69 THE VIRGINIANS HAD A PLAN   **PTJ**, I, 27–31.

69 THEY WOULD NOT IMPORT OR CONSUME   Ibid. The signatories to this agreement pledged "to be frugal in the use and consumption of **British** manufactures" in the hope that "the merchants and manufacturers of **Great-Britain** may, from motives of interest, friendship, and justice, be engaged to exert themselves to obtain for us a redress of those grievances under which the trade and inhabitants of **America** at present labour." (Ibid., 28.) A provocative document, but in the spring of 1769 Jefferson, who signed it, and most of his colleagues were still far from revolution. In the Apollo Room after the adoption of the Nonimportation Resolutions, the assembled legislators drank toasts to the royal family, to Lord Botetourt, to "a speedy and lasting union between **Great-Britain** and her colonies," and to the author of the **Letters from a Farmer in Pennsylvania**. (Ibid., 31.) It was, to say the least, a confusing time.

70 ACCOMPANYING HIS MOTHER   Parton, **Life**, 99.

70 THE SLAVE REPLIED   **TDLTJ**, 43.

70 THE BURNED BOOKS   **PTJ**, I, 35.

70 "WOULD TO GOD"   Ibid.

71 DESPERATE, EVEN FRANTIC   Ibid., 34–38.

71 HE CONTEMPLATED MOVING   Ibid., 35. "If this conflagration, by which I am burned out of a

home," he said, "had come before I had advanced so far in preparing another, I do not know but I might have cherished some treasonable thoughts of leaving these my native hills." (Ibid.)

71 HE BLEAKLY ALLUDED TO IT   Ibid.

72 THE SUMMIT OF HIS MOUNTAIN   **GB,** 16–19.

72 CREATED AN ORCHARD   Ibid., 15. His thought was to build and move into a house he described to his uncle as "another habitation which I am about to erect, and on a plan so contracted as that I shall have but one spare bedchamber for whatever visitants I may have." He was ready for a demanding pace: "Nor have I reason to expect at any future day to pass a greater proportion of my time at home." What he called the "way to and from Williamsburg" was to be a familiar one. (**PTJ,** I, 24.)

72 "YOU BEAR YOUR MISFORTUNE"   **PTJ,** I, 38.

72 "CARRY ON, AND PRESERVE"   Ibid. John Page sensed, too, that Jefferson was applying his reading of the ancients to the destruction of a whole domestic world. "I have heard of your loss and heartily condole with you, but am much pleased with the philosophy you manifest." (Ibid.) As philosophical as Jefferson tried to be, the pain was still there, and his thoughts turned to other hearths and other lives. He idealized his brother-in-law's situation. Dabney Carr, he told Page, "speaks, thinks, and dreams of nothing but his young son. This friend of ours, Page, in a very small house, with a table, half a dozen chairs,

and one or two servants, is the happiest man in the universe." (Ibid., 36.)

72 AN ADVERTISEMENT JEFFERSON PLACED Ibid., 33.

73 WOULD OWN MORE THAN 600 SLAVES Stanton, **"Those Who Labor for My Happiness,"** 106. Writing of the difficulties of historical work on slavery at Monticello, Stanton noted: "To reconstruct the world of Monticello's African Americans is a challenging task. Only six images of men and women who lived there in slavery are known, and their own words are preserved in just four reminiscences and a handful of letters. Archaeological excavations are unearthing fascinating evidence of the material culture of Monticello's black families, and since 1993, steps have been taken to record the oral histories of their descendants. Without the direct testimony of most of the African American residents of Monticello, we must try to hear their voices in the sparse records of Jefferson's Farm Book and the often biased accounts and letters dealing with labor management and through the inherited memories of those who left Monticello for lives of freedom." (Ibid.) See also Cassandra Pybus, "Thomas Jefferson and Slavery," in Cogliano, ed., **A Companion to Thomas Jefferson,** 271–83. A new work is Henry Wiencek, **Master of the Mountain: Thomas Jefferson and His Slaves** (New York, 2012). Wiencek was kind to share a galley of his book with me; he offers a bracing

argument about Jefferson and slavery—one that is of a piece with my contention that Jefferson was driven to control and exert power over the world around him. "The regime at Monticello was far crueler than we have been led to believe; but more important, Jefferson's financial letters and accounts reveal his icy calculus of slavery's profits. He calculated he was getting a 4% increase in capital assets per year on the births of black children. He urged a neighbor to invest in slaves. He financed the rebuilding of Monticello with a $2,000 'slave-equity' loan from a Dutch banking house. Far from being stuck or ensnared in slavery, Jefferson embraced it. He modernized slavery, diversified it, industrialized it. Through him we can see why slavery survived the Revolution and how it emerged as a robust and adaptable component of the American economy." (Henry Wiencek to author, June 27, 2012.)

73 INHERITED 150   Stanton, "Those Who Labor for My Happiness," 106.

73 BOUGHT ROUGHLY 20   Ibid.

73 MOST OF THE OTHERS WERE BORN INTO SLAVERY ON HIS LANDS   Ibid.

73 FROM 1774 TO 1826   Ibid.

74 "I MADE ONE EFFORT"   Jefferson, Writings, 5.

74 CRAFTED A BILL   JHT, I, 121–22, and John C. Miller, The Wolf by the Ears: Thomas Jefferson and Slavery (Charlottesville, Va., 1991), 4–5.

74 UNILATERAL AUTHORITY TO FREE A SLAVE Miller, Wolf by the Ears, 4. Miller wrote: "For

half a century, manumission had been permitted only with the consent of the governor and council; Jefferson sought to give every slaveowner the right to free his slaves if he so desired." (Ibid.)

74 "MERITORIOUS SERVICES" Gordon-Reed, **Hemingses of Monticello,** 109. As Gordon-Reed wrote, the statute governing manumission, in effect since 1723, stated: "No negro, mulatto or Indian slaves shall be set free upon any pretense whatsoever, except for some meritorious services, to be adjudged and allowed by the governor and council." (Ibid.)

74 JEFFERSON ASKED RICHARD BLAND Miller, **Wolf by the Ears,** 5.

75 THE CASE OF SAMUEL HOWELL V. WADE NETHERLAND Ibid., 4–5. See also Gordon-Reed, **Hemingses of Monticello,** 99–101.

75 "EVERYONE COMES INTO" Gordon-Reed, **Hemingses of Monticello,** 100.

75 LOST THE CASE Miller, **Wolf by the Ears,** 5–6.

76 "I REFLECT OFTEN" **PTJ,** 35–36.

FIVE · A World of Desire and Denial

77 "HARMONY IN THE MARRIAGE" **PTJ,** XXX, 15.

77 "A LITHE AND EXQUISITELY" **TDLTJ,** 43.

77 "HER COMPLEXION WAS BRILLIANT" Randall, **Jefferson,** I, 63–64.

77 "GOOD SENSE AND GOOD NATURE" **PTJ,** I, 66.

77 ONE KINSMAN THOUGHT THE JEFFERSONS "A COUPLE" Ibid., 84. The kinsman was Robert

Skipwith, who married a sister of Martha's. By
the middle of 1771, Jefferson was writing Skipwith at the Forest: "Offer prayers for me too at
that shrine to which, tho' absent, I pay continual
devotion." (Ibid., 78.) In reply, on September 20,
1771, Skipwith said: "My sister Skelton, Jefferson I wish it were, with the greatest fund of good
nature has all that sprightliness and sensibility
which promises to ensure you the greatest happiness mortals are capable of enjoying." (Ibid., 84.)

78 "THE BEGINNINGS OF KNOWLEDGE" Parton,
Life, 128.

78 HE CONFIDED IN HER ABOUT POLITICS **PTJ,** I,
247.

78 PATTY'S "PASSIONATE ATTACHMENT" **TDLTJ,**
343.

78 JEFFERSON'S "CONDUCT AS A HUSBAND" Ibid.

78 PATTY ONCE COMPLAINED THAT SOME INSTANCE
Ibid.

78 "BUT IT WAS ALWAYS SO" Ibid.

78 LIKED HAVING HER WAY Kukla, **Mr. Jefferson's
Women,** 72.

78 JEFFERSON ONCE GENTLY REBUKED **TDLTJ,**
343.

78 "MY DEAR, A FAULT IN SO YOUNG" Ibid., 344.

78 "WARM GUSH OF GRATITUDE" Ibid.

79 "MY GRANDMOTHER JEFFERSON" TJF, http://
www.monticello.org/site/jefferson/martha-wayles
-skelton-jefferson (accessed 2012).

79 "MUCH BETTER . . . IF OUR COMPANION VIEWS A
THING" **PTJ,** XXX, 15.

79 HAD RISEN FAR IN VIRGINIA Gordon-Reed, **Hemingses of Monticello,** 57–90, is a brilliant, groundbreaking account of John Wayles's background in England, his life in Virginia, and his relationship with Elizabeth Hemings.

80 POOR, UNDISTINGUISHED FAMILY Ibid., 59.

80 THE CHILD LIVED BUT THE MOTHER DID NOT Ibid., 77. The first Mrs. Wayles lost a set of twins before giving birth to Patty. (Ibid.)

80 NEVER WANTED HER OWN CHILDREN TO FACE Ibid., 145. Gordon-Reed wrote: "Her reported words do not appear to have been motivated by a desire to die knowing that her husband would in some perverse way always belong just to her. This was not about him. It was about her children. She was concerned about the prospect of her daughters' growing up under the control of a woman who was not their mother." (Ibid.)

80 WAYLES WAS A DEBT COLLECTOR Ibid., 68–69.

80 "MR. WAYLES WAS A LAWYER" Jefferson, **Writings,** 5.

81 PROVOKED ANXIETY AMONG THE PLANTERS Gordon-Reed, **Hemingses of Monticello,** 69–71. One day Wayles was trying to track down Jefferson kinsman Thomas Mann Randolph only to be informed that Randolph had (conveniently, given the nature of Wayles's business) "gone to some springs on the frontiers to spend the summer." (Ibid.)

81 A MOCKING POEM Ibid., 74.

81 A CONTROVERSIAL MURDER TRIAL Ibid., 74–76.

In the frenzy of the hour, Wayles clearly had enemies with a motive to say the most extreme and negative things they could. He did, however, come from obscurity—there are suggestions in the written record that he arrived in America as a "servant boy" to a richer family—and debt collecting and slave trading were not considered entirely gentlemanly lines of work. (Ibid., 75.)

Understanding that he was not engaged in business calculated to endear him to the elite of his time and place—an elite to which he very much wanted to belong—Wayles had a political sense of his own. One of the things political people do (whether they are political in the vote-seeking sense or simply in the context of seeking status among one's neighbors) is take advantage of whatever avenue may be at hand. Along with the purchase and sale of slaves, the church was one of the most widely shared aspects of life among rich Virginians. Believers or not, prominent men—including Jefferson—were expected to play a role in the life of one's parish. Wayles apparently decided that he would assume such a role, thus building up social capital among those who may have seen him mainly as the face of the creditor enemy or as, in the words from **The Virginia Gazette,** "ill-bred." He took pains to help fill the pulpit on different occasions. (Ibid., 67.)

82 UNDERTOOK LEGAL WORK FOR WAYLES **MB,** I, 64.

82 MARRIED BATHURST SKELTON   JHT, I, 157.

82 AND THEIR SON, JOHN, DIED   TJF, http://www
.monticello.org/site/jefferson/martha-wayles-skel
ton-jefferson (accessed 2012).

82 AN ATTRACTIVE WIDOW   TDLTJ, 43.

82 SUITORS LURKED ABOUT   Ibid., 44.

82 QUESTIONS OF BLOOD, SEX, AND DOMINION   As
noted, Gordon-Reed, **Hemingses of Monticello,**
is the masterwork on this subject. I also learned
much from Lewis and Onuf, **Sally Hemings and
Thomas Jefferson;** Joshua D. Rothman, **Noto-
rious in the Neighborhood: Sex and Families
Across the Color Line in Virginia, 1787–1861**
(Chapel Hill, N.C., 2003); and Elise Lemire,
"Miscegenation": Making Race in America
(Philadelphia, 2002).

83 A MAN NAMED HEMINGS   Lewis and Onuf,
Sally Hemings and Thomas Jefferson, 255. The
source is Madison Hemings's oral history. See
also Gordon-Reed, **Hemingses of Monticello,**
49–50.

83 THE EPPES FAMILY OF BERMUDA HUNDRED
Gordon-Reed, **Hemingses of Monticello,** 50–51.

83 MOVED TO THE FOREST   Ibid., 57.

83 GAVE BIRTH TO SEVERAL CHILDREN   Ibid., 59.

83 HIS DAUGHTER'S TWO STEPMOTHERS   JHT, I,
432–33. Wayles's two other wives were Tabitha
Cocke and Elizabeth Lomax.

83 "TAKEN BY THE WIDOWER WAYLES"   Lewis and
Onuf, **Sally Hemings and Thomas Jefferson,**
255.

83 ELIZABETH HEMINGS BORE FIVE CHILDREN Gordon-Reed, **Hemingses of Monticello,** 80.

83 IN 1773 CAME A SIXTH Ibid.

84 "ANY LADY IS ABLE" Ibid., 346. As Gordon-Reed notes, the members of a white master's official family—that is, the one sanctioned by custom and law and the church—would pretend that the head of their household was not doing what he was self-evidently doing. And so mixed-race children lived in a cultural twilight in which they were denied yet fought over as white family members worried that guilt or love or duty (or all three) would lead the master to give his nonwhite children some part of his estate. (Ibid.)

84 THE YEAR HE TURNED UP **MB,** I, 209.

84 A "ROMANTIC, POETICAL" DESCRIPTION **PTJ,** I, 65.

84 AN ELDERLY WOMAN Ibid., 66.

84 DESTINED FOR EACH OTHER **TDLTJ,** 44.

86 "I HAVE WHAT I HAVE BEEN TOLD" **PTJ,** I, 62.

86 ORDERED A CLAVICHORD Ibid., 71.

86 "LET THE CASE BE" Ibid.

87 HALF-DOZEN WHITE SILK COTTON STOCKINGS Ibid., 71–72.

87 THE REVEREND WILLIAM COUTTS **MB,** I, 285. See also Gordon-Reed, **Hemingses of Monticello,** 101.

87 THE VIRGINIA GAZETTE REPORTED THE MARRIAGE **The Virginia Gazette,** January 2, 1772.

87 REFERRED TO HER AS A "SPINSTER" **PTJ**, I, 86–87.

88 BORN AT ONE O'CLOCK IN THE MORNING **MB**, I, 294.

88 THE JEFFERSONS REMAINED AT THE FOREST **GB**, 35.

88 SNOW HAD GROWN TOO DEEP Randall, **Jefferson**, I, 64.

88 PRESSED ON THROUGH THE FORESTS Ibid.

88 AT SUNSET Ibid.

88 FIRES WERE OUT Ibid.

89 "THE HORRIBLE DREARINESS" Ibid.

89 DISCOVERED PART OF A BOTTLE OF WINE Ibid., 65. On the subject of Monticello, Jefferson had been worried for some months about the seeming inadequacy of the nascent estate to receive a new bride. "I have here but one room, which, like the cobbler's, serves me for parlor for kitchen and hall," Jefferson said on Wednesday, February 20, 1771. "I may add, for bed chamber and study too. My friends sometimes take a temperate dinner with me and then retire to look for beds elsewhere. I have hopes however of getting more elbow room this summer." (**PTJ**, I, 63.) His vision for Monticello was mythic. "Come to the new Rowanty," he wrote in August 1771. "A spring, centrically situated, might be the scene of every evening's joy. There we should talk over the lessons of the day, or lose them in music, chess, or the merriments of our family companions. The heart thus lightened, our pillows would be

soft, and health and long life would attend the happy scene." (Ibid., 78.)

89 MOVED ON TO ELK HILL   MB, I, 286.

89 AT ITS PEAK ELK HILL WAS 669 ACRES   Ibid., 366.

89 "THE TENDER AND THE SUBLIME"   PTJ, I, 96.

89 OSSIAN'S EPIC IMAGERY   Thomas M. Curley, Samuel Johnson, the Ossian Fraud and the Celtic Revival in Great Britain and Ireland (New York, 2009) offers a full-scale treatment of the literary deception.

90 "AS TWO DARK STREAMS"   Jefferson's Literary Commonplace Book, ed. Douglas L. Wilson (Princeton, N.J., 1989), 142–43.

90 A CAREFUL HOUSEKEEPER   Scharff, Women Jefferson Loved, 93–94.

90 "MRS. JEFFERSON WOULD"   Bear, Jefferson at Monticello, 3.

91 A CALLER AT MONTICELLO   VTM, 8.

91 "COPIOUS AND WELL-CHOSEN"   Ibid.

91 "AS ALL VIRGINIANS"   Ibid., 9.

91 CARR DIED OF A "BILIOUS FEVER"   MB, I, 340.

92 SKETCHING OUT HIS PLANS   TDLTJ, 47.

93 JOHN WAYLES DIED   MB, I, 329.

93 TO MOVE ELIZABETH HEMINGS   Gordon-Reed, Hemingses of Monticello, 92.

94 THE HEMINGS FAMILY   See, for instance, ibid.; Lucia Stanton, Free Some Day: The African-American Families of Monticello (Charlottesville, Va., 2000); and TJF, http://www.mon

ticello.org/site/plantation-and-slavery/hemings
-family (accessed 2012).

SIX · Like a Shock of Electricity

96 "THE AMERICANS HAVE MADE A DISCOVERY" "Speech on Townshend Duties, 19 April 1769," **The Writings and Speeches of Edmund Burke,** II, ed. Paul Langford (Oxford, 1980), 231. See also Virginia History, Government, and Geography Service, **Road to Independence: Virginia 1763–1783** (Memphis, Tenn., 2010), 33.

99 "THINGS SEEM TO BE HURRYING"   **PTJ**, I, 111.

99 THE EARLY AFTERNOON HOURS Ibid., 104. Writing from Williamsburg, John Blair told Jefferson that there had been "a very moderate trembling of the earth [in Williamsburg], so moderate that not many perceived it, but Dr. Gilmer informs me it was a pretty smart shock with you." (Ibid.)

99 REPUTEDLY MENTALLY DISABLED SISTER Brodie, **Thomas Jefferson,** 48, 71.

99 A SPRINGTIME SNOWSTORM   **GB,** 55.

99 KILLED "ALMOST EVERYTHING"   Ibid.

99 "THIS FROST WAS GENERAL"   Ibid.

100 A SECOND DAUGHTER ON SUNDAY   **MB,** I, 372.

100 SHE HAD BEEN PREGNANT For accounts of the toll of childbirth on women in these years, see Catherine M. Scholten, " 'On the Importance of the Obstetrick Art': Changing Customs of

Childbirth in America, 1760 to 1825," **William and Mary Quarterly,** 3d ser., 34, no. 3 (July 1977): 426–45, and **Childbearing in American Society: 1650–1850** (New York, 1985), 42–49; Mary Beth Norton, **Liberty's Daughters: The Revolutionary Experience of American Women, 1750–1800** (Ithaca, N.Y., 1996), 71–84; Judith Walzer Leavitt, **Brought to Bed: Childbearing in America, 1750 to 1950** (New York, 1986), 36–63; Marie Jenkins Schwartz, **Birthing a Slave: Motherhood and Medicine in the Antebellum South** (Cambridge, Mass., 2006), 143–86.

100 THE PURCHASE OF "BREAST PIPES" Scharff, **Women Jefferson Loved,** 93. See also **MB,** I, 373.

101 THE TOWNSHEND ACTS Morgan, **Birth of the Republic,** 34–35.

101 THE BOSTON TEA PARTY Middlekauff, **Glorious Cause,** 231–37.

101 NONIMPORTATION AGREEMENTS **PTJ,** I, 27–31, is one example.

101 THE POSSIBLE ARREST OF AMERICANS Middlekauff, **Glorious Cause,** 219–20. In 1772, New England radicals had burned a British ship on customs duty, the HMS **Gaspee,** after it had run aground in Narragansett Bay. When no one was arrested in the case, London announced a special investigation and said that anyone apprehended in the matter would be tried in England. For the colonists the decree was infuriating and terrifying. Here was a grave imperial threat. (Ibid.)

101 COMMITTEES OF CORRESPONDENCE   Ibid., 221.

101 HE ORDERED A "ROBE"   Imogene E. Brown, **American Aristides,** 86.

102 "OUR SALE OF SLAVES GOES"   **PTJ,** I, 96.

102 TO REBEL QUITE ANOTHER   Isaac Samuel Harrell, **Loyalism in Virginia: Chapters in the Economic History of the Revolution** (Durham, N.C., 1926), 1. It was not a clear-cut call. "Despite the events of the preceding decade, in 1773 loyalism was the logical state of mind in Virginia; loyalism called for the maintenance of the long established social, religious, and political order," wrote Harrell. "In religion, in social customs, in personal contact, Virginia, of all the colonies in North America, was most closely akin to the mother country." (Ibid.) In terms of Virginia's predominant position, Harrell believed the March 1773 session, which was prorogued, to be "the beginning of the end" of royal rule. (Ibid., 30–31.)

Middlekauff, **Glorious Cause,** 30–52, offers an intriguing account of the roots of revolution. "Why these Americans engaged in revolution had much to do with the sort of people they were." (Ibid., 31.) Middlekauff argued that the combination of the Protestant emphasis on the centrality of the individual and the Whig sense of history created the climate for revolution. (Ibid., 30–52.)

For Jefferson, whether it was Crown or Parliament, the consistent theme was usurpation.

Even Loyalists were willing to acknowledge London bore some blame; their point was that the constitution could, with effort, be brought back into balance. For example, in June and July 1774, in William Rind's **Virginia Gazette**, Thomson Mason, brother of George, argued that the English constitution was "the wisest system of legislation that ever did, or perhaps ever will, exist." To Mason, the "monarchy, aristocracy, and democracy [each] possessed of their distinct powers, checked, tempered, and improved each other. . . . The honor of the monarchy tempered the impetuosity of democracy, the moderation of aristocracy checked the ardent aspiring honor of monarchy, and the virtue of democracy restrained the one, impelled the other, and invigorated both." (Virginia History, Government, and Geography Service, **Road to Independence,** 37.) The problem, Mason said, was that the aristocracy had knocked the system off balance by usurping power through Parliament.

Looking back from the perspective of 1926, Charles M. Andrews also argued that the central motivation came from rivalries between the colonial assemblies and Parliament:

Primarily, the American Revolution was a political and constitutional movement and only secondarily one that was either financial, commercial, or social. At bottom the fundamental issue was the political inde-

pendence of the colonies, and in the last
analysis the conflict lay between the British Parliament and the colonial assemblies,
each of which was probably more sensitive,
self-conscious, and self-important than was
the voting population that it represented.
For many years these assemblies had fought
the prerogative successfully and would have
continued to do so, eventually reducing it
to a minimum, as the later self-governing
dominions have done; but in the end it was
Parliament, whose powers they disputed,
that became the great antagonist. (Andrews,
"American Revolution," 230.)

Reflecting on the American Revolution from
the perspective of 1790, William Smith, Jr., the
New York-born chief justice of Canada, wrote
Lord Dorchester:

The truth is that the country had outgrown
its government, and wanted the true remedy
for more than half a century before the rup-
ture commenced. . . . To expect wisdom and
moderation from near a score of petty Par-
liaments, consisting in effect of only one of
the three necessary branches of a Parliament,
must, after the light brought by experience,
appear to have been a very extravagant expectation. . . . An American Assembly, quiet
in the weakness of their infancy, could not

but discover in their elevation to prosperity, that themselves were the substance, and the governor and Board of Council were shadows in their political frame. All America was thus, at the very outset of the plantations, abandoned to democracy. And it belonged to the Administrations of the days of our fathers to have found the cure, in the erection of a Power upon the continent itself, to control all its own little republics, and create a Partner in the Legislation of the Empire, capable of consulting their own safety and the common welfare. (Sir Charles Prestwood Lucas, **A History of Canada, 1763–1812** [Oxford, 1909], 256.)

Proposals for reconciliation were considered but none really seemed practicable. The most prominent was that of Joseph Galloway. (Middlekauff, **Glorious Cause,** 257–58.) And there was John Randolph's, described and reprinted in Mary Beth Norton, "John Randolph's 'Plan of Accommodations,' " **William and Mary Quarterly,** 3d ser., 28, no. 1 (January 1971): 103–20.

102 HIS COUSIN JOHN RANDOLPH Samuel Willard Crompton, "Randolph, John," February 2000, American National Biography Online, http://www.anb.org/articles/01/01–00767.html (accessed 2011). In London, Mary Beth Norton wrote, John Randolph was "one of the most active and respected refugees, playing a major role

in each of the three organizations formed by the American exiles. In 1779 he was selected to present to George III a petition on the American war signed by 105 loyalists; a few months later he led a group of loyalists who offered their services to the king in the event of a French invasion of Great Britain; and in 1783 he was named chairman of the committee established by Virginia refugees to review the property claims they intended to submit to the British government." (Norton, "John Randolph's 'Plan of Accommodations,' " 104.) For more on Loyalists and the Revolution, see Wilbur H. Siebert, "The Dispersion of the American Tories" in Wright, **Causes and Consequences of the American Revolution,** 249–58; Harrell, **Loyalism in Virginia;** Richard Archer, **As If an Enemy's Country: The British Occupation of Boston and the Origins of Revolution** (New York, 2010); Thomas B. Allen, **Tories: Fighting for the King in America's First Civil War** (New York, 2010); and Paul H. Smith, "The American Loyalists: Notes on Their Organization and Numerical Strength," **William and Mary Quarterly,** 3d ser., 25, no. 2 (April 1968): 259–77.

102 ABOUT A FIFTH OF WHITE AMERICAN COLONISTS Gordon S. Wood, **American Revolution,** 113. The usual figure for the number of Loyalists in America during the Revolution is a third, but recent scholarship based on militia recruitment puts the estimate at closer to a fifth. Sixty to

eighty thousand Loyalists left America during the war. (Ibid.) I am indebted to Wood for insights on this point.

102 "Non solum nobis" MB, I, 37.

102 For the elite, revolution was Michael A. McDonnell, **The Politics of War: Race, Class, and Conflict in Revolutionary Virginia** (Chapel Hill, N.C., 2007), 1–15, delineates the tensions that divided Virginians by class before and during the war. "The way patriot leaders organized for war and reacted to the demands of those they expected to fight it depicts a conservative, anxious, sometimes fearful group clinging to traditional notions of hierarchy, deference, and public virtue in an attempt to maintain its privileged position within an increasingly challenged and challenging social and political culture," McDonnell wrote. (Ibid., 6.)

103 Virginia's public finances Harrell, **Loyalism in Virginia,** 22–25.

103 The money that planters owed creditors Ibid., 26–29.

103 Such debts were now "hereditary" Ibid., 26.

103 Virginians owed at least Ibid.

103 Nearly half the total Ibid.

103 In May 1774, Jefferson and Patrick Henry Ibid., 26–27. The measure failed, Harrell wrote, because the "conservatives . . . were not yet ready for the leadership of these radicals. In October, 1777, when the principles of rifle democracy were

supreme, a law was passed which provided in part for the sequestration of these debts." (Ibid., 27.)

103 JOHN WAYLES DIED IN 1773 Sloan, **Principle and Interest,** 14.

103 ESTATE WORTH £30,000 Ibid.

103 LARGEST CREDITOR, FARELL AND JONES Ibid. There was also a contested £6,000 charge against Wayles over a shipment of slaves. (Ibid., 14.)

103 DECIDED TO BREAK UP Ibid., 15.

103 JEFFERSON'S LIABILITY Ibid., 16.

103 WAS NOT SOLELY ECONOMIC The economic issues at play in the Revolution are, of course, a subject of long and ferocious debate. The "progressive interpretation" (or the "Beardian interpretation" after the historian Charles Beard), can be summarized, as Esmond Wright pointed out in 1966, with the following quotation from Louis M. Hacker: "The struggle was not over high-sounding political and constitutional concepts: over the power of taxation and, in the final analysis, over natural rights: but over colonial manufacturing, wild lands and furs, sugar, wine, tea and English merchant capitalism within the imperial-colonial frame-currency, all of which meant, simply, the survival or collapse of work of the mercantilist system." (Wright, **Causes and Consequences of the American Revolution,** 114–15.) Arthur M. Schlesinger, Sr., offered a more nuanced view, arguing that the emphasis of interpretation should be on "the clashing of economic interests and the interplay

of mutual prejudices, opposing ideals and personal antagonisms—whether in England or in America—which made inevitable in 1776 what was unthinkable in 1760." (Ibid., 103.) For selections of Hacker's and Schlesinger's arguments, see ibid., 103–42.

My own view is that economics clearly—even self-evidently—played a critical role for Jefferson and many others. It would be folly to deny this, for arguments about power and rights are obviously of a piece with matters of property and wealth. I do not believe, however, that the American Revolution was only about the rich preserving their riches. Harrell (to whom I am indebted for his work on this subject in relation to Virginia) put it well, noting that pointing out the economic factors was not to

> underestimate the political theories involved in the American Revolution, to question the devotion of Washington, the patriotism of Henry, or the political astuteness of Jefferson. But an examination of the constitutional principles that appealed to leading citizens does not afford a complete explanation of the momentous movement which transformed Virginia, the most ultra-British colony in North America, into a staunch supporter of the Revolutionary doctrines. Lands to the west, claimed by Virginia under charters, won from France partly by Virginia men and

with Virginia money, and sorely needed by
Virginia in 1775, were being exploited by
an irresponsive government—bartered and
pawned to court favorites, politicians, and
speculators. The rapid contraction of the
currency to meet the demands of the British trading interests and the ruinous trend
of Virginia exchange accentuated the diverse
economic interests of the colony and the
mother country. The planters were hopelessly in debt to the British merchants. Current political theories in the colonies and
the economic interests of the planters were
in harmony. (Harrell, **Loyalism in Virginia,**
28–29.)

Also illuminating is Jack P. Greene, "William
Knox's Explanation for the American Revolution," **William and Mary Quarterly,** 3d ser., 30,
no. 2 (April 1973): 293–306.

104 BEFORE 1729, NO ROYAL GOVERNOR   Harrell,
Loyalism in Virginia, 4. I am indebted to Harrell for these statistics.

104 GOVERNORS INTERVENED FEWER THAN   Ibid.

105 BETWEEN 1764 AND 1773, THERE WERE   Ibid.

105 ANNOUNCED THE BOSTON PORT ACT   **PTJ,** I,
106.

105 AGREED "WE MUST BOLDLY"   Ibid.

105 JOINED JEFFERSON IN THE CAPITOL'S COUNCIL
CHAMBER   Ibid.

105 "WE WERE UNDER [THE] CONVICTION"   Ibid.

"No example of such a solemnity had existed since the days of our distresses in '55, since which a new generation had grown up," Jefferson said, alluding to a difficult period in the French and Indian War.

107 "RUMMAGED" THROUGH RUSHWORTH'S COLLECTION   Ibid.

107 "COOKED UP A RESOLUTION"   Ibid.

107 FROM "THE EVILS OF CIVIL WAR"   Ibid. The proclamation passed on Tuesday the twenty-fourth; on Thursday the twenty-sixth, Lord Dunmore called the House to the Council Room where the document had originated. The governor was direct. "I have in my hand a paper published by order of your House, conceived in such terms as reflect highly upon his Majesty and the Parliament of Great Britain; which makes it necessary for me to dissolve you; and you are dissolved accordingly." (Ibid.) Off the burgesses went to the Raleigh, from which, on May 27, 1774, they called for a "general congress . . . to deliberate on those general measures which the united interests of America may from time to time require." (Ibid., 108.)

Then, on Sunday the twenty-ninth, came a plea from Boston: All the colonies, Massachusetts hoped, would join in what amounted to an economic boycott of Great Britain through nonimportation and nonexportation agreements. (Ibid., 110.) At ten o'clock on Monday morning, Peyton Randolph summoned the remaining burgesses to the Raleigh (there were, both the resolution and **The Virginia Gazette** reported, twenty-five still in the area), where the group chose a moderate course. Under Randolph's leadership, the Virginians said they would schedule a meeting of "the late Members of the House of Burgesses" for August 1. An "Association against Importations," the Monday caucus said, would "probably be entered into" once enough burgesses arrived back in Williamsburg, and "perhaps against Exportations also after a certain time." (Ibid.) With so many burgesses out of town, the remaining legislators could not risk the appearance of usurpation nor were they yet ready to contemplate all-out war. On that day in late May 1774, Peyton Randolph, Thomas Jefferson, George Washington, and others were declining to commit themselves until they absolutely had to. The exports—tobacco, really—were the key. To end that trade would cost Virginia untold economic and political pain. Before leaving Williamsburg, Jefferson added his name to the call for the August 1 meeting: "We fixed this distant day in hopes of accommodating the meeting to every gentleman's private affairs, and that they might, in the meantime, have an opportunity of collecting the sense of their respective counties." (Ibid., 111.)

107 AWARE OF THE STAKES   Ibid., 111.

107 MONTICELLO'S CHERRIES HAD RIPENED   **GB,** 55.

107 A LETTER TO THEIR CONSTITUENTS PTJ, I, 116–17.

107 THE REVEREND CHARLES CLAY Ibid., 117.

107 "THE NEW CHURCH" ON THE HARDWARE RIVER Ibid., 116.

108 THE "PLACE . . . THOUGHT THE MOST" Ibid.

108 "THE PEOPLE MET GENERALLY" Jefferson, **Writings**, 9.

108 THE FREEHOLDERS OF ALBEMARLE PTJ, I, 117–19.

108 COMPOSED BY JEFFERSON Ibid., 119.

108 "THE COMMON RIGHTS OF MANKIND" Ibid., 117.

108 "WE WILL EVER BE READY" Ibid.

108 AN IMMEDIATE BAN Ibid., 117–18. As he drafted the Albemarle resolutions he also wrote a proposed Declaration of Rights for the approaching August 1 meeting. (Ibid., 119–20.)

109 FRESH CUCUMBERS AND LETTUCE **GB**, 56.

109 INSTRUCTIONS TO THE DELEGATES PTJ, I, 121–37. See also Anthony M. Lewis, "Jefferson's 'Summary View' as a Chart of Political Union," **William and Mary Quarterly**, 3d ser., 5, no. 1 (January 1948): 34–51. Kristofer Ray, "Thomas Jefferson and 'A Summary View of the Rights of British North America,'" in Cogliano, ed., **A Companion to Thomas Jefferson**, 32–43, is also valuable.

109 WITH THESE PAGES PTJ, I, 121–37.

109 "THAT OUR ANCESTORS" Jefferson, **Writings**, 105–6.

109 CONCLUDED WITH A PASSAGE Ibid., 121.

110 "IT IS NEITHER OUR WISH" Ibid., 121–22.

110 STRICKEN WITH DYSENTERY Ibid., 9.

110 WITH TWO COPIES Ibid.

111 THANKS TO CLEMENTINA Martha J. King, "Rind, Clementina"; http://www.anb.org/articles/01-01143.html; **American National Biography Online** Feb. 2000 (accessed 2012).

111 THE ASSEMBLED BURGESSES APPLAUDED **PTJ**, I, 671.

111 HAND-PULLED PRESS Colonial Williamsburg Foundation, http://www.history.org/almanack/life/trades/tradepri.cfm (accessed 2012).

111 "WITHOUT THE KNOWLEDGE" **PTJ**, I, 672.

111 "IT IS THE INDISPENSABLE DUTY" Ibid.

111 GEORGE WASHINGTON PAID 3s 9d Ibid.

112 LOANED HIS TO WILLIAM PRESTON Ibid.

112 URGING HIM TO READ "THE ENCLOSED" Ibid.

112 TOO STARKLY FOR SOME AT THAT HOUR Randall, **Jefferson,** I, 90. See also Hayes, **Road to Monticello,** 159. One man was apparently unimpressed: Patrick Henry. "Whether Mr. Henry disapproved the ground taken, or was too lazy to read it (for he was the laziest man in reading I ever knew) I never learned; but he communicated it to nobody," wrote Jefferson. (Jefferson, **Writings,** 9.) In the way of politics, the **Summary View**'s most immediate practical use for Virginia lay in the fact that it was not adopted; it instead served as a warning. "It will evince to the world the moderation of our late convention,

who have only touched with tenderness many of the claims insisted on in this pamphlet, though every heart acknowledged their justice," read the editors' preface of Jefferson's pamphlet. Translation: Take care, Your Majesty, for things could be worse. (**PTJ**, I, 672.)

Still, in private, Jefferson was furious that his draft had had so little impact at Williamsburg. Using the language of the General Confession of Sin in the Anglican Book of Common Prayer, he said: "We have done those things which we ought not to have done. And we have not done those things which we ought to have done." Writing on a copy of the final "Instructions" as passed, Jefferson was merciless, listing four technical "defects" on the import/export question. More broadly, he was unhappy with the failure of rhetoric and what was to his mind a fatal political flaw. "The American grievances are not defined," he wrote. Without them, he believed, such a document lost potency. Looking ahead to the Continental Congress about to assemble in Philadelphia, he wrote: "We are to conform to such resolutions only of the Congress as our deputies assent to: which totally destroys that union of conduct in the several colonies which was the very purpose of calling a Congress." (Ibid., 143.)

112 ADDED TO A BILL OF ATTAINDER IN LONDON Jefferson, **Writings**, 10. See also **JHT**, I, 189–90.

113 "DEATH IS THE WORST" **Jefferson's Literary**

Commonplace Book, 87. See also Garrett Ward Sheldon, **The Political Philosophy of Thomas Jefferson** (Baltimore, Md., 1993), 19–21.

114 "A VERY HANDSOME PUBLIC PAPER" Randall, **Jefferson,** I, 188.

SEVEN · There Is No Peace

115 "BLOWS MUST DECIDE" John Ferling, **Almost a Miracle: The American Victory in the War of Independence** (New York, 2009), 28.

115 THE PEACH TREES WERE BLOSSOMING GB, 66. Jefferson noted the blossoms on March 10, 1775. (Ibid.)

115 PREPARING TO LEAVE FOR RICHMOND MB, I, 392.

115 ST. JOHN'S JHT, I, 194. See also Mayer, **Son of Thunder,** 241. The church, Henry Mayer wrote, was "a spare wooden building with a peaked roof and squat belfry." (Ibid.)

115 A HILLTOP WOODEN ANGLICAN CHURCH Virginia Writers' Project, **Virginia: A Guide to the Old Dominion** (Richmond, Va., 1992), Virginia State Library and Archives. See also Lewis W. Burton, **Annals of Henrico Parish** (Richmond, Va., 1904), 18–19.

115 THE LARGEST STRUCTURE IN RICHMOND Robert Douthat Meade, **Patrick Henry: Practical Revolutionary** (Philadelphia, 1969), 17–18.

115 SAT BEHIND THE COMMUNION RAIL Burton, **Annals of Henrico Parish,** 22.

116 THE TOUGH-MINDED, SCOTTISH-BORN Benjamin Quarles, "Lord Dunmore as Liberator," **William and Mary Quarterly,** 3d ser., 15, no. 4 (October 1958): 494–507.

116 HAD FORBIDDEN VIRGINIANS John E. Selby, **The Revolution in Virginia, 1775–1783** (Williamsburg, Va., 1988), 1–2.

116 NEITHER SIDE SHOWED JHT, I, 194. Militia were also forming across Virginia. (Ibid.)

116 WARM ENOUGH FOR THE WINDOWS Meade, **Patrick Henry,** 23.

116 CALLED ON VIRGINIA Mayer, **Son of Thunder,** 243–47.

116 STANDING IN PEW 47 Burton, **Annals of Henrico Parish,** 23–24.

116 THE EASTERN AISLE Ibid. Henry "stood, according to tradition, near the present corner of the east transept and the nave, or more exactly, as it is commonly stated, in pew 47, in the east aisle of the nave, the third one from the transept aisle. He . . . faced the eastern wall of the transept, where were then two windows." (Ibid.)

116 "GENTLEMEN MAY CRY" Mayer, **Son of Thunder,** 245.

117 "HIS ELOQUENCE WAS PECULIAR" **The Writings and Speeches of Daniel Webster,** XVII, ed. Fletcher Webster (Boston, 1903), 367.

117 A COMMITTEE THAT INCLUDED JEFFERSON **JHT,** I, 195.

117 THE COMMITTEE RESOLVED **PTJ,** I, 161. In Richmond, Jefferson also wrote a resolution au-

thorizing the creation of a committee to investigate Lord Dunmore's March 21 proclamation on lands, writing George Wythe, who was in Williamsburg, for counsel. (Ibid., 115–16, 162–63.)

118 POSSIBLE FISSURES   Ibid., 159.

118 DRINKING AT MRS. YOUNGHUSBAND'S   MB, I, 392.

118 DINING AT GUNN'S   Ibid.

118 BUYING BOOK MUSLIN   Ibid.

118 ELECTED AS A DEPUTY   Ibid. He was to serve if, as expected, Peyton Randolph had to be in Richmond for the revision of the Virginia constitution. (Ibid.)

118 THE FIRST CONGRESS HAD BEEN CALLED "America During the Age of Revolution, 1764–1775," LOC, http://memory.loc.gov/ammem/collections/continental/timeline1e.html (accessed 2012). See also Jack N. Rakove, **The Beginnings of National Politics: An Interpretive History of the Continental Congress** (New York, 1979).

118 BRITISH TROOPS TOOK CONTROL OF POWDER MAGAZINES   Middlekauff, **Glorious Cause,** 270. "During the autumn and winter [Gage] had received a series of surprises which persuaded him that only force could bring the Americans to heel," Middlekauff wrote. (Ibid.)

118 "FORCE," THE GOVERNMENT ADVISED GAGE   Ibid., 272.

119 LEAVE VIRGINIA IN "EVIDENT DANGER"   PTJ, I, 160.

119 AT LEXINGTON AND CONCORD   Middlekauff,

Glorious Cause, 273–81. See also George F. Scheer and Hugh F. Rankin, **Rebels and Redcoats** (New York, 1957), 17–40.

119 A SHIFTING SIXTEEN-MILE FRONT Middlekauff, **Glorious Cause,** 279.

119 273 BRITISH AND 95 AMERICAN CASUALTIES Ibid.

119 THE EXACT SEQUENCE OF THE BATTLE IS UNCLEAR Ibid., 276.

119 ANY "LAST HOPES OF RECONCILIATION" Ibid., 281. See also **PTJ,** I, 165.

119 "A FRENZY OF REVENGE" Middlekauff, **Glorious Cause,** 279.

119 "THE FLAME OF CIVIL WAR" Scheer and Rankin, **Rebels and Redcoats,** 45.

119 CONTENDING WITH SLAVE VIOLENCE McDonnell, **Politics of War,** 47–53. See also Quarles, "Lord Dunmore as Liberator."

119 SUPPLIES OF GUNPOWDER McDonnell, **Politics of War,** 49–50.

120 WHITES WERE "ALARMED" Ibid., 47.

120 IN NORTHUMBERLAND COUNTY Ibid., 49.

120 AS THURSDAY, APRIL 20, 1775 Ibid., 52–54.

120 ROYAL MARINES REMOVED FIFTEEN HALF BARRELS Ibid.

120 A FURIOUS CROWD OF COLONISTS Ibid. Peyton Randolph and others won some time before violence could break out by convincing the Virginians to allow a delegation to confront Dunmore for an explanation. (Ibid.)

120 AT THE PALACE, DUNMORE ANNOUNCED Ibid.

120 "ONE OF THE HIGHEST INSULTS" Ibid.

120 "UNDER THE MUSKETS" Ibid.

120 TWO DAYS LATER DUNMORE ARRESTED Ibid.

120 ANNOUNCED THAT "BY THE LIVING GOD" Ibid., 55. Dunmore also said he would rally "a majority of white people and all the slaves on the side of the government." (Ibid.)

121 SWIFT AND PREDICTABLE Ibid., 56. According to McDonnell, Dunmore, with some evident satisfaction, said: "My declaration that I would arm and set free such slaves as should assist me if I was attacked has stirred up fears in them which cannot easily subside." (Ibid.)

121 "HELL ITSELF" Quarles, "Lord Dunmore as Liberator," 495. Of Dunmore, George Washington wrote to Richard Henry Lee: "If that man is not crushed before spring, he will become the most formidable enemy America has; his strength will increase as a snow ball by rolling: and faster, if some expedient cannot be hit upon, to convince the slaves and servants of the impotency of his designs." (Ibid.)

Just how impotent those designs were was now the prevailing question. Jefferson was worried enough to speculate on how to evacuate his clan. On December 2, 1775, John Hancock called on Washington to "effectually repel [Dunmore's] violences and secure the peace and safety of that colony." On December 4 the Congress as a whole urged Virginia to resist the governor "to the utmost." (Ibid.)

121 "But for God's sake" **PTJ**, I, 167. He lined out the sentence in a draft of the letter. (Ibid.)

121 "Within this week" Ibid., 165.

121 seemed to doom Ibid.

121 the militia declared McDonnell, **Politics of War,** 61–62.

122 the particular manifestation In a section of the letter he composed but deleted from the version he sent to Small, Jefferson said:

> It is a lamentable thing that the persons entrusted by the king with the administration of government should have kept their employers under . . . constant delusion. It appears now by their letters laid before the Parliament that from the beginning they have labored to make the ministry believe that the whole ferment has been raised and constantly kept up by a few ~~hot headed demagogues~~ principal men in every colony, and that it might be expected to subside in a short time either of itself, or by the assistance of a coercive power. The reverse of this is most assuredly the truth: the utmost efforts of the more intelligent people having been requisite and exerted to moderate the almost ungovernable fury of the people. That the abler part has been pushed forward to support their rights in the field of reason is true; and it was there alone they wished to decide the contest. (**PTJ**, I, 166–67.)

Jefferson thought "principal men" such as himself could ultimately control the Virginians. There was no central command, however, and different counties dispatched—or threatened to dispatch—troops to Williamsburg. Dunmore took no chances, sending his wife and children to live on board the HMS **Fowey.** (McDonnell, **Politics of War,** 61–62, 73–74.) Jefferson also held the king responsible for the haughty tone and tough tactics of the British. "It is a lamentable circumstance that the only mediatory power acknowledged by both parties"—that is, George III—"instead of leading to a reconciliation [of] his divided people, should pursue the incendiary purpose of still blowing up the flames as we find him constantly doing in every speech and public declaration," Jefferson wrote Small. "This may perhaps be intended to intimidate into acquiescence, but the effect has been unfortunately otherwise." (**PTJ,** I, 165.)

122 "A LITTLE KNOWLEDGE" **PTJ,** I, 165–66.

122 A SPIRITED SESSION McDonnell, **Politics of War,** 71. They were there at Dunmore's invitation—or, more precisely, at the invitation of Lord North's ministry, which had directed each colonial governor to convene the local legislatures. The business at hand: Consideration of conciliatory proposals from North. London was asking that the colonists contribute toward the common defense and the support of the imperial government in each colony. In exchange, Britain

would not tax the colonists for these services beyond the initial amount. (Ibid.)

122 CONCILIATORY PROPOSALS   Ibid.

122 THREE VIRGINIA COLONISTS   Ibid., 72–73.

122 DUNMORE FELT THE SITUATION   Ibid., 73. Dunmore said that his "house was kept in continual alarm and threatened every night with an assault." (Ibid.)

122 SEEKING REFUGE ABOARD THE HMS **Fowey** Quarles, "Lord Dunmore as Liberator," 497.

123 A MEASURED TONE   **PTJ**, I, 170–74.

123 AS JEFFERSON RECALLED IT   Jefferson, **Writings**, 10–11.

123 PEYTON RANDOLPH, WHO BELIEVED   Ibid., 11. Randolph was just back from Philadelphia, where the sense of the Continental Congress opposed London's proposals. It would be useful, then, for Virginia to be in the forefront of the movement against the overtures. Randolph, Jefferson said, "was anxious that the answer of our assembly . . . should harmonize with what he knew to be the sentiments and wishes of the body he had recently left." (Ibid.)

124 "LONG AND DOUBTFUL"   Ibid.

124 UNITY AMONG THE COLONIES   **PTJ**, I, 173. In closing, Jefferson asked: "What then remains to be done?" Virginia deferred the matter to the Congress in Philadelphia, praying for "the even-handed justice of that being who doth no wrong, earnestly beseeching him to illuminate the coun-

cils and prosper the endeavors of those to whom America hath confided her hopes." (Ibid.)

EIGHT · The Famous Mr. Jefferson

125 "As our enemies have found"   PTJ, I, 186.

125 "The present crisis"   Ibid., 224.

125 Lodging on Chestnut   MB, I, 399.

125 sent accounts of the military situation   PTJ, I, 246–47.

125 Benjamin Franklin's proposal   Ibid., 177–82.

125 recorded the "Financial and Military"   Ibid., 182–84.

126 new ideas, new people, new forces   For portraits of Philadelphia as it was in these years, see McCullough, **John Adams**, 78–85; and Paul H. Smith, ed., **Letters of Delegates to Congress, 1774–1789, IV, May 16-August 15, 1776** (Washington, D.C., 1976), 123–24; 194–95; 307–8; 311–12.

126 were "a people, thrown together"   United States National Park Service, **Independence: A Guide to Independence National Historical Park, Philadelphia, Pennsylvania** (Washington, D.C., 1982), 20.

126 "The poorest laborer"   Ibid. America's connection to larger forces was also self-evident. "French vessels frequently arrive here," wrote Josiah Bartlett, a delegate from New Hampshire. "Two came up to this city yesterday, their

loading chiefly cotton, molasses, sugar, coffee, canvass etc. Last Saturday an American vessel arrived from the French West Indies with 7400 lb. of powder, 149 stand of arms." (Paul H. Smith, **Letters of Delegates to Congress**, IV, 124.)

127 JOHN ADAMS OF MASSACHUSETTS **PTJ**, I, 175. Jefferson reported Washington's selection as what he called "Generalissimo of all the Provincial troops in North-America," adding: "The Congress have directed 20,000 men to be raised and hope by a vigorous campaign to dispose our enemies to treaty." (Ibid.) See also Scheer and Rankin, **Redcoats and Rebels,** 68–73. As Adams described the nomination, "Mr. Washington, who happened to sit near the door, as soon as he heard me allude to him, from his usual modesty, darted into the library-room." (Ibid., 70–71.)

127 THE BATTLE AT BUNKER HILL Scheer and Rankin, **Redcoats and Rebels,** 52–64.

127 RECORDED SEEING "THE FAMOUS MR. JEFFERSON" Hayes, **Road to Monticello**, 167.

127 "JEFFERSON IS THE GREATEST" Kaminski, **Founders on the Founders,** 286.

127 ADAMS AND JEFFERSON See, for instance, McCullough, **John Adams**, 110–17; Ferling, **Adams vs. Jefferson**; and Lester J. Cappon, ed., **The Adams-Jefferson Letters: The Complete Correspondence Between Thomas Jefferson and Abigail and John Adams** (Chapel Hill, N.C., 1987), for accounts of the relationship be-

tween the two men, and between Jefferson and Abigail Adams and their larger families.

128 BORN IN BRAINTREE, MASSACHUSETTS, IN 1735 McCullough, **John Adams,** 30.

128 "I CONSIDER YOU AND HIM" Ibid., 604.

128 AN INTENSE ADMIRATION He had already personally contributed toward the support of Boston during the Port Act siege (**MB,** I, 396), but now his appreciation rose to a new level. "The adventurous genius and intrepidity of those people is amazing," Jefferson said of the New Englanders in early July 1775. (**PTJ,** I, 185.)

129 CONGRESS AUTHORIZED AN INVASION OF CANADA Middlekauff, **Glorious Cause,** 309–14. From the Declaration of Causes: "We have received certain intelligence that General Carleton, the Governor of Canada, is instigating the people of that province and the Indians to fall upon us; and we have but too much reason to apprehend that schemes have been formed to excite domestic enemies against us." (**PTJ,** I, 217.)

129 MONTREAL SURRENDERED BUT QUEBEC HELD OUT Paul S. Boyer and Melvyn Dubofsky, eds., **The Oxford Companion to United States History** (New York, 2001) 285.

129 "NOBODY NOW ENTERTAINS" **PTJ,** I, 186.

129 JEFFERSON AND JOHN DICKINSON **MB,** I, 400. See also **PTJ,** I, 187–219.

130 DECLARATION OF THE CAUSES **PTJ,** I, 187–219. The audience was a trans-atlantic one. Jefferson

argued that America was not the aggressor and that all was not yet lost. Americans, he said, "mean not in any wise to affect that union with [Great Britain] in which we have so long and so happily lived, and which we wish so much to see again restored." (Pauline Maier, **American Scripture: Making the Declaration of Independence** [New York, 1997], 19–20.) They did not wish to "disquiet the minds of our Friends and fellow subjects in any part of the empire." He offered a triptych of declarative assertions to support his case: "We did not embody a soldiery to commit aggression on them; we did not raise armies for glory or for conquest. We did not invade their island carrying death or slavery to its inhabitants." Americans took up arms in defense only, Jefferson said, and longed for a reconciliation to "deliver us from the evils of a civil war." (**PTJ**, I, 203.)

130 RODE THE FERRY TO THE WOODLANDS **MB**, I, 401.

130 MADE A TRIP TO THE FALLS Ibid., 403.

130 EXTENDED ITS HAND TO THE KING **PTJ**, I, 219–23.

130 "ELOQUENCE IN PUBLIC ASSEMBLIES" Kaminski, **Founders on the Founders**, 287.

131 "A PUBLIC SPEAKER" Ibid.

131 "FEW PERSONS CAN BEAR" Ibid.

131 "THE CONTINUANCE AND THE EXTENT" **PTJ**, I, 223–24.

132 FACED A "DEFICIENCY" Ibid., 224.

132 AFTER A VISIT TO ROBERT BELL'S SHOP **MB**, I, 402.

132 LEFT PHILADELPHIA FOR VIRGINIA Ibid., 403–4.

132 STOPPED ALONG THE ROAD Ibid.

133 "FOR GOD'S SAKE" Morgan, **Virginians at Home,** 50.

133 NEVER STOPPED HUMMING Bear, **Jefferson at Monticello,** 13.

133 AN AEOLIAN HARP **MB**, I, 28.

133 "MRS. JEFFERSON WAS SMALL" Bear, **Jefferson at Monticello,** 5.

133 SUPERVISING THE SLAUGHTER OF DUCKS Stein, **Worlds of Thomas Jefferson at Monticello,** 15–16.

133 MANAGED THE SLAVES IN THE HOUSE Ibid., 16.

134 "THE HOUSE WAS BUILT" Ibid., 14.

134 HE ACQUIRED A CHESSBOARD Jefferson bought books, he bought clothes, he bought tickets to plays—then he bought punch at the playhouse. He spent money to make himself handsome, comfortable, entertained, and engaged. **MB**, I, 28, records the examples here, and the Memorandum Books and **PTJ**—as well as the extant collections at Monticello—record a life of acquisition and consumption.

134 "A COPIOUS AND WELL-CHOSEN" Stein, **Worlds of Thomas Jefferson at Monticello,** 14.

134 HIS ARCHITECTURAL SENSE **MB**, I, 24.

134 THE PAINTING SCHEME Ibid., 27.

134 ORDERED A COPY Ibid., 35.

134 SENT FOR A CLOTHESPRESS   Ibid., 29.

135 JOINED THE PHILOSOPHICAL SOCIETY   Ibid., 338–39. See also Ibid., 525.

135 PUBLISHED A BOOK   Ibid., 341.

135 HIS KINSMAN JOHN RANDOLPH   **PTJ**, I, 240–43. For details on John Randolph's violin, see Hayes, **Road to Monticello**, 104, and **MB**, I, 77.

135 WAS FASCINATED BY GARDENING   TJF, http://www.monticello.org/site/houses-and-gardens/jefferson-scientist-and-gardener (accessed 2012).

135 EXPRESSING REGRET   **PTJ**, I, 241. Jefferson cast the issue in personal terms. "There may be people to whose tempers and dispositions contention may be pleasing. . . . But to me it is of all states but one the most horrid." He added: "My first wish is a restoration of our just rights; my second a return of the happy period when, consistently with duty, I may withdraw myself totally from the public stage and pass the rest of my days in domestic ease and tranquility, banishing every desire of afterwards even hearing what passes in the world." (Ibid.) The longing for withdrawal was something of a conventional trope for public men in the eighteenth century, men whose idealized model of service was that of Cincinnatus, the Roman general who was summoned, reluctantly, to power from his plow.

136 CONCENTRATED WITHIN "A SMALL FACTION"   Ibid.

136 "THEY HAVE TAKEN IT"   Ibid. "Even those in Parliament who are called friends to America

seem to know nothing of our real determinations," he told Randolph. The British seemed to think that Americans "did not mean to insist rigorously on the terms they held out," said Jefferson, but "continuance in this error may perhaps have very ill consequences." In fact, the offer of the Congress of 1774 amounted to "the lowest terms they thought possible to be accepted in order to convince the world they were not unreasonable." Those conditions, however, had been set out "before blood was spilt." Now Jefferson could make no promises. "I cannot affirm, but have reason to think, these terms would not now be accepted," he told Randolph. (Ibid.) Jefferson also made bold to suggest that Britain's imperial destiny might be in the balance. "If indeed Great Britain, disjoined from her colonies, be a match for the most potent nations of Europe with the colonies thrown into their scale, they may go on securely," he told Randolph. "But if they are not assured of this, it would be certainly unwise, by trying the event of another campaign, to risk our accepting a foreign aid which perhaps may not be obtainable but on a condition of everlasting avulsion from Great Britain." (Ibid., 242.)

136 DRAFTED BUT DELETED   Ibid., 243. Yet he remained defiant, telling Randolph that he would "lend my hand to sink the whole island in the ocean" if Britain did not satisfy American demands. (Ibid., 242.) The conflict felt inescapably personal, for the North Atlantic world was

a comparatively small one. After a trip to London in 1772, Alexander McCaul, a merchant friend, wrote Jefferson: "I saw several of our old Virginia friends and on the Change of London you would meet with many faces you had seen before." There was an assumption of enduring common ties. "It is happy for the natives of Britain [that] they have such a resource as North America, for there, if they happen to be reduced, they may always have bread with industry," McCaul wrote Jefferson. "The Virginia planters may thank their stars they have so good a country to cultivate, though many of them are not sensible of the happiness they enjoy." (Ibid., 93.)

137 TO USE HIS DEPARTING KINSMAN   Ibid.

137 PARTED ON A WARM NOTE   Ibid., 242–43.

138 "THOUGH WE MAY POLITICALLY DIFFER"   Ibid., 244.

138 2ND EARL OF DARTMOUTH   Ibid., 243.

138 HIS DAUGHTER JANE   Randall, **Jefferson**, I, 383.

138 ONLY A YEAR AND A HALF OLD   Ibid. According to Jefferson's notes in his Book of Common Prayer, Jane was born on April 3, 1774, and died in September 1775. (Ibid.)

138 ON CHESTNUT STREET   **MB**, I, 407.

139 "I HAVE SET APART"   **PTJ**, I, 251.

139 "I HAVE NEVER RECEIVED"   Ibid., 252.

139 CANNONS EN ROUTE   Ibid., 247.

139 COMING "AT THE EXPRESS"   Ibid. The British, Jefferson reported to Francis Eppes, had a

continental strategy ready. Ten thousand more troops—raised from the garrison at Gibraltar and from Ireland—were due in the spring. While in control of New York, Albany, St. John's, and Quebec they would use their naval vessels as communication channels to keep these cities and Boston in contact. The feared effect, according to Jefferson: The British would "distress us on every side acting in concert with one another." (Ibid.)

139 AT ROXBOROUGH, THE COUNTRY HOUSE MB, I, 407.

140 RANDOLPH SUFFERED A STROKE Ibid.

140 "OUR MOST WORTHY SPEAKER" PTJ, I, 268.

140 AT HAMPTON, NEAR NORFOLK Ibid., 249.

140 THE BRITISH TRIED TO LAND Ibid.

140 UNDERTAKING EXPEDITIONS AGAINST CANADA Ibid. See also Middlekauff, Glorious Cause, 309–14. "We are all impatience to hear from Canada," said Robert Carter Nicholas on November 10, 1775. (PTJ, I, 256.)

141 CREATED A COMMITTEE OF SAFETY McDonnell, Politics of War, 92–97. The committee's duties, McDonnell noted, included the "sole power to direct the movement of the army and to call out the minutemen and militia into service, to call for assistance from other colonies, and to purchase any arms outside the colony. All officers in every branch of the armed forces were specifically ordered to obey the Committee of Safety; no military officers whatsoever could sit

on it." (Ibid., 97.) See also Middlekauff, **Glorious Cause,** 565–66.

141 THE ELEVEN MONTHS PRECEDING THE DECLARATION   In August, Jefferson had written John Randolph that he "would rather be in dependence on Great Britain, properly limited, than on any nation upon earth, or than on no nation." (**PTJ,** I, 242.) The flummoxing phrase, though, was "properly limited": What did that mean? As 1775 fell away, month by month, to stand alone as a nation was not yet the chief desire of Jefferson's heart, or of the broad American public's. (See Maier, **American Scripture,** 21.) So what happened? George III and Lord Dunmore, two men cloaked in the ancient authority of the Old World, chose this season to assert themselves in ways that proved inflammatory and decisive. On Thursday, October 26, 1775, George III told Parliament that the American course was "manifestly carried on for the purpose of establishing an independent Empire." It was a "desperate conspiracy" whose "authors and supporters . . . meant only to amuse, by vague expressions of attachment to the parent State, and the strongest protestations of loyalty to me, whilst they were preparing for a general revolt." (Ibid.) London now intended "to put a speedy end to these disorders by the most decisive exertions." The words gave the king's unhappy subjects no apparent opening for negotiation, and little reason to think that they might avert total

war. (Ibid.) And then Dunmore struck in Virginia.

141 DEPREDATIONS OF A SUPERIOR MILITARY FORCE
PTJ, I, 260. "Former labors in various public
employments now appear as recreations compared with the present," Edmund Pendleton
wrote. (Ibid.)

141 "WE CARE NOT FOR OUR TOWNS" Ibid., 259.
Page continued: "I have not moved many of my
things away—indeed nothing but my papers,
a few books, and some necessaries for housekeeping. I can declare without boasting that I
feel such indignation against the authors of our
grievances and the scoundrel pirates in our rivers and such concern for the public at large that
I have not and cannot think of my own puny
person and insignificant affairs." (Ibid.)

142 FROM HIS SHIPBOARD QUARTERS Quarles,
"Lord Dunmore as Liberator," 494.

142 DECLARED MARTIAL LAW McDonnell, **The
Politics of War,** 134.

142 ANY SLAVE OR INDENTURED SERVANT Ibid.
Dunmore proclaimed: "And I do hereby further
declare all indented servants, Negroes, or others
(appertaining to the Rebels,) free that are able
and willing to bear arms [and join] His Majesty's Troops, as soon as may be, for the more
speedily reducing this Colony to a proper sense
of their duty, to His Majesty's crown and dignity." (Ibid.)

142 SAW THEIR MOST FEVERED PTJ, I, 266–67. In

a letter to the Virginia delegates in Philadelphia, Robert Carter Nicholas wrote of "the unhappy situation of our country." It was worse than ever, Nicholas said: "A few days since was handed to us from Norfolk Ld. D's infamous proclamation, declaring the law martial in force throughout this colony and offering freedom to such of our slaves, as would join him." Dunmore allies were "plying up the rivers, plundering plantations and using every art to seduce the negroes. The person of no man in the colony is safe, when marked out as an object of their vengeance; unless he is immediately under the protection of our little army." (Ibid.)

142 "I HAVE WRITTEN TO PATTY" Ibid., 264.

143 SWEPT UP AND DOWN Quarles, "Lord Dunmore as Liberator," 494–97. On December 8, 1775, Edward Rutledge wrote that Dunmore's proclamation had done "more effectually to work an eternal separation between Great Britain and the Colonies, than any other expedient, which could possibly have been thought of." (Ibid., 495.)

143 "FOR GOD'S SAKE" PTJ, I, 265–66.

143 "SOME RASCALS, ALL FOREIGNERS" Ibid., 271.

143 "NO COUNTRY EVER REQUIRED" Ibid., 268. Jefferson was committed to doing all he could to prepare for the worst. For him, the period between the end of August, when he wrote John Randolph his calculated letter about American determination, and late November was

one of unremitting strife. Sitting down to write Randolph again on November 29, 1775, three months after his first charming message, Jefferson held out less hope that there was anything London might do to reach reconciliation.

He opened with a rosy account of American success in Canada, noting "in a short time we have reason to hope the delegates of Canada will join us in Congress and complete the American Union as far as we wish to have it completed." He then turned to Dunmore, blaming him for the violence in Virginia. "You will have heard before this reaches you that Lord Dunmore has commenced hostilities in Virginia," Jefferson wrote. "That people bore with everything till he attempted to burn the town of Hampton. They opposed and repelled him with considerable loss on his side and none on ours. It has raised our country into [a] perfect frenzy." He spoke of George III. "It is an immense misfortune to the whole empire to have a king of such a disposition at such a time. We are told and everything proves it true that he is the bitterest enemy we have. His minister is able, and that satisfies me that ignorance or wickedness somewhere controls him." Unlike August, this time Jefferson's message was more militant. "Believe me, Dear Sir, there is not in the British empire a man who more cordially loves a Union with Great Britain than I do," he said. "But by the God that made me I will cease to exist before I yield to a connection on such terms as the British Parliament propose and in this I think I speak the sentiments of America. We want neither inducement nor power to declare and assert a separation. It is will alone which is wanting and that is growing apace under the fostering hand of our king." (Ibid., 269.)

143 NAMED TO A COMMITTEE Ibid., 272–75.

144 "THE CONTINENTAL FORCES BY SEA AND LAND" Ibid., 272.

144 ETHAN ALLEN HAD BEEN CAPTURED Ibid., 276–77.

144 "WE DEPLORE THE EVENT" Ibid., 276.

144 CONGRESS DEFERRED ANY DECISION Ibid., 277.

144 LEAVING PHILADELPHIA MB, I, 411.

145 OPENED A CASK OF 1770 MADEIRA Ibid., 413.

145 WAS SENT A NEW PAMPHLET PTJ, I, 286.

145 "THE CAUSE OF AMERICA" Craig Nelson, **Thomas Paine: Enlightenment, Revolution, and the Birth of Modern Nations** (New York, 2006), 85.

NINE · The Course of Human Events

146 "FOR GOD'S SAKE" PTJ, I, 287.

146 THE BELLS RUNG Harlow Giles Unger, **John Hancock: Merchant King and American Patriot** (New York, 2000), 242.

146 ABOUT SEVEN O'CLOCK MB, I, 415.

146 ASKED THE REVEREND CHARLES CLAY Ibid.

146 BURIED AT MONTICELLO Kern, **Jeffersons at Shadwell**, 243–44.

147 AN "ATTACK OF MY PERIODICAL HEADACHE" **TDLTJ**, 184.

147 HE WAS "OBLIGED TO AVOID READING" **PTJ**, VI, 570.

148 STRANGE TIME Ibid., I, 287. A week after his mother's death, Jefferson received letters from Williamsburg about declaring independence. "The notion of independency seems to spread fast in this colony," said James McClurg on April 6, 1776. (Ibid.)

148 LIVED WITH THE HEADACHE Ibid., 296.

148 PAYING A MIDWIFE TO DELIVER **MB**, I, 416.

148 COLLECTING MONEY Ibid.

148 LEFT MONTICELLO FOR PHILADELPHIA Ibid., 417.

148 ARRIVING SEVEN DAYS LATER Ibid., 418.

148 "I AM HERE" **PTJ**, I, 292.

148 ON MAY 23 HE TOOK Ibid., 293. See also **MB**, I, 418.

148 THREE-STORY HOUSE Thomas Donaldson, **The House in Which Thomas Jefferson Wrote the Declaration of Independence** (Philadelphia, 1898), examines the sundry claims of different houses but concludes Graff's establishment was home to Jefferson as he wrote. For details about the house, see John H. Hazelton, **The Declaration of Independence: Its History** (New York, 1970), 149–54.

148 HE INITIALLY FELT OUT OF PHASE PTJ, I, 293. "I have been so long out of the political world that I am almost a new man in it," Jefferson wrote Page on May 17, 1776. (Ibid.) But he knew this: Not every colony was in the same place in terms of its determination to declare independence, an irrevocable step. Foreign alliances were essential to the success of the American cause, and "for [independence] several colonies, and some of them weighty, are not yet quite ripe. I hope ours is and that they will tell us so." (Ibid., 294.)

148 THAT THE "UNITED COLONIES" Ibid., 298–99.

149 BEGAN THE NEXT DAY Ibid., 309.

149 SOME REPRESENTATIVES ARGUED Ibid. Jefferson heard John Dickinson and James Wilson of Pennsylvania, Robert Livingston of New York, Edward Rutledge of South Carolina, and others argue for delay. The chief issue lay with the middle colonies—Pennsylvania, Maryland, Delaware, New Jersey, and New York. (South Carolina, too, was reluctant.) Recording the thrust of the argument, Jefferson wrote that they said the time was not yet right, for they believed the Congress should not "take any capital step till the voice of the people drove us into it." (Ibid.) The reaction had been bad enough the previous month with John Adams's May 15 resolution "for suppressing the exercise of all powers derived from the crown [which] had shown, by the ferment into which it had thrown these middle colonies, that they had not yet accom-

modated their minds to a separation from the mother country." (Ibid.)

149 A PRECIPITOUS DECLARATION   Ibid., 309–10.

149 "FOREIGN POWERS WOULD"   Ibid., 310. There was an even darker possibility: How could the Congress be confident that Britain's rivals would be inclined to throw themselves in the balance with a newly independent America? Surely, the anti-declaration members suggested, "France and Spain had reason to be jealous of that rising power which would one day certainly strip them of all their American possessions," which could mean that "it was more likely they should form a connection with the British court, who, if they should find themselves unable otherwise to extricate themselves from their difficulties, would agree to a partition of our territories, restoring Canada to France, and the Floridas to Spain, to accomplish for themselves a recovery of these colonies." (Ibid.)

149 JOHN ADAMS, RICHARD HENRY LEE, GEORGE WYTHE   Ibid., 311.

149 "NO GENTLEMAN"   Ibid. Arguing that the only truly problematic colonies were Pennsylvania and Maryland, the pro-declaration delegates suggested "the backwardness of these two colonies might be ascribed partly to the influence of proprietary power and connections, and partly to their having not yet been attacked by the enemy." (Ibid., 312.)

149 A COMPROMISE WAS PROPOSED   Ibid., 313.

Adams, Wythe, Lee, and their allies were practical men. Understanding how quickly opinion was moving, they did not try to force their will on the Congress—at least not that day.

149 WERE "NOT YET MATURED" Ibid.

150 ADAMS THOUGHT JEFFERSON SHOULD DO IT Kaminiski, **Founders on the Founders,** 287–88.

150 A SECRET CONVERSATION Hazelton, **Declaration of Independence,** 9–11.

150 "WE WERE ALL SUSPECTED" Ibid., 10.

151 "THIS WAS PLAIN DEALING" **The Works of John Adams,** II, ed. Charles Francis Adams (Boston, 1856), 513.

152 "YOU INQUIRE WHY SO YOUNG A MAN" Ibid.

153 THE ENSUING CONVERSATION WITH JEFFERSON Ibid.

154 WAS "NOT TO FIND OUT" TJ to Henry Lee, May 8, 1825. Extract published at Papers of Thomas Jefferson Retirement Series Digital Archive, http://www.monticello.org/familyletters (accessed 2011).

154 AT JACOB GRAFF'S HOUSE Hazelton, **Declaration of Independence,** 149–51. Robert G. Parkinson, "The Declaration of Independence," in Cogliano, ed., **A Companion to Thomas Jefferson,** 44–59, is a valuable essay; it is particularly good on the (necessarily, given the practical demands of the political moment) collaborative nature of the writing of the Declaration.

154 A SMALL WOODEN DESK http://americanhistory

.si.edu/collections/object.cfm?key=35&objkey =8968 (accessed 2012).

154 "Neither aiming at originality" TJ to Henry Lee, May 8, 1825. Extract published at Papers of Thomas Jefferson Retirement Series Digital Archive, http://www.monticello.org/fam ilyletters (accessed 2011).

154 "When in the course of human events" PTJ, I, 315, 413–33.

155 "self-evident" was Benjamin Franklin's Isaacson, Benjamin Franklin, 312.

156 be sent "to the several assemblies" Maier, American Scripture, 130.

156 Constituencies included readers Ibid., 130–32.

156 some of which were obscure Ibid., 107.

156 Jefferson's influences were manifold See, for instance, Maier, American Scripture; Garry Wills, Inventing America: Jefferson's Declaration of Independence (Garden City, N.Y., 1978); and Carl Becker, The Declaration of Independence: A Study in the History of Political Ideas (New York, 1970).

156 James Wilson's pamphlet Hatzenbuehler, "Growing Weary in Well-Doing," 12–14.

156 George Mason's Declaration of Rights Ibid., 14–20.

156 "The enclosed paper" PTJ, I, 404.

156 whose gout and boils Isaacson, Benjamin Franklin, 310.

157 "A MEETING WE ACCORDINGLY HAD" The Works of John Adams, II, ed. Charles Francis Adams, 514.

157 INTRODUCED ON FRIDAY, JUNE 28 PTJ, I, 313–14.

157 "THE PUSILLANIMOUS IDEA" Ibid., 314.

158 "THE CLAUSE, TOO, REPROBATING" Ibid., 314–15.

158 HE FAIRLY WRITHED Isaacson, Benjamin Franklin, 313.

158 FRANKLIN TRIED TO SOOTHE HIS YOUNG COLLEAGUE Ibid. Franklin deployed an old anecdote about a hatmaker who had wanted a sign that read "John Thompson, hatter, makes and sells hats for ready money," with a picture of a hat. His friends so pecked away at the sign it wound up with only the hatmaker's name and the picture of a hat. (Ibid.)

158 "I HAVE MADE IT A RULE" Ibid., 310.

159 "POLITICS AS WELL AS RELIGION" Randall, Jefferson, I, 177–78

159 VOTED TO ADOPT THE RESOLUTION William Hogeland, Declaration: The Nine Tumultuous Weeks When America Became Independent, May 1-July 4, 1776 (New York, 2012), 173.

159 THE TEMPERATURE WAS 76 JHT, I, 229.

159 RECORDED PURCHASES Ibid.

159 OVERNIGHT THE PHILADELPHIA PRINTER JOHN DUNLAP "Transcript of Publishing the Declaration of Independence," LOC, http://www.loc

.gov/rr/program/journey/declaration-transcript.html (accessed 2012).

159 BENJAMIN TOWNE, PUBLISHER OF THE PENNSYLVANIA EVENING POST Ibid.

159 THE NEWS WAS ANNOUNCED Ibid.

159 IN FRONT OF THE STATE HOUSE Hogeland, **Declaration**, 179.

159 "GOD BLESS THE FREE STATES" Ibid.

159 HORSEFLIES BUZZED THROUGH Parton, **Life**, 191.

160 "THE SILK-STOCKINGED LEGS" Ibid.

160 JEFFERSON LOVED THE STORY Randall, **Jefferson**, I, 153.

160 "GERRY, WHEN THE HANGING COMES" Ibid.

160 "A THEATRICAL SHOW" Kaminski, **Founders on the Founders**, 315.

160 "JEFFERSON RAN AWAY" Ibid.

160 BENTHAM SCOFFED David Armitage, **The Declaration of Independence: A Global History** (Cambridge, Mass., 2007), 173–86, reprints the text of Bentham's "Short Review of the Declaration," which was originally published in London in 1776.

161 "ABSURD AND VISIONARY" Ibid., 173.

161 " 'ALL MEN' " Ibid., 174.

161 "YOU WILL JUDGE" **PTJ**, I, 456. The colleague was Richard Henry Lee. In reply, Lee said that he wished "the manuscript had not been mangled as it is. It is wonderful, and passing pitiful, that the rage of change should be so unhappily

applied. However the **thing** is in its nature so good, that no cookery can spoil the dish for the palates of freemen." (Ibid., 471.)

161 "I AM HIGHLY PLEASED" Ibid., 470. See also Robert M. S. McDonald, "Thomas Jefferson's Changing Reputation as Author of the Declaration of Independence: The First Fifty Years," **Journal of the Early Republic** 19, no. 2 (Summer, 1999): 169–95.

TEN · The Pull of Duty

162 "I PRAY YOU TO COME" **PTJ,** I, 477.

162 "REBELLION TO TYRANTS" Ibid., 677–79.

162 SUFFERED A DISASTROUS MISCARRIAGE Scharff, **Women Jefferson Loved,** 118. By now Patty's health was a perennial issue for Jefferson. "I am sorry the situation of my domestic affairs renders it indispensably necessary that I should solicit the substitution of some other person here in my room," Jefferson wrote on June 30, 1776. "The delicacy of the House will not require me to enter minutely into the private causes which render this necessary: I trust they will be satisfied I would not have urged it again were it not necessary." (**PTJ,** I, 408.)

162 "I WISH I COULD" **PTJ,** I, 458.

163 "A FAVORITE WITH" TJF, http://www.monti cello.org/site/jefferson/martha-wayles-skelton -jefferson (accessed 2012).

163 THE ONSLAUGHT OF MILITARY REPORTS   PTJ, I, 433–74.

163 FRAUGHT WITH FEARS   Ibid., 475–76, describes the case of Carter Braxton, a Virginia politician who had fallen from popular favor. Braxton's wife's family, the Corbins, held sympathies for the Crown. Rumors in Williamsburg, William Fleming reported to Jefferson, alleged unspecified instances of "extreme[ly] imprudent, and inimical conduct" on the part of Mrs. Braxton, which "affected his political character exceedingly." (Ibid., 475.) The conduct appears to have been remarks protesting the imprisonment of a brother in Williamsburg. (Alonzo Thomas Dill, **Carter Braxton, Virginia Signer: A Conservative in Revolt** [Lanham, Md., 1983], 69–73.)

164 A LOYALIST PLOT IN NEW YORK   Ibid., 412–13. "One fact is known of necessity, that one of the General's lifeguard being thoroughly convicted was to be shot last Saturday," wrote Jefferson on July 1. (Ibid., 412.)

164 THE MAYOR OF NEW YORK   Chernow, **Washington,** 903–4.

164 THE BRITISH, MEANWHILE, WERE   PTJ, I, 412. "General Howe with some ships (we know not how many) is arrived at the Hook, and, as is said, has landed some horse on the Jersey shore," wrote Jefferson. (Ibid.)

164 "OUR CAMPS RECRUIT SLOWLY"   Ibid., 477. There was a delay in the flow of British troops

to serve under Howe, but Jefferson noted that "our army [in] Canada" was "in a shattered condition." He was frustrated by the pace of the Congress's post-declaration business of forming a government. "The minutiae of the Confederation have hitherto engaged us; the great points of representation, boundaries, taxation etc being left open," he told Lee. It was time, he said, for Lee to relieve him. "For God's sake, for your country's sake, and for my sake, come." (Ibid.) There was one welcome piece of news from Virginia: the defeat of Dunmore at Gwynn's Island. "This was a glorious affair," John Page told Jefferson on July 15, 1776. "Lord Dunmore has had a most complete Drubbing." (Ibid., 462.) Richard Henry Lee cheered the "disgrace of our African Hero at Gwynn's Island." (Ibid., 471.)

164 "It is a painful situation" Ibid., 412.

164 "If any doubt" Ibid., 412–13. The vicissitudes of politics were much in evidence, and the defeat of two Virginia delegates for reelection to the Congress troubled some observers. "We are now engaged beyond the power of withdrawing, and I think cannot fail of success in happiness, if we do not defeat ourselves by intrigue and canvassing to be uppermost in offices of power and lucre," Edmund Pendleton wrote Jefferson. There was, Pendleton said, "much of this" in the sessions at Williamsburg in which Benjamin Harrison and Carter Braxton were denied new terms. (Ibid., 471–72.) Harrison was eliminated for fairly mun-

dane reasons: He had championed the appointment of an official physician opposed by another
faction, and his foes took him out. (Ibid., 475.)

165 A WAR WITH THE CHEROKEES Anthony F. C.
Wallace, **Jefferson and the Indians: The Tragic
Fate of the First Americans** (Cambridge, Mass.,
1999), 54–60.

165 JEFFERSON'S VIEWS OF NATIVE AMERICANS
Ibid., 1–20, offers a good overview. See also Francis Paul Prucha, **The Great Father: The United
States Government and the American Indians**,
I (Lincoln, Neb., 1984), 5–88, for an account
of the colonial, revolutionary, and early post-
revolutionary periods. Jefferson believed Indians
more capable than blacks. (Jefferson, **Writings**,
266.) "The Indians . . . will often carve figures
on their pipes not destitute of design and merit,"
Jefferson wrote in Query XIV of **Notes on the
State of Virginia.** "They will crayon out an animal, a plant, or a country, so as to prove the existence of a germ in their minds which only wants
cultivation. They astonish you with strokes of
the most sublime oratory; such as to prove their
reason and sentiment strong, their imagination
glowing and elevated. But never yet could I find
that a black had uttered thought above the level
of plain narration; never see even an elementary
trait of painting or sculpture." (Ibid.) See also
Andrew Cayton, "Thomas Jefferson and Native
Americans," in Cogliano, ed., **A Companion to
Thomas Jefferson**, 237–52.

165 A GENUINE CURIOSITY Jefferson, **Writings,** 218–29.

165 "NOTHING WILL REDUCE" **PTJ,** I, 485–86.

166 A PROPOSED CONSTITUTION FOR VIRGINIA Ibid., 329–86.

166 HE CLOSELY FOLLOWED THE CONGRESS'S DEBATES Jefferson, **Writings,** 24–32.

166 "THE ARTICLES OF CONFEDERATION" Ibid., 24.

166 DRAFT RULES OF PROCEDURE FOR THE CONGRESS **PTJ,** I, 456–58.

166 HE AND JOHN ADAMS ONCE DISAGREED McCullough, **John Adams,** 113–14.

167 "I RECEIVE BY EVERY POST" **PTJ,** I, 477.

167 A POSTSCRIPT BEGGING LEE Ibid. The next day, writing John Page, he said: "I purpose to leave this place the 11th of August, having so advised Mrs. Jefferson by last post, and every letter brings me such an account of the state of her health, that it is with great pain I can stay here till then." (Ibid., 483.) Lee was delayed, preventing Jefferson from keeping his promise to Patty to leave on August 11. (Ibid., 486.)

167 TO KEEP VIRGINIA'S QUORUM Ibid., 483.

167 "I AM UNDER THE PAINFUL NECESSITY" Ibid., 486. There was some talk that Patty was on the mend. "I wish you as pleasant a journey as the season will admit," wrote Edmund Pendleton, "and hope you'll find Mrs. Jefferson recovered, as I had the pleasure of hearing in Goochland she was better." (Ibid., 508.)

167 A SEAL FOR THE NEW NATION Ibid., 494–97.

168 "Pharaoh sitting in an open chariot" Ibid., 495.

168 So why did the colonists   I am indebted to **EOL**; J. G. A. Pocock, **The Machiavellian Moment: Florentine Political Thought and the Atlantic Republican Tradition** (Princeton, N.J., 1975); Joyce Oldham Appleby, **Liberalism and Republicanism in the Historical Imagination** (Cambridge, Mass., 1992); and Wood, **Radicalism of the American Revolution.**

171 longed to be in the thick of shaping the government   **PTJ**, I, 292.

171 her frequent pregnancies   Gordon-Reed, **Hemingses of Monticello**, 141–43.

171 "I hope you'll get cured"   **PTJ**, I, 489.

172 to use the Wythe house   Ibid., 585.

172 the handsome brick house   Colonial Williamsburg Foundation, http://www.history.org/almanack/places/hb/hbwythe.cfm (accessed 2011).

ELEVEN · An Agenda for Liberty

175 "Those who expect"   Thomas Paine, **The American Crisis**, No. 4, September 11, 1777.

177 "It is error alone"   Jefferson, **Writings**, 286.

177 chose to entrust the mission   **PTJ**, I, 521–22.

177 Russia might dispatch   Ibid., 522.

177 "to acquaint me"   Ibid., 523.

177 asked the messenger to await   Ibid., 524. The messenger bearing Hancock's letter arrived

on October 8, 1776; Jefferson's reply to Hancock is dated October 11. (Ibid.)

177 PATTY COULD BE WITH HIM   Ibid., 604. See also **MB**, I, 426.

178 "IT WOULD ARGUE"   **PTJ**, I, 524.

179 "NO CARES FOR MY OWN PERSON"   Ibid. Jefferson was so anxious about missing out on the service in France that he told Silas Deane, who was to serve with Franklin, "I feel within myself the same kind of desire of an hour's conversation with yourself or Dr. Franklin which I have often had for a confabulation with those who have passed the irredeemable bourne." (Ibid., II, 25.) By framing the matter in such terms—equating time with Deane and Franklin with unobtainable time with the dead—he invested the work in France with the highest possible meaning, equal to his love for his parents, his sister Jane, Dabney Carr, Peyton Randolph, and his lost children. He felt the loss of the French opportunity that deeply.

180 A REMARKABLE LEGISLATIVE AGENDA FOR LIBERTY   **JHT**, I, 235–85.

180 "THE STRENGTH OF THE GENERAL PULSE"   Randall, **Jefferson**, I, 199.

180 A STRIKE AGAINST ENTAIL   **JHT**, I, 247–60. "To annul this privilege, and instead of an aristocracy of wealth . . . to make an opening for the aristocracy of virtue and talent . . . was deemed essential to a well-ordered republic," Jefferson said. "To effect it, no violence was necessary, no

deprivation of natural right, but rather an enlargement of it by a repeal of the law. For this would authorize the present holder to divide the property among his children equally, as his affections were divided; and would place them, by natural generation, on the level of their fellow citizens." (Jefferson, **Writings**, 32–33.)

181 "A DISTINCT SET OF FAMILIES" Jefferson, **Writings**, 32.

181 ALTERING CRIMINAL JUSTICE Ibid., 270.

181 GENERAL PUBLIC EDUCATION Randall, **Jefferson**, I, 223–26.

181 THE NATURALIZATION OF THE FOREIGN-BORN Ibid., 202.

181 A NEWCOMER ON THE POLITICAL SCENE Ibid., 198.

181 BORN IN 1751 For background on Madison, see Ralph Ketcham, **James Madison: A Biography** (Charlottesville, Va., 1990). Richard Brookhiser, **James Madison** (New York, 2011), is an interesting recent work, as is Andrew Burstein and Nancy Isenberg, **Madison and Jefferson** (New York, 2010).

181 MADISON "ACQUIRED A HABIT" Randall, **Jefferson**, I, 198.

182 "BUT A WITHERED LITTLE APPLE-JOHN" "James Madison," The White House, http://www.white house.gov/about/presidents/jamesmadison (accessed 2012).

182 "NEVER WANDERING FROM" Randall, **Jefferson**, I, 198.

182 FREEDOM OF RELIGION   PTJ, I, 525–58.

182 HAD BECOME A READER   Thomas Jefferson, **Jefferson's Extracts from the Gospels: "The Philosophy of Jesus" and "The Life and Morals of Jesus,"** ed. Dickinson W. Adams and Ruth W. Lester (Princeton, N.J., 1983). I have long found the introduction to this volume essential reading on the subject of Jefferson and religion. See also Eugene R. Sheridan, **Jefferson and Religion** (Charlottesville, Va., 1998); Paul K. Conkin, "The Religious Pilgrimage of Thomas Jefferson," in **Jeffersonian Legacies,** ed. Peter S. Onuf (Charlottesville, Va., 1993), 19–49; Edwin S. Gaustad, **Sworn on the Altar of God: A Religious Biography of Thomas Jefferson** (Grand Rapids, Mich., 1996); and Charles B. Sanford, **The Religious Life of Thomas Jefferson** (Charlottesville, Va., 1984). I also explored aspects of Jefferson's views on religion in my **American Gospel: God, the Founding Fathers, and the Making of a Nation** (New York, 2006).

183 HONEST ABOUT HIS STATE'S ABYSMAL RECORD Jefferson, **Writings,** 283–87.

183 HEARD BAPTIST MINISTERS PREACHING   William Lee Miller, **The First Liberty: America's Foundation in Religious Freedom** (Washington, D.C., 2003), 6. For more on Madison's work in Virginia on liberty of conscience, especially on the distinction between "liberty" and "toleration," see ibid., 4–8; Robert A. Rutland, **George Mason: Reluctant Statesman** (Baton Rouge,

La., 1980), 60; and Ketcham, **James Madison,** 71–73.

183 In 1767, Jefferson was involved   **MB,** I, 22. In another matter, sincerely devoted to helping a friend who longed to be ordained an Anglican priest, Jefferson wrote several letters on the subject, including a plea for Peyton Randolph's influence, yet marveled at what he believed to be the inherent limitations of minds defined by Christian factionalism. His friend's father was a Presbyterian minister in Aberdeen, Scotland, who received his son on a visit with joy—until he discovered his son's mission. "Yet, so wonderful is the dominion of bigotry over her votaries that on the first information of his purpose to receive episcopal ordination he shut him from his doors and abjured every parental duty," Jefferson told Randolph. (**PTJ,** I, 49–51.)

183 "spiritual tyranny"   Jefferson, **Writings,** 34.

183 "our Savior chose not to propagate"   **PTJ,** I, 544.

184 Jefferson's notes on the issue   Ibid., 537.

184 petitioned the assembly for relief   **JHT,** I, 274–80.

184 "brought on the severest contests"   Jefferson, **Writings,** 34.

184 "honest men, but zealous"   Ibid.

184 statute for religious liberty   Ibid., 40. See also John A. Ragosta, "The Virginia Statute for Establishing Religious Freedom," in Cogliano, ed., **A Companion to Thomas Jefferson,** 75–90.

184 "MEANT TO COMPREHEND" Jefferson, **Writings**, 34.

185 AN AMENDMENT STIPULATING "THE FREEDOM" Ibid., 44. See also Randall, **Jefferson,** I, 227, and Miller, **Wolf by the Ears,** 19–22.

185 "IT WAS FOUND THAT" Jefferson, **Writings,** 44.

185 "YET THE DAY IS NOT DISTANT" Ibid. Two acts did succeed in 1778 and in 1782 in Virginia: An abolition of the slave trade and a liberalization of manumission laws—what Miller called "the only concrete legislative achievements of the war years with a direct bearing upon slavery. For Jefferson, it was a disappointing performance: He had hoped that Virginia would take the lead among the states in providing for the eventual abolition of slavery and in arranging for the resettlement of the freed blacks outside the United States after peace had been restored." (Miller, **Wolf by the Ears,** 22.)

186 "THE ENEMY" **PTJ,** I, 659.

186 "NO MAN . . . EVER HAD" Ferling, **Almost a Miracle,** 167.

186 REPORTS THAT GERMANY **PTJ,** II, 13–14.

186 "10,000 MEN CHIEFLY GERMANS" Ibid., 14.

186 "THE SOUTHERN AND MIDDLE COLONIES" Ibid.

187 GAVE BIRTH TO A SON **MB,** I, 447.

187 LIVED ONLY SEVENTEEN DAYS Ibid.

187 IF THE JEFFERSONS GAVE HIM A NAME Ibid.

187 AT HOME ON THE FIRST OF AUGUST Ibid., 468.

187 RECORDING THE DOMESTIC DETAILS Martha

Wayles Skelton Jefferson Account Book. http://lcweb2.loc.gov/ammem/collections/jefferson_papers/ser7vol1.html#mwsj (accessed 2012).

187 HANDWRITING WAS STRONG AND CLEAR Author observation.

187 THERE ARE DOODLES, TOO Ibid.

187 "FREE FROM BLOT" TJF, http://www.monticello.org/site/jefferson/martha-wayles-skelton-jefferson (accessed 2012).

187 "TOLD OF NEATNESS" Ibid.

188 TO SEW CLOTHES AND SUPPLY THE ARMY PTJ, III, 532. See also Scharff, **Women Jefferson Loved,** 134–35. Scharff reported that at least one additional letter from Mrs. Jefferson on the subject has been located in recent years, which changes the historical consensus that the communication to Eleanor Conway Madison was the only surviving letter of Patty Jefferson's. (Ibid., 419.)

188 "MRS. WASHINGTON HAS" **PTJ,** III, 532.

188 "COULD WE BUT GET" Ibid., II, 3.

188 "THEY PLAY THE VERY DEVIL" Ibid.

188 "WE HAVE PRETTY CERTAIN" Ibid., 264. See also Randall, **Jefferson,** I, 245. A different kind of war was at hand. "I am of opinion the enemy have pretty well lost sight of conquering America by arms; for instead of drawing their force to a point, and making an effort against our grand army, it seems to be their plan to carry on a kind of piratical war in detached parties, by burning our towns, plundering our sea coasts, and dis-

tressing individuals," William Fleming wrote Jefferson on May 22, 1779. (**PTJ**, II, 268.)

189 ELECTED GOVERNOR OF VIRGINIA **PTJ**, II, 277–78.

189 "IN A VIRTUOUS AND FREE STATE"   Ibid.

189 THE BALLOTING HAD PITTED   Ibid.

189 JEFFERSON AND JOHN PAGE WERE COMPELLED Ibid., 278–79.

190 "AS THIS IS THE FIRST"   Ibid., 279.

191 ISAAC GRANGER JEFFERSON RECALLED   Bear, **Jefferson at Monticello**, 4.

TWELVE · A Troublesome Office

192 "THEY CERTAINLY MEAN"   **PTJ**, II, 236.

192 "I AM THOROUGHLY"   Ibid., III, 405.

192 "THEY FORMED IN LINE"   Bear, **Jefferson at Monticello**, 8.

193 THE THREAT AND THEN THE REALITY   Overall, optimism about America's military prospects grew in 1779–80. France and Spain were now with the United States; these allies were able to pressure Britain in the Atlantic, the Caribbean, and the Mediterranean. The British faced wars as far away as southern India. (Jeremy Black, **Crisis of Empire: Britain and America in the Eighteenth Century** [London, 2008], 159.) The difficulties Britain confronted globally, though, did not immediately translate into fatal weakness in America. By turning more attention and force to the South—to Georgia, to the Carolinas, and to

Governor Jefferson's Virginia—the British were able to bring terror to the American interior.

For a revisionist view of Jefferson's performance as governor, see Emory G. Evans, "Executive Leadership in Virginia, 1776–1781: Henry, Jefferson, and Nelson," in **Sovereign States in an Age of Uncertainty,** ed. Ronald Hoffman and Peter J. Albert (Charlottesville, Va., 1981), 185–225.

193 GEORGIA HAD COLLAPSED   Ferling, **Almost a Miracle,** 384–85.

193 SOUTH CAROLINA WAS NEXT   Ibid.

193 A TWO-FRONT WAR   **PTJ,** III, 29–30. As Richard Henry Lee told Jefferson: "In Virginia we have properly two frontiers, one bordered by a wilderness, the other by a sea. Into both of these issue savages, and into the latter the most savage." (Ibid.)

194 YEARS OF "INTENSE LABOR"   Ibid., 298.

194 "I WILL NOT CONGRATULATE YOU"   Ibid., III, 11.

195 CAPTURE OF HENRY HAMILTON   Ibid., 287. See also ibid., 292–95, for the actual orders about the irons. Under attack from the British about the treatment of Hamilton, Jefferson, who detested such attacks, put the matter to George Washington. "The importance of this question in a public view, and my own anxiety under a charge of a violation of national faith, [as] the Executive of this Commonwealth, will I hope apologize for my adding this to the many, many troubles with which I know you to be burdened," Jeffer-

son wrote Washington on July 17, 1779. (Ibid., III, 41.) Washington's reply was moderate in tone. "Whether it may be expedient to continue him in his present confinement from motives of policy and to satisfy our people, is a question I cannot determine; but if it should, I would take the liberty to suggest that it may be proper to publish all the cruelties he has committed or abetted . . . and the evidence in support of the charges." (Ibid., 61.)

195 "THE HAIR BUYER GENERAL" Ibid.

195 IN MAY 1778 HE HAD DRAFTED A BILL OF AT-
TAINDER Ibid., 189–93. See also W. P. Trent, "The Case of Josiah Philips," **American Histori-cal Review** 1, no. 3 (April 1896): 444–54.

195 FOR "COMMITTING MURDERS" **PTJ**, II, 189–90. As Jefferson recalled the episode, "Philips was a mere robber, who availing himself of the troubles of the times, collected a banditti, retired to the Dismal swamp, and from thence sallied forth, plundering and maltreating the neighboring inhabitants, and covering himself, without authority, under the name of a British subject." (Ibid., 191.)

195 AN EXTRAORDINARY EXPRESSION OF POWER
Ibid., 191–93. In **PTJ**, Julian P. Boyd wrote:

The Bill that TJ drew, though it was indeed an attainder limited by the condition that Philips surrender himself before a certain date to be tried according to regular judicial procedure, nevertheless was an assumption by the legislature that (1) Philips was a common criminal and was not acting under a British commission, and (2) that the legislature could of right make such a distinction affecting the life and liberty of an individual. Since this was assuming to the legislature a power over the rights of an individual usually regarded as belonging within the province of the judiciary and under protection of established legal procedures, the least that can be said about the Bill of Attainder of 1778 is that it was an extreme violation of TJ's belief in the principle of the separation of powers of government. (Ibid., 192.)

Leonard Levy uses the case in his argument against Jefferson's record on civil liberties. (Leonard W. Levy, **Jefferson and Civil Liberties: The Darker Side** [Chicago, 1989].)

195 "COMMUTE A GOOD PART" Ibid., 194. The problem of recruitment was a recurring one. Jefferson's tendency to cast reality in congenial ways at the price of strict accuracy was on display in a letter he wrote to Benjamin Franklin. At a time of disturbing rumors about the commitment of different American states to the cause of an independent nation, Jefferson wanted to impress Franklin with Virginia's fealty. "With respect to the state of Virginia in particular, the people seem to have deposited the monar-

chial and taken up the republican government with as much ease as would have attended their throwing off an old and putting on a new suit of clothes," Jefferson said on August 13, 1777. "Not a single throe has attended this important transformation." (Ibid., 26.)

195 "UNSUCCESSFUL BEYOND ALL" Ibid., III, 39.

195 TOURING VIRGINIA'S GUNNERY **MB,** I, 437.

196 PLANNED AN EXPEDITION Ibid., 321.

196 CLARK WAS A TALL For major treatments of George Rogers Clark see Lowell H. Harrison, **George Rogers Clark and the War in the West** (Lexington, Ky., 1976); John Bakeless, **Background to Glory: The Life of George Rogers Clark** (Philadelphia, 1957); and Temple Bodley, **George Rogers Clark: His Life and Public Services** (Boston, 1926). See also Richard M. Ketchum, "Men of the Revolution: 11. George Rogers Clark," **American Heritage** 25, no. 1 (December 1973): 32–33; 78; Gregory Fremont Barnes and others, eds., **The Encyclopedia of the American Revolutionary War: A Political, Social, and Military History,** I, A-D, 222–24.

196 HE CAPTURED KASKASKIA Barnes and others, **Encyclopedia of the American Revolutionary War,** I, 223.

196 AND VINCENNES Ibid.

196 SECURED AMERICAN INFLUENCE Ketchum, "Men of the Revolution: 11. George Rogers Clark," 78.

196 AFTER SEVERELY BURNING HIS LEG Ibid.

197 "WELL, IS IT OFF?" Ibid.

197 "THE WANT OF MEN" **PTJ**, III, 321.

197 "THERE IS REASON" Ibid., 317. Jefferson was unflinching. "I am sorry to hear that there are persons in your quarters so far discontented with the present government as to combine with its enemies to destroy it. . . . The measures they are now taking expose them to the pains of the law, to which it is our business to deliver them." Try them for treason, he advised William Preston on March 21, 1780. Failing conviction on capital grounds, Jefferson also advised Preston not to give up, for "perhaps it may be sufficient to convict them of a misprision of treason which is punishable by fine and imprisonment at the pleasure of the court." (Ibid., 325.)

198 THE COLDEST WINTER Ibid., 343. "We have had all over N. America a winter so severe as to exceed everything conceivable in our respective climates," Jefferson told Mazzei. "In this state our rivers were blocked up to their mouths with ice for six weeks. People walked over York river at the town of York, which was never before done, since the discovery of this country. Regiments of horse with their attendant wagons marched in order over Patowmack at Howe's ferry, and James river at Warwick." (Ibid.)

198 SHIFTING THE CAPITAL OF VIRGINIA Ibid., 333–34.

198 A HOUSE ON RICHMOND'S SHOCKOE HILL **MB**, I, 495.

198 CLIMATE OF EXTREME EMERGENCY **PTJ**, III, 335. "Among the various conjectures of alarm and distress which have arisen in the course of the revolution, it is with pain I affirm to you, Sir, that no one can be singled out more truly critical than the present," James Madison wrote Jefferson from Philadelphia on March 27, 1780. (Ibid.) While the Congress begged Virginia for men and matériel, Madison also complained to Jefferson about the feeble national government. "They can neither enlist, pay, nor feed a single soldier," Madison wrote Jefferson on May 6, 1780. (Ibid., 370.)

198 CHARLESTON FELL TO THE BRITISH Ferling, **Almost a Miracle**, 426–28. From Paris, Mazzei commiserated about Charleston. "Bad news have long legs," he wrote Jefferson on June 22, 1780, reporting the glee over the South Carolina reports in British circles. "It is amazing the impression such an event makes in Europe," Mazzei said. "The greater the distance, the more it will be magnified in men's own imagination." There was much talk of the significance of Charleston, and the talk fed upon itself. "Men of liberal sentiments consider all other causes as secondary, and of little moment, in comparison to the establishment of a free asylum for mankind," he said. "Want of information makes them apprehensive of consequences too bad, and very distant from probability." John Adams was "almost worn out" from reassuring allies and friends.

(**PTJ**, III, 458–60.) Yet Jefferson's belief in the cause, however troubled the cause might be, was abiding.

198 "While we are" **PTJ**, III, 447.

198 another Tory uprising Ibid., 479. On August 8, 1780, William Preston wrote: "A most horrid conspiracy amongst the Tories in this Country being providentially discovered about ten days ago." (Ibid., 533.) Jefferson had specific thoughts about how to fight such rebellions: "It will probably be better to seek the insurgents and suppress them in their own settlements than to await their coming, as time and space to move in will perhaps increase their numbers," he told Preston on July 3. (Ibid., 481.)

198 more Indian violence Ibid., 544.

198 Elected to a second Ibid., 410. Jefferson was pleased and gratified. "I receive with great satisfaction this testimony of the public approbation," he said on June 4, 1780. (Ibid., 417.)

198 Cornwallis routed the American general Middlekauff, **Glorious Cause**, 460–63. See also **PTJ**, III, 558–59. Edward Stevens told Jefferson to "picture it as bad as you possible can and it will not be as bad as it really is." The militia had performed miserably. "Their cowardly behavior has indeed given a mortal wound to my feelings," Stevens said. (Ibid.) While John Page thought Gates was to blame ("Did not the General venture on too boldly, relying too much on a continuance of his for-

mer good fortune?" [Ibid., 576]), Jefferson felt a personal responsibility for the loss and was humiliated by the reports of the Virginia militia's performance. "I am extremely mortified at the misfortune incurred in the South and the more so as the militia of our state concurred so eminently in producing it," Jefferson wrote to Gates on September 3, 1780. (Ibid., 588.) To Edward Stevens, Jefferson tried to make the best of things. "I sincerely condole with you on our late misfortune which sits the heavier on my mind as being produced by my own countrymen," he wrote. "Instead of considering what is past, however, we are to look forward and prepare for the future." (Ibid., 593.) It was a mature point of view, but he could not hide his embarrassment.

He wanted out—or thought he did. "The application requisite to the duties of the office I hold is so excessive, and the execution of them after all so imperfect, that I have determined to retire from it at the close of the present campaign," Jefferson wrote to Richard Henry Lee on September 13, 1780. "I wish a successor to be thought of in time who to sound whiggism can join perseverance in business, and an extensive knowledge of the various subjects he must superintend. Such a one may keep up above water even in our present moneyless situation." (Ibid., 643.) He repeated his thoughts about standing down early to John Page, suggesting that perhaps Page should take his place. Page was having none of it, telling Jefferson that "should you resign, you will give me great uneasiness, and will greatly distress your country." (Ibid., 655.)

199 CITING THE "DISASTER" PTJ, III, 564.

199 BENEDICT ARNOLD, THE AMERICAN GENERAL Boyer and Dobofsky, **Oxford Companion to United States History,** 50. See also **MB,** I, 504–5. Jefferson's anger at Arnold was intense and personal. "You will readily suppose that it is above all things desirable to drag him from those under whose wing he is now sheltered," Jefferson wrote General Peter Muhlenberg on January 31, 1781.

Jefferson wanted Arnold dead. "I shall be sorry to suppose that any circumstances may put it out of their power to bring him off alive after they shall have taken him and of course oblige them to put him to death," Jefferson wrote in lines he deleted from the final version of the letter to Muhlenberg. "Should this happen . . . I must give my approbation to their putting him to death." (**PTJ,** IV, 487.)

199 WORD OF THE BRITISH Michael Kranish, **Flight from Monticello: Thomas Jefferson at War** (New York, 2010), 166. Kranish's account is invaluable.

199 A SERIES OF INVASION RUMORS Hoffman and Albert, **Sovereign States,** 214–15.

199 CREATED "DISGUST" WHEN THE MILITIAMEN Ibid.

199 HE DECLINED TO SUMMON Kranish, **Flight from Monticello**, 166–67.

199 A MESSENGER FOUND HIM Ibid., 166.

199 JEFFERSON HAD ISSUED Ibid., 174–75.

200 ROBERT HEMINGS AND JAMES HEMINGS Bear, **Jefferson at Monticello**, 6.

200 PROPERTY JEFFERSON OWNED ON FINE CREEK Ibid., 124.

200 AT ABOUT ONE O'CLOCK Kranish, **Flight from Monticello**, 191.

200 TOOK OFF THE TOP OF A BUTCHER'S HOUSE Bear, **Jefferson at Monticello**, 7.

200 "IN TEN MINUTES" Ibid., 7–8.

200 "THE BRITISH WAS DRESSED IN RED" Ibid., 8.

200 SPENT THE HOURS OF THE INVASION Kranish, **Flight from Monticello**, 190.

200 BROUGHT ALONG HANDCUFFS Bear, **Jefferson at Monticello**, 9.

200 A BRITISH OFFICER ASKED Ibid., 8.

201 HIS FATHER HAD "PUT ALL THE SILVER" Ibid.

201 "LIKE AN EARTHQUAKE" Ibid., 9.

201 "MEN OF ENTERPRISE" **PTJ**, IV, 487. See also **JHT**, I, 340–41.

201 UNHAPPY AND SKEPTICAL McDonnell, **Politics of War**, 399–477, is a brilliant account of the actual politics of the hour in Virginia. Militiamen disliked being too long away from home (ibid., 404–5), were uncomfortable serving under Continental officers (ibid., 405–10), and resisted draft orders from the Continental army (ibid., 411–19). "By this point, many Virginians were

reluctant to aid the patriot cause in any way," wrote McDonnell. "Many were tired of giving supplies—through both impressments and taxes—and getting little back." (Ibid., 442.)

202 "MILD LAWS, A PEOPLE" **PTJ**, V, 113.

202 RISKING THE WRATH OF THE PEOPLE McDonnell, **Politics of War**, 452.

THIRTEEN · Redcoats at Monticello

203 "SUCH TERROR AND CONFUSION" JHT, I, 358–59.

203 RETREATED FROM RICHMOND McDonnell, **Politics of War**, 462–63.

203 THE DEATH OF YET ANOTHER CHILD MB, I, 508.

203 JEFFERSON CHOSE TO STAY Scharff, **Women Jefferson Loved**, 139.

204 THERE WERE RIOTS OVER A DRAFT McDonnell, **Politics of War**, 453–61.

204 REDUCED TO ASKING GEORGE WASHINGTON PTJ, VI, 32–33.

204 HIS "LONG DECLARED" Ibid., 33.

204 "THE LABORS OF" Ibid.

205 HE SPENT SATURDAY, JUNE 2, 1781 Ibid., 78.

205 ELECT THOMAS NELSON, JR. Hayes, **Road to Monticello**, 231.

205 FOR A "UNION OF" Ibid.

205 CORNWALLIS HAD ORDERED TARLETON Ibid.

206 RIDING FAST, THE BRITISH DRAGOONS Virginius Dabney, "Jouett Outrides Tarleton, and

Saves Jefferson from Capture," **Scribner's Maga-zine,** June 1928, 690.

206 IT WAS LATE   Ibid., 691.

206 A GIANT OF A VIRGINIA MILITIAMAN   Ibid.

206 "THE BEST AND FLEETEST OF FOOT"   Ibid.

206 CRASHED THROUGH THE WILDERNESS   Ibid.

206 HIS FACE WAS "CRUELLY LASHED"   Ibid., 691–92.

206 BROKE THEIR MARCH AT A PLANTATION   Ibid., 692.

206 FOR ABOUT THREE HOURS   Ibid.

206 TO SET FIRE TO A WAGON TRAIN   Ibid. "Tarle-ton says in his account of the expedition that he burned the wagons with their contents, instead of taking them with him, in order that no time might be lost," wrote Dabney. "He adds: 'Soon after daybreak some of the principal gentlemen of Virginia who had fled to the borders of the mountains for security, were taken out of their beds. . . . In the neighborhood of Doctor [Thomas] Walker's a member of the Continental Congress was made prisoner, and the British light troops, after a halt of half an hour to refresh the horses, moved on toward Charlottesville.' " (Ibid.)

206 JOUETT ARRIVED AT MONTICELLO   Ibid. "The raiders were still many miles away," wrote Dabney. "Jack gave the alarm to the governor. . . . He then spurred his all-but-exhausted mount to Charlottesville, two miles farther on, and warned the legislature. He had beaten the British by about three hours. Paul Revere's fifteen-mile

jaunt over fairly good roads in the moonlight seems almost nothing by comparison." (Ibid.)

206 COOLLY, JEFFERSON ORDERED BREAKFAST Ibid.

207 PATTY AND THE TWO CHILDREN Kranish, **Flight from Monticello,** 279.

207 HIDING SILVER IN ANTICIPATION Bear, **Jefferson at Monticello,** 8. See also Kranish, **Flight from Monticello,** 284.

207 "IN PREPARING FOR FLIGHT" **PTJ,** VI, 84.

207 TO A NEIGHBORING PEAK Dabney, "Jouett Outrides Tarleton," 693.

207 TOOK HIS SPYGLASS Ibid.

207 LOOKING OUT AT CHARLOTTESVILLE Ibid.

207 HE TURNED TO GO Ibid.

207 HIS SWORD CANE Ibid.

207 AS HE RETRIEVED IT, HIS CURIOSITY Ibid.

207 HE SAW THE BRITISH Ibid.

207 MOUNTED HIS BEST HORSE Kranish, **Flight from Monticello,** 283.

207 THE REDCOATS ARRIVED Ibid., 284.

207 ONE COCKED A PISTOL Ibid.

207 "FIRE AWAY, THEN" Ibid.

207–8 DRANK SOME OF JEFFERSON'S WINE Ibid.

208 LEGEND HAS IT Hayes, **Road to Monticello,** 284.

208 ESPECIALLY ELK HILL **MB,** I, 515–16. See also **PTJ,** VI, 224–25.

208 TWENTY-THREE OF JEFFERSON'S SLAVES I am grateful to Lucia Stanton for these figures. See also Stanton, **"Those Who Labor for My Happiness,"** 132–33.

208 RIDING AWAY FROM MONTICELLO   MB, I, 510.

208 AT POPLAR FOREST   Joan L. Horn, **Thomas Jefferson's Poplar Forest: A Private Place** (Forest, Va., 2002), 22.

208 EXPRESSED ITS GRATITUDE   Dabney, "Jouett Outrides Tarleton," 694–95. "What would have been the fate of Jefferson, Henry, Lee, Harrison, and Nelson had they been taken captive by Tarleton?" wrote Dabney. "Some are of the opinion that Jefferson, at least, would have been tried in England as a traitor and hanged, but it is quite unlikely that such severe punishment would have been meted out to him. It is probably safe to assume, however, that these leaders in the revolutionary movement would have been treated as harshly as any civilian Americans who could have fallen into British hands. If the career of Jefferson alone had been cut short or substantially altered at this period of his life, the history of the United States would have been vastly changed. It is conceivable that, if he had been made prisoner, this country would have been deprived for all time of the services of the American who did most to burst the fetters which bound the souls of men 150 years ago, and to fix the principles upon which democracy in the Republic rests today. Nor should we forget that the capture of the author of the Declaration of Independence, three of its signers, and Patrick Henry would have been a severe blow to the struggling colonials." (Ibid., 697.)

208 IT ALSO PASSED A RESOLUTION   PTJ, VI, 88–90.

208 "RESOLVED, THAT AT THE NEXT SESSION" Ibid., 88.

209 "COULD NOT BE INTENDED"   Ibid., 105.

209 TIME HAD COME FOR A "DICTATOR"   McDonnell, **Politics of War**, 465.

210 NEEDED TO BE "ARMED"   Ibid.

210 THE MOTION FAILED   Ibid.

210 ACCOUNTS OF JEFFERSON'S TERRIBLE TIME For a sympathetic view, see Evans, "Executive Leadership in Virginia," 215–16. "In evaluating Thomas Jefferson's governorship, historians have more often than not focused on his last five months in office and especially on the few days in late December and early January 1781," wrote Evans.

> The result is that, in the popular mind, he is considered not to have been a very good chief executive. Nothing could be further from the truth. It is true, of course, that the governor did not respond as quickly as he should have on December 31 to the news that a "fleet of 27 sail" had been sighted at the mouth of the James River. . . . Invasion scares and raids during the past several years had made both the public and its leaders less alert than they should have been. But the demands on the state were now tremendous, and the governor did not want to take any action that would strain its resources unnecessarily. . . . Under

the circumstances the conclusion must be
that he did remarkably well. (Ibid., 215–18.)

210 THE HOUSE INQUIRY WAS SHORT-LIVED McDonnell, **Politics of War,** 465. Jefferson believed
Patrick Henry, an emerging political rival, was
the motivating force behind the censure. "The
trifling body who moved this matter was below
contempt; he was more an object of pity," Jefferson said of George Nicholas. "His natural ill-
temper was the tool worked by another hand.
He was like the minnows which go in and out of
the fundament of the whale. But the whale himself was discoverable enough by the turbulence
of the water under which he moved." (**PTJ,** VI,
143.)

210 "NO FOUNDATION" **PTJ,** VI, 143.

211 "TAKEN MY FINAL LEAVE" Ibid., 118.

211 "A DESIRE TO LEAVE PUBLIC OFFICE" Ibid.

211 THE AMERICANS TRIUMPHED AT YORKTOWN
At Yorktown on October 17, 1781, a European
soldier fighting with Cornwallis described the
siege. "At daybreak the enemy bombardment re-
sumed, more terribly strong than ever before,"
he wrote. "They fired from all positions without let-up. . . . There was nothing to be seen but
bombs and cannonballs raining down on our
entire line." (Black, **Crisis of Empire,** 166.)

211 "THERE WAS TREMENDOUS FIRING" Bear, **Jefferson at Monticello,** 10–11.

212 "LET ME DESCRIBE TO YOU" **TDLTJ,** 58–60.

213 "STOOD ARRAIGNED" **PTJ**, VI, 185. In May 1782, Patty Jefferson gave birth to another daughter, also Lucy Elizabeth. As a result of the birth Mrs. Jefferson was quite ill. Two days before the birth of the daughter, Jefferson had informed the Speaker of the House of Delegates, John Tyler, that he declined his recent election to the House of Delegates. (See **JHT**, I, 393–97; **PTJ**, VI, 179–87; and Willard Sterne Randall, **Thomas Jefferson,** 347.)

Speaker Tyler responded with a possible threat that Jefferson might be arrested and forced to attend. James Monroe also sent a letter to Jefferson on May 11, 1782, urging him to attend. According to the historian Dumas Malone's account, Jefferson wrote Monroe what Julian P. Boyd called a long "embittered" letter of May 20 spelling out in "extreme anxiety" why he would not attend. (See **JHT**, I, 394–97; and **PTJ**, VI, 184–87.)

In a footnote to this letter, the editors of the Monroe papers wrote: "Jefferson, still smarting from the criticism of his conduct as governor and gravely concerned about the dangerous state of his wife's health, declined to serve in the House of Delegates, following his election as a delegate. He used this response to JM's letter of 11 May as a means of communicating to the House the justification for his decision not to serve." There is no indication that they actually arrested or seized Jefferson to compel his attendance. There was only the threat. Patty Jefferson, of course, died four months later on September 6, 1782. (**The Papers of James Monroe**, II, ed. Daniel Preston and Marlena C. Delong [Westport, Conn., 2003-], 36.)

213 "Mrs. Jefferson has added" Ibid., 186.

FOURTEEN · To Burn on Through Death

214 "Mrs. Jefferson has at last" Scharff, **Women Jefferson Loved**, 151.

214 may have suffered from tuberculosis **MB**, I, 521. See also Gordon Jones and James A. Bear, "Thomas Jefferson: A Medical History," unpublished manuscript, Thomas Jefferson Foundation, Charlottesville, Va.

214 Jefferson "was never out of calling" **TDLTJ**, 63.

214 helping her take medicines Ibid.

215 Either at her bed Ibid.

215 craved Jefferson's company Randall, **Jefferson**, I, 380.

215 some lines from Sterne **PTJ**, VI, 196–97.

216 "I have been much" Scharff, **Women Jefferson Loved**, 148.

216 "the house servants" Bear, **Jefferson at Monticello**, 99.

216 "have often told my wife" Ibid.

216 "When she came to the children" Ibid., 99–100.

217 he gave his promise Ibid., 100.

217 TO HELP THE GRIEVING HUSBAND TDLTJ, 63.

218 "THE SCENE THAT FOLLOWED" Ibid.

218 A PALLET TO LIE ON Ibid.

218 "HE KEPT HIS ROOM" Ibid.

219 "WHEN AT LAST" Ibid.

219 "I HAD HAD SOME THOUGHTS" PTJ, VI, 197.

219 RUMOR HAD JEFFERSON Ibid., 199.

219 "I EVER THOUGHT HIM" Scharff, Women Jefferson Loved, 151.

219 HIS EPITAPH FOR PATTY Randall, Jefferson, I, 383.

220 THE POSSIBILITY OF SUICIDE PTJ, VI, 198–99.

220 HE KNEW HIS DUTY Ibid. "The care and instruction of our children indeed affords some temporary abstractions from wretchedness and nourishes a soothing reflection that if there be beyond the grave any concern for the things of this world there is one angel at least who views these attentions with pleasure and wishes continuance of them while she must pity the miseries to which they confine me," Jefferson wrote. (Ibid.)

221 HE WAS A LONG WAY Ibid., 198. He neglected Elk Hill, saying that he was "finding myself absolutely unable to attend to anything like business." (Ibid.)

FIFTEEN · Return to the Arena

222 "I KNOW NO DANGER SO DREADFUL" PTJ, VI, 248.

225 "The states will go to war" Ibid.

226 Musing on the perils of fame Ibid., 204–5.

226 "If you meant" Ibid., 205.

227 asked him to serve Ibid., 202. According to James Madison, "the act took place in consequence of its being suggested that the death of Mrs. J had probably changed the sentiments of Mr. J with regard to public life, and that all the reasons which led to his original appointment still existed." (Ibid.) See also ibid., 210–15.

227 "I had two months before" Ibid., 210.

228 Visiting Ampthill, the plantation Ibid., 206–7.

228 "pursue the object of my mission" Ibid., 206.

228 "I shall lose no moment" Ibid.

228 "a little emerging" Ibid., 203.

229 published a notice in The Virginia Gazette Ibid., 210.

229 He and Patsy expected to sail Ibid., 211.

229 took rooms at Mary House's MB, I, 527.

229 charming political company Ibid.

229 Eliza House Trist PTJ, VI, 375. "Your character was great in my estimation long before I had the pleasure of your acquaintance personally, for I always understood your country was greatly benefited by your counsels; and I value you now because I know you are good," she wrote him in late 1783. (Ibid.)

229 Madison's wooing of fifteen-year-old Ibid., 262–64. See also Gordon-Reed, Hem-

ingses of Monticello, 309–12. Gordon-Reed made an illuminating point about the marriageable ages of women in these years, noting that men of Jefferson and Madison's generation often pursued teenaged girls. Hence Jefferson and Sally Hemings and Madison and Kitty Floyd. There are other examples: John Marshall was twenty-five when he set out to win Polly Ambler—who was fourteen at the time. (Ibid., 311.) Thomas Mann Randolph, Sr., was to marry a seventeen-year-old when he was fifty. (Ibid.) "Much as it may assault present-day sensibilities, fifteen- and sixteen-year-old girls were in Hemings's time thought eligible to become seriously involved with men, even men who were substantially older," wrote Gordon-Reed. (Ibid., 309.)

230 TOOK DETAILED NOTES   Ibid., 212–13.

230 "HAD I JOINED YOU"   Ibid., 217.

230 "MY INDIVIDUAL TRIBUTE"   Ibid., 222. Jefferson understood, he wrote to Washington, "you must receive much better intelligence from the gentlemen whose residence there has brought them into a more intimate acquaintance with the characters and views of the European courts, yet I shall certainly presume to add my mite." (Ibid., 222–23.)

231 JEFFERSON RETURNED TO VIRGINIA Ibid., 259–61. His mission suspended, he left Philadelphia for Virginia on April 12. Madison kept him apprised of romantic and political developments. "Before you left us," Madison wrote of

Kitty Floyd, "I had sufficiently ascertained her sentiments. Since your departure the affair has been pursued." (Ibid., 262.) On his way home Jefferson stopped in Richmond. For two weeks he reacquainted himself with the minutiae of Virginia, "associating and conversing with as many" legislators as he could. It was his first sustained period of time among these men since the end of the gubernatorial crisis, and Jefferson seems to have hurled himself back into the action with enthusiasm. He wrote Madison with his impressions of possible candidates for the Congress—and of his sense of how the state's leadership viewed the fundamental question of national power. Jefferson confided this political intelligence in a letter written from Tuckahoe on the morning of Wednesday, May 7, 1783. (Ibid., 265–67.)

231 "SHOULD THE CALL BE MADE" Ibid., 267.

231 "MR. JEFFERSON WAS PLACED" Ibid.

231 THE CONGRESS TO WHICH JEFFERSON WAS ELECTED Boyer and Dubofsky, **Oxford Companion to United States History**, 51, summarizes the powers of the Confederation Congress (and the lack thereof).

233 DEVISE A "VISIBLE HEAD" **PTJ**, VI, 516–29.

233 "THIS WAS THEN IMPUTED" Randall, **Jefferson**, I, 394–95.

233 "OUR PLAN BEST, I BELIEVE, COMBINES" Ibid.

233 A POWER OF CENTRAL **PTJ**, VI, 248. "We have substituted a Congress of deputies from every

state to perform this task," Jefferson wrote, "but we have done nothing which would enable them to enforce their decisions. What will be the case? They will not be enforced. . . . Can any man be so puffed up with his little portion of sovereignty as to prefer this calamitous accompaniment to the parting of a little of his sovereign right and placing it in a council from all the states, . . . who being chosen by himself annually, [are] removable at will?" (Ibid.)

233 HAD TO LAY THEIR "SHOULDERS" Ibid., 249.

234 "I HAVE LONG THOUGHT" **PTJ**, X, 272. Jay made such points often. "An uneasiness prevails through the country and may produce untoward events," he wrote on July 14, 1786. "Time alone can decide this and many other doubts, for nations, like individuals, are more frequently guided by circumstances than circumstances by them." (Ibid., 135.) Through the years, they got along, but only just. In Madison's view, expressed in 1785, the Congress had thus far "kept the vessel from sinking, but it has been by standing constantly at the pump, not by stopping the leaks which have endangered her." (Ibid., VIII, 579.)

234 "THERE NEVER WILL BE MONEY" Ibid., 225.

234 "WHAT, THEN, IS THE AMERICAN" J. Hector St. John de Crèvecoeur, **Letters from an American Farmer; and, Sketches of Eighteenth-Century America,** ed. Albert E. Stone (New York, 1986), 69.

234 IN 1780, THE MARQUIS DE BARBÉ-MARBOIS PTJ, IV, 166–67.

234 NOTES ON THE STATE OF VIRGINIA Jefferson, **Writings**, 123–325. See also David Tucker, **Enlightened Republicanism: A Study of Jefferson's Notes on the State of Virginia** (Lanham, Md., 2008), and " 'I have known': Thomas Jefferson, Experience, and 'Notes on the State of Virginia,' " in Cogliano, ed., **A Companion to Thomas Jefferson**, 60–74.

235 "AN EXACT DESCRIPTION" Jefferson, **Writings**, 127.

235 "THE PARTICULAR CUSTOMS" Ibid., 288. When John Adams read the **Notes**, he praised them highly. "It is our meditation all the day long," Adams wrote to Jefferson. "I cannot now say much about it, but I think it will do its author and his country great honor." (**PTJ**, VIII, 160.) Adams added that the passages on slavery were "worth diamonds." (Ibid.)

235 IN AN EVENING'S CONVERSATION PTJ, VI, 377.

236 TWO LARGELY NEGLECTED PIECES Irving Brant, "Two Neglected Madison Letters," **William and Mary Quarterly**, 3d ser., 3, no. 4 (October 1946): 569–87.

236 KITTY FLOYD BROKE OFF PTJ, VI, 333. Writing obliquely to Jefferson, Madison said that "the object I was . . . pursuing has been brought [to an end] by one of those incidents to which such affairs are liable." (Ibid.)

236 "I SINCERELY LAMENT" Ibid., 335–36.

236 "Parliamentary news is interesting" PTJ, VI, 317.

sixteen · A Struggle for Respect

239 "Foreign civil arrangement" PTJ, VI, 470.

239 three hundred Continental soldiers Ibid., 318–19. It was only after the legislature's departure, Madison told Jefferson, that "the mutineers surrendered their arms and impeached some of their officers, the two principal of whom have escaped to sea." (Ibid., 318.)

239 Pennsylvania officials Peter S. Onuf, ed., **Congress and the Confederation** (New York, 1991), 70–71.

240 to "prevent any inferences" PTJ, VI, 319.

240 remained at Princeton See Varnum Lansing Collins, **The Continental Congress at Princeton** (Whitefish, Mont., 2005).

240 moved to Annapolis Edith Rossiter Bevan, "Thomas Jefferson in Annapolis, November 25, 1783-May 11, 1784," **Maryland Historical Magazine** 41, no. 2 (1946): 115–24, offers some commentary and an accounting of daily expenditures.

240 to secure him a room PTJ, VI, 336.

240 left Monticello on Thursday, October 16, 1783 **MB**, I, 536.

240 offered "scanty accommodations" PTJ, VI, 319.

240 A "VILLAGE WHERE THE PUBLIC BUSINESS" Ibid., 337.

240 As "THE UNITED STATES" Ibid., 369.

240 "IT IS NOW ABOVE A FORTNIGHT" Ibid., 381.

240 "THE RIOT OF PHILADELPHIA" Ibid.

241 THE TREATY OF PARIS JHT, II, 414–17.

241 STILL NO QUORUM IN THE CONGRESS PTJ, VI, 388. "I am sorry to say that I see no immediate prospect of making up nine states, so careless are either the states or their delegates to their particular interests as well as the general good which would require that they be all constantly and fully represented in Congress," Jefferson told Benjamin Harrison on December 17, 1783. (Ibid.)

241 "I CANNOT HELP" Ibid., 419.

241 "ALL THAT CAN BE SAID" Ibid. With France distracted by a continental war, America would be in a weakened bargaining position—a fact Jefferson understood and feared. (Ibid.) Jefferson was determined that Congress abide by its own rules and hold off on ratification until what he called "the danger of not having nine states" was overcome. (Ibid., 420.) The making of treaties was "an act of so much energy and substance" that to settle for seven states only would be "a breach of faith in us, a prostitution of our seal, and a future ground . . . of denying the validity of a ratification." (Ibid., 424–25.)

241 "I HAVE HAD VERY ILL HEALTH" Ibid., 438.

242 JEFFERSON SOUGHT A COMPROMISE Ibid., 441–

42. In Jefferson's words, those members of the "opinion that 9 having ratified the Provisional treaty and instructed their ministers to enter into a definitive one conformable thereto, which is accordingly done, seven may under these particular circumstances ratify what has been so declared by 9 to have their approbation." (Ibid., 441.)

242 CONNECTICUT AND NEW JERSEY AT LENGTH ARRIVED   Ibid., 461.

242 HE CALLED ON "ALL THE GOOD"   Ibid., 463.

242 "THAT WERE IT CERTAIN"   Ibid., 386–87.

243 "I HAVE BEEN JUST ABLE"   Ibid., 466.

243 "THE DIFFERENT SPECIES OF BONES"   Ibid., 371.

243 THE COMTE DE BUFFON   MB, I, 549.

243 "UNCOMMONLY LARGE PANTHER SKIN"   Ibid.

243 "I FIND THEY HAVE SUBSCRIBED"   PTJ, VI, 371.

244 A MECHANICAL COPYING DEVICE   Ibid., 373.

SEVENTEEN · Lost Cities and Life Counsel

245 THE GOVERNOR IS   PTJ, VII, 303.

245 ALL THE TALK WAS OF BALLOONS   Ibid., 57.

245 GRAND BALLOONING EXPERIMENTS   Jefferson and Hopkinson are referring to a series of experimental balloon flights that were conducted in Paris in late 1783. In June 1783, the brothers Montgolfier—Joseph-Michel and Jacques-Étienne, who had developed the first hot-air balloons—conducted the first public launching

of a balloon in Paris. Then, on November 21, 1783, Jean-François Pilâtre de Rozier made a manned flight in a balloon in Paris. Pilâtre de Rozier was killed on June 15, 1785, when he and a companion, Pierre-Ange Romain, "plummeted over 1,000 feet to their deaths near Boulogne when the double balloon in which they were attempting to cross the English Channel caught fire and partially collapsed." (L. H. Butterfield, Wendell D. Garrett, and Marjorie E. Sprague, eds., **Adams Family Correspondence**, VI, 181.) Jefferson refers to the Pilâtre de Rozier crash in a letter of June 19, 1785. (**PTJ**, VIII, 237.) Jefferson also mentioned the crash in a letter to Abigail Adams on June 21, 1785. "This will damp for a while the ardor of the Phaetons of our race who are endeavoring to learn us the way to heaven on wings of our own," he wrote. (Ibid., 241.)

245 THE REVOLUTIONARY POSSIBILITIES **PTJ**, VI, 542.

246 TEN YEARS LATER **MB**, I, 548–49.

246 "A HIGH FLYING POLITICIAN" **PTJ**, VII, 20.

246 "A SUBTERRANEOUS CITY" Ibid., 123.

247 "THE BRITISH ROBBED ME" Ibid., VI, 507.

247 "YOU HAVE NO DOUBT" Ibid., 508.

247 "IN SOME OF THE REMOTEST SETTLEMENTS" Ibid., 509.

247 BUFFON'S THEORY OF HEAT Ibid., 436–37.

247 "I HAVE ALWAYS THOUGHT" Ibid., XVIII, 98.

248 HE WROTE THE MARQUIS DE BARBÉ-MARBOIS Ibid., VI, 373–74. "The plan of reading which

I have formed for her is considerably different from what I think would be most proper for her sex in any other country than America," he wrote Marbois. "I am obliged in it to extend my views beyond herself, and consider her as possibly at the head of a little family of her own. The chance that in marriage she will draw a blockhead I calculate at about fourteen to one, and of course that the education of her family will probably rest on her own ideas and direction without assistance." He was thus pressing her harder than he otherwise would have. "With the best poets and prosewriters I shall therefore combine a certain extent of reading in the graver sciences. However I scarcely expect to enter her on this till she returns to me. Her time in Philadelphia will be chiefly occupied in acquiring a little taste and execution in such of the fine arts as she could not prosecute to equal advantage in a more retired situation." (Ibid., 374.)

248 "THE ACQUIREMENTS WHICH I HOPE" Ibid., 359.

248 "CONSIDER THE GOOD LADY" Ibid., 359–60. As he traveled as a member of the Congress, Jefferson kept an eye on his daughters. On the road, this time to Annapolis, he wrote James Monroe that he was leaving Patsy in Philadelphia "having had it in my power to procure for her the best tutors in French, dancing, music, and drawing." (Ibid., 355.)

Also to Patsy, who was apparently caught up

in an enthusiasm about the coming of the apocalypse in the wake of a severe earthquake, Jefferson advised caution and perspective. "I hope you will have good sense enough to disregard those foolish predictions that the world is to be at an end soon," he wrote her on December 11, 1783. "The Almighty has never made known to anybody at what time he created it, nor will he tell anybody when he means to put an end to it, if ever he means to do it." (Ibid., 380.)

249 "With respect to the distribution" Ibid., 360.

249 "You are now old enough" Ibid., 379.

250 to become "a man" Ibid.

250 "Our future connection with Spain" Ibid., VIII, 408.

250 "Fix reason firmly" Ibid., XII, 15.

250 "Monroe is buying" Kaminski, **Founders on the Founders,** 291.

251 "Though the different walks of life" **PTJ,** XXXI, 118.

251 The note, Donald told Jefferson, "was so friendly" Kaminski, **Founders on the Founders,** 294–95.

251 "Admonition after admonition" **PTJ,** VI, 546.

252 "Among other legislative" Ibid., 549.

252 to warn of "encroachments" Ibid., 511–12.

252 "gives a picture" Ibid., VII, 15–16.

253 "an attack of my periodical headache" Ibid., VI, 570.

253 "I suppose the crippled state" Ibid., VII, 25.

253 for prewar debts EOL, 112, and Charles Pinnegar, **Virginia and State Rights, 1750–1861** (Jefferson, N.C., 2009), 53.

253 at least two elements EOL, 112.

253 a trade route connecting PTJ, VI, 548. See also Joel Achenbach, **The Grand Idea: George Washington's Potomac and the Race to the West** (New York, 2004), 31–37.

253 "This is the moment" PTJ, VII, 26–27.

254 fascinated Washington Achenbach, **Grand Idea,** 37. See also Stuart Leibiger, **Founding Friendship: George Washington, James Madison, and the Creation of the American Republic** (Charlottesville, 1999), 37.

254 "I have no expectation" PTJ, VII, 49.

254 where a portage road Achenbach, **Grand Idea,** 28, 112–20.

254 Washington supervised improvements Leibiger, **Founding Friendship,** 46. See also Achenbach, **Grand Idea,** 129–35.

254 Chesapeake & Ohio Canal Leibiger, **Founding Friendship,** 46–47.

254 "opinion of the Institution of the Society of Cincinnati" PTJ, VII, 88.

255 "is interesting, and, so far as" Ibid., 105–7.

255 "The way to make friends quarrel" Ibid., 106.

256 taken Jefferson's counsel seriously Ibid., 109. See also Markus Hünemörder, **The Society**

of the Cincinnati: Conspiracy and Distrust in Early America (New York, 2006), 28–29.

256 "MIGHT DRAW INTO THE ORDER" Hünemörder, Society of the Cincinnati, 47.

256 "I SEE THE BEST EFFECTS" PTJ, VI, 548–49.

256 CONGRESS ACCEPTED THE VIRGINIA CESSION Ibid., 571–80.

256 A PLAN TO CREATE NEW STATES Ibid., 581–617.

256 HAD NAMES FOR THEM Ibid., 591.

256 ORDINANCE OF 1784 Ibid., 581–617.

257 "FOREVER REMAIN A PART" Ibid., 614.

257 "THEIR RESPECTIVE GOVERNMENTS" Ibid.

257 BANNED THE EXPANSION OF SLAVERY Miller, Wolf by the Ears, 27.

257 THE PLAN FAILED BY A SINGLE VOTE Ibid., 28.

257 A DELEGATE FROM NEW JERSEY WAS TOO ILL Ibid.

257 "THUS WE SEE THE FATE" Ibid.

257 WOULD NO LONGER RISK HIS "USEFULNESS" Ibid., 89.

257 THE NORTHWEST ORDINANCE OF 1787 Ibid., 29. See also Boyer and Dubofsky, Oxford Companion to United States History, 557–58; Adam Rothman, Slave Country: American Expansion and the Origins of the Deep South (Cambridge, Mass., 2005), 18–19; and EOL, 121–22.

258 THE MORNING AND INTO THE AFTERNOON PTJ, VII, 221–30.

258 AFTER THE REGULAR POST HAD LEFT ANNAPOLIS Ibid., 229.

258 "I am now to take"   Ibid., 233.

258 "At the close of every session"   Ibid.

259 "a tender legacy"   Ibid., 233–34.

259 a farewell to the Virginia House   Ibid., 244.

260 "foolish World in Paris"   Ibid., 257.

260 gathered intelligence on the commerce   Ibid., 323–55.

260 "might in some degree"   Ibid., 358.

260 four o'clock on the Monday morning   MB, I, 554.

EIGHTEEN · The Vaunted Scene of Europe

262 "He is full of honor and sincerity"   William Howard Adams, The Paris Years of Thomas Jefferson (New Haven, Conn., 2000), 184.

265 "A coward is much more"   PTJ, VII, 640.

265 remembered the "good company"   TDLTJ, 73.

265 "The winds were so favorable"   MB, I, 555.

266 He was determined   Lawrence S. Kaplan, Jefferson and France: An Essay on Politics and Political Ideas (Westport, Conn., 1980), 19–20.

266 Jefferson viewed France in the context   Ibid. I agree with Kaplan's argument, one supported by Jefferson's more astute contemporaries. For the case against Jefferson on the French question, see Conor Cruise O'Brien, The Long Affair: Thomas Jefferson and the French

Revolution, 1785–1800 (Chicago, 1996). Iain McLean, "The Paris Years of Thomas Jefferson," in Cogliano, ed., **A Companion to Thomas Jefferson,** 110–27, is a fine survey of the period.

267 HARES, RABBITS, AND PARTRIDGES **PTJ,** VII, 383–84.

267 STILTON CHEESES Ibid., 384. In the end, he could not send the cheeses. (Ibid., 429.)

267 "VERY THICK WEATHER" Ibid., 508.

267 A FEVER STRUCK PATSY Ibid.

267 "THROUGH A COUNTRY" Ibid.

267 "THE MOST AGREEABLE COUNTRY" Roy and Alma Moore, **Thomas Jefferson's Journey to the South of France** (New York, 1999), 16.

267 JEFFERSON NEGOTIATED TREATIES ON WHALE OIL Kaplan, **Jefferson and France,** 30. See also **JHT,** II, 196–97, and Merrill D. Peterson, "Thomas Jefferson and Commercial Policy, 1783–1793," **William and Mary Quarterly,** 3d ser., 22, no. 4 (October 1965): 599–600.

267 HE KEPT A WARY EYE Kaplan, **Jefferson and France,** 33. I am indebted to Kaplan for these points. See also **PTJ,** VIII, 339 and 373–74.

267 THE PURCHASE OF AMERICAN EXPORTS Ibid. See also **PTJ,** XIV, 304–5; ibid., XV, 502.

267 TO THE OPENING OF ST. DOMINGUE Kaplan, **Jefferson and France,** 33. See also **PTJ,** XV, 456.

268 "I BEG YOU'D PUT" **PTJ,** VII, 376.

268 A CHATTY, DETAILED MEMORANDUM Kaplan, **Jefferson and France,** 33. See also **PTJ,** VII, 386–91.

268 THE MARQUIS DE CONDORCET William Howard Adams, **Paris Years of Thomas Jefferson**, 7.

268 JEFFERSON TOOK UP RESIDENCE Ibid., 47–48.

269 "FOR THE ARTICLES OF HOUSEHOLD FURNITURE" **PTJ**, VIII, 230.

269 "MR. ADAMS' COLLEAGUE" **Adams Family Correspondence**, VI, 78.

269 "AN AGREEABLE MAN" McCullough, **John Adams**, 312.

269 "AS MUCH YOUR BOY" Ibid., 311.

269 "EVERY DAY ENLARGING" William Howard Adams, **Paris Years of Thomas Jefferson**, 41.

269 HOUSES, THEATERS, THE WALL OF THE FARMERS-GENERAL Ibid., 43–45.

270 THE PALAIS ROYAL Ibid., 59.

270 THIS "GREAT AND GOOD" COUNTRY Jefferson, **Writings**, 98.

270 "SO ASK THE TRAVELLED INHABITANT" Ibid.

270 THE BARBARY STATES **EOL**, 633–39. See also Robert W. Tucker and David C. Hendrickson, **Empire of Liberty: The Statecraft of Thomas Jefferson**, 294–99; Frank Lambert, **The Barbary Wars: American Independence in the Atlantic World** (New York, 2005); and Joseph Wheelan, **Jefferson's War: America's First War on Terror, 1801–1805** (New York, 2003).

271 "THESE STATES ARE NOTED" David Adams, **Geography; Or, A Description of the World** (Boston, 1820), 306.

271 "TO PURCHASE THEIR PEACE" **PTJ**, VII, 511.

271 "YET FROM SOME GLIMMERINGS" Ibid.

271 "SURELY OUR PEOPLE" Ibid., 511–12.

271 CAPTURE OF AN AMERICAN SHIP Ibid., 639–40.

271 PRESSED AGAIN FOR A WARLIKE RESPONSE Ibid. John Jay had other, more conventional ideas, transmitting instructions from the Congress directing Jefferson, Franklin, and Adams to treat with the Barbary States, and even raising the possibility that American funds might be used to bribe the right people in order to make peace. A deal was necessary, Jay wrote, "because the continuance of . . . hostilities must constantly expose our free citizens to captivity and slavery." (Ibid., VIII, 20.) If the diplomats found it wise to buy influence, then so be it. "At courts where favoritism as well as corruption prevails, it is necessary that attention be paid even to men who may have no other recommendation than their influence with their superiors." (Ibid., 21.)

271 "THESE ARE FRAMED" Ibid., 644. He was soon confronted with a conflict with Spain over the American West. On Thursday, July 22, 1784, at New Orleans, Spain closed the Mississippi to navigation. Madrid's offer to Americans—to allow some maritime traffic down the river, but to prohibit American exportation from New Orleans—was a poor one, and Jefferson needed to know how hard he should push the matter. "I would wish you to sound your acquaintances on the subject and to let me know what they think of it; and whether if nothing more can be

obtained, this or no treaty, that is to say, this or war would be preferred." (Ibid., 510.)

From home Charles Thomson had disagreeable news about the Committee of the States, the quasi-executive body Jefferson had helped bring into being. The committee had adjourned without "the harmony and good humor that could have been wished," Thomson reported on October 1, 1784. (Ibid., 432.) The price to be paid was not limited to the domestic scene. "I am apprehensive it will have an ill aspect in the eyes of European nations and give them unfavorable impressions, which will require all your address and abilities to remove," he wrote Jefferson. (Ibid.) The Congress had a difficult time even choosing a home. "If Congress should not be able to make a majority . . . to determine on any one place of fixed residence (a case very likely to happen)," Francis Hopkinson wrote Jefferson, "will they not be in a situation like that of Mahomet's Tomb—suspended between Heaven and Earth and belonging to neither!" (Ibid., 535.)

By November Jefferson's fears about America's loss of face because of the weak Confederacy were confirmed. "All respect for our government is annihilated on this side [of] the water, from an idea of its want of tone and energy," Jefferson wrote Elbridge Gerry. "It is a dangerous opinion to us, and possibly will bring on insults which will force us into war." (Ibid., 502.)

272 "HE HAS A PRINCIPLE" William Howard

Adams, **Paris Years of Thomas Jefferson**, 184–85. English policy on trade was so stringent, Jefferson believed it "a nation so totally absorbed in self interest that nothing will force them to be just but rigorous retaliation." (**PTJ**, VII, 516; also see ibid., 509–10.)

Jefferson always maintained a tough line with Britain. "Nothing will bring them to reason but physical obstruction applied to their bodily senses," he told Madison on March 18, 1785. "We must show that we are capable of foregoing commerce with them before they will be capable of consenting to an equal commerce." Tobacco was America's ally in this case: "Our tobacco they must have from whatever place we make its deposit, because they can get no other whose quality so well suits the habits of their people." (Ibid., VIII, 40.)

272 INVENTED A FICTITIOUS FRENCH OFFICER   **PTJ**, VII, 540–45. The "officer lately returned" allowed that there had been a few incidents: the Philadelphia Mutiny ("Yet in this mutiny there neither was blood shed nor a blow struck"); a riot in Charleston; the passage of some resolutions in town meetings protesting various articles of the Treaty of Paris; and, in Virginia, the call to halt payment of the British debts until there was restitution for the confiscated slaves.

Yet the disturbances in America, Jefferson's officer wrote, were nothing compared to the recent violence in London under Lord Gordon.

"Where is there any country of equal extent with the U.S. in which fewer disturbances have happened in the same space of time? . . . With respect to the people their confidence in their rulers in general is what common sense will tell us it must be, where they are of their own choice annually, unbribed by money, undebauched by feasting, and drunkenness. It would be difficult to find one man among them who would not consider a return under the dominion of Great Britain as the greatest of all possible miseries." (Ibid., 540–42.)

The difficulty facing Jefferson in answering widely distributed attacks was formidable. "The views and designs, the intrigues and projects, of courts are let out by insensible degrees and with infinite art and delicacy in the gazettes," said John Adams. "The English papers are an engine by which everything is scattered all over the world. . . . Of these papers, the French emissaries in London, even in time of war—but especially in time of peace, make a very great use; they insert in them things which they wish to have circulated far and wide." (Ibid., 544.)

272 "NOTHING IS KNOWN" Ibid., 540.

273 HE WAS DISPATCHING BARRELS OF BRANDY Ibid., 500–501.

273 LUCY, AGE TWO, WAS DEAD Ibid., 441.

273 DESCRIBED AS A "CONVULSIVE STRANGULATING" Robert Hooper, **Quincy's Lexicon-Medicum: A New Medical Dictionary** (Philadelphia, 1817),

611. See also Nicholas Bakalar, "First Mention; Pertussis, 1913," **The New York Times,** April 13, 2010.

273 "It's impossible to paint" **PTJ,** VII, 441.

274 "both suffered as much pain" Ibid., 441–42.

274 "Present me affectionately" Ibid., 636.

274 "Mr. J. is a man of great sensibility" William Howard Adams, **Paris Years of Thomas Jefferson,** 181.

274 "Behold me at length" **PTJ,** VIII, 568.

274 "My God! How little do" Ibid., 233.

275 walking up to six or eight miles a day Ibid., 90.

275 "I must have Polly" Ibid., 141.

275 "I think I have somewhere" Kaminski, **Founders on the Founders,** 292–93.

276 "Our country is getting" **PTJ,** VIII, 357.

276 "We have intelligence" Ibid., 293.

277 "It is said that Great Britain" Ibid., 196.

277 "Our governments" Ibid.

NINETEEN · The Philosophical World

278 "Will you take the trouble" **PTJ,** IX, 158.

278 shopping in France **MB,** I, 565 and ff.

278 attended masquerade balls Ibid., 600.

279 a forward baroness Ibid., 611.

279 made his way to Versailles Ibid., 562.

279 He also visited Patsy Cynthia A. Kierner,

Martha Jefferson Randolph, Daughter of Monticello: Her Life and Times (Chapel Hill, N.C., 2012), 51–59.

279 "A HOUSE OF EDUCATION" PTJ, XI, 612. See also Kierner, Martha Jefferson Randolph, 54.

279 HE TRIED TO PLAY CHESS MB, I, 610.

279 "I HAVE HEARD HIM SAY" Ibid.

279 CALLED ON THE COMTESSE D'HOUDETOT AT SANNOIS PTJ, VIII, 241. See also William Howard Adams, Paris Years of Thomas Jefferson, 75.

279 "IN ALL ITS PERFECTION" PTJ, VIII, 241.

280 THE COMMISSIONING OF A STATUE Ibid., VII, 378. "The intention of the assembly is that the statue should be the work of the most masterly hand," Harrison told Jefferson. "I shall therefore leave it to you to find out the best in any of the European states." (Ibid.)

280 COME TO AMERICA "FOR THE PURPOSE" Ibid., 567. "I trust that having given to your country so much of your time heretofore, you will add the short space which this operation will require to enable them to transmit to posterity the form of the person whose actions will be delivered to them by History. Monsieur Houdon is at present engaged in making a statue of the king of France. A bust of Voltaire executed by him is said to be one of the first in the world." (Ibid.)

280 "AN IMPROVEMENT IS MADE HERE" Ibid., VIII, 455.

281 "TO COMMUNICATE TO ME" Ibid., 301.

281 DOCUMENTS ABOUT FRENCH MARINES Ibid., XI, 31.

281 TO CONVINCE THE COMTE DE BUFFON Ibid., IX, 158.

281 TRAVELED TO A SCHOOL FOR THE BLIND MB, I, 595.

281 EXCHANGED AMERICAN NUTS AND BERRIES Ibid., 599.

281 THE AMERICAN EXPLORER JOHN LEDYARD Ibid., 586.

281 LEDYARD WAS PLANNING A JOURNEY JHT, II, 67–68.

281 "IT IS CERTAINLY OF GREAT IMPORTANCE" PTJ, VIII, 73.

282 "HAS THE ABBÉ ROCHON" Ibid., 75.

282 HE PURCHASED A PORCELAIN MARS Ibid., 548.

282 THE FIGURINES WERE ACCIDENTALLY DESTROYED Ibid., IX, 126.

282 HE ONCE SENT CORSETS Ibid., XI, 45–46.

282 "HE WISHES THEY MAY" Ibid.

282 ENGLISH TAILORING AND SHOEMAKING NEEDS Ibid., XII, 484–85. Jefferson's direct contact was William Stephens Smith, the Adamses' son-in-law. (Ibid.)

282 "I HAVE AT LENGTH" Ibid., VIII, 473.

283 HÔTEL DE LANGEAC MB, I, 594.

283 "I CULTIVATE IN MY OWN GARDEN" PTJ, XII, 135.

283 "I AM NOW OF AN AGE" Ibid., VIII, 500.

283 "I OBSERVED THAT" William Howard Adams, **Paris Years of Thomas Jefferson**, 185–86.

283 "HE IS EVERYTHING" Kaminksi, **Founders on the Founders**, 293.

283 "MR. JEFFERSON IS A MAN" Ibid., 294.

284 A PORTRAIT OF THE DAILY ROUTINE **PTJ**, XI, 122–23.

285 "THE POLITICS OF EUROPE" Ibid., IX, 264.

285 FOR "A HUNDRED OR TWO" Ibid., 267.

285 A CONVENTION TO DEAL Ibid., 335.

286 "I ALMOST DESPAIR" Ibid.

286 PAINE VISITED JEFFERSON IN PARIS **JHT**, II, 142–43.

286 THE SON OF A CORSET MAKER Christopher Hitchens, **Thomas Paine's Rights of Man: A Biography** (New York, 2006), 20–21.

286 WAS BORN IN THETFORD Craig Nelson, **Thomas Paine**, 14.

286 YOUNG PAINE WAS BAPTIZED Ibid., 16–17. "Having been raised in two religions simultaneously during a period when competing doctrines waged armed warfare against one another could have triggered Paine's adult tendency to question all received wisdom," wrote Nelson. (Ibid., 17.)

286 MORE THAN HALF A MILLION COPIES Susan Jacoby, **Freethinkers: A History of American Secularism** (New York, 2004), 35.

286 **THE RIGHTS OF MAN** Ibid., 38–39.

286 **THE AGE OF REASON** Ibid., 41–43.

286 PAINE AND JEFFERSON BECAME FRIENDS Wood,

Idea of America, 213–28, examines Paine and Jefferson in detail. Referring to historical indictments of Jefferson on questions of slavery and of the racial inferiority passages in the **Notes on the State of Virginia,** Wood writes: "Paine may be able to help redeem Jefferson. Since it is clear that Jefferson and Paine thought alike on virtually every issue, Paine's radical and democratic credentials may allow historians, especially those of the left, to see Jefferson in a somewhat more favorable light, or at least see him in light of the eighteenth century, and not in today's light." (Ibid., 227.) See also Seth Cotlar, **Tom Paine's America: The Rise and Fall of Transatlantic Radicalism in the Early Republic** (Charlottesville, Va., 2011).

In 1801, Jefferson offered Paine passage from France to the United States on a U.S. Navy vessel after Paine had spent time in prison for opposing the execution of Louis XVI. By now president, Jefferson argued to Madison that the author of **Common Sense** deserved special attention. "There is a clear enough line between Thomas Paine and citizens in general," he told Madison. (**PTJ,** XXXV, 125.) Paine declined Jefferson's offer and ultimately arrived in the United States in November 1802. (Ibid., 126.)

286 A SERIES OF MEETINGS   **PTJ,** IX, 285–88.

286 LARGE PIPES OF TOBACCO   Ibid. See also Abigail Adams 2d to John Quincy Adams, **Adams Family Correspondence,** VII, 41–42.

287 "WHAT HAS BEEN ALREADY" **PTJ**, IX, 295. "I am so impressed and distressed with this affair that I will go to New York or to Algiers or first to one and then to the other . . . rather than it should not be brought to a conclusion." (Ibid.) For Adams's correspondence with John Jay on these matters, see **The Works of John Adams, Second President of the United States: With a Life of the Author, Notes, and Illustrations, by His Grandson Charles Francis Adams**, VIII (Boston, 1853), 372–79.

287 IN A LETTER DATED TUESDAY Ibid.

287 HE WOULD BE BACK BEFORE Ibid., 318.

287 AT A LONDON DINNER Ibid., 398–99.

287 "HE WAS SERIOUS IN THIS" Ibid., 399.

288 "I KNOW OF NO GENTLEMAN" Ibid., 555.

288 "IMPOSSIBLE FOR ANYTHING" Jefferson, **Writings,** 57.

289 "THEY TEEM WITH EVERY HORROR" **PTJ**, VIII, 548.

289 "IT WOULD HAVE ILLY SUITED ME" Ibid.

289 SURVEYING ENGLISH GARDENS Ibid., IX, 369–75; McCullough, **John Adams**, 356–62.

289 "MY ANXIETIES ON THIS SUBJECT" **PTJ**, VIII, 451. "I must now repeat my wish to have Polly sent to me next summer," Jefferson wrote Francis Eppes on August 30, 1785. "With respect to the person to whose care she should be trusted, I must leave it to yourself and Mrs. Eppes altogether," Jefferson said. "Some good lady passing from America to France, or even England, would

be most eligible; but a careful gentleman who would be so kind as to superintend her would do." (Ibid.)

289 A SIMPLE LETTER ARRIVED   Ibid., 517.

290 "I WISH SO MUCH TO SEE YOU"   Ibid., 532–33.

290 "I WILL VENTURE TO ASSERT"   Ibid., IX, 380.

TWENTY · His Head and His Heart

291 "WE ARE NOT IMMORTAL OURSELVES"   PTJ, X, 451.

291 "A GOLDEN-HAIRED, LANGUISHING"   Helen Duprey Bullock, **My Head and My Heart: A Little History of Thomas Jefferson and Maria Cosway** (New York, 1945), 14.

291 BORN NEAR FLORENCE   Ibid., 15. My portrait of Cosway relies on ibid.; William Howard Adams, **Paris Years of Thomas Jefferson;** and Stephen Lloyd, "The Accomplished Maria Cosway: Anglo-Italian Artist, Musician, Salon Hostess and Educationalist (1759–1838)," **Journal of Anglo-Italian Studies** 2 (1992): 108–39. Adams's book is especially thorough and engaging.

291 WAS BARELY RESCUED   Ibid., 14.

292 IN THE GLAMOROUS CIRCLES   Ibid., 15–16.

292 THE WRITER JAMES BOSWELL   Gordon Trumbull, "Boswell, James (1740–1795)," in **Oxford Dictionary of National Biography**, 729–40.

292 SIR JOSHUA REYNOLDS   Jane Turner, ed., **The Dictionary of Art**, XXVI (New York, 1996), 270–81.

292 ANGELICA KAUFFMANN   Wendy Wassyng Roworth, "Kauffman, (Anna Maria) Angelica Catharina (1741–1807)," in **Oxford Dictionary of National Biography**, XXX, 914–17.

292 THE COLLECTOR CHARLES TOWNLEY   B. F. Cook, "Townley, Charles (1737–1805)," in **Oxford Dictionary of National Biography**, LV, 115–17.

292 "A WELL-MADE LITTLE MAN"   Kukla, **Mr. Jefferson's Women**, 89.

292 WON THE PATRONAGE OF THE PRINCE OF WALES   William Howard Adams, **Paris Years of Thomas Jefferson**, 101, 225.

292 SET UP HOUSEKEEPING AT SCHOMBERG HOUSE   Ibid., 225.

292 "HIS NEW HOUSE"   Bullock, **My Head and My Heart**, 18.

292 FURNITURE WAS ORNATELY CARVED   Ibid. I am indebted to Bullock for the details of the Cosways' interior design. Her quotation of John Thomas Smith was critical to capturing the ethos of the Cosway world.

293 WILLIAM HAZLITT HAD WRITTEN   William Howard Adams, **Paris Years of Thomas Jefferson**, 225.

293 HORACE WALPOLE, THE WRITER   Ibid., 225–26.

293 MADEMOISELLE LA CHEVALIÈRE D'EON, KNOWN IN HER DAY   Ibid., 226.

293 ONE COSWAY FRIEND   Ibid., 224–25.

293 HUGUES AND THE COSWAYS   Ibid., 103.

293 THE ARTIST JOHN TRUMBULL   Turner, **Dictionary of Art**, XXXI, 391–92.

293 THE MEN WHO HAD DESIGNED THE DOME   William Howard Adams, **Paris Years of Thomas
Jefferson**, 62–63.

294 ALLOWING LIGHT TO POUR THROUGH   Ibid.,
62. Adams wrote: "To [Jefferson's] eye, the light-
filled room seemed to manifest the idealism of
the age. It was a recurring image that he could
not shake. The marriage of practical engineer-
ing and aesthetic beauty was a relationship that
would often inspire his architectural fantasies."
(Ibid., 62–63.)

294 "THE MOST SUPERB THING"   Ibid. Adams added:
"The halle's sparkling glass and thin wooden ribs
somehow captured for Jefferson the spirit of an
'enlightened space' that was both symbolic and
utilitarian." (Ibid., 63.)

294 No. 6 RUE ST.-FLORENTIN   Michael Gallet,
**Paris Domestic Architecture of the 18th Cen-
tury** (London, 1972), 21.

294 VOLUPTUOUS LIPS   Bullock, **My Head and My
Heart**, 13–14, offers a vivid description of Mrs.
Cosway; the effect of her lips are evident from
portraits of her.

294 DIPLOMATIC DISPATCHES HAD ARRIVED   PTJ,
X, 445. See also Bullock, **My Head and My
Heart**, 21.

294 "EVERY SOUL OF YOU"   **PTJ**, X, 445.

294 HER ENGLISH WAS NOT PARTICULARLY FLUENT
See, for instance, **PTJ**, X, 494–96.

294 HAD DINNER TOGETHER   Bullock, **My Head and My Heart**, 21. The details of the day come from this account of Bullock's, who drew them from Jefferson's "Head and Heart" letter. See also **PTJ**, X, 443–55.

295 TREATED "MEN LIKE DOGS"   Bullock, **My Head and My Heart**, 2o.

295 "EVERY MOMENT WAS FILLED"   **PTJ**, X, 446.

295 A FONDNESS FOR GETAWAY SPOTS   William Howard Adams, **Paris Years of Thomas Jefferson**, 244–47, describes the Jefferson-Cosway excursions in detail.

296 "HOW GRAND THE IDEA"   Ibid., 244.

296 "THE WHEELS OF TIME"   Ibid.

296 JEFFERSON DISLOCATED HIS RIGHT WRIST   Bullock, **My Head and My Heart**, 24. See also **PTJ**, X, 431–33.

296 "IT WAS BY ONE OF THOSE FOLLIES"   **PTJ**, X, 478.

296 "I ONLY MENTION MY WISH"   Ibid., 394.

296 "I HAVE PASSED"   Ibid., 431–32.

297 "I AM VERY, VERY SORRY"   Ibid., 433.

297 "MR. AND MRS. COSWAY ARRIVED"   Ibid., 438.

297 HIS "LAST SAD OFFICE"   Ibid., 443.

297 "SEATED BY MY FIRESIDE"   Ibid., 444.

302 "YOUR LETTER COULD EMPLOY ME"   Ibid., 494.

TWENTY-ONE · Do You Like Our New Constitution?

304 "CHERISH THEREFORE THE SPIRIT" PTJ, XI, 49.

304 DEBT-RIDDEN, FRANCE FACED A SUPREME TEST Sylvia Neely, **A Concise History of the French Revolution** (Lanham, Md., 2008), 1–54, is instructive. See also Bailey Stone, **Reinterpreting the French Revolution: A Global-Historical Perspective** (New York, 2002), 14–61, and William Doyle, **The Oxford History of the French Revolution** (New York, 2002), 66–85.

304 PARTLY BECAUSE OF ITS SPENDING ON THE AMERICAN REVOLUTION Neely, **Concise History of the French Revolution**, 40–42.

304 JEFFERSON WAS SHOCKED PTJ, XI, 415.

304 TAXES WERE UNEQUAL Neely, **Concise History of the French Revolution**, 7–12.

305 "IT IS IMPOSSIBLE" Ibid., 45.

305 THE KING SUMMONED AN ASSEMBLY OF NOTABLES PTJ, XI, 31–32. "You will have seen in the public papers that the king has called an Assembly of the Notables of his country," Jefferson told John Jay in January 1787. "This has not been done for 160 years past." (Ibid., 31.)

305 "OF COURSE" Ibid.

305 "SHOULD THEY ATTEMPT" JHT, II, 182.

305 THE ASSEMBLY OF NOTABLES FAILED Neely, **Concise History of the French Revolution**, 47.

305 ONE FROM THE MARQUIS DE LAFAYETTE Ibid.

305 CREATED IN THE MIDDLE AGES   Ibid., 6.

305 ITS LAST MEETING HAD BEEN HELD IN 1614
Ibid.

305 "WE TALKED ABOUT THE ESTABLISHMENT"
Ibid., 57.

306 "THE INEFFICACY OF OUR GOVERNMENT"   PTJ,
X, 488.

306 A GROUP LED BY DANIEL SHAYS   Wilentz, **Rise
of American Democracy,** 30–32. See also **EOL,**
111; William Hogeland, **The Whiskey Rebellion: George Washington, Alexander Hamilton, and the Frontier Rebels Who Challenged
America's Newfound Sovereignty** (New York,
2006), 52–53; and Don Higginbotham, "War
and State Formation in Revolutionary America" in Gould and Onuf, **Empire and Nation,**
67. There were international sources for the discontent. Several of the eastern states, Jefferson
wrote, "depended before the war chiefly on their
whale oil and fish. The former was consumed in
London, but being now loaded there with heavy
duties, cannot go there. Much of their fish went
up the Mediterranean, now shut to us by the piratical states. Their debts therefore press them,
while the means of payment have lessened."
(PTJ, X, 631.)

306 "A SPIRIT OF LICENTIOUSNESS"   **PTJ,** X, 488.
Ezra Stiles of Yale wrote Jefferson about the rebellion on September 14, 1786: "Our enemies
are fomenting discord among us and have succeeded to excite some tumults and popular in-

surrections." (Ibid., 386.) Liberty would be safe, Stiles said, so long as "property in the United States is so minutely partitioned and transfused among the inhabitants." (Ibid.)

John Jay also sent Jefferson newspaper accounts of the unrest. "A reluctance to taxes, an impatience of government, a rage for property, and little regard to the means of acquiring it, together with a desire of equality in all things, seem to actuate the mass of those who are uneasy in their circumstances," Jay wrote. (Ibid., 489.)

To Stiles, Jefferson replied: "The commotions which have taken place in America, as far as they are yet known to me, offer nothing threatening. They are a proof that the people have liberty enough, and I would not wish them less than they have. If the happiness of the mass of the people can be secured at the expense of a little tempest now and then, or even of a little blood, it will be a precious purchase. **Malo libertatum periculosam quam quietam servitutem.** Let common sense and common honesty have fair play and they will soon set things to rights." (Ibid., 629.)

306 SOUGHT TO REASSURE JEFFERSON Ibid., 557. Contradicting her husband on the Shays violence, Abigail Adams had a different, darker view, writing Jefferson: "With regard to the tumults in my native state . . . Instead of that laudable spirit which you approve, which makes a people watchful over their liberties and alert in

the defense of them, these mobbish insurgents are for sapping the foundation, and destroying the whole fabric at once." (Ibid., XI, 86.)

306 "I CAN NEVER FEAR" Ibid., 619.

307 THERE MIGHT BE CANADIAN DESIGNS Ibid., 596.

307 AN "IDEA THAT MAY DO" Ibid. William S. Smith was explicit about the connection between the British and Indians. "I hope there will not be any necessity for [the] spilling of blood, for there is no knowing where it will end," Smith wrote Jefferson. "If there is an appearance of it, may we not shelter ourselves from the horror and inconvenience of internal commotion by turning the tide on these Britons by a formal declaration of war[?] They are at the bottom of it, and merit our highest indignation." (Ibid., XI, 90.)

307 "THE BASIS OF OUR GOVERNMENTS" Ibid., XI, 49.

308 A LETTER TO MADISON Ibid., 92–97.

309 "I HOLD IT THAT A LITTLE REBELLION" Ibid., 93.

309 JOURNEY THROUGH THE SOUTH Ibid., 415–64. See also TJF, http://www.monticello.org/site/research-and-collections/journey-through-france-and-italy-1787 (accessed 2011).

309 "ARCHITECTURE, PAINTING, SCULPTURE" PTJ, XI, 215.

309 "I AM NOW IN THE LAND" Ibid., 247.

309 THE CONSTITUTIONAL CONVENTION HAD BEGUN Middlekauff, Glorious Cause, 642–44.

310 SKEPTICAL OF A PROPOSAL   Ibid., 480–81.

310 POLLY DID NOT WANT TO PART WITH THE MAN
Ibid., 501–2.

310 "THE OLD NURSE WHOM YOU"   Ibid., 502.

310 APPEARED NEARLY WHITE   Bear, **Jefferson at
Monticello,** 4. The source is Isaac Granger Jefferson, who said: "Sally Hemings's mother Betty
was a bright mulatto woman, and Sally mighty
near white." (Ibid.)

310 "VERY HANDSOME, [WITH] LONG HAIR STRAIGHT
DOWN HER BACK"   Ibid.

311 WAS WELL DEVELOPED   Gordon-Reed, **Hemingses of Monticello,** 194–95. I am indebted
to Gordon-Reed for her insights on possibilities
suggested by Abigail Adams's account of receiving Sally Hemings.

311 ABIGAIL ADAMS GUESSED   Ibid.

311 RAMSEY WAS HOPING   Ibid., 197–208.

311 "I TELL HER THAT I DID NOT"   Ibid., 502.

311 SHOULD COME FETCH HIS YOUNGER DAUGHTER
Ibid.

312 "AS CONTENTED . . . AS SHE WAS MISERABLE"
Ibid., 503.

312 "THE GIRL WHO IS WITH [POLLY]"   Ibid.

312 JEFFERSON THANKED ABIGAIL   Ibid., 514–15.

312 CRYING AND "THROWN INTO ALL"   Ibid., 551.

312 POLLY JEFFERSON AND SALLY HEMINGS ARRIVED
MB, I, 674.

312 "SHE HAD TOTALLY FORGOTTEN"   **PTJ,** XI,
592.

313 "HER READING, HER WRITING"   Ibid., 634.

313 "It is really" Ibid., XII, 69.

313 "Nothing can exceed" Ibid., 103.

314 "The report of an intention" Dunbar, **Study of "Monarchical" Tendencies**, 96.

314 Hamilton was said to believe Ibid., 97.

314 alleged plan of Hamilton's "that had in view" Ibid., 96–97.

314 "At this moment there is not" Douglas Brymner, **Report on Canadian Archives, 1890** (Ottawa, 1891), 97–98. Lord Dorchester sent this report to Lord Sydney on April 10, 1787.

315 "They are divided into three" Ibid., 99.

316 a crisis in the United Netherlands **JHT**, II, 184–87.

316 "It conveys to us the important lesson" Ibid., 184.

316 "We are, therefore, never safe" Ibid., 187.

316 George Washington dispatched **PTJ**, XII, 149–50.

316 Benjamin Franklin sent one Ibid., 236–37.

316 letters about the Constitution flowed See, for example, ibid., 252–257. "It has in my mind great faults, but . . . it is fairly to be concluded that this is a better scheme than can be looked for from another experiment," wrote Edward Carrington. (Ibid., 255.) St. John de Crèvecoeur told Jefferson, "I trust that every man who [is] attached to the glory and happiness of his country, as well as to his property, will be for it." (Ibid., 332.)

316 it "seems to be" Ibid., 335.

317 "How do you like" Ibid., 350–51.

317 "He may be reelected from" Ibid., 351.

317 "the world has at length" Ibid., 356.

317 "We have had 13 states" Ibid., 356–57.

318 "The want of facts" Ibid., 357.

318 he reacted to the Constitution Ibid., 438–43.

318 "freedom of religion" Ibid., 440.

319 "After all, it is my principle" Ibid., 442.

319 Jefferson suggested that Ibid., 569–70. "I sincerely wish that the 9 first conventions may receive, and the 4 last reject it," he wrote Madison in February 1788. "The former will secure it finally, while the latter will oblige them to offer a declaration of rights in order to complete the union. We shall thus have all its good, and cure its principal defect." (Ibid.) Madison disagreed. He believed full ratification was the essential first step.

Some in Virginia wanted a conditional ratification like the one Jefferson had suggested earlier or a call for a new convention to take matters up again. "In either event, I think the Constitution and the Union will be both endangered," Madison wrote Jefferson in April 1788. (Ibid., XIII, 98.)

319 "There are indeed some faults" Ibid., XIII, 174. Jefferson was brought into the debate over the ratification of the Constitution by proxy on Monday, June 9, 1788, by Patrick Henry, who sought to turn Jefferson's skepticism about parts

of the Constitution into wholehearted opposition. (Ibid., 354–55.)

"I might go farther," Henry told the Virginia ratifying convention, "I might say, not from public authority, but good information, that his opinion is, that you reject this government. His character and abilities are in the highest estimation; he is well acquainted, in every respect, with this country. . . . This illustrious citizen advises you to reject this government till it be amended. . . . At a great distance from us, he remembers and studies our happiness. Living in splendor and dissipation, he thinks yet of bills of rights—thinks of those little, despised things called **maxims.** Let us follow the sage advice of this common friend of our happiness." (Ibid., 354.)

Madison had had enough of Henry. "I believe that, were that gentleman now on this floor, he would be for the adoption of this Constitution. I wish his name had never been mentioned. I . . . know that the delicacy of his feelings will be wounded when he will see in print what has and may be said concerning him on this occasion." (Ibid., 355.)

The problem was that Henry's interpretation of Jefferson's position was plausible—but Henry was interpreting Jefferson's **February** position in **June,** after Jefferson had moved to an affirmative view of the Constitution. Jefferson was now largely in agreement with Francis Hopkinson, who observed: "Whether **this** is the best possible system of government, I will not pretend to say. Time must determine; but I am well persuaded that without an efficient federal government, the states must in a very short time sink into contempt and the most dangerous confusion." (Ibid., 370.) Because of the distance, however, no one could know that Jefferson had reached this conclusion, which made Madison's rescue mission all the more difficult. But the mission succeeded.

319 JEFFERSON FOLLOWED THE POLITICS OF RATIFICATION Ibid., 159–61.

320 THE SIGNIFICANCE OF THE PRESIDENCY Ibid., 352.

320 GLIMPSED MARIA COSWAY'S HANDWRITING Ibid., 103–4.

320 "AT HEIDELBERG I WISHED" Ibid., 104.

320 HE SHARED A JOKE WITH HER Ibid. See also Gordon-Reed, **Hemingses of Monticello**, 281–82.

320 FASCINATED BY A 1699 PAINTING Gordon-Reed, **Hemingses of Monticello**, 281–83. Fawn Brodie was the first observer to point out the implications of Jefferson's interest in an image of a patriarchal figure being given a young slave woman for sexual purposes while Sally Hemings was living with Jefferson in Paris. (Ibid.)

320 THE PICTURE, JEFFERSON SAID, WAS "DELICIOUS" **PTJ**, XIII, 103.

321 "PARIS IS NOW BECOME" Ibid., 151.

TWENTY-TWO · A Treaty in Paris

322 "He desired to bring my mother" Lewis and Onuf, **Sally Hemings and Thomas Jefferson,** 256.

322 there was Sally Hemings Gordon-Reed, **Hemingses of Monticello,** 326–28.

322 had been paid some small wages Ibid., 236.

322 twelve livres a month for ten months Ibid., 236–41.

323 had bought clothing Ibid., 259–60.

323 had her inoculated Ibid., 213–23.

323 James was trained as a chef Ibid., 169–90.

323 may have served the Jefferson daughters Ibid., 211–13.

324 "the strongest of the human passions" Burstein, **Jefferson's Secrets,** 171.

324 "light colored and decidedly good-looking" TJF, http://www.monticello.org/site/plantation-and-slavery/appendix-h-sally-hemings-and-her-children (accessed 2012).

324 at the times she was likely to have conceived TJF, http://www.monti cello.org/site/plantation-and-slavery/v-assessment-possible-paternity-other-jeffersons (accessed 2012).

324 enslaved persons could apply for their liberty Gordon-Reed, **Hemingses of Monticello,** 172–82.

324 he had once advised a fellow slave owner Ibid., 182–83.

324 "Mr. Jefferson's concubine" Lewis and

Onuf, **Sally Hemings and Thomas Jefferson,**
256.

325 WAS PREGNANT WHEN JEFFERSON WAS PREPAR-
ING   Ibid.

325 "SHE WAS JUST BEGINNING"   Ibid.

325 SHE, NOT HE, WAS IN CONTROL   Gordon-Reed,
Hemingses of Monticello, 339. "Whether she
had had time in her young life to learn this fact
about him or not, the truth is that few things
could have disturbed the very thin-skinned, pos-
sessive, and controlling Jefferson more deeply
than having persons in his inner circle take the
initiative and express their willingness to remove
themselves from it," wrote Gordon-Reed. (Ibid.)

326 "TO INDUCE HER TO DO SO"   Lewis and Onuf,
Sally Hemings and Thomas Jefferson, 256.

326 "IN CONSEQUENCE OF HIS PROMISE"   Ibid.

326 THEIR FATHER KEPT THE PROMISE   Ibid.

326 "WE ALL BECAME FREE"   Ibid., 256. Here is a
summary of the Jefferson-Hemings children and
their fates, from Lucia C. Stanton, Shannon Senior Research Historian at Monticello:

Sally Hemings had at least six children,
who are now believed to have been fathered
by Thomas Jefferson years after his wife's
death. According to Jefferson's records, four
survived to adulthood. Beverly (b. 1798), a
carpenter and fiddler, was allowed to leave
the plantation in late 1821 or early 1822
and, according to his brother, passed into

white society in Washington, D.C. Harriet
(b. 1801), a spinner in Jefferson's textile shop,
also left Monticello in 1821 or 1822, probably with her brother, and passed for white.
Madison Hemings (1805–1878), a carpenter
and joiner, was given his freedom in Jefferson's will; he resettled in southern Ohio in
1836, where he worked at his trade and had
a farm. Eston Hemings (1808-ca. 1856), also
a carpenter, moved to Chillicothe, Ohio, in
the 1830s. There he was a well-known professional musician before moving about 1852 to
Wisconsin, where he changed his surname to
Jefferson along with his racial identity. Both
Madison and Eston Hemings made known
their belief that they were sons of Thomas
Jefferson. (TJF, http://www.monticello.org/
site/plantation-and-slavery/sally-hemings [ac-
cessed 2012].)

326 THE CALLING OF THE ESTATES-GENERAL JHT,
II, 193.

326 "I IMAGINE YOU HAVE HEARD" PTJ, XIII, 358.

327 THE TWO MEN MET IN AMSTERDAM JHT, II,
187–92, and Peterson, **Thomas Jefferson and
the New Nation,** 367–68, are useful on these
issues.

327 THE FIRST TREATY TO BE RATIFIED JHT, II,
199–202; **PTJ,** XIV, 66–180.

328 WASHINGTON WAS TO BE PRESIDENT PTJ,
XIV, 3–4. To Jefferson, William S. Smith re-

ported on a (failed) anti-Federalist scheme to roil the new government. The purported plan: Have Virginia refuse to vote for Washington for president, which would then, in this scenario, make Adams president. It was a result, Smith told Jefferson, "which would not be consistent with the wish of the country and could only arise from the finesse of antifederal electors with a view to produce confusion and embarrass the operations of the Constitution, against which many have set their faces." (Ibid., 559–60.)

328 "IT IS . . . DOUBTFUL"   Ibid., XIII, 502.

328 "HANCOCK IS WEAK"   Ibid., XIV, 17.

329 AN "ILL UNDERSTANDING"   Ibid., 275.

329 "WHO HAD BEEN UTTERLY AVERSE"   Ibid., 301. Humphreys concluded: "Still, all the more reasonable men saw that the remedy would be infinitely worse than the disease." (Ibid.)

329 JEFFERSON WANTED TO COME HOME   Ibid., 189. "I consider as no small advantage the resuming the tone of mind of my constituents, which is lost by long absence, and can only be recovered by mixing with them." (Ibid.)

329 ESPECIALLY INTERESTED IN ESTABLISHING Ibid., 332. "I shall hope . . . for the pleasure of personal conferences with your Excellency on the subjects of this letter and others interesting to our country, of getting my own ideas set to rights by a communication of yours, and of taking again the tone of sentiment of my own coun-

try which we lose in some degree after a certain absence." (Ibid.)

329 "By the bye, you have been often" Ibid., 324.

329 the spirit of faction Richard Hofstadter, **The Idea of a Party System: The Rise of Legitimate Opposition in the United States, 1780–1840** (Berkeley, Calif., 1969), viii. (The first 121 pages of Hofstadter are on point.) The Founders, Hofstadter wrote, "did not believe in political parties as such, scorned those that they were conscious of as historical models, had a keen terror of party spirit and its evil consequences, and yet, almost as soon as their national government was in operation, found it necessary to establish parties." (Ibid., viii.) See also Wood, **Radicalism of the American Revolution**, 298–301.

329 "I am not" **PTJ**, XIV, 650.

330 "My great wish" Ibid., 651.

330 "J. Adams espoused the cause" Ibid., XV, 147–48.

330 Jefferson called Adams's proposal Ibid., 315. In May 1789, Madison tucked an intriguing point in the middle of a letter. "I have been asked whether any appointment at home would be agreeable to you. Being unacquainted with your mind I have not ventured on an answer." (Ibid., 153.)

330 a brutally cold winter in France **JHT**, II, 205.

330 "Our new constitution" PTJ, XIV, 420.
Kaplan, **Jefferson and France,** makes an interesting point, arguing that Jefferson's reactions to
events both in France and in America were colored by his consistent belief in the centrality of
the French alliance. "Fear of alienating the support of French liberals rising to power with the
Revolution made him look upon the suppression
of Shays' Rebellion and the creation of the Constitution as threats to America's republicanism
and hence to America's continued friendship
with France." (Ibid., 35.) Jefferson hoped that
France would peaceably find its way to a kind
of English constitution with defined individual
rights. He hoped, too, that reform would come
with relative ease and that France might "within
two or three years, be in enjoyment of a tolerably free constitution, and that without its having cost them a drop of blood." It was, of course,
not to be. (William Howard Adams, **Paris Years
of Thomas Jefferson,** 252; JHT, II, 193.)

331 riots in Paris killed about one hundred
people **PTJ,** XV, 104.

331 interpreted the violence in the most benign light Ibid., 111. By way of explanation,
Kaplan wrote: "With the future of his own country in mind, Jefferson gave wholehearted support
to the revolutionists in their struggle against the
internal hostility of the privileged classes and the
external enmity of the rest of Europe." (Kaplan,
Jefferson and France, 36.)

331 JEFFERSON HAD SKETCHED A CHARTER OF RIGHTS **PTJ,** XV, 167–68.

331 THE FRUSTRATED THIRD ESTATE Doyle, **Oxford History of the French Revolution,** 104–7.

332 HIS HOUSE WAS ROBBED Ibid., 260. "My hotel having lately been robbed, for the third time, I take the liberty of uniting my wish with that of the inhabitants of this quarter" in hoping for "the protection of a guard," he wrote the Comte de Montmorin on July 8, 1789. (Ibid.)

332 HE MONITORED A STREET BATTLE Ibid., 273.

332 HE WAS AT HIS FRIEND MADAME DE CORNY'S William Howard Adams, **Paris Years of Thomas Jefferson,** 287.

332 "THE TUMULTS IN PARIS" **PTJ,** XV, 276–77.

332 "THE HEAT OF THIS CITY" Ibid., 277.

333 "A MORE DANGEROUS SCENE OF WAR" Ibid., 279.

333 "HERE IN THE MIDST OF TUMULT" Ibid., 305.

333 "BREAK EVERY ENGAGEMENT" Ibid., 354.

333 ADOPTED THE DECLARATION Larry E. Tise, **The American Counterrevolution: A Retreat from Liberty, 1783–1800** (Mechanicsburg, Pa., 1998), 440–41. In addition, the Comte de Mirabeau, Emmanuel-Joseph Sieyès, and Jean-Joseph Mounier each played a part in determining its final form. (David P. Forsythe, **Encyclopedia of Human Rights,** I [Oxford, 2009], 406.)

333 INFLUENCED BY THE DECLARATION Peter Hanns Reill and Ellen Judy Wilson, **Encyclopedia of the Enlightenment** (New York, 1996),

143. Other influences included the 1776 Virginia Declaration of Rights (ibid.) and the U.S. state constitutions, especially those of Virginia, Maryland, and Massachusetts. (Forsythe, **Encyclopedia of Human Rights,** I, 406.)

333 HAD COUNSELED Forsythe, **Encyclopedia of Human Rights,** I, 406. Before writing the Declaration, Lafayette consulted with Thomas Paine, Benjamin Franklin, and Alexander Hamilton. Jefferson sent Madison a copy of the draft, which Gouverneur Morris also reviewed while in Paris. (Ibid.)

333 BEGAN AT FOUR **PTJ,** XV, 355.

333 "A SILENT WITNESS" Ibid. He knew that he was in a dangerous position—an American diplomat appearing to meddle in the internal politics of his host nation. The next morning, Jefferson went to Montmorin to confess and perform the "duties of exculpation." The count, though, was ahead of Jefferson—or chose to pretend that he was. "He told me he already knew everything which had passed, that, so far from taking umbrage at the use made of my house on that occasion, he earnestly wished I would habitually assist at such conferences, being sure I should be useful in moderating the warmer spirits, and promoting a wholesome and practicable reformation only." (Ibid.)

334 AGREED TO A STRUCTURE Ibid. "The result was an agreement that the king should have a suspensive veto on the laws, that the legislature should be composed of a single body only, and that to

be chosen by the people." The decisions made by the Assembly that evening "reduced the Aristocracy to insignificance and impotence." (Ibid.)

334 "DECIDED THE FATE OF THE [FRENCH] CONSTITUTION" Ibid.

334 WHO HAD SENT GEORGE WASHINGTON THE KEY TO THE BASTILLE TJF, http://www.monticello.org/site/jefferson/marquis-de-lafayette (accessed 2012).

334 PATSY JEFFERSON RECALLED STANDING AT THE WINDOW Mrs. O. J. Wister and Miss Agnes Irwin, eds., **Worthy Women of Our First Century** (Philadelphia, 1877), 22. See also TJF, http://www.monticello.org/site/jefferson/marquis-de-lafayette (accessed 2012).

334 FIRST CAME THE ROYAL COACH, AND A CHAMBERLAIN BOWED Ibid.

334 RESEMBLED "THE BELLOWINGS OF THOUSANDS OF BULLS" Ibid.

334 "LAFAYETTE! LAFAYETTE!" Ibid.

334 NOTICING PATSY WATCHING FROM THE WINDOW, BOWED TO HER Ibid.

334 A MARK OF RESPECT SHE NEVER FORGOT Ibid.

334 ALL HER LIFE SHE KEPT A TRICOLORED COCKADE Ibid.

334 "SO FAR IT SEEMED" **PTJ**, XVI, 293. The letter was written in 1790.

335 A LONG LETTER TO JAMES MADISON Ibid., XV, 384–99.

336 HE DID NOT SERIOUSLY PRESS Consider, for instance, a letter Jefferson wrote later, in 1816.

I am certainly not an advocate for frequent and untried changes in laws and constitutions. I think moderate imperfections had better be borne with; because, when once known, we accommodate ourselves to them, and find practical means of correcting their ill effects. But I know also that laws and institutions must go hand in hand with the progress of the human mind. As that becomes more developed, more enlightened, as new discoveries are made, new truths disclosed, and manners and opinions change with the change of circumstances, institutions must advance also, and keep pace with the times. We might as well require a man to wear still the coat which fitted him when a boy, as civilized society to remain ever under the regimen of their barbarous ancestors. (TJ to Samuel Kercheval, July 12, 1816, Thomas Jefferson Papers, LOC.)

336 CLAY WAS SEEKING A CONGRESSIONAL SEAT **PTJ**, XVI, 129.

336 "YOU ARE TOO WELL INFORMED" Ibid.

337 THE ISSUE OF RIFLE MANUFACTURING Ibid., XV, 422.

337 "THE SPIRIT OF PHILOSOPHICAL" Ibid., XVI, 150.

338 JEFFERSON LEFT PARIS Ibid., XV, 487.

338 HOW TO MEASURE THE WIDTH Ibid., 493.

338 TUTORED POLLY IN SPANISH Ibid., 497.

338 He also set out "roving through"   Ibid., 509.

338 "On our return"   Ibid.

338 purchasing "a chienne bergere"   TJF, http://www.monticello.org/site/house-and-gardens/dogs (accessed 2012).

339 "the most careful intelligent dogs"   Ibid.

TWENTY-THREE · A New Post in New York

343 "In general, I think it necessary"   PTJ, XVI, 493.

343 "fine autumn weather"   Ibid., XV, 552.

343 at a quarter to one   Ibid., 560.

343 an offer from the president   Ibid., 519. "In the selection of characters to fill the important offices of government in the United States," George Washington wrote Jefferson, "I was naturally led to contemplate the talents and disposition which I knew you to possess and entertain for the service of your country." (Ibid.)

Madison underscored Washington's message. "I take for granted that you will . . . have known the ultimate determination of the President on your appointment," he wrote Jefferson on January 24, 1790. "All that I am able to say on the subject is that a universal anxiety is expressed for your acceptance; and to repeat my declarations that such an event will be more conducive to the general good, and perhaps to the very objects you have in view in Europe, than your return to your former station." (Ibid., XVI, 126.) Madison had been consistent. "It is of infinite importance that you should not disappoint the public wish on this subject," he had written when the nomination was approved. (Ibid., 169.)

344 "CRITICISMS AND CENSURES" Ibid., XVI, 34.

344 WASHINGTON LEFT THE TACTICAL WORK Ibid., 118. All in all, Jefferson said, he preferred to return to France. "But it is not for an individual to choose his post," Jefferson wrote Washington. "You are to marshal us as may best be for the public good. . . . Be so good only as to signify to me by another line your ultimate wish, and I shall conform to it cordially." (Ibid., 34–35.)

345 WAS NOT TO BE IN CHARGE OF ALL DOMESTIC AFFAIRS Ibid. "I was sorry to find him so little biased in favor of the domestic service allotted to him," Madison wrote Washington on Monday, January 4, 1790, "but was glad that his difficulties seemed to result chiefly from what I take to be an erroneous view of the kind and quantity of business annexed to that which constituted the foreign department." There was a domestic component to the job, but Madison expected it to be minimal. (Ibid.)

345 A STRONG CASE FOR THE CABINET Ibid., 116.

345 WASHINGTON WANTED AN ANSWER Ibid., 118. As Jefferson considered his course, he replied to an "Address" the people of Albemarle County had presented to him expressing their thanks

and respect on his return from abroad. (Ibid., 167–80.) "At an early period of your life and a very critical era of public affairs we elected you our representative in the general Assembly. . . . In that station your virtues and talents became known to your country, by whom they were afterwards made more extensively beneficial to the community at large." (Ibid., 177.)

As noted above, his reply encapsulated the creed he had forged through experience and contemplation in the quarter century since his first session of the House of Burgesses:

We have been fellow-laborers and fellow-sufferers, and heaven has rewarded us with a happy issue from our struggles. It rests now with ourselves alone to enjoy in peace and concord the blessings of self-government, so long denied to mankind: to show by example the sufficiency of human reason for the care of human affairs and that the will of the majority, the natural law of every society, is the only sure guardian of the rights of man. Perhaps even this may sometimes err. But its errors are honest, solitary and short-lived.—Let us then, my dear friends, forever bow down to the general reason of the society. We are safe with that, even in its deviations, for it soon returns again to the right way. These are lessons we have learnt together. (Ibid., 178.)

346 HE ACCEPTED WASHINGTON'S OFFER   Ibid., 184.

346 SPOKE IN PRACTICAL POLITICAL TERMS   Ibid., 228–29.

346 DECIDED TO MARRY HER THIRD COUSIN   JHT, II, 250–52. See also Kierner, **Martha Jefferson Randolph,** 76–82.

346 THEY HAD MET WHEN PATSY WAS A CHILD   Kierner, **Martha Jefferson Randolph,** 76–77.

346 AMBITIOUS, WELL EDUCATED, AND BLACK-HAIRED   Ibid., 77. "My daughter, on her arrival in Virginia, received the addresses of a young Mr. Randolph, the son of a bosom friend of mine," Jefferson wrote Madame de Corny. (**PTJ,** XVI, 290.)

346 "THOUGH HIS TALENTS"   **PTJ,** XVI, 290.

347 TO ARRANGE PATSY'S MARRIAGE SETTLEMENT Ibid., 182.

347 THE WEDDING TOOK PLACE   Ibid., 189–91.

347 WAS PERHAPS REACTING TO HER FATHER'S LIAISON   Gordon-Reed, **Hemingses of Monticello,** 422. For Gordon-Reed's complete discussion of Patsy's courtship and marriage—including the fact that Jefferson did not follow custom and give Sally Hemings, a familiar figure, to either of his daughters on the occasions of their marriages—see ibid., 414–27.

347 RANDOLPH WAS INTERESTED IN FARMING   **PTJ,** XVI, 370. "The necessity I am under of turning my attention to the cultivation of my little farm has inclined my thoughts of late towards agriculture," Thomas Mann Randolph, Jr., wrote Jeffer-

son. "To one as fond as I am of physical research, and so much accustomed to exercise, such an inclination might be dangerous: but however enticing the subject, however pleasing the employment, I am resolved it shall never seduce me from the study of the law, and the attempt to acquire political knowledge." (Ibid.)

Jefferson was intimately engaged with the lives of his daughters. Patsy's marriage did not change that. Randolph's father gave the couple an estate southeast of Richmond, called Varina. Both of the newlyweds came to prefer Edgehill, a place near Monticello, but they could not yet afford it. Jefferson offered his counsel, but his own financial affairs were such that he could not offer much more. (Ibid., 386–87. See also **JHT**, II, 252–53.) "No circumstance ever made me feel so strongly the thralldom of Mr. Wayles's debt," he told his eldest daughter. "Were I liberated from that, I should not fear but that Col. Randolph and myself . . . could effect fixing you there." (**PTJ**, XVI, 387.) The Randolphs ultimately bought Edgehill.

347 THE CARE AND TENDING Gordon-Reed, **Hemingses of Monticello**, 247–48.

347 THE PRECISE LOCATION OF HER LIVING QUARTERS I am indebted to Monticello's Lucia Stanton and Susan Stein for this information.

348 MULBERRY ROW I am indebted to Susan Stein for this description of Mulberry Row.

348 SLOW AND AT TIMES SNOWY **PTJ**, XVI, 277–78.

348 "The Congress under the new constitution" Ibid., XV, 91.

348 Jefferson could not find quarters Ibid., XVI, 278–79.

349 "an indifferent one" Ibid., 300.

349 "Mr. Jefferson is here" Cappon, **Adams-Jefferson Letters,** xxxix.

349 then relatively remote neighborhood **JHT,** II, 259.

349 Leopold II, the Holy Roman Emperor Jeremy Black, **From Louis XIV to Napoleon** (London, 1999), 159.

349 the Declaration of Pillnitz Ibid.

349 declared war on Austria Ibid., 160.

349 a thirteen-year series of wars **EOL,** 175.

349 drew Britain and Spain into war For a very general overview, see U.S. Department of State, Office of the Historian, "The United States and the French Revolution, 1789–1799," http://history.state.gov/milestones/1784–1800/FrenchRev (accessed 2012).

350 On Sunday, March 21, 1790 **PTJ,** XVI, 288.

350 a "daily, confidential and cordial" **PTJRS,** VII, 103.

350 after Washington sat for a portrait **JHT,** II, 259.

351 "Nothing can excel Mr. Jefferson's abilities" **PTJ,** XIV, 223.

351 "I have found Mr. Jefferson" Ibid., XV, 498.

351 "You can scarcely have heard" Ibid., VII, 383.

351 "He was incapable of fear" PTJRS, VII, 101.

352 "His mind was great" Ibid.

352 "His temper was naturally" Ibid.

352 was struck by See PTJ, XVI, 416; 432; 435–36; 487.

353 "Be so good as to say" Ibid., 286.

353 "The transaction of business" Ibid., 379.

353 "He had a rambling, vacant look" **Journal of William Maclay: United States Senator from Pennsylvania, 1789–1791** (New York, 1965), 272.

354 he was "lofty and erect" TJF, http://www.monticello.org/site/research-and-collections/physical-descriptions-jefferson (accessed 2011).

354 "His information was equally polite" TJF, http://www.monticello.org/site/research-and-collections/jefferson-conversation (accessed 2011).

354 "When the hour of dinner" PTJ, XX, 646–47.

355 "Perhaps their conduct" Ibid., XVIII, 80.

355 "wonder and mortification" Ibid., XVI, 237.

355 "for the most part" Ibid.

355 The quasi-regal air around the president JHT, II, 256–68.

356 essays entitled **Discourses on Davila** PTJ, XVI, 238–39.

356 JEFFERSON ARRANGED FOR FENNO TO PUBLISH Ibid., 238–41.

357 FENNO BECAME ENTIRELY A CREATURE Ibid., 240–41.

357 "I HAVE BUT ONE SYSTEM OF ETHICS" Ibid., 291.

357 A LATE SNOW IN NEW YORK Ibid., 405.

357 WASHINGTON BECAME SO ILL Ibid., 429. "On Monday last the President was taken with a peripneumony of threatening appearance," Jefferson wrote Patsy on May 16, 1790. "Yesterday (which was the 5th day) he was thought by the physicians to be dying. However about 4 o'clock in the evening a copious sweat came on, his expectoration, which had been thin and ichorous, began to assume a well digested form, his articulation became distinct, and in the course of two hours it was evident he had gone through a favorable crisis. He continues mending today, and from total despair we are now in good hopes of him. Indeed he is thought quite safe." (Ibid.)

357 A FISHING TRIP OFF SANDY HOOK Ibid., 2.

357 WOULD "CARRY OFF THE REMAINS" Ibid., 475.

357 JEFFERSON RAN INTO ALEXANDER HAMILTON Ibid., XVII, 205–7.

357 BORN IN 1755 Chernow, **Alexander Hamilton,** 17. See ibid., 7–40, for details of Hamilton's early life.

358 ENROLLING AT KING'S COLLEGE Ibid., 41–61.

358 QUICK WITH HIS PEN Ibid., 58–61.

358 HE BECAME A TOP AIDE Ibid., 85–129.

358 MARRIED INTO A POWERFUL NEW YORK FAMILY Ibid., 128–32.

358 A DELEGATE TO THE CONSTITUTIONAL CONVENTION Ibid., 222–42.

358 SAID TO BE "AMAZINGLY FOND" Julian P. Boyd, **Number 7: Alexander Hamilton's Secret Attempts to Control American Foreign Policy** (Princeton, N.J., 1964), 23.

358 IN A SPEECH Chernow, **Alexander Hamilton,** 233.

360 "THE EYE SETTLED WITH A DEEPER INTEREST" Randall, **Jefferson,** III, 336.

360 "FOUND THE TREASURY SECRETARY 'SOMBER'" **PTJ,** XVII, 205.

360 IN HIS **REPORT ON THE PUBLIC CREDIT** IN EARLY 1790 Sharp, **American Politics in the Early Republic,** 34–35.

360 BY TARIFFS ON IMPORTS AND EXCISE TAXES ON DISTILLED SPIRITS Ibid., 34.

360 FUNDING THE DEBT Ibid., 35.

361 SHREWDER SPECULATORS, MADISON TOLD JEFFERSON Ibid.

361 THE SECOND ELEMENT OF HAMILTON'S PLAN Ibid., 36.

361 INSTANTLY DIVIDED THE NATION Ibid. In Sharp's estimation, "Hamilton's assumption proposal threatened to destroy the newly organized government." (Ibid.)

362 VOTED DOWN FEDERAL ASSUMPTION Ibid.

362 HE ASKED FOR A WORD **PTJ,** XVII, 205.

362 "IT WAS A REAL FACT" Ibid., 206. Jefferson also

said: "And . . . it has become probable that unless they can be reconciled by some plan of compromise, there will be no funding bill agreed to, our credit . . . will burst and vanish, and the states separate to take care everyone of itself." (Ibid., XVI, 537.)

362 Unlike many of his fellow Virginians Sharp, **American Politics in the Early Republic,** 36. Sharp quoted "Light-Horse Harry" Lee on the subject. Lee said he "had rather myself submit to all the hazards of war and risk the loss of everything dear to me in life than to live under the rule of an . . . insolent northern majority." One hope, Lee noted, was moving the capital to "the territorial center" of the country. (Ibid.)

362 The location of the national capital JHT, II, 287–99, is a good account of the politics of the decision about the capital.

363 "The Potomac stands a bad chance" Ibid., 298.

363 he convened a dinner Ibid., 301. "On considering the situation of things," Jefferson said, "I thought the first step towards some conciliation of views would be to bring Mr. Madison and Col. Hamilton to a friendly discussion of the subject." (Ibid., 298.)

363 "men of sound heads" Ibid.

363 "that if everyone retains" PTJ, XVI, 540. Sharp, **American Politics in the Early Republic,** 37, describes Jefferson's thinking as well.

363 MADISON AGREED TO EASE HIS OPPOSITION JHT, II, 301.

364 "AS THE PILL WOULD BE A BITTER ONE" PTJ, XVII, 207. "This is the real history of the assumption," Jefferson said. (Ibid.)

364 "THE LEAST BAD OF ALL THE TURNS" Ibid., XVI, 575.

364 "IT IS MUCH TO BE WISHED" Ibid., VIII, 399. He added: "No man can have a natural right to enter on a calling by which it is at least ten to one he will ruin many better men than himself. Yet these are the actual links which hold us whether we will or no to Great Britain." (Ibid.)

364 "EVERY HUMAN BEING, MY DEAR" Ibid., XVII, 215.

365 "ONE PARTY CHARGES THE CONGRESS" Ibid., XVIII, 131.

TWENTY-FOUR · Mr. Jefferson Is Greatly Too Democratic

366 "I OWN IT IS MY OWN OPINION" PTJ, XXII, 38.

366 NOOTKA SOUND, A DISTANT INLET ON THE WESTERN COAST JHT, II, 310–14.

367 "BEEN AMONGST SUCH INSOLENT BULLIES" PTJ, XVI, 414.

367 JEFFERSON FRETTED ABOUT A SPRAWLING WAR JHT, II, 310–11. Jefferson was cold-eyed about the threat. "I am so deeply impressed with the magnitude of the dangers which will attend our

government if Louisiana and the Floridas be added to the British empire," he wrote Washington in August 1790, "that in my opinion we ought to make ourselves parties in the **general war** expected to take place, should this be the only means of preventing the calamity." (**PTJ**, XVII, 129.)

368 War, Jefferson said   **PTJ**, XVII, 127.

368 encirclement by the British   **JHT**, II, 310. See also **PTJ**, XVII, 138.

368 Vice President Adams agreed   **PTJ**, XVII, 138. Adams wrote: "The consequences . . . on the general security and tranquility of the American confederation of having them in our rear, and on both our flanks, with their navy in front, are very obvious." (Ibid.)

368 Secretary of War Knox believed   Ibid., 140.

368 to march through U.S. territory   Ibid., 128–29.

368 "a middle course"   Ibid., 130.

368 "war is full of chances"   Ibid., 129.

368 campaign against the Shawnee and Miami Indians   Ibid., 131–32.

369 should keep the Indian mission   Ibid., 131.

369 Alexander Hamilton had already   Ibid., 133.

369 George Beckwith, who had played a role   Scheer and Rankin, **Rebels and Redcoats**, 379–84, is a general account of the Arnold treason. See Frank T. Reuter, " 'Petty Spy' or Effective

Diplomat: The Role of George Beckwith," **Journal of the Early Republic** 10 (Winter 1990), 471–92, for more on Beckwith.

369 HAMILTON'S RELATIONSHIP WITH   As the title suggests, Julian P. Boyd's **Number 7: Alexander Hamilton's Secret Attempts to Control American Foreign Policy** (Princeton, N.J., 1964) offers a considered indictment of Hamilton's conduct. See also Chernow, **Alexander Hamilton,** 294–95, for a kinder interpretation than Boyd's.

369 "I HAVE ALWAYS PREFERRED"   Boyd, **Number 7,** 24. At stake, perhaps, were the British West Indies, which Hamilton noted would be protected in an alliance with London but endangered if the Americans were more closely linked with France. (Ibid., 24–25.)

369 AMERICA'S "NAVAL EXERTIONS"   Ibid., 25.

369 "MAY BE DEPENDED UPON"   Ibid. One of the questions raised by the Nootka Sound episode was about control of the British forts along the western borders of the United States. Despite the provisions of the Treaty of Paris, London had refused to give them up. Now the British were interested in taking advantage of any fighting related to Nootka Sound to secure their hold on the forts and possibly expand their influence within the United States—a sign that the war between America and Britain was not fully and forever over. (Ibid., 34–35.)

369 "MR. JEFFERSON . . . IS GREATLY TOO DEMO-CRATIC"   Ibid., 27.

370 "Mr. Jefferson . . . is a man" Ibid., 32.

370 spain backed down JHT, II, 310.

370 stopped at Mount Vernon PTJ, XVIII, 2. In August 1790 Jefferson had joined Washington for a journey to Rhode Island. Beginning on August 15, 1790, they enjoyed "a very pleasant sail of two days going and two days returning" through Long Island Sound, and at Newport and Providence the president was received with what Jefferson called "great cordiality." (Ibid., XVII, 402.)

371 "The richest ground" Ibid., 45. "The grain, though small, is always plump," Jefferson wrote. "The President is so excellent a farmer that I place full confidence in his recommendation." (Ibid.)

371 Leasing a four-story brick house from Thomas Leiper Ibid., XVII, 309–10.

371 ordered shipments of wine Ibid., 493.

371 three separate but related issues See PTJ, XVIII, 220, 310, 369.

371 The proposal for a national bank EOL, 143–45.

372 Jefferson and Madison objected JHT, II, 338. See also PTJ, XIX, 275–82.

372 the bank bill's constitutionality PTJ, XIX, 281.

372 "To take a single step beyond" Ibid., 276.

372 "If the pro and the con hang so even" Ibid., 280.

373 HAMILTON REPLIED BRILLIANTLY **JHT**, II, 347.

373 "AN ADHERENCE TO THE LETTER" Ibid.

373 WASHINGTON HAD MADISON DRAFT A VETO MESSAGE **EOL**, 144.

373 "CONGRESS MAY GO HOME" **JHT**, II, 340.

373 RECORDED THE BURST OF COLORS **PTJ**, XX, 250.

373 "WE ARE RUINED, SIR" Ibid., 236.

374 "MRS. TRIST HAS OBSERVED" Ibid.

374 JONATHAN B. SMITH, A PHILADELPHIA MERCHANT Ibid., 290. Also see ibid., 268–313. In defense of his father in the face of Jefferson's "heresies" remark, John Quincy Adams launched a counterattack ("took up the cudgels," in Jefferson's phrase) in the newspapers under the pseudonym Publicola. (Ibid.) Adams himself was long believed to be the author, but it was his son's work, and the Publicola assaults on Jefferson were powerful. Publicola, Madison reported to Jefferson, "is probably the manufacture of his son out of materials furnished by himself. . . . There is more of method also in the arguments, and much less of clumsiness and heaviness in the style, than characterize [the senior Adams's] writings." (Ibid., 298–99.)

By midsummer 1791 the controversy over Jefferson's attack on Adams had expanded to include the secretary of state's antagonism to Hamilton as well. The tensions at the highest levels of government were palpable. "A host of writers have risen in favor of Paine, and prove that in this quarter at least the spirit of republicanism is sound," Jefferson told Monroe on July 10, 1791. "The contrary spirit of the high officers of government is more understood than I expected. Col. Hamilton, avowing that he never made a secret of his principles, yet taxes the imprudence of Mr. Adams in having stirred the question and agrees that 'his business is done.' " (Ibid., 297.)

Jefferson was flummoxed. What to do about Adams, whom he had unquestionably attacked in the note about the **Rights of Man**? He wanted to explain himself to the vice president but wavered about how to go about it. "I have a dozen times taken up my pen to write to you and as often laid it down again, suspended between opposing considerations," Jefferson wrote Adams on July 17, 1791. "I determine however to write from a conviction that truth, between candid minds, can never do harm."

Yes, he had written the words attributed to him; and yes, he believed Adams's views to be among the "heresies" he mentioned. What Jefferson regretted most, he told Adams, was how they had been "thrown on the public stage as public antagonists. That you and I differ in our ideas of the best form of government is well known to us both: but we have differed as friends should do, respecting the purity of each other's motives, and confining our difference of opinion to private conversation. And I can declare with truth in the presence of the Almighty that nothing was further from my intention or expectation than to have had either my own or your name brought before the public on this occasion." (Ibid., 302.)

Adams accepted the thrust of Jefferson's explanation, but his anguished reply shows how far-reaching the implications of the affair had become. The publisher who printed Jefferson's note, Adams said, "has sown the seeds of more evils than he can ever atone for. The pamphlet, with your name . . . was generally considered as a direct and open personal attack upon me, by countenancing the false interpretation of my writings as favoring the introduction of hereditary monarchy and aristocracy into this country."

Adams's sensitivity about **Davila** was self-evident. "The question everywhere was what heresies are intended by the Secretary of State?" he told Jefferson. "The answer in the newspapers was, the Vice President's notions of a limited monarchy, an hereditary government of king and lords, with only elective commons." The charge had set off a "hue and cry [among] all my enemies and rivals," Adams said. "It is thought by some, that Mr. Hancock's friends are preparing the way, by my destruction, for his election to the place of Vice President, and that of Mr. Samuel Adams to be Governor of this Commonwealth, and then [the anti-Adams faction] will be sure of all the loaves and fishes in the national government and the state government as they hope." In sum, it had been a miserable summer for the vice president. (Ibid., 305–7.)

All in all, Jefferson drew some comfort from the episode, for the public reaction tended to favor Paine over **Davila** or Publicola. The people, Jefferson wrote Paine on July 29, 1791, "appear firm in their republicanism, notwithstanding the contrary hopes and assertions of a sect here, high in names, but small in numbers." (Ibid., 308.)

374 HE WAS "EXTREMELY PLEASED"   Ibid.

375 "THAT I HAD IN MY VIEW"   Ibid., 291.

375 "TO TAKE OFF A LITTLE OF THE DRYNESS"   Ibid., 293.

375 "OPPOSITION TO THE GOVERNMENT"   Ibid., 294.

375 "MEANT FOR THE ENEMIES OF THE GOVERNMENT"   Ibid.

375 "I HAVE REASON TO THINK"   Ibid., 300.

375 A CONTEST BETWEEN JEFFERSON AND HAMILTON   See, for instance, Claude G. Bowers, **Jefferson and Hamilton: The Struggle for Democracy in America** (Boston, 1966).

377 "WE WERE EDUCATED IN ROYALISM"   PTJ, XIV, 661.

377 "COURTS LOVE THE PEOPLE ALWAYS"   Ibid., 431.

377 "IF THE DUKE OF ANGOULEME"   Ibid., XII, 220–21.

378 "IN SHORT, MY DEAR FRIEND"   Ibid., 221.

378 "The politics of the western country" Dunbar, **Study of "Monarchical" Tendencies**, 106. Wilkinson added that only a "high toned monarchy" could remedy the Confederation government's "imbecility, distraction and capricious policy." (Ibid.)

378 "There is such a rooted aversion" **PTJ**, XIII, 461–62.

378 In a report of a conversation "Governor Simcoe's Conversation with Peirce Duffy," June 1793, Niagara, Simcoe Family Foundations, Archives of Ontario. George Beckwith also reported that an American informant had told him that there was no gentleman "who does not view the present government with contempt, who is not convinced of its inefficiency, and who is not desirous of changing it for a Monarchy." (Boyd, **Number 7**, 7.)

379 "To my mind a true estimate" Hamilton, **Writings**, 978. The quotation is found in the course of a revealing letter of Hamilton's to James Bayard about Jefferson, Burr, and the 1800 election. (Ibid., 977–81.)

380 In 1790 and in 1791 **EOL**, 200–201, 533–34. See also Herring, **From Colony to Superpower**, 62–63.

380 fought to win the liberties Miller, **Wolf by the Ears**, 133.

381 "The situation of the Saint-Domingue fugitives" **PTJ**, XXVI, 503.

381 "It is high time" Ibid.

381 THE LONG-DREADED SLAVE WAR   Miller, **Wolf by the Ears,** 133–34.

381 "EVERY ACCOUNT OF THE SUCCESS"   Edward Thornton to Lord Hawkesbury, May 1, 1802, FO 5/35, National Archives of the United Kingdom, Kew.

381 MIGHT BECOME THE ASYLUM   Miller, **Wolf by the Ears,** 132–33.

381 THE LEADERSHIP OF TOUSSAINT-LOUVERTURE   Herring, **From Colony to Superpower,** 105–6.

382 REASSESS ITS AMBITIONS   Ibid.

382 "I WRITE TODAY"   **PTJ,** XX, 342–43.

382 A TRIP OF THEIR OWN   Ibid., 434–73, covers the journey and its sundry purposes. See also Andrea Wulf, **The Founding Gardeners,** 90–110. In New York, Sir John Temple, the British consul general, told London that Jefferson's "party and politics" were popular. (**PTJ,** XVIII, 240–41.) Robert Troup, a Hamiltonian, told the Treasury secretary that he believed the Jefferson interest, which in his view included Chancellor Robert R. Livingston and Aaron Burr—was moving toward total war. "There was every appearance of a passionate courtship between the Chancellor—Burr—Jefferson and Madison when the latter two were in town," Troup wrote Hamilton on June 15, 1791. "**Delenda est Carthago** [Carthage must be destroyed] I suppose is the maxim adopted with respect to you." (Ibid., XX, 434.)

382 IN THEIR BRIEF TIME TOGETHER   Ibid., 435.

382 PHILIP FRENEAU, A WRITER   Ibid., 453, 657, and 718. For the full account of the Freneau chapter in early national Jeffersonian politics, see ibid., 718–59. See also Philip M. Marsh, "Philip Freneau and His Circle," **Pennsylvania Magazine of History and Biography** 63, no. 1 (January 1939): 37–59, and Marsh, "Freneau and Jefferson: The Poet-Editor Speaks for Himself About the **National Gazette** Episode," **American Literature** 8 (May 1936): 180–89.

382 WHOM MADISON HAD KNOWN   Marsh, "Philip Freneau and His Circle," 39.

382 SUBSIDIZED BY THE DEPARTMENT OF STATE   Ibid., 45–47. "I should have given him the perusal of all my letters of foreign intelligence and all foreign newspapers; the publication of all proclamations and other public notices within my department, and the printing of the laws, which added to his salary would have been a considerable aid," Jefferson wrote Madison on July 21, 1791. (**PTJ**, XX, 657.)

382 A CRITICAL STEP   Todd Estes, "Jefferson as Party Leader," in Cogliano, ed., **A Companion to Thomas Jefferson,** 132–34.

383 JOHN BECKLEY   Ibid., 139.

383 "DESTINED FOR COMMANDS"   Bailey, "From 'Floating Ardor' to the 'Union of Sentiment:' Jefferson on the Relationship between Public Opinion and the Executive" in ibid., 194. The context was the enforcement of the embargo in 1807, but as Bailey notes, the remark "reveals

nicely the relationship between executive action and public judgment." (Ibid.)

383 "NOTHING NEW IS TALKED OF HERE" **PTJ,** XX, 617.

383 "YOU MENTIONED FORMERLY" Ibid., 706.

383 JEFFERSON AND HAMILTON SPOKE PRIVATELY Ibid., XXII, 38–39. Hamilton added of the republican experiment: "The success indeed so far is greater than I had expected, and therefore at present success seems more possible than it had done heretofore, and there are still other stages of improvement which, if the present does not succeed, may be tried and ought to be tried before we give up the republican form altogether, for that mind must be really depraved which would not prefer the equality of political rights which is the foundation of pure republicanism, if it can be obtained with order." (Ibid.)

384 "WHETHER THESE MEASURES" Peterson, **Thomas Jefferson and the New Nation,** 436.

384 "THE PEOPLE IN YOUR QUARTER" Ibid., 437.

384 "THERE IS A VAST MASS" Ibid., 436.

384 LAWMAKERS WERE BECOMING FINANCIALLY ENMESHED **PTJ,** XXIII, 537–41. See also ibid., XXIV, 25–27. On a separate but related matter, **EOL,** 299, alludes to Jefferson's broader concerns about the corrupting possibilities of patronage.

TWENTY-FIVE · Two Cocks in the Pit

385 "How unfortunate . . . that whilst" PTJ, XXIV, 317.

385 Dinner was over PTJRS, III, 305.

385 President Washington was out of town Ibid.

385 dominated by a "collision of opinion" Ibid.

386 in his view "if some of its" Ibid.

386 "it was the most perfect model" Ibid. See also Chernow, **Alexander Hamilton**, 393–94.

386 Sir Francis Bacon, John Locke, and Sir Isaac Newton PTJRS, III, 305.

386 Hamilton asked Jefferson Ibid.

386 "I told him" Ibid.

386 Hamilton paused Ibid.

386 "The greatest man" Ibid.

386 "Mr. Adams was honest" Ibid.

387 Jefferson was running late PTJ, XXIII, 184.

387 "doubling the velocity" Ibid.

387 for "the Treasury possessed already" Ibid. Jefferson continued "that even future Presidents (not supported by the weight of character which [he] himself possessed) would not be able to make head against this department." It was a gentle, effective way to flatter Washington and to raise his concerns about Hamilton to Washington, who did not mind tributes to his own character. (Ibid.)

387 not one of "personal interest" Ibid.

388 THE PRESIDENT THEN BROUGHT THE TALK Ibid. During "that pause of conversation which follows a business closed," Jefferson later wrote, Washington "said in an affectionate tone that he had felt much concern at an expression which dropt from me yesterday, and which marked my intention of retiring" when Washington did. (Ibid.)

388 WASHINGTON SAID HE INTENDED Ibid., 184–85.

388 "I TOLD HIM THAT NO MAN" Ibid., 185.

389 "HAD SET OUT WITH" Ibid., 186.

389 "ONLY A SINGLE SOURCE" Ibid.

389 "DELUGING THE STATES WITH PAPER-MONEY" Ibid.

390 "FEATHERED THEIR NESTS" Ibid. Jefferson had asked Madison to supply a list of the names of lawmakers who held public securities or stock in the Bank of the United States. He wanted it, he said, to show the president "that I have not been speaking merely at random." Jefferson ultimately did not use any such list in arguments with Washington. (Ibid., XXIV, 26.)

390 HIS FOES "HAD NOW" Ibid., 187. Washington asked what, specifically, Jefferson was talking about. "I answered . . . that in the Report on Manufactures which, under color of giving **bounties** for the encouragement of particular manufactures, meant to establish the doctrine that the power given by the Constitution to collect taxes to provide for the **general welfare** of

the U.S. permitted Congress to take everything under their management which **they** should deem for the **public welfare,** and which is susceptible to the application of money." (Ibid.)

390 "DAILY PITTED IN THE CABINET LIKE TWO COCKS" **PTJRS,** II, 272.

390 JEFFERSON NOTICED THAT **PTJ,** XXIII, 259.

390 "HE SAID THAT HE DID NOT LIKE" Ibid., 263. "He stopped here," Jefferson continued, "and I kept silence to see whether he would say anything more in the same line, or add any qualifying expression to soften what he had said. But he did neither." (Ibid.)

391 THE PUBLIC DEBT, PAPER MONEY Ibid., 535–41. On first hearing Washington raise the possibility of retiring after a single term, Jefferson had chosen to remain silent on the question. He knew, he said, "we were some day to try to walk alone, and if the essay should be made while you should be alive and looking on, we should derive confidence from that circumstance, and resource if it failed." (Ibid., 536.) In May, Jefferson used a letter urging Washington to reconsider stepping down to marshal his case against Hamilton. Washington's possible retirement after a single term, Jefferson said, was "a subject of inquietude to my mind." (Ibid., 535.)

391 THE "ULTIMATE OBJECT" Ibid., 537.

391 "THAT THIS WAS CONTEMPLATED" Ibid.

391 IT "WILL BE THE INSTRUMENT" Ibid.

392 THE "MONARCHIAL FEDERALISTS" Ibid., 538.

Jefferson was practical about what could be rescued. A new Congress, he said, "will not be able
to undo all which the two preceding legislatures,
and especially the first, have done. . . . But some
parts of the system may be rightfully reformed;
a liberation from the rest unremittingly pursued
as fast as right will permit, and the door shut in
future against similar commitments of the nation." (Ibid.) Such a moderate approach, however, depended on a Republican Congress. If the
majority of the next legislature "be still in the
same principles with the present," Jefferson said,
"it is not easy to conjecture what would be the
result, nor what means would be resorted to for
correction of the evil." (Ibid.)

392 "I CAN SCARCELY CONTEMPLATE"   Ibid.

392 "THE CONFIDENCE OF THE WHOLE UNION"
Ibid., 539. Jefferson continued: "If the first corrective of a numerous representation should fail
in its effect, your presence will give time for trying others not inconsistent with the union and
peace of the states." (Ibid.)

392 GIVE US A FEW YEARS   Ibid.

392 JEFFERSON DINED AT WASHINGTON'S   Ibid.,
XXIV, 50. Two days later, at what Jefferson described as a "dinner of Jay-ites," the financier
Robert Morris raised the prospect of a challenge
to John Adams in the 1792 election for vice president. "R.M. mentioned to the company that
[George] Clinton was to be vice-president, that
the Antis intended to set him up." (Ibid.)

392 "I was not displeased"   Ibid.

393 "Too many of these"   Ibid., 85.

393 Washington gently tried to calm   Ibid., 210–12. Washington added: "That there might be a few who wished [a monarchy] in the higher walks of life, particularly in the great cities. But that the main body of the people in the Eastern states were as steadily for republicanism as in the Southern." (Ibid., 210.) Washington also claimed to have been always ambivalent about the ceremonial pomp of the presidency.

According to an account of the administration's first days in New York that passed from Washington's personal secretary Tobias Lear to Attorney General Edmund Randolph to Jefferson, Washington "resisted for 3 weeks the efforts to introduce **levees**" before agreeing to them, and he left the details to his aide David Humphreys and others. After "an Antichamber and Presence room were provided, and those who were to pay their court were assembled, the President set out, preceded by Humphreys." They walked through the outer room, entered the second, and Humphreys preceded Washington, "first calling out with a loud voice 'the President of the US.' The President was so much disconcerted with it that he did not recover it the whole time of the levee, and when the company was gone he said to Humphreys, 'Well, you have taken me in once, but by God you shall never take me in a second time.' " (Ibid., XXV, 208.)

393 "How unfortunate" Ibid., 317.

394 Jefferson replied with passion Ibid., 351–60.

394 "That I have utterly" Ibid., 353.

394 "flowed from principles adverse to liberty" Ibid.

394 "He undertook" Ibid., 354. Jefferson added: "These views thus made to prevail, their execution fell of course to me; and I can safely appeal to you, who have seen all my letters and proceedings, whether I have not carried them into execution as sincerely as if they had been my own, though I ever considered them as inconsistent with the honor and interest of our country." (Ibid.)

395 "newspaper contests" Randall, **Jefferson,** II, 82.

395 "I will not suffer" **PTJ,** XXIV, 358.

395 "thought it important" Ibid., 434.

395 "did not believe" Ibid., 435.

395 "there were many more" Ibid.

396 "For I will frankly" Ibid., 499. Washington also found the congressional corruption charge overwrought. "He said that as to that interested spirit in the legislature, it was what could not be avoided in any government, unless we were to exclude particular descriptions of men, such as the holders of the funds, from all office. I told him there was a great difference between the little accidental schemes of self interest which would take place in every body of men and influence their

votes, and a regular system for forming a corps of interested persons who should be steadily at the orders of the Treasury." (Ibid., 435.)

396 "Why, then," Ibid.

396 worried about rebellion Ibid., 383–85.

397 the secretary of state's signature Ibid., 385.

397 "Should Congress adopt" Dunbar, **Study of "Monarchical" Tendencies**, 105.

398 "there was no stability" **PTJ**, XXIV, 607.

398 revelations of an affair Ibid., 751. See also notes to ibid., XVIII, 611–88.

398 Giles of Virginia introduced resolutions Ibid., XXV, 311–12. As the editors of the **PTJ** write: "Nevertheless, Jefferson's covert support of the House Republican drive against Hamilton in 1793 remains a highly significant benchmark in his public career, marking a crucial stage in his gradual shift from the role of a statesman standing above the clash of conflicting political parties to the more partisan role that eventually propelled him to the presidency, that of chief leader of the Republican party." (Ibid., 292.) See also Todd Estes, "Jefferson as Party Leader," in Cogliano, ed., **A Companion to Thomas Jefferson,** 128–44.

399 Giles "and one or two others" **PTJ**, XXV, 311.

399 "bank directors" Ibid.

399 "The public will see" Ibid., 314.

399 until "those who troubled" Ibid., 137.

399 "When they suffer" Ibid.

400 Reports of rising violence in France
Neely, **Concise History of the French Revolution,** 189–220.

400 the September 1793 declaration of the
Reign of Terror Ibid., 191–97, 254–55.

400 "We were all strongly attached to France"
EOL, 174–75.

400 From the autumn of 1792 forward Ibid.,
176–77. As Wood wrote:

> Now some Federalists began to see in France
> the terrifying possibilities of what might
> happen in America if popular power were
> allowed to run free. The rioting in Paris and
> elsewhere, the horrific massacres in Septem-
> ber 1792 of over fourteen hundred prisoners
> charged with being enemies of the Revo-
> lution, the news that Lafayette had been
> deserted by his troops and his allies in the
> Assembly and had fled France—all these
> events convinced the Federalists that the
> French Revolution was sliding into popular
> anarchy. . . . When Americans learned that
> the thirty-eight-year-old king Louis XVI, the
> ruler who had helped them win their inde-
> pendence from the British a decade earlier,
> had been executed for treason on January 21,
> 1793, and that the French Republic had de-
> clared war on England on February 1, 1793,
> their division into Federalists and Republi-

cans intensified. The meaning of the French Revolution now became entwined in the quarrel that Americans were having among themselves over the direction of their own revolution. (Ibid.)

400 HE LOST FRIENDS TO THE GUILLOTINE William Howard Adams, **Paris Years of Thomas Jefferson,** 295–97. See also O'Brien, **Long Affair.**

400 LAFAYETTE SPENT FIVE YEARS Paul S. Spalding, **Lafayette: Prisoner of State** (Columbia, S.C., 2012).

400 "IN THE STRUGGLE WHICH WAS NECESSARY" **PTJ,** XXV, 14.

401 PRO-FRENCH ORGANIZERS IN BOSTON Charles Warren, **Jacobin and Junto; or, Early American Politics as Viewed in the Diary of Dr. Nathaniel Ames, 1758–1822** (New York, 1968), 46.

402 "A NUMBER OF CITIZENS" Ibid.

402 CONSIDER RETURNING TO PARIS **PTJ,** XXV, 243–45. Washington, who characteristically took a moderate position, tended to be warmer toward the French in his conversations with Jefferson. The president, Jefferson wrote on January 3, 1793, said "he considered **France as the sheet anchor of this country and its friendship as a first object.** There are in the U.S. some characters of opposite principles; some of them are high in office, others possessing great wealth, and all of them hostile to France and looking fondly to

England as the staff of their hope. . . . The little party above mentioned have espoused it only as a stepping stone to monarchy, and have endeavored to approximate it to that in its administration, in order to render its final transition more easy." (Ibid., 14–15.)

402 WASHINGTON'S REPLY WAS POINTED   Ibid., 244.

402 JEFFERSON STRUCK BACK   Ibid.

402 ASKED JEFFERSON "TO CONSIDER MATURELY" Ibid.

TWENTY-SIX · The End of a Stormy Tour

404 "I FEEL FOR YOUR SITUATION"   **PTJ**, XXVI, 133.

404 THE PLANTATION WAS CALLED BIZARRE   See Cynthia A. Kierner, **Scandal at Bizarre: Rumor and Reputation in Jefferson's America** (New York, 2004), for details and analysis of the episode.

405 "NEVER THROW OFF THE BEST AFFECTIONS" **PTJ**, XXV, 621.

405 "IN THE COURSE OF OUR CONVERSATION"   Ibid., 301–2.

406 SHOULD NOT "SUFFER YOURSELF"   Ibid., 304.

406 "MR. JEFFERSON [IS] . . . DISTINGUISHED AS" **The Words of Thomas Jefferson** (Charlottesville, Va., 2008), 200. On the public debt, Jefferson said he believed "the only difference which I can see between the two parties is that the republican one wish it could be paid tomorrow,

the fiscal party wish it to be perpetual, because they find in it an engine for corrupting the legislature." (**PTJ**, XXV, 318.) For a list of stockholders in the Congress, see ibid., 432–35.

Civility was strained. "I understood on Saturday from the Attorney General," Hamilton wrote Jefferson, "that it was your wish a meeting should be had—to which I replied, in substance, that I considered it in your power to convene one; and should attend if called upon; but that I did not perceive the utility of one at this time." (Ibid., 440.)

406 A HOUSE ON THE SCHUYLKILL RIVER **PTJ**, XXV, 353.

406 "FROM MONTICELLO YOU" Ibid., 444.

406 "OUR REPUBLIC" Ibid., XXVI, 101.

407 "YOUR MIN. PLEN." Ibid.

407 "CERTAINLY OURS WAS A REPUBLICAN" Ibid., 101–2.

407 "KNOX TOLD SOME" Ibid., 554–55.

407 "MAKE HIM BELIEVE" Ibid., 522.

407 "HE WAS EVIDENTLY SORE" Ibid., 102.

408 THE FRENCH REPUBLIC DECLARED WAR ON BRITAIN **EOL**, 177.

408 "IT HAS BEEN ASKED" **PTJ**, XXVI, 272–73.

408 "UNCONSTITUTIONAL AND IMPROPER" Ibid., 382. "I am extremely afraid that the P. may not be sufficiently aware of the snares that may be laid out for his good intentions by men whose politics at bottom are very different from his own," Madison wrote in June 1793. "An assumption of

prerogatives not clearly found in the Constitution and having the appearance of being copied from a monarchial model will beget animadversion equally mortifying to him, and disadvantageous to the government." (Ibid., 273.)

408 "WE HAD NOT OBJECTED"   Ibid., XXVII, 400.

409 "OTHER QUESTIONS AND ANSWERS"   Ibid., 401.

409 "THOUGH IT WOULD BE A GOOD THING"   Ibid., 428.

409 EDMOND-CHARLES GENET   Ibid., XXV, 469–70. Washington, who was to be away, told Jefferson that Genet "should unquestionably be received, but he thought not with too much warmth or cordiality." Jefferson "wondered at first at this restriction; but. . . . became satisfied it was a small sacrifice to the opinion of Hamilton." (Ibid.)

409 "LENGTHY CONSIDERATIONS"   Ibid., 469

409 JEFFERSON HOPED AN ENTHUSIASTIC PUBLIC RECEPTION   Ibid., 619. On April 28, 1793, Jefferson wrote Madison: "We expect Mr. Genet here within a few days. It seems as if his arrival would furnish an occasion for the **people** to testify their affections without respect to the cold caution of their government." (Ibid.)

409 THE ENVOY WAS ORGANIZING PRIVATEERS **EOL**, 185–89.

409 "HOTHEADED, ALL IMAGINATION"   **PTJ**, XXVI, 444.

409 INDEED GENET DID   **EOL**, 188.

410 "NOT AS SECRETARY OF STATE"   Ibid.

410 TO RECALL GENET **PTJ,** XXVI, 598, 685–715. There was a second element to the decision: that Genet be informed of the requested recall. Jefferson disagreed with the last, thinking "it would render him extremely active in his plans, and endanger confusion. But I was overruled by the other three gentlemen and the President." (Ibid., 598.)

410 HAMILTON HAD WON THIS BATTLE Ibid., 502–3. "H., sensible of the advantage they have got, is urging a full appeal by the government to the people" to have Genet recalled to France, Jefferson said. "Such an explosion would manifestly endanger a dissolution of the friendship between the two nations." (Ibid.)

410 "HE WILL SINK" Ibid., 606.

410 "TO MY FELLOW-CITIZENS" Ibid., 239.

410 "THE MOTION OF MY BLOOD" Ibid., 240.

410 "WORN DOWN" Ibid., 240–41.

411 "TORN TO PIECES AS WE ARE" Ibid., 552.

411 A RUMOR REACHED JEFFERSON Ibid., 219.

411 WHAT WERE CALLED DEMOCRATIC-REPUBLICAN SOCIETIES Ibid., 601–3.

411 "THE PRESIDENT WAS MUCH INFLAMED" Ibid., 602–3.

412 JEFFERSON WANTED OUT Ibid., 593–94, 660. For a benign view of Jefferson's motivations, see Philip M. Marsh, "Jefferson's Retirement as Secretary of State," **Pennsylvania Magazine of History and Biography** 69, no. 3 (July 1945): 220–24.

412 HE PAID A CALL   Ibid., 627–30. For Jefferson's successor at the Department of State, Washington's mind seemed to be on the politics of the moment. He liked Robert R. Livingston of New York, but "to appoint him while Hamilton was in and before it should be known he was going out, would excite a newspaper conflagration, as the ultimate arrangement would not be known." (Ibid., 629.)

412 THE "PARTICULAR UNEASINESS"   Ibid., 628.

412 "THE CONSTITUTION WE HAVE"   Ibid.

413 "MEN NEVER CHOSE TO DESCEND"   Ibid., 630.

413 YELLOW FEVER STRUCK   Ibid., XXVII, 7.

413 "IT HAS NOW GOT"   Ibid.

413 "VIEWING WITH SORROW"   Ibid., 334.

414 "HAMILTON IS ILL OF THE FEVER"   Ibid., 62.

414 "I WOULD REALLY GO AWAY"   Ibid.

414 "WITH SINCERE REGRET"   Ibid., XXVIII, 3.

414 "LET A CONVICTION"   Ibid.

415 "THAT RICHMOND IS MY NEAREST PORT"   Ibid., XXVII, 661.

415 "COVERED WITH GLORY"   Ibid., XXVIII, 7.

415 THE MARVEL OF HOW WELL   Adams, ed., **Letters of John Adams**, II, 240.

415 "JEFFERSON WENT OFF"   **Words of Thomas Jefferson**, 201.

415 "MY PRIVATE BUSINESS"   **PTJ**, XXVIII, 14.

TWENTY-SEVEN · In Wait at Monticello

419 "To preserve the freedom" PTJ, XXXI, 128.

421 "I live on my horse" Ibid., XXVIII, 332.

421 "I think it is Montaigne" Ibid., 15. Despite his protestations, he remained in touch with the times. Acknowledging his obsession with the Hamilton–congressional axis, Jefferson said: "I indulge myself on one political topic only, that is, in disclosing to my countrymen the shameless corruption of a portion of the representatives in the 1st and 2nd Congresses and their implicit devotion to the treasury. I think I do good in this, because it may produce exertions to reform the evil on the success of which the form of the government is to depend." (Ibid., 15–16.)

421 "I could not have supposed" Ibid., 21–22.

422 "I congratulate you" Ibid., 50.

422 "Instead of writing" Ibid., 57.

422 "My countrymen are groaning" Ibid.

423 might soon "get out" Ibid., 72.

424 dispatched John Jay Ibid., 69–71.

424 "may extricate us from" Ibid., 75.

424 "The spirit of war" Ibid., 55.

424 he decided to pull down JHT, III, 221–22, details the story of the two Monticellos.

424 "We are now living" PTJ, XXVIII, 181.

424 "He is a very long time" JHT, III, 221.

425 "Architecture is my delight" Ibid., 222.

425 MULBERRY ROW   TJF, http://www.monticello
.org/mulberry-row/places (accessed 2012).

425 NEW SLAVE QUARTERS, A SMOKEHOUSE, DAIRY
Ibid.

425 A NAILERY   FB, 426–53.

425 "AS HE CANNOT"   Ibid., xiv.

425 COMPLETED IN 1809   TJF, http://www.monti
cello.org/mulberry-row/places (accessed 2012).

425 WERE MOVED HERE   Ibid.

425 KITCHEN, ICE CELLAR, STORE ROOMS   Beiswanger, **Thomas Jefferson's Monticello**, 68.

426 "IN INCESSANT TORMENT"   **PTJ**, XXVIII, 155.

426 "JEFFERSON IS VERY ROBUST"   Ibid., 249.

426 HIS MOUNTS TENDED TO HAVE NOBLE NAMES
TJF, http://www.monticello.org/site/research-and
-collections/horses (accessed 2012). See also **FB**,
87–109.

426 "BELOW THE OLD DAM"   TJF, http://www.mon
ticello.org/site/research-and-collections/fishing
(accessed 2012).

426 OUTINGS ON THE SCHUYLKILL RIVER   Ibid.

426 A DAY AT LAKE GEORGE   Ibid. See also **PTJ**,
XX, 463–64.

427 "A FAR LESS PLEASANT WATER"   **PTJ**, XX, 464.

427 HE KEPT GUNS   TJF, http://www.monticello
.org/site/research-and-collections/firearms (accessed 2012).

427 TRAVELED ARMED   Ibid.

427 HE ONCE LEFT BEHIND   Ibid.

427 BEST FORM OF EXERCISE   Ibid.

427 OFTEN RECOMMENDED IT   Ibid.

427 RIDING WAS THE GREAT SOLACE AND ACTIVITY Ibid.

427 JEFFERSON HUNTED "SQUIRRELS AND PARTRIDGES" Bear, **Jefferson at Monticello,** 17–18. See also TJF, http://www.monticello.org/site/research-and-collections/hunting (accessed 2012).

427 "OLD MASTER WOULDN'T SHOOT" Bear, **Jefferson at Monticello,** 18.

427 WOULD "SCARE . . . UP" PARTRIDGES Ibid.

427 DRIVE HUNTERS AWAY FROM MONTICELLO'S DEER PARK Ibid., 21.

427 A "TWO SHOT-DOUBLE BARREL" TJF, http://www.monticello.org/site/research-and-collections/firearms (accessed 2012).

427 A SET OF TURKISH PISTOLS Ibid.

427 "20 INCH BARRELS" Ibid.

427 "EVERY AMERICAN WHO WISHES" Ibid.

427 A "GUN-MAN" Ibid.

427 "I AM A GREAT FRIEND" Ibid.

428 "PERSONALITIES, WHICH LESSEN THE PLEASURES" **PTJ,** XXVIII, 24.

428 THE NEXT WEEK JAMES MONROE Ibid., 29–31. Jefferson made no secret of his own opinions. In an April 1794 letter, he weighed in on the Treasury, rumors of war with Britain, an issue about the French islands, naval and land armaments, and marine fortifications. Then came the obligatory denial of his own interest in the questions in which he had just expressed his interest: "I find my mind totally absorbed in my rural occupations," he told Madison. (Ibid., 49–50.) A telling

reaction to Federalism came in late March, when the House of Representatives created a Ways and Means Committee as a check on Hamilton. In the debate over whether to establish the panel, "the fiscal party," Madison said, "perceiving their danger, offered a sort of compromise," but the measure failed, and the committee was created. The House now had the institutional means to manage money matters more carefully. (Ibid., 46.)

428 LEGISLATION TO CREATE A NEW ARMY Ibid., 38.

428 WAS "FOUNDED UPON THE IDEA" Ibid., 41.

429 "A CHANGE SO EXTRAORDINARY" Ibid.

429 TO RENOUNCE ANY HEREDITARY TITLES Ibid., 245.

429 "YOU WANT TO HOLD US UP" Ibid.

429 GILES'S AMENDMENT PASSED; DEXTER'S FAILED Ibid.

430 HIS ANNUAL MESSAGE Ibid., 213.

430 THE WHISKEY REBELLION IN THE WEST See Hogeland, **Whiskey Rebellion.**

430 ATTACKS ON BOWER HILL Ibid., 147–50, 152–83.

430 GENERAL JOHN NEVILLE Ibid., 97–105.

430 JAMES MCFARLANE, WAS SHOT AND KILLED Ibid., 154–56.

430 THE DEMOCRATIC-REPUBLICAN SOCIETIES Eugene P. Link, **Democratic-Republican Societies, 1790–1800** (New York, 1973), is a full account. See also Philip S. Foner, ed., **The**

Democratic-Republican Societies, 1790–1800: A Documentary Sourcebook of Constitutions, Declarations, Addresses, Resolutions, and Toasts (Westport, Conn., 1976); and **PTJ**, XXVIII, 220–22.

430 "THE ATTEMPT WHICH HAS BEEN" **PTJ**, XXVIII, 219.

431 "THE DENUNCIATION OF" Ibid., 228.

431 "THERE WAS INDEED" Ibid., 229.

431 HE WOULD USE A WHITE CAMBRIC HANDKERCHIEF **TDLTJ**, 48–49.

431 "THE ONLY IMPATIENCE OF TEMPER" Randall, **Jefferson**, III, 675.

432 WHEN JEFFERSON ORDERED **TDLTJ**, 321.

432 "TELL JUPITER TO COME" Ibid.

432 "IN TONES AND WITH A LOOK" Ibid.

432 TWO FERRYMEN HAD BEEN FIGHTING Ibid.

432 "HIS EYES FLASHING" Ibid., 322.

433 "AND THEY DID ROW" Ibid.

433 "IF YOU VISIT ME" **PTJ**, XXVIII, 337.

433 "COME THEN . . . AND LET US" Ibid., 368.

433 "YOU OUGHT TO BE" Ibid., 315. Jefferson had suggested Madison should consider his own possible candidacy, a scenario Madison dismissed: "Perhaps it will be best, at least for the present to say in brief, that reasons of **every** kind, and some of them of the most **insuperable** as well as **obvious** kind, shut my mind against the admission of any idea such as you seem to glance at." In fact, Madison implied, the time was coming when he and Jefferson would have to speak privately

and in person about Jefferson's political future. (Ibid.)

433 JEFFERSON ADMITTED THAT THE SUBJECT   Ibid., 338–40. This letter of April 27, 1795, has been the subject of intriguing scholarly attention. James Roger Sharp, "Unraveling the Mystery of Jefferson's Letter of April 27, 1795," **Journal of the Early Republic** 6, no. 4 (Winter 1986): 411–18, explores an important textual change in the copy of the letter that Jefferson kept. Jefferson wrote that as he would not seek the office, "my sole object is to avail myself of the first opening ever given me from a friendly quarter (and I could not with decency do it before), of preventing any division or loss of votes, which might be fatal to the Southern interest." Yet someone— Jefferson himself, perhaps, or Thomas Jefferson Randolph (who edited his grandfather's papers in the 1820s) or Nicholas P. Trist, who worked with Randolph—changed the word "Southern" in the letter to read "Republican."

Anxious to present the Jeffersonian political movement as a national, not a sectional, undertaking, whoever changed the phrase was evidently attempting to protect Jefferson from appearing to be anything less than a firm nationalist. States'-rights and national tensions existed from the start, and the prolific Jefferson proved a useful source of quotations and inspiration for sectionalist (and even secessionist) elements in America in his lifetime and long afterward. The preponderance of his life and work, though, put Jefferson on the side of the American union.

It seems likely that his use of the word "Southern" in 1795 was more of a reference to the choice of candidate to lead the Republican interest than it was a wholesale characterization of Republicanism as a regional phenomenon. Consider the sentences following the use of the phrase "Southern interest": "If that [the Southern interest] has any chance of prevailing, it must be by avoiding the loss of a single vote, and by concentrating all its strength on one object. **Who** [emphasis mine] this should be is a question I can more freely discuss with anybody than yourself. In this I painfully feel the loss of Monroe. Had he been here I should have been at no loss for a channel through which to make myself understood." (**PTJ**, XXVIII, 339.)

My reading of this is that Jefferson is still trying to encourage Madison to seek the presidency, in part because Jefferson loved Madison and believed in him, but also because Jefferson would prefer a Republican president from the South to a Republican president from the middle states or New England.

433 "CONTINUAL INSINUATIONS" Ibid., 338.

434 "THE LITTLE SPICE OF AMBITION" Ibid., 339.

435 "I AM CONVINCED" **PTJ**, XXXVI, 676.

435 "MAKE ME UP A SET" Ibid., XXVIII, 377.

436 "A FUGITIVE PUBLICATION" Ibid., 387.

436 WILLIAM BRANCH GILES ANNOUNCED Noble E.

Cunningham, **The Jeffersonian Republicans: The Formation of Party Organization, 1789–1801** (Chapel Hill, N.C., 1957), 86.

436 IN THE FALL, AARON BURR OF NEW YORK Ibid., 86–87.

436 FEDERALIST CHARGES THAT THE TWO MEN Ibid.

436 A BRIEF VISIT ON JEFFERSON'S MOUNTAINTOP Isenberg, **Fallen Founder:** 145–46. As Isenberg noted, "There is no record of what Jefferson and Burr discussed during this brief visit. . . . The two men had little time to plan, and it is highly unlikely that they accomplished anything so momentous as cementing the Republican ticket. Still, Burr **was** actively campaigning. He had made the long trip not just to consult with Jefferson but to show in the flesh his commitment to the Virginia Republicans." (Ibid., 146.)

437 THE TREATY, WHICH PRESIDENT WASHINGTON RECEIVED **PTJ**, XXVIII, 400.

437 ANGRY CROWDS BURNED JAY IN EFFIGY **EOL,** 198. For more on reaction to the Jay Treaty, see Warren, **Jacobin and Junto.**

437 TALK OF IMPEACHING WASHINGTON Ibid. See also Michael Beschloss, **Presidential Courage: Brave Leaders and How They Changed America 1789–1989** (New York, 2007), 1.

437 JEFFERSON DESPISED THE TREATY **PTJ**, XXVIII, 55. By August, Jefferson was writing Madison about Hamilton's maneuvers in New York. "You will perceive by the enclosed that Hamilton

has taken up his pen in support of the treaty. . . . He spoke on its behalf in the meeting in New York, and his party carried a decision in favor of it by a small majority. But the Livingstonians appealed to stones and clubs and beat him and his party off the ground. This from a gentleman just from Philadelphia." (Ibid., 430.) Madison later corrected Jefferson on the details of the anecdote, almost none of which was accurate. (Ibid., 432.)

437 "From North to South"   Ibid., 435.

437 mid-August floods   Ibid., 439.

437 "So general a burst of"   Ibid., 449.

437 "really a colossus to the antirepublican party"   Ibid., 475.

438 fretting about "the quietism"   Ibid., 476. The storm stirred Jefferson's allies. Rutledge, telling him the obligation to serve outweighed his concern about his reputation: "The experience of every day evinces that the service of our country, like the practice of virtue, must bring with it its own reward: whoever expects that gratitude to be the fruit of patriotism expects a vain thing, and disappointment, or mortification will be his portion." (Ibid., 502.)

Rutledge's son delivered the letter personally and stayed at Monticello for a time. "He found me in a retirement I dote on, living like an Antediluvian patriarch among my children and grandchildren, and tilling my soil," Jefferson wrote the senior Rutledge afterward. On the question of public life, Jefferson was apparently unwavering. "You hope I have not abandoned entirely the service of our country: after a five and twenty years continual employment in it, I trust it will be thought I have fulfilled my tour, like a punctual soldier, and may claim my discharge." Yet he could not avoid politics, adding: "I join with you in thinking the treaty an execrable thing." It was, Jefferson said, an "infamous act, which is really nothing more than a treaty of alliance between England and the Anglomen of this country against the legislature and people of the United States." (Ibid., 541–42.)

438 "A BOLDER PARTY-STROKE WAS NEVER STRUCK" JHT, IV, 247.

438 THE HOUSE NEEDED TO APPROVE FUNDING John C. Miller, **The Federalist Era, 1789–1801** (Prospect Heights, Ill., 1998), 172–76. James Madison mounted a bid to bring the treaty before the House of Representatives. Madison's argument, one with which Jefferson had much sympathy, was that the House should have a voice in a treaty that touched on so many matters that also fell under House jurisdiction. The treaty did require House approval of an appropriations measure to fund parts of the treaty, and the measure passed over Madison's objection. (Ibid.)

438 "A SUPERCILIOUS TYRANT" Warren, **Jacobin and Junto,** 63.

438 "RULER WHO TRAMPLES" Ibid.

438 "Never, till a few months" Ibid., 64.

439 "This was the first time" Ibid.

439 "The N. England States" **PTJ**, XXIX, 95.

440 "Two parties then do exist" Ibid., XXVIII, 508–9.

441 Jefferson wrote Bache Ibid., 560–61.

441 Though he had hardly left the arena Joseph J. Ellis, **American Sphinx**, 184, fixes the **Aurora** moment as the one that marks Jefferson's reentry into politics. As noted, I do not believe Jefferson ever left, but Ellis makes an interesting point: Asking the editors for the papers put Jefferson back on the stage in the eyes of those most politically engaged of men—the newspaper editors of the eighteenth century.

442 "You will have seen" Ibid., XXIX, 124.

443 Jefferson had read a report Ibid., 127–30. "That to your particular friends and connections, you have described, and they have announced to me, as a person under a dangerous influence; and that, if I would listen **more** to some **other** opinions all would be well," Washington said. He continued:

> My answer invariably has been that I had
> never discovered any thing in the conduct of
> Mr. Jefferson to raise suspicions, in my mind,
> of his insincerity; that if he would retrace my
> public conduct while he was in the Admin-
> istration, abundant proofs would occur to
> him, that truth and right decisions, were the

sole objects of my pursuit; that there were as many instances within his **own** knowledge of my having decided **against,** as in **favor of** the opinions of the person evidently alluded to; and moreover, that I was no believer in the infallibility of the politics or measures of **any man living.** In short, that I was no party man myself, and the first wish of my heart was, if parties did exist, to reconcile them. (Ibid., 142.)

443 "EVERYTHING SACRED AND HONORABLE" Ibid., 127.

443 MAY "TRY TO SOW TARES" Ibid.

443 "AS YOU HAVE MENTIONED" Ibid., 142.

444 PATRICK HENRY TO STAND APE, I, 36. See also Kidd, **Patrick Henry,** 234–35.

444 "TO INFORM YOU THAT THE PEOPLE" Ibid., 169.

444 "I HAVE NOT THE ARROGANCE" Ibid., 199.

TWENTY-EIGHT · To the Vice Presidency

445 "THERE IS A DEBT OF SERVICE" PTJ, XXIX, 233.

445 "YOU AND I HAVE FORMERLY SEEN" Ibid., 456–57.

445 WASHINGTON'S FAREWELL ADDRESS APE, I, 38–39.

446 "A SIGNAL, LIKE DROPPING A HAT" Ibid., 70. See also Ferling, **Adams vs. Jefferson,** 85. Word spread quickly. "I rejoice at the news" of Wash-

ington's retirement, a correspondent wrote Jefferson, "because I consider him as a man dangerous to the liberties of this country. Misled himself, he lends his influence to others, and by his name gives a sanction to the most dangerous measures." (**PTJ**, XXIX, 185.)

446 Presidential elections in the first decades   In the mysterious way these things became clear in presidential elections from 1796 until Andrew Jackson was nominated for reelection by a national party convention thirty-six years later, it was instantly understood that John Adams and Thomas Jefferson were the leading candidates to succeed Washington.

446 Until the ratification of the Twelfth Amendment   **EOL**, 285. See also Bruce Ackerman, **The Failure of the Founding Fathers: Jefferson, Marshall, and the Rise of Presidential Democracy** (Cambridge, Mass., 2007), which is a fascinating study.

446 **The Columbian Mirror and Alexandria Gazette**   PTJ, XXIX, 193.

447 John Taylor of Caroline   Ibid., 194.

447 describing a 1794 conversation   Ibid. The Republicans immediately sensed the political possibilities of the Taylor report about Adams's remarks. John Mason, son of George, asked for a certified copy of the account, saying Adams's comments would "do more good than anything which has yet been spoken of." (Ibid., 194–95.)

447 Campaign literature read   **APE**, I, 40.

447 "Thomas Jefferson is a firm republican" Ferling, **Adams vs. Jefferson**, 90.

447 THE RISING PROSPECT OF WAR WITH FRANCE Ibid., 93. Pierre Adet, a French diplomat, publicly suggested the Federalists were too favorably disposed toward the British and that Jefferson would be the wiser choice in terms of relations with France. The Federalists in turn used this quasi endorsement against Jefferson. (**APE**, I, 30.)

448 A LATE-AUTUMN COLD SPELL **PTJ**, XXIX, 211.

448 "Few will believe" Ibid.

448 HAMILTON, WHO OPPOSED BOTH **APE**, I, 40.

448 A FASCINATING STRATEGY Ibid. As Page Smith wrote in **APE**, I:

> The plan called for the Federalist electors in New England to cast all their votes for Adam and Pinckney for President and Vice-President while the electors in South Carolina, Pinckney's home state, would throw away a few Adams votes and thus give the Presidency to the man plainly intended to be Vice-President, leaving Adams in that office. Had it succeeded and the Federalist candidate for Vice-President become President by a ruse, the Federalist party would have been split beyond hope of repair. Adams would almost certainly have resigned as Vice-President, leaving that office presumably to Jefferson or Burr. Equally likely was the election of Jefferson as President. (Ibid.)

448 ADAMS "TOO HEADSTRONG"   PTJ, XXIX, 214.
If Pinckney succeeded, Madison also said, "It
is to be hoped that P[inckney] may equally disappoint those who expect to make . . . use of
him. . . . and there is always the chance of a de-
volution of the business on the House of Reps.
which will I believe decide it as it ought to be
decided." (Ibid.)

    And there was a chance Jefferson could even
place third: "The prevailing idea is that Pinckney will have the greatest number of votes: and
I think that Adams will be most likely to stand
next." (Ibid., 218.)

448 "YOU MUST RECONCILE"   Ibid., 218.

449 "A DIFFICULTY FROM WHICH"   Ibid, 223.

449 "FULLY TO SOLICIT ON MY BEHALF"   Ibid.

449 PINCKNEY FADED TO THIRD   APE, I, 41.

449 "IT IS EXPECTED"   PTJ, XXIX, 226. Madison
wrote Jefferson of Adams:

> You know that his feelings will not enslave
> him to the example of his predecessor. It is
> certain that his censures of our paper system
> and the intrigues at New York for setting
> P. above him have fixed an enmity with the
> British faction. Nor should it pass for noth-
> ing, that the true interest of New England
> particularly requires reconciliation with
> France as the road to her commerce. Add
> to the whole that he is said to speak of you
> now in friendly terms and will no doubt be

soothed by your acceptance of a place subordinate to him. It must be confessed however that all these calculations are qualified by his political principles and prejudices. But they add weight to the obligation from which you must not withdraw yourself. (Ibid., 226–27.)

450 ADAMS WON, BARELY **APE**, I, 41.

450 "O LORD!" Miller, **Federalist Era**, 264–65.

450 BELIEVED DEEPLY IN "THE SENSE" Ibid.

450 "I VALUE THE LATE VOTE HIGHLY" **PTJ**, XXIX, 258. He was always a precise vote counter: "In this point of view the difference between 68 and 71 votes is little sensible, and still less that between the real vote which was 69 and 70 because one real elector in Pennsylvania was excluded from voting by the miscarriage of the votes, and one who was not an elector was admitted to vote." (Ibid.)

450 "I KNEW IT WAS IMPOSSIBLE" Ibid., 232. To Edward Rutledge, Jefferson wrote: "You have seen my name lately tacked to so much of eulogy and of abuse, that I daresay you hardly thought it meant for your old acquaintance of 76. In truth I did not know myself under the pens either of my friends or foes. It is unfortunate for our peace that unmerited abuse wounds, while unmerited praise has not the power to heal. These are hard wages for the services of all the active and healthy years of one's life." (Ibid.)

His supporters braced him for the inevitable

criticism that was to come during the administration, in part by portraying the attackers as agents of what Jefferson hated and feared most. "It is true that you have been abused," James Sullivan, a Republican lawyer and politician in Massachusetts, wrote Jefferson from Boston on January 12, 1797. "But this abuse came from a party who are determined to abuse every one who will not, with them, bow in adoration to the British monarchy. If the abuse and calumny of these men can deprive the public of the services of those on whom they may confide with safety, there will be an end to our free constitutions: and the enemies of an elective republic will obtain a complete triumph." (Ibid., 262.)

450 "THE HONEYMOON WOULD BE" Ibid.

451 "THIS IS CERTAINLY NOT A MOMENT" Ibid.

451 WHISPERS OF POSSIBLE SECESSION Ibid., 364.

451 THE THREE-FIFTHS CLAUSE Ibid. See also Garry Wills, "Negro President": Jefferson and the Slave Power (New York, 2003), for a discussion of the role of the three-fifths clause in the politics of the early republic.

451 "WE SHALL NEVER" PTJ, XXIX, 364.

452 "I HAVE NO AMBITION" Ibid., 235. Benjamin Rush believed, with Jefferson, that it had been a lucky thing to lose the top post for now. "Accept of my congratulations upon your election to the Vice President's Chair of the United States, and upon your escape of the Office of President," Rush wrote. "In the present situation of our

country it would have been impossible for you to have preserved the credit of republican principles, or your own character for integrity, had you succeeded to the **New York** administration of our government. The seeds of British Systems in everything have at last ripened. What a harvest of political evils is before us!" (Ibid., 251.)

452 A DRAFT OF THE LETTER   Ibid., 247–51. See also McCullough, **John Adams,** 465–66.

452 MADISON REPLIED WITH A SIX-POINT CASE **PTJ,** XXIX, 263–65.

453 HE WOULD NOT MAIL   Ibid., 280–81. A significant moment in the exchange with Madison over the virtues of the letter to Adams lies in a philosophical passage of Jefferson's—a passage informed by a sense of tragedy. "In truth I do not recollect in all the animal kingdom a single species but man which is eternally and systematically engaged in the destruction of its own species," Jefferson wrote. "What is called civilization seems to have no other effect on him than to teach him to pursue the principle of **bellum omnium in omnia** [an allusion to Thomas Hobbes's notion of "the war of all against all"] on a larger scale, and in place of the little contests of tribe against tribe, to engage all the quarters of the earth in the same work of destruction." (Ibid., 248.)

453 JEFFERSON REACHED PHILADELPHIA **MB,** II, 954–55.

453 ADAMS, WHO LODGED AT FRANCIS'S **PTJ,** XXIX, 551.

453 REPAID THE COURTESY THE NEXT MORNING Ibid.

453 CLOSING THE DOOR BEHIND HIM Ibid.

454 WAS GLAD JEFFERSON WAS ALONE Ibid.

454 HAD MUCH TO TALK ABOUT Ibid.

454 JEFFERSON AGREED THAT HE SHOULD Ibid., 552.

454 "HE SAID THAT IF MR. MADISON" Ibid.

454 THE CEREMONIAL PROCEEDINGS McCullough, **John Adams**, 467–70.

454 DELIVERED A SHORT SPEECH **PTJ**, XXIX, 310–12. Should any lawmaker find fault with his rulings from the chair, Jefferson said, he would "rely on the liberality and candor of those from whom I differ to believe that I do it on pure motives." (Ibid., 311.) Faced with his primary duty—that of presiding over the Senate—he turned to his oldest teacher for guidance on his newest work, writing George Wythe for thoughts on parliamentary procedure. (Ibid., 275–76.)

455 TO THE MORTALITY OF THE PRESIDENT Ibid., 311.

455 ONE NEW YORK REPUBLICAN Matthew Livingston Davis attributed this statement to George Clinton. (Davis Memorandum Book, 10–11, Rufus King Papers, New York Historical Society.)

455 INAUGURATION OF JOHN ADAMS McCullough, **John Adams**, 466–70.

455 WASHINGTON SEEMED CHEERFUL Ferling, **Adams vs. Jefferson**, 98.

455 "THE PRESIDENT IS FORTUNATE" PTJ, XXIX, 255. Washington's retirement from power was an epochal event for the country and for those who had fought for him and with him in war and peace. Jefferson assessed his old chief with a cold eye:

> Such is the popularity of the President that the people will support him in whatever he will do, or will not do, without appealing to their own reason or to any thing but their feelings towards him: his mind had been so long used to unlimited applause that it could not brook contradiction, or even advice offered unasked. To advice, when asked, he is very open. I have long thought therefore it was best for the republican interest to soothe him by flattery where they could approve his measures, and to be silent where they disapprove, that they may not render him desperate as to their affections, and entirely indifferent to their wishes; in short, to lie on their oars while he remains at the helm, and let the bark drift as his will and a superintending providence shall direct. (Ibid., 252.)

455 "THE SECOND OFFICE" Ibid., 362. "When I retired from this place and the office of Secretary of State, it was in the firmest contemplation of never more returning here," Jefferson told Gerry. "There had indeed been suggestions in the public

papers that I was looking towards a succession to the President's chair. But feeling a consciousness of their falsehood, and observing that the suggestions came from hostile quarters, I considered them as intended merely to excite public odium against me. I never in my life exchanged a word with any person on the subject till I found my name brought forward generally in competition with that of Mr. Adams." (Ibid.)

From Massachusetts, Elbridge Gerry wrote of his pleasure at Jefferson's election and offered the kind of wisdom most readily available from those familiar with politics but distant from the unfolding drama of the day. "Thus circumstanced, give me leave to express my apprehensions that the consequence of this election will be repeat[ed stratagems, to] weaken or destroy the confidence of the P and VP in each other, from an assurance that if it continues to the end of the President's administration the VP will be his successor and perhaps from a dread of your political influence." (Ibid., 326.)

455 ADAMS AND JEFFERSON DINED Ibid., 552.

456 "HE IMMEDIATELY SAID" Ibid. Responding specifically to the suggestion that there might be tensions between him and Adams, Jefferson said: "These machinations will proceed from the Hamiltonians by whom he is surrounded, and who are only a little less hostile to him than to me. . . . I cannot help fearing that it is impossible for Mr. Adams to believe that the state of

my mind is what it really is; that he may think I view him as an obstacle in my way." (Ibid., 362.)

456 HE FOUGHT TO KEEP THE PEACE EOL, 272–75.

456 THE QUASI-WAR WITH FRANCE Ibid., 245–46.

456 "THE HALF WAR WITH FRANCE" Ibid., 245.

456 RETAINED WASHINGTON'S CABINET McCullough, **John Adams,** 471–72.

456 THIS PROVED PROBLEMATIC It was, McCullough wrote, "one of the most fateful steps of his presidency." (Ibid., 471.)

457 REFLECTING ON THE EVENING CONVERSATION Ibid.

457 PATSY RANDOLPH HAD THREE CHILDREN Kierner, **Martha Jefferson Randolph,** 102.

457 "CONSTANTLY RESIDES WITH HER FATHER" Anne Hollingsworth Wharton, **Social Life in the Early Republic** (Williamstown, Mass., 1970), 110.

457 THE NEXT YEAR POLLY MARRIED JOHN WAYLES EPPES TJF, http://www.monticello.org/site/jefferson/maria-jefferson-eppes (accessed 2012).

457 EIGHT MONTHS AND THREE WEEKS LATER Gordon-Reed, **Hemingses of Monticello,** 530–36. As Gordon-Reed noted, the original William Beverley had been a great Virginian who had known Peter Jefferson and had negotiated the Treaty of Lancaster, the instrument by which Virginia took vast swaths of lands in the West from the Six Nations of the Iroquois. Naming his son Beverly honored Virginia and two other

things of immense importance to Jefferson: his father and his vision of a boundless West. (Ibid.)

458 "I HAVE BEEN FOR SOME TIME" **PTJ**, XXX, 129.

458 "A FEW INDIVIDUALS OF NO FIXED SYSTEM" Ibid., XXIX, 437–38. Yet Jefferson still sought a degree of harmony and civility. "Political dissension is doubtless a less evil than the lethargy of despotism: but still it is a great evil, and it would be as worthy the efforts of the patriot as of the philosopher, to exclude its influence if possible, from social life," he wrote. (Ibid., 404.)

459 "A DETERMINATION NEVER TO DO" Randall, **Jefferson,** I, 22–23.

460 "WHEN THIS IS IN RETURN" Ibid.

460 A CATACLYSMIC REACTION IN FRANCE **EOL**, 239.

460 "I ANTICIPATE THE BURNING" **PTJ**, XXIX, 404–5.

461 MAZZEI PUBLICIZED THE WASHINGTON LETTER Ibid., 73–88.

461 "THE PASSIONS ARE TOO HIGH" Ibid., 456.

462 USING A NEW YELLOW FEVER EPIDEMIC Ibid., XXIX, 592. "Ambition is so vigilant, and where it has a model always in view as in the present case"—Madison and Jefferson thought that Adams saw himself in a monarchial light—"is so prompt in seizing its advantages, that it cannot be too closely watched, or too vigorously checked." (Ibid.)

462 "Damn 'em, Damn 'em"   Ibid., 593.

462 " 'For my part . . . I avow myself a monarchist' "   Ibid., 596.

twenty-nine · The Reign of Witches

463 "No, I think a party is necessary"   PTJ,
XXX, 420.

463 a disturbing story about 1787   Ibid., 13–14.

464 the failure of the new government   Ibid.
"They wished things to get more and more into
confusion to justify the violent measure they
proposed." (Ibid., 14)

464 spat in the face of another   James Morton
Smith, **Freedom's Fetters: The Alien and Sedi-
tion Laws and American Civil Liberties** (Ithaca,
N.Y., 1966), 223–24. See also **EOL**, 227–30.

464 after Griswold insulted Lyon's courage
James Morton Smith, **Freedom's Fetters**, 223–24.

464 An effort to expel Lyon   Ibid.

464 attacked Lyon with a cane   **EOL**, 229.

464 seized some fireplace tongs   Ibid.

464 brawled on the House floor   Ibid.

464 a diplomatic mission to France had failed
Ibid., 243.

464 "produced such a shock"   Ibid.

465 a message calling on Americans   John
Adams, "Special Message," March 19, 1798, The
American Presidency Project, http://www.presi
dency.ucsb.edu/ws/?pid=65650 (accessed 2012).

465 "adopt with promptitude"   Ibid.

465 "OUR SEAFARING AND COMMERCIAL CITIZENS" Ibid.

465 KNOWN AS THE ALIEN AND SEDITION ACTS EOL, 249, 259. See also Risjord, **Jefferson's America, 1760–1815,** 292–96.

466 "WRITE, PRINT, UTTER OR PUBLISH" EOL, 259.

466 "EVERYONE HAS A RIGHT" **PTJ,** XXX, 434–35.

466 "HOW INCREDIBLE WAS IT" Ibid., XXXI, 445.

467 FINES UP TO $2,000 AND UP TO TWO YEARS IN PRISON EOL, 259.

467 "FOR MY OWN PART" **PTJ,** XXX, 560.

467 THE DANGER OF WAR WAS REAL EOL, 259. "There existed a domestic—what shall I call it?—a conspiracy, a faction leagued with a foreign power to effect a revolution or a subjugation of this country, by the arms of that foreign power," said Robert Goodloe Harper. (Ibid.)

467 "THE MANAGEMENT OF FOREIGN RELATIONS" **PTJ,** XXX, 348.

468 JEFFERSON DINED WITH ADAMS Ibid., 113.

468 "WITHOUT WISHING TO DAMP" Ibid., XXXI, 129. Of Adams, James Madison said: "His language to the young men of Philadelphia is the most abominable and degrading that could fall from the lips of the first magistrate of an independent people, and particularly from a Revolutionary patriot. . . . The abolition of royalty was it seems not one of his Revolutionary principles." (Ibid., XXX, 359.)

469 "I AM AMONG THOSE" Ibid., 127.

469 THESE WERE "BRANCHES OF SCIENCE" Ibid.

469 "THE GENERATION WHICH IS GOING OFF" Ibid., 128.

469 A PARADE OF ABOUT 1,200 SUPPORTERS Ibid., XXX, 341–42.

470 A FAST DAY Ibid.

470 VIOLENCE BROKE OUT Ibid.

470 "ADAMS' FAST" Warren, **Jacobin and Junto**, 75.

470 "A FRAY ENSUED" **PTJ**, XXX, 341.

470 CONSPIRATORIAL FRAME OF MIND Ibid., 353. He understood that Adams was attempting to orchestrate public opinion. "All sorts of artifices have been descended to, to agitate the popular mind," Jefferson wrote Madison on May 17, 1798. "The President received 3 anonymous letters (written probably by some of the war-men) announcing plots to burn the city on the fast-day. He thought them worth being made known, and great preparations were proposed by way of caution. . . . Many weak people packed their most valuable movables to be ready for transportation." (Ibid.)

470 "I KNOW THAT ALL MY MOTIONS" Ibid., 484.

470 FEARED HIS MAIL Ibid., 588. "Yet the infidelities of the post office and the circumstances of the times are against my writing fully and freely, whilst my own indispositions are as much against writing mysteries innuendoes and half confidences," Jefferson said. "I know not which mortifies me most, that I should fear to write what I think, or my country bear such a state of things." (Ibid.)

470 "EXECUTED WITH UNRELENTING FURY" Ibid., 440.

470 HAMILTON WAS TO BECOME Ibid., 300.

470 HAMILTON ULTIMATELY DECLINED Ibid., 302.

470 "POLITICS AND PARTY HATREDS" Ibid., 355.

471 JEFFERSON WAS PRESSED FOR CASH Ibid., 277.

471 "MR. B's HABITUAL INTOXICATION" Ibid., 15.

471 ANNOUNCED THE DEATH OF HARRIET HEMINGS Ibid., 43.

471 JEFFERSON COMPOSED A LETTER Ibid., XXXI, 172–74.

471 PREGNANT WITH ANOTHER CHILD Gordon-Reed, **Hemingses of Monticello,** 73, 195.

472 "THE X. Y. Z. FEVER" Ibid., 559–60.

472 MONCK WAS A NOBLEMAN WHO BACKED THE RESTORATION For more of the letter that alluded to the Oliverians and to Monck, see **PTJ,** XXX, 559–60.

472 BENJAMIN FRANKLIN BACHE James Morton Smith, **Freedom's Fetters,** 188–204.

472 JAMES THOMSON CALLENDER Ibid., 334–58.

473 MATTHEW LYON Ibid., 225–46.

473 A LETTER HE HAD WRITTEN Ibid., 226.

473 "CONTINUAL GRASP FOR POWER" Ibid.

473 "A SEDITIOUS FOREIGNER" Ibid.

473 LYON WAS INDICTED, TRIED, AND CONVICTED Ibid., 229–38. Stevens Thomson Mason reported public reaction to Jefferson on November 23, 1798: "Lyon's trial has produced a very strong sensation here, and many who have valued themselves on being friends of order and sup-

porters of government admit that this is going too far." (**PTJ**, XXX, 586.)

473 FOUR MONTHS IN JAIL   Ibid., 235.

473 FINED HIM $1,000   Ibid. Paterson also charged Lyon court costs of $60.96.

473 "MATTHEW LYON, AS A MEMBER"   Ibid.

473 "I KNOW NOT"   Ibid., 237.

473 SOUGHT REELECTION   Ibid., 238–42.

473 "WHAT PERSON WHO REMEMBERS"   **PTJ**, XXXI, 57.

474 "PRAY, MY DEAR SIR"   Ibid., XXX, 641.

474 SECRETLY DRAFTED RESOLUTIONS   Ibid., 529–56.

475 BALKED AT THE NULLIFICATION LANGUAGE   Ibid., XXXI, 266–68.

475 "IN THE SENATE," WROTE BRECKINRIDGE   Ibid., 266.

475 "I THINK WE SHOULD"   Ibid., XXX, 580.

476 "IN EVERY FREE AND DELIBERATING SOCIETY"   Ibid., 388–89.

476 "NO ONE CAN KNOW"   Margaret Bayard Smith, **First Forty Years**, 406.

477 "I AM FOR FREEDOM OF RELIGION"   **PTJ**, XXX, 646–47.

478 HE SOLICITED FRIENDS   Ibid., 661.

478 DISCUSSED PUBLIC-OPINION STRATEGIES   Ibid., XXXI, 10. One example: "A piece published in Bache's paper on **foreign influence** has had the greatest currency and effect," Jefferson wrote Madison on February 5, 1799. (Ibid.)

478 "SENSIBLE THAT THIS SUMMER"   Ibid.

478 "I WISH YOU TO GIVE THESE" **APE**, I, 63.
He begged Madison to write letters he could
then circulate. "You can render such incalculable services in this way." (**PTJ**, XXXI, 10.)
The mobilization of public sentiment was a
powerful weapon. On February 13, 1799, Jefferson wrote: "A wonderful and rapid change
is taking place in Pennsylvania, Jersey and N.
York. Congress is daily plied with petitions
against the Alien and Sedition laws and standing armies. . . . The materials now bearing on
the public mind will infallibly restore it to its
republican soundness in the course of the present summer, if the knowledge of facts can only
be disseminated among the people." Jefferson
repeated the point to Pendleton the next day.
(Ibid., 35–39.)

478 "A DECIDED CHARACTER" **PTJ**, XXXI, 40.

THIRTY · Adams vs. Jefferson Redux

479 "I SHOULD BE UNFAITHFUL" **PTJ**, XXXII,
126. Jefferson continued: "The first wish of my
heart is to see them so guarded as to be safe in
any hands, and not to depend on the personal
disposition of the depository: and I hope this to
be practicable as long as the people retain the
spirit of freedom. . . . Our chief object at present
should be to reconcile the divisions which have
been artificially excited and to restore society to
its wonted harmony." (Ibid., 126–27.)

479 "THAT NOT A WORD SHOULD BE SPOKEN" Ibid., XXXI, 64.

480 THE FEDERALISTS "BEGAN TO ENTER" Ibid.

480 "IT WAS IMPOSSIBLE TO PROCEED" Ibid.

480 WAS GOING TO RAISE A "PRESIDENTIAL ARMY" Ibid., 97.

480 JOHN RANDOLPH OF ROANOKE Ibid., 305–6, 314.

480 THE NEXT EVENING TWO MARINES Ibid., 314.

480 "JOSTLED AND [HAD] HIS COAT PULLED" Ibid. Characteristically, Randolph refused to drop the matter, petitioning President Adams to dismiss the marines "to afford a remedy, and to restrain men . . . from giving personal abuse and insult." Nothing came of the petition. (Ibid., 306–7)

480 A "REIGN OF WITCHES" Ibid., XXX, 389.

480 REPORTED THAT HAMILTON HAD LED Ibid., XXXI, 337–38.

481 "NO MORTAL CAN FORESEE" Ibid., 465.

481 "WILL NEVER PERMIT" APE, I, 68.

481 "GOD—AND A RELIGIOUS PRESIDENT" Ferling, **Adams vs. Jefferson,** 154.

481 "BECAUSE HE IS NOT A FANATIC" APE, I, 68.

481 HAD "HARANGUED" A GRAND JURY PTJ, XXXI, 589. The familiar Federalist claim that Jefferson was a nonbeliever was on Chase's mind in part because of a dinner Jefferson had planned to give on a Sunday. (Ibid.)

482 JAMES THOMSON CALLENDER, A VIRULENT REPUBLICAN Ibid., 589–90.

482 **THE PROSPECT BEFORE Us** For discussions

of the book, see Ferling, **Adams vs. Jefferson,** 136–37.

482 "The reign of Mr. Adams" James Morton Smith, **Freedom's Fetters,** 339.

482 "cannot fail to produce" **APE,** I, 63.

482 Abigail and John Adams seethed Cappon, **Adams-Jefferson Letters,** 273.

482 George Washington died **JHT,** III, 442.

483 Jefferson had been dishonest Willard Sterne Randall, **George Washington: A Life** (New York, 1997), 480–81.

483 "Perhaps no man in this community" **JHT,** III, 443.

483 Freneau wrote some verses Ibid.

484 "The horrors which" **PTJ,** XXXI, 524.

484 "The batteries of slander" Ibid., 526.

484 "Our opponents perceive" Ibid., 536.

484 "madness and extravagance" Ibid., 546–47.

485 "The people through all the states" Ibid., 547.

485 Adams made some cabinet changes Ibid., 581. See also McCullough, **John Adams,** 537–39.

485 Adams also disbanded **PTJ,** XXXI, 581.

485 "are, on the approach of an election" Ibid.

485 published rumors that Jefferson had died Ibid., XXXII, 42.

486 "I thought I had lost" Ibid.

486 a small gathering Ibid., 58–59.

487 Jefferson denied it all Ibid., 98–99.

487 Jefferson had to count Ibid., 97. One sign

of the tensions of the moment: Jefferson, who did not know McGregory, sent the reply through another Connecticut friend, noting that "the stratagems of the times [are] very multifarious" and he wanted to be sure that no "improper use" would be made of the letter. No one was to be trusted. (Ibid.)

487 A SLAVE NAMED GABRIEL Ibid., 131–32. For Monroe on the revolt, see ibid., 144–45. See also **EOL,** 534–42; Miller, **Wolf by the Ears,** 126–29; and Brodie, **Thomas Jefferson,** 342–43. James Sidbury, **Ploughshares into Swords: Race, Rebellion, and Identity in Gabriel's Virginia, 1730–1810** (New York, 1997), is also illuminating.

487 HANGING TWENTY-SIX CONSPIRATORS **PTJ,** XXXII, 145. Once reassured the rebellion had been broken up, Jefferson took a moderate tone. "There is a strong sentiment that there has been hanging enough," he wrote to James Monroe, then governor. "The other states and the world at large will forever condemn us if we indulge in a principle of revenge, or go one step beyond absolute necessity." (Ibid., 160.)

487 "THEIR PLAN WAS TO MASSACRE" Ibid., 137.

488 A PANIC Ibid., XXXVII, 335–36. Gabriel's conspiracy was in 1800; the subsequent episodes during what John C. Miller called the "Great Fear" (Miller, **Wolf by the Ears,** 127) included one in Norfolk in 1802. (**PTJ,** XXXVII, 335–36.)

Jefferson linked St. Domingue to the American situation. "The course of things in the neighboring islands of the West Indies appears to have given a considerable impulse to the minds of the slaves in different parts of the U.S.," Jefferson wrote Rufus King on July 13, 1802.

A great disposition to insurgency has manifested itself among them, which, in one instance, in the state of Virginia broke out into actual insurrection. This was easily suppressed: but many of those concerned, (between 20. and 30. I believe) fell victims to the law. So extensive an execution could not but excite sensibility in the public mind, and beget a regret that the laws had not provided, for such cases, some alternative, combining more mildness with equal efficacy. The legislature of the state, at a subsequent meeting, took the subject into consideration, and have communicated to me through the Governor of the state, their wish that some place could be provided, out of the limits of the U.S. to which slaves guilty of insurgency might be transported; and they have particularly looked to Africa as offering the most desirable receptacle. We might, for this purpose, enter into negotiations with the natives, on some part of the coast, to obtain a settlement, and, by establishing an African company, combine with it commercial operations, which might not only reimburse expenses but procure profit also. (Ibid., XXXVIII, 54.)

488 THE STATE'S HOUSE OF DELEGATES ASKED JEFFERSON   Ibid., XXXVIII, 56.

488 A FOREIGN LAND   Ibid.

488 AN APPROACH WAS MADE   Miller, **Wolf by the Ears,** 128. Jefferson had suggested Sierra Leone to Monroe. (**PTJ,** XXXVIII, 56.) Abolitionists had resettled some African American slaves in Serra Leone. See Simon Schama, **Rough Crossings** (New York, 2006), 11. The slaves who settled in Freetown, Sierra Leone, had joined the British during the Revolutionary War and had briefly lived in Nova Scotia before making the journey to Sierra Leone. (Ibid., 3–5, 269–81.)

488 HAMILTON WAS UNHAPPY   **APE,** I, 60–61.

488 NEW YORK ELECTION RESULTS   **PTJ,** XXXI, 509.

488 LEGISLATURES CHOSE PRESIDENTIAL ELECTORS   **APE,** I, 61.

488 "A MOST AUSPICIOUS GLOOM"   **PTJ,** XXXI, 554.

488 APPEALED TO JOHN JAY   **APE,** I, 61. See also Walter Stahr, **John Jay: Founding Father** (New York, 2005), 360–61.

488 "IN TIMES LIKE THIS"   **APE,** I, 61.

489 "PROPOSING A MEASURE"   Ibid.

489 JEFFERSON MET WITH ADAMS   **PTJRS,** III, 306.

490 TALK OF FIELDING   **PTJ**, XXXI, 509. See also **APE**, I, 61–62.

490 ANTI-ADAMS FEDERALISTS SUCH AS HAMILTON **APE**, I, 61.

491 "TO SUPPORT **ADAMS** AND **PINCKNEY**"   Ibid.

491 "HOCUS-POCUS MANEUVERS"   **PTJ**, XXXI, 561.

491 AN ATTACK ON THE SECOND PRESIDENT   Ibid., XXXII, 238–39.

491 "OUR ENEMIES ARE"   **Life and Correspondence of Rufus King,** III, ed. Charles R. King (New York, 1971), 331.

491 "IF WE MUST HAVE"   Ferling, **Adams vs. Jefferson,** 141. Troup, Hamilton's old college roommate, echoed the point to Rufus King on December 4, 1800: "General Hamilton makes no secret of his opinion that Jefferson should be preferred to Adams." (**Life and Correspondence of Rufus King,** III, 340.)

492 "I HAVE SOMETIMES ASKED MYSELF"   **PTJ**, XXXII, 122.

492 RESULTS FROM THE STATES REACHED MONTICELLO   See, for instance, ibid., 225–26, in which Stevens Thomson Mason reported the Maryland tallies. See also ibid., 263. Jefferson was relieved at the results of the different state elections. "Whatever may be the event of the Executive election, the Legislative one will give us a majority in the H. of R. and all but that in the Senate," he wrote. "The former alone will keep the government from running wild, while

a reformation in our state legislatures will be working and preparing a complete one in the Senate. A President can then do little mischief." (Ibid., 227.)

492 "DEMOCRATIC PRINCIPLES SEEM" **Life and Correspondence of Rufus King,** III, 353.

492 "I HAVE NEVER HEARD" **APE,** I, 128.

493 "I BELIEVE WE MAY CONSIDER" **PTJ,** XXXII, 300.

493 "TEMPESTS AND TORNADOES" Caesar A. Rodney to Joseph H. Nicholson, February 19, 1801, Joseph H. Nicholson Papers, LOC.

493 "HIGHFLYING FEDERALISTS" **PTJ,** XXXII, 306–7.

493 "HAS PRODUCED GREAT DISMAY" Ibid., 322.

493 "SOME OF THE JACOBINS" **Life and Correspondence of Rufus King,** III, 354.

494 "OUR TORIES BEGIN TO GIVE" John Randolph to Joseph Nicholson, December 16, 1800, Joseph H. Nicholson Papers, LOC.

494 SHOWED NO OUTWARD SIGNS Isenberg, **Fallen Founder,** 216–20.

494 "I DO NOT . . . APPREHEND" **PTJ,** XXXII, 343.

494 THERE IS NO EVIDENCE Ibid. Joanne Freeman points out, however, something that clearly bothered the Jeffersonians. "In the end, Burr kept his word [about not working against Jefferson in the House] but left things open; he didn't court the Presidency, but once the tie was announced, he said nothing about declining the office if offered, an ambiguity that kept Federalist hopes alive

until the final hour." (Freeman, "A Qualified Resolution: The Presidential Election of 1800," in Cogliano, ed., **A Companion to Thomas Jefferson,** 155.)

494 JEFFERSON SOON CAME TO BELIEVE "Notes on a Conversation with Aaron Burr, January 26, 1804," Thomas Jefferson Papers, LOC.

494 THE EVENTUAL OUTCOME **PTJ,** XXXII, 347.

495 "THE PRESIDENT, I AM TOLD" **Life and Correspondence of Rufus King,** III, 366–67.

495 "THE DREAD NOW" J. Preston to John Breckenridge, December 28, 1800, Breckinridge Family Papers, LOC.

495 "THE FEDS APPEAR" **PTJ,** XXXII, 358.

496 THEY CAME TO JEFFERSON Ibid., 367.

496 "WHERE," MCHENRY ASKED **Life and Correspondence of Rufus King,** III, 362.

THIRTY-ONE · A Desperate State of Affairs

497 "RUMORS ARE VARIOUS" Horn, Lewis, and Onuf, **Revolution of 1800,** 65.

497 "IT IS EXTREMELY UNCERTAIN" **The Papers of John Marshall,** VI, ed. Herbert A. Johnson and others (Chapel Hill, N.C., 1974-), 41.

497 SIX OR SEVEN BOARDINGHOUSES **Records of the Columbia Historical Society.,** Vol. 25, 1923, 198–99.

497 A PHILADELPHIA BOOT MAKER **National Intelligencer,** February 6. 1801.

497 A BOOKSTORE Ibid., February 16, 1801.

497 BENJAMIN W. MORRIS AND CO. GROCERIES **Washington Federalist,** February 17, 1801.

497 WILD, WOODED, AND FILLED WITH GAME Margaret Bayard Smith, **First Forty Years,** 10. "Conrad's boarding house was on the south side of Capitol Hill and commanded an extensive and beautiful view," Margaret Bayard Smith wrote. "It was on the top of the hill, the precipitous sides of which were covered with grass, shrubs, and trees in their wild uncultivated state." (Ibid.) There was only one church in the city. "At this time the only place for public worship in our new city was a small, a very small frame building at the bottom of Capitol Hill. It had been a tobacco-house belonging to Daniel Carroll and was purchased by a few Episcopalians for a mere trifle and fitted up as a church in the plainest and rudest manner. During the first winter, Mr. Jefferson regularly attended service on the Sabbath-day in the humble church." (Ibid., 13.)

498 "THE ELECTION" **PTJ,** XXXII, 385.

498 BURR "WAS HEARD TO INSINUATE" Ibid., 400.

498 "SOME OF OUR FRIENDS" Ibid., 399.

498 "THERE WOULD BE REALLY CAUSE" Dunn, **Jefferson's Second Revolution,** 198.

498 "WHAT WILL BE THE PLANS" Ibid., 204.

498 "JEFFERSON AS A POLITICIAN" Roger Griswold to Fanny Griswold, January 22, 1801, William Griswold Lane Memorial Collection, Manuscripts and Archives, Yale University Library.

498 On Sunday, January 11, 1801 Ibid., January 11, 1801.

499 "opens upon us" **PTJ**, XXXII, 318.

499 told by "high authority" Ibid., XXXIV, 21.

499 "Some strange reports" Ibid., XXXII, 403.

500 debating whether to remain Ibid.

500 "Unfriendly foreign ministers" Ibid., 425–26.

500 the Judiciary Act of 1801 Kathryn Turner, "Federalist Policy and the Judiciary Act of 1801," **William and Mary Quarterly**, 3rd ser., 22 (January 1965): 3–32. See also Miller, **Federalist Era**, 275. John Marshall described things to Rufus King this way on January 18, 1801: "The Congress are probably about to pass a bill reorganizing our judicial system. The principal feature in the new bill is the separation of the supreme from the circuit courts." (**Papers of John Marshall**, VI, 57.)

501 "The Judiciary bill has been" Stevens Thomson Mason to John Breckinridge, February 12, 1801, Breckinridge Family Papers, LOC.

501 a "parasitical plant" **EOL**, 420.

501 had "retired into the judiciary" Ibid.

501 "midnight judges" Miller, **Federalist Era**, 275.

501 to name John Marshall Kathryn Turner, "The Appointment of Chief Justice Marshall," **William and Mary Quarterly**, 3rd ser., 17 (April 1960): 143–63.

501 MET IN JANUARY 1801 Simon, **What Kind of Nation**, 134.

501 THOUGH ADAMS HAD SOUGHT TO REENLIST JOHN JAY Ibid.

502 "WHO SHALL I NOMINATE NOW?" Ibid.

502 HE TOLD THE PRESIDENT THAT HE HAD NO COUNSEL TO GIVE Ibid.

502 "I BELIEVE I MUST NOMINATE YOU" Ibid.

502 MARSHALL RECALLED BEING "PLEASED" Ibid.

502 CONFIRMED THE PRESIDENT'S NOMINATION Ibid.

502 "MR. JEFFERSON IS UNDOUBTEDLY" Caesar A. Rodney to Joseph H. Nicholson, February 17, 1801, Joseph H. Nicholson Papers, LOC.

502 JEFFERSON HIMSELF WAS WORRIED ENOUGH **PTJRS**, III, 306. The ensuing scene is drawn from this account of Jefferson's.

503 "INTEREST, CHARACTER, DUTY" **PTJ**, XXXII, 432.

504 "BUT SHOULD IT BE POSSIBLE" Ibid.

504 "IF BAD MEN WILL DARE" Ibid., 433.

504 THE PENNSYLVANIA MILITIA WAS TO BE READIED Ibid., XXXIII, 391.

504 A FEW FIRES Ibid., XXXII, 435.

504 "THE BURNING OF THE WAR-OFFICE" Ibid.

504 "IT SEEMS HEAVEN" Roger Griswold to Fanny Griswold, January 20, 1801, William Griswold Lane Memorial Collection, Manuscripts and Archives, Yale University Library.

505 "I LONG TO BE" **PTJ**, XXXII, 475.

505 "THE APPROACH OF THE 11TH FEB." Ibid., 559.

505 NOTES JEFFERSON MADE   Ibid., 583.

505 BAYARD SOON SHIFTED TACK   Sharp, **Deadlocked Election of 1800**, 161.

506 "THIS IS ABSOLUTELY FALSE"   **Anas**, 238–39.

506 DID JEFFERSON STRIKE A DEAL   See, for instance, **EOL**, 285; **JHT**, IV, 487–93; Sharp, **Deadlocked Election of 1800**, 159–62; Joanne B. Freeman, "Corruption and Compromise in the Election of 1800: The Process of Politics on the National Stage" in Horn, Lewis, and Onuf, **Revolution of 1800**, 87–120; Chernow, **Alexander Hamilton**, 637–38; Wilentz, **Rise of American Democracy**, 93–94 ("After discussions with two of Jefferson's supporters—though not with the candidate himself—Bayard was persuaded that Jefferson had made specific concessions about preserving the public credit," wrote Wilentz.)

507 "HE STOPPED ME"   **Anas**, 239.

507 STANDING ON THE STEPS   Ibid.

507 "I TOLD HIM"   Ibid.

507 "IT WAS UNDERSTOOD"   Ibid., 239–40.

507 JEFFERSON HAD SIMILAR EXCHANGES   Ibid., 240.

508 "I DO NOT RECOLLECT"   Ibid.

508 "JEFFERSON IS TO BE PREFERRED"   **JHT**, III, 500.

508 "IS AS LIKELY"   Kaminski, **Founders on the Founders**, 308.

508 "MR. JEFFERSON IS A MAN"   Ibid., 307–8.

509 LAWMAKERS SLEPT ON PALLETS   Margaret Bayard Smith, **First Forty Years**, 23–24.

509 AN AILING REPRESENTATIVE   Ibid., 24.

509 CARRIED THROUGH THE SNOW   Ibid.

509 HIS WIFE HELPED GUIDE HIS HAND   Ibid.

509 AT ONE P.M. ON TUESDAY, FEBRUARY 17, 1801
PTJ, XXXII, 578. See also Freeman, "A Qualified Revolution: The Presidential Election of
1800," in Cogliano, ed., **A Companion to
Thomas Jefferson**, 145–63.

509 "THE CONSPIRATORS"   Margaret Bayard Smith,
First Forty Years, 25.

509 "HURRIED TO THEIR LODGINGS"   Ibid.

509 "TO GO WITHOUT A CONSTITUTION"   **PTJ**,
XXXIII, 4.

509 "IN THE EVENT OF A USURPATION"   Ibid., 230.

510 "WHEN I LOOK BACK"   Ibid., XXXIV, 258–59.

510 IN ALEXANDRIA, THIRTY-TWO ROUNDS WERE
FIRED   Ibid., XXXIII, 3.

510 IN RICHMOND, THERE WERE FIREWORKS   Ibid.,
46.

510 RANG BELLS FROM BEFORE NOON TO SUNDOWN
Ibid., 28.

510 "OUR PEOPLE IN THIS COUNTY"   Noble E. Cun-
ningham, **Jeffersonian Republicans in Power:
Party Operations, 1801–1809** (Chapel Hill,
N.C., 1963), 6.

510 "MANY DECLARE YOU AN ATHEIST"   **PTJ**,
XXXIV, 39.

511 "THE STRANGE REVOLUTION"   **Papers of John
Marshall**, VI, 82.

511 "THE COURSE TO BE PURSUED"   Ibid.

511 WOULD "EXCITE THE RESENTMENT" Ibid., 83.

511 ASKED THE VICE PRESIDENT TO DINNER Mc-Cullough, **John Adams,** 558.

511 "MR. JEFFERSON DINES WITH US" Ibid.

511 SHE WAS TO LEAVE WASHINGTON Ibid., 561.

511 JEFFERSON "MADE ME A VISIT" Ibid., 559.

512 "I CANNOT REGRET" **PTJ,** XXXIII, 37.

512 "AS TO THE FUTURE" Ibid., 32.

512 "TO YOU, SIR, DOTH" Ibid., 42.

512 "IF WE SPEND" Ibid., XXXV, 90.

512 THE "DUTY OF THE CHIEF MAGISTRATE" **EOL,** 283. Jefferson articulated this particular view after he left office, in 1810.

513 "I SINCERELY THANK YOU" **PTJ,** XXXIII, 422.

THIRTY-TWO · The New Order of Things Begins

515 "ALL . . . WILL BEAR IN MIND" **PTJ,** XXXIII, 149.

517 "YOU ALWAYS HAD THE PEOPLE" Ibid., 127.

517 "I KNOW INDEED" Ibid., 465.

517 "AS THE TWO HOUSES" Ibid., 119.

517 MARSHALL REPLIED Ibid., 120–21.

518 HAD MADE PLANS McCullough, **John Adams,** 565.

518 LEAVE WASHINGTON ON THE FOUR A.M. **Papers of John Marshall,** VI, 89.

518 HE WENT THROUGH NEW YORK, IT WAS SAID Miller, **Federalist Era,** 276.

518 "Sensible, moderate men" McCullough, **John Adams**, 564. Also see Sharp, **Deadlocked Election of 1800**, 165–66.

518 he was more than ready McCullough, **John Adams**, 564–66. McCullough makes the case that, contrary to the conventional view, there is "no evidence" that Adams was "downcast, [and] bitter." Sharp agrees, writing that "there is little evidence that an enraged and ill-tempered Adams [was] skulking out of Washington at the last moment to avoid public humiliation." (Sharp, **Deadlocked Election of 1800**, 165–66.)

518 cannon fire **National Intelligencer,** March 6, 1801.

518 the District of Columbia's artillery corps Ibid.

518 Samuel Harrison Smith called on Jefferson Margaret Bayard Smith, **First Forty Years**, 26. "Mr. Jefferson had given [S. H. Smith] a copy [of the inaugural address] early in the morning, so that on coming out of the house, the paper was distributed immediately," Margaret Bayard Smith wrote Miss Susan B. Smith on March 4, 1801. "Since then there has been a constant succession of persons coming for the papers." (Ibid.)

518 written in Jefferson's small, neat hand Ibid. "The original in Jefferson's handwriting is among the papers of Mr. J. Henley Smith; also his second inaugural address in his handwriting and signed." (Ibid.)

518 AT TEN O'CLOCK   **National Intelligencer,** March 6, 1801.

518 SHORTLY BEFORE NOON   **Alexandria Times,** March 6, 1801.

518 A DELEGATION OF CONGRESSMEN   **National Intelligencer,** March 6, 1801.

519 FOLLOWED A GROUP OF OFFICERS   **Alexandria Times,** March 6, 1801.

519 THEIR SWORDS DRAWN   Ibid.

519 PARTED TO ALLOW JEFFERSON THROUGH   Ibid.

519 STOOD, SALUTING   Ibid.

519 AFTER ANOTHER BLAST OF CANNON   **National Intelligencer,** March 6, 1801.

519 ABOUT A THOUSAND PEOPLE   Cunningham, **Jeffersonian Republicans in Power,** 3.

519 "MAGNIFICENT IN HEIGHT"   Byrd, **The Senate, 1789–1989: Addresses on the History of the United States Senate,** 406.

519 THE ROOM WAS 86 BY 48 FEET   Ibid.

519 EACH SENATOR HAD   Ibid.

519 "SO CROWDED THAT"   Margaret Bayard Smith, **First Forty Years,** 26. It was, the **National Intelligencer** reported, "the largest concourse of citizens ever assembled here." (**National Intelligencer,** March 6, 1801.)

519 ROSE IN DEFERENCE TO JEFFERSON   **National Intelligencer,** March 6, 1801.

519 AFTER MARSHALL ADMINISTERED THE OATH   Wilentz, **Rise of American Democracy,** 99, offers this memorable image: "The first thing that Thomas Jefferson saw as president was the

dark face of John Marshall, the chief justice of the Supreme Court, who had just sworn him into office. The two were second cousins, related through the august Randolph family of Virginia—and they intensely disliked each other's politics." (Ibid.) See also Jean Edward Smith, **John Marshall: Definer of a Nation** (New York, 1996). For more on the rivalry between the two Virginians, see R. Kent Newmyer, **John Marshall and the Heroic Age of the Supreme Court** (Baton Rouge, La., 2001), 146–209, which focuses on Jefferson's presidential years, and James F. Simon, **What Kind of Nation: Thomas Jefferson, John Marshall, and the Epic Struggle to Create a United States** (New York, 2002).

519 IN HIS WEAK VOICE   Margaret Bayard Smith, **First Forty Years**, 26.

519 "ALL . . . WILL BEAR IN MIND"   PTJ, XXXIII, 149–51.

521 "TODAY THE NEW POLITICAL YEAR"   **Papers of John Marshall**, VI, 89.

521 "THE DEMOCRATS ARE DIVIDED"   Ibid.

521 "IF HE ARRANGES HIMSELF"   Ibid.

521 RETURNING TO HIS LETTER WRITING AT FOUR P.M.   Ibid.

522 "YOU WILL BEFORE THIS"   Ibid.

522 "IN POLITICAL SUBSTANCE"   Ibid., 137.

522 "VIRTUALLY A CANDID RETRACTION"   Dunn, **Jefferson's Second Revolution**, 225.

522 "OLD FRIENDS WHO HAD BEEN"   PTJ, XXXIII, 261.

522 "IT IS NOT POSSIBLE"   Ibid., 426.

523 "WE REFLECT"   Ibid., 290.

523 "PURSUING STEADILY MY OBJECT"   Ibid., XXX-
VII, 296–97. "Nero wished all the necks of
Rome united in one, that he might sever them at
a blow," Jefferson had written in his second year
in office. So it was, he said, with his foes, who,
"wishing to have a single representative of all the
objects of their hatred, honor me with that post,
and exhibit against me such atrocities as no nation has ever before heard or endured. I shall
protect them in the right of lying and calumni-
ating, and shall go on to merit the continuance
of it." (Ibid., 296.)

523 "I FEEL A GREAT LOAD"   Ibid., XXXIII, 181.

524 THE AUTHORITY OF THE PRESIDENTIAL OFFICE
Robert M. Johnstone, Jr., **Jefferson and the
Presidency: Leadership in the Young Republic**
(New York, 1978), stated the case well. "It is a
central thesis of this book that Jefferson's presidency marked the pioneering effort in erecting a
working model of presidential leadership characterized by persuasion and the cultivation of influence. Jefferson was the first president willing
to implement the bargaining relationships that
could enhance presidential influence, and he did
so with great natural skill and patience." (Ibid.,
14.) McDonald, in Cogliano, ed., **A Companion
to Thomas Jefferson,** 164–83, explores issues of
Jefferson and executive power. "A commonsense
understanding of Jefferson's presidency as a ref-

erendum on the issues and ideas that secured his election in 1800 and 1801 holds that, although he sometimes broke rules that he advocated as opposition leader, he never abandoned the goal of a strictly limited and thoroughly republican government," McDonald writes, and I agree: Such was always his goal, even if his means to the end of securing republicanism were not always strictly republican. (Ibid., 165.) Sorting through the scholarship of Leonard White, Jeremy D. Bailey, and Johnstone, McDonald also notes: "Leonard White may be correct to observe that 'Jefferson fully maintained in practice the Federalist conception of the executive power'. . . , but Johnstone believes that his similar actions were governed by different justifications. So does Jeremy Bailey . . . , who argues that Jefferson, who had long supported executive vigor, strengthened the presidency by envisioning it as the one branch representative of—and subject to—all of the nation's voters. The fact that Jefferson, as Johnstone writes, 'combined the constitutional power of the presidency with a "political" power grounded on popular support' made this mode of leadership republican. . . . The fact that it was Jefferson who accomplished the feat made it Republican." (Ibid., 178.)

524 REPUBLICAN CONGRESSIONAL MAJORITIES http://artandhistory.house.gov/house_history/partydiv.aspx (accessed 2012).

524 THE SENATE MARGIN http://www.senate.gov/

pagelayout/history/one_item_and_teasers/party
div.htm (accessed 2012).

525 SENT A REASSURING SIGNAL **PTJ**, XXXIII, 14.

525 "ONE IMPUTATION" Ibid.

525 BROUGHT THE NATIONAL DEBT DOWN FROM $83 MILLION TO $57 MILLION Robert M. S. McDonald, "The (Federalist?) Presidency of Thomas Jefferson," in Cogliano, ed., **A Companion to Thomas Jefferson,** 170.

526 REDUCING MILITARY EXPENDITURES Ibid.

526 THE QUASI-WAR ENDED **EOL**, 275.

526 PREWAR LEVELS Between 1800 and 1802, combined spending by the Department of War and the Navy went from $6 million to $2.1 million. In 1797, it had been $1.4 million. (Davis Rich Dewey, **Financial History of the United States** [New York, 1922], 111, 119–20, 124.) These peacetime military reductions were inseparable from Jefferson's broad plan of small government and reduced taxes. Secretary of the Treasury Albert Gallatin noted they were necessary "in order to render a repeal of all the internal duties practicable," if the country was to simultaneously pay down the debt. (**PTJ**, XXXIII, 275.)

526 DOWNSIZED THE NAVY He also docked all but six frigates. These were the maximum reductions then permitted by law, and he would have otherwise docked all but three ships. (**JHT**, III, 102–3. See also **PTJ**, XXXIV, 384–85.)

526 NAVAL POWERS OF EUROPE Before the Battle of Trafalgar in 1805, these were England, France,

and Spain. Afterwards, England became the sole naval power.

526 ONE OF DEFENSE This also informed Jefferson's preference for smaller gunboats over frigates as tensions increased with England and France, a preference for which he was criticized toward the end of his presidency. [Ian W. Toll, **Six Frigates** (New York, 2006) 284–87.]

526 BARBARY PIRATES See Cappon, **Adams-Jefferson Letters,** 324–25, 584–85.

526 DECLINED TO WEAR A CEREMONIAL SWORD **PTJ,** XXXIII, 134.

526 DINNER AS USUAL Margaret Bayard Smith, **First Forty Years,** 12–13.

526 COACHES AND SILVER HARNESSES Seale, **President's House,** I, 90.

527 ABIGAIL ADAMS HUNG LAUNDRY IN THE EAST ROOM Stein, **Worlds of Thomas Jefferson at Monticello,** 54.

527 "GREAT UNFINISHED AUDIENCE-ROOM" Ibid.

527 JEFFERSON NOW INSTALLED HIS SECRETARY Ibid., 56.

527 IN THE SOUTHWEST CORNER OF THE FIRST FLOOR Ibid.

527 DRAWERS FOR JEFFERSON'S TOOLS AND KNICK-KNACKS Ibid.

527 HE KEPT GERANIUMS IN THE WINDOW AND MOCKINGBIRDS AT HAND Margaret Bayard Smith, **First Forty Years,** 384–85.

527 HE WAS USUALLY HUMMING Stein, **Jefferson at Monticello,** 13.

527 JEFFERSON KEPT PET MOCKINGBIRDS TJF, http://www.monticello.org/site/research-and-col lections/mockingbirds (accessed 2012).

527 "LEARN ALL THE CHILDREN" PTJ, XXVI, 250.

527 A BIRD HE NAMED DICK TJF, http://www .monticello.org/site/research-and-collections/ mockingbirds (accessed 2012). As Lucia Stanton noted, "Dick" is a little disappointing given the standard set by Jefferson's noble and often mythological names for his horses, but there we are. (Ibid.)

527 HANGING ITS CAGE IN THE WINDOW Margaret Bayard Smith, First Forty Years, 385.

528 ORDERED THE DEMOLITION William Seale, The President's House: A History, I (Washington, D.C., 1986), 88.

528 "WATER CLOSETS . . . OF SUPERIOR CONSTRUCTION" Ibid.

528 WHICH PIECES OF FURNITURE Ibid.

528 HIS CHIEF DOMESTIC, RAPIN PTJ, XXXIII, 96–98.

529 HENRY DEARBORN FROM MASSACHUSETTS Ibid., 13.

529 BORN IN GENEVA IN 1761 Henry Adams, Life of Albert Gallatin, is full of primary documents. See also "Albert Gallatin, (1761–1849)," Biographical Dictionary of the United States Congress, 1774-Present, http://bioguide.con gress.gov/scripts/biodisplay.pl?index=g000020 (accessed 2012).

529 LOUIS-ANDRÉ PICHON TOLD PARIS Louis-

André Pichon to Ministère des Affaires étrangères [s.d.], **Correspondence Poltique,** vol. 52, Les Archives Diplomatiques.

529 "ONE CANNOT HELP"   Ibid.

529 "HENCEFORTH, WE CAN PREDICT"   Ibid.

530 "INVARIABLY OPPOSED"   Ibid.

530 "THE STORM THROUGH WHICH"   **PTJ,** XXXIII, 196.

530 "WE CAN NO LONGER"   Ibid., 394.

530 "I AM SENSIBLE HOW FAR"   Ibid., 506.

531 REFERRED TO THE FEDERALISTS AS MADMEN   Ibid., XXXIV, 262. See also ibid., XXXIII, 403.

531 "THEIR LEADERS ARE A HOSPITAL"   Ibid., XXXIV, 262.

531 "**POLITICS WILL NOT MAKE YOU**"   Ibid., XXXIII, 568.

531 IN ESSENTIAL HARMONY   Ibid., 254. "It will be a great blessing to our country if we can once more restore harmony and social love among its citizens," Jefferson told Gerry. Yet he understood the political realities. "I was not deluded by the eulogisms of the public papers in the first moments of change. If they could have continued to get all the loaves and fishes, that is if I would have gone over to them, they would continue to eulogize. But I well knew that the moment that such removals should take place, as the justice of the preceding administration ought to have executed, their hue and cry would be set up and they would take their old stand." (Ibid., 491.)

531 "MANY FRIENDS MAY GROW COOL"   Ibid., 127.

532 "THE DANGERS TO OUR FORM OF GOVERN-MENT" Ibid., 636.

532 "THE EJECTED PARTY" Ibid., XXXIV, 228.

532 A RANGE OF ISSUES AND PROBLEMS See, for instance, ibid., XXXIII, 585–94.

532 LIKE "TWO MICE IN A CHURCH" **The Selected Letters of Dolley Payne Madison**, ed. David B. Mattern and Holly C. Shulman (Charlottesville, Va., 2003), 39. See also **PTJ**, XXXIV, 200.

532 "I AM STILL AT A GREAT LOSS" **PTJ**, XXXIII, 260.

533 BE "A REAL FAVOR" Ibid., XXXIV, 242.

533 "THE CITY IS RATHER SICKLY" Ibid., XXXV, 109.

533 "IT IS SUBSTITUTING" Ibid.

533 "WE FIND THIS A VERY AGREEABLE" **JHT**, IV, 42.

533 ISSUED PRESIDENTIAL PARDONS James Morton Smith, **Freedom's Fetters**, 268.

533 HIS OLD ALLY JAMES THOMSON CALLENDER **PTJ**, XXXIII, 309–10.

533 CALLENDER HAD THREE CHILDREN Ibid., 216.

534 "HURT" BY THE "DISAPPOINTMENT" Ibid., 573.

534 "I NOW BEGIN" Ibid., 575.

534 HE ASKED ALBERT GALLATIN TO REPLY Ibid., 372.

534 HAD BEEN OUT OF FAVOR Brodie, **Thomas Jefferson**, 322–23. "His first writings here had fallen far short . . . and the scurrilities of his subsequent ones began evidently to do mischief," Jefferson wrote Monroe. Callender felt the dis-

tance and resented it. He knew, he said, that Jefferson "had on various occasions treated me with such ostentatious coolness and indifference that I could hardly say that I was able to love or trust him." (Ibid., 323.)

535 "Mr. Jefferson has not returned" Ibid., 345.

535 "The money was refused" Ibid.

535 "Do you know that" Claude G. Bowers, **Jefferson in Power: The Death Struggle of the Federalists** (Boston, 1936), 67.

536 dispatched Meriwether Lewis to give Callender Brodie, **Thomas Jefferson**, 345–46.

536 he sent a note to his cabinet PTJ, XXXV, 576–78.

537 papers "conveying information" Ibid., 606.

THIRTY-THREE · A Confident President

538 "The measures recommended" Bowers, **Jefferson in Power**, 89.

538 "Here are so many wants" PTJ, XXXVI, 176.

538 "a steady and uniform course" Ibid., XXXV, 677.

538 "an interval of 4 hours" Ibid.

538 a ride or a walk Ibid., XXXVI, 99.

538 "engaged with company" Ibid.

539 "mechanics, mathematics, philosophy" TJ to Thomas Paine, January 13, 1803, Thomas Jefferson Papers, LOC.

539 "I HAD GOOD REASON" **PTJ**, XXXVII, 475.

539 TENSION WITH A SUPPORTER TJ to Nathaniel Macon, March 22, 1806, Thomas Jefferson Papers, LOC.

539 "THIS EVENING MY COMPANY" Ibid.

539 WHOM HE KNEW HE WOULD NOT SEE AGAIN TJ to Ellen Wayles Randolph, October 19, 1807, Coolidge Collection of Thomas Jefferson Manuscripts, Massachusetts Historical Society.

540 THE MADISONS STAYED BRIEFLY **Selected Letters of Dolley Payne Madison,** 39–40.

540 ON PENNSYLVANIA AVENUE FOUR BLOCKS Ibid., 40.

540 AT 1333 F STREET Ibid.

540 ESTABLISHED A HOSPITABLE SALON See Catherine Allgor, **A Perfect Union: Dolley Madison and the Creation of the American Nation** (New York, 2006).

540 THEIR THREE-STORY BRICK HOUSE **Selected Letters of Dolley Payne Madison,** 40.

540 "FASHIONABLE TALK" Ibid., 54.

540 "AS GAY AS IN THE WINTER" Margaret Bayard Smith, **First Forty Years,** 27.

540 MRS. SMITH SAT NEXT TO JEFFERSON Ibid., 29.

540 THE TWO "WERE SO EASY" Ibid.

540 ON M STREET NEAR THIRTY-SECOND Bowers, **Jefferson in Power,** 9.

540 "HER PERSON IS FAR LESS ATTRACTIVE" Ibid., 9–10.

541 "THE PRESIDENT'S DINNERS" Cunningham, **Jeffersonian Republicans in Power,** 96.

541 "IF THE MEMBERS ARE TO KNOW NOTHING" Ibid., 90.

542 "WHAT SORT OF GOVERNMENT" Margaret Bayard Smith, **First Forty Years**, 397.

542 "ONE, SIRE" Ibid.

542 VISITED JEFFERSON IN THE CABINET ROOM Ibid., 396.

542 "WHY ARE THESE LIBELS ALLOWED?" Ibid., 397.

542 "PUT THAT PAPER IN YOUR POCKET" Ibid.

542 "MR. JEFFERSON HAS PUT ASIDE" Louis-André Pichon to Ministère des Affaires étrangères, 26 Pluviôse an 10, **Correspondence Politique**, vol. 54, Les Archives Diplomatiques.

543 JEFFERSON WORE DIFFERENT COMBINATIONS **JHT**, IV, 371.

543 FOUND THAT THE PRESIDENT "BEHAVED VERY CIVILLY" Augustus Foster to Elizabeth Cavendish, December 30, 1804, Augustus Foster Papers, LOC.

543 "HE IS DRESSED" Ibid.

543 JOSEPH STORY OF MASSACHUSETTS **JHT**, IV, 373.

544 THE "LEVELING SPIRIT" OF REPUBLICANISM Edward Thornton to Lord Hawkesbury, December 9, 1801, FO 5/32, National Archives of the United Kingdom, Kew.

544 JOHN QUINCY ADAMS BELIEVED **Memoirs of John Quincy Adams**, I, 403.

545 "YOU WILL FIND [IT]" **PTJ**, XXXVI, 20.

545 AT A CABINET MEETING Ibid., XXXIV, 114–15.

545 TO "SEARCH FOR AND DESTROY" Abraham D. Sofaer, **War, Foreign Affairs, and Constitutional Power: The Origins** (Cambridge, Mass., 1976), 209.

545 TO "PLACE [HIS] SHIPS" Ibid., 210.

546 "TOO LONG . . . HAVE THOSE BARBARIANS" **PTJ**, XXXVI, 3.

546 JEFFERSON DESCRIBED THE AMERICAN VICTORY Sofaer, **War, Foreign Affairs, and Constitutional Power**, 212.

546 ASKED CONGRESS TO AUTHORIZE Ibid. "I communicate all material information on this subject, that, in the exercise of this important function confided by the Constitution to the Legislature exclusively, their judgment may form itself on a knowledge and consideration of every circumstance of weight," he told Congress. (Ibid.)

546 CONGRESS FELL INTO JEFFERSON'S HANDS Ibid., 214–16.

546 JEFFERSON ATTEMPTED AN ELABORATE OPERATION Ibid., 216–21.

547 FIRST ANNUAL MESSAGE TO CONGRESS **PTJ**, XXXVI, 52–68.

547 SAVE FOR THE BARBARY STATES Ibid., 58.

547 "A TESTIMONY TO THE WORLD" Ibid., 59.

548 "NOTHING CAN EXCEED" John Taylor to John Breckinridge, December 22, 1801, Breckinridge Family Papers, LOC.

548 "VIRGINIA LITERALLY DOMINATES" **Life and Correspondence of Rufus King,** IV, 103. Troup also said: "Congress are now engaged in repeal-

ing almost all the internal taxes, and the whiskey drinkers particularly will be in spirits." (Ibid.)

548 "UNDER THIS ADMINISTRATION" Cunningham, **Jeffersonian Republicans in Power,** 10.

549 SHOULD "ALARM ALL WHO ARE" Bowers, **Jefferson in Power,** 90.

549 "MINE IS AN ODD DESTINY" Ibid., 94–95.

549 "EVERY DAY WE SEE VANISH" Louis-André Pichon to Ministère des Affaires étrangères, 7 Frimaire an 11, **Correspondence Politique,** vol. 55, Les Archives Diplomatique. In political terms, President Jefferson's personality projected a prevailing sense of calm except in the chambers or newspaper offices of unforgiving Federalists. "The two parties . . . at least are not here as they are in Europe, the haves and the have-nots; it's rather the division into two great interests, maritime and agricultural; the first has dominated since independence, and the second dominates in turn. But Mr. Jefferson, although leader of the second, will do nothing which might displease the friends he has in the first group, or make his enemies there revolt," wrote Pichon. "He will be able to indulge in some manias which offend conventions and shock the ideas of the most educated men of the East; but at bottom, his administration will certainly be prudent, economic, [and] conservative at home and abroad." (Ibid.)

550 A VAST CHEESE ARRIVED **PTJ,** XXXVI, 246–52. Jefferson understood from whence it came. "It is an ebullition of republicanism in a state

where it has been under heavy oppression," he wrote John Wayles Eppes on January 1, 1802. (Ibid., 261.)

550 THE DANBURY BAPTIST ASSOCIATION HAD ASSEMBLED   Ibid., 253–58.

550 "BELIEVING WITH YOU"   Ibid., 258.

550 "I AGREE WITH YOU"   Ibid., XXXII, 205.

551 "THE TERRIBLE EVILS OF DEMOCRACY"   **Life and Correspondence of Rufus King,** IV, 11.

551 ABOLISH ALL INTERNAL TAXES   **EOL,** 293.

551 AUTHORIZED MILITARY FORCE   Ibid., 637.

551 EASE NATURALIZATION RULES   Ibid., 291.

551 REPEAL THE JUDICIARY ACT OF 1801   Ibid., 420–21.

551 "WOULD TO GOD"   **Life and Correspondence of Rufus King,** IV, 109.

551 SEEMINGLY UNCONTROLLABLE   Isenberg, **Fallen Founder,** 230. "Burr was not immediately abandoned by the Jefferson administration," wrote Isenberg. "It happened gradually over the first year of the president's term." (Ibid., 229.)

552 THE COMPLICATIONS OF NEW YORK STATE POLITICS   Ibid., 226–31.

552 JEFFERSON CHOSE TO THWART BURR'S AMBITIONS   Ibid., 229–31.

552 ONE BURRITE, MATTHEW L. DAVIS, CALLED ON THE PRESIDENT   Gustavus Myers, **The History of Tammany Hall** (Ann Arbor, Mich., 2005), 15. In Myers's version of the story, Davis had been talking about the "immense influence" of New York in the moments before Jefferson caught the

fly. The president then asked Davis if he had ever noticed the difference in size between "one portion of the insect and its body." As Myers has it, "The hint was not lost on Davis, who, though not knowing whether Jefferson referred to New York or to him, ceased to talk on the subject." (Ibid.) My own view is that snatching a fly out of the air would leave a distinct enough impression even without additional commentary.

552 "THERE IS HARDLY A MAN" Isenberg, **Fallen Founder,** 231.

552 "THERE IS CERTAINLY" **Life and Correspondence of Rufus King,** IV, 133.

552 "MR. BURR WILL SURELY ARRIVE" Louis-André Pichon to Ministère des Affaires étrangères, 4 Ventôse an 10, French Archives, Ministère des Affaires étrangères, **Correspondence Politique,** vol. 54, Les Archives Diplomatiques. "He is a man against whom you know all there is to say, but what is certain is that he would take the reins of business; if the Federalists consent, you can rely that this nation takes on an appearance that it has not had before," Pichon added. (Ibid.)

552 A CELEBRATORY FEDERALIST DINNER **Life and Correspondence of Rufus King,** IV, 103.

553 ON THE FOURTH **PTJ,** XXXVIII, 121.

553 "THE SPECIAL FEASTS" Ibid., 89.

553 "THE PRINCIPLES WHICH DIRECT IT" Louis-André Pichon to Ministère des Affaires étrangères, 4 Ventôse an 10, **Correspondence Politique,** vol. 54, Les Archives Diplomatiques.

554 "That would scarcely happen" Ibid.

554 "Jefferson is the idol" **Life and Correspondence of Rufus King,** IV, 103–4.

554 A decade later **PTJ,** XXV, 75–84.

554 a threat from the British James P. Ronda, **Jefferson's West: A Journey with Lewis and Clark** (Charlottesville, Va., 2000), 26–27. For a standard account of Jefferson and the Lewis and Clark expedition, see Donald Jackson, **Thomas Jefferson and the Stony Mountains: Exploring the West from Monticello** (Norman, Okla., 1993).

554 "it requires only the countenance" Alexander Mackenzie, **Voyages from Montreal, on the River St. Laurence: Through the Continent of North America, to the Frozen and Pacific Oceans; in the Years 1789 and 1793** (New York, 1814), 388.

555 "Many political reasons" Ibid., 392.

555 "I am afraid" Ronda, **Jefferson's West,** 21.

555 a theater of contention Ibid., 33–37, describes some of the political and diplomatic factors at work, including counsel from Gallatin and Attorney General Levi Lincoln.

555 Meriwether Lewis, his private secretary TJF, http://www.monticello.org/site/research-and-collections/meriwether-lewis (accessed 2012).

555 Born in 1774 at Locust Hill Ibid.

555 ten miles from Monticello Ibid.

555 his own "neighborhood" Ibid.

555 blue-eyed Marshall Smelser, **The Democratic Republic, 1801–1815** (New York, 1968), 125.

555 A LIEUTENANT IN THE U.S. ARMY   TJF, http://
www.monticello.org/site/research-and-collec
tions/meriwether-lewis (accessed 2012).

556 "KNOWLEDGE OF THE WESTERN COUNTRY"
Ibid.

556 APPARENTLY DREW ON LEWIS'S SENSE   Ibid.

556 CONGRESS SECRETLY AGREED   PTJ, XXXIX,
588. "You know we have been many years wishing to have the Missouri explored and whatever
river, heading with that, runs into the Western
ocean," Jefferson wrote Benjamin S. Barton
from Washington in February 1803. "Congress,
in some secret proceedings, have yielded to a
proposition I made them for permitting me to
have it done. It is to be undertaken immediately
with a party of about ten, and I have appointed
Capt. Lewis, my secretary, to conduct it." (Ibid.)

556 THE PRESIDENT ASKED FOR   TJF, http://www
.monticello.org/site/jefferson/jeffersons-confi
dential-letter-to-congress (accessed 2012).

556 FIFTEEN TIMES THAT AMOUNT   Jackson, **Letters
of Lewis and Clark,** II, 428. The best estimate
of the cost is $38,722.25. I am grateful to Bar-
bara Oberg and to Gary Moulton for their help
on this point.

556 "CAPT. LEWIS IS BRAVE"   **PTJ,** XXXIX, 599.

556 LEWIS ASKED WILLIAM CLARK   TJF, http://
www.monticello.org/site/jefferson/expedition
-timeline (accessed 2012).

THIRTY-FOUR · Victories, Scandal, and a Secret Sickness

557 "BY THIS WENCH SALLY" PTJ, XXXVIII, 324.

557 IT WAS AN IDEAL OF THE AGE Wood, **Radicalism of the American Revolution,** 298–301.

557 HAD WARNED AGAINST PARTISAN SPIRIT George Washington, **Writings,** ed. John H. Rhodehamel (New York, 1997), 962–77.

557 WERE NEVER TO BE REALIZED Jefferson himself came to see that total unity of interest was simply not an element of the political condition. He would later tell John Adams that all societies in all times had been divided roughly along Whig and Tory (or Republican and Federalist) lines. In his **Origins of American Politics,** Bernard Bailyn quotes a 1733 essay in the New York **Gazette** on the practicalities of partisanship. "I may venture to say that some opposition, though it proceed not entirely from a public spirit, is not only necessary in free governments but of great service to the public. Parties are a check upon one another, and by keeping the ambition of one another within bounds, serve to maintain the public liberty. Opposition is the life and soul of public zeal which, without it, would flag and decay for want of an opportunity to exert itself. . . . It may indeed proceed from wrong motives, but still it is necessary." (Ibid., 126.)

Bailyn found a Pennsylvania writer saying much the same thing in 1738 and a New York writer in 1748 arguing that "regard for liberty has always made me think that parties in a free state ought rather to be considered as an advantage to the public than an evil. Because while they subsist I have viewed them as so many spies upon one another, ready to proclaim abroad and warn the public of any attack or encroachment upon the public liberty and thereby rouse the members thereof to assert those rights they are [entitled?] to by the laws." (Ibid., 127.) Such sentiments were the exception, not the rule, but Jefferson articulated similar views.

557 "You may suppose" Cunningham, **Jeffersonian Republicans in Power,** 102.

558 "The men of the different parties" Ibid.

558 "No tavern or boarding house" Ibid., 103.

558 "Nothing shall be spared" Ibid., 8.

558 "The attempt at reconciliation" Ibid., 9.

558 "There is nothing to which a nation" **PTJ,** XXXIII, 234.

559 "gloomy days of terrorism" **PTJRS,** III, 227.

559 "The country is so totally" **Diary of John Quincy Adams, 1794–1845: American Political, Social, and Intellectual Life from Washington to Polk,** ed. Allan Nevins (New York, 1969), 21.

559 "Mr. Jefferson doesn't at all" Louis-André Pichon to Ministère des Affaires étrangères, 27 Vendémiaire an 10, **Correspondence Politique,** vol. 53, Les Archives Diplomatiques.

560 THE NEW JUDICIARY ACT OF 1802 See, for instance, Richard E. Ellis, The Jeffersonian Crisis: Courts and Politics in the Young Republic (New York, 1971), and Johnstone, **Jefferson and the Presidency**, 164–80.

560 PROCEEDED WITH CAUTION Johnstone, **Jefferson and the Presidency**, 170–73. While Richard E. Ellis argued that **Marbury v. Madison** triggered Jefferson's push for judicial reform (Ellis, **Jeffersonian Crisis**, 40–45), Johnstone believed that "the little evidence available . . . seems to point to the conclusion that while the **Marbury** 'show cause' order did galvanize Republicans into demands for immediate action and may well have convinced Jefferson to agree to put repeal first on the Senate's agenda at the December session of Congress, the president's basic commitment for repeal had already been made." (Johnstone, **Jefferson and the Presidency**, 172.)

561 DRILY WROTE THAT THE "JUDICIAL SYSTEM" Johnstone, **Jefferson and the Presidency**, 173. On Saturday, February 20, 1802, in a seven-hour speech, James Bayard attacked the repeal of the 1801 act. (**PTJ**, XXXVI, 618–19.) "There are many," he said, "very many who believe, if you strike this blow, you inflict a mortal wound on the Constitution. There are many now willing to spill their blood to defend that Constitution. Are gentlemen disposed to risk the consequences?" (Ibid., 619.) Jefferson reacted coolly—and hoped his equanimity would be noticed. "They expect

to frighten us: but are met with perfect sang-froid," Jefferson told Thomas Mann Randolph, Jr., the day after Bayard's remarks. (Ibid., 618.)

561 THE REPEAL PASSED PTJ, XXXVII, 72–74.

561 THE HOUSE VOTE REFLECTED Johnstone, **Jefferson and the Presidency,** 175.

561 A SINGLE VOTE Ibid.

561 ELIMINATED THE NEW CIRCUIT JUDGESHIPS http://www.fje.gov/history/home.nsf/page/land mark04.html (accessed 2012).

561 THE FEDERALISTS WERE HORRIFIED "If the principle becomes settled which is established by this decision of the Legislature, I shall hereafter consider the Constitution of no value," Roger Griswold wrote on Friday, March 5, 1802. (Letter of Roger Griswold, March 5, 1802, William Griswold Lane Memorial Collection. Manuscripts and Archives, Yale University.)

561 "THE JUDGE'S INVETERACY IS PROFOUND" Henry Adams, **History,** 132.

561 THE CASE OF **MARBURY V. MADISON** Simon, **What Kind of Nation,** 173–90.

562 PICKERING WAS UNSTABLE Irving Brant, **Impeachment: Trials and Errors** (New York, 1972), 46–57, is good on Pickering's alcoholism. Also see Lynn W. Turner, "The Impeachment of John Pickering," **American Historical Review** 54 (April 1949), 485–507, and Eleanore Bushnell, **Crimes, Follies, and Misfortunes: The Federal Impeachment Trials** (Urbana, Ill., 1992), 43–55.

562 THE EFFORT AGAINST CHASE Brant, **Impeachment,** 58–83, and Richard Ellis, "The Impeachment of Samuel Chase" in **American Political Trials,** ed. Michael R. Belknap (Westport, Conn., 1981), 57–78.

562 "WHERE THE LAW IS UNCERTAIN" Henry Adams, **History,** 402.

563 "OUGHT THIS SEDITIOUS AND OFFICIAL ATTACK" Ibid., 402–3.

563 "I ASK THESE QUESTIONS" Ibid.

563 THE SENATE CONVICTED JOHN PICKERING **EOL,** 422.

563 THE HOUSE IMPEACHED SAMUEL CHASE Ibid., 422–24.

563 AN ACQUITTAL FROM THE SENATE Ibid., 424.

563 AN "ELECTIONEERING PARTISAN" Henry Adams, **History,** 456.

563 HOPES "THAT YOUR EXCELLENCY" **PTJ, XXXV,** 477.

563 ASKED "TO GO TO WASHINGTON" Ibid., XXXVI, 581.

563 "YOU ARE IN DANGER" Ibid., 641.

564 "AN ENERGETIC TONE" Ibid., XXXIII, 257.

564 "AT LENGTH" Ibid., 208. See also **The Hutchinson Illustrated Encyclopedia of British History,** ed. Simon Hall (Chicago, 1999), 224, and Edward Hale, **The Fall of the Stuarts and Western Europe from 1678 to 1697** (New York, 1913), 36–37.

565 A MODERATE TONE **PTJ,** XXXIII, 208–9.

565 "WE MUST BE EASY" Ibid., 423.

565 HE DID NOT FAIL TO TAKE DECISIVE ACTION Carl E. Prince, "The Passing of the Aristocracy: Jefferson's Removal of the Federalists, 1801–1805," **The Journal of American History** 57, no. 3 (December 1970): 563–75. See also Carl Russell Fish, "Removal of Officials by the Presidents of the United States," in **Annual Report of the American Historical Association for the Year 1899,** I (Washington, D.C., 1900), 67–70.

565 HE DISPLACED ABOUT Prince, "Passing of the Aristocracy," 565–66.

565 THE STRONG MAJORITY OF WHOM Ibid.

565 THE HISTORICAL COMPANY OF ANDREW JACKSON Ibid., 566.

565 HARD ON ADAMS'S LAST-MINUTE DECISIONS **PTJ,** XXXIII, 428. "The nominations crowded in by Mr. Adams after he knew he was not appointing for himself, I treat as mere nullities," Jefferson said on March 24, 1801. (Ibid.)

565 THAT OF ELIZUR GOODRICH Ibid., XXXIV, 90–94.

565 A REMONSTRANCE AGAINST GOODRICH'S REMOVAL Ibid., 381–84. Also see ibid., 301–2.

565 "DECLARATIONS BY MYSELF" Ibid., 555–56.

566 THE NATURE OF THE ENTERPRISE Louis-André Pichon to Ministère des Affaires étrangères, 27 Vendémiaire an 10, **Correspondence Politique,** vol. 53, Les Archives Diplomatiques. From the perspective of an outsider, Louis-André Pichon clearly got the message Jefferson was sending. To Pichon, the New Haven matter left "no doubt

about the course which he proposes to follow during his administration." (Ibid.)

566 "THE INFAMOUS AND SEDITIOUS LIBELS" **PTJ**, XXXIX, 473.

566 "ON THE SUBJECT OF PROSECUTIONS" Ibid., 553.

567 "IT IS WELL KNOWN THAT" Ibid., XXXVIII, 323–25. The editors of **PTJ** cite: Richmond **Recorder**, 15, 22, 29 Sep., 20 Oct., 10, 17 Nov., 8 Dec. 1802; anb, s.v. "Hemings, Sally"; Durey, **Callender**, 157–63; Annette Gordon-Reed, **Thomas Jefferson and Sally Hemings: An American Controversy** (Charlottesville, Va., 1997), 59–77; Joshua D. Rothman, "James Callender and Social Knowledge of Interracial Sex in Antebellum Virginia," in Jan Ellen Lewis and Peter S. Onuf, eds., **Sally Hemings and Thomas Jefferson: History, Memory, and Civic Culture** (Charlottesville, Va., 1999), 87–113.

568 HE CORRECTED THOSE HE MISSED Ibid., 325.

568 "THE LICENSE THAT HAS BEEN INDULGED" Louis-André Pichon to Ministère des Affaires étrangères, 22 Vendémiaire an 11, **Correspondence Politique**, vol. 55, Les Archives Diplomatiques.

568 AN 1805 LETTER Thomas Jefferson to Robert Smith, Washington, July 1, 1805, Thomas Jefferson Collection, HM 5759, The Huntington Library, San Marino, Calif.

568 IT IS POSSIBLE, THOUGH, THAT JEFFERSON WAS NOT ADDRESSING TJF, http://www.monticello

.org/site/plantation-and-slavery/iii-review-doc umentary-sources (accessed 2012).

569 "CALLENDER AND SALLY" McCullough, **John Adams,** 581. Jefferson's friends hurried to reassure him. "I would at this time only remark that as to the case of the lady there is not a **gentleman** in the U. States of either party who does not hold in detestation the pitiful propagations of so pitiful a tale," Smith replied from Baltimore on July 4, 1805. "Your country by their approving voice at the last election have passed sentence on all the allegations that malice has exhibited against you."

Of Callender in particular, John Quincy Adams wrote Rufus King on October 8, 1802: "He writes under the influence of personal resentment and revenge, but the effect of his publications upon the reputation of the President has been considerable." (**Life and Correspondence of Rufus King,** IV, 176.)

569 WAS FOUND DROWNED Lewis and Onuf, **Sally Hemings and Thomas Jefferson,** 104.

569 IN THREE FEET OF WATER Hyland, **In Defense of Thomas Jefferson,** 9–10.

569 OBSERVED WANDERING DRUNKENLY Ibid.

569 THE INQUEST DISCOVERED NO EVIDENCE Ibid.

569 IN 1806 THOMAS MOORE, AN IRISH POET Stanton, "Those Who Labor for My Happiness," 27–29.

569 **"The weary statesman"** Ibid., 29.

569 Patsy and a former Jefferson secretary Ibid., 30.

569 "obnoxious passages" Ibid.

569 laughed them off Ibid. Patsy and Burwell, it was reported, ultimately "joined heartily in the merriment." (Ibid.)

570 "My health has always been" **PTJ**, XXXVI, 178.

570 "I have said as much" Ibid.

570 The complaint was diarrhea JHT, IV 186.

570 a "disease characterized by" Robley Dunglison, **Medical Lexicon: A Dictionary of Medical Science** (Philadelphia, 1846), 244.

571 "Mrs. Eppes is beautiful" Margaret Bayard Smith, **First Forty Years**, 34.

571 "gave me an account" Ibid., 35.

571 "I have only time" Mary Jefferson Eppes to John Wayles Eppes, November 25, 1802. Extract published at Papers of Thomas Jefferson Retirement Series Digital Archive, http://www.monticello.org/familyletters (accessed 2012).

572 "Adieu once more" **PTJ**, XXXIX, 309–10.

572 Jefferson set about acquiring TJ to Martha Jefferson Randolph, May 6, 1805, MA 1029.1-173, The Morgan Library & Museum, New York.

572 observed the president sitting Margaret Bayard Smith, **First Forty Years**, 396.

572 "I will catch you" **PTJ**, XXXVIII, 111.

572 "I have wrought" Ibid., XVIII, 499–500.

573 SEEKING CONGRESSIONAL SEATS Kierner, **Martha Jefferson Randolph**, 124. See also TJF, http://www.monticello.org/site/jefferson/john-wayles-eppes (accessed 2012).

THIRTY-FIVE · The Air of Enchantment!

574 "THE NEWS OF THE CESSION" Margaret Bayard Smith, **First Forty Years**, 38.

574 "THE FAME OF YOUR POLITICAL WISDOM" Horatio Gates to TJ, July 7, 1803, Thomas Jefferson Papers, LOC.

574 THE THIRD TREATY OF SAN ILDEFONSO See Walter Nugent, **Habits of Empire: A History of American Expansionism** (New York, 2008), 57.

574 GLORIOUS EIGHTEENTH-CENTURY PALACE **International Dictionary of Historic Places**, III, eds. Trudy Ring and Robert M. Salkin (Chicago, 1995), "La Granja de San Ildefonso (Segovia, Spain)," Elizabeth Brice, 300–3.

575 "WORKS MOST SORELY" **PTJ**, XXXVII, 264.

575 "I AM WILLING TO HOPE" Joseph J. Ellis, **American Creation**, 212–13.

575 "I BELIEVE THAT THE DESTINIES" **PTJ**, XXXVII, 298.

575 "THERE IS ON THE GLOBE ONE SINGLE SPOT" Ibid., 264.

575 IN A CONVERSATION "OF SOME LENGTH" Edward Thornton to Lord Hawkesbury, March 6, 1802, FO 3/35, National Archives of the United Kingdom, Kew.

575 "THE OCCUPATION OF THIS COUNTRY" Ibid.

575 "THE INEVITABLE CONSEQUENCES" Ibid.

576 "THE DAY THAT FRANCE TAKES POSSESSION" **PTJ**, XXXVII, 264.

577 WILLING TO SHIFT HIS SYMPATHIES Joseph J. Ellis, **American Creation**, 213.

577 "FRANCE PLACING HERSELF" **PTJ**, XXXVII, 264.

577 A COPY OF A SUBSEQUENT TREATY Nugent, **Habits of Empire**, 57.

577 A TUTORIAL ON THE PRACTICALITIES OF POWER **PTJ**, XXXVII, 372–75.

578 "A MOST IMPORTANT PIECE OF POLITICAL BUSINESS" **Selected Letters of Dolley Payne Madison**, 52.

578 "IN THIS SITUATION" TJ to James Monroe, January 10, 1803, James Monroe Papers, LOC.

578 A SNOWSTORM AND UNFAVORABLE WINDS James Monroe to TJ, March 7, 1803, Thomas Jefferson Papers, LOC.

578 "I HOPE THE FRENCH GOVT." Ibid.

578 A DRAWING ROOM GATHERING IN PARIS Robert R. Livingston to TJ, March 12, 1803, Thomas Jefferson Papers, LOC.

579 "WHEN THE FIRST CONSUL" Ibid.

579 "YOU MAY EASILY SURMISE THE SENSATION" Ibid.

580 NAPOLEON WAS IN HIS BATH Joseph J. Ellis, **American Creation**, 220–21.

580 "YOU WILL HAVE NO NEED" Ibid.

580 "I RENOUNCE LOUISIANA" Ibid.

580 "THE FIELD OPEN TO US" Ibid.

580 HE AND MONROE . . . NEGOTIATED A TREATY
Jon Kukla, **A Wilderness So Immense: The
Louisiana Purchase and the Destiny of Amer-
ica** (New York, 2004), 265–83.

580 WORD REACHED JEFFERSON Ibid., 285.

581 A TREATY WITH FRANCE ON APRIL 30 TJ to
Thomas Mann Randolph, Jr., July 5, 1803,
Thomas Jefferson Papers, LOC.

581 "IT IS SOMETHING LARGER" Ibid.

581 "THIS REMOVES FROM US" Ibid.

581 "IT MUST . . . STRIKE" Horatio Gates to TJ,
July 7, 1803, Thomas Jefferson Papers, LOC.

581 "EVERY FACE" Andrew Jackson to TJ, August 7, 1803, Thomas Jefferson Papers, LOC.

581 "THE THING IS NEW" Arthur Campbell to TJ,
January 17, 1804, Letters of Application and
Recommendation, 1801–1809, General Records
of the Department of State, National Archives.

582 HE WROTE MERIWETHER LEWIS TJ to Meriwether Lewis, July 4, 1803, Clark Family Collection, Missouri History Museum, St. Louis.
Jefferson wrote:

> In the journey which you are about to un-
> dertake for the discovery of the course and
> source of the Mississippi, and of the most
> convenient water communication from
> thence to the Pacific ocean, your party being
> small, it is to be expected that you will en-
> counter considerable dangers from the In-

dian inhabitants. Should you escape those
dangers and reach the Pacific ocean, you
may find it imprudent to hazard a return
the same way, and be forced to seek a passage round by sea, in such vessels as you may
find on the Western coast. But you will be
without money, without clothes, and other
necessaries; as a sufficient supply cannot be
carried with you from hence. Your resource
in that case can only be in the credit of the
U.S. for which purpose I hereby authorize
you to draw on the Secretaries of State, of
the Treasury, of War and of the Navy of
the U.S. according as you may find your
draughts will be most negotiable, for the
purpose of obtaining money or necessaries
for yourself and your men: and I solemnly
pledge the faith of the United States that
these draughts shall be paid punctually at
the date they are made payable. I also ask of
the Consuls, agents, merchants and citizens
of any nation with which we have intercourse
or amity to furnish you with those supplies
which your necessities may call for, assuring
them of honorable and prompt retribution.
And our own Consuls in foreign parts where
you may happen to be, are hereby instructed
and required to be aiding and assisting to
you in whatsoever may be necessary for procuring your return back to the United States.
And to give more entire satisfaction and

confidence to those who may be disposed to aid you, I, Thomas Jefferson, President of the United States of America, have written this letter of general credit for you with my own hand, and signed it with my name. (Ibid.)

582 JEFFERSON HAD WRITTEN DETAILED INSTRUC-TIONS Ronda, **Jefferson's West,** 36–39.

582 FILLED WITH FESTIVE CALLERS Margaret Bayard Smith, **First Forty Years,** 38–39.

583 "ENLIVENED TOO BY THE PRESENCE" Ibid., 39.

583 "THE FUTURE INHABITANTS" TJ to John Breckinridge, August 12, 1803, Thomas Jefferson Papers, LOC.

583 "I VERY EARLY SAW" TJ to Joseph Priestley, January 29, 1804, Thomas Jefferson Papers, LOC.

583 "HAVE YOU SEEN THE NEW WORK OF MALTHUS" Ibid.

584 HAD TO BE RATIFIED BY SUNDAY, OCTOBER 30, 1803 **The Louisiana Historical Quarterly,** XXXI (New Orleans, 1948), 269.

584 "GREAT AND WEIGHTY MATTERS" Proclamation for Special Session of Congress, 1803, portfolio 227, no. 3, Broadside Collection, LOC.

584 REQUIRED A CONSTITUTIONAL AMENDMENT **PTJ,** XXXIX, 327–28. "There is no constitutional difficulty as to the acquisition of territory: and whether, when acquired, it may be taken into the union by the constitution as it now stands, will become a question of expediency," Jefferson had written Gallatin in January

1803. "I think it will be safer not to permit the enlargement of the Union but by amendment of the constitution." (Peterson, **Jefferson and the New Nation,** 770.)

584 "This treaty must of course" TJ to John Breckinridge, August 12, 1803, Thomas Jefferson Papers, LOC.

584 "The Executive in seizing" Ibid.

585 "It is the case" Ibid.

585 "I wrote you" TJ to John Breckinridge, August 18, 1803, Breckinridge Family Papers, LOC.

585 The unwelcome letter received on Wednesday, August 17 TJ to Albert Gallatin, August 23, 1803, Gallatin Papers, MS 238 New-York Historical Society, New York City. The key letter itself is Robert R. Livingston to TJ, June 2, 1803, Thomas Jefferson Papers, LOC.

586 "You will find that" Ibid.

586 "Whatever Congress shall think" TJ to Wilson Cary Nicholas, September 7, 1803, Thomas Jefferson Papers, LOC.

586 "Is there not danger" **PTJ,** XXXIX, 304.

586 Thomas Paine suggested Thomas Paine to TJ, September 23, 1803, Thomas Jefferson Papers, LOC. Paine also wrote Jefferson a compelling brief against seeking an amendment for Louisiana. "It appears to me to be one of those cases with which the Constitution had nothing to do, and which can be judged of only by the circumstances of the times when such a case

shall occur," Paine wrote from Stonington, Connecticut, on September 23, 1803. (Ibid.)

587 "I CONFESS . . . I THINK IT" TJ to Wilson Cary Nicholas, September 7, 1803, Thomas Jefferson Papers, LOC. He also had to figure out how to pay the bills. To Robert Smith, he wrote:

> You know the importance of our being enabled to announce in the message that the interest of the Louisiana purchase (800,000.d) can be paid without a new tax, and what advantage the necessity of a new tax would give the opposition to the ratification of the treaty, where two or three desertions would reject it. To avoid a new tax we had a deficiency (on the estimates as given in) of about 400,000. D. Our colleagues have set their shoulders heartily to the work: Mr. Madison has struck us off 100,000. D. Genl Dearborn something upwards of that, and we still want 180,000. D. to be quite secure. The estimate received from your office, which I enclose you, amounts probably to 770, or 780. And were it possible to reduce it to 600. it would place us at ease. (TJ to Robert Smith, October 10, 1803, Thomas Jefferson Papers, LOC.)

588 UP TO TWO HUNDRED THOUSAND SQUARE MILES Wallace, **Jefferson and the Indians**, 239.

588 ENCOURAGE WHITE SETTLEMENT Ibid., 206–7.

588 THE INDIANS "WILL IN TIME" Ibid., 273.

588 ANY ATTACKING TRIBES BY "SEIZING" Ibid.

589 "OUR BUSINESS IS TO MARCH" TJ to George Clinton, December 31, 1803, Thomas Jefferson Papers, LOC.

589 "THE [REPUBLICANS] HAVE" Gouverneur Morris to Roger Griswold, November 25, 1803, William Griswold Lane Memorial Collection, Manuscripts and Archives, Yale University Library. Of a planned festival to celebrate the Purchase, Simeon Baldwin wrote on January 22, 1804: "It will be a great day among the Democrats here. Few or none of the Federalists will join them—they are not yet satisfied there is occasion for joy—They fear the effect of so great an extension of our territory. . . . They fear the easy introduction of French men, French politics and French intrigue. Northern men fear the influence of such an additional weight to the politics of the South." Simeon Baldwin to Elizabeth Baldwin, January 22, 1804, Baldwin Family Papers, Yale University.

589 "IF, I SAY, FEDERALISM IS CRUMBLING" Pickering to George Cabot, January 29, 1804, Henry Adams, ed., **Documents Relating to New-England Federalism: 1800–1815** (Boston, 1905), 341.

589 "A REUNION OF THE NORTHERN STATES" Ibid., 357.

589 "THE PEOPLE OF THE EAST" Ibid., 339.

590 "MANY PERSONS ARE AT THIS MOMENT" Letter

of Roger Griswold, January 10, 1804, William
Griswold Lane Memorial Collection, Manuscripts and Archives, Yale University Library.

THIRTY-SIX · The People Were Never More Happy

591 "IF WE CAN KEEP" TJ to Elbridge Gerry, March
3, 1804, Thomas Jefferson Papers, LOC.

591 "I THINK YOU OUGHT" Anonymous to TJ, on
or before June 15, 1804, Thomas Jefferson Papers, LOC.

591 AROUND THREE THIRTY OR FOUR O'CLOCK
JHT, IV, 370.

591 HE ENTERTAINED CONSTANTLY Merry Ellen
Scofield, "The Fatigues of His Table: The Politics of Presidential Dining During the Jefferson
Administration," Journal of the Early Republic
26, no. 3 (Fall 2006): 449–69. Scofield made a
particular study of records of Jefferson's dinner
guests from 1804 to 1809.

592 SOCIABILITY WAS ESSENTIAL See, for instance,
Wood, Revolutionary Characters, 105–7.

592 JEFFERSON DISLIKED CONFRONTATION Scofield, "Fatigues of His Table," 465–66.

593 HE PREFERRED "PELL-MELL" Selected Letters
of Dolley Payne Madison, 44.

593 REVELED IN HIS FIRST DINNER TJF, http://
www.monticello.org/site/research-and-collec
tions/dinner-etiquette (accessed 2011). Louisa
Catherine Adams, wife of John Quincy, was also

impressed. "The entertainment was handsome," she said. "French servants in livery, a French butler, a French cuisine, and a buffet full of choice wine." (JHT, IV, 374.) Margaret Bayard Smith saw the Jefferson dinners as democratic metaphors. "At Mr. Jefferson's table the conversation was general; every guest was entertained and interested in whatever topic was discussed," she wrote. "To each an opportunity was offered for the exercise of his colloquial powers and the stream of conversation thus enriched by such various contributions flowed on full, free and animated." (Margaret Bayard Smith, **First Forty Years,** 389.)

593 "IT IS A LONG TIME SINCE" TJF, http://www .monticello.org/site/research-and-collections/din ner-etiquette (accessed 2011).

594 THE RAPIDLY DEPLETING NUMBER OF TREES Margaret Bayard Smith, **First Forty Years,** 11.

594 "SUCH AS GREW" Ibid.

594 "HOW I WISH" Ibid.

594 "AND HAVE YOU NOT" Ibid., 12.

594 "NO," SAID JEFFERSON Ibid.

594 HAD BEGUN HIS WASHINGTON CAREER Lynn W. Turner, "Thomas Jefferson Through the Eyes of a New Hampshire Politician," **Mississippi Valley Historical Review** 30, no. 2 (September 1943): 205–14, charts Plumer's shifting opinion of Jefferson. "At the end of his five years in Congress," Turner writes, "he had sloughed off most of [his] bias and was, indeed, about to transfer

his political allegiance to Jefferson's party. Because he recorded this transformation in shrewd and faithful detail, Plumer's story provides an interesting study of the impact of Jefferson's personality upon his own." (Ibid., 206.)

595 "I HAVE A CURIOSITY" Ibid., 211.

595 JEFFERSON GAVE PLUMER SOME PECANS Ibid., 210.

595 "I SHALL, THEN" Ibid., 211.

596 THE WIFE OF THE MAYOR OF GEORGETOWN Margaret Bayard Smith, **First Forty Years**, 390.

596 SHE ASKED JEFFERSON IF HE LIVED NEAR CARTERS MOUNTAIN Ibid.

596 "VERY CLOSE" Ibid.

596 "I SUPPOSE IT'S" Ibid.

596 "WHY, YES" Ibid., 391.

596 DESCRIBED AS "DISTINGUISHED PERSONS" Ibid., 389.

596 "EARNEST AND ANIMATED" Ibid.

596 ONE GUEST, WHO HAD LIVED IN EUROPE Ibid.

596 "SILENT AND UNNOTICED" Ibid.

596 "A STRANGER IN HIS OWN COUNTRY" Ibid.

597 "To YOU, MR. C., WE ARE INDEBTED" Ibid. The guest was Nathaniel Cutting.

597 SUDDENLY ATTENTION WARMED Ibid., 389–90.

597 "YES, SIR" Ibid., 390.

597 "A PERSON OF IMPORTANCE" Ibid.

597 ANTHONY MERRY, THE NEW MINISTER FROM BRITAIN JHT, IV, 367–92, covers the Merry affair.

597 THE PRESIDENT'S RECEPTION   Henry Adams, **History,** 549–51.

598 MRS. MADISON WAS THE HOSTESS   Ibid., 551–52.

598 "A VIRAGO, AND IN THE SHORT COURSE"   TJ to James Monroe, January 8, 1804, James Monroe Papers, LOC. The Madisons asked the Merrys to dinner after the evening at the president's; the secretary of state also practiced "pell-mell," but the Merrys were not to be stymied a second time. As Jefferson heard the story, Mrs. Merry was "not to be the foremost," prompting her husband to action. Merry "seized her by the hand, led her to the head of the table, where Mrs. Gallatin . . . politely offered her place to Mrs. Merry, who took it without . . . apology." That was enough for Mrs. Merry, who thereafter, Jefferson said, "declined dining, except at one or two private citizens', where it is said there were previous stipulations." (TJ to William Short, January 23, 1804, John Work Garrett Library, Johns Hopkins University, Baltimore.)

598 "WE SAY TO THEM, NO"   TJ to William Short, January 23, 1804, John Work Garrett Library, Johns Hopkins University, Baltimore.

598 "WE ARE NOT AS FRIENDLY NOW"   TJ to James Monroe, January 8, 1804, James Monroe Papers, LOC.

598 "THIS IS TOTALLY WITHOUT FOUNDATION"   Ibid.

599 HE WAS RENOMINATED   APE, I, 83.

599 SENATOR TIMOTHY PICKERING SAT DOWN
Timothy Pickering to Theodore Lyman, February 11, 1804, Timothy Pickering Papers, Massachusetts Historical Society.

599 "TO RESIST THE TORRENT"   Ibid.

599 "IT IS NOT UNUSUAL FOR TWO FRIENDS"   Ibid.

600 "WE ARE DEMOCRATIC ALTOGETHER"   Adams,
Documents Relating to New-England Federalism, 346.

600 "I AM DISGUSTED"   **Life and Correspondence of Rufus King**, IV, 364.

600 "THAT THE SHORTEST AND BEATEN ROAD"
Ibid., 438.

600 "OUGHT TO FIX THE ATTENTION"   Henry
Adams, **History**, 422. On the evening of Sunday, April 8, 1804, John Quincy Adams called on King in New York. There he joined King and Pickering in King's library. The subject was separation. Pickering took his leave; afterward, King made himself clear to Adams. "I disapprove entirely of the project; and so, I am happy to tell you, does General Hamilton." (Ibid., 425.)

600 MERRY HEARD THEM AND REPORTED   JHT,
IV, 406.

601 "THE POSSIBILITY OF A DIVISION"   Augustus
Foster to Elizabeth Cavendish, June 30, 1805, Augustus Foster Papers, LOC.

601 BURR CALLED ON JEFFERSON   Notes on a Conversation with Aaron Burr, January 26, 1804, Thomas Jefferson Papers, LOC. "He began by

recapitulating summarily that he had come to N. Y. a stranger some years ago, that he found the country in possession of two rich families, (the Livingstons and Clintons), that his pursuits were not political and he meddled not," Jefferson wrote of their conversation. "When the crisis however of 1800 came on, they found their influence worn out, and solicited his aid with the people. He lent it without any views of promotion that his being named a candidate for V.P. was unexpected by him. He acceded to it with a view to promote my fame and advancement, and from a desire to be with me whose company and conversation had always been fascinating to him."

Jefferson drily observed later, "Col. Burr must have thought I could swallow strong things in my own favor, when he founded his acquiescence in the nomination as V.P. to his desire of promoting my honor, the being with me whose company and conversation had always been fascinating to him etc. I had never seen Col. B. till he came as a member of Senate. His conduct very soon inspired me with distrust." (Ibid.)

601 "MANY LITTLE STORIES" Ibid.

601 JEFFERSON'S REPLY Ibid.

602 "THAT GREAT OPPOSITION" TJ to Thomas McKean, January 17, 1804, Thomas McKean Papers, Historical Society of Pennsylvania.

602 A FIRE HAD DEVASTATED NORFOLK TJ to Thomas Newton, March 5, 1804, Thomas Jefferson Papers, LOC.

602 "A THOUSAND JOYS TO YOU" TJ to Mary Jefferson Eppes, February 26, 1804, Edgehill-Randolph Papers, University of Virginia Library.

602 HIGH WINDS AND ICE John Wayles Eppes to TJ, March 9, 1804, Edgehill-Randolph Papers, University of Virginia Library.

602 "I FEEL DREADFULLY" John Wayles Eppes to TJ, March 19, 1804, Edgehill-Randolph Papers, University of Virginia.

603 THE U.S. FRIGATE **PHILADELPHIA** In his Message to Congress on March 20, 1804, Jefferson said: "I communicate to Congress a letter received from Capt. Bainbridge Commander of the **Philadelphia** frigate informing us of the wreck of that vessel on the coast of Tripoli and that himself, his officers and men had fallen into the hands of the Tripolitans. This accident renders it expedient to increase our force and enlarge our expenses in the Mediterranean beyond what the last appropriation for the Naval service contemplated. I recommend therefore to the consideration of Congress such an addition to that appropriation as they may think the exigency requires." [Message to Congress, March 20, 1804, LOC, http://hdl.loc.gov/loc.mss/mtj.mtjbib013280 (accessed 2012).]

603 STEPHEN DECATUR LED A COURAGEOUS EXPEDITION Lambert, **Barbary Wars**, 142–44. See also **EOL**, 637–39.

603 "THE MOST BOLD AND DARING" Sofaer, **War, Foreign Affairs, and Constitutional Power**, 217.

603 "In general I am mortified"　TJ to James Madison, April 15, 1804, James Madison Papers, LOC.

603 took charge of her care　TJ to James Madison, April 9, 1804, James Madison Papers, LOC. Jefferson wrote Madison:

> I found my daughter Eppes at Monticello, whither she had been brought on a litter by hand; so weak as barely to be able to stand, her stomach so disordered as to reject almost everything she took into it, a constant small fever, and an imposthume rising in her breast. The indulgence of her friends had permitted her to be uninformed of the importance of strict attention to the necessity of food, and its quality. I have been able to regulate this, and for some days she has taken food enough to support her, and of the kind only which her stomach bears without rejection. . . . Her spirits and confidence are favorably affected by my being with her, and aid the effects of regimen. (Ibid.)

603 "Our spring is remarkably"　TJ to James Madison, April 13, 1804, James Madison Papers, LOC.

604 Jefferson wrote to Dearborn　TJ to Henry Dearborn, April 17, 1804, Coolidge Collection of Thomas Jefferson Manuscripts, Massachusetts Historical Society.

604 POLLY DIED   Cappon, **Adams-Jefferson Letters,** 265.

604 "HOW THE PRESIDENT"   Thomas Mann Randolph, Jr., to Caesar A. Rodney, April 16, 1804, Andre De Coppet Collection, Princeton University.

604 "A LETTER FROM THE PRESIDENT"   **Selected Letters of Dolley Payne Madison,** 53.

604 "I ARRIVED HERE"   TJ to Martha Jefferson Randolph, May 14, 1804, MA 1029.1-173, The Morgan Library & Museum, New York.

605 "IT HAS BEEN SOME TIME"   Abigail Adams to TJ, May 20, 1804, Literary and Historical Manuscripts Morgan Library & Museum, New York. The complete correspondence between Abigail Adams and Jefferson, along with editorial commentary, can be found in Cappon, **Adams-Jefferson Letters,** 265–82. Jefferson sent the letter to John Wayles Eppes, saying that it proved the enduring attachment between the two families—and that he was going to reply to express his own esteem and "with a frank declaration that one act of his life, and never but one, gave me personal displeasure, his midnight appointments." (TJ to John Wayles Eppes, June 4, 1804, Thomas Jefferson Collection, HM 5747, The Huntington Library, San Marino, Calif.) Eppes wrote his father-in-law a warm, insightful reply. "I re-enclose to you Mrs. Adams's letter—If I may judge of its excellence from the sensibility excited by its perusal, it contains the generous

effusions of an excellent heart. . . . In expressing towards her the sentiments of your heart you
will of course know no limit but the extent of
your feelings." Eppes's political counsel, however, echoed what Madison had advised Jefferson six years before, in the aftermath of the 1796
election. "How far under existing circumstances
it may be prudent to indulge in the expression of
any private feeling towards Mr. Adams is to me
extremely doubtful—No possible event could I
imagine excite in his bosom sympathy towards
you—The thread of friendship between you is
on his part broken never more to be united—He
is extremely odious to your warmest friends and
admirers." (John Wayles Eppes to TJ, June 14,
1804, Coolidge Collection of Thomas Jefferson
Manuscripts, Massachusetts Historical Society.)

605 JEFFERSON REPLIED, POLITELY Cappon, **Adams-
Jefferson Letters**, 269–71.

605 ABIGAIL ADAMS WROTE HIM AGAIN Ibid, 271–
74.

607 JEFFERSON REPLIED Ibid., 274–76.

607 JOHN ADAMS LEARNED OF IT Ibid., 282. On
November 19, 1804, Adams wrote: "The whole
of this correspondence was begun and conducted
without my knowledge or suspicion. Last evening
and this morning at the desire of Mrs. Adams I
read the whole. I have no remarks to make upon
it at this time and in this place." (Ibid.)

607 IN WEEHAWKEN, NEW JERSEY Chernow, **Alexander Hamilton**, 700–705.

607 THE PUBLIC REACTION TO HAMILTON'S DEATH Ibid., 710–14.

608 "THE GREATEST AND MOST VIRTUOUS" JHT, IV, 425–26.

608 HIS HUGE NEW YORK FUNERAL Chernow, Alexander Hamilton, 711–13.

608 "SEIZED THE MOMENT" Cappon, Adams-Jefferson Letters, 488.

608 "WE HAD INDEED" JHT, IV, 430.

608 MORE PRESSING ISSUE WAS BURR David O. Stewart, American Emperor: Aaron Burr's Challenge to Jefferson's America (New York, 2011), 124–33.

609 BURR WANTED TO "EFFECT" Anthony Merry to Lord Hawkesbury, August 6, 1804, FO 5/42, National Archives of the United Kingdom, Kew.

609 "I SINCERELY REGRET" TJ to Elbridge Gerry, March 3, 1804, Thomas Jefferson Papers, LOC.

609 GEORGE CLINTON REPLACED BURR APE, I, 82–83.

609 THE CHILD OF IRISH IMMIGRANTS Bowers, Jefferson in Power, 257–58.

610 FIELDED CHARLES COTESWORTH PINCKNEY APE, I, 83–84.

610 THE PRESIDENT WAS REELECTED Ibid.

610 "THERE IS A PLOT" "A Friend of the Constitution" to TJ, December 6, 1804, Thomas Jefferson Papers, LOC.

610 "THE POWER OF THE ADMINISTRATION" Bowers, Jefferson in Power, 266.

611 "WE HAVE BUT FEW"   TJ to Martha Jefferson Randolph, January 7, 1805, MA 1029.1-173, The Morgan Library & Museum, New York.

611 "WE ENTERED YOUNG"   TJ to John Langdon, January 9, 1805, Thomas Jefferson Papers, LOC.

612 WAS DRESSED WELL   **William Plumer's Memorandum of Proceedings in the United States Senate, 1803–1807,** ed. Everett Somerville Brown (New York, 1969), 211–13.

612 "HE WAS TODAY RESERVED"   Ibid.

612 "WE DROVE THEM"   Augustus Foster to Elizabeth Cavendish, December 2, 1805, Augustus Foster Papers, LOC.

612 VICE PRESIDENT BURR TOOK HIS LEAVE   Isenberg, **Fallen Founder,** 279–82.

613 "HE CAN NEVER"   **William Plumer's Memorandum,** 213.

613 "ALL IS NOW BUSINESS"   TJ to John Glendy, March 3, 1805, Thomas Jefferson Papers, LOC.

613 "THE SUCCESSOR OF MONTEZUMA"   Augustus Foster to Frederick Foster, July 1, 1805, Augustus Foster Papers, LOC.

613 DRESSED IN BLACK   Ibid.

613 ON HORSEBACK   Ibid.

613 SPEAKING TOO SOFTLY   Ibid.

613 "DURING THIS COURSE"   Inaugural Address, March 4, 1805, LOC.

614 "ALL WHO CHOSE ATTENDED"   Augustus Foster to Frederick Foster, July 1, 1805, Augustus Foster Papers, LOC.

614 SOME MUSIC CAPPED THE DAY   Ibid.

614 "MY OPINION ORIGINALLY"   TJ to John Taylor, January 6, 1805, Thomas Jefferson Papers, LOC.

614 "I HAVE SINCE BECOME"   Ibid.

615 "IT BEING THE WISH"   William Clark to TJ, April 3, 1805, Thomas Jefferson Papers, LOC.

615 "I CAN FORESEE NO MATERIAL"   Meriwether Lewis to TJ, April 7, 1805, Thomas Jefferson Papers, LOC.

616 A COLLECTION OF ARTIFACTS   Invoice of Articles Sent by Lewis and Clark Expedition, April 7, 1805, Thomas Jefferson Papers, LOC. See also TJF, http://www.monticello.org/site/jefferson/trail-to-monticello (accessed 2012).

616 "THE VOYAGE OF DISCOVERY"   William Eustis to TJ, August 17, 1805, Thomas Jefferson Papers, LOC.

616 CLARK STAKED THE CLAIM   **The Journals of Lewis and Clark,** ed. John Bakeless (New York, 2002), 283. See also Smelser, **Democratic Republic,** 128.

617 FROM LONDON HE ORDERED   List of Items to be Acquired in London, TJ to William Tunnicliff, April 25, 1805, Thomas Jefferson collection, HM 575, The Huntington Library, San Marino, Calif.

617 A ROOM IN THE MANSION FOR FOSSILS   TJ to Caspar Wistar, Jr., March 20, 1808, Thomas Jefferson Papers, LOC.

617 SKULLS, JAWBONES AND TEETH   Ibid.

617 "ONE HORN OF A COLOSSAL ANIMAL" Ibid.

617 "THE BONES ARE SPREAD" Ibid.

617 PURCHASED TWO BEAR CUBS Zebulon Pike to TJ, February 3, 1808, Editorial Files, Papers of Thomas Jefferson, Princeton University.

617 "I WOULD RECOMMEND IF PRACTICABLE" Ibid.

618 "I PUT THEM TOGETHER WHILE HERE" TJ to Charles Willson Peale, February 6, 1808, Thomas Jefferson Papers, LOC.

618 "WE CERTAINLY ARE NOT TO DENY" TJ to Daniel Salmon, February 15, 1808, Thomas Jefferson Papers, LOC.

618 "THE ACTUAL PRESIDENT" **Life and Correspondence of Rufus King**, IV, 509.

619 "A JEALOUS SENSE OF PRAISE AND CENSURE" Edward Thornton to Lord Hawkesbury, August 4, 1802, FO 5/35, National Archives of the United Kingdom, Kew.

619 "WELL-PLACED TO BE CONSIDERED" Ibid.

619 "I REALLY BELIEVE" Ibid.

619 "WILL YOU COME AND TAKE" TJ to John Breckinridge, March 5, 1806, Albert W. Whelpley Autographs Collection, W567, Box 3, Folder 99, Item 0515, Cincinnati Museum Center.

620 THE CROAKING OF FROGS JHT, V, 122–24.

620 "AGRICULTURE, GARDENING" Margaret Bayard Smith, **First Forty Years**, 50.

620 "WHAT WOULD YOU THINK" TJ to James Madison, Albert Gallatin, and Henry Dearborn, February 28, 1806, Thomas Jefferson Papers, LOC.

620 SUGGESTIONS FOR THE YOUNG   TJ to John Carr, April 28, 1807, Carr-Cary Papers, University of Virginia Library.

621 TENSIONS WITH SPAIN   EOL, 374–75.

621 THE FATE OF THE FLORIDAS   Ibid.

621 FINANCIAL CLAIMS   Harry Ammon, **James Monroe** (Charlottesville, 1990), 238–44.

621 MISSION OF MONROE'S TO THE SPANISH CAPITAL   Message to Congress on Spanish and French Spoliations, December 6, 1805, LOC.

621 RISK A BROADER WAR   Ibid. See also **EOL**, 375.

621 "OUR CONSTITUTION IS"   **JHT**, V, 76.

622 HARASSING AMERICAN SHIPS   John M. Murrin and others, **Liberty, Equality, Power** 6th ed. (Boston, 2012), 218.

622 VICTORY AT AUSTERLITZ   **EOL**, 621.

622 TRIUMPH AT TRAFALGAR   Ibid.

622 ALLEGEDLY PLOTTING AGAINST \THE UNITED STATES   Isenberg, **Fallen Founder**, 271–316. "Personal friendship for you and the love of my country induce me to give you a warning about Col. Burr's intrigues," an anonymous correspondent wrote Jefferson in a letter received on the first day of December 1805.

You admit him at your table, and you held a long, and private conference with him a few days ago after dinner at the very moment he is meditating the overthrow of your administration and what is more conspiring against the state. . . . A foreign agent, now at Washington, knows since February last his plans and has seconded them beyond what you are aware of. Mistrust Burr's opinions, and advice: be thoroughly persuaded B. is a new Catilina. Watch his connections with Mr. M——y and you will find him a British pensioner, and agent. (Anonymous to TJ, received December 1, 1805, Thomas Jefferson Papers, LOC.)

A related development was the arrival in New York of the Spanish officer Francisco de Miranda, a Venezuelan-born adventurer who dreamed of building a New World empire out of all the Spanish territories. A second note from the "Friend" said:

I had forgot in my last to mention the arrival at N. York of General Miranda. This event forms a link in Burr's maneuvers. His instructions like those of Burr come from the same source . . . the same plans, or others similar in their tendency are to be offered to you . . . Be careful; although ostensibly directed against a foreign power, the destruction of our government, your ruin, and the material injury of the Atlantic states are their true object. ("A Friend" to TJ, received after December 1, 1805, Thomas Jefferson Papers, LOC.)

622 "What an awful spectacle" TJ to Thomas Lomax, January 11, 1806, Thomas Jefferson Papers, LOC.

THIRTY-SEVEN · A Deep, Dark, and Widespread Conspiracy

623 "The designs of" TJ to Caesar A. Rodney, December 5, 1806, Editorial Files, Papers of Thomas Jefferson, Princeton University.

623 brightened by Patsy's family's JHT, V, 65.

623 Dolley Madison had helped Patsy Martha Jefferson Randolph to TJ, October 26, 1805, Coolidge Collection of Thomas Jefferson Manuscripts, Massachusetts Historical Society.

623 to tend to his cellar TJ to Jean P. Reibelt, November 16, 1805, Thomas Jefferson Papers, LOC.

624 Randolph of Roanoke broke with Jefferson See, for instance, EOL, 375.

624 a long-standing dispute involving Cunningham, Jeffersonian Republicans in Power, 78–79. See also EOL, 128–29.

624 "He considered Great Britain" William Plumer's Memorandum, 443–44.

624 struck again the next day Ibid., 444.

625 "Sit down, Sir, I say sit down" Irving Brant, James Madison, IV (New York, 1961), 316.

625 "astonished all his hearers" Ibid., 315.

625 as either the "Quids" EOL, 428. The new division in Washington worried some Republi-

cans. " 'We are all Republicans, we are all Federalists' read extremely well at the time, and I thought much good would come out of it, but I have found none," Thomas Leiper wrote Jefferson from Philadelphia in March 1806. "Everything you do is wrong with the Leaders of that party and John Randolph." (Thomas Leiper to TJ, March 23, 1806, Thomas Jefferson Papers, LOC.) Jefferson refused to overreact to the Randolph defection. "The H. of R. is as well disposed as I ever saw one," he wrote Wilson Cary Nicholas in April. "The defection of so prominent a leader threw them into dismay and confusion for a moment, but they soon rallied to their own principles, and let him go off with 5 or 6 followers only." (TJ to Wilson Cary Nicholas, April 13, 1806, MA 6006, Literary and Historical Manuscripts, Morgan Library & Museum, New York.)

625 OR THE "OLD REPUBLICANS" JHT, V, 150.

626 THE FIRST PRESIDENT TO CALL FOR Margaret G. Myers, **A Financial History of the United States** (New York, 1970), 106. "The real impetus to federal participation in internal improvements came from . . . Thomas Jefferson, when he announced happily in his second Inaugural address in 1805 that the end of the public debt was in sight, and that 'the revenue thereby liberated, may . . . be applied, in time of peace, to rivers, canals, roads, arts, manufacturers, education, and other great objects within each State.' " (Ibid.)

626 PUBLIC WORKS   See Joseph H. Harrison, Jr., " 'Sic Et Non': Thomas Jefferson and Internal Improvement," **Journal of the Early Republic 7,** no. 4 (Winter, 1987): 335–49.

626 "EDUCATION, ROADS, RIVERS, CANALS"   Ibid., 341.

626 "BY THESE OPERATIONS"   Ibid.

626 LANDMARK REPORT   Henry Adams, **Life of Albert Gallatin,** 350–51. See also **Report of the Secretary of the Treasury, on the Subject of Public Roads and Canals; Made in Pursuance of a Resolution of Senate, of March 2d, 1807** (Washington, 1816).

626 WITH THE EMBARGO   Harrison, " 'Sic Et Non:' Thomas Jefferson and Internal Improvement," 343. Harrison wrote: "By the time that Gallatin's Report on Roads and Canals . . . was submitted to the Senate in April 1808, the Embargo had dried up the revenues needed to put its recommendations into effect." (Ibid.)

626 TENSIONS WITH ENGLAND   Mayer, **Constitutional Thought of Thomas Jefferson,** 219. "Except for a Senate resolution calling on Gallatin to submit a report on a comprehensive plan of national roads and canals, Congress did not act on Jefferson's proposal: the continuing risk of war forced both the administration and Congress to shelve the plan." (Ibid.)

626 WITHOUT THE CONSTITUTIONAL AUTHORITY   Harrison, " 'Sic Et Non,' " 343. Harrison wrote: "His constitutional amendments, in that last

winter of his presidency, were effectively undercut by Joseph B. Varnum of Massachusetts, who . . . consigned the amendments to a committee headed by [John] Randolph. It was a death sentence: the committee never reported." (Ibid.)

626 NEARLY EVERY PROJECT Myers, **A Financial History,** 106–108.

626 CUMBERLAND OR NATIONAL ROAD See Theodore Sky, **The National Road and the Difficult Path to Sustainable National Investment** (Lanham, Md., 2011).

626 "NEVER, IN MY OPINION" John Randolph to James M. Garnett, Jr., October 28, 1806, John Randolph Papers, LOC.

627 "SECRET ENEMIES" Ibid.

627 "DAMNING WITH FAINT PRAISE" Ibid. "What a tissue of intrigue, conspiracy and cabal does every day open to our view!" Randolph added.

627 "IS THE PRESENT EXECUTIVE PERFECT?" Ibid.

627 "THE MASK WHICH AMBITION HAS WORN" John Randolph to James M. Garnett, Jr., September 4, 1806, John Randolph Papers, LOC.

627 "THE OLD REPUBLICAN PARTY" John Randolph to James Monroe, March 26, 1808, John Randolph Papers, LOC.

627 THE TELLTALE HEADACHE WAS BACK JHT, V, 143.

627 HMS **LEANDER** WAS SCREENING JHT, V, 143. "A letter from the Mayor of N.Y. complains of the murder lately committed, and the trespasses

by the **Leander, Cambrian** and **Driver,** and asking for a naval force," Jefferson wrote in his notes on a cabinet meeting where the administration formulated a response. Notes on a Cabinet Meeting, May 1, 1806, Thomas Jefferson Papers, LOC.

627 ORDERING THE THREE   Ibid.

627 CALLED FOR THE ARREST   Ibid.

627 "MY PRESENT MALADY"   TJ to George Logan, March 12, 1806, Thomas Jefferson Papers, LOC.

628 "A LAMENESS IN THE KNEE"   TJ to Lucy Lewis, May 26, 1806, Coolidge Collection of Thomas Jefferson Manuscripts, Massachusetts Historical Society.

628 "I HAVE GOTTEN"   TJ to John Wayles Eppes, May 24, 1806, Thomas Jefferson Collection HM 5770, The Huntington Library, San Marino, Calif.

628 HAD RISEN AS USUAL   Chadwick, **I Am Murdered,** 3. See also Gordon-Reed, **Hemingses of Monticello,** 592–94.

628 EATEN BREAKFAST   Ibid., 14–15.

628 SICK TO HIS STOMACH   Ibid., 15.

628 A MIXED-RACE TEENAGER NAMED MICHAEL   Ibid., 16.

628 WAS SUSPICIOUS AND ORDERED AN AUTOPSY   William Duval to TJ, June 4, 1806, Thomas Jefferson Papers, LOC.

629 "I AM MURDERED"   Chadwick, **I Am Murdered,** 16.

629 WYTHE "MENTIONED NO NAME"   William

Duval to TJ, June 8, 1806, Thomas Jefferson Papers, LOC.

629 WYTHE'S PRIVATE LIFE I am indebted to Gordon-Reed, **Hemingses of Monticello,** 592–94, for this account.

629 LYDIA BROADNAX, A FREE WOMAN OF COLOR Ibid., 592.

629 IN WYTHE'S WILL Ibid., 592–93. Wythe had also left "property to another former slave Benjamin, who predeceased Wythe." (Ibid., 592.)

629 PROVISIONS ASKING JEFFERSON TO OVERSEE THE EDUCATION Ibid., 593. Wythe also left Brown "bank stock." (Ibid.)

629 THAT BROWN WAS THE SON OF BROADNAX AND WYTHE Ibid. "The exact nature of Michael Brown's connection to Wythe and Broadnax is unknown," wrote Gordon-Reed. "It has often been assumed that he was Wythe's son and that Broadnax was his mother. No evidence exists to support either conclusion, however, though Wythe's treatment of the pair was extraordinary." (Ibid.)

629 "WHETHER BROWN" Ibid.

629 WYTHE LEFT JEFFERSON Chadwick, **I Am Murdered,** 162.

629 "GRATIFIED ME UNCEASINGLY" Gordon-Reed, **Hemingses of Monticello,** 593.

630 "SUCH AN INSTANCE OF DEPRAVITY" TJ to William Duval, June 14, 1806, Thomas Jefferson Papers, LOC. Violence had cost him his friend. Soon it threatened to strike even closer to home.

One day in the House of Representatives, where Thomas Mann Randolph, Jr., had kept largely to himself, speaking rarely, a quarrel sprang up involving—unsurprisingly—John Randolph of Roanoke. Words were exchanged, and Thomas Mann Randolph, Jr., believed himself so insulted that only a duel could resolve matters. (TJ to James Ogilvie, June 23, 1806, Coolidge Collection of Thomas Jefferson Manuscripts, Massachusetts Historical Society.) The possibility both horrified and terrified Jefferson.

"It is with an aching heart I take up my pen, and this circumstance must apologize for my interference in the present case but where everything which I hold dear in this world is at stake, where the future happiness of our whole family, or their future misery unmixed and unabating, are hanging in even suspense, it must be justifiable to urge our rights to a due share of weight in your deliberations," Jefferson wrote his son-in-law on June 23. (TJ to Thomas Mann Randolph, Jr., June 23, 1806, Edgehill-Randolph Papers, University of Virginia Library.)

A duel was madness, Jefferson believed, sheer madness, but he understood he had to be delicate with his sensitive son-in-law. "Certainly I would not wish you to do what might lessen you in the esteem of the world," Jefferson said. "But I wish you to estimate correctly the public opinion in such a case, and not to volunteer beyond what that might require or approve." He could not keep his own emotions in check. "How different is the stake which you two would bring into the field!" Jefferson said. "On his side, unentangled in the affections of the world a single life, of no value to himself or others. On yours, yourself, a wife, and a family of children all depending, for all their happiness and protection in this world on you alone." (Ibid.)

Finally tempers cooled sufficiently, and the matter went away. But for a time it had been yet another source of stress and strain for Jefferson—a cause of personal worry at a time of public anxiety.

630 A DEBILITATING DROUGHT   TJ to James Madison, July 26, 1806, James Madison Papers, LOC.

630 "BURR IS UNQUESTIONABLY"   TJ to Thomas Mann Randolph, Jr., November 3, 1806, Coolidge Collection of Thomas Jefferson Manuscripts, Massachusetts Historical Society.

631 WAS ALLEGEDLY   Stewart, **American Emperor,** 134–42. "We learn that he is actually building 10 or 15 boats able to take a large gun and fit for the navigation of those waters. We give him all the attention our situation admits: as yet we have no legal proof of any overt act which the law can lay hold of." (TJ to Thomas Mann Randolph, Jr., November 3, 1806, Coolidge Collection of Thomas Jefferson Manuscripts, Massachusetts Historical Society.)

631 "THIS IS INDEED"   James Wilkinson to TJ, November 12, 1806, in **Report of the Commit-**

tee Appointed to Inquire into the Conduct of General Wilkinson (Washington, D.C., 1811), 425–28.

631 TO ISSUE A PROCLAMATION Proclamation on Military Expeditions against Spain, November 27, 1806, Thomas Jefferson Papers, LOC.

631 WHAT WAS BURR DOING? For details, see Isenberg, **Fallen Founder,** and Stewart, **American Emperor.**

632 PLUMER DINED WITH JEFFERSON **William Plumer's Memorandum,** 543–44.

632 INCRIMINATING PAPERS **JHT,** V, 264.

632 DRAFTED A BILL "AUTHORIZING" TJ to John Dawson, December 19, 1806, Thomas Jefferson Papers, LOC. "On the whole, this squall, by showing with what ease our government suppresses movements which in other countries requires armies, has greatly increased its strength by increasing the public confidence in it," Jefferson said in February 1807. "It has been a wholesome lesson, too, to our citizens, of the necessary obedience to their government." (Johnstone, **Jefferson and the Presidency,** 198.)

633 "STRICT LINE OF THE LAW" Message to Congress, January 22, 1807, LOC.

633 "GUILT IS PLACED BEYOND QUESTION" Sofaer, **War, Foreign Affairs, and Constitutional Power,** 191.

633 JEFFERSON PAID CAREFUL ATTENTION TJ to Caesar A. Rodney, March 22, 1807, Private Collection of William I. Davis, Newark, Ohio;

Papers of Thomas Jefferson, Editorial Files, Princeton University. "Burr, as a prisoner under a guard of 10 men, passed Coweta 800 miles from here, on the 3d inst.," Jefferson wrote Rodney.

> At 30 miles a day he will be at Cartersville on James River on Thursday the 26th. There is not therefore one moment to be lost in deciding and acting on these questions. 1. Must he not be ordered from Cartersville down to Richmond for trial? 2. Should not an express go off instantly to meet him at Cartersville? Will Mr. Rodney be so good as to call on me between 8. and 9. this morning to consult on the above? I ask him thus early, because between 9 and 10 my headache comes on which renders me incapable of business. (Ibid.)

633 "No man's history" TJ to Levi Lincoln, March 25, 1807, Coolidge Collection of Thomas Jefferson Manuscripts, Massachusetts Historical Society.

633 "leaves me but an hour" Ibid.

634 in the Eagle Tavern Joseph Wheelan, **Jefferson's Vendetta: The Pursuit of Aaron Burr and the Judiciary** (New York, 2006), 6–7.

634 filibusters were not illegal Simon, **What Kind of Nation**, 232–33.

634 messenger from Richmond JHT, V, 320–25.

634 subpoenaing the president TJ to George

Hay, June 20, 1807, Thomas Jefferson Papers, LOC.

635 MARSHALL'S DECISIONS AND DEMEANOR EOL, 439–40.

635 "THE NATION WILL JUDGE" TJ to William Branch Giles, April 20, 1807, Thomas Jefferson Papers, LOC.

636 "I AM NOW IN THE 7TH DAY" TJ to Martha Jefferson Randolph, March 20, 1807, Edgehill-Randolph Papers, University of Virginia Library.

636 "I AM TIRED OF" TJ to John Dickinson, January 13, 1807, Historical Society of Pennsylvania.

636 "THE BRITISH COMMISSIONERS" TJ to James Monroe, March 21, 1807, James Monroe Papers, LOC.

637 JEFFERSON INVITED JOHN WAYLES EPPES TJ to Thomas Mann Randolph, Jr., February 18, 1807, Thomas Jefferson Papers, LOC.

637 "WHAT ACTS OF MINE" Ibid.

637 "YOUR RETURN TO THE HOUSE" Ibid.

637 "REALLY LOVING YOU" TJ to Thomas Mann Randolph, Jr., February 19, 1807, Edgehill-Randolph Papers, University of Virginia Library.

638 DISPATCHED A RETAINER TJ to Thomas Mann Randolph, Jr., February 28, 1807, Thomas Jefferson Papers, LOC.

638 "I CERTAINLY WOULD NOT" Ibid.

638 JEFFERSON KEPT TRACK TJ to Martha Jefferson Randolph, March 12, 1807, MA 1029.1-173, The Morgan Library & Museum, New York.

THIRTY-EIGHT · This Damned Embargo

639 "Never since" TJ to Pierre-Samuel du Pont de Nemours, July 14, 1807, Thomas Jefferson Papers, LOC.

639 "Something now occurs" TJ to Albert Gallatin, July 10, 1807, Gallatin Papers, New-York Historical Society, New York City.

639 attack on the USS Chesapeake Bowers, **Jefferson in Power,** 427–28.

640 "After I had read" John Keehmle to TJ, June 29, 1807, Thomas Jefferson Papers, LOC. The correspondent, John Keehmle, added: "This unexpected attack on one of our national vessels, has realized my anticipations and fears of the hostile disposition of the **British Government** toward us. They have now cast the die, and struck the blow; it rests with you as the head of our nation to resent the unexpected murder of our citizens, in a spirited and manly manner, and you may rely and depend on the hearty support and approbation of all true Americans." (Ibid.)

640 "I am sorry to be" Bowers, **Jefferson in Power,** 428.

640 "I am so much fatigued" Ibid.

640 of appearing at Jefferson's annual levee Ibid., 431.

640 patriotic toasts Ibid.

641 banning armed British ships Proclamation on British Armed Vessels, July 2, 1807, Thomas Jefferson Papers, LOC. "At length a deed tran-

scending all we have hitherto seen or suffered, brings the public sensibility to a serious crisis, and our forbearance to a necessary pause," he said. (Ibid.)

641 HE DECIDED TO CALL Notes on Cabinet Meeting, July 5, 1807, Thomas Jefferson Papers, LOC. He was receiving reassuring counsel from voices outside the administration. "The late outrage by the British on the **Chesapeake,** has produced everywhere, within our range of intelligence at this place, a degree of emotion bordering on rage," wrote James Wilkinson from Richmond on June 29. And yet, Wilkinson wrote, "The present is no moment for precipitancy or a stretch of power. On the contrary the British being prepared for war and we not, a sudden appeal to hostilities will give them a great advantage. . . . The prevalent, I might say almost universal, sentiment here is embargo, and to you, Sir, every honest eye is directed in full confidence." (James Wilkinson to TJ, June 29, 1807, Thomas Jefferson Papers, LOC.)

641 ORDERED THE PURCHASE **PTJRS,** III, 100. "After the affair of the Chesapeake, we thought war a very possible result," he wrote afterward. "Our magazines were illy provided with some necessary articles, nor had any appropriations been made for their purchase. We ventured, however, to provide them, and to place our country in safety." (Ibid.)

641 "THE MOMENT OUR PEACE" Annual Message

to Congress, October 27, 1807, President's Messages, Records of the United States Senate, National Archives. See also Sofaer, **War, Foreign Affairs and Constitutional Power,** 172.

641 THE PRESIDENCY WAS FURTHER STRENGTHENED Sofaer, **War, Foreign Affairs and Constitutional Power,** 172–73.

641 "A STRICT OBSERVANCE" **PTJRS,** III, 99.

642 A SHIP—THE USS **REVENGE**—WAS DISPATCHED Jon Latimer, **1812** (Cambridge, Mass., 2007), 21.

642 "TO THE TORIES" George Clinton to TJ, July 9, 1807, Thomas Jefferson Papers, LOC.

642 "THE SPIRIT AND ENTERPRISE" William Duane to TJ, July 8, 1807, Thomas Jefferson Papers, LOC. Still, Jefferson was determined to maintain his perspective amid the storm. He described his plan to John Page in July 1807:

1. The usage of civilized nations requires that an opportunity of reparation shall always be given. If a word and a blow were the practice there would never be peace.

2. We should procrastinate 3 or 4 months, were it only to give time to our merchants to get in their vessels, property and seamen, which are the identical materials with which the war is to be carried on.

3. It is our duty to do no act which may com[mit] the legislature to war, rather than non-intercourse or any other measure they may prefer. They will probably be called in

time to receive the answer of England. Before that they would be acting in the dark. (TJ to John Page, July 9, 1807, Thomas Jefferson Papers, LOC.)

642 "REASON AND THE USAGE"   TJ to John Wayles Eppes, July 12, 1807, Thomas Jefferson Papers, LOC. A correspondent signing himself "An Indignant American" wrote: "The time will come, if it has not already, when the American people will feel indignant at the **pusillanimity** of their chief Magistrate. Remember Carters Mountain, and now that you have an opportunity, convince the world that you are not what you have been always supposed to be a **coward**." ("An Indignant American" to TJ, July 1807, Thomas Jefferson Papers, LOC.)

643 " 'REPARATION FOR' "   TJ to Pierre-Samuel du Pont de Nemours, July 14, 1807, Thomas Jefferson Papers, LOC.

643 CALLED FOR THE OCTOBER SPECIAL SESSION **JHT,** V, 435.

643 INCREASED THE MAIL SERVICE   Thomas Jefferson to Egbert Benson, July 31, 1807, Thomas Jefferson Papers, LOC. At Monticello he surveyed a world scene that seemed more and more complex and demanding. "I never expected to be under the necessity of wishing success to Bonaparte. But the English being equally tyrannical at sea as he is on land, and that tyranny bearing on us

in every point of either honor or interest, I say, 'down with England,' and as for what Bonaparte is then to do to us, let us trust to the chapter of accidents. I cannot, with the Anglomen, prefer a certain present evil to a future hypothetical one," he wrote Thomas Leiper on August 21. (TJ to Thomas Leiper, August 21, 1807, Thomas Jefferson Papers, LOC.)

His trip back to Washington was something of a disaster. He nearly lost his horse crossing the Rapidan River. Then, two days after reaching the President's House, he came down with the flu. It was going to be that kind of season. (TJ to Martha Jefferson Randolph, October 12, 1807, MA 1029.1-173, The Morgan Library & Museum, New York.)

643 JEFFERSON HAD GUESSED   TJ to Thomas Mann Randolph, Jr., July 5, 1807, Thomas Jefferson Papers, LOC. "The power of declaring war being in Congress," Jefferson had written, "the Executive should do no act committing them to war, when it is very probable they may prefer a nonintercourse to war." (Ibid.)

644 AT DINNER ONE DAY   **Diary of John Quincy Adams,** 48.

644 "I SUPPOSE [THIS] WILL TAKE"   Ibid.

644 "IF THERE WAS ANY SINCERITY"   Ibid.

644 QUESTION OF THE MOMENT   TJ to Thomas Mann Randolph, Jr., November 30, 1807, Thomas Jefferson Papers, LOC.

645 "The members, as far as" TJ to Thomas Mann Randolph, Jr., October 26, 1807, Thomas Jefferson Papers, LOC.

645 news from Paris and London JHT, V, 481.

645 Jefferson proposed Message to Congress, December 17, 1807, LOC. See also JHT, V, 482.

645 "making every preparation" Ibid.

645 "The war fever is past" TJ to Martha Jefferson Randolph, November 23, 1807, MA 1029.1-173, The Morgan Library & Museum, New York.

646 "In every point of view" Albert Gallatin to TJ, December 18, 1807, Thomas Jefferson Papers, LOC.

646 "What is good" JHT, V, 476.

646 "The embargo keeping" TJ to John Taylor, January 6, 1808, Washburn Collection, Massachusetts Historical Society.

647 legislation had passed quickly Robert W. Tucker and David C. Hendrickson, Empire of Liberty (New York, 1992), 204.

647 struck by "a tooth-ache" TJ to Martha Jefferson Randolph, December 29, 1807, Literary and Historical Manuscripts, MA 1029.1-173, The Morgan Library & Museum, New York.

647 the weapons of economic war Burton Spivak, Jefferson's English Crisis: Commerce, Embargo, and the Republican Revolution (Charlottesville, Va., 1979), x.

648 "Our people have" Ibid., 8.

648 "Confidence now seems" Timothy Pickering

to T. Williams, January 18, 1808, Timothy Pickering Papers, Massachusetts Historical Society.

648 "IMPLICIT, BLIND CONFIDENCE" Ibid.

648 "OUR EMBARGO, WHICH HAS BEEN" TJ to the Marquis de Lafayette, February 24, 1809, Thomas Jefferson Papers, LOC.

649 THERE WERE PROTESTS Bowers, **Jefferson in Power,** 465–67.

649 ESSENTIALLY INVITED SHIPS Louis Martin Sears, **Jefferson and the Embargo** (Durham, N.C., 1927), 70.

649 SMUGGLING WAS AN ENORMOUS PROBLEM Wilentz, **Rise of American Democracy,** 131–32.

649 THOSE "COMBINING AND CONFEDERATING" Proclamation on the Embargo, April 19, 1808, Thomas Jefferson Papers, LOC.

649 CONNECTICUT BECAME A BASTION Sears, **Jefferson and the Embargo,** 185–86.

650 "ANY OTHER MEASURE" Ibid., 142.

650 "THE EMBARGO IS" TJ to Benjamin Rush, January 3, 1808, Thomas Jefferson Papers, LOC.

650 HISTORY HAS NOT BEEN KIND See, for instance, Henry Adams, **History,** 1160–252; Johnstone, **Jefferson and the Presidency,** 254–306; William M. Goldsmith, **The Growth of Presidential Power: A Documented History,** I, **The Formative Years** (New York, 1974), 466–81.

651 "I HAVE BEEN HAPPY" TJ to Thomas Leiper, May 25, 1808, Thomas Jefferson Papers, LOC.

651 "YOU INFERNAL VILLAIN" John Lane Jones to TJ, August 8, 1808, Thomas Jefferson Collec-

tion, HM 9018, The Huntington Library, San Marino, Calif.

652 "YOU ARE THE DAMDEST" Anonymous to TJ, on or before August 25, 1808, Thomas Jefferson Papers, LOC.

652 "THY DEStruction is" Anonymous to TJ, on or before June 10, 1808, Thomas Jefferson Papers, LOC.

653 "IN AN OPEN, FREE-HEARTED" Bowers, **Jefferson in Power,** 432.

653 "SHOULD HAVE HIS HEAD" Ibid.

653 VILLAGERS BURNED Ibid., 450.

653 "THE ATTEMPT IS" James Sullivan to TJ, April 2, 1808, Thomas Jefferson Papers, LOC. Three days later, reporting on Federalist maneuvering, Sullivan added: "The deep-laid plot of Pickering's letter, added to the embargo, gave them fresh confidence . . . and they have done the most wonderful things with them. They came out, however, openly, and avowedly upon the position of a dissolution of the national government, and a separation of the Northern from the Southern States. They expect this arrangement to be supported by the court of London, and however you may treat the idea with neglect, it is on the request of this party, in New England, that seven ships of the line, and ten thousand troops are on their way to Halifax." (Ibid., April 5, 1808.)

653 MADISON WAS NOMINATED FOR PRESIDENT APE, I, 96. See also TJ to Thomas Mann Ran-

dolph, Jr., January 26, 1808, Thomas Jefferson Papers, LOC. In that letter, Jefferson wrote:

A caucus was held on Saturday by the members of Congress at which 89. attended. Mr. Madison had 83. votes, Clinton 3. Monroe 3. as president, and Clinton had 79. as V. President. But one member from N. York attended, and but 1. federalist, J.Q. Adams who voted for Mr. Madison. Of the Virginia members in town J. Randolph, Garnett, Gray, Trigg and Bassett declined attending, the last because disapproving the manner of calling the Caucus, but avowedly in favor of Mr. Madison. The vote for Clinton as V.P. was under a firm belief he had declared he would not accept it. It is now believed he will accept. . . . But his acceptance will in my opinion prevent all opposition to Mr. Madison, and whether he does or not it is believed that N.Y. will vote for Mr. Madison. His election is considered as out of all question. (Ibid.)

653 "I SEE WITH INFINITE GRIEF" TJ to James Monroe, February 18, 1808, James Monroe Papers, LOC.

654 THE ELECTION OF 1808 APE, I, 92–122.

654 ECHOES OF OLD REFRAINS Ibid., 93–94.

654 122 ELECTORAL VOTES TO PINCKNEY'S 47 Ibid., 92.

654 MOVEMENT TOWARD ENDING   For a full treatment of legislative action in this period, see Spivak, **Jefferson's English Crisis**, 188–97.

655 "THE MONARCHISTS OF THE NORTH" TJ to Thomas Mann Randolph, Jr., January 2, 1809, Thomas Jefferson Papers, LOC. Jefferson watched Massachusetts closely. "Their Republican members think that if we will fix by law a day when the embargo shall cease (as some day in June), that this will satisfy so great a portion of their people as to remove the danger of a convention," he told Randolph. "This will probably be consented to with an addition that letters of marque and reprisal shall issue the same day. . . . For if war takes place with England, we have no security that she will not offer neutrality and commerce to N. England and that the latter will not accept it," Jefferson said. To Charles Bankhead, Jefferson wrote: "In the mean time the disquietude in the North is extreme, and we are uncertain what extent of conflagration a spark might occasion." (TJ to Charles L. Bankhead, January 19, 1809, Manuscripts, Mss 2 J3595 a43, Virginia Historical Society, Richmond.)

655 "A LINE SEEMS NOW TO BE"   TJ to Charles L. Bankhead, January 19, 1809, Manuscripts, Mss 2 J3595 a43, Virginia Historical Society, Richmond.

THIRTY-NINE · A Farewell to Ultimate Power

656 "CONSIDERING THE EXTRAORDINARY CHARACTER" Annual Message to Congress, November 8, 1808, President's Messages, Records of the United States Senate, National Archives.

656 "THE DISEASED JAW BONE" TJ to Martha Jefferson Randolph, January 10, 1809, MA 1029.1-173, The Morgan Library & Museum, New York.

656 "I AM ALREADY SENSIBLE" TJ to Charles Thomson, December 25, 1808, Charles Thomson Papers, LOC.

656 INVENTORIED THE FURNITURE TJ to Thomas Claxton, February 19, 1809, Thomas Jefferson Papers, LOC.

657 HOW TO PAY HIS BILLS JHT, VI, 3.

657 ARGONAUTS OF OLD Cappon, **Adams-Jefferson Letters,** 614.

657 "NATURE INTENDED ME" TJ to Pierre-Samuel du Pont de Nemours, March 2, 1809, Thomas Jefferson Papers, LOC.

657 HE INSPIRED AS MUCH DIVISION Positive verdicts, of course, pleased Jefferson. "It is a common observation that the present is a time of political phenomena," wrote William Jarvis from Lisbon on February 18, 1809. "The extraordinary events which have occurred within the last thirty years, on both sides of the Atlantic, will without doubt amply justify the assertion: but

the United States has been the only country during this period and unhappily for mankind almost any other where the good of the people has been the sole seed of government. In the attainment of this philanthropic object, your administration will perhaps stand unrivalled in the history of the world." (William Jarvis to TJ, February 18, 1809, Thomas Jefferson Papers, LOC.)

657 "A FEW FLEETING" Allegany County, Maryland, Citizens to TJ, February 20, 1809, Thomas Jefferson Papers, LOC.

658 "THOU STRANGE INCONSISTENT MAN!" William Penn to TJ, February 24, 1809, Thomas Jefferson Papers, LOC.

658 "YOU HAVE BROUGHT" "Cassandra" to TJ, February 28, 1809, Thomas Jefferson Papers, LOC.

658 "I SUPPOSE INDEED" TJ to Richard M. Johnson, March 10, 1808, Thomas Jefferson Papers, LOC. Jefferson's recommended books:

Volney's Lessons of history.
Millot's antient history.
Anacharsis
Middleton's life of Cicero.
Gibbon's decline of the Roman empire.
Millot's Modern history.
Russel's history of Modern Europe.
Millot's history of France.
Davila's history of the civil wars of France.
Sully's Memoirs.

The French revolution by Rabaut and La Cretelle.

The Revolution of France by Desodards.

Voltaire's historical works.

Robertson's Charles V.

Historical works of Frederic king of Prussia.

Segur's history of Frederic William II.

Ruthere's History of Poland.

Tooke's life of Catharine II.

Memoires Secrets de la Russie.

Baxter's history of England (this is Hume's text republicanised.)

Ld. Orrery's history of England.

Ld. Bacon's history of Henry VIII.

Macaulay's history.

Ludlow's memoirs.

Anecdotes of the life of Chatham.

Belsham's history and Memoirs.

Robertson's history of Scotland.

Mosheim's Ecclesiastical history

Priestley's corruptions of Christianity. (Ibid.)

659 "I became of course"   Ibid.
659 "In the character of Marcus Aurelius"   David Bailie Warden to TJ, December 4, 1807, Thomas Jefferson Papers, LOC.
659 "We are all politics"   TJ to Charles L. Bankhead, November 26, 1808, Coolidge Collection of Thomas Jefferson Manuscripts, Massachusetts Historical Society.

659 "The Congressional campaign"   TJ to Levi Lincoln, November 13, 1808, Thomas Jefferson Papers, LOC.

660 "Here, everything is"   TJ to Thomas Mann Randolph, Jr., December 13, 1808, Thomas Jefferson Papers, LOC.

660 "Never will it be"   JHT, V, 666.

660 left the President's House   Ibid.

660 departed the mansion by themselves   Ibid.

660 thought the setting   Bowers, **Jefferson in Power,** 504–5.

661 Mrs. Madison looked   Margaret Bayard Smith, **First Forty Years,** 58.

661 stood at the drawing room door   Ibid.

661 crowded with carriages   Ibid.

661 a half hour's wait   Ibid.

661 Jefferson saw Margaret Bayard Smith   Ibid.

661 reached for her hand   Ibid., 58–59.

661 "Remember the promise"   Ibid., 59.

661 Mrs. Smith, of course, reassured him   Ibid.

661 "You have now resigned"   Ibid.

661 "Yes indeed"   Ibid.

661 told that "the ladies"   Ibid.

661 "That is right"   Ibid.

661 he joined celebrating Republicans   Ibid., 60–61.

662 "The crowd was excessive"   **Diary of John Quincy Adams,** 58.

662 "I am full of plans"   TJ to Charles Thomson,

December 25, 1808, Charles Thomson Papers, LOC.

662 HE HAD SUGGESTED Martha Jefferson Randolph to TJ, March 2, 1809, Coolidge Collection of Thomas Jefferson Manuscripts, Massachusetts Historical Society.

662 "AS TO AUNT MARKS" Ibid.

662 ORDERED AN ABRIDGMENT **MB**, II, 1242.

663 SENT A GERANIUM **PTJRS**, I, 29.

663 ARRANGED PAYMENT **MB**, II, 1242–43.

663 BACON HAD COME TO WASHINGTON Bear, **Jefferson at Monticello,** 104–8. See also **MB**, II, 1243.

663 JEFFERSON REACHED MONTICELLO **MB**, II, 1243.

664 JULIEN CAME TO SET UP Ibid., 1244.

FORTY · My Body, Mind, and Affairs

667 "I STEER MY BARK" Cappon, **Adams-Jefferson Letters,** 467.

669 "AMIDST THE DIN OF WAR" **PTJRS**, I, 359.

669 RED BED CURTAINS HUNG James A. Bear, Jr., "The Last Few Days in the Life of Thomas Jefferson," **Magazine of Albemarle County History** 32 (1974): 63–79. See especially page 68.

669 THE ROOMS WERE PEACEFUL Author observation. My description of Jefferson's quarters and his routine owe much to the kindness of the president, the trustees, and the staff of the

Thomas Jefferson Foundation. At my request I was granted unusual access to Monticello in the overnight and early morning hours in order to observe as closely as possible the material culture in which Jefferson lived and worked, including the sounds he heard and the possible play of light as he awoke in the mornings. I am particularly indebted to Susan R. Stein for her counsel and for her "Notes on Jefferson's Bed Chamber," Memorandum to author, November 10, 2011.

669 A 1790 CLOCK MOUNTED BETWEEN TWO OBE-LISKS "Notes on Jefferson's Bed Chamber," Memorandum of Susan R. Stein to author.

669 HUNG A SWORD Bear, "Last Few Days in the Life of Thomas Jefferson," 68.

669 "A LONG FORGOTTEN ARABIAN PRINCE" Ibid.

669 JEFFERSON'S UBIQUITOUS MOCKINGBIRDS "Notes on Jefferson's Bed Chamber," Memorandum of Susan R. Stein to author.

670 OVERNIGHT THE SILENCE OF THE CHAMBER Author observation.

670 THE TICK-TICK-TICK OF THE TALL CLOCK Ibid.

670 HIS WIFE'S WALNUT DRESSING TABLE "Notes on Jefferson's Bed Chamber," Memorandum of Susan R. Stein to author. I am also grateful to Elizabeth Chew of the Monticello curatorial office for showing me the dresser.

670 JEFFERSON HAD HIS OWN PRIVY JUST STEPS AWAY Ibid.

670 HE USED PIECES OF SCRAP PAPER Ibid.

670 EXAMPLES WERE COLLECTED FROM HIS PRIVY

Ibid. The papers can be found on Reel 15, Nicholas Philip Trist Papers, Manuscript Division, LOC.

670 FIVE TO EIGHT HOURS OF SLEEP A NIGHT Randall, **Jefferson**, III, 450.

670 READING FOR HALF AN HOUR Ibid.

670 DIFFICULTY HEARING DIFFERENT VOICES Ibid.

670 SUFFERING FROM EXTREMELY RARE FEVERS Ibid., 451.

670 "NOW TO HAVE LEFT ME" Ibid.

670 IN THE SUN'S DIRECT PATH Author observation.

670 MUCH OF HIS FIRST SENSE OF LIGHT Ibid.

671 ELEVEN-THOUSAND-SQUARE-FOOT, THIRTY-THREE-ROOM HOUSE TJF, http://www.monticello.org/site/house-and-gardens/monticello-house-faq (accessed 2012).

671 TEN OTHER ROOMS IN THE PAVILIONS AND UNDER THE SOUTH TERRACE Ibid.

671 WALKING INTO THE ENTRANCE HALL My descriptions of the rooms in the house are the result of my observation; Stein, **Worlds of Thomas Jefferson at Monticello**; and the very fine digital records and accounts at TJF, http://www.monticello.org/site/house-and-gardens (accessed 2012).

671 THE FLOOR WAS GREEN Stein, **Worlds of Thomas Jefferson at Monticello**, 63. Her complete account of the entrance hall is on pages 61–71.

671 WHITEWASHED WITH A YELLOW-ORANGE DADO

TJF, http://www.monticello.org/site/house-and -gardens/entrance-hall (accessed 2012).

671 ANTLERS OF MOOSE AND ELK   Ibid.

671 THE UPPER JAWBONE OF A MASTODON   Ibid.

671 FORTY INDIAN OBJECTS   Ibid.

672 CARVED STONE SCULPTURES   Ibid.

672 SMALL PORTRAIT OF A YOUNG SACK CHIEF   Ibid.

672 THE FRY-JEFFERSON MAP OF VIRGINIA   Ibid.

672 OF NORTH AMERICA, EUROPE, AFRICA, AND ASIA   Ibid.

672 WAS A SCALE MODEL OF THE PYRAMID OF CHE-OPS   Ibid.

672 A SCULPTURE, **ARIADNE**   Ibid.

672 LONG MISTOOK FOR ONE OF CLEOPATRA   Ibid.

672 **ST. JEROME IN MEDITATION AND JESUS IN THE PRAETORIUM**   Ibid.

672 "JESUS . . . STRIPPED OF THE PURPLE"   TJF, http://www.monticello.org/site/house-and-gar dens/jesus-praetorium-painting (accessed 2012).

672 THERE WERE PORTRAITS   TJF, http://www .monticello.org/site/house-and-gardens/ entrance-hall (accessed 2012).

672 TWO ENGRAVINGS   Ibid.

672 AND BUSTS OF   Ibid.

672 "MEMORIALS OF THOSE WORTHIES"   TJ to James Bowdoin, April 27, 1805, Thomas Jefferson Pa-pers, LOC.

673 A PLASTER RELIEF OF AN EAGLE   TJF, http:// www.monticello.org/site/house-and-gardens/ plaster-eagle-and-stars (accessed 2012).

673 UNDER A BRASS ARGAND-STYLE LAMP   TJF,

http://www.monticello.org/site/house-and-gardens/entrance-hall (accessed 2012).

674 FLOOR OF CHERRY AND BEECH   TJF, http://www.monticello.org/site/house-and-gardens/parlor (accessed 2012).

674 JEFFERSON PERSONALLY DESIGNED   Ibid.

674 THE PARLOR IS EIGHTEEN FEET, TWO INCHES   Ibid.

674 CARD TABLES, CHAIRS, SOFAS, A CHESS SET   Ibid.

674 "PORTRAITS—24"   Ibid.

674 HERE HUNG PAINTINGS AND HERE SAT SCULPTURES   Ibid.

675 THE BRILLIANTLY YELLOW DINING ROOM   TJF, http://www.monticello.org/site/house-and-gardens/monticello-dining-room (accessed 2012).

675 DOUBLE POCKET DOORS ON ROLLERS   TJF, http://www.monticello.org/site/house-and-gardens/tea-room (accessed 2012).

675 THE SMALL OCTAGONAL TEA ROOM   Ibid.

675 HE CALLED HIS "MOST HONORABLE SUITE"   Ibid.

675 BUSTS OF WASHINGTON, FRANKLIN, LAFAYETTE, AND JOHN PAUL JONES   Ibid.

675 PATSY HAD A BLUE SITTING ROOM   TJF, http://www.monticello.org/site/house-and-gardens/monticello-south-square-room (accessed 2012).

675 A NORTH OCTAGONAL ROOM   TJF, http://www.monticello.org/site/house-and-gardens/north-octagonal-room (accessed 2012).

675 DOME ROOM ATOP THE HOUSE   TJF, http://www.monticello.org/site/house-and-gardens/dome-room (accessed 2012).

675 A SERIES OF SMALL BEDROOMS Author observation.

675 "IF IT HAD NOT BEEN CALLED MONTICELLO" Stein, **Worlds of Thomas Jefferson at Monticello,** 50. See also Andrew Burstein, "Jefferson in Retirement," in Cogliano, ed., **A Companion to Thomas Jefferson,** 218–33.

675 HIS "CHEERFULNESS AND AFFECTION" Randall, **Jefferson,** III, 349.

675 LIKE A "PATRIARCH OF OLD" TDLTJ, 374.

675 "OUR MOTHER EDUCATED ALL" Ibid., 342.

676 THEY FOLLOWED HIM ON GARDEN WALKS Randall, **Jefferson,** III, 349.

676 "WOULD VIOLATE ONE OF HIS RULES" Ibid.

676 HE NEVER HAD TO RAISE HIS VOICE Ibid.

676 HE PICKED FRUIT FOR THEM Ibid.

676 HE ORGANIZED AND PRESIDED OVER RACES Ibid.

676 ON SOME SUMMER NIGHTS Ellen Wayles Randolph Coolidge to Henry S. Randall, February 22, 1856. Extract published at Papers of Thomas Jefferson Retirement Series Digital Archive, http://www.monticello.org/familyletters (accessed 2011).

676 IT HAD BEEN MADE BY JOHN HEMINGS Ibid.

677 "WHEN IT GREW TOO DARK TO READ" Randall, **Jefferson,** III, 350.

677 "CROSS QUESTIONS AND CROOKED ANSWERS" Ibid.

677 "I LOVE MY LOVE WITH A" Ibid. See also http://www.monticello.org/site/jefferson/fun-fact:4 (accessed 2012).

677 THE ARRIVAL OF CANDLES Randall, **Jefferson,** III, 350.

677 CONSTRUCTED VENETIAN PORCHES Gordon-Reed, **Hemingses of Monticello,** 613–14.

677 WHEN HE WAS SNOWED IN AT POPLAR FOREST **PTJRS,** III, 394.

677 ON JOURNEYS TO BEDFORD Randall, **Jefferson,** III, 344.

678 SHE HAD NEVER HAD A SILK DRESS Ibid., 350.

678 HE MIGHT HEAR A CHILD Ibid., 348–49.

678 "OUR GRANDFATHER SEEMED TO READ" **TDLTJ,** 345.

678 "SO EMINENTLY SYMPATHETIC" Ibid., 344.

679 "MR. JEFFERSON CALLED" Elizabeth Trist to [Elizabeth Kortright Monroe], April 3, 1809. Published at Papers of Thomas Jefferson Retirement Series Digital Archive, http://www.monticello.org/familyletters (accessed 2011).

679 "THE SUN NEVER SEES HIM" **PTJRS,** I, 392–93.

679 "THERE IS A TRANQUILITY ABOUT HIM" Ibid., 395.

679 "WE HAVE BEEN PERMITTED" Ibid., 4.

679 "YOU HAVE, IN YOUR PUBLIC CAPACITY" Ibid., 69.

680 "THOUGH I AM CONVINCED" Ibid., 263.

680 "NO ONE KNOWS BETTER" Ibid., 471.

680 "WHAT WOULD BECOME OF MANKIND" Ibid., III, 58.

680 WROTE WITH HIS LEGS STRETCHED OUT I am grateful to Elizabeth Chew of the Monticello curatorial office for this detail.

680 "My present course of life" **PTJRS**, III, 304.

680 samplings of the English mulberry Ibid., I, 40, 467.

681 "I am now on horseback" Ibid., III, 315. See also Lucia Stanton, "Thomas Jefferson: Planter and Farmer," in Cogliano, ed., **A Companion to Thomas Jefferson**, 253–70.

681 "I feel a much greater interest" Randall, **Jefferson**, III, 450.

681 "If there be a God" **PTJRS**, III, 315.

681 He subscribed to the papers Ibid., I, 214. Jefferson offered counsel to Madison from time to time, but the third president's influence over the fourth has sometimes been exaggerated. See Roy J. Honeywell, "President Jefferson and His Successor," **American Historical Review** 46, no. 1 (October 1940): 64–75. They exchanged at least 39 letters in Madison's first year as president (Madison wrote 22, Jefferson 17), but the number dropped off as the years passed. Madison appears to have written Jefferson just eight times during the second term. The two men spoke personally when they could, of course, but such contact was necessarily limited by Madison's duties and Jefferson's decision to stay largely at home in retirement. (Ibid., 66.)

681 "reading the newspapers" **PTJRS**, I, 154.

681 the "ineffable luxury" Ibid., 475.

682 "The bundle being too large" Ibid., 327–28. See also ibid., 510, for Jefferson's note of

thanks to Clark for the sheepskin and an Indian blanket.

682 OVERSAW THE ENGLISH TRANSLATION Ibid., III, 3–25.

682 DEBATED THE ORIGINS OF THE POTATO Ibid., I, 196.

682 WROTE FOR VINE CUTTINGS Ibid., 586.

682 MUSED ON THE ROLE OF LIBRARIES Ibid., 205.

682 JOHN WALKER, HIS ONETIME FRIEND Ibid., 498–99.

682 HE SENT A GIFT OF A BASKET OF RIPE FIGS Ibid., 500.

683 VIRGINIA HAD ALWAYS CONTRIBUTED "ABOVE PAR" Ibid., 383.

683 THE BRUTAL DEATH OF HIS OLD SECRETARY MERIWETHER LEWIS Ibid., 602–4.

683 AS JEFFERSON HEARD THE STORY Ibid., 632–33. For a biographical sketch of Lewis, see ibid., 436.

683 AN UNSPARING ACCOUNT OF JEFFERSON Ibid., III, 610.

684 RECORDED THE BIRTHS OF HEMINGS'S CHILDREN Gordon-Reed, **Hemingses of Monticello,** 15–16.

684 "HE WAS NOT IN THE HABIT" Lewis and Onuf, eds., **Sally Hemings and Thomas Jefferson,** 24.

684 "AFFECTIONATE TOWARD HIS WHITE GRANDCHILDREN" Ibid.

684 "THE ENJOYMENT OF" Lemire, **"Miscegenation": Making Race in America,** 11.

684 IN A LETTER TO JAMES PARTON Gordon-Reed, **Thomas Jefferson and Sally Hemings,** 254–57.

684 Randolph "said in one case" Ibid., 254.

685 "a gentleman dining with Mr. Jefferson" Ibid.

685 a theory ultimately disproved by DNA research TJF, http://www.monti cello.org/site/plantation-and-slavery/report-research-com mittee-thomas-jefferson-and-sally-hemings (accessed 2012).

685 "I asked Col. R[andolph]" Gordon-Reed, **Thomas Jefferson and Sally Hemings**, 255.

685 "The secrets of an old Virginia manor" Ibid., 256.

686 "I am little able" **PTJRS**, IV, 35.

686 "It is wonderful to me" Ibid., 87–88.

686 "How do you do?" Ibid., 100.

686 "Such an intercourse" Ibid., III, 278. See also Cappon, **Adams-Jefferson Letters**, 283–89.

687 "You remember the machinery" **PTJRS**, III, 305.

687 "Many are the evils" Ibid., 356.

687 The second president spent two days Ibid., IV, 314. The ensuing scene is drawn from this source.

688 "This is enough for me" Ibid., 313.

688 Rush sent word of Jefferson's sentiments Ibid., 389–91.

688 "A letter from you" Ibid., 428–29.

689 When Adams answered Ibid., 483–85.

689 "On the subject of the history" Cappon, **Adams-Jefferson Letters**, 452.

690 "So many subjects crowd upon me" **PTJRS**, VI, 277.

690 "You and I ought not to die before" Ibid., 297.

690 "Mr. Adams and myself" Ibid., V, 670.

690 "My reputation has been" Ibid., VI, 227.

690 "The summum bonum with me" Ibid., 231.

690 "Men have differed" Cappon, **Adams-Jefferson Letters**, 335.

691 "And shall you and I" Ibid., 337.

691 "I believe in the integrity" **PTJRS**, V, 3.

692 "The natural aristocracy" Ibid., VI, 563.

692 "I have thus" Ibid., 566–67.

693 exchanged a total of 329 letters Cappon, **Adams-Jefferson Letters**, xxix.

693 "We have had a wretched winter" **PTJRS**, III, 437.

693 "The rancor of party" Ibid., 473.

694 "War however may become" Ibid., I, 61. As ever, Jefferson worried about Congress. "I know no government which would be so embarrassing in war as ours," he wrote Madison on March 17, 1809. "This would proceed very much from the lying and licentious character of our papers; but much also from the wonderful credulity of the members of Congress in the floating lies of the day. And in this no experience seems to correct them. I have never seen a Congress during the last 8 years a great majority of which I would not implicitly rely on in any question, could their

minds have been purged of all errors of fact."
(Ibid.)

694 News of a British frigate and sloop of war
Ibid., IV, 133.

694 "Our country has twice" Ibid., 103.

694 Jefferson returned home Ibid., V, 82.

694 "Your declaration of war" Ibid.

695 sent a war-preparation message to Congress
EOL, 659–700.

695 "We are to have war then?" PTJRS, IV,
472.

695 "Your message had all" Ibid., 376–77.

FORTY-ONE · To Form Statesmen, Legislators and Judges

696 "In a republican nation" TJ to David Hard-
ing, April 20, 1824. Extract published at Papers
of Thomas Jefferson Retirement Series Digital
Archive, http://www.monticello.org/familyletters
(accessed 2011).

696 As late as 1810 EOL, 667.

696 "The people will not" Ibid.

697 the War of 1812 was disastrous Ibid.,
659–700. See also JHT, VI, 107–36; Anthony
S. Pitch, **The Burning of Washington: The British Invasion of 1814** (Annapolis, Md., 1998), is
a vivid account of the attack on the American
capital.

697 "No government can be maintained"
PTJRS, VII, 648.

697 VICTORIES AT BALTIMORE AND AT PLATTSBURGH EOL, 690–91.

697 THE HARTFORD CONVENTION Ibid., 692–95. See also JHT, VI, 126–27. Richard Buel, Jr., **America on the Brink: How the Political Struggle Over the War of 1812 Almost Destroyed the Young Republic** (New York, 2005), chronicles the depth of the Federalist opposition to the Republican project in the first decade and a half of the nineteenth century.

697 "THE CEMENT OF THE UNION" JHT, VI, 126.

698 IN 1814 THE EPISCOPAL BISHOP OF SOUTH CAROLINA PTJRS, VII, 368.

698 PATSY GUESSED Randall, **Jefferson**, III, 332.

698 THE SMASHING OF GLASS ALERTED Ibid., 331.

698 STRANGERS HOPING FOR A GLIMPSE Ibid.

699 "APPROACH WITHIN A DOZEN YARDS" Ibid.

699 HENRY RANDALL ONCE WALKED OVER Ibid., 332.

699 A VIRGINIA GENTLEMAN WHO HAD FALLEN OUT Ibid., 333.

700 HIS HEARING WAS FAILING A BIT Ibid., 426.

700 ILL IN EARLY 1818 Ibid., 445.

700 HE WROTE WARMLY TO JOHN ADAMS Ibid., 446.

701 CHRONIC FINANCIAL TROUBLE See, for instance, JHT, VI, 453–56.

701 APPEARS TO HAVE DRUNK TOO MUCH Alan Pell Crawford, **Twilight at Monticello: The Final Years of Thomas Jefferson** (New York, 2008), 138.

701 IS SAID TO HAVE GROWN JEALOUS   Ibid., 137–38.

701 THREE TERMS AS GOVERNOR   JHT, VI, 341. See also TJF, http://www.monticello.org/site/ jefferson/thomas-mann-randolph (accessed 2012).

701 FELL OUT OVER THE FATE OF EDGEHILL   Gordon-Reed, **Hemingses of Monticello,** 418.

701 SAID HE WAS "MORE FEROCIOUS"   Ibid., 417.

701 CHARLES L. BANKHEAD   PTJRS, III, 633–34. See also Anne Z. Cockerham, Arlene W. Keeling, and Barbara Parker, "Seeking Refuge at Monticello: Domestic Violence in Thomas Jefferson's Family." **Magazine of Albemarle County History** 64 (2006): 29–52.

702 "HE WAS A FINE-LOOKING"   Bear, **Jefferson at Monticello,** 94.

702 "I HAVE SEEN HIM"   Ibid.

702 JEFFERSON TOOK BANKHEAD TO POPLAR FOREST Crawford, **Twilight at Monticello,** 70–72. See also Randall, **Jefferson,** III, 264.

702 TO TREAT HIS OWN SON   Ibid., 126–27. "Nothing less than his good, and the hope of restoring happiness to his family and friends and to yourself particularly could have induced me to the pain of this communication," Jefferson wrote the senior Bankhead. (Ibid., 127.)

702 "IN A STATE APPROACHING INSANITY"   Ibid., 127.

702 COULD BE VICIOUS   Ibid.

703 FOR REFUSING TO HAND OVER THE KEYS   Bear, **Jefferson at Monticello,** 94.

703 PATSY TRIED TO CALM   Ibid.

703 BANKHEAD GOT INTO A FIGHT   Crawford, **Twilight at Monticello,** 166–67.

704 "WITH RESPECT TO BANKHEAD"   Ibid., 171.

704 "I THINK, WITH YOU"   Cappon, **Adams-Jefferson Letters,** 467.

704 "I STEER MY BARK"   Ibid.

704 "I DARE NOT LOOK BEYOND"   **PTJRS,** VII, 217–18.

704 "SOME MEN LOOK"   TJ to H. Tompkinson (Samuel Kercheval), July 12, 1816. Extract published at Papers of Thomas Jefferson Retirement Series Digital Archive, http://www.monticello.org/familyletters (accessed 2011).

705 "THE FACT IS"   TJ to Benjamin Waterhouse, March 3, 1818. Extract published at Papers of Thomas Jefferson Retirement Series Digital Archive, http://www.monticello.org/familyletters (accessed 2011).

706 BURNING OF THE ROUGHLY 3,000 BOOKS   **JHT,** VI, 172.

706 6,487 VOLUMES   Ibid., 176.

706 "FOR ITS SELECTION"   Ibid., 177.

706 IT WAS A UNIVERSITY   Randall, **Jefferson,** III, 462–63, details the organizational foundations.

707 TO "FORM THE STATESMEN"   Thomas Jefferson and the University of Virginia Commissioners: The Rockfish Gap Report, August 4, 1818. Extract published at Papers of Thomas Jefferson Retirement Series Digital Archive, http://www.monticello.org/familyletters (accessed 2011).

707 "I know of no"   TJ to William C. Jarvis, September 28, 1820. Extract published at Papers of Thomas Jefferson Retirement Series Digital Archive, http://www.monticello.org/familyletters (accessed 2011).

707 "I think by far"   **PTJ**, X, 244–45. In 1814, he told Thomas Cooper: "I have long had under contemplation, and been collecting materials for the plan of a university in Virginia which should comprehend all the sciences useful to us, and none others." (**PTJRS**, VII, 127.)

708 "This institution will be"   TJ to William Roscoe, December 27, 1820. Extract published at Papers of Thomas Jefferson Retirement Series Digital Archive, http://www.monticello.org/familyletters (accessed 2011).

708 "For here we are not"   Ibid.

708 "If our legislature"   TJ to Joseph C. Cabell, January 22, 1820. Extract published at Papers of Thomas Jefferson Retirement Series Digital Archive, http://www.monticello.org/familyletters (accessed 2011). Jefferson initially hoped the university would be the capstone of a broader system of public education, a cause to which he had been devoted for decades. "Were it necessary to give up either the Primaries or the University, I would rather abandon the last," he said in January 1823. "Because it is safer to have a whole people respectably enlightened, than a few in a high state of science and the many in ignorance. This last is the most dangerous state in which a

nation can be. The nations and governments of Europe are so many proofs of it." (Ibid., January 13, 1823.)

708 RODE THROUGH "A PERFECT HURRICANE" Elizabeth Trist to Nicholas P. Trist, March 9, 1819. Published at Papers of Thomas Jefferson Retirement Series Digital Archive, http://www .monticello.org/familyletters (accessed 2011).

708 SAID TO HAVE INSTALLED A TELESCOPE Randall, **Jefferson**, III, 473.

709 THE STATE'S RELIGIOUS WORLD REACTED Ibid., 465.

709 HE OFFERED A BRILLIANT PLAN Ibid., 468–69.

710 "I REJOICE THAT" TJ to Benjamin Waterhouse, June 26, 1822. Extract published at Papers of Thomas Jefferson Retirement Series Digital Archive, http://www.monticello.org/familyletters (accessed 2011).

710 "IS BECOME THE FAVORITE BEVERAGE" TJ to Edmund Rogers, February 14, 1824. Extract published at Papers of Thomas Jefferson Retirement Series Digital Archive, http://www .monticello.org/familyletters (accessed 2011).

710 "WERE I TO BE THE FOUNDER" TJ to Thomas B. Parker, May 15, 1819. Extract published at Papers of Thomas Jefferson Retirement Series Digital Archive, http://www.monticello.org/family letters (accessed 2011).

711 A FORTY-SIX-PAGE WORK **The Jefferson Bible**, 17. This Smithsonian edition is an elegant and engaging volume.

711 THE PHILOSOPHY OF JESUS Randall, **Jefferson**, III, 654.

711 A MORE AMBITIOUS WORK **The Jefferson Bible**, 26–31.

711 "THE RELIGION OF JESUS" TJ to Jared Sparks, November 4, 1820, Thomas Jefferson Papers, LOC.

711 A CHURCHGOER WHO CARRIED Meacham, **American Gospel**, 278.

711 "OF A SECT BY MYSELF" Ibid., 4.

711 JEFFERSON HOPED THAT Johann N. Neem, "A Republican Reformation: Thomas Jefferson's Civil Religion and the Separation of Church from State" in Cogliano, ed. **A Companion to Thomas Jefferson**, 91–109, is an excellent essay on the complexities of Jefferson's thinking on these matters.

712 "THE TRUTH IS THAT" Cappon, **Adams-Jefferson Letters**, 594.

712 "MAY WE MEET THERE AGAIN" Neem, "A Republican Reformation: Thomas Jefferson's Civil Religion and the Separation of Church from State" in Cogliano, ed. **A Companion to Thomas Jefferson**, 97.

712 "THE DOCTRINES OF JESUS ARE SIMPLE" Ibid., 103.

713 "IS KNOWN TO" Randall, **Jefferson**, III, 440.

713 "BOLD IN THE PURSUIT" PTJRS, VII, 191.

713 "IT IS TOO LATE IN THE DAY" Ford, **Writings**, IX, 412–14.

713 DONATED MONEY TO THE AMERICAN BIBLE SO-
CIETY **PTJRS**, VII, 178.

714 HE WAS FELLED Randall, **Jefferson**, III, 453.

714 "THE BOISTEROUS SEA OF LIBERTY" TJ to Richard Rush, October 20, 1820. Extract published
at Papers of Thomas Jefferson Retirement Series
Digital Archive, http://www.monticello.org/
familyletters (accessed 2011).

FORTY-TWO · The Knell of the Union

715 "FROM THE BATTLE OF BUNKER'S HILL" Randall, **Jefferson**, III, 454. .

715 "I HAVE MUCH CONFIDENCE" TJ to François
Barbé de Marbois, June 14, 1817. Extract published at Papers of Thomas Jefferson Retirement
Series Digital Archive, http://www.monticello
.org/familyletters (accessed 2011).

716 "LIKE A FIRE BELL IN THE NIGHT" TJ to John
Holmes, April 22, 1820. Extract published at Papers of Thomas Jefferson Retirement Series Digital Archive, http://www.monticello.org/family
letters (accessed 2011).

716 "THE CESSION OF THAT KIND" Randall, **Jefferson**, III, 456.

717 "THE BANKS, BANKRUPT LAW" Cappon, **Adams-
Jefferson Letters**, 548–49.

717 THE RESOLUTION WAS A COMPROMISE Howe,
Wrought, 147–60. See also Wilentz, **Rise of
American Democracy**, 231–40, and Robert

Pierce Forbes, **The Missouri Compromise and Its Aftermath: Slavery and the Meaning of America** (Chapel Hill, N.C., 2007).

717 "IT IS NOT A MORAL QUESTION" TJ to the Marquis de Lafayette, December 26, 1820. Extract published at Papers of Thomas Jefferson Retirement Series Digital Archive, http://www.monti cello.org/familyletters (accessed 2011).

718 "THE LEADERS OF FEDERALISM" Randall, **Jefferson**, III, 457. "They are taking advantage of the virtuous feelings of the people to effect a division of parties by a geographical line; they expect that this will insure them, on local principles, the majority they could never obtain on principles of Federalism," said Jefferson. (Ibid.)

718 "A HIDEOUS BLOT" TJ to William Short, September 8, 1823. Extract published at Papers of Thomas Jefferson Retirement Series Digital Archive, http://www.monticello.org/familyletters (accessed 2011).

718 "THIS, MY DEAR SIR" **PTJRS**, VII, 604. The plan had been proposed by Edward Coles.

719 "THERE IS NOTHING I WOULD NOT SACRIFICE" Ibid., 652.

719 "NOTHING IS MORE CERTAINLY WRITTEN" Jefferson, **Writings**, 44.

719 AN INTRINSIC "DEGRADATION" **PTJRS**, VII, 603.

720 RENDERING MORAL JUDGMENTS IN RETROSPECT I am indebted to Arthur Schlesinger, Jr., for

this insight. "Self-righteousness in retrospect is easy—also cheap," he used to say.

720 BEGINNING WITH ROBERT CARTER See Andrew Levy, **The First Emancipator: The Forgotten Story of Robert Carter, the Founding Father Who Freed His Slaves** (New York, 2005).

720 THE POLITICIANS OF THE NORTH Wilentz, **Rise of American Democracy**, 218–22. See also Eric Foner, **The Story of American Freedom** (New York, 1998), 84–94.

721 "THE SOUTHERN INTEREST" Sharp, "Unraveling the Mystery of Jefferson's Letter of April 27, 1795," 411–18.

721 "I DO NOT SAY THIS" Randall, **Jefferson**, III, 499.

721 "WHERE THE DISEASE IS MOST" Ford, **Writings**, IX, 516.

722 "THE MARCH OF EVENTS" TJ to Frances Wright, August 7, 1825. Extract published at Papers of Thomas Jefferson Retirement Series Digital Archive, http://www.monticello.org/family letters (accessed 2011).

722 PERSONAL DEBT WAS ANOTHER ENDURING IRONY Herbert E. Sloan, **Principle and Interest: Thomas Jefferson and the Problem of Debt** (New York, 1995), is the standard account. See also TJF, http://www.monticello.org/site/research-and-collections/debt (accessed 2012); and Gordon-Reed, **Hemingses of Monticello**, 629–35.

722 PLANTERS OF HIS TIME AND PLACE   Robert E. Brown and B. Katherine Brown, **Virginia, 1705–1786: Democracy or Aristocracy?** (East Lansing, Mich., 1964), 96–124.

722 THE GROWING OF TOBACCO   See, for instance, T. H. Breen, **Tobacco Culture: The Mentality of the Great Tidewater Planters on the Eve of Revolution** (Princeton, N.J., 1987); and TJF, http://www.monticello.org/site/plantation-and -slavery/crops-monticello (accessed 2012).

723 SHIFTED AWAY   TJF, http://www.monticello.org/ site/plantation-and-slavery/crops-monticello (ac- cessed 2012).

723 ALWAYS GREW THE CROP   **FB,** 255–310.

723 A CONFLUENCE OF FACTORS   TJF, http://www .monticello.org/site/plantation-and-slavery/crops -monticello (accessed 2012). See also Gordon- Reed, **Hemingses of Monticello,** 316–17.

723 WORTH £4,000   Sloan, **Principle and Interest,** 18.

723 SKYROCKETING INFLATION   Ibid., 16.

723 "BUT A SHADOW"   Ibid.

723 THE DEBT REMAINED   Virginia law protected him from British creditors, even under the Treaty of Paris. The signing of the Constitution, however, made him vulnerable to collection, and is probably part of the reason he asked to return from France in late 1788. At home he would be better able to manage the farming at Monti- cello and to bring his finances into order. (Ibid., 16–17, 21.) See also TJF, http://www.monticello

.org/site/research-and-collections/debt (accessed 2012) and Gordon-Reed, **Hemingses of Monticello,** 629–35.

723 "BY THE SMOOTH HANDLE" Randall, **Jefferson,** III, 525.

723 THE PROSPECT OF RUIN WAS REAL Sloan, **Principle and Interest,** 3–12. See also Gordon-Reed, **Hemingses of Monticello,** 629–35, and **JHT,** VI, 301–16 and 473–78.

724 EVEN MORE EAGER TJF, http://www.monti cello.org/site/jefferson/quotations-university-vir ginia (accessed 2012).

724 "AS WELL AS HE DID 10 YEARS AGO" Elizabeth Trist to Nicholas P. Trist, March 9, 1819. Extract published at Papers of Thomas Jefferson Retirement Series Digital Archive, http://www.monti cello.org/familyletters (accessed 2011).

724 "THE PAPERS TELL US" Randall, **Jefferson,** III, 476.

725 HE PUT A FOOT WRONG Ibid., 486–87.

725 "DURING SUMMER" Ibid., 476.

725 "LIKE OTHER YOUNG PEOPLE" Cappon, **Adams-Jefferson Letters,** 613–14.

725 "WE HAVE BEEN TOO CARELESS" Randall, **Jefferson,** III, 488.

726 CROSSING THE RIVANNA Virginia J. Randolph (Trist) to Nicholas Philip Trist, May 13, 1823. Extract published at Papers of Thomas Jefferson Retirement Series Digital Archive, http://www .monticello.org/familyletters (accessed 2011).

727 IN OCTOBER 1823 HE ANSWERED Randall,

Jefferson, III, 491. See also T. R. Schellenberg, "Jeffersonian Origins of the Monroe Doctrine," **Hispanic American Historical Review** 14 (February 1934): 1–31.

727 "The question presented" Randall, **Jefferson,** III, 491.

728 "You are not to believe" Ibid., 495.

728 Jefferson favored Crawford Howe, **Wrought,** 203. See also **JHT,** VI, 431–32.

729 Jackson's charges of a "corrupt bargain" See, for instance, Wilentz, **Rise of American Democracy,** 254–57.

729 Arriving at Monticello TJF, http://www .monticello.org/site/research-and-collections/la fayettes-visit-to-monticello-1824 (accessed 2012). I am indebted to these accounts for my portrait of the visit. See also Randall, **Jefferson,** III, 503. For a general account of Lafayette's journey to America, see Howe, **Wrought,** 304–5.

729 At a banquet in Lafayette's honor Randall, **Jefferson,** III, 504.

730 "His deeds in the war" Ibid.

730 "Born and bred among your fathers" Ibid.

731 "In conversation" Ibid., 506.

731 "I feel much alarmed" Ibid.

732 "I cannot pretend" Ibid., 507.

732 cosigned a note for $20,000 Ibid., 533–35. Randall is my source for the Nicholas episode.

734 The market was bad For the story of the lottery, see **JHT,** VI, 473–82, 488, 495–96, 511.

734 HE HAD BEEN, PATSY SAID Ibid., 473.

734 IN AN APPEAL TO THE GENERAL ASSEMBLY Ibid., 473–78.

734 TO HIS HORROR Ibid., 479.

734 WAS IN CHARGE OF THE ARRANGEMENTS Ibid.

734 ASKED TO SEND COUNSEL TO A YOUNG NAMESAKE Randall, **Jefferson,** III, 524–25.

737 IN A BIZARRE EPISODE Ibid., 540.

737 "THE REVOLUTION IN PUBLIC OPINION" Jefferson, **Writings,** 1516. The occasion was a letter to James Heaton dated May 20, 1826.

737 "IT IS NOW THREE WEEKS" Bear, "Last Few Days in the Life of Thomas Jefferson," 63–79.

737 STILL, HE REFUSED TO GIVE UP Randall, **Jefferson,** III, 538.

738 ORGANIZERS OF THE WASHINGTON CELEBRATIONS Jefferson, **Writings,** 1516.

738 "ALL EYES ARE OPENED" Ibid., 1517.

738 "TAKE CARE OF ME WHEN DEAD" Ibid., 1515.

738 A DIFFERENT PASSION: WINE J. Jefferson Looney, "Thomas Jefferson's Last Letter," **Virginia Magazine of History and Biography** 112, no. 2 (2004): 178–84.

739 HE CONTINUED TO READ Randall, **Jefferson,** III, 539.

FORTY-THREE · No, Doctor, Nothing More

740 "THE LOSS OF MR. JEFFERSON" Randall, **Jefferson,** III, 551.

740 JEFFERSON PAINFULLY PUT PEN TO PAPER   Bear, "Last Few Days in the Life of Thomas Jefferson," 65.

740 THE DOCTOR SAID HE WAS "APPREHENSIVE" Ibid.

741 HIS DAUGHTER SAT WITH HIM DURING THE DAY Randall, **Jefferson**, III, 543.

741 THOMAS MANN RANDOLPH, JR., THE MAN WHO Bear, "Last Few Days in the Life of Thomas Jefferson," 66.

741 "HIS MIND WAS ALWAYS CLEAR"   Randall, **Jefferson**, III, 543.

741 JEFFERSON TOLD HIS GRANDSON   Ibid., 544.

741 LEE WAS ON A MISSION   **VTM**, 108.

741 PATSY STOPPED LEE   Ibid., 108–9.

741 HE WAS "NEVER MORE TO BEHOLD"   Ibid., 109.

742 JEFFERSON, LYING IN HIS BED   Ibid.

742 "MY EMOTIONS AT APPROACHING"   Ibid.

742 JEFFERSON COULD NOT HELP LEE   Ibid., 108–9.

742 AN INTRIGUING DETAIL   Ibid., 109–10.

742 "MRS. RANDOLPH AFTERWARDS TOLD ME" Ibid., 110.

743 HE SAID GOOD-BYE   Randall, **Jefferson**, III, 543–44.

743 "GEORGE DOES NOT"   Ibid., 544.

743 "LORD, NOW LETTEST THOU THY SERVANT" Ibid., 547.

743 THOMAS JEFFERSON RANDOLPH SUGGESTED Ibid., 543.

743 "DO NOT IMAGINE FOR A MOMENT"   Ibid.

743 "THAT ETERNAL SLEEP" TJ to William Short, May 5, 1816. Extract published at Papers of Thomas Jefferson Retirement Series Digital Archive, http://www.monticello.org/familyletters (accessed 2012).

743 HE AWOKE TO A NOISE Randall, **Jefferson**, III, 543.

743 HE HAD COMPOSED A POEM **TDLTJ**, 429. Also see Bear, "Last Few Days in the Life of Thomas Jefferson," 73.

744 MUSED ABOUT THE REVOLUTION Randall, **Jefferson**, III, 543.

744 HIS BED CURTAINS, HE NOTED Ibid.

744 "A FEW HOURS MORE" Ibid.

744 AT FIVE FORTY-FIVE P.M. ON THE SECOND Bear, "Last Few Days in the Life of Thomas Jefferson," 73.

745 HE SLEPT FITFULLY Ibid.

745 THEN, ON THE EVENING OF THE THIRD Randall, **Jefferson**, III, 548.

745 JEFFERSON TOOK WHAT WOULD BE Bear, "Last Few Days in the Life of Thomas Jefferson," 73.

745 "OH GOD" Nicholas P. Trist to Joseph Coolidge, "His Bedside, July 4th, 1826," Correspondence of Ellen Wayles Randolph Coolidge, University of Virginia Library.

745 "NO, DOCTOR, NOTHING MORE" Bear, "Last Few Days in the Life of Thomas Jefferson," 74.

745 THE REMAINING THREE HOURS Ibid., 75.

745 "THIS IS THE FOURTH?" Ibid.

745 TRIST COULD NOT BRING HIMSELF   Ibid.

745 MURMURING ABOUT THE REVOLUTIONARY COM-
MITTEE OF SAFETY   Ibid., 74–75.

746 "WARN THE COMMITTEE"   Randall, **Jefferson,**
III, 546.

746 AT FOUR O'CLOCK IN THE MORNING   Bear, "Last
Few Days in the Life of Thomas Jefferson," 75.

746 AT TEN HE STIRRED   Ibid.

746 IT WAS BURWELL COLBERT   Randall, **Jefferson,**
III, 544. Also see Gordon-Reed, **Hemingses of
Monticello,** 650–51.

746 AT TEN MINUTES BEFORE ONE O'CLOCK   Randall, **Jefferson,** III, 542.

746 HE DIED WITH HIS EYES OPEN   Ibid., 544.

746 THOMAS JEFFERSON RANDOLPH TOUCHED
Ibid.

747 NICHOLAS TRIST QUIETLY CLIPPED   Bear, "Last
Few Days in the Life of Thomas Jefferson," 76.

747 THE WOODEN COFFIN BUILT BY JOHN HEMINGS
Gordon-Reed, **Hemingses of Monticello,** 651.

747 THE COFFIN WAS TAKEN TO THE PARLOR   Bear,
"Last Few Days in the Life of Thomas Jefferson," 77.

747 "TO ME HE HAS BEEN MORE"   Randall, **Jefferson,** III, 551.

747 "HE LIVES AND WILL LIVE"   Ibid., 550.

747 "HE OUGHT TO BE REVERED"   **VTM,** 102–3.

747 WORMLEY HUGHES, THE GARDENER, DUG
Gordon-Reed, **Hemingses of Monticello,** 652.

747 THE WEATHER HAD BEEN WET   Bear, "Last Few
Days in the Life of Thomas Jefferson," 77.

747 GOT A LATE START Ibid., 78.

747 A SMALL GROUP Ibid., 77–78.

748 READ THE BURIAL OFFICE Ibid., 78.

748 " 'I AM THE RESURRECTION AND THE LIFE' " Ibid.

748 IN HIS LIFE AND IN HIS WILL JEFFERSON Gordon-Reed, **Hemingses of Monticello,** 649–51.

748 THE FOUR CHILDREN OF JEFFERSON AND SALLY'S TJF, http://www.monticello.org/site/plantation-and-slavery/sally-hemings (accessed 2012). This article is based on the research of Lucia Stanton.

748 "HARRIET MARRIED A WHITE MAN" TJF, http://www.monticello.org/site/plantation-and-slavery/harriet-hemings (accessed 2012).

748 MADISON WAS FREED IN JEFFERSON'S WILL TJF, http://www.monticello.org/site/plantation-and-slavery/sally-hemings (accessed 2012).

748 MOVED TO OHIO Ibid.

748 SETTLED IN WISCONSIN Ibid.

748 CHANGED HIS NAME Ibid.

748 DECLARED HIMSELF TO BE WHITE Ibid.

748 IN HIS WILL JEFFERSON ALSO FREED Gordon-Reed, **Hemingses of Monticello,** 647.

748 NO OTHER SLAVES Ibid., 657.

748 SOON MOVED TO CHARLOTTESVILLE Ibid., 659.

749 JEFFERSON DID NOT NAME HER IN HIS WILL Ibid., 657.

749 THERE IS EVIDENCE THAT HIS WISHES Ibid. "Sally Hemings's situation was convoluted and mysterious, as it had been since her return to

America, but one can piece together what happened," wrote Gordon-Reed. "Many years later, in 1873, Israel Gillette stated that Jefferson had freed seven slaves, including Sally Hemings and all her children. Of course, he freed only five people in his will. Beverly and Harriet Hemings simply left Monticello as white people with no formal emancipation. Who were the other two? Jefferson evidently made oral bequests of freedom as well. Members of his family told Henry Randall that Jefferson had directed his daughter to free forty-five-year-old Wormley Hughes, if he wanted to be free. For very obvious reasons, no one in the family would report to a historian an oral instruction from Jefferson to free Sally Hemings if she wanted it. Eight years after her father's death, Martha Randolph directed that two of her father's slaves, Sally Hemings and Wormley Hughes, and one of her own Randolph slaves, Betsy, the wife of Peter Hemings, be given 'their time,' even though all had been living as free people since Jefferson's death." (Ibid.)

749 GAVE SALLY HEMINGS "HER TIME" Ibid. " 'Giving time' was a customary way of emancipation that avoided having to make a request to the legislature or county court to allow the enslaved person to remain in the state," wrote Gordon-Reed. (Ibid.)

749 SHE BEQUEATHED SOME MEMENTOS Ibid., 653.

749 THE LOTTERY HE HAD HOPED JHT, VI, 496.

749 BETWEEN $1 MILLION AND $2 MILLION TJF,

http://www.monticello.org/site/research-and
-collections/debt (accessed 2012).

749 MONTICELLO AND HIS SLAVES HAD TO BE SOLD
Gordon-Reed, **Hemingses of Monticello,**
655–62. (Gordon-Reed rightly describes the
post-Jefferson Monticello as "the final catastro-
phe." [Ibid., 655.]) See also Randall, **Jefferson,**
III, 561–63; **JHT, VI,** 504–14; and Crawford,
Twilight at Monticello, 247–61. For an account
of the fate of the Monticello mansion itself, see
Marc Leepson, **Saving Monticello: The Levy
Family's Epic Quest to Rescue the House That
Jefferson Built** (New York, 2001).

749 "VISIBLE AND PALPABLE MARKS" **Diary of John
Quincy Adams,** 360.

749 ONE MORNING BEFORE BREAKFAST Robert V.
Remini, **Daniel Webster: The Man and His
Time** (New York, 1997), 263. Webster described
how he wrote the speech to Millard Fillmore.
(Ibid.)

750 ON A BEAUTIFUL DAY IN BOSTON Ibid., 264.

750 "ON OUR FIFTIETH ANNIVERSARY" **The Writings and Speeches of Daniel Webster,** I, 289.

750 "THOMAS JEFFERSON SURVIVES" McCullough,
John Adams, 646. The manuscript source is
Susan Boylston Adams Clark to Abigail Louisa
Smith Adams Johnson, July 9, 1826, A. B. John-
son Papers, Massachusetts Historical Society.

EPILOGUE · All Honor to Jefferson

751 "JEFFERSON'S PRINCIPLES ARE SOURCES OF LIGHT" Woodrow Wilson, **College and State Educational Literary and Political Papers (1875–1913)**, II, ed. Ray Stannard Baker and William E. Dodd (New York, 1925), 428.

751 HE SURVIVES AS HE LIVED Jack N. Rakove, "Our Jefferson" in Lewis and Onuf, **Sally Hemings and Thomas Jefferson**, 210. "Jefferson remains alive for us—'us' being both scholars and the public—to an extent and with an attractive power that none of his contemporaries can rival: not Madison, with his more deeply probing intellect; not Washington, struggling with the importance of being George; not even Franklin, the other self-fashioned sage whose inner life rivals Jefferson's in its elusiveness." (Ibid., 210.)

751 "TO HAVE BEEN THE INSTRUMENT" Edward Everett, **An Address Delivered at Charlestown, August 1, 1826, In Commemoration of John Adams and Thomas Jefferson** (Boston, 1826), 134.

752 "MR. JEFFERSON MEANT" Merrill D. Peterson, **The Jefferson Image in the American Mind** (Charlottesville, Va., 1998), 284.

752 ELLEN WAYLES COOLIDGE WAS EN ROUTE Ellen Wayles Coolidge to Henry S. Randall, May 16, 1857, Correspondence of Ellen Wayles Coolidge, University of Virginia Library. Extract published at Papers of Thomas Jefferson Retirement Series

Digital Archive, http://www.monticello.org/fam
ilyletters (accessed 2012).

754 "If Jefferson was wrong"   Parton, **Life**, iii.

755 "Man . . . feels that"   TJ to Joseph C. Cabell,
February 2, 1816, Extract published at Papers of
Thomas Jefferson Retirement Series Digital Archive, http://www.monticello.org/familyletters
(accessed 2012).

756 "The leadership he sought"   Henry Adams,
History, 363.

757 "The principles of Jefferson"   **The Collected Works of Abraham Lincoln**, III, ed.
Roy P. Basler (New Brunswick, N.J., 1953–55),
375–76. The letter is dated April 6, 1859.

758 "All honor to Jefferson"   Ibid., 376.

758 "It is not necessary for us"   Franklin D.
Roosevelt, "Address at Jefferson Day Dinner in
St. Paul, Minnesota," April 18, 1932, The American Presidency Project, http://www.presidency
.ucsb.edu/ws/index.php?pid=88409   (accessed
2012).

759 In September 1948, at the Bonham High
School   Harry S. Truman, "Address at Bonham, Texas," September 27, 1948, The American Presidency Project, http://www.presidency
.ucsb.edu/ws/?pid=13021 (accessed 2012).

759 "I have a profound faith"   Ibid.

760 Saluting Jefferson's "transforming genius"
Ronald Reagan, "Remarks and a Question-and-
Answer Session at the University of Virginia in
Charlottesville," December 16, 1988, The Amer-

ican Presidency Project, http://www.presidency
.ucsb.edu/ws/?pid=35272 (accessed 2012).

761 "PRESIDENTS KNOW ABOUT THIS" Ibid.

761 "HE KNEW HOW" Ibid.

762 ACHIEVEMENTS HE ORDERED CARVED TJ, un-
dated memorandum on epitaph, Thomas Jefferson Papers, LOC.

763 "AND I HAVE OBSERVED" TJ to William Ludlow, September 6, 1824. Extract published at
Papers of Thomas Jefferson Retirement Series
Digital Archive, http://www.monticello.org/fam
ilyletters (accessed 2012).

763 HE WAS BORNE Bear, "Last Few Days in the
Life of Thomas Jefferson," 65.

763 WHEN DUSK COMES I am an indebted to Fraser D. Neiman of Monticello, who generously
checked my observation that the cemetery remained in sunlight longer than Shadwell, the
Rivanna, Monticello itself, Mulberry Row, and
the main gardens and orchards.

Fraser and his team ran a solar radiation
simulation in a geographical information system (ArcGIS), using a digital elevation model
of Monticello Mountain and the surrounding
topography, including Montalto. The simulation took into account the effects of topography. The simulation estimated the amount of
solar radiation that hit the ground surface between the hours of seven and eight p.m. on July
6, 1826. The result showed that the ground surface at the cemetery remains in direct sunlight

after the ground surfaces around the mansion and around the houses on Mulberry Row have passed into shadow. The northwestern slope of the mountain is the only portion of Jefferson's five thousand acres that remain in light after the cemetery itself passes into shadow.

BIBLIOGRAPHY

MANUSCRIPT COLLECTIONS

Adams Family Papers, Massachusetts Historical Society, Boston

Baldwin Family Papers, Manuscripts and Archives, Yale University Library, New Haven, Conn.

Breckinridge Family Papers, Library of Congress, Washington, D.C.

Colonel John Brown and Major General Preston Brown Papers, Manuscripts and Archives, Yale University Library, New Haven, Conn.

Aaron Burr Papers, New York Public Library

William A. Burwell Papers, Library of Congress, Washington, D.C.

Clark Family Collection, Missouri History Museum, St. Louis

Coolidge Collection of Thomas Jefferson Manuscripts, Massachusetts Historical Society, Boston

Correspondance politique/Affaires politiques jusqu'en 1896: des États-Unis, Archives des affaires étrangères, La Courneuve, France

Correspondence of Ellen Wayles Randolph Coolidge, Special Collections, University of Virginia Library, University of Virginia, Charlottesville, Va.

The David Library of the American Revolution, Washington Crossing, Penn.

Henry Dearborn Papers, Massachusetts Historical Society, Boston

Robley Dunglison Papers, College of Physicians of Philadelphia, Philadelphia

Edgehill-Randolph Papers, Special Collections, University of Virginia Library, University of Virginia, Charlottesville, Va.

William Eustis Papers, Library of Congress, Washington, D.C.

Augustus Foster Papers, Library of Congress, Washington, D.C.

Albert Gallatin Papers, New-York Historical Society

John Work Garrett Library, Johns Hopkins University, Baltimore

Gratz Collection, Historical Society of Pennsylvania, Philadelphia

The Huntington Library, San Marino, Calif.

Andrew Jackson Papers, Library of Congress, Washington, D.C.

Thomas Jefferson Papers, Library of Congress, Washington, D.C.

Papers of Thomas Jefferson, Editorial Files, Princeton University, Princeton, N.J.

Papers of Thomas Jefferson: Retirement Series, Thomas Jefferson Foundation, http://www.monticello.org/site/research-and-collections/papers (accessed March 25, 2012)

Papers of Thomas Jefferson: Retirement Series Digital Archive, Thomas Jefferson Foundation, www.monticello.org/familyletters (accessed March 25, 2012)

Jessup Family Foundations, Archives of Ontario, Toronto

Edward Jessup Papers, Archives of Ontario, Toronto

William Griswold Lane Memorial Collection, Manuscripts and Archives, Yale University Library, New Haven, Conn.

Rufus King Papers, New-York Historical Society

Levi Lincoln Papers, Massachusetts Historical Society, Boston

Literary and historical manuscripts, Pierpont Morgan Library, New York, N.Y.

Matthew Livingston Davis Papers, New-York Historical Society, New York, N.Y.

The Loyalist Collection, University of New Brunswick, Fredericton, New Brunswick

James Madison Papers, Library of Congress, Washington, D.C.

James Madison Papers, New York Public Library

James Monroe Papers, Library of Congress, Washington, D.C.

James Monroe Papers, New York Public Library

National Archives of the United Kingdom, FO 5/14 and 32–58, 353/30 and 60, Kew, Richmond, Surrey, London.

Joseph H. Nicholson Papers, Library of Congress, Washington, D.C.

Harrison Gray Otis Papers, Massachusetts Historical Society, Boston

Timothy Pickering Papers, Massachusetts Historical Society, Boston

William Dummer Powell and Family Collection, Library and Archives, Ottawa, Ontario

John Randolph of Roanoke Papers, Library of Congress, Washington, D.C.

Russell Family Papers, Archives of Ontario, Toronto

John Rutledge Papers, Southern Historical Collection, Wilson Library, University of North Carolina at Chapel Hill

John Graves Simcoe Papers, Devon Record Office, Exeter, Devon, United Kingdom

Simcoe Family Foundations, Archives of Ontario, Toronto

Samuel Smith Family Papers, Library of Congress, Washington, D.C.

Albert W. Whelpley Autographs Collection, Cincinnati Museum Center

BOOKS CONSULTED

Abernethy, Thomas P. **A History of the South**. Vol. 4, **The South in the New Nation, 1789–1819**. Baton Rouge: Louisiana State University Press, 1961.

———. **Western Lands and the American Revolution**. New York: Russell and Russell, 1959. First published in 1937 by D. Appleton-Century.

Achenbach, Joel. **The Grand Idea: George Washington's Potomac and the Race to the West**. New York: Simon and Schuster, 2004.

Ackerman, Bruce. **The Failure of the Founding Fathers: Jefferson, Marshall, and the Rise of Presi-**

dential Democracy. Cambridge, Mass.: Belknap Press of Harvard University Press, 2007.

————. We the People. Vol. 1, Foundations. Cambridge, Mass.: Belknap Press of Harvard University Press, 1991.

Adair, Douglass. Fame and the Founding Fathers: Essays. Edited by Trevor Colbourn. Indianapolis: Liberty Fund, 1998. First published in 1974 by W. W. Norton.

Adams, Daniel. Geography; or, A Description of the World. 5th ed. Boston: Lincoln and Edmands, 1820.

Adams, Henry. Documents Relating to New-England Federalism: 1800–1815. Boston: Little, Brown, 1905.

————. History of the United States of America During the Administrations of Thomas Jefferson. Edited by Earl N. Harbert. The Library of America, no. 31. New York: Literary Classics of the United States, 1986.

————. The Life of Albert Gallatin. Philadelphia: J. B. Lippincott, 1880. Reprint, LaVergne, Tenn.: Kessinger, 2009. Page numbers are to the 2009 edition.

Adams, John. The Political Writings of John Adams. Edited by George Wescott Carey. Conservative Leadership Series, no. 6. Washington, D.C.: Regnery, 2000.

————. The Works of John Adams, Second President of the United States: With a Life of the Author, Notes, and Illustrations, by His Grandson

Charles Francis Adams. 10 vols. Boston: Little, Brown, 1850–56.

Adams, John Quincy. **The Diary of John Quincy Adams, 1794–1845: American Political, Social, and Intellectual Life from Washington to Polk**. Edited by Allan Nevins. American Classics. New York: Frederick Ungar, 1969. First published in 1928 by Longmans, Green.

———. **Memoirs of John Quincy Adams, Comprising Portions of His Diary from 1795 to 1848**. Edited by Charles Francis Adams. 12 vols. Philadelphia: J. B. Lippincott, 1874–77.

Adams, William Howard. **The Paris Years of Thomas Jefferson**. New Haven, Conn.: Yale University Press, 2000.

———, ed. **The Eye of Thomas Jefferson**. Charlottesville, Va.: Thomas Jefferson Memorial Foundation, 1992. First published in 1976 by the National Gallery of Art.

Albanese, Catherine L. **Sons of the Fathers: The Civil Religion of the American Revolution**. Philadelphia: Temple University Press, 1976.

Allen, Thomas B. **Tories: Fighting for the King in America's First Civil War**. New York: HarperCollins, 2010.

Allgor, Catherine. **A Perfect Union: Dolley Madison and the Creation of the American Nation**. New York: Henry Holt, 2006.

Allison, Robert J. **The Crescent Obscured: The United States and the Muslim World, 1776–1815**. New York: Oxford University Press, 1995.

Ames, Fisher. **Works of Fisher Ames: With a Selection from His Speeches and Correspondence**. Edited by Seth Ames. Vol. 1. Boston: Little, Brown, 1854.

Ammon, Harry. **James Monroe: The Quest for National Identity**. Charlottesville: University Press of Virginia, 1990. First published in 1971 by McGraw-Hill.

Anderson, Dice Robins. **William Branch Giles: A Study in the Politics of Virginia and the Nation from 1790 to 1830**. Menasha, Wis.: George Banta, 1914. Reprint, LaVergne, Tenn.: BiblioBazaar, 2010.

Anderson, Fred. **Crucible of War: The Seven Years' War and the Fate of Empire in British North America, 1754–1766**. New York: Vintage Books, 2001.

Anderson, William L., ed. **Cherokee Removal: Before and After**. Athens: University of Georgia Press, 1991.

Andrews, Charles M. **The Colonial Background of the American Revolution: Four Essays in American Colonial History**. Rev. ed. New Haven, Conn.: Yale University Press, 1931.

Andrews, William L., ed. **Journeys in New Worlds: Early American Women's Narratives**. Wisconsin Studies in American Autobiography. Madison: University of Wisconsin Press, 1990.

Appleby, Joyce. **Liberalism and Republicanism in the Historical Imagination**. Cambridge, Mass.: Harvard University Press, 1992.

———. **Thomas Jefferson**. The American Presidents. New York: Times Books, 2003.

Archer, Richard. **As If an Enemy's Country: The British Occupation of Boston and the Origins of Revolution**. New York: Oxford University Press, 2010.

Armitage, David. **The Declaration of Independence: A Global History**. Cambridge, Mass.: Harvard University Press, 2007.

Bailyn, Bernard. **The Ideological Origins of the American Revolution**. Enlarged ed. Cambridge, Mass.: Belknap Press of Harvard University Press, 1992.

————. **The Origins of American Politics**. Charles K. Colver Lectures, Brown University. New York: Alfred A. Knopf, 1968.

————. **To Begin the World Anew: The Genius and Ambiguities of the American Founders**. New York: Alfred A. Knopf, 2003.

Bakeless, John. **Background to Glory: The Life of George Rogers Clark**. Philadelphia: J. B. Lippincott, 1957.

Balogh, Brian. **A Government Out of Sight: The Mystery of National Authority in Nineteenth-Century America**. Cambridge: Cambridge University Press, 2009.

Banning, Lance. **The Jeffersonian Persuasion: Evolution of a Party Ideology**. Ithaca, N.Y.: Cornell University Press, 1978.

————. **The Sacred Fire of Liberty: James Madison and the Founding of the Federal Republic**. Ithaca, N.Y.: Cornell University Press, 1995.

Baron, Robert C., and Conrad Edick Wright, eds.

The Libraries, Leadership, and Legacy of John Adams and Thomas Jefferson. Boston: Massachusetts Historical Society, 2010.

Barratt, Carrie Rebora, and Ellen G. Miles. Gilbert Stuart. New Haven, Conn.: Yale University Press, 2004.

Bayard, James A. Letters of James Asheton Bayard, 1802–1814. Letters to Caesar A. Rodney. Papers of the Historical Society of Delaware, no. 31. Wilmington: Historical Society of Delaware, 1901.

————. Papers of James A. Bayard, 1796–1815. Edited by Elizabeth Donnan. New York: Da Capo Press, 1971. First published in 1915 by the Government Printing Office.

Bear, James A., Jr., ed. Jefferson at Monticello. Charlottesville: University of Virginia Press, 1967.

Becker, Carl. The Declaration of Independence: A Study in the History of Political Ideas. New York: Vintage Books, 1970. First published in 1942 by Alfred A. Knopf.

Beckley, John James. Justifying Jefferson: The Political Writings of John James Beckley. Edited by Gerard W. Gawalt. Washington, D.C.: Library of Congress, 1995.

Beeman, Richard R. Patrick Henry: A Biography. New York: McGraw-Hill, 1974.

————. Plain, Honest Men: The Making of the American Constitution. New York: Random House, 2009.

Beiswanger, William L., Peter J. Hatch, Lucia Stanton, and Susan R. Stein. Thomas Jefferson's Monticello. Chapel Hill: University of North Carolina Press, 2001.

Belknap, Michal R., ed. **American Political Trials**. Contributions in American History, no. 94. Westport, Conn.: Greenwood Press, 1981.

Bemis, Samuel Flagg. **Jay's Treaty: A Study in Commerce and Diplomacy**. Rev. ed. New Haven, Conn.: Yale University Press, 1962.

Beran, Michael Knox. **Jefferson's Demons: Portrait of a Restless Mind**. New York: Free Press, 2003.

Bercovitch, Savan, ed. **The Cambridge History of American Literature**. Vol. 1, **1590–1820**. Cambridge: Cambridge University Press, 1997.

Berlin, Ira. **Many Thousands Gone: The First Two Centuries of Slavery in North America**. Cambridge, Mass.: Belknap Press of Harvard University Press, 1998.

Bernstein, R. B. **Thomas Jefferson**. New York: Oxford University Press, 2005.

———. **Thomas Jefferson: The Revolution of Ideas**. Oxford Portraits. New York: Oxford University Press, 2004.

Beschloss, Michael. **Presidential Courage: Brave Leaders and How They Changed America 1789–1989**. New York: Simon and Schuster, 2007.

Beveridge, Albert J. **The Life of John Marshall**. 4 vols. Boston: Houghton Mifflin, 1916–19.

Binder, Frederick M. **The Color Problem in Early National America as Viewed by John Adams, Jefferson, and Jackson**. Studies in American History, no. 7. The Hague: Mouton, 1969.

Black, Jeremy. **Crisis of Empire: Britain and America in the Eighteenth Century**. London: Continuum, 2008.

———. **From Louis XIV to Napoleon: The Fate of a Great Power**. London: UCL Press, 1999.

Blackburn, Joyce. **George Wythe of Williamsburg**. New York: Harper and Row, 1975.

Blakeley, Phyllis R, and John N. Grant, eds. **Eleven Exiles: Accounts of Loyalists of the American Revolution**. Toronto: Dundurn Press, 1982.

Bobrick, Benson. **Angel in the Whirlwind: The Triumph of the American Revolution**. New York: Simon and Schuster, 1997.

Bodley, Temple. **George Rogers Clark: His Life and Public Services**. Boston: Houghton Mifflin, 1926.

Boles, John B., and Randal L. Hall, eds. **Seeing Jefferson Anew: In His Time and Ours**. Charlottesville: University of Virginia Press, 2010.

Borden, Morton. **The Federalism of James A. Bayard**. Columbia Studies in the Social Sciences, no. 584. New York: Columbia University Press, 1955.

Bowers, Claude G. **Jefferson and Hamilton: The Struggle for Democracy in America**. Boston: Houghton Mifflin, 1966.

———. **Jefferson in Power: The Death Struggle of the Federalists**. Boston: Houghton Mifflin, 1936.

Boyd, Julian P. **Number 7: Alexander Hamilton's Secret Attempts to Control American Foreign Policy, with Supporting Documents**. Princeton, N.J.: Princeton University Press, 1964.

Boyer, Paul S., and Melvyn Dubofsky, eds. **The Oxford Companion to United States History. New York: Oxford University Press, 2001.

Brant, Irving. Impeachment: Trials and Errors. New York: Knopf, 1972.

Breen, T. H. American Insurgents, American Patriots: The Revolution of the People. New York: Hill and Wang, 2010.

———. Tobacco Culture: The Mentality of the Great Tidewater Planters on the Eve of Revolution. Princeton, N.J.: Princeton University Press, 1987.

Bridenbaugh, Carl. The Spirit of '76: The Growth of American Patriotism Before Independence. New York: Oxford University Press, 1975.

Brodie, Fawn M. Thomas Jefferson: An Intimate History. New York: W. W. Norton, 1998.

Brookhiser, Richard. James Madison. New York: Basic Books, 2011.

Brown, Imogene E. American Aristides: A Biography of George Wythe. Rutherford, N.J.: Fairleigh Dickinson University Press, 1981.

Brown, Kathleen M. Good Wives, Nasty Wenches, and Anxious Patriarchs: Gender, Race, and Power in Colonial Virginia. Chapel Hill: Published for the Institute of Early American History and Culture by the University of North Carolina Press, 1996.

Brown, Robert E., and B. Katherine Brown. Virginia, 1705–1786: Democracy or Aristocracy? East Lansing: Michigan State University Press, 1964.

Brown, Wallace. The Good Americans: The Loyalists in the American Revolution. New York: William Morrow, 1969.

———. The King's Friends: The Composition and Motives of the American Loyalist Claimants. Providence, R.I.: Brown University Press, 1965.

Brown, Wallace, and Hereward Senior. Victorious in Defeat: The American Loyalists in Exile. New York: Facts on File, 1984.

Bruce, William Cabell. John Randolph of Roanoke, 1773–1833: A Biography Based Largely on New Material. 2 vols. New York: G. P. Putnam's Sons, 1922.

Brymner, Douglas. Report on Canadian Archives, 1890. Ottawa: Brown Chamberlin, 1891.

Buel, Richard, Jr. America on the Brink: How the Political Struggle Over the War of 1812 Almost Destroyed the Young Republic. New York: Palgrave Macmillan, 2005.

Bullock, Helen Duprey. My Head and My Heart: A Little History of Thomas Jefferson and Maria Cosway. New York: G. P. Putnam's Sons, 1945.

Burgh, James. Political Disquisitions; or, An Enquiry into Public Errors, Defects, and Abuses. 3 vols. American Revolutionary War Series. Carlisle, Mass.: Applewood Books, 2009. First published in 1774–75 by E. and C. Dilly.

Burke, Edmund. The Writings and Speeches of Edmund Burke. Edited by Paul Langford. Vol. 2. Oxford: Clarendon Press, 1980.

Burns, James MacGregor. The Vineyard of Liberty.

The American Experiment. New York: Alfred A. Knopf, 1982.

Burstein, Andrew. **Jefferson's Secrets: Death and Desire at Monticello**. New York: Basic Books, 2005.

Burstein, Andrew, and Nancy Isenberg. **Madison and Jefferson**. New York: Random House, 2010.

Burt, Alfred LeRoy. **The Evolution of the British Empire and Commonwealth, from the American Revolution**. Boston: Heath, 1956.

Burton, Louis W. **Annals of Henrico Parish**. Edited by J. Staunton Moore. Richmond, Va.: Williams Printing, 1904.

Bushnell, Eleanore. **Crimes, Follies, and Misfortunes: The Federal Impeachment Trials**. Urbana: University of Illinois Press, 1992.

Butterfield, L. H., Wendell D. Garrett, and Marjorie E. Sprague, eds. **Adams Family Correspondence**. 10 vols. to date. The Adams Papers. 2d ser. Cambridge, Mass.: Belknap Press of Harvard University Press, 1963–.

Byrd, William. **The Commonplace Book of William Byrd II of Westover**. Edited by Kevin Berland, Jan Kirsten Gilliam, and Kenneth A. Lockridge. Chapel Hill: Published for the Omohundro Institute of Early American History and Culture, Williamsburg, Va., by the University of North Carolina Press, 2001.

Calhoon, Robert M. **The Loyalist Perception and Other Essays,** Columbia: University of South Carolina Press, 1989.

———. **The Loyalists in Revolutionary America,**

1760–1781. The Founding of the American Republic. New York: Harcourt Brace Jovanovich, 1973.

Cappon, Lester J., ed. **The Adams-Jefferson Letters: The Complete Correspondence Between Thomas Jefferson and Abigail and John Adams**. Chapel Hill: Published for the Omohundro Institute of Early American History and Culture, Williamsburg, Va., by the University of North Carolina Press, 1987. First published in 1959 by the University of North Carolina Press.

Carter, Susan B. **Historical Statistics of the United States: Earliest Times to the Present**. Millennial ed. 5 vols. Cambridge: Cambridge University Press, 2006.

Cerami, Charles A. **Jefferson's Great Gamble: The Remarkable Story of Jefferson, Napoleon and the Men Behind the Louisiana Purchase**. Naperville, Ill.: Sourcebooks, 2003.

Chadwick, Bruce. **I Am Murdered: George Wythe, Thomas Jefferson, and the Killing That Shocked a New Nation**. Hoboken, N.J.: John Wiley and Sons, 2009.

Chernow, Ron. **Alexander Hamilton**. New York: Penguin Press, 2004.

———. **Washington: A Life**. New York: Penguin Press, 2010.

Chinard, Gilbert. **Thomas Jefferson: The Apostle of Americanism**. 2d ed., rev. Ann Arbor: University of Michigan Press, 1966. First published in 1929 by Little, Brown.

Cogliano, Francis D. **Thomas Jefferson: Reputation**

and Legacy. Jeffersonian America. Charlottesville: University of Virginia Press, 2006.

————, ed. **A Companion to Thomas Jefferson**. Oxford: Wiley-Blackwell, 2011.

Colbourn, Trevor. **The Lamp of Experience: Whig History and the Intellectual Origins of the American Revolution**. Indianapolis: Liberty Fund, 1998. First published in 1965 by the University of North Carolina Press.

Colbourn, Trevor, and James T. Patterson, eds. **The American Past in Perspective**. Vol. 1, **To 1877**. Boston: Allyn and Bacon, 1970.

Collins, Varnum Lansing. **The Continental Congress at Princeton**. Whitefish, Mont.: Kessinger, 2005. First published in 1908 by the Princeton University Library.

Conway, Stephen. **The British Isles and the War of American Independence**. New York: Oxford University Press, 2000.

Corwin, Edward S., Randall W. Bland, Theodore T. Hindson, and Jack W. Peltason. **The President: Office and Powers, 1787–1984; History and Analysis of Practice and Opinion**. 5th rev. ed. New York: New York University Press, 1984.

Côté, Richard N. **Strength and Honor: The Life of Dolley Madison**. Mt. Pleasant, S.C.: Corinthian Books, 2005.

Cotlar, Seth. **Tom Paine's America: The Rise and Fall of Transatlantic Radicalism in the Early Republic**. Jeffersonian America. Charlottesville: University of Virginia Press, 2011.

Cousins, Norman, ed. "In God We Trust": The Religious Beliefs and Ideas of the American Founding Fathers. New York: Harper and Brothers, 1958.

Crawford, Alan Pell. Twilight at Monticello: The Final Years of Thomas Jefferson. New York: Random House, 2008.

Cruikshank, E. A., ed. The Correspondence of Lieut. Governor John Graves Simcoe: With Allied Documents Relating to His Administration of the Government of Upper Canada. 5 vols. Toronto: Ontario Historical Society, 1923–31.

Cunliffe, Marcus. American Presidents and the Presidency. 2d ed., rev. and enlarged. New York: McGraw-Hill, 1976.

————. George Washington: Man and Monument. Rev. ed. A Mentor Book. New York: New American Library, 1982. First published in 1958 by Little, Brown.

Cunningham, Noble E. The Jeffersonian Republicans in Power: Party Operations, 1801–1809. Chapel Hill: Published for the Institute of Early American History and Culture at Williamsburg, Virginia, by the University of North Carolina Press, 1963.

————. The Jeffersonian Republicans: The Formation of Party Organization, 1789–1801. Chapel Hill: Published for the Institute of Early American History and Culture at Williamsburg, Virginia, by the University of North Carolina Press, 1957.

Curley, Thomas M. Samuel Johnson, the Ossian Fraud and the Celtic Revival in Great Britain and

Ireland. Cambridge: Cambridge University Press, 2009.

Cutler, William Parker, and Julia Perkins Cutler. **Life, Journals and Correspondence of Rev. Manasseh Cutler, LL.D.** 2 vols. Cincinnati: Robert Clarke, 1888. Reprint, LaVergne, Tenn.: Kessinger, 2009.

Dangerfield, George. **The Awakening of American Nationalism, 1815–1828.** The New American Nation Series. New York: Harper and Row, 1965.

Daniels, Jonathan. **The Randolphs of Virginia.** Garden City, N.Y.: Doubleday, 1972.

Daughan, George C. **1812: The Navy's War.** New York: Basic Books, 2011.

Dawson, Matthew Q. **Partisanship and the Birth of America's Second Party, 1796–1800: Stop the Wheels of Government.** Contributions in Political Science, no. 387. Westport, Conn.: Greenwood Press, 2000.

DeConde, Alexander. **This Affair of Louisiana.** New York: Charles Scribner's Sons, 1976.

Dewey, Davis Rich. **Financial History of the United States,** 8th ed. New York: Longmans, Green and Company, 1922.

Dewey, Frank L. **Thomas Jefferson, Lawyer.** Charlottesville: University Press of Virginia, 1987.

Dickerson, Oliver M. **The Navigation Acts and the American Revolution.** Philadelphia: University of Pennsylvania Press, 1951.

Dickinson, H. T., ed. **Britain and the American Revolution.** London: Addison Wesley Longman, 1998.

Dill, Alonzo Thomas. **Carter Braxton, Virginia**

Signer: A Conservative in Revolt. Lanham, Md.: University Press of America, 1983.

Donaldson, Thomas. **The House in Which Thomas Jefferson Wrote the Declaration of Independence**. Philadelphia: Avil Printing, 1898.

Dowd, Gregory Evans. **War Under Heaven: Pontiac, the Indian Nations, and the British Empire**. Baltimore: Johns Hopkins University Press, 2004.

Dowdey, Clifford. **The Virginia Dynasties: The Emergence of "King" Carter and the Golden Age**. Boston: Little, Brown, 1969.

Downes, Paul. **Democracy, Revolution, and Monarchism in Early American Literature**. Cambridge: Cambridge University Press, 2002.

Doyle, William. **The Oxford History of the French Revolution**. 2d ed. New York: Oxford University Press, 2002.

Dreisbach, Daniel L. **Thomas Jefferson and the Wall of Separation Between Church and State**. Critical America. New York: New York University Press, 2002.

Dunbar, Louise Burnham. **A Study of "Monarchical" Tendencies in the United States from 1776 to 1801**. New York: Johnson Reprint Corp., 1970. First published in 1922 by the University of Illinois.

Dunglison, Robley. **Medical Lexicon: A Dictionary of Medical Science**. 5th ed. Philadelphia: Lea and Blanchard, 1845.

Dunn, Susan. **Jefferson's Second Revolution: The Election Crisis of 1800 and the Triumph of Republicanism**. Boston: Houghton Mifflin, 2004.

Eckenrode, H. J. The Randolphs: The Story of a Virginia Family. Indianapolis: Bobbs-Merrill, 1946.

Edling, Max M. A Revolution in Favor of Government: Origins of the U.S. Constitution and the Making of the American State. New York: Oxford University Press, 2003.

Elkins, Stanley, and Eric McKitrick. The Age of Federalism. New York: Oxford University Press, 1993.

Ellis, Joseph J. American Creation: Triumphs and Tragedies at the Founding of the Republic. New York: Alfred A. Knopf, 2007.

————. American Sphinx: The Character of Thomas Jefferson. New York: Alfred A. Knopf, 1997.

————. Passionate Sage: The Character and Legacy of John Adams. New York: W. W. Norton, 1993.

Ellis, Richard E. The Jeffersonian Crisis: Courts and Politics in the Young Republic. New York: Oxford University Press, 1971.

————. The Union at Risk: Jacksonian Democracy, States' Rights, and the Nullification Crisis. New York: Oxford University Press, 1989.

Evans, Dorinda. The Genius of Gilbert Stuart. Princeton, N.J.: Princeton University Press, 1999.

Everett, Edward. An Address Delivered at Charlestown, August 1, 1826, in Commemoration of John Adams and Thomas Jefferson. Boston: W. L. Lewis, 1826.

Fatton, Robert, Jr., and R. K. Ramazani, eds. Religion, State, and Society: Jefferson's Wall of Separation in Comparative Perspective. New York: Palgrave Macmillan, 2009.

Fauquier, Francis. **The Official Papers of Francis Fauquier, Lieutenant Governor of Virginia, 1758–1768**. Edited by George Reese. 3 vols. Charlottesville: University Press of Virginia for the Virginia Historical Society, 1980–83.

Feigenbaum, Gail. **Jefferson's America and Napoleon's France: An Exhibition for the Louisiana Purchase Bicentennial**. Edited by Victoria Cooke. New Orleans: New Orleans Museum of Art, 2003.

Ferguson, Robert A. **The American Enlightenment, 1750–1820**. Cambridge, Mass.: Harvard University Press, 1997.

Ferling, John. **Adams vs. Jefferson: The Tumultuous Election of 1800**. Pivotal Moments in American History. New York: Oxford University Press, 2004.

———. **Almost a Miracle: The American Victory in the War of Independence**. New York: Oxford University Press, 2009.

———. **Independence: The Struggle to Set America Free**. New York: Bloomsbury Press, 2011.

———. **Setting the World Ablaze: Washington, Adams, Jefferson, and the American Revolution**. New York: Oxford University Press, 2000.

Field, James A., Jr. **America and the Mediterranean World, 1776–1882**. Princeton, N.J.: Princeton University Press, 1969.

Fischer, David Hackett. **America, a Cultural History**. Vol. 1, **Albion's Seed: Four British Folkways in America**. New York: Oxford University Press, 1989.

———. **Paul Revere's Ride**. New York: Oxford University Press, 1994.

———. **Washington's Crossing**. Pivotal Moments in American History. New York: Oxford University Press, 2004.

Flavell, Julie. **When London Was Capital of America**. New Haven, Conn.: Yale University Press, 2010.

Flexner, James Thomas. **George Washington and the New Nation, 1783–1793**. Boston: Little, Brown, 1970.

Flower, Milton E. **John Dickinson: Conservative Revolutionary**. Charlottesville: Published for the Friends of the John Dickinson Mansion by the University Press of Virginia, 1983.

Foner, Eric. **The Story of American Freedom**. New York: W. W. Norton, 1998.

Foner, Philip S., ed. **The Democratic-Republican Societies, 1790–1800: A Documentary Sourcebook of Constitutions, Declarations, Addresses, Resolutions, and Toasts**. Westport, Conn.: Greenwood Press, 1976.

Forbes, Robert Pierce. **The Missouri Compromise and Its Aftermath: Slavery and the Meaning of America**. Chapel Hill: University of North Carolina Press, 2007.

Forsythe, David P., ed. **Encyclopedia of Human Rights**. Vol. 1, **Afghanistan—Democracy and Right to Participation**. New York: Oxford University Press, 2009.

Franklin, Benjamin. **A Benjamin Franklin Reader**. Edited by Walter Isaacson. New York: Simon and Schuster, 2003.

Freeman, Douglas Southall, John Alexander Carroll, and Mary Wells Ashworth. **George Washington: A Biography.** 7 vols. New York: Charles Scribner's Sons, 1948–57.

Freeman, Joanne B. **Affairs of Honor: National Politics in the New Republic.** New Haven, Conn.: Yale Nota Bene, 2002.

Fremont-Barnes, Gregory. **The Wars of the Barbary Pirates: To the Shores of Tripoli; The Rise of the US Navy and Marines.** Essential Histories, no. 66. Oxford: Osprey, 2006.

Fremont-Barnes, Gregory, Richard Alan Ryerson, James Arnold, and Roberta Wiener, eds. **The Encyclopedia of the American Revolutionary War: A Political, Social, and Military History.** 5 vols. Santa Barbara, Calif.: ABC-CLIO, 2006.

Frey, Sylvia R. **Water from the Rock: Black Resistance in a Revolutionary Age.** Princeton, N.J.: Princeton University Press, 1991.

Fryer, Mary Beacock, and Christopher Dracott. **John Graves Simcoe, 1752–1806: A Biography.** Toronto: Dundurn Press, 1998.

Gaines, James R. **For Liberty and Glory: Washington, Lafayette, and Their Revolutions.** New York: W. W. Norton, 2007.

Gallatin, Albert. **Biographical Memoir of Albert Gallatin.** New York: J. and H. G. Langley, 1843. Reprint, LaVergne, Tenn.: Kessinger, 2009. Page numbers are to the 2009 edition.

———. **Report of the Secretary of the Treasury, or**

the Subject of Public Roads and Canals, Made in Pursuance of a Resolution of Senate of March 2d, 1807. Washington, D.C.: William A. Davis, 1816.

———. Selected Writings of Albert Gallatin. Edited by E. James Ferguson. The American Heritage Series. Indianapolis: Bobbs-Merrill, 1967.

Gardner, Jared. Master Plots: Race and the Founding of an American Literature, 1787–1845. Baltimore: Johns Hopkins University Press, 1998.

Gaustad, Edwin S. Faith of the Founders: Religion and the New Nation, 1776–1826. Waco, Tex.: Baylor University Press, 2004. Reprint of 2d edition, which was published in 1993 as Neither King Nor Prelate: Religion and the New Nation, 1776–1826 by William B. Eerdmans.

———. Sworn on the Altar of God: A Religious Biography of Thomas Jefferson. Library of Religious Biography. Grand Rapids, Mich.: William B. Eerdmans, 1996.

Gibbs, George. Memoirs of the Administrations of Washington and John Adams, Edited from the Papers of Oliver Wolcott, Secretary of the Treasury. 2 vols. New York: Printed for the Subscribers [W. Van Norden, Printer], 1846.

Gillespie, Michael Allen. The Theological Origins of Modernity. Chicago: University of Chicago Press, 2008.

Gipson, Lawrence Henry. The British Empire Before the American Revolution. 15 vols. New York: Alfred A. Knopf, 1939–70.

Godson, Susan H. The College of William and

Mary: A History. 2 vols. Williamsburg, Va.: King and Queen Press, Society of the Alumni, College of William and Mary in Virginia, 1993.

Goldsmith, William M. **The Growth of Presidential Power: A Documented History**. Vol. 1, **The Formative Years**. New York: Chelsea House, 1974.

Gordon-Reed, Annette. **The Hemingses of Monticello: An American Family**. New York: W. W. Norton, 2008.

———. **Thomas Jefferson and Sally Hemings: An American Controversy**. Charlottesville: University Press of Virginia, 1997.

Gorn, Elliott J., Randy Roberts, and Terry D. Bilhartz, eds. **Constructing the American Past: A Source Book of a People's History**. 5th ed. Vol. 1. New York: Pearson / Longman, 2005.

Gould, Eliga H. **The Persistence of Empire: British Political Culture in the Age of the American Revolution**. Chapel Hill: Published for the Omohundro Institute of Early American History and Culture, Williamsburg, Va., by the University of North Carolina Press, 2000.

Gould, Eliga H., and Peter S. Onuf, eds. **Empire and Nation: The American Revolution in the Atlantic World**. Anglo-America in the Transatlantic World. Baltimore: Johns Hopkins University Press, 2005.

Green, Michael D. **The Politics of Indian Removal: Creek Government and Society in Crisis**. Lincoln: University of Nebraska Press, 1982.

Greene, Jack P. **The Quest for Power: The Lower Houses of Assembly in the Southern Royal Colo-**

nies, 1689–1776. New York: W. W. Norton, 1972. First published in 1963 by the University of North Carolina Press.

Griffin, Patrick. **American Leviathan: Empire, Nation, and Revolutionary Frontier**. New York: Hill and Wang, 2007.

Halliday, E. M. **Understanding Thomas Jefferson**. New York: HarperCollins, 2001.

Hamilton, Alexander. **The Papers of Alexander Hamilton**. Edited by Harold C. Syrett and Jacob E. Cooke. 27 vols. New York: Columbia University Press, 1961–87.

———. **Writings**. The Library of America, no. 129. New York: Literary Classics of the United States, 2001.

Hammond, John Craig. **Slavery, Freedom, and Expansion in the Early American West**. Jeffersonian America. Charlottesville: University of Virginia Press, 2007.

Harrell, Isaac Samuel. **Loyalism in Virginia: Chapters in the Economic History of the Revolution**. Duke University Publications. Durham, N.C.: Duke University Press, 1926.

Harrison, Lowell H. **George Rogers Clark and the War in the West**. Lexington: University Press of Kentucky, 1976.

Hast, Adele. **Loyalism in Revolutionary Virginia: The Norfolk Area and the Eastern Shore**. Studies in American History and Culture, no. 34. Ann Arbor, Mich.: UMI Research Press, 1982.

Hatch, Nathan O. **The Sacred Cause of Liberty: Republican Thought and the Millennium in Revolutionary New England**. New Haven, Conn.: Yale University Press, 1977.

Hatfield, April Lee. **Atlantic Virginia: Intercolonial Relations in the Seventeenth Century**. Philadelphia: University of Pennsylvania Press, 2003.

Hayes, Kevin J. **The Road to Monticello: The Life and Mind of Thomas Jefferson**. New York: Oxford University Press, 2008.

Hazelton, John H. **The Declaration of Independence: Its History**. New York: Da Capo Press, 1970. First published in 1906 by Dodd, Mead.

Herring, George C. **From Colony to Superpower: U.S. Foreign Relations Since 1776**. The Oxford History of the United States. New York: Oxford University Press, 2008.

Higginbotham, Don. **War and Society in Revolutionary America: The Wider Dimensions of Conflict**. American Military History. Columbia: University of South Carolina Press, 1988.

Hitchens, Christopher. **Thomas Paine's Rights of Man**. Books That Changed the World. New York: Atlantic Monthly Press, 2006.

Hoffman, Ronald, and Peter J. Albert, eds. **Sovereign States in an Age of Uncertainty**. Perspectives on the American Revolution. Charlottesville: Published for the United States Capitol Historical Society by the University Press of Virginia, 1981.

Hofstadter, Richard. **The American Political Tradi-**

tion and the Men Who Made It. New York: Vintage Books, 1989. First published in 1948 by Alfred A. Knopf.

———. Anti-Intellectualism in American Life. New York: Vintage Books, 1963.

———. The Idea of a Party System: The Rise of Legitimate Opposition in the United States, 1780–1840. Jefferson Memorial Lectures. Berkeley: University of California Press, 1969.

———. The Paranoid Style in American Politics and Other Essays. Cambridge, Mass.: Harvard University Press, 1996. First published in 1965 by Alfred A. Knopf.

Hogeland, William. Declaration: The Nine Tumultuous Weeks When America Became Independent, May 1–July 4, 1776. New York: Simon and Schuster, 2010.

———. The Whiskey Rebellion: George Washington, Alexander Hamilton, and the Frontier Rebels Who Challenged America's Newfound Sovereignty. New York: Simon and Schuster, 2006.

Holton, Woody. Abigail Adams. New York: Free Press, 2010.

———. Forced Founders: Indians, Debtors, Slaves, and the Making of the American Revolution in Virginia. Chapel Hill: Published for the Omohundro Institute of Early American History and Culture, Williamsburg, Va., by the University of North Carolina Press, 1999.

Hooper, Robert. Quincy's Lexicon-Medicum: A

New Medical Dictionary. Philadelphia: E. and R. Parker, Griggs, 1817.

Hormats, Robert D. The Price of Liberty: Paying for America's Wars. New York: Times Books, 2007.

Horn, James. Adapting to a New World: English Society in the Seventeenth-Century Chesapeake. Chapel Hill: Published for the Institute of Early American History and Culture, Williamsburg, Va., by the University of North Carolina Press, 1994.

Horn, James, Jan Ellen Lewis, and Peter S. Onuf, eds. The Revolution of 1800: Democracy, Race, and the New Republic. Jeffersonian America. Charlottesville: University of Virginia Press, 2002.

Horn, Joan L. Thomas Jefferson's Poplar Forest: A Private Place. Forest, Va.: Corporation for Jefferson's Poplar Forest, 2002.

Horwitz, Robert H., ed. The Moral Foundations of the American Republic. 3d ed. Charlottesville: University Press of Virginia, 1986.

Howard, Hugh. Houses of the Founding Fathers. New York: Artisan, 2007.

Howe, Daniel Walker. What Hath God Wrought: The Transformation of America, 1815–1848. The Oxford History of the United States. New York: Oxford University Press, 2007.

Hunt, Lynn. Inventing Human Rights: A History. New York: W. W. Norton, 2007.

Hyland, William G., Jr. In Defense of Thomas Jefferson: The Sally Hemings Sex Scandal. New York: Thomas Dunne Books, 2009.

Imbarrato, Susan Clair. **Declarations of Independency in Eighteenth-Century American Autobiography**. Knoxville: University of Tennessee Press, 1998.

Irving, Washington. **George Washington: A Biography**. Abridged and edited by Charles Neider. Garden City, N.Y.: Doubleday, 1976. First published in 5 volumes from 1855–59 by G. P. Putnam.

Isaacson, Walter. **Benjamin Franklin: An American Life**. New York: Simon and Schuster, 2003.

Isenberg, Nancy. **Fallen Founder: The Life of Aaron Burr**. New York: Penguin Books, 2008.

Jackson, Donald. **Thomas Jefferson and the Stony Mountains: Exploring the West from Monticello**. Norman: University of Oklahoma Press, 1993. First published in 1981 by the University of Illinois Press.

Jacob, Margaret, and James Jacob, eds. **The Origins of Anglo-American Radicalism**. London: Allen and Unwin, 1984.

Jacoby, Susan. **Freethinkers: A History of American Secularism**. New York: Metropolitan Books, 2004.

Jasanoff, Maya. **Liberty's Exiles: American Loyalists in the Revolutionary World**. New York: Alfred A. Knopf, 2011.

Jayne, Allen. **Jefferson's Declaration of Independence: Origins, Philosophy, and Theology**. Lexington: University Press of Kentucky, 1998.

Jefferson, Thomas. **The Complete Anas of Thomas Jefferson**. Edited by Franklin B. Sawvel. New York: Round Table Press, 1903. Reprint, LaVergne, Tenn.: BiblioLife, 2009. Page numbers are to the 2009 edition.

———. **Jefferson Abroad.** Edited by Douglas L. Wilson and Lucia Stanton. New York: Modern Library, 1999.

———. **The Jefferson Bible: The Life and Morals of Jesus of Nazareth.** Boston: Beacon Press, 1989. First published in 1904 by the Government Printing Office.

———. **The Jefferson Bible: The Life and Morals of Jesus of Nazareth, Extracted Textually from the Gospels in Greek, Latin, French and English.** With essays by Harry R. Rubenstein, Barbara Clark Smith, and Janice Stagnitto Ellis. Washington, D.C.: Smithsonian Books, 2011.

———. **Jefferson's Extracts from the Gospels: "The Philosophy of Jesus" and "The Life and Morals of Jesus."** Edited by Dickinson W. Adams and Ruth W. Lester. The Papers of Thomas Jefferson. 2d ser. Princeton, N.J.: Princeton University Press, 1983.

———. **Jefferson's Literary Commonplace Book.** Edited by Douglas L. Wilson. The Papers of Thomas Jefferson. 2d ser. Princeton, N.J.: Princeton University Press, 1989.

———. **Jefferson's Memorandum Books: Accounts, with Legal Records and Miscellany, 1767–1826.** Edited by James A. Bear, Jr., and Lucia C. Stanton. 2 vols. The Papers of Thomas Jefferson. 2d ser. Princeton, N.J.: Princeton University Press, 1997.

———. **Light and Liberty: Reflections on the Pursuit of Happiness.** Edited by Eric S. Petersen. New York: Modern Library, 2004.

———. **The Papers of Thomas Jefferson.** Edited by

Julian P. Boyd and others. 38 vols. to date. Princeton, N.J.: Princeton University Press, 1950–.

———. **The Papers of Thomas Jefferson. Retirement Series.** Edited by J. Jefferson Looney and others. 8 vols. to date. Princeton, N.J.: Princeton University Press, 2004–.

———. **Thomas Jefferson's Farm Book: With Commentary and Relevant Extracts from Other Writings.** Edited by Edwin Morris Betts. Charlottesville: University Press of Virginia, 1976. First published in 1953 by Princeton University Press.

———. **Thomas Jefferson's Garden Book, 1766–1824: With Relevant Extracts from His Other Writings.** Edited by Edwin Morris Betts. Philadelphia: American Philosophical Society, 1944.

———. **The Words of Thomas Jefferson.** Charlottesville, Va: Thomas Jefferson Foundation, 2008.

———. **Writings.** Edited by Merrill D. Peterson. The Library of America, no. 17. New York: Literary Classics of the United States, 1984.

———. **The Writings of Thomas Jefferson.** Edited by Paul Leicester Ford. 10 vols. New York: G. P. Putnam's Sons, 1892–99. Reprint, LaVergne, Tenn.: Kessinger, 2009.

Johnstone, Robert M., Jr. **Jefferson and the Presidency: Leadership in the Young Republic.** Ithaca, N.Y.: Cornell University Press, 1978.

Jones, Howard Muford. **America and French Culture, 1750–1848.** Westport, Conn.: Greenwood Press, 1973. First published in 1927 by the University of North Carolina Press.

Jones, Hugh. **The Present State of Virginia**. London: Printed for J. Clarke, 1724.

Jones, Robert F. **George Washington**. Rev. ed. New York: Fordham University Press, 1986.

Jordan, Daniel P. **Political Leadership in Jefferson's Virginia**. Charlottesville: University Press of Virginia, 1996.

Kaminski, John P. **The Great Virginia Triumvirate: George Washington, Thomas Jefferson, and James Madison in the Eyes of Their Contemporaries**. Charlottesville: University of Virginia Press, 2010.

———, ed. **The Founders on the Founders: Word Portraits from the American Revolutionary Era**. Charlottesville: University of Virginia Press, 2008.

Kaplan, Lawrence S. **Jefferson and France: An Essay on Politics and Political Ideas**. Westport, Conn.: Greenwood Press, 1980. First published in 1967 by Yale University Press.

Kastor, Peter J. **The Great Acquisition: An Introduction to the Louisiana Purchase**. Great Falls, Mont.: Lewis and Clark Interpretive Association, 2003.

Kern, Susan. **The Jeffersons at Shadwell**. The Lamar Series in Western History. New Haven, Conn.: Yale University Press, 2010.

Ketcham, Ralph. **James Madison: A Biography**. Charlottesville: University Press of Virginia, 1990. First published in 1971 by Macmillan.

———, ed. **The Anti-Federalist Papers and the Constitutional Convention Debates**. New York: Signet Classic, 2003.

Ketchum, Richard M. **Divided Loyalties: How the**

American Revolution Came to New York. New York: Henry Holt, 2002.

Kidd, Thomas S. Patrick Henry: First Among Patriots. New York: Basic Books, 2011.

Kierner, Cynthia A. Martha Jefferson Randolph, Daughter of Monticello: Her Life and Times. Chapel Hill: University of North Carolina Press, 2012.

————. Scandal at Bizarre: Rumor and Reputation in Jefferson's America. New York: Palgrave Macmillan, 2004.

Kimball, Marie. Jefferson: The Road to Glory, 1743–1776. New York: Coward-McCann, 1943.

————. Jefferson: The Scene of Europe, 1784–1789. New York: Coward-McCann, 1950.

————. Jefferson: War and Peace, 1776–1784. New York: Coward-McCann, 1947.

————. Thomas Jefferson's Cook Book. Charlottesville: University Press of Virginia, 1976.

King, Rufus. The Life and Correspondence of Rufus King: Comprising His Letters, Private and Official, His Public Documents, and His Speeches. 6 vols. Edited by Charles R. King. New York: Da Capo Press, 1971. First published in 1894–1900 by G. P. Putnam's Sons.

Koch, Adrienne. The Philosophy of Thomas Jefferson. Chicago: Quadrangle Books, 1964. First published in 1943 by Columbia University Press.

Kolodny, Annette. The Land Before Her: Fantasy and Experience of the American Frontiers, 1630–

1860. Chapel Hill: University of North Carolina Press, 1984.

Kranish, Michael. **Flight from Monticello: Thomas Jefferson at War**. New York: Oxford University Press, 2010.

Kukla, Jon. **Mr. Jefferson's Women**. New York: Alfred A. Knopf, 2007.

————. **A Wilderness So Immense: The Louisiana Purchase and the Destiny of America**. New York: Anchor Books, 2004.

Labaree, Leonard Woods. **Conservatism in Early American History**. Ithaca, N.Y.: Cornell University Press, 1965. First published in 1948 by New York University Press.

LaCroix, Alison L. **The Ideological Origins of American Federalism**. Cambridge, Mass.: Harvard University Press, 2010.

Lambert, Frank. **The Barbary Wars: American Independence in the Atlantic World**. New York: Hill and Wang, 2005.

Lancaster, Bruce. **The American Heritage Book of the Revolution**. Edited by Richard M. Ketchum. New York: American Heritage, 1958.

Lancaster, Robert A., Jr. **Historic Virginia Homes and Churches**. Philadelphia: J. B. Lippincott, 1915.

Landau, Barry H. **The President's Table: Two Hundred Years of Dining and Diplomacy**. New York: Collins, 2007.

Langguth, A. J. **Patriots: The Men Who Started**

the American Revolution. New York: Simon and Schuster, 1988.

————. Union 1812: The Americans Who Fought the Second War of Independence. New York: Simon and Schuster, 2006.

Leavitt, Judith Walzer. Brought to Bed: Childbearing in America, 1750 to 1950. New York: Oxford University Press, 1986.

Lee, Henry. Observations on the Writings of Thomas Jefferson: With Particular Reference to the Attack They Contain on the Memory of the Late Gen. Henry Lee; In a Series of Letters. N.p.: Nabu Press, 2010. First published in 1832 by C. De Behr.

Leepson, Marc. Saving Monticello: The Levy Family's Epic Quest to Rescue the House That Jefferson Built. Charlottesville: University of Virginia Press, 2001.

Lemire, Elise. "Miscegenation": Making Race in America. Philadelphia: University of Pennsylvania Press, 2002.

Levy, Andrew. The First Emancipator: The Forgotten Story of Robert Carter, the Founding Father Who Freed His Slaves. New York: Random House, 2005.

Levy, Leonard W. Jefferson and Civil Liberties: The Darker Side. Elephant paperback ed. Chicago: Ivan R. Dee, 1989. First published in 1963 by Harvard University Press.

————. Origins of the Bill of Rights. Contemporary Law Series. New Haven, Conn.: Yale University Press, 1999.

Lewis, Jan Ellen, and Peter S. Onuf, eds. **Sally Hemings and Thomas Jefferson: History, Memory, and Civic Culture**. Jeffersonian America. Charlottesville: University of Virginia Press, 1999.

Lincoln, Abraham. **The Collected Works of Abraham Lincoln**. Edited by Roy P. Basler. 9 vols. New Brunswick, N.J.: Rutgers University Press, 1953–55.

Link, Eugene P. **Democratic-Republican Societies, 1790–1800**. New York: Octagon Books, 1973. First published in 1942 by Columbia University Press.

Lucas, Sir Charles Prestwood. **A History of Canada, 1763–1812**. Oxford: Clarendon Press, 1909.

Lukes, Steven, ed. **Power**. Readings in Social and Political Theory. New York: New York University Press, 1986.

Lyon, E. Wilson. **The Man Who Sold Louisiana: The Career of François Barbé-Marbois**. Norman: University of Oklahoma Press, 1942.

Mackenzie, Alexander. **Voyages from Montreal, on the River St. Laurence: Through the Continent of North America, to the Frozen and Pacific Oceans; In the Years 1789 and 1793**. 2 vols. in 1. New York: W. B. Gilley, 1814.

Mackie, John Milton. **John Milton Mackie's "The Administration of President Washington."** Edited by Frank E. Grizzard, Jr. Buena Vista, Va.: Mariner, 2006.

Maclay, William. **The Journal of William Maclay, United States Senator from Pennsylvania, 1789–1791**. American Classics. New York: F. Ungar,

1965. Reprinted from the 1927 edition by A. and C. Boni; first published in 1890 by D. A. Appleton.

Madison, Dolley. **The Selected Letters of Dolley Payne Madison.** Edited by David B. Mattern and Holly C. Shulman. Charlottesville: University of Virginia Press, 2003.

Madison, James. **James Madison: A Biography in His Own Words.** Edited by Merrill D. Peterson. 2 vols. The Founding Fathers. New York: Newsweek, 1974.

———. **The Papers of James Madison: Presidential Series.** Edited by Robert A. Rutland and others. 6 vols. to date. Charlottesville: University Press of Virginia, 1984–.

Maier, Pauline. **American Scripture: Making the Declaration of Independence.** New York: Alfred A. Knopf, 1997.

———. **Ratification: The People Debate the Constitution, 1787–1788.** New York: Simon and Schuster, 2010.

Malone, Dumas. **Jefferson and His Time.** 6 vols. Boston: Little, Brown, 1948–81. Vol. 1, **Jefferson the Virginian,** 1948. Vol. 2, **Jefferson and the Rights of Man,** 1951. Vol. 3, **Jefferson and the Ordeal of Liberty,** 1962. Vol. 4, **Jefferson the President: First Term, 1801–1805,** 1970. Vol. 5, **Jefferson the President: Second Term, 1805–1809,** 1974. Vol. 6, **The Sage of Monticello,** 1981.

———. **Thomas Jefferson as Political Leader.** Jefferson Memorial Lectures. Berkeley: University of California Press, 1963.

Mapp, Alf J., Jr. Thomas Jefferson: Passionate Pilgrim; The Presidency, the Founding of the University, and the Private Battle. Lanham, Md.: Rowman and Littlefield, 2008. First published in 1991 by Madison Books.

Marshall, John. The Papers of John Marshall. Edited by Herbert A. Johnson and others. 12 vols. to date. Chapel Hill: University of North Carolina Press, 1974–.

———. Writings. Edited by Charles F. Hobson. The Library of America, no. 198. New York: Library of America, 2010.

Marshall, P. J. The Making and Unmaking of Empires: Britain, India, and America, c. 1750–1783. New York: Oxford University Press, 2005.

Matrana, Marc R. Lost Plantations of the South. Jackson: University Press of Mississippi, 2009.

Matthew, H. C. G., and Brian Harrison, eds., Oxford Dictionary of National Biography: In Association with the British Academy; From the Earliest Times to the Year 2000. New York: Oxford University Press, 2004.

Matthews, Richard K. The Radical Politics of Thomas Jefferson: A Revisionist View. Lawrence: University Press of Kansas, 1984.

May, Henry F. The Enlightenment in America. New York: Oxford University Press, 1976.

Mayer, David N. The Constitutional Thought of Thomas Jefferson. Constitutionalism and Democracy. Charlottesville: University Press of Virginia, 1994.

Mayer, Henry. **All on Fire: William Lloyd Garrison and the Abolition of Slavery**. New York: St. Martin's Press, 1998.

———. **A Son of Thunder: Patrick Henry and the American Republic**. New York: Grove Press, 2001. First published in 1986 by Franklin Watts.

McClinton, Arthur T., and J. Winston Coleman, Francis F. Wayland, John Walter Wayland, and Thomas Lewis. **The Fairfax Line: A Historic Landmark**. Edinburg, Va.: Shenandoah County Historical Society, 1990. First published in 1925 by Henkel Press.

McConville, Brendan. **The King's Three Faces: The Rise and Fall of Royal America, 1688–1776**. Chapel Hill: Published for the Omohundro Institute of Early American History and Culture, Williamsburg, Va., by the University of North Carolina Press, 2006.

McCormick, Richard P. **The Presidential Game: The Origins of American Presidential Politics**. New York: Oxford University Press, 1982.

McCoy, Drew R. **The Elusive Republic: Political Economy in Jeffersonian America**. Chapel Hill: Published for the Institute of Early American History and Culture, Williamsburg, Va., by the University of North Carolina Press, 1980.

———. **The Last of the Fathers: James Madison and the Republican Legacy**. Cambridge: Cambridge University Press, 1989.

McCullough, David. **The Greater Journey: Americans in Paris**. New York: Simon and Schuster, 2011.

———. **John Adams**. New York: Simon and Schuster, 2001.

———. **1776**. New York: Simon and Schuster, 2005.

McDonald, Forrest. **The Presidency of Thomas Jefferson**. American Presidency Series. Lawrence: University Press of Kansas, 1976.

———. **States' Rights and the Union: Imperium in Imperio, 1776–1876**. American Political Thought. Lawrence: University Press of Kansas, 2000.

McDonnell, Michael A. **The Politics of War: Race, Class, and Conflict in Revolutionary Virginia**. Chapel Hill: Published for the Omohundro Institute of Early American History and Culture, Williamsburg, Va., by the University of North Carolina Press, 2007.

McDougall, Walter A. **Freedom Just Around the Corner: A New American History, 1585–1828**. New York: HarperCollins, 2004.

McPherson, James M., ed. **"To the Best of My Ability": The American Presidents**. Rev. U.S. ed. New York: DK, 2004.

Meacham, Jon. **American Gospel: God, the Founding Fathers, and the Making of a Nation**. New York: Random House, 2006.

Meade, Robert Douthat. **Patrick Henry: Practical Revolutionary**. Philadelphia: J. B. Lippincott, 1969.

Meckler, Michael, ed. **Classical Antiquity and the Politics of America: From George Washington to George W. Bush**. Waco, Tex.: Baylor University Press, 2006.

Merli, Frank J., and Theodore A. Wilson, eds. **Makers**

of American Diplomacy, from Benjamin Franklin to Henry Kissinger. 2 vols. New York: Charles Scribner's Sons, 1974.

Merrill, Boynton, Jr. **Jefferson's Nephews: A Frontier Tragedy**. Lincoln: University of Nebraska Press, 2004. First published in 1976 by Princeton University Press.

Middlekauff, Robert. The **Glorious Cause: The American Revolution, 1763–1789**. Rev. and expanded ed. The Oxford History of the United States. New York: Oxford University Press, 2005.

Milkis, Sidney M., and Michael Nelson. **The American Presidency: Origins and Development, 1776–2007**. 5th ed. Washington, D.C.: CQ Press, 2008.

Miller, Douglas T. **The Birth of Modern America, 1820–1850**. New York: Pegasus, 1970.

Miller, John C. **The Federalist Era, 1789–1801**. Prospect Heights, Ill.: Waveland Press, 1998. First published in 1960 by Harper and Row.

———. **The Wolf by the Ears: Thomas Jefferson and Slavery**. Charlottesville: Thomas Jefferson Memorial Foundation and the University Press of Virginia, 1991. First published in 1977 by the Free Press.

Miller, William Lee. **The First Liberty: America's Foundation in Religious Freedom**. Expanded and updated ed. Washington, D.C.: Georgetown University Press, 2003.

Monroe, James. **The Papers of James Monroe**. Edited by Daniel Preston and Marlena C. DeLong. 4 vols. to date. Westport, Conn.: Greenwood Press, 2003–.

Montross, Lynn. The Reluctant Rebels: The Story of the Continental Congress, 1774–1789. New York: Harper and Brothers, 1950.

Moody, William B. B. Monarchism in America. Livermore, Calif.: WingSpan Press, 2009.

Moore, Christopher. The Loyalists: Revolution, Exile, Settlement. Toronto: Macmillan of Canada, 1984.

Moore, John Hammond. Albemarle, Jefferson's County, 1727–1976. Charlottesville: Published for the Albemarle County Historical Society by the University Press of Virginia, 1976.

Moore, Roy, and Alma Moore. Thomas Jefferson's Journey to the South of France. New York: Stewart, Tabori and Chang, 1999.

Morgan, Edmund S. American Slavery, American Freedom: The Ordeal of Colonial Virginia. New York: W. W. Norton, 1975.

———. The Birth of the Republic, 1763–89. Rev. ed. Chicago History of American Civilization, no. 14. Chicago: University of Chicago Press, 1977.

———. The Gentle Puritan: A Life of Ezra Stiles, 1727–1795. New Haven, Conn.: Published for the Institute of Early American History and Culture, Williamsburg, Va., by Yale University Press, 1962.

———. Inventing the People: The Rise of Popular Sovereignty in England and America. New York: W. W. Norton, 1988.

———. Virginians at Home: Family Life in the Eighteenth Century. Williamsburg in America Series, no. 2. Charlottesville, Va: Dominion Books, 1963.

First published in 1952 by Colonial Williamsburg, Williamsburg, Va.

Morgan, Edmund S., and Helen M. Morgan. **The Stamp Act Crisis: Prologue to Revolution**. With a new preface by Edmund S. Morgan. Chapel Hill: Published for the Institute of Early American History and Culture at Williamsburg, Va., by the University of North Carolina Press, 1995. First published in 1953 by the University of North Carolina Press.

Morton, Louis. **Robert Carter of Nomini Hall: A Virginia Tobacco Planter of the Eighteenth Century**. Charlottesville, Va.: Dominion Books, 1969. First published in 1941 by Colonial Williamsburg, Williamsburg, Va.

Morton, Richard L. **Colonial Virginia**. Vol. 2, **Westward Expansion and Prelude to Revolution, 1710–1763**. Chapel Hill: Published for the Virginia Historical Society by the University of North Carolina Press, 1960.

Mullin, Gerald W. **Flight and Rebellion: Slave Resistance in Eighteenth-Century Virginia**. New York: Oxford University Press, 1972.

Murrin, John M., and others. **Liberty, Equality, Power: A History of the American People**. 6th ed. Boston: Wadsworth Cengage Learning, 2012.

Myers, Gustavus. **The History of Tammany Hall**. Ann Arbor: University of Michigan Library, 2005. First published in 1901 by the author.

Myers, Margaret G. **A Financial Hisotry of the United States**. New York: Columbia University Press, 1970.

Nagel, Paul C. **John Quincy Adams: A Public Life, a Private Life**. New York: Alfred A. Knopf, 1997.

Nash, Gary B. **The Unknown American Revolution: The Unruly Birth of Democracy and the Struggle to Create America**. New York: Viking, 2005.

Neely, Sylvia. **A Concise History of the French Revolution**. Lanham, Md.: Rowman and Littlefield, 2008.

Nelson, Craig. **Thomas Paine: Enlightenment, Revolution, and the Birth of Modern Nations**. New York: Viking, 2006.

Nelson, Michael, ed. **The Presidency and the Political System**. Washington, D.C.: CQ Press, 1984.

Nelson, William H. **The American Tory**. Oxford: Clarendon Press, 1961.

Newmyer, R. Kent. **John Marshall and the Heroic Age of the Supreme Court**. Baton Rouge: Louisiana State University Press, 2001.

Niven, John. **Martin Van Buren: The Romantic Age of American Politics**. New York: Oxford University Press, 1983.

Noll, Mark A. **America's God: From Jonathan Edwards to Abraham Lincoln**. New York: Oxford University Press, 2002.

Norton, Mary Beth. **The British-Americans: The Loyalist Exiles in England, 1774–1789**. Boston: Little, Brown, 1972.

———. **Liberty's Daughters: The Revolutionary Experience of American Women, 1750–1800**. Ithaca, N.Y.: Cornell University Press, 1996.

Novak, Michael. **Choosing Presidents: Symbols**

of Political Leadership. 2d ed. New Brunswick, N.J.: Transaction, 1992. Rev. ed. of Choosing Our King: Powerful Symbols in Presidential Politics, published in 1974 by Macmillan.

Nugent, Walter. Habits of Empire: A History of American Expansion. New York: Alfred A. Knopf, 2008.

O'Brien, Conor Cruise. The Long Affair: Thomas Jefferson and the French Revolution, 1785–1800. Chicago: University of Chicago Press, 1996.

O'Lalor, Peter Joseph. The Never Realized Republic: Political Economy and Republican Virtue. 2d ed., rev. N.p.: Booksurge, 2005.

Onuf, Peter S. Jefferson's Empire: The Language of American Nationhood. Jeffersonian America. Charlottesville: University Press of Virginia, 2000.

———. The Mind of Thomas Jefferson. Charlottesville: University of Virginia Press, 2007.

———. Statehood and Union: A History of the Northwest Ordinance. Midwestern History and Culture. Bloomington: Indiana University Press, 1987.

———, ed. Congress and the Confederation. Vol. 4 of The New American Nation, 1775–1820. New York: Garland, 1991.

———, ed. Jeffersonian Legacies. Charlottesville: University Press of Virginia, 1993.

Onuf, Peter S., and Nicholas P. Cole, eds. Thomas Jefferson, the Classical World, and Early America. Jeffersonian America. Charlottesville: University of Virginia Press, 2011.

Onuf, Peter S., and Nicholas Onuf. **Federal Union, Modern World: The Law of Nations in an Age of Revolutions, 1776–1814.** Madison, Wis.: Madison House, 1993.

Onuf, Peter S., and Leonard J. Sadosky. **Jeffersonian America.** Problems in American History, no. 5. Malden, Mass.: Blackwell, 2002.

Osborne, J. A. **Williamsburg in Colonial Times: Incidents in the Lives of the English Colonists in Virginia During the 17th and 18th Centuries as Revealed in Old Documents and Files of "The Virginia Gazette."** Richmond, Va.: Dietz Press, 1936.

Paine, Thomas. **Collected Writings.** The Library of America, no. 76. New York: Library of America, 1995.

Palmer, Gregory. **Biographical Sketches of Loyalists of the American Revolution.** Westport, Conn.: Meckler, 1984. Rev. ed. of the 2d ed. of work by Lorenzo Sabine and published in 1864 by Little, Brown.

———, ed. **A Bibliography of Loyalist Source Material in the United States, Canada, and Great Britain.** Westport, Conn.: Meckler, 1982.

Palmer, R. R. **The Age of the Democratic Revolution: A Political History of Europe and America, 1760–1800.** 2 vols. Princeton, N.J.: Princeton University Press, 1965.

Parent, Anthony S., Jr. **Foul Means: The Formation of a Slave Society in Virginia, 1660–1740.** Chapel Hill: Published for the Omohundro Institute of Early American History and Culture, Williamsburg, Va., by the University of North Carolina Press, 2003.

Parkman, Francis. **Montcalm and Wolfe: The French and Indian War.** With a foreword by C. Vann Woodward. New York: Da Capo Press, 1995. First published in 1884 by Little, Brown.

Parton, James. **Life of Thomas Jefferson.** The American Scene, Comments and Commentators. New York: Da Capo Press, 1971. First published in 1874 as **Life of Thomas Jefferson, Third President of the United States** by J. R. Osgood.

Pasley, Jeffrey L. **"The Tyranny of Printers": Newspaper Politics in the Early American Republic.** Jeffersonian America. Charlottesville: University of Virginia Press, 2003.

Patterson, C. Perry. **Presidential Government in the United States: The Unwritten Constitution.** Chapel Hill: University of North Carolina Press, 1947.

Perkins, Bradford. **Prologue to War: England and the United States, 1805–1812.** Berkeley: University of California Press, 1961.

Peterson, Merrill D. **The Great Triumvirate: Webster, Clay, and Calhoun.** New York: Oxford University Press, 1987.

———. **The Jefferson Image in the American Mind.** Charlottesville: Thomas Jefferson Memorial Foundation and the University Press of Virginia, 1998. First published in 1960 by Oxford University Press.

———. **Thomas Jefferson and the New Nation: A Biography.** New York: Oxford University Press, 1970.

————, ed. **Visitors to Monticello**. Charlottesville: University Press of Virginia, 1989.

Phillips, Kevin. **The Cousins' Wars: Religion, Politics, and the Triumph of Anglo-America**. New York: Basic Books, 1999.

Piecuch, Jim. **Three Peoples, One King: Loyalists, Indians, and Slaves in the Revolutionary South, 1775–1782**. Columbia: University of South Carolina Press, 2008.

Pierard, Richard V., and Robert D. Linder. **Civil Religion and the Presidency**. Grand Rapids, Mich.: Academie Books, 1988.

Pitch, Anthony S. **The Burning of Washington: The British Invasion of 1814**. Annapolis, Md.: Naval Institute Press, 1998.

Plumer, William. **William Plumer's Memorandum of Proceedings in the United States Senate, 1803–1807**. Edited by Everett Somerville Brown. New York: Da Capo Press, 1969. First published in 1923 by Macmillan.

Pocock, J. G. A. **The Machiavellian Moment: Florentine Political Thought and the Atlantic Republican Tradition**. Princeton, N.J.: Princeton University Press, 1975.

Pollak, Louis H., ed. **The Constitution and the Supreme Court: A Documentary History**. Vol. 1. Cleveland: World, 1966.

Potts, Gwynne Tuell, and Samuel W. Thomas. **George Rogers Clark: Military Leader in the Pioneer West and Locust Grove; The Croghan Homestead**

Honoring Him. Louisville, Ky.: Historic Locust Grove, 2006.

Prucha, Francis Paul. **The Great Father: The United States Government and the American Indians.** 2 vols. Lincoln: University of Nebraska Press, 1984.

Rakove, Jack N. **The Beginnings of National Politics: An Interpretive History of the Continental Congress.** New York: Alfred A. Knopf, 1979.

————. **Revolutionaries: A New History of the Invention of America.** Boston: Houghton Mifflin Harcourt, 2010.

Randall, Henry S. **The Life of Thomas Jefferson.** 3 vols. The American Scene. New York: Da Capo Press, 1972. First published in 1858 by Derby and Jackson.

Randall, Willard Sterne. **Ethan Allen: His Life and Times.** New York: W. W. Norton, 2011.

————. **George Washington: A Life.** New York: Henry Holt, 1997.

————. **Thomas Jefferson: A Life.** New York: Henry Holt, 1993.

Randolph, John. **Considerations on the Present State of Virginia.** Edited by E. G. Swem. Heartman's Historical Series, no. 32. New York: C. F. Heartman, 1919. Reprint, LaVergne, Tenn.: BiblioLife, 2010.

————. **A Letter from the Virginia Loyalist John Randolph to Thomas Jefferson, Written in London in 1779.** Edited by Leonard L. Mackall. Reprinted from the **Proceedings of the American Antiquarian Society** for April 1920. Worcester, Mass.: American Antiquarian Society, 1921.

Randolph, Sarah N. **The Domestic Life of Thomas Jefferson**. New York: Harper and Brothers, 1871.

Reardon, John J. **Edmund Randolph: A Biography**. New York: Macmillan, 1975.

————. **Peyton Randolph, 1721–1775: One Who Presided**. Durham, N.C.: Carolina Academic Press, 1982.

Remini, Robert V. **Daniel Webster: The Man and His Time**. New York: W. W. Norton, 1997.

Reps, John W. **Tidewater Towns: City Planning in Colonial Virginia and Maryland**. Williamsburg Architectural Studies. Charlottesville: University Press of Virginia, 1972.

Richard, Carl J. **The Founders and the Classics: Greece, Rome, and the American Enlightenment**. Cambridge, Mass.: Harvard University Press, 1994.

————. **The Golden Age of the Classics in America: Greece, Rome, and the Antebellum United States**. Cambridge, Mass.: Harvard University Press, 2009.

————. **Greeks and Romans Bearing Gifts: How the Ancients Inspired the Founding Fathers**. Lanham, Md.: Rowman and Littlefield, 2009.

Richter, Daniel K. **Before the Revolution: America's Ancient Pasts**. Cambridge, Mass.: Belknap Press of Harvard University Press, 2011.

————. **Facing East from Indian Country: A Native History of Early America**. Cambridge, Mass.: Harvard University Press, 2001.

Risjord, Norman K. **Jefferson's America, 1760–1815**. 3d ed. Lanham, Md.: Rowman and Littlefield, 2010.

Rivers, Isabel, and David L. Wykes, eds. **Joseph Priestley: Scientist, Philosopher, and Theologian.** New York: Oxford University Press, 2008.

Ronda, James P. **Jefferson's West: A Journey with Lewis and Clark.** Monticello Monograph Series. Charlottesville, Va.: Thomas Jefferson Foundation, 2000.

Rosenfeld, Richard N. **American Aurora: A Democratic-Republican Returns; The Suppressed History of Our Nation's Beginnings and the Heroic Newspaper That Tried to Report It.** New York: St. Martin's Press, 1997.

Rossiter, Clinton. **The American Presidency.** Rev. ed. New York: New American Library, 1960.

Rothman, Adam. **Slave Country: American Expansion and the Origins of the Deep South.** Cambridge, Mass.: Harvard University Press, 2005.

Rothman, Joshua D. **Notorious in the Neighborhood: Sex and Families Across the Color Line in Virginia, 1787–1861.** Chapel Hill: University of North Carolina Press, 2003.

Rutland, Robert A. **George Mason: Reluctant Statesman.** Baton Rouge: Louisiana State University Press, 1980. First published in 1961 by Colonial Williamsburg, Williamsburg, Va.

———. **James Madison: The Founding Father.** Columbia: University of Missouri Press, 1997. First published in 1987 by Macmillan.

Sabine, Lorenzo. **The American Loyalists; or, Biographical Sketches of Adherents to the British**

Crown in the War of the Revolution. Boston: Charles C. Little and James Brown, 1864.

Sabine, William H. W., ed. **Historical Memoirs of William Smith**. 2 vols. New York: Arno Press, 1969. Reprint of the 3d ed., which began publication in 1956.

Sandoz, Ellis. **Political Sermons of the American Founding Era, 1730–1805**. 2 vols. Indianapolis: Liberty Fund, 1998.

Sanford, Charles B. **The Religious Life of Thomas Jefferson**. Charlottesville: University Press of Virginia, 1984.

Scadding, Henry, ed. **Letter to Sir Joseph Banks (President of the Royal Society of Great Britain) Written by Lieut.-Governor Simcoe in 1791**. Copp, Clark, 1890.

Schama, Simon. **Citizens: A Chronicle of the French Revolution**. New York: Vintage Books, 1990.

———. **Rough Crossings: Britain, the Slaves and the American Revolution**. New York: Ecco, 2006.

Scharff, Virginia. **The Women Jefferson Loved**. New York: Harper, 2010.

Scheer, George F., and Hugh F. Rankin. **Rebels and Redcoats**. New York: World, 1957.

Schlesinger, Arthur M., Jr. **War and the American Presidency**. New York: W. W. Norton, 2004.

Scholten, Catherine M. **Childbearing in American Society, 1650–1850**. The American Social Experience Series, no. 2. New York: New York University Press, 1985.

Schwartz, Marie Jenkins. **Birthing a Slave: Motherhood and Medicine in the Antebellum South**. Cambridge, Mass.: Harvard University Press, 2006.

Scott, K. Anthony. **Thomas Jefferson and Alexander Hamilton: A Defining Political Debate**. Boca Raton, Fla.: Universal, 2008.

Seale, William. **The President's House: A History**. Vol. 1. Washington, D.C.: White House Historical Association with the cooperation of the National Geographic Society, 1986.

Sears, Louis Martin. **Jefferson and the Embargo**. Durham, N.C.: Duke University Press, 1927.

Selby, John E. **The Revolution in Virginia, 1775–1783**. Williamsburg, Va.: Colonial Williamsburg Foundation, 1988.

A Selection of Eulogies Pronounced in the Several States, in Honor of Those Illustrious Patriots and Statesmen, John Adams and Thomas Jefferson. Hartford, Conn.: D. F. Robinson, 1826. Reprint, N.p.: General Books, 2009.

Sharp, James Roger. **American Politics in the Early Republic: The New Nation in Crisis**. New Haven, Conn.: Yale University Press, 1993.

———. **The Deadlocked Election of 1800: Jefferson, Burr, and the Union in the Balance**. American Presidential Elections. Lawrence: University Press of Kansas, 2010.

Sheehan, Bernard W. **Seeds of Extinction: Jeffersonian Philanthropy and the American Indian**. New York: Published for the Institute of Early American History and Culture at Williamsburg, Va., by

W. W. Norton, 1974. First published in 1973 by the University of North Carolina Press.

Sheldon, Garrett Ward. **The Political Philosophy of Thomas Jefferson**. Baltimore: Johns Hopkins University Press, 1993.

Shepherd, Jack. **The Adams Chronicles: Four Generations of Greatness**. Boston: Little, Brown, 1975.

Sheridan, Eugene R. **Jefferson and Religion**. Charlottesville, Va.: Thomas Jefferson Memorial Foundation, 1998.

Shortt, Adam, and Arthur G. Doughty, eds. **Documents Relating to the Constitutional History of Canada, 1759–1791**. 2d and rev. ed. Vol. 2. Ottawa: J. de L. Taché, 1918.

Shuffelton, Frank, ed. **The Cambridge Companion to Thomas Jefferson**. Cambridge Companions to American Studies. Cambridge: Cambridge University Press, 2009.

Sidbury, James. **Ploughshares into Swords: Race, Rebellion, and Identity in Gabriel's Virginia, 1730–1810**. New York: Cambridge University Press, 1997.

Sidney, Algernon. **Discourses Concerning Government**. Edited by Thomas G. West. Indianapolis: Liberty Classics, 1990. First published in 1698 by J. Toland.

Simon, James F. **What Kind of Nation: Thomas Jefferson, John Marshall, and the Epic Struggle to Create a United States**. New York: Simon and Schuster, 2002.

Skowronek, Stephen. **The Politics Presidents Make: Leadership from John Adams to George Bush**.

Cambridge, Mass.: Belknap Press of Harvard University Press, 1997.

Sky, Theodore. **The National Road and the Difficult Path to Sustainable National Investment.** Lanham, Md.: University of Delaware Press, 2011.

Sloan, Herbert E. **Principle and Interest: Thomas Jefferson and the Problem of Debt.** New York: Oxford University Press, 1995.

Smelser, Marshall. **The Democratic Republic, 1801–1815.** The New American Nation Series. New York: Harper and Row, 1968.

Smith, Culver H. **The Press, Politics, and Patronage: The American Government's Use of Newspapers, 1789–1875.** Athens: University of Georgia Press, 1977.

Smith, James Morton, **Freedom's Fetters: The Alien and Sedition Laws and American Civil Liberties.** Ithaca, N.Y.: Cornell University Press, 1966.

——, ed. **The Republic of Letters: The Correspondence Between Thomas Jefferson and James Madison, 1776–1826.** 3 vols. New York: W. W. Norton, 1995.

Smith, Jean Edward. **John Marshall: Definer of a Nation.** New York: Henry Holt, 1996.

Smith, Margaret Bayard. **The First Forty Years of Washington Society in the Family Letters of Margaret Bayard Smith.** Edited by Gaillard Hunt. American Classics. New York: Frederick Ungar, 1965. First published in 1906 by Charles Scribner's Sons.

Smith, Paul H. **Loyalists and Redcoats: A Study in**

British Revolutionary Policy. Chapel Hill: Published for the Institute of Early American History and Culture at Williamsburg, Va., by the University of North Carolina Press, 1964.

———, ed. **Letters of Delegates to Congress, 1774–1789**. 26 vols. Washington, D.C.: Library of Congress, 1976–2000.

Smith, William. **The Diary and Selected Papers of Chief Justice William Smith, 1784–1793**. Edited by L. F. S. Upton. 2 vols. The Publications of the Champlain Society, nos. 41 and 42. Toronto: Champlain Society, 1963–65.

Smith-Rosenberg, Carroll. **This Violent Empire: The Birth of an American National Identity**. Chapel Hill: Published for the Omohundro Institute of Early American History and Culture, Williamsburg, Va., by the University of North Carolina Press, 2010.

Sofaer, Abraham D. **War, Foreign Affairs, and Constitutional Power: The Origins**. Cambridge, Mass.: Ballinger, 1976.

Spalding, Paul S. **Lafayette: Prisoner of State**. Columbia, S.C.: University of South Carolina Press, 2010.

Spivak, Burton. **Jefferson's English Crisis: Commerce, Embargo, and the Republican Revolution**. Charlottesville: University Press of Virginia, 1979.

Stahr, Walter. **John Jay: Founding Father**. New York: Hambledon and London, 2005.

Stanton, Lucia. **Free Some Day: The African-American Families of Monticello**. Monticello

Monograph Series. Charlottesville, Va.: Thomas Jefferson Foundation, 2000.

———. **Slavery at Monticello.** Monticello Monograph Series. Charlottesville, Va.: Thomas Jefferson Memorial Foundation, 1996.

———. **"Those Who Labor for My Happiness": Slavery at Thomas Jefferson's Monticello.** Jeffersonian America. Charlottesville: University of Virginia Press, 2012.

Stein, Susan R. **The Worlds of Thomas Jefferson at Monticello.** New York: H. N. Abrams, in association with the Thomas Jefferson Memorial Foundation, 1993.

Stevens, John Austin. **Albert Gallatin: An American Statesman.** Honolulu, Hawaii: University Press of the Pacific, 2000. First published in 1883 by Houghton, Mifflin.

Stewart, David O. **American Emperor: Aaron Burr's Challenge to Jefferson's America.** New York: Simon and Schuster, 2011.

———. **The Summer of 1787: The Men Who Invented the Constitution.** New York: Simon and Schuster, 2007.

St. John de Crèvecoeur, J. Hector. **Letters from an American Farmer; and, Sketches of Eighteenth-Century America.** Edited by Albert E. Stone. New York: Penguin Books, 1986.

Stoll, Ira. **Samuel Adams: A Life.** New York: Free Press, 2009.

Stone, Bailey. **Reinterpreting the French Revolution:**

A Global-Historical Perspective. New York: Cambridge University Press, 2002.

Sydnor, Charles S. Gentlemen Freeholders: Political Practices in Washington's Virginia. Chapel Hill: Published for the Institute of Early American History and Culture at Williamsburg, Va., by the University of North Carolina Press, 1952.

Taylor, Alan. American Colonies. The Penguin History of the United States. New York: Penguin Books, 2002.

————. The Civil War of 1812: American Citizens, British Subjects, Irish Rebels, and Indian Allies. New York: Alfred A. Knopf, 2010.

Thomas, Isaiah. The History of Printing in America: With a Biography of Printers and an Account of Newspapers. 2d ed. Edited by Marcus A. McCorison. New York: Crown, 1970.

Tise, Larry E. The American Counterrevolution: A Retreat from Liberty, 1783–1800. Mechanicsburg, Penn.: Stackpole Books, 1998.

Toll, Ian W. Six Frigates: The Epic History of the Founding of the U.S. Navy. New York: W. W. Norton, 2006.

Troy, Gil, Arthur M. Schlesinger, Jr., and Fred L. Israel, eds. History of American Presidential Elections, 1789–2008. 4th ed. Vol. 1, 1789–1868. New York: Facts on File, 2010.

Tucker, David. Enlightened Republicanism: A Study of Jefferson's "Notes on the State of Virginia." Lanham, Md.: Lexington Books, 2008.

Tucker, George. **The Life of Thomas Jefferson: Third President of the United States**. Vol. 1. London: Charles Knight, 1837. Reprint, Lexington, Ky.: Adamant Media Corp., 2006.

Tucker, Robert W., and David C. Hendrickson. **Empire of Liberty: The Statecraft of Thomas Jefferson**. New York: Oxford University Press, 1992.

Turner, Jane, ed. **The Dictionary of Art**. 34 vols. New York: Grove's Dictionaries, 1996.

Tyler, Lyon Gardiner. **Williamsburg: The Old Colonial Capital**. Richmond, Va.: Whittet and Shepperson, 1907.

Unger, Harlow Giles. **John Hancock: Merchant King and American Patriot**. New York: John Wiley and Sons, 2000.

United States National Park Service. Division of Publications. **Independence: A Guide to Independence National Historical Park, Philadelphia, Pennsylvania**. National Park Handbook, no. 115. Washington, D.C.: National Park Service, U.S. Dept. of the Interior, 1982.

Upton, L. F. S. **The Loyal Whig: William Smith of New York and Quebec**. Toronto: University of Toronto Press, 1969.

Van Buren, Martin. **The Autobiography of Martin Van Buren**. Edited by John C. Fitzpatrick. Vol. 2 of the **Annual Report of the American Historical Association for the Year 1918**. Washington, D.C.: Government Printing Office, 1920.

———. **Inquiry into the Origin and Course of Political Parties in the United States**. Reprints of

Economic Classics. New York: A. M. Kelley, 1967. First published in 1867 by Hurd and Houghton.

Varg, Paul A. **Foreign Policies of the Founding Fathers**. Baltimore: Penguin Books, 1970.

Virginia. General Assembly. House of Burgesses. **Journals of the House of Burgesses of Virginia, 1619–[1776]**. 13 vols. Volumes for 1619–1761 edited by H. R. McIlwaine; volumes for 1761–76 edited by John Pendleton Kennedy. Richmond, Va.: Colonial Press, E. Waddey, 1905–15. Reprint, LaVergne, Tenn.: BiblioLife, 2010.

Virginia History, Government, and Geography Service. **Road to Independence: Virginia, 1763–1783**. Memphis, Tenn.: General Books, 2010. First published in 1975 by the Virginia Division of Secondary Education.

Virginia Writers' Project. **Virginia: A Guide to the Old Dominion**. Richmond, Va.: Virginia State Library and Archives in cooperation with the Virginia Center for the Book, 1992. First published in 1940 by Oxford University Press.

Waldstreicher, David. **In the Midst of Perpetual Fetes: The Making of American Nationalism, 1776–1820**. Chapel Hill: Published for the Omohundro Institute of Early American History and Culture, Williamsburg, Va., by the University of North Carolina Press, 1997.

Wallace, Anthony F. C. **Jefferson and the Indians: The Tragic Fate of the First Americans**. Cambridge, Mass.: Belknap Press of Harvard University Press, 1999.

Wallace, W. Stewart. The United Empire Loyalists: A Chronicle of the Great Migration. Chronicles of Canada. Toronto: Glasgow, Brook, 1920.

Warren, Charles. Jacobin and Junto; or, Early American Politics as Viewed in the Diary of Dr. Nathaniel Ames, 1758–1822. New York: Blom, 1968. First published in 1931 by Harvard University Press.

Washburn, Wilcomb E. The Governor and the Rebel: A History of Bacon's Rebellion in Virginia. Chapel Hill: Published for the Institute of Early American History and Culture at Williamsburg, Va. by the University of North Carolina Press, 1957.

Washington, George. Writings. Edited by John H. Rhodehamel. The Library of America, no. 91. New York: Library of America, 1997.

Webster, Daniel. The Writings and Speeches of Daniel Webster. Edited by Fletcher Webster. 18 vols. Boston: Little, Brown, 1903.

Wharton, Anne Hollingsworth. Social Life in the Early Republic. Williamstown, Mass.: Corner House, 1970. First published in 1902 by J. B. Lippincott.

Wheelan, Joseph. Jefferson's Vendetta: The Pursuit of Aaron Burr and the Judiciary. New York: Carroll and Graf, 2006.

———. Jefferson's War: America's First War on Terror, 1801–1805. New York: Carroll and Graf, 2003.

White, Leonard D. The Jeffersonians: A Study in Administrative History, 1801–1829. New York: Macmillan, 1951.

Wiencek, Henry. Master of the Mountain: Thomas

Jefferson and His Slaves. New York: Farrar, Straus and Giroux, 2012.

Wilentz, Sean. Chants Democratic: New York City and the Rise of the American Working Class, 1788–1850. New York: Oxford University Press, 1984.

———. The Rise of American Democracy: Jefferson to Lincoln. New York: W. W. Norton, 2005.

———, ed. Major Problems in the Early Republic, 1787–1848: Documents and Essays. Major Problems in American History Series. Lexington, Mass.: D. C. Heath, 1992.

Wills, Garry. Inventing America: Jefferson's Declaration of Independence. America's Political Enlightenment. Garden City, N.Y.: Doubleday, 1978.

———. Negro President: Jefferson and the Slave Power. Boston: Houghton Mifflin, 2003.

Wilson, Ellen Judy. Encyclopedia of the Enlightenment. Edited by Peter Hanns Reill. New York: Facts on File, 1996.

Wilson, James. Considerations on the Nature and the Extent of the Legislative Authority of the British Parliament. Philadelphia: William and Thomas Bradford, 1774.

Wilson, Richard Guy, ed. Thomas Jefferson's Academical Village: The Creation of an Architectural Masterpiece. Rev. ed. Charlottesville: University of Virginia Press, 2009.

Wilson, Woodrow. College and State, Educational, Literary and Political Papers (1875–1913). Edited by Ray Stannard Baker and William E. Dodd. 2

vols. The Public Papers of Woodrow Wilson, Authorized Edition. New York: Harper and Brothers, 1925.

Wiltse, Charles M. The Jeffersonian Tradition in American Democracy. American Century Series. New York: Hill and Wang, 1960. First published in 1935 by the University of North Carolina Press.

Winik, Jay. The Great Upheaval: America and the Birth of the Modern World, 1788–1800. New York: HarperCollins, 2007.

Winterer, Caroline. The Culture of Classicism: Ancient Greece and Rome in American Intellectual Life, 1780–1910. Baltimore: Johns Hopkins University Press, 2004.

Wirt, William. Sketches of the Life and Character of Patrick Henry. 25th ed. Philadelphia: Claxton, Remsen and Haffelfinger, 1878.

Wister, Mrs. O. J., and Miss Agnes Irwin, eds. Worthy Women of Our First Century. Philadelphia: Lippincott, 1877.

Wood, Gordon S. The American Revolution: A History. New York: Modern Library, 2003.

———. The Creation of the American Republic, 1776–1787. Chapel Hill: Published for the Institute of Early American History and Culture at Williamsburg, Va., by the University of North Carolina Press, 1998. First published in 1969 by the University of North Carolina Press.

———. Empire of Liberty: A History of the Early Republic, 1789–1815. The Oxford History of the

United States. New York: Oxford University Press, 2009.

————. The Idea of America: Reflections on the Birth of the United States. New York: Penguin Press, 2011.

————. The Radicalism of the American Revolution. New York: Vintage Books, 1993.

————. Revolutionary Characters: What Made the Founders Different. New York: Penguin Press, 2006.

Wright, Esmond, ed. Causes and Consequences of the American Revolution. Chicago: Quadrangle Books, 1966.

Wulf, Andrea. Founding Gardeners: The Revolutionary Generation, Nature, and the Shaping of the American Nation. New York: Alfred A. Knopf, 2011.

Yokota, Kariann Akemi. Unbecoming British: How Revolutionary America Became a Postcolonial Nation. New York: Oxford University Press, 2011.

Young, Alfred F., and Gregory H. Nobles. Whose American Revolution Was It? Historians Interpret the Founding. New York: New York University Press, 2011.

Young, Alfred F., ed. Beyond the American Revolution: Explorations in the History of American Radicalism. DeKalb: Northern Illinois University Press, 1993.

Young, James Sterling. The Washington Community, **1800–1828**. New York: Columbia University Press, 1968.

Zacks, Richard. **The Pirate Coast: Thomas Jefferson, the First Marines, and the Secret Mission of 1805**. New York: Hyperion, 2005.

Zagarri, Rosemarie. **Revolutionary Backlash: Women and Politics in the Early American Republic**. Early American Studies. Philadelphia: University of Pennsylvania Press, 2007.

ARTICLES, ESSAYS, REVIEWS, AND WEB PAGES

"America During the Age of Revolution, 1764–1775." Documents from the Continental Congress and the Constitutional Convention, 1774–89. Library of Congress, American Memory. http://memory.loc .gov/ammem/collections/continental/timeline1e .html (accessed March 25, 2012).

Andrews, Charles M. "The American Revolution: An Interpretation." **The American Historical Review** 31, no. 2 (January 1926): 219–32.

"Appendix H: Sally Hemings and Her Children." Thomas Jefferson Foundation. http://www.mon ticello.org/site/plantation-and-slavery/appendix-h -sally-hemings-and-her-children (accessed May 18, 2012).

Ayres, S. Edward. "Albemarle County, Virginia, 1744–1770: An Economic, Political, and Social Analysis." **Magazine of Albemarle County History** 25 (1966–67): 37–72.

Bakalar, Nicholas. "First Mention: Pertussis, 1913." **The New York Times,** April 13, 2010.

Balleck, Barry J. "When the Ends Justify the Means: Thomas Jefferson and the Louisiana Purchase." **Presidential Studies Quarterly** 22 (Fall 1992): 679–96.

Bear, James A., Jr. "The Last Few Days in the Life of Thomas Jefferson." **Magazine of Albemarle County History** 32 (1974): 63–79.

————. "Wine." Thomas Jefferson Encyclopedia, Thomas Jefferson Foundation. http://www.monti cello.org/site/research-and-collections/wine (accessed March 24, 2012).

Belohlavek, John M. "Economic Interest Groups and the Formation of Foreign Policy in the Early Re-public." **Journal of the Early Republic** 14 (Winter 1994): 476–84.

Berdahl, Clarence A. "Presidential Selection and Democratic Government." **The Journal of Politics** 11 (February 1949): 14–41.

Beschloss, Michael, and Hugh Sidey. "James Madison." The White House. http://www.whitehouse.gov/about/presidents/jamesmadison (accessed March 24, 2012).

Bevan, Edith Rossiter. "Thomas Jefferson in Annapolis, November 25, 1783–May 11, 1784." **Maryland Historical Magazine** 41, no. 2 (1946): 115–24.

Borden, Morton. "A Neo-Federalist View of the Jef-fersonians." Review of **The Presidency of Thomas Jefferson,** by Forrest McDonald. **Reviews in American History** 5 (June 1977): 196–202.

Bowman, Albert H. "Jefferson, Hamilton and American Foreign Policy." **Political Science Quarterly** 71 (March 1956): 18–41.

Boyd, Julian P. "Two Diplomats Between Revolutions: John Jay and Thomas Jefferson." **Virginia Magazine of History and Biography** 66 (April 1958): 131–46.

Boyett, Gene W. "Developing the Concept of the Republican Presidency, 1787–1788." **Presidential Studies Quarterly** 7 (Fall 1977): 199–208.

Brant, Irving. "Two Neglected Madison Letters." **The William and Mary Quarterly,** 3d ser., 3 (October 1946): 569–87.

Brown, Wallace. "The View at Two Hundred Years: The Loyalists of the American Revolution." **Proceedings of the American Antiquarian Society** 101 (April 1970): 25–47.

Bullock, Helen D., ed. "A Dissertation on Education in the Form of a Letter from James Maury to Robert Jackson, July 17, 1762." **Papers of the Albemarle County Historical Society** 2 (1941–42): 36–60.

Caldwell, L. K. "Thomas Jefferson and Public Administration." **Public Administration Review** 3 (Summer 1943): 240–53.

Calhoon, Robert M. "William Smith Jr.'s Alternative to the American Revolution." **The William and Mary Quarterly,** 3d ser., 22 (January 1965): 105–18.

Carson, David A. "Jefferson, Congress, and the Question of Leadership in the Tripolitan War." **Virginia Magazine of History and Biography** 94 (October 1986): 409–24.

Casper, Gerhard. "Executive-Congressional Separation of Power During the Presidency of Thomas Jefferson." **Stanford Law Review** 47 (February 1995): 473–97.

Chan, Michael D. "Alexander Hamilton on Slavery." **The Review of Politics** 66 (Spring 2004): 207–31.

Charles, Joseph. "Adams and Jefferson: The Origins of the American Party System." **The William and Mary Quarterly,** 3d ser., 12 (July 1955): 410–46.

Cockerham, Anne Z., Arlene W. Keeling, and Barbara Parker. "Seeking Refuge at Monticello: Domestic Violence in Thomas Jefferson's Family." **Magazine of Albemarle County History** 64 (2006): 29–52.

Cohen, Morris L. "Thomas Jefferson Recommends a Course of Law Study." **University of Pennsylvania Law Review** 119 (April 1971): 823–44.

Cohen, William. "Thomas Jefferson and the Problem of Slavery." **The Journal of American History** 56 (December 1969): 503–26.

Crompton, Samuel Willard. "Randolph, John." February 2000. American National Biography Online. http://www.anb.org/articles/01/01-00767.html (accessed 2011).

———. "Randolph, Sir John." American National Biography Online. http://www.anb.org/articles/01/01-00769.html (accessed 2011).

"Crops at Monticello." Thomas Jefferson Encyclopedia, Thomas Jefferson's Monticello. http://www.monticello.org/site/plantation-and-slavery/crops-monticello (accessed April 8, 2012).

Cunliffe, Marcus. "Thomas Jefferson and the Dangers of the Past." **The Wilson Quarterly** 6 (Winter 1982): 96–107.

Curtis, George M., III. "Sphinx Without a Riddle: Joseph Ellis and the Art of Jefferson Biography." **Indiana Magazine of History** 95 (June 1999): 178–201.

Dabney, Virginius. "Jouett Outrides Tarleton, and Saves Jefferson from Capture." **Scribner's Magazine,** June 1928, 690–98.

"Dabney Carr (1743–1773)." Thomas Jefferson Encyclopedia, Thomas Jefferson Foundation. http:// www.monticello.org/site/research-and-collections/ dabney-carr-1743-1773 (accessed March 23, 2012).

"Debt." Thomas Jefferson Encyclopedia, Thomas Jefferson Foundation. http://www.monticello.org/site/ research-and-collections/debt (accessed April 8, 2012).

Deutsch, Herman J. "Economic Imperialism in the Early Pacific Northwest." **Pacific Historical Review** 9 (December 1940): 377–88.

"Dinner Etiquette." Thomas Jefferson Encyclopedia, Thomas Jefferson Foundation. http://www.monti cello.org/site/research-and-collections/dinner-eti quette (accessed April 7, 2012).

"Dome Room." Thomas Jefferson Encyclopedia, Thomas Jefferson Foundation. http://www.monti cello.org/site/house-and-gardens/dome-room (accessed April 7, 2012).

Dorfman, Joseph. "The Economic Philosophy of Thomas Jefferson." **Political Science Quarterly** 55 (March 1940): 98–121.

Dufour, Ronald P. "Pepperrell, Sir William." American National Biography Online. http://www.anb.org/articles/01/01-00717.html (accessed 2011).

Dumbauld, Edward. "Thomas Jefferson and the City of Washington." **Records of the Columbia Historical Society** 50 (1980): 67–80.

"Entrance Hall." Thomas Jefferson Encyclopedia, Thomas Jefferson Foundation. http://www.monticello.org/site/house-and-gardens/entrance-hall (accessed April 7, 2012).

Evans, Emory G. "Trouble in the Backcountry: Disaffection in Southwest Virginia During the American Revolution." In **An Uncivil War: The Southern Backcountry During the American Revolution,** edited by Ronald Hoffman, Thad W. Tate, and Peter J. Albert, 179–212. Perspectives on the American Revolution. Charlottesville: Published for the U.S. Capitol Historical Society by the University Press of Virginia, 1985.

Evans, Howard V. "The Nootka Sound Controversy in Anglo-French Diplomacy—1790." **The Journal of Modern History** 46 (December 1974): 609–40.

"Expedition Timeline." Thomas Jefferson Foundation. http://www.monticello.org/site/jefferson/expedition-timeline (accessed April 4, 2012).

Fa, Bernard. "Early Party Machinery in the United States: Pennsylvania in the Election of 1796." **The Pennsylvania Magazine of History and Biography** 60 (October 1936): 375–90.

Finer, Herman. "Jefferson, Hamilton, and American Democracy." **Economica,** no. 18 (November 1926): 338–44.

"Firearms." Thomas Jefferson Encyclopedia, Thomas Jefferson Foundation. http://www.monticello.org/site/research-and-collections/firearms (accessed April 2, 2012).

Fish, Carl Russell. "Removal of Officials by the Presidents of the United States." In **Annual Report of the American Historical Association for the Year 1899**. Vol. 1, 67–86. Washington, D.C.: Government Printing Office, 1900.

"Fishing." Thomas Jefferson Encyclopedia, Thomas Jefferson Foundation. http://www.monticello.org/site/research-and-collections/fishing (accessed April 2, 2012).

"Francis Fauquier (bap. 1703–1768)." **Encyclopedia Virginia**, http://www.encyclopedia virginia.org/fauquier_francis_bap_1703-1768 (accessed March 24, 2012).

"Gallatin, Albert, (1761–1849)." Biographical Directory of the United States Congress, 1774–Present. http://bioguide.congress.gov/scripts/biodisplay.pl?index=g000020 (accessed March 24, 2012).

"George Wythe House." Colonial Williamsburg, Colonial Williamsburg Foundation. http://www.history.org/almanack/places/hb/hbwythe.cfm (accessed March 25, 2012).

Gibbs, D. D. "Sir John Floyer, M.D. (1649–1734.)" **British Medical Journal** 1 (January 25, 1969): 242–45.

Gould, Eliga H. "A Virtual Nation: Greater Britain and the Imperial Legacy of the American Revolution." **The American Historical Review** 104 (April 1999): 476–89.

Greene, Jack P. "William Knox's Explanation for the American Revolution." **The William and Mary Quarterly,** 3d ser., 30 (April 1973): 293–306.

Griffin, Patrick. "In Retrospect: Lawrence Henry Gipson's 'The British Empire Before the American Revolution.' " Review of **The British Empire Before the American Revolution,** by Lawrence Henry Gipson. **Reviews in American History** 31, no. 2 (June 2003): 171–83.

Grigg, Milton L. "Thomas Jefferson and the Development of the National Capital." **Records of the Columbia Historical Society** [42] (1953/1956): 81–100.

Hammond, John Craig. " 'They Are Very Much Interested in Obtaining an Unlimited Slavery': Rethinking the Expansion of Slavery in the Louisiana Purchase Territories, 1803–1805." **Journal of the Early Republic** 23 (Autumn 2003): 353–80.

Hansen, Dagny B. "Captain James Cook's First Stop on the Northwest Coast: By Chance or by Chart?" **Pacific Historical Review** 62 (November 1993): 475–84.

Harling, Philip. "The Duke of York Affair (1809) and the Complexities of War-Time Patriotism." **The Historical Journal** 39, no. 4 (December 1996): 963–84.

Harrison, Joseph H., Jr. " 'Sic Et Non': Thomas Jefferson and Internal Improvement." **Journal of the Early Republic** 7 (Winter 1987): 335–49.

Hatch, Peter J. "Thomas Jefferson's Favorite Vegetables." Thomas Jefferson Foundation. http://www.monticello.org/site/house-and-gardens/thomas-jeffersons-favorite-vegetables (accessed March 23, 2012).

Hatzenbuehler, Ronald L. "Growing Weary in Well-Doing: Thomas Jefferson's Life Among the Virginia Gentry." **Virginia Magazine of History and Biography** 101 (January 1993): 5–36.

Hickey, Donald R. "America's Response to the Slave Revolt in Haiti, 1791–1806." **Journal of the Early Republic** 2 (Winter 1982): 361–79.

Hickish, Edgar C. "Peter Jefferson, Gentleman." Unpublished manuscript. Thomas Jefferson Foundation, Charlottesville, Va.

Higgenbotham, Don. "Virginia's Trinity of Immortals: Washington, Jefferson, and Henry, and the Story of Their Fractured Relationships." **Journal of the Early Republic** 23 (Winter 2003): 521–43.

Hodin, Stephen B. "The Mechanisms of Monticello: Saving Labor in Jefferson's America." **Journal of the Early Republic** 26 (Fall 2006): 377–418.

Holland, Matthew S. " 'To Close the Circle of Our Felicities': 'Caritas' and Jefferson's First Inaugural." **The Review of Politics** 66 (Spring 2004): 181–205.

Honeywell, Roy L. "President Jefferson and His Successor." **The American Historical Review** 46 (October 1940): 64–75.

"House and Gardens." Thomas Jefferson Foundation. http://www.monticello.org/site/house-and-gardens (accessed April 7, 2012).

Howard, Seymour. "Thomas Jefferson's Art Gallery for Monticello." **Art Bulletin** 59 (December 1977): 583–600.

Howe, John R., Jr. "Republican Thought and Political Violence of the 1790s." **American Quarterly** 19, no. 2 (Summer 1967): 147–65.

Hoxie, R. Gordon. "Inaugurating the Presidency and the President." **Presidential Studies Quarterly** 23 (Spring 1993): 213–19.

"Hunting." Thomas Jefferson Encyclopedia, Thomas Jefferson Foundation. http://www.monticello.org/site/research-and-collections/hunting (accessed April 2, 2012).

Irwin, Douglas A. "The Aftermath of Hamilton's 'Report on Manufactures.' " **The Journal of Economic History** 64 (September 2004): 800–821.

Jasanoff, Maya. "The Other Side of Revolution: Loyalists in the British Empire." **The William and Mary Quarterly**, 3d ser., 65 (April 2008): 205–32.

Jefferson, Thomas. "Jefferson's Confidential Letter to Congress." Thomas Jefferson Foundation. http://www.monticello.org/site/jefferson/jeffersons-confidential-letter-to-congress (accessed April 4, 2012).

"Jefferson: The Scientist and Gardener." Thomas Jefferson Foundation. http://www.monticello.org/site/house-and-gardens/jefferson-scientist-and-gardener (accessed May 18, 2012).

Jennings, Francis. "Johnson, Sir William." American National Biography Online. http://www.anb.org/articles/01/01-00458.html (accessed 2011).

"John Randolph, 'The Tory.' " Colonial Williamsburg, Colonial Williamsburg Foundation. http://www.history.org/almanack/people/bios/bioratjr.cfm (accessed March 22, 2012).

Johnson, Ludwell H., III. "Sharper Than a Serpent's Tooth: Thomas Jefferson and His Alma Mater." **Virginia Magazine of History and Biography** 99 (April 1991): 145–62.

Johnson, Odai. "Thomas Jefferson and the Colonial American Stage." **Virginia Magazine of History and Biography** 108, no. 2 (2000): 139–54.

Jones, Gordon W., and James A. Bear. "Thomas Jefferson's Medical History." Unpublished manuscript. Thomas Jefferson Foundation, Charlottesville, Va.

Jones, James F., Jr. "Montesquieu and Jefferson Revisited: Aspects of a Legacy." **The French Review** 51 (March 1978): 577–85.

"Journal of a French Traveller in the Colonies, 1765." Parts 1 and 2. **The American Historical Review** 26 (July 1921): 726–47; 27 (October 1921): 70–89.

"Journey Through France and Italy (1787)." Thomas Jefferson Encyclopedia, Thomas Jefferson Foundation. http://www.monticello.org/site/research-and -collections/journey-through-france-and-italy-1787 (accessed March 31, 2012).

Kelly, James C., and B. S. Lovell. "Thomas Jefferson: His Friends and Foes." **Virginia Magazine of History and Biography** 101 (January 1993): 133–57.

Ketchum, Richard M. "Men of the Revolution: 11. George Rogers Clark." **American Heritage** 25, no. 1 (December 1973): 32–33, 78.

Kimball, Fiske. "The Life Portraits of Jefferson and

Their Replicas." **Proceedings of the American Philosophical Society** 88 (December 28, 1944): 497–534.

Kimball, Marie. "A Playmate of Thomas Jefferson." **North American Review** 213 (February 1921): 145–56.

"Lafayette's Visit to Monticello (1824)." Thomas Jefferson Encyclopedia, Thomas Jefferson Foundation. http://www.monticello.org/site/research-and-collections/lafayettes-visit-to-monticello-1824 (accessed April 8, 2012).

Landin, Harold W. "Some Letters of Thomas Paine and William Short on the Nootka Sound Crisis." **The Journal of Modern History** 13 (September 1941): 357–74.

Leibiger, Stuart. "Thomas Jefferson and the Missouri Crisis: An Alternative Interpretation." **Journal of the Early Republic** 17 (Spring 1997): 121–30.

Lerche, Charles O., Jr. "Jefferson and the Election of 1800: A Case Study in the Political Smear." **The William and Mary Quarterly,** 3d ser., 5 (October 1948): 467–91.

Lewis, Anthony M. "Jefferson's Summary View As a Chart of Political Union." **The William and Mary Quarterly,** 3d ser., 5, no. 1 (January 1948): 34–51.

Lind, Michael. "Hamilton's Legacy." **The Wilson Quarterly** 18 (Summer 1994): 40–52.

Lloyd, Stephen. "The Accomplished Maria Cosway: Anglo-Italian Artist, Musician, Salon Hostess and Educationalist (1759–1838)." **Journal of Anglo-Italian Studies** 2 (1992): 108–39.

Looney, J. Jefferson. "Thomas Jefferson's Last Letter." **Virginia Magazine of History and Biography** 112, no. 2 (2004): 178–84.

Magnis, Nicholas E. "Thomas Jefferson and Slavery: An Analysis of His Racist Thinking as Revealed by His Writings and Political Behavior." **Journal of Black Studies** 29 (March 1999): 491–509.

Marsh, Philip M. "Freneau and Jefferson: The Poet-Editor Speaks for Himself About the **National Gazette** Episode." **American Literature** 8 (May 1936): 180–89.

———. "Jefferson's Retirement as Secretary of State." **The Pennsylvania Magazine of History and Biography** 69 (July 1945): 220–24.

———. "Philip Freneau and His Circle." **The Pennsylvania Magazine of History and Biography** 63, no. 1 (January 1939): 37–59.

"Martha Wayles Skelton Jefferson." Thomas Jefferson Encyclopedia, Thomas Jefferson Foundation. http://www.monticello.org/site/jefferson/martha-wayles-skelton-jefferson (accessed 2012).

Matthewson, Tim. "Jefferson and Haiti." **The Journal of Southern History** 61 (May 1995): 209–48.

———. "Jefferson and the Nonrecognition of Haiti." **Proceedings of the American Philosophical Society** 140 (March 1996): 22–48.

McDonald, Robert M. S. "Thomas Jefferson's Changing Reputation as Author of the Declaration of Independence: The First Fifty Years." **Journal of the Early Republic** 19, no. 2 (Summer 1999): 169–95.

Mead, Walter Russell. "First Principals: Alexander

Hamilton and the American Founders." Review of **Alexander Hamilton,** by Ron Chernow. **Foreign Affairs** 83 (July–August 2004): 133–35.

"Meriwether Lewis." Thomas Jefferson Encyclopedia, Thomas Jefferson Foundation. http://www.monti cello.org/site/research-and-collections/meriwether -lewis (accessed April 4, 2012).

Meschutt, David. " 'A Perfect Likeness': John H. I. Browere's Life Mask of Thomas Jefferson." **American Art Journal** 21 (Winter 1989): 4–25.

Miroff, Bruce. "Alexander Hamilton: The Aristocrat as Visionary." **International Political Science Review** 9 (January 1988): 43–54.

Mitchell, Broadus. "Alexander Hamilton, Executive Power and the New Nation." **Presidential Studies Quarterly** 17 (Spring 1987): 329–43.

"Mockingbirds." Thomas Jefferson Encyclopedia, Thomas Jefferson Foundation. http://www.mon ticello.org/site/research-and-collections/mocking birds (accessed April 2, 2012).

"Monticello Dining Room." Thomas Jefferson Encyclopedia, Thomas Jefferson Foundation. http:// www.monticello.org/site/house-and-gardens/ monticello-dining-room (accessed April 7, 2012).

"Monticello (House) FAQ." Thomas Jefferson Encyclopedia, Thomas Jefferson Foundation. http:// www.monticello.org/site/house-and-gardens/ monticello-house-faq#rooms (accessed April 7, 2012).

"Monticello South Square Room." Thomas Jefferson Encyclopedia, Thomas Jefferson Foundation. http://

www.monticello.org/site/house-and-gardens/south-square-room (accessed April 7, 2012).

Morgan, James Morris. "How President Jefferson Was Informed of Burr's Conspiracy." **The Pennsylvania Magazine of History and Biography** 27, no. 1 (1903): 56–59.

Morse, Anson D. "Alexander Hamilton." **Political Science Quarterly** 5 (March 1890): 1–23.

Newbold, Stephanie P. "Statesmanship and Ethics: The Case of Thomas Jefferson's Dirty Hands." **Public Administration Review** 65 (November–December 2005): 669–77.

Norris, John M. "The Policy of the British Cabinet in the Nootka Crisis." **The English Historical Review** 70 (October 1955): 562–80.

"North Octagonal Room." Thomas Jefferson Encyclopedia, Thomas Jefferson Foundation. http://www.monticello.org/site/house-and-gardens/north-octagonal-room (accessed April 7, 2012).

Norton, Mary Beth. "John Randolph's 'Plan of Accommodations.' " **The William and Mary Quarterly**, 3d ser., 28 (January 1971): 103–20.

Oberg, Barbara. Review of **Thomas Jefferson**, by Joyce Appleby. **The Pennsylvania Magazine of History and Biography** 128 (October 2004): 406–8.

Parkinson, Robert G. "First from the Right: Massive Resistance and the Image of Thomas Jefferson in the 1950s." **Virginia Magazine of History and Biography** 112, no. 1 (2004): 2–35.

"Parlor." Thomas Jefferson Encyclopedia, Thomas Jefferson Foundation. http://www.monticello.org/site/house-and-gardens/parlor (accessed April 7, 2012).

Peterson, Merrill D. "Thomas Jefferson and Commercial Policy, 1783–1793." **The William and Mary Quarterly,** 3d ser., 22 (October 1965): 584–610.

"Physical Descriptions of Jefferson." Thomas Jefferson Encyclopedia, Thomas Jefferson Foundation. http://www.monticello.org/site/research-and-collections/physical-descriptions-jefferson (accessed March 31, 2012).

"Plantation and Slavery." Thomas Jefferson Foundation. http://www.monticello.org/site/plantation-and-slavery (accessed April 2, 2012).

Prince, Carl E. "The Passing of the Aristocracy: Jefferson's Removal of the Federalists, 1801–1805." **The Journal of American History** 57 (December 1970): 563–75.

"Printer and Binder." Colonial Williamsburg, Colonial Williamsburg Foundation. http://www.history.org/almanack/life/trades/tradepri.cfm (accessed March 24, 2012).

Quarles, Benjamin. "Lord Dunmore as Liberator." **The William and Mary Quarterly,** 3d ser., 15 (October 1958): 494–507.

Rahe, Paul A. "Thomas Jefferson's Machiavellian Political Science." **The Review of Politics** 57 (Summer 1995): 449–81.

Rakove, Jack N. "Presidential Selection: Electoral Fallacies." **Political Science Quarterly** 119 (Spring 2004): 21–37.

Randolph, John. "Letters of John Randolph, of Roanoke, to General Thomas Marsh Forman." **Virginia Magazine of History and Biography** 49 (July 1941): 201–16.

Ranlet, Philip. "Johnson, John." American National Biography Online. http://www.anb.org/articles/03/03-00247.html (accessed 2011).

Reagan, Ronald. "Remarks and a Question-and-Answer Session at the University of Virginia in Charlottesville," December 16, 1988. The American Presidency Project. http://www.presidency.ucsb.edu/ws/?pid=35272 (accessed April 8, 2012).

"Report of the Research Committee on Thomas Jefferson and Sally Hemings." Thomas Jefferson Foundation. http://www.monticello.org/site/plantation-and-slavery/report-research-committee-thomas-jefferson-and-sally-hemings (accessed March 23, 2012).

Reuter, Frank T. " 'Petty Spy' or Effective Diplomat: The Role of George Beckwith." **Journal of the Early Republic** 10 (Winter 1990): 471–92.

Riordan, Liam. "Loyalism." **Oxford Bibliographies,** Oxford University Press. http://oxfordbibliographiesonline.com/view/document/obo-9780199730414/obo-9780199730414-0118.xml (accessed March 22, 2012).

Roosevelt, Franklin D. "Address at Jefferson Day Dinner in St. Paul Minnesota," April 18, 1932. The American Presidency Project. http://www.presidency.ucsb.edu/ws/?pid=88409 (accessed April 8, 2012).

Rosano, Michael J. "Liberty, Nobility, Philanthropy,

and Power in Alexander Hamilton's Conception of Human Nature." **The American Journal of Political Science** 47 (January 2003): 61–74.

"Sally Hemings." Thomas Jefferson Encyclopedia, Thomas Jefferson Foundation. http://www.monticello.org/site/plantation-and-slavery/sally-hemings (accessed April 7, 2012).

Schellenberg, T. R. "Jeffersonian Origins of the Monroe Doctrine." **Hispanic American Historical Review** 14 (February 1934): 1–31.

Scherr, Arthur. "The Significance of Thomas Pinckney's Candidacy in the Election of 1796." **The South Carolina Historical Magazine** 76 (April 1975): 51–59.

Scheuerman, William E. "American Kingship? Monarchical Origins of Modern Presidentialism." **Polity** 37 (January 2005): 24–53.

Schmitt, Gary J. "Jefferson and Executive Power: Revisionism and the 'Revolution of 1800.'" **Publius** 17 (Spring 1987): 7–25.

Scholten, Catherine M. "'On the Importance of the Obstetrick Art': Changing Customs of Childbirth in America, 1760 to 1825." **The William and Mary Quarterly,** 3d ser., 34 (July 1977): 426–45.

Scofield, Merry Ellen. "The Fatigues of His Table: The Politics of Presidential Dining During the Jefferson Administration." **Journal of the Early Republic** 26 (Fall 2006): 449–69.

Selby, John E. "Murray, John." American National Biography Online. http://www.anb.org/articles/01/01-00242.html (accessed 2011).

————. "Randolph, Peyton." American National Biography Online. http://www.anb.org/articles/01/01-00768.html (accessed 2011).

Self, Robert L., and Susan R. Stein. "The Collaboration of Thomas Jefferson and John Hemings: Furniture Attributed to the Monticello Joinery." **Winterthur Portfolio** 33 (Winter 1998): 231–48.

Shalhope, Robert E. "Thomas Jefferson's Republicanism and Antebellum Southern Thought." **The Journal of Southern History** 42 (November 1976): 529–56.

Sharp, James Roger. "Unraveling the Mystery of Jefferson's Letter of April 27, 1795." **Journal of the Early Republic** 6, no. 4 (Winter 1986): 411–18.

Sheehan, Bernard W. " 'The Famous Hair Buyer General': Henry Hamilton, George Rogers Clark, and the American Indian." **Indiana Magazine of History** 79 (March 1983): 1–28.

Sheehan, Colleen A. "Madison v. Hamilton: The Battle Over Republicanism and the Role of Public Opinion." **American Political Science Review** 98 (August 2004): 405–24.

Shepard, E. Lee. "Randolph, Edmund." American National Biography Online. http://www.anb.org/articles/02/02-00269.html (accessed 2011).

Shippen, Rebecca Lloyd. "Inauguration of President Thomas Jefferson, 1801." **The Pennsylvania Magazine of History and Biography** 25 (April 1901): 71–76.

Smelser, Marshall. "The Federalist Period as an Age

of Passion." **American Quarterly** 10 (Winter 1958): 391–419.

Smith, Paul H. "The American Loyalists: Notes on Their Organization and Numerical Strength." **The William and Mary Quarterly,** 3d ser., 25, no. 2 (April 1968): 259–77.

Sofka, James R. "The Jeffersonian Idea of National Security: Commerce, the Atlantic Balance of Power, and the Barbary War, 1786–1805." **Diplomatic History** 21 (Fall 1997): 519–44.

Stanton, Lucia. "Looking for Liberty: Thomas Jefferson and the British Lions." **Eighteenth-Century Studies** 26 (Summer 1993): 649–68.

Swanson, Donald F. "Thomas Jefferson on Establishing Public Credit: The Debt Plans of a Would-Be Secretary of the Treasury?" **Presidential Studies Quarterly** 23 (Summer 1993): 499–508.

"Tea Room." Thomas Jefferson Encyclopedia, Thomas Jefferson Foundation. http://www.monticello.org/site/house-and-gardens/tea-room (accessed April 7, 2012).

Temperley, H. W. V. "Debates on the Declaratory Act and the Repeal of the Stamp Act, 1766." **The American Historical Review** 17 (April 1912): 563–86. Reprint, LaVergne, Tenn.: Nabu Public Domain Reprints, 2010.

Thomas, Milton Halsey. "Alexander Hamilton's Unfought Duel of 1795." **The Pennsylvania Magazine of History and Biography** 78 (July 1954): 342–52.

"Thomas Mann Randolph." Thomas Jefferson Encyclopedia, Thomas Jefferson Foundation. http://www.monticello.org/site/jefferson/thomas-mann-randolph (accessed April 8, 2012).

Thornton, Anna Maria Brodeau. "Diary of Mrs. William Thornton, 1800–1863." **Records of the Columbia Historical Society** 10 (1907): 88–226.

Trent, W. P. "The Case of Josiah Philips." **The American Historical Review** 1, no. 3 (April 1896): 444–54.

Truman, Harry S. "Address at Bonham, Texas," September 27, 1948. The American Presidency Project. http://www.presidency.ucsb.edu/ws/?pid=13021 (accessed April 8, 2012).

Tucker, Robert W., and David C. Hendrickson. "Thomas Jefferson and American Foreign Policy." **Foreign Affairs** 69 (Spring 1990): 135–56.

Tucker, Spencer C., and Frank T. Reuter. "The Chesapeake-Leopard Affair." **Naval History** 10 (March/April 1996): 40–44.

Turner, Kathryn. "The Appointment of Chief Justice Marshall." **The William and Mary Quarterly,** 3d ser., 17 (April 1960): 143–63.

——. "Federalist Policy and the Judiciary Act of 1801." **The William and Mary Quarterly,** 3d ser., 22 (January 1965): 3–32.

Turner, Lynn W. "The Impeachment of John Pickering." **The American Historical Review** 54 (April 1949): 485–507.

——. "Thomas Jefferson Through the Eyes of a New Hampshire Politician." **Mississippi Valley Historical Review** 30, no. 2 (September 1943): 204–14.

Verner, Coolie. "Mr. Jefferson Makes a Map." **Imago Mundi** 14 (1959): 96–108.

Wallace, D. D. "Jefferson's Part in the Purchase of Louisiana." **The Sewanee Review** 19 (July 1911): 328–38.

Walling, Karl. "Was Alexander Hamilton a Machiavellian Statesman?" **The Review of Politics** 57 (Summer 1995): 419–47.

Wells, Jane Flaherty. "Thomas Jefferson's Neighbors: Hore Browse Trist of 'Birdwood' and Dr. William Bache of 'Franklin.' " **Magazine of Albemarle County History** 47 (1989): 1–13.

"William Small." Thomas Jefferson Encyclopedia, Thomas Jefferson Foundation. http://www.monti cello.org/site/jefferson/william-small (accessed March 24, 2012).

Wilson, Douglas L. "The Evolution of Jefferson's 'Notes on the State of Virginia.' " **Virginia Magazine of History and Biography** 112, no. 2 (2004): 98–133.

Wilson, Gaye. "Horses." Thomas Jefferson Encyclopedia, Thomas Jefferson Foundation. http://www .monticello.org/site/research-and-collections/horses (accessed April 2, 2012).

Wrabley, Raymond B., Jr. "Anti-Federalism and the Presidency." **Presidential Studies Quarterly** 21 (Summer 1991): 459–70.

"Wren Building." Colonial Williamsburg, Colonial Williamsburg Foundation. http://www.history.org/ almanack/places/hb/hbwren.cfm (accessed March 24, 2012).

Young, Alfred F. "English Plebeian Culture and Eighteenth-Century American Radicalism." In **The Origins of Anglo-American Radicalism**, edited by Margaret Jacob and James Jacob, 185–212. London: Allen and Unwin, 1984.

DISSERTATION

Giunta, Mary A. "The Public Life of William Branch Giles, Republican, 1790–1815." Ph.D. diss., Catholic University of America, 1980.

MAGAZINES, JOURNALS, AND NEWSPAPERS

The Aberdeen (Scotland) **Journal**
Alexandria (Va.) **Advertiser and Commercial Intelligencer**
Alexandria (Va.) **Times**
American Art Journal
The American Historical Review
The American Journal of Political Science
American Political Science Review
American Quarterly
Art Bulletin
The Caledonian Mercury (Edinburgh, Scotland)
Cobbett's Political Register (London)
Diplomatic History
Economica
Eighteenth-Century Studies
The English Historical Review
Foreign Affairs

The French Review
Hispanic American Historical Review
The Historical Journal
The Hull (England) Packet and Original Weekly Commercial, Literary and General Advertiser
Imago Mundi
Indiana Magazine of History
International Political Science Review
The Ipswich (England) Journal
The Journal of American History
Journal of Black Studies
The Journal of Economic History
The Journal of Modern History
The Journal of Politics
The Journal of Southern History
Journal of the Early Republic
Magazine of Albemarle County History
The Morning Chronicle (London)
National Intelligencer (Washington, D.C.)
Naval History
The New York Times
North American Review
Oxford Bibliographies
Pacific Historical Review
Papers of the Albemarle County Historical Society
The Pennsylvania Magazine of History and Biography
Political Science Quarterly
Polity
Presidential Studies Quarterly
Proceedings of the American Antiquarian Society

Proceedings of the American Philosophical Society
Public Administration Review
Publius
Records of the Columbia Historical Society
The Review of Politics
Reviews in American History
The Sewanee Review
The South Carolina Historical Magazine
Stanford Law Review
University of Pennsylvania Law Review
The Virginia Gazette (Williamsburg)
Virginia Magazine of History and Biography
Washington (D.C.) Federalist
The William and Mary Quarterly
The Wilson Quarterly
Winterthur Portfolio

ILLUSTRATION CREDITS

ENDPAPERS

MONTICELLO, FIRST VERSION (ELEVATION). Drawing by Thomas Jefferson, probably before March 1771. N48; K23. Original manuscript from the Coolidge Collection of Thomas Jefferson Manuscripts. Massachusetts Historical Society.

TITLE PAGE AND PART-TITLE PAGES

iv–v   MONTICELLO WEST FRONT AND GARDEN: 1825, by Jane Pitford Braddick Peticolas; © Thomas Jefferson Foundation at Monticello

xxxviii–1   MAP OF VIRGINIA AND MARYLAND: drawn by Joshua Fry and Peter Jefferson, printed by Sayer and Jefferys, c. 1776; © Thomas Jefferson Foundation at Monticello, photograph by Edward Owen

96–97   DECLARATION OF INDEPENDENCE: by John Trumbull, 1818; Rotunda of the U.S. Capitol/Architect of the Capitol

174–75   THE TAKING OF YORKTOWN: by Turgis of Paris; Library of Congress Prints and Photographs Division, Washington, D.C.

222–23   EXPERIMENT AT VERSAILLES OF THE MONT-GOLFIER BROTHERS WITH THE FLIGHT IN A "MONTGOLFIERE" HOT-AIR BALLOON OF A

COCK, A DUCK, AND A SHEEP ON SEPTEM-
BER 19, 1783: Bibliothèque des Arts Déco-
ratifs, Paris, France/Archives Charmet/The
Bridgeman Art Library

262–63 HALLE AUX BLÉS, PARIS, VIEW OF THE
WHEAT MARKET AND THE CUPOLA: after
Pierre Courvoisier/Bibliothèque Nationale,
Paris, France/Giraudon/The Bridgeman Art
Library

340–41 INAUGURATION OF GEORGE WASHINGTON:
(nineteenth-century lithograph); © Collection of the New-York Historical Society,
USA/The Bridgeman Art Library

418–19 PRESIDENTIAL CAMPAIGN BANNER: 1800;
The Granger Collection, NYC

514–15 LOUISIANA PURCHASE MAP: U.S.40–4, Old
Map File, Record Group 49: Records of the
Bureau of Land Management (General Land
Office), Cartographic Section, National Ar-
chives at College Park, MD

666–67 VIEW OF THE UNIVERSITY OF VIRGINIA,
CHARLOTTESVILLE, AND MONTICELLO
FROM LEWIS MOUNTAIN: 1856, by C.
Bohn/The Granger Collection, NYC

SECTION 1

- WILLIAM RANDOLPH: American School (late seventeenth century); Virginia Historical Society, Richmond, Virginia, USA/The Bridgeman Art Library

- MARY ISHAM RANDOLPH: American School (eighteenth century); Virginia Historical Society, Richmond, Virginia, USA/The Bridgeman Art Library
- PEYTON RANDOLPH: Library of Congress Prints and Photographs Division, Washington, D.C.
- WREN HALL, THE COLLEGE OF WILLIAM AND MARY: engraving by Crump, after a painting by Thomas Millington, c. 1850; The Colonial Williamsburg Foundation, Museum Purchase, 1975–264
- PORTRAIT OF GEORGE III IN HIS CORONATION ROBES: c. 1760 by Allan Ramsay; Private Collection/The Bridgeman Art Library
- PORTRAIT OF FRANCIS FAUQUIER, LIEUTENANT GOVERNOR OF VIRGINIA IN THE AMERICAN COLONIES: c. 1757, by Richard Wilson; © Coram in the care of the Foundling Museum, London/The Bridgeman Art Library
- PORTRAIT OF WILLIAM SMALL (DETAIL): by Tilly Kettle; The College of William and Mary in Virginia
- GEORGE WYTHE: 1888, by Albert Rosenthal, after William S. Leney; The Granger Collection, NYC
- PATRICK HENRY MAKING HIS FAMOUS SPEECH IN THE HOUSE OF BURGESSES: after Peter Fred Rothermel; Private Collection/The Stapleton Collection/The Bridgeman Art Library
- PORTRAIT OF JOHN MURRAY, 4TH EARLY OF DUNMORE: 1929, by Charles Xavier Harris (copy of original by Sir Joshua Reynolds); Virginia Histori-

cal Society, Richmond, Virginia, USA/The Bridgeman Art Library

- DAUGHTER MARTHA JEFFERSON RANDOLPH: 1823, by James Westhall Ford; © Thomas Jefferson Foundation at Monticello, photograph by Edward Owen

- THOMAS MANN RANDOLPH, JR.: American School (eighteenth century); Virginia Historical Society, Richmond, Virginia, USA/The Bridgeman Art Library

- DRAWING OF SLAVE QUARTERS AT MONTICELLO: 1770, by Thomas Jefferson; The Granger Collection, NYC

- PORTRAIT OF JOHN ADAMS: after Gilbert Stuart; Musée franco-américaine du Château de Blérancourt, Chauny, France/The Bridgeman Art Library

- TITLE PAGE OF A SUMMARY VIEW OF THE RIGHTS OF BRITISH AMERICA BY THOMAS JEFFERSON: 1774; Rare Books and Special Collections Division of the Library of Congress, Washington, D.C.

- HOUSE OF JACOB GRAFF, JR., WHERE JEFFERSON WROTE THE DECLARATION OF INDEPENDENCE IN 1776: by Benjamin Ridgway Evans; courtesy of the Historical Society of Pennsylvania Medium Graphics Collection

- "ORIGINAL ROUGH DRAFT" OF THE DECLARATION OF INDEPENDENCE: June 1776; Thomas Jefferson Papers, Manuscript Division, Library of Congress, Washington, D.C.

- WRITING THE DECLARATION OF INDEPENDENCE IN 1776: by Jean Leon Gerome Ferris; Virginia

Historical Society, Richmond, Virginia, USA/The Bridgeman Art Library

- SIEGE OF YORKTOWN, OCTOBER 17, 1781: 1836, by Louis Charles Auguste Couder; Château de Versailles, France/Giraudon/The Bridgeman Art Library
- TITLE PAGE OF NOTES ON THE STATE OF VIRGINIA BY THOMAS JEFFERSON: © Thomas Jefferson Foundation at Monticello

SECTION 2

- THOMAS JEFFERSON: 1791, by Charles Willson Peale; The Granger Collection, NYC
- THOMAS JEFFERSON AS U.S. AMBASSADOR TO FRANCE, 1786: by Mather Brown; Private Collection/Peter Newark Pictures/The Bridgeman Art Library
- JEFFERSON SKETCH OF THE FIRST HOUSE, OR MONTICELLO I: © Thomas Jefferson Foundation at Monticello
- MONTICELLO, SECOND VERSION (PLAN AND WEST ELEVATION): by Robert Mills, 1803; N155, K156/ original manuscript from the Coolidge Collection of Thomas Jefferson Manuscripts, Massachusetts Historical Society
- BUILDING THE HÔTEL DE SALM PARIS IN 1786 (DETAIL): artist unknown; Musée Carnavalet Paris/ Alfredo Dagli Orti/The Art Archive at Art Resource, NY
- CHRISTOPHER COLUMBUS, AFTER A PAINTING IN

THE UFFIZI, FLORENCE: 1788, by Calendi, Giuseppe; © Massachusetts Historical Society, Boston, MA, USA/The Bridgeman Art Library

- AMERICUS VESPUCIUS, BY UNKNOWN ARTIST: 1788; Massachusetts Historical Society
- SIR WALTER RALEIGH: 1787, by or after Edward Alcock; © Thomas Jefferson Foundation at Monticello/photograph by Edward Owen
- FRANCIS BACON, VISCOUNT ST. ALBAN: by Johan van der Banck, 1731, after an unknown artist (c. 1618); © National Portrait Gallery, London/NPG 1904
- SIR ISAAC NEWTON: by Sir Godfrey Kneller, Bt, 1702; © National Portrait Gallery, London/NPG 2881
- JOHN LOCKE: 1789, attributed to Stewart after Sir Godfrey Kneller; © Thomas Jefferson Foundation at Monticello/photograph by Edward Owen
- SURRENDER OF GENERAL LORD CORNWALLIS AT YORKTOWN, OCTOBER 19, 1781: 1820, by John Trumbull; United States Capitol Building, The Art Archive at Art Resource, NY
- GEORGE WASHINGTON: 1784–86, by Joseph Wright and John Trumbull; © Massachusetts Historical Society, Boston, MA, USA/The Bridgeman Art Library
- BENJAMIN FRANKLIN: attributed to Jean Valade, after 1778 original by Joseph-Silfrede Duplessis; © Thomas Jefferson Foundation at Monticello
- JAMES MONROE: 1817, by Gilbert Stuart; The Granger Collection, NYC

- JOHN ADAMS: 1788, by Mather Brown; © Boston Athenaeum, USA/The Bridgeman Art Library
- ABIGAIL ADAMS: 1785, by Mather Brown; The Granger Collection, NYC
- PORTRAIT OF JAMES MADISON BY GILBERT STUART: 1804; The Colonial Williamsburg Foundation, Gift of Mrs. George S. Robbins, 1945–23
- DOLLEY PAYNE MADISON BY GILBERT STUART: 1804; White House Historical Association (White House Collection)
- MARQUIS MARIE-JOSEPH PAUL YVES ROCH GILBERT DU MOTIER DE LAFAYETTE: 1790, by Joseph Boze; © Massachusetts Historical Society, Boston, MA, USA/The Bridgeman Art Library
- NAPOLEON CROSSING THE ALPS: by Jacques-Louis David; Château de Versailles, France/Peter Willi/The Bridgeman Art Library
- MARIA COSWAY: engraving by Valentine Green, after Maria Cosway self-portrait, 1787; Carol Burnell Collection
- KING LOUIS XVI OF FRANCE ON HIS CORONATION DAY, JUNE 11, 1775: c. 1787; The Granger Collection, NYC
- PORTRAIT OF MARIE ANTOIÂNETTE, QUEEN OF FRANCE: 1775, by Jean-Baptiste André Gautier D'Agoty; Chateau de Versailles, France/Giraudon/The Bridgeman Art Library
- DESCENT FROM THE CROSS: mid-sixteenth century, by Frans Floris; © Thomas Jefferson Foundation at Monticello/photograph by Edward Owen
- HERODIAS BEARING THE HEAD OF ST. JOHN THE

Baptist: copy after Guido Reni original, c. 1631; © Thomas Jefferson Foundation at Monticello/ photograph by Edward Owen

- Jesus in the Praetorium: copy after Jan Gossaert original, 1527; © Thomas Jefferson Foundation at Monticello/photograph by Edward Owen

- Sarah Presents Hagar to Abraham: copy of the painting in Munich, Alte Pinakothek, dated 1699, by Adriaen van der Werff; Louvre, Paris, France/Erich Lessing/Art Resource, NY

- Young Chief of the Sack Nation: 1802; © Thomas Jefferson Foundation at Monticello/photograph by Edward Owen

- Natural Bridge Engraving: 1808, after William Roberts; © Thomas Jefferson Foundation at Monticello

- Lewis and Clark on the Lower Columbia River: 1905, by Charles Marion Russell; Private Collection/Peter Newark American Pictures/The Bridgeman Art Library

- "A Philosophic Cock": 1804, American School (nineteenth century); American Antiquarian Society, Worcester, Massachusetts, USA/The Bridgeman Art Library

- Alexander Hamilton: 1806, by John Trumbull; The Granger Collection, NYC

- Aaron Burr: by John Vanderlyn, early nineteenth century; The Granger Collection, NYC

- Portrait of Timothy Pickering: by Gilbert Stuart; courtesy of M. S. Rau Antiques, New Orleans

- TRIPOLITAN WAR: 1804, from a painting by Dennis Malone Carter; The Granger Collection, NYC
- THOMAS JEFFERSON RANDOLPH: c. 1808, by Charles Willson Peale; © Thomas Jefferson Foundation at Monticello/photograph by Edward Owen
- JEFFERSON'S WRITING DESK: Division of Political History, National Museum of American History, Smithsonian Institution, Washington, D.C.
- POPLAR FOREST: by L. Diane Johnson, 1999; courtesy of Thomas Jefferson's Poplar Forest, Bedford County, Virginia
- UNIVERSITY OF VIRGINIA ROTUNDA AND LAWN: engraving by J. Serz, published by C. Bohn, 1856; Accession #RG-30/1/8.801, University of Virginia Visual History Collection, Special Collections, University of Virginia Library, Charlottesville, VA

SECTION 3

- ENGRAVING OF GRILLE DE CHAILLOT, which shows Hôtel de Langeac, where Jefferson lived in Paris; © Thomas Jefferson Foundation at Monticello
- THE TAKING OF THE BASTILLE, JULY 14, 1789: French School (eighteenth century); Château de Versailles, France/Giraudon/The Bridgeman Art Library
- THOMAS JEFFERSON DEED OF MANUMISSION TO JAMES HEMINGS, FEBRUARY 5, 1796: accession

#5589, Special Collections, University of Virginia Library, Charlottesville, VA

- WASHINGTON WITH JEFFERSON AND HAMILTON: 1872, by Constantino Brumidi; Senate Reception Room of the U.S. Capitol/Architect of the Capitol
- JOHN JAY: 1794, by Gilbert Stuart; The Granger Collection, NYC
- RUFUS KING: 1820, by Gilbert Stuart; National Portrait Gallery, Smithsonian Institution, Washington, D.C./Art Resource, NY
- PRESIDENTIAL CAMPAIGN BANNER: 1800; The Granger Collection, NYC
- A VIEW OF THE PRESIDENT'S HOUSE IN THE CITY OF WASHINGTON AFTER THE CONFLAGRATION OF AUGUST 24, 1814: engraver William Strickland, artist George Munger; Library of Congress Prints and Photographs Division, Washington, D.C.
- DESIGN FOR THE PRESIDENT'S HOUSE COMPETITION: c. 1792, by Thomas Jefferson; The Granger Collection, NYC
- PORTRAIT OF ELIZABETH MERRY, WIFE OF ANTHONY MERRY: 1805, by Gilbert Stuart; Fundación Lázaro Galdiano, Madrid
- MARGARET BAYARD SMITH: After the portrait by Charles Bird King, in the possession of her grandson, J. Henley Smith, Washington, from **The First Forty Years of Washington Society** by Gaillard Hunt (ed.)
- TREATY BETWEEN THE UNITED STATES AND FRANCE FOR THE CESSION OF LOUISIANA, APRIL 30,

Westhall Ford, 1823; © Thomas Jefferson Foundation at Monticello/photograph by Katherine Wetzel

- EPITAPH BY THOMAS JEFFERSON: c. March, 1826; Thomas Jefferson Papers, Manuscript Division, Library of Congress, Washington, D.C.

INDEX

Abraham (prophet), 320

Adams, Abigail, 55, 127,
    415, 450, 482, 511,
    518, 527, 971n
  death of, 700
  Polly Jefferson and,
    310–11
  TJ's correspondence
    with, 269–70,
    274–75, 282–83,
    289, 349–50, 604–6,
    1112n–1113n

Adams, Charles, 518–19

Adams, Charles Francis,
  794n

Adams, Henry, ix, 752,
  756, 782n

Adams, John, xviii–xix,
  xxi–xxii, xxv, xxxv,
  114, 127–28, 160,
  166–67, 230, 240,
  258, 269, 279, 282,
  286–89, 313, 327,
  330, 351, 368,
  377–79, 406,
  422–23, 450,
  452–54, 462,
  480–82, 507, 526,
  547–48, 556, 561,
  565, 593, 607, 657,
  672, 673, 724–26,
  729, 749–50, 751,
  756, 765–66, 768,
  802n–3n, 902n,
  926n, 944n, 956n,
  959n, 1049n–50n,
  1107n
  Alien and Sedition
    Acts and, 465–67
  background of, 128
  cabinet of, 485
  Charles Adams's death
    and, 517–18, 522–23
  death of, 749–50
  Declaration of
    Independence and,
    149–53
  on democracy, 356
  on draft Constitution,
    316–17
  1800 election and,
    490–91, 501–3,
    1037n, 1038n
  elected president, 450

Adams, John
(**continued**)
final words of, 750
inauguration of, 454
Judiciary Act signed
by, 500–1
in mission to Great
Britain, 275
New York lodgings of,
348
as president, 456–57
on public speaking,
130–31
on Shays's Rebellion,
306–7
TJ contrasted with,
127–28
TJ's correspondence
with, 608–9, 667,
686–93, 712–13,
716, 724–25,
1004n–5n, 1087n
TJ's friendship with,
127–28, 415, 489,
511, 686–87
TJ's unmailed letter to,
452–53
XYZ affair and,
464–65
Adams, John, Sr., 128
Adams, John Quincy,
xxi, 270, 538, 544,
559, 610, 644, 652,
660, 688, 727, 749,
788n, 1003n, 1139n
Adams, Louisa
Catherine, 644
Adams, Nabby, **see**
Smith, Abigail
Adams
Adams, Samuel, 152,
1005n
Adams, Thomas, 86
Addison, Joseph, 12, 65
Aeschylus, 739
Age of Reason, The
(Paine), 286
Albany Plan of Union,
41–42, 830n–31n
Alberti, Francis, 65
Alexander I, Tsar of
Russia, 674
Alexander VI, Pope, 366
Algiers, 270
Alien and Sedition Acts,
465–70, 479–80,
524, 529, 647, 687
Federalists and, 467,
469–70, 479–81
Madison on, 467–68
prosecutions under,
472–73

Republicans and, 465–66, 470, 479–81

TJ's opposition to, 473–78

TJ's pardons under, 533–35

Allen, Ethan, 144

Ambler, Betsy, 203

Ambler, Jacquelin, 38

Ambler, Polly, 941n

America (Ogilby), 12

American Bible Society, 713–14

American Philosophical Society, 135, 554

American Revolution, xxxii, 198–99, 241, 828n–48n

Albany Plan of Union in, 41–42

boycott in, 101, 107, 118

British threat to arm slaves in, 122, 123, 142–43

Dunmore's seizure of gunpowder in, 116, 121–22

early conflicts in, 102–4

English history and tradition in, 42–44

French Revolution and, 400–1

hatred of George III in, xxxiii–xxxiv

legacy of English Civil War and, 168–69

liberal tradition in, 169

Navigation Acts and, 41, 46

roots of, 866n–67n

Stamp Act and, 48–51, 59, 68, 106, 179

Sugar Act and, 46

Summary View and, 109–14, 118

western lands and, 46, 104, 196–97

see also Paris, Treaty of

Ames, Fisher, 445

Ames, Nathaniel, 470

Ampthill (plantation), 228

Anacharsis, 620

Anburey, Thomas, 9

Andrews, Charles M., 866n

Anglican Church, 183

Annapolis Convention
of 1786, 296
Anson, George, Lord,
12, 30
Aranjuez, Treaty of, 577
**Architecture of A-
Palladio,** 134
Argonaut, HMS, 367
Arnold, Benedict, 140,
199, 201, 205, 212,
225, 369, 411, 423,
929n
Articles of
Confederation, 125,
222
Franklin's proposal of,
232–33
**Art of Cookery Made
Plain and Easy**
(Glasse), 134
Artois, Comte d', 295
Assembly of Notables,
French, 305, 326
Aurelius, Marcus, 659
Aurora, 441, 443, 472,
1035n
Austerlitz, Battle of,
622
Austria, 349
Autobiography
(Jefferson), 80

Bache, Benjamin
Franklin, 435, 441,
472
Bacon, Edmund, xxiii,
216, 663, 702
Bacon, Francis, 26, 352,
386, 674
Bainbridge, William,
1109n
Baldwin, Abraham, 463
Baldwin, Simeon, 558,
1103n
ballooning experiments,
245–46, 947n
Baltimore **American,**
485
Bankhead, Ann Cary
Randolph, 404, 659,
701–2, 704
Bankhead, Charles L.,
659, 701–3, 1140n
Bank of the United
States, 547, 587–88,
1012n
Barbary States, 287, 423,
545–47, 955n
Dale mission to,
545–46
Philadelphia episode
and, 603, 1110n
Barbé-Marbois, Marquis

de, 234, 248, 580, 715, 948n–49n
Barlow, Joel, 644
Barron, James, 639
Barton, Benjamin S., 1086n
Baxter (author), 617, 620–21
Bayard, Andrew, 784n
Bayard, James, 498, 505–6, 509, 522, 784n, 795n, 1007n, 1089n
Bayard, John, 795n
Beckley, John, 374, 383
Beckwith, George, 314, 369, 1000n, 1007n
Beggar's Opera, The (Gay), 65
Bell, John, 663
Bell, Robert, 132
Bentham, Jeremy, 160
Bergere (Jefferson's dog), xxv
Berkeley, Sir William, 9
Berlin Decree, 645
Bermuda, 587
Bernard, John, 354
Beverley, William, 1046n
Bible, 739

Bingham, William, 454
Bishop, Samuel, 565
Bizarre (plantation), 404
Bland, Martha, 133
Bland, Richard, 74, 844n
Bland, Theodorick, Jr., 132
Bolingbroke, Henry St. John, Viscount, 42
Bolling, John, 471
Bolling, Mary Jefferson, 471
Bonaparte, Joséphine, 578–79
Book of Kings, The, xxv
Boston Port Act, 105, 108, 118, 889n
Boston Tea Party, 101, 105, 123
Boswell, James, 292, 295
Botetourt, Norborne Berkeley, Lord, 66, 69, 116, 851n
Braxton, Carter, 909n, 910n
Breckinridge, John, 475, 495, 583, 619
Broadnax, Lydia, 629, 1125n
Brown, Mather, 674

Brown, Michael, 628–29, 1125n

Buffon, Comte de, 243, 247, 281

Bunker Hill, Battle of, 127, 715

Burgh, James, 132

Burgoyne, John, 186

Burke, Edmund, 96, 168

Burkin, Elizabeth, 60

Burnaby, Andrew, xxxviii

Burr, Aaron, xviii, 382, 444, 459, 623, 1107–8n, 1032n, 1060n–62n, 1108n–9n, 1118n–19n
  arrest and trial of, 633–36
  background of, 436
  conspiracy and plotting of, 622, 630–32
  1800 election and, 488, 493–95, 498, 504, 505, 508
  1804 election and, 601, 608–9
  Hamilton slain by, 607
  Plumer on, 612–13
  TJ's presidency and, 551–53

Burr, Aaron, Sr., 436

Burr, Elizabeth Edwards, 436

Burr, Theodosia (daughter), 436

Burr, Theodosia Prevost, 436

Burwell, Lewis, Jr., 35

Burwell, Rebecca Lewis, 35–38, 56, 62, 64, 69, 82, 147, 203

Burwell, William A., 569

Bush, George H. W., 768

Bushnell, David, 281

Byrd, William, II, 6, 10–11, 826n

Cabot, George, 493–94, 551, 600

Caesar, Julius, 386, 563

Calhoun, John C., 728

Callender, James Thomson, 472, 482, 573, 605, 607, 1077n, 1093n
  pardon issue and, 533–36

Sally Hemings controversy and, 566–70

Cambrian, HMS, 627

Camden, Battle of, 199

Campbell, Arthur, 1098n

Canada, xxxiv, 129, 141, 307, 367, 397, 554, 587, 649, 839n, 899n, 903n

capitalism, 169

Caractacus (Jefferson's horse), 207

Carey, Henry, 65

Carleton, General, 889n

Carlton (plantation), 702

Carr, Dabney, 20, 56, 91–93, 113, 249, 259, 741, 852n, 914n

Carr, Dabney, Jr., 740, 747

Carr, Martha Jefferson, 56, 59, 88, 91, 93, 217, 249, 258, 484

Carr, Peter, 249, 259, 685

Carroll, Daniel, 1062n

Carter, Robert, 720

Carters Mountain, 596

Cary, Archibald, 228, 278, 281

Castiglioni, Luigi, 283

Ceracchi, Giuseppe, 360

Ceres, 265, 267

Cervantes, Miguel de, 248

Charles I, King of England, 42

Charles II, King of England, 472, 769

Charlotte, Queen of England, 288

Chase, Samuel, 481–82, 562
  impeachment of, 563, 635

Chastellux, Marquis de, 211–13, 228

Chatsworth (estate), 21

Cherokee Indians, 165

Chesapeake, USS, 639–43, 1131n

Chesapeake & Ohio Canal, 254

Chestnut, Mary Boykin, 83–84

Chevalière d'Eon, Mademoiselle, 293

Christianity, TJ's views on, 710–11

Cicero, 111, 334

Cincinnatus, 388

Claggett, Thomas, 499
Clark, George Rogers,
    196–97, 226, 244,
    554–56
Clark, William, 197,
    556, 582, 615–17,
    681
Clarke, General, 287
Clay, Charles, 107, 146,
    336
Clay, Henry, 728
Clermont, 343
Clinton, George, 462,
    589, 609, 642,
    1014**n**, 1139**n**
Cobbett, William, 439
Cocke, William, 444
Coercive Acts, 118
Colbert, Burwell, 703,
    737, 746
Coles, Edward, 688
Coles, John, 64
College of William and
    Mary, 21–22, 62,
    182, 247, 818**n**
**Columbian Mirror and
    Alexandria Gazette,
    The,** 446
Columbus, Christopher,
    673, 674
Common Sense (Paine),

47, 145, 286, 374,
    964**n**
Concord, Battle of,
    xxxiii, 119, 123
Condorcet, Marquis de,
    268
Congress,
    Confederation, 241,
    475
    Committee of States
    of, 233, 957**n**
    powerlessness of,
    232–33, 239–40,
    251–52
    ratification of Treaty of
    Paris in, 240–43
    sites of, 239–40
    Virginia's cession of
    territory and, 256
Congress, Continental,
    33, 107–9, 118, 129,
    309–10, 673, 878**n**,
    886**n**, 893**n**
    Committee of
    Unfinished Business
    of, 143–44
    Declaration of
    Independence in,
    153–60
    independence debate
    in, 148–49, 169–70

national government
debate in, 166
official seal and,
167–68
Olive Branch petition
and, 130
Second, 115–17,
118–19, 124,
125–27
Congress, U.S., 319,
348, 372, 430, 436,
454, 462, 500, 539,
546, 551, 556, 586,
633, 651, 706, 946n,
956n, 957n, 1013n,
1014n, 1110n
Chesapeake
controversy and,
642–43
corruption issue and,
384, 391
embargo issue and,
646–48, 654–55
Jay Treaty in, 439
Missouri statehood
issue in, 715–17
TJ's first annual
address to, 547
see also House of
Representatives, U.S.;
Senate, U.S.

Connecticut, 186, 242,
361, 565, 599, 649
Connecticut Courant,
451
Considerations on the
Nature and Extent of
the Authority of the
British Parliament
(Wilson), 156
Constitution, French,
334
Constitution, U.S., xviii,
328, 368, 372,
408–9, 429, 468,
477, 562, 610, 615,
687, 691, 693,
694–95, 984n,
1012n, 1022n
drafting of, 315–19
first treaty under,
327–28
Louisiana Purchase
and, 583–89, 1101n
ratification of, 319–20,
976n
three-fifths clause of,
451
TJ's reaction to,
317–19
Twelfth Amendment
to, 446, 602, 1037n

Constitutional Convention of 1787, xxxiv, 285–86, 309–10, 318, 391
  Hamilton at, 358–59
  monarchism and, 464
  nascent royalism and, 314–15
Constitutional Settlement of 1689–1701, 43
Cook, James, 367
Coolidge, Ellen Randolph, 79, 539, 676, 752–54
Cooper, Thomas, 708–9
Copley, John Singleton, 119
Cornwallis, Charles, Lord, 198–99, 203–6, 208, 212, 225, 423, 936n
Corny, Madame de, 332
Corps of Volunteers for North West Discovery, see Lewis and Clark expedition
Cosway, Maria Hadfield, xxxi, 291–302, 320, 333, 675
  background and description of, 294
  TJ's "Head and Heart" letter to, 297–303
  TJ's liaison with, 295–303
Cosway, Richard, 292–93, 295
Coutts, William, 87
Coxe, Tench, 428, 462, 500, 532
Crawford, William, 728
Creek Indians, 624
Crèvecoeur, J. Hector St. John de, 235, 247, 268, 975n
Cromwell, Oliver, 42
Cutting, John Brown, 378
Cutting, Nathaniel, 351

Dale, Richard, 545–46
Danbury Baptist Association, 550
Dandridge, Nathaniel, 34, 48
Dante Alighieri, 226
Dartmouth, William Legge, Lord, 138
Davies, Samuel, 65

Davis, Matthew L., 552, 1083n
Dawson, John, 633
Day of Fasting and Prayer resolution, 106–7, 112, 179, 576
Deane, Silas, 33, 177, 914n
Dearborn, Henry, 529, 604, 620
de Calonne, Charles-Alexandre, 305
Decatur, Stephen, 603
Declaration of Independence, xx, 18, 44, 53, 142, 146–61, 170, 179–80, 200, 225, 244, 246, 260, 492, 576, 641, 672, 707, 744, 757, 762
  Adams on, 149–53
  editing of, 155–56
  Enlightenment vision of, 154, 156–57, 163
  50th anniversary of, 738, 804n
  Franklin and, 155–58
  French Revolution and, 333
  influences on, 156–57
  Page on, 161
  ratification of, 159–60
  slavery question and, 158, 185–86
  TJ and drafting of, 150–56
Declaration of Pillnitz, 349
Declaration of Rights, British, 43, 156
Declaration of the Rights of Man and of the Citizen, 333, 380
Declaratory Act, British, 59
Dehon, Theodore, 698
Delaware, 149, 902n
De l'influence de la révolution de l'Amérique sur l'Europe (Condorcet), 268
democracy, 356, 372–73, 392, 484, 600
  in TJ-Adams correspondence, 691–93
Democratic-Republicans, 411, 422
  Whiskey Rebellion and, 430

de Staël, Madame, xxv
Dexter, Samuel, 429,
    485
Dick (pet bird), 527–28,
    1075n
Dickinson, John, 67,
    129, 466, 512, 530,
    636, 902n
Discourses on Davila
    (Adams), 356, 375,
    383, 1005n
Dissertation on
    Education (Maury),
    21
Dixon, John, 54
Donald, Alexander,
    251
Don Quixote
    (Cervantes), 248
Dorchester, Lord, 314,
    867n–68n
Douglas, William, 19
Douglas (home), 65
Driver, HMS, 627
Drummer (Addison), 65
Drummond, Mrs., 84
Duane, William, 642
Duché, Jacob, 126
Duffy, Peirce, 378–79
Dunbar, Louise
    Burnham, 800n

Dunglison, Robley, 570,
    740, 745
Dunlap, John, 159
Dunlap, William, 620
Dunmore, John Murray,
    Lord, 116, 119–21,
    123, 139–42, 193,
    880n, 883n, 898n,
    910n
  House of Burgesses
    dissolved by, 69, 141,
    875n
du Pont de Nemours,
    Pierre-Samuel,
    485–86, 575, 577,
    657, 680
Duval, William, 630

East India Company,
    105
Edgehill (plantation),
    701, 993n
Edgeworth, Maria, 702
Edwards, Jonathan, 436
Eisenhower, Dwight D.,
    768
election of 1796, 445–54
  fear of war with France
    and, 446–47
  Republican-Federalist
    conflict in, 447–50

three-fifths clause and,
451
TJ on politics of, 450
TJ's unmailed letter to
Adams in, 452–53
election of 1800,
xvii–xxi, 437, 452,
480, 497–98, 545,
560, 566, 659,
686–87, 1071n–72n
Adams and, 489–91,
502–3, 1038n
Alien and Sedition
Acts and, 484
Burr and, 488,
493–98, 504, 505,
508
Federalists and, 494,
500, 501, 509
House vote in, 509
Judiciary Act and,
500–2
New York State returns
in, 488, 492
in Pennsylvania,
503–4
results of, 492–93
TJ-Adams exchanges
and, 502–3, 507–8
TJ's satisfaction with,
512–13

election of 1804:
Burr and, 601, 608–9
Federalists and, 610
Hamilton's death and,
607–9
results of, 610
TJ's renomination in,
599
elections:
of 1792, 462
of 1796, see election of
1796
of 1800, see election of
1800
of 1804, see election of
1804
of 1808, 618, 653,
1138n–39n
of 1824, 728
of 1828, 729
Elk Hill (plantation),
208
Ellsworth, Oliver, 501
English Civil War, 42,
105, 466, 472, 564
legacy of, 168, 768
Enlightenment, xxiv,
154, 386, 802n
Declaration of
Independence and,
154, 156, 163

entail, 180

Enterprize, USS,
546

Eppes, Elizabeth, 220,
228, 258, 273–74,
313, 343

Eppes, Francis, 80, 229,
258, 273, 289, 343,
894n, 965n

Eppes, John Wayles, 457,
495, 573, 602, 628,
637, 642, 693, 697,
1112n

Eppes, Polly Jefferson,
187, 217, 220, 228,
258, 274, 289, 322,
343, 373, 383, 512,
532, 568, 571–72,
743, 825n, 965n,
1170n
  children of, 602
  death of, 603–4
  in journey to France,
    310–13
  marriage of, 457

Erskine, David
  Montagu, 644

Estates-General, French,
305, 326, 331–32

Euripides, 32, 739

Eustis, William, 616

Everett, Edward, 751

Excursion (Mallet), 92

**Experiments upon
  the Human Bile**
  (McClurg), 135

Farmer's Letters, 67

Farrell and Jones
  (merchant house), 80,
  103

Fauquier, Francis, 24,
51, 66–67, 126, 193,
823n

Federalists, xix, 329,
355–57, 380–83,
398, 400, 411, 422,
428–29, 443–44,
456–57, 484–86,
490, 524, 526–27,
529, 531, 548,
559–61, 563–65,
592, 640, 652,
655, 687, 718, 728,
803n, 1018n, 1038n,
1060n, 1082n
  Alien and Sedition
    Acts and, 467, 469,
    479–80
  disunion movement
    and, 599–600
  1800 election and,

493–95, 500, 501, 509
1804 election and, 610–11
1808 election and, 653
Hartford Convention and, 697
Jay Treaty and, 439
Judiciary Act of 1801 and, 500, 560
Louisiana Purchase and, 588
Mazzei letter controversy and, 461
1796 election and, 446–50
TJ's assessments of, 441–42, 531–32
TJ's presidency criticized by, 548–54, 559–60, 563–65, 594–95
Twelfth Amendment and, 602
War of 1812 and, 697
Fenno, John, 356–57, 375
First Great Awakening, 169
Fitzhugh, William, 509

Flat Hat Club (FHC), 35
Fleming, William, 909n
Fletcher, Elijah, 683
Florida, Spanish, 367, 621, 839n, 903n, 999n
Floyd, Catherine "Kitty," 229, 236, 941n
Floyd, William, 229
Forest (plantation), 82–84, 88
Fort Detroit, 194–96
Fossett, Joe, 748
Foster, Augustus J., 543, 600–1, 612, 613, 644
Foster, Dwight, 508
Fowey, HMS, 122, 885n–86n
Frame, David, 60
France, xxiii, xxiv, 152, 177, 179, 211, 225, 229–30, 247, 315–16, 322, 359, 367, 369, 394, 447, 454, 553, 621–22, 659, 687, 840n, 903n, 920n, 946n, 983n–84n, 1038n
Jay Treaty and, 460–61, 464

France, (continued)
  Louisiana Purchase
    and, 575–81,
    584–85
  St. Domingue slave
    insurrection and,
    380–81
  slavery and, 322
  Third Treaty of San
    Ildefonso and,
    574–77
  TJ's mission to, see
    France, Jefferson's
    mission to
  U.S. embargo and,
    646–49, 650–51
  U.S. Quasi-War with,
    456, 465, 529–30
  U.S. relationship with,
    265–68, 327–28,
    400–3
  XYZ affair and, 464,
    472, 564
France, Jefferson's
    mission to, 260–339
  art and science
    interests in, 279–81,
    291–95
  chess playing in, 279
  Cosway liaison in,
    294–303, 333

French Revolution in,
    304–5, 331–33
intellectual society in,
    279
literary world in,
    292–93
Paris in, 269–70
Patsy Jefferson in, 260,
    265–67, 268–69,
    275, 279, 287, 289,
    311, 334
philosophical world in,
    281
public and Parisian life
    in, 283–85
return to U.S. in,
    338–39, 343
TJ's acquisitions in,
    278
TJ's interests and
    studies in, 270
TJ's lodgings in,
    268–69
TJ's view of France
    and, 265–66
trip to Great Britain in,
    287–89
U.S.-France relations
    and, 266–68
voyage to France in,
    259–60, 265–67

"Frankfort advice,"
151–52
Franklin, Benjamin, 41,
125, 131, 167–68,
177, 230, 240,
252–53, 258, 268,
280, 316, 327, 328,
460, 661, 674, 675,
830n–31n, 905n–6n,
914n, 923n, 956n,
986n
Articles of
Confederation
proposed by, 232–33
Declaration of
Independence and,
155–56, 158
Frederick II (the Great),
King of Prussia, xxv,
840n
Frederick William II,
King of Prussia, 316,
349
French and Indian War,
45, 129, 696, 839n
French Revolution,
265–66, 307, 327,
331, 1018n
American Revolution
and, 400
Declaration of

Independence and,
333
European wars and,
349
financial and political
differences in, 304–5
onset, 332–33
Reign of Terror in,
332, 349, 400
French West Indies, 423
Freneau, Philip, 382,
407, 483–84
Fry, Joshua, 6
Furman, Richard, 553

Gabriel (slave), 487–88,
1056n
Gage, Thomas, 118
Gallatin, Albert, 428,
479, 498, 529, 534,
557, 540–41, 552,
557–58, 586, 604,
620, 626, 639–40,
646, 784n, 1100n,
1107n, 1122n
Gallatin, Hannah, 529,
540–41, 784n, 1107n
Galloway, Joseph, 868n
Gaspee, HMS, 864n
Gates, Horatio, 199, 415,
574, 581, 927n

Gay, John, 65

Gazette de Leide, 356–57

Gazette of the United States, 356, 382, 406, 481, 485

General Assembly, Virginia, 183, 185, 203, 236, 364–65, 734
TJ in, 180–81

General Court, Virginia, 25

Genet, Edmond-Charles, 409, 428, 1022n

Geography: Or a Description of the World (Adams), 271

George III, King of England, xxxiii, 49, 52, 54, 109, 115, 156, 168, 170, 208, 288, 472, 481, 597, 645, 869n, 885n, 896n, 899n

Georgia, 158, 193, 361, 624

Germania (Tacitus), 44

Germany, 186

Gerry, Elbridge, xx, 58, 160, 452, 477, 499, 609, 957n, 1044n, 1075n

Ghent, Treaty of, xxxiii, 697, 728

Gibbon, Edward, 658

Gibbs, James, 134

Gil Blas (Lesage), 248

Giles, William Branch, 398–99, 429–30, 433, 436, 532, 636

Glasse, Hannah, 134

Glorious Revolution of 1688, 42–44

Goodrich, Elizur, 565

Gordon, Lord, 958n

Gordon-Reed, Annette, 629

Graff, Jacob, Jr., 148, 154

Granger, George, 200

Great Britain, xx, xxxii–xxxiii, 48, 67, 69, 110, 136, 165, 177, 225, 315, 359, 370, 379, 394, 397, 428–29, 554, 612, 621–22, 636, 673, 687, 768, 840, 851, 896n, 920n, 959n, 972n

Adams as minister to, 275

American Revolution and history of, 42–44

imports boycott and, 624

impressment practice of, 371, 636, 645, 696

Jay Treaty and, 437–38, 460

Nootka Sound episode and, 366–68, 370, 1001n

Olive Branch petition and, 130

TJ's antipathy for, 272, 276, 350, 355

TJ's visit to, 287–89

Treaty of Paris and, 231, 241–43, 253

U.S. Embargo and, 643–55

War of 1812 and, xxxiii, 649–50, 697

at war with France, 408, 423, 460

Great War for the Empire, 45

Grenville, George, 46–47

Griswold, Roger, 464, 498–99, 504, 548, 589, 1090n

Grizzle (Jefferson's dog), xxv

habeas corpus, 318

Haiti, see St. Domingue

Hamilton, Alexander, xxi, xxxv, 366, 428, 462, 468, 470, 480, 525, 552, 587, 633, 672, 673, 726, 758, 765, 788n, 803n, 986n, 1001n, 1003n–4n, 1008n, 1013n, 1017n, 1021n, 1024n, 1032n–33n

background of, 357–58

Burr's slaying of, 607–9

at Constitutional Convention, 358–59

corruption issue and, 384

debt assumption issue and, 360–65

1800 election and, 488–89, 491, 508

excise tax proclamation of, 396–97

Hamilton, Alexander,
   (continued)
 Genet affair and, 409
 Jay Treaty and,
    438–39
 monarchist sympathies
    of, 369, 390
 national bank proposal
    of, 371–72
 Reynolds affair and,
    398
 Rights of Man note of,
    374–75
 1796 election and, 448
 TJ contrasted with,
    375–76
 TJ's ideological conflict
    with, 375–80,
    383–95, 406–7, 411
 on TJ's inaugural
    address, 522
 on Washington's death,
    483
Hamilton, Henry,
    195–97, 921n
Hamilton, William, 130
Hammond, George, 390
Hancock, John, 177–78,
    328, 883n, 1005n
Handel, George Frideric,
    278

Harper, Robert
    Goodloe, 534
Harrison, Benjamin,
    160, 910n
Harrison, William
    Henry, 588
Hartford Convention of
    1814–15, 697, 728
Harvard College, 708
Hatch, Frederick, 743,
    748
Hay, George, 634
Hazlitt, William, 293
Hemings, Captain, 83
Hemings, Critta, 83
Hemings, Elizabeth, 83,
    87, 93–94, 148, 216,
    217, 1174n
Hemings, Eston, 326,
    748, 799n, 981n
Hemings, Harriet, 326,
    471, 748, 799n,
    980n, 1174n
Hemings, James, 83, 94,
    191, 200, 258, 260,
    323, 338, 343
Hemings, John, 94, 148,
    676, 747, 748
Hemings, Madison, 83,
    322, 324–26, 684,
    748, 980n–981n

Hemings, Martin, 191, 207, 211

Hemings, Peter, 83, 1173n

Hemings, Robert, 83, 94, 191, 200

Hemings, Sarah "Sally," xxxi–xxxii, 83, 94, 217, 320, 322–26, 338, 532, 992n
Callender's exposé of, 557, 567–69
children of, 323–26, 457, 471–72, 684–85, 719–20, 748, 796n–800n, 980n–81n, 1174n
death of, 749
description of, 310–11
DNA analysis of descendents of, 765, 798n
emancipation of, 748–49, 1174n
in journey to France, 310–12
Monticello life of, 347–48, 648
TJ's liaison with, 322–26, 347–48, 434, 765, 940n–41n

Hemings, Thenia, 83

Hemings, William Beverly, 326, 457, 748, 980n, 1174n

Hemings family, 83–84
in move to Monticello, 93–94

Henry, Patrick, 34, 48, 54, 103, 105, 111, 116–17, 126, 127, 189, 209, 405, 444, 877n, 934n, 976n–77n
Fifth Resolution and, 48–52

Hichborn, Benjamin, 498

Hill, Henry, 140

History of England (Baxter), 617

History of England (Rapin-Thoyras), 12

Hobbes, Thomas, 1041n

Home, John, 65

Homer, 113, 219

Honest Yorkshireman, The (Carey), 65

Hopkinson, Francis, 245–46, 248, 329, 947n, 957n, 977n

Hopkinson, Mrs.
Thomas, 248
Horace, 620
Houdetot, Comtesse d',
279
Houdon, Jean-Antoine,
280, 675, 961n
House, Mary, 229, 240
House, Samuel, 244
House of Burgesses,
Virginia, 7, 8, 22,
41, 59, 99, 105, 122,
126, 157, 185, 434,
541, 744, 845n, 991n
dissolution of, 69, 141,
875n
Fifth Resolution debate
in, 48–52
Journal of, 69
slavery question and,
74–75
TJ elected to, 68
TJ's first session in,
100–1
House of Commons,
British, 46–47, 168,
844n
House of Delegates,
Virginia, 488
House of Representatives,
U.S., xix, 353,
390–91, 449, 479–80,
529, 531, 624, 1034n,
1126n
Alien and Sedition Acts
petition in, 479–80
debt assumption issue
in, 362
1800 election and,
xx–xxi, 505, 509–10
1824 election and,
728–29
Giles's resolution in,
398–99
Griswold-Lyons brawl
in, 464
Jay Treaty and, 439
Missouri statehood
issue in, 715–16
Ways and Means
Committee of, 1028n
Howe, William, 909n
Howell, Samuel, 75
Hughes, Wormley, 699,
747, 1173n
Hugues, Pierre-François,
293
Humboldt, Alexander
von, 542
Hume, David, 621
Humphreys, David, 329,
1015n

Iliad (Homer), 220
impressment, 371, 637,
    645, 696
Indiana Territory, 588
Indians, xxxiii, 45, 104,
    165, 423, 551, 554,
    588–89, 719, 889n,
    911n, 973n
  in American
    Revolution, 193, 198
  Northwest Territories
    mission and, 368–69
  TJ's view of, 165
Intolerable Acts, 105
Irving, Washington, 182
Isle of Wight, 267
Italy, 309
Izard, Ralph, 277

Jackson, Andrew, xxi,
    565, 581, 728,
    731–32, 788n,
    1037n
James, Duke of York,
    564
Jamestown colony,
    xxxii, 6
Jarvis, William, 1141n
Jay, John, 230–31, 234,
    241, 277, 280–81,
    328, 392, 424, 437,

488–89, 501, 609,
    943n, 956n, 972n
Jay Treaty, 437–38, 442,
    447
  France's reaction to,
    460
  Mazzei letter
    controversy and, 461
Jefferson, Elizabeth, 16,
    99, 107
Jefferson, Field, 798n–
    99n
Jefferson, George, 799n
Jefferson, Isaac Granger,
    xxiii, 90–91, 133,
    191, 192, 200–1, 211,
    427, 797n–98n
Jefferson, Isham, 799n
Jefferson, Jane
    (daughter), 100, 138
Jefferson, Jane (sister),
    15, 19, 133, 179, 218,
    229, 815n, 914n
  death of, 56–57, 92
Jefferson, Jane Randolph
    (mother), 3, 8, 10,
    13–18, 807n, 815n,
    816n
  death of, 146–48
  TJ influenced by,
    15–18

Jefferson, John Garland,
799n
Jefferson, Lilburne, 799n
Jefferson, Lucy Elizabeth
(first), 203, 213
Jefferson, Lucy Elizabeth
(second), 213, 214,
217, 220, 228, 937n
death of, 273–74
Jefferson, Martha
(daughter), see Carr,
Martha Jefferson
Jefferson, Martha Wayles
Skelton (Patty),
77–91, 100, 142,
171–72, 178, 180,
200, 311
background of, 80–82
British occupation of
Monticello and, 200,
208
death of, 214–20, 227,
938n
health of, 138–41, 162,
167, 171, 179, 187,
213, 908n
personality of, 187–88
TJ's courtship of,
84–87
TJ's deathbed vow to,
216–17

TJ's married life with,
88–91, 133, 187–88
TJ's relationship with,
77–79, 132–33
Jefferson, Mary, see
Bolling, Mary
Jefferson
Jefferson, Patsy, see
Randolph, Patsy
Jefferson
Jefferson, Peter (father),
3–8, 13, 62, 111,
128, 807n,
812n–13n, 1046n
background of, 6–8
death of, 15
library of, 11–12, 43
Jefferson, Polly, see
Eppes, Polly Jefferson
Jefferson, Randolph,
797n–99n
Jefferson, Robert, 799n
Jefferson, Thomas:
achievement of, 762
aging of, 686–87,
724–26, 729–31,
737–38
ambition of, 194, 344
anger displays of, 432
antimonarchism of,
xxxiv–xxxv

architectural sense of,
134–35
and art of living well,
27–29
assessment of, 751,
754–62, 766–67
authority as viewed by,
194–95
on balloon flight,
245–46
birth of, 4
book collection of,
706
British invasion of
Virginia and, 201–2
British occupation
of Monticello and,
206–8
Burwell courtship
fiasco and, 35–38
bust of, 260
celebrity of, 114
charm of, xxix–xxx
Chastellux's assessment
of, 212
as chess player, 545,
891n
childhood of, 5–8,
11–16
at College of William
and Mary, 23–35

commonplace book of,
90, 113
as conversationalist,
xxix–xxxi, 55–56,
594–98, 698, 731
curiosity of, 246–47,
619–20, 686
death threats against,
563–64, 610
decline and death of,
738–47
descriptions of, xvii,
xxxiii, 353–54,
542–43, 683,
781n– 82n
dress of, 543–44, 593,
612
education of,
19–35
1800 election and,
xvii–xxi
eightieth birthday of,
727
elected to Congress,
232
elected to House of
Burgesses, 68
as emblem of liberty,
757–60
Enlightenment and,
xxiv–xxv, 26–27

Jefferson, Thomas:
(**continued**)
envoy to Paris offer
and, 227–28
extended family of,
701–4
family background of,
3–10, 11–12
as father, 100, 248–49
fear of failure and
criticism of, 344
ferry crossing incident
and, 432
final words of, 746
finances of, 103, 471,
628, 657, 678, 720,
722–23, 732–34,
749, 993n, 1166n
in first journey outside
Virginia, 57
first memory of,
12–13, 812n
fishing practice of,
426–27
forty-seventh birthday
of, 353
as friend, 251
fundamental
republicanism of, 379
garden book of, 57, 67,
100

gardening interest of,
130, 135, 289, 620
as governor of Virginia,
189–93, 198
as grandfather, 675–78
gravesite of, 747, 763
gun collection of, 427
headaches of, 38–39,
147, 253, 352, 357,
366, 627–28, 633,
636, 670
health of, xvii, 243,
335, 426, 434,
570–71, 627–28,
647, 670, 700, 714,
724–25, 737
history as interest of,
41–43, 564
horses owned and
disciplined by, 426,
431–32
hunting practice of,
427
as husband, 100
Indians as viewed by,
165
on kinds of
government, 307–9
Lafayette's assessment
of, 351
landscaping and, 130

law career of, 31–32,
59, 70
leadership of, xxiii,
53–54, 113, 114,
179–80, 762
legacy of, 766–68
on living a virtuous
life, 734–36
lottery idea of, 734, 749
Lucy Jefferson's death
and, 273–74
Maclay's description of,
353
memorandum book of,
100, 102, 891n
Monocrats term of,
376, 380, 431
mother's death and,
146–48
music as interest of,
85–86, 91
named secretary of
state, 343–46
new states favored by,
256–57
official seal design and,
167–68
outings and activities
of, 426–27
on partisanship,
1087n–88n

Patty Jefferson's death
and, 216–21
pet bird of, 527–28,
669, 1075n
political maturation of,
53–55
political style of, 126,
459–60
political vision of,
xxi–xxii, xxvi–xxx
politics as interest
of, 24, 35, 40–41,
47–48, 170, 434–35,
459, 681
politics of personal
relationships and,
354–55
politics-philosophy
duality and, 336–37
Polly's death and, 604
Potomac river project
and, 253–54
pragmatism of, 106
presidency of, see
Jefferson, Thomas,
presidency of
public speaking and,
55, 130–31
religion and, 14, 106,
166, 182–84, 250,
481–82, 708–14

Jefferson, Thomas:
(continued)
as Renaissance man,
xxvi
resigns as secretary of
state, 414–16
Revolution and,
105–13
Rivanna River project
and, 52–53
and rumors of death
and dishonesty,
485–87
Sally Hemings's liaison
with, see Hemings,
Sarah "Sally"
scientific interests of,
246–47, 469, 617–20,
681–82
1796 election and,
445–47, 449–50
on sex, 324
sexuality and, 38–39,
826n–28n
Shadwell fire and,
70–71
slavery question and,
72–76, 185–86,
257, 716–22, 737,
853n–54n
slaves freed by, 748

sleep habits of,
670–71
spiritual beliefs of,
710–14
Thornton's assessment
of, 619
tombstone of, 762
U.S. as envisioned by,
469
as vice-president,
454–58, 464
violin studied by, 66,
85, 91
Virginia legislature's
inquiry into conduct
of, 208–13
wedding of, 87–88
western lands interest
of, 243–44, 253
women and,
xxviii–xxxi, 35–39,
61–65, 76, 826n–27n
as writer, 55
Jefferson, Thomas,
presidency of,
515–664
Burr case subpoena in,
634–35
Burr schism in,
551–53, 554
cabinet in, 528–29

Chesapeake crisis in, 639–42

death threats in, 563–64, 610

disunion movement in, 599–601

domestic policy in, 547–48, 551

end of, 656–58

expansion and exploration of U.S. in, see Lewis and Clark expedition; Louisiana Purchase

family life in, 532–33, 571–73

federal appointments in, 564–65

Federalists' criticism of, 548–54, 559–60, 564–66, 594–95

first annual message to Congress in, 547–49

first inaugural address in, xxiii, 515, 519–22, 557, 1069n

foreign policy in, 546–47, 551, 621–22, 636–37, 642–51

governing style of, 541–43, 544

hospitality and entertainment in, 591–98

idealism and realism in, 530–31

insurrection legislation in, 632

and journey to Monticello, 663

judiciary in, 560–63

living style in, 543–44

military policy in, 546

newspaper attacks in, 566–67

partisanship in, 557–59, 594–96

pet birds and, 527–28

presidential office in, 528

privacy and, 539

religion issue in, 550–51

Republican agenda in, 559–60

Sally Hemings controversy in, 567–70

scientific inquiry in, 617–19

Jefferson, Thomas,
    presidency of,
    (continued)
  second inaugural
    address in, 613–15,
    1115n
  taxes in, 551–52
  TJ's inauguration in,
    517–18, 528
  TJ's leadership in, 611,
    1071n
  TJ's personal dress
    style in, 542–44
  TJ's working habits in,
    538–39
  western exploration in,
    554–55
Jefferson, Thomas, Jr.,
    799n
Jefferson, Thomas
    (grandfather), 6–7,
    798n
Jefferson Memorial, 761
Jesus of Nazareth,
    710–12
Johnson, William, 725
Johnson, William
    Samuel, 369
Jones, John Lane, 651
Jones, John Paul, 675
Jordan, Daniel P., 796n

Jouett, Jack, 206, 211
Judaism, 710
Judiciary Act (1801),
    500, 635, 1062n
  repeal of, 551, 560–62,
    1089n
Judiciary Act (1802),
    560–61
Julien (chef), 664
Jupiter (slave), 39, 40,
    94, 110–11, 432

Karamanli, Hamet, 547
Kauffmann, Angelica,
    292
Keehmle, John, 1131n
Kennedy, John F., ix
Kentucky, 474, 757
King, Rufus, 411, 491,
    493, 496, 511, 548,
    552–54, 577, 581,
    600, 1057n, 1062n,
    1094n, 1108n
Knox, Henry, 328, 351,
    354, 368, 385, 405,
    407, 411
Krumpholtz, Johann
    Baptist, 295

Lafayette, Marquis de,
    202, 283, 305,

331–35, 351, 393, 400, 648, 674, 675, 681, 717, 728, 729, 987n, 1018n

Lancaster, Treaty of, 1046n

Langdon, John, 447, 611

Latrobe, Benjamin H., 593

Leander, HMS, 627

Lear, Tobias, 1015n

Ledyard, John, 281

Lee, Henry (son), 741–43

Lee, Henry "Light-Horse Harry," 430, 741, 998n

Lee, Richard Henry, 105, 148, 152, 162, 164, 167, 186, 192, 907n, 921n, 928n

Legrand, Jacques-Guillaume, 293–94

Leiper, Thomas, 371, 1121n

Lemaire, Etienne, 528

Leopard, HMS, 639–40, 642, 645

Leopold II, Holy Roman Emperor, 349

Lesage, Alain-René, 248

Letter from Alexander Hamilton, Concerning the Public Conduct and Character of John Adams, Esq., President of the United States, 491

Letters from a Farmer in Pennsylvania (Dickinson), 129

Letters from an American Farmer (Crèvecoeur), 234

Lewis, Meriwether, 197, 527, 532, 536, 547, 582, 615–16
  death of, 683
  TJ's instructions to, 1098n–1100n

Lewis, Nicholas, 229, 283

Lewis, Warner, 251

Lewis and Clark expedition, xxvii, 196, 754
  achievement of, 616
  artifacts from, 615–17
  cost of, 1086n

Lewis and Clark
expedition,
(continued)
Louisiana Purchase
and, 582–83
onset of, 582
Lexington, Battle of,
xxxiii, 119, 123
Leyden Gazette, 273
Library of Congress,
670, 706
Life and Morals of
Jesus of Nazareth
Extracted Textually
from the Gospels in
Greek, Latin, French
& English, The
(Jefferson), 711
Lincoln, Abraham, 74,
766
TJ as viewed by,
757–58
Lincoln, Levi, 529, 586,
659, 686
Linn, Dr., 505
Livingston, Edward,
488, 505
Livingston, Robert R.,
382, 384, 406, 474,
578, 585, 902n,
1008n, 1024n

Livy, 620
Locke, John, 26, 156,
169, 183, 352, 386,
674
Logan, George, 628
Louisiana Purchase,
xxvii, 574–84, 610,
650, 716
constitutionality
question and,
584–89, 1101n–2n
Federalists' reaction to,
589–90
Franco-Spanish treaty
and, 574–75
Lewis and Clark
expedition and, 582
Monroe mission and,
576, 578–81
Napoleon and,
575–80, 583
St. Domingue slave
uprising and,
579–80
TJ's reaction to,
581–84
Louis XVI, King of
France, 266, 304,
313, 334, 349, 400,
408, 674, 964n,
1018n

Luke, Book of, 743
Luzerne, Chevalier de la, 262, 272
Lyman, Theodore, 599
Lyon, Matthew, 464, 473, 476

McCaul, Alexander, 894n
McClurg, James, 135
McFarlane, James, 430
McGregory, Uriah, 486–87
McHenry, James, 283, 485, 496, 551
Machiavelli, Niccolò, 169
McKean, Thomas, 509, 566, 602
Mackenzie, Alexander, 554–55
Maclay, William, 353, 373
Macon, Nathaniel, 539
Macpherson, James, 89
Madison, Dolley, 471, 540, 578, 598, 604, 623, 661, 675, 694, 697
Madison, Eleanor Conway, 188
Madison, James, xxi, 181–82, 183, 219, 231, 239, 240, 241, 246, 259, 328, 344–46, 352, 361, 362, 540, 578, 580, 614, 618, 624, 634, 650, 657, 674, 675, 679, 680, 691, 699–700, 706, 747, 786n, 1012n, 1030n, 1032n–33n, 1038n–39n, 1053n, 1151n, 1155n
on Alien and Sedition Acts, 467–68
background of, 181–82
Callender pardon issue and, 535–36
debt assumption issue and, 363–64
1808 election and, 653–54
inauguration of, 660–62
Kitty Floyd courtship and, 229–30, 236, 941n
as secretary of state, 528–29

Madison, James,
(continued)
TJ's correspondence
with, 250, 251–52,
256, 258–59,
285–86, 308–9, 313,
318, 335–38, 375,
377, 408–10, 414,
421, 431, 433, 434,
438, 439, 448–49,
452–53, 455, 479,
484, 493, 603–4,
620, 681–82, 695,
738, 786n, 926n,
941n–42n,
989n–90n, 1022n,
1029n, 1111n
in trip to New
England, 382–83
War of 1812 and,
695
Madison, Rev. James,
247, 281
Magdalen, HMS, 120
Magellan, Ferdinand,
674
Malesherbes,
Guillaume-Chrétien
de, 281
Mallet, David, 92
Malta, 579

Malthus, Thomas,
583–84
Marbury, William,
561–62
Marbury v. Madison,
561, 1089n
Marie-Antoinette,
Queen of France,
xxv, 266, 334, 349
Mark, Book of, 672
Marks, Anne Scott, 662
Marshall, John, 24, 400,
405, 485, 495, 497,
500, 501–2, 511–12,
519, 521–22, 706,
941n
Burr trial and, 635
TJ's dislike of, 561,
1070n
Washington biography
of, 725
Martínez, Esteban José,
367
Mary II, Queen of
England, 43, 769
Maryland, 11, 58–59,
149, 186, 361, 495,
902n, 986n
Mason, George, 156,
235
Mason, John, 1037n

Mason, Stevens Thomson, 501, 1059n

Mason, Thomson, 866n

Massachusetts, 68–69, 150–51, 252, 306, 361, 599, 600, 655, 829n, 986n, 1140n
first revolutionary clashes in, 119

Massachusetts Spy, 518

Maury, James, 19–20, 62, 250, 783n

Mazzei, Philip, 268, 461, 686, 926n

Medical Lexicon: A Dictionary of Medical Science (Dunglison), 570

Mémoires de la Comtesse de la Motte, Les, xxv

Mémoires de la Princesse de Bareith, xxv

Memoirs of the War (Lee), 741

Mercer, James, 123–24

Merchant of Venice (Shakespeare), 65, 85

Merry, Anthony, 597–99, 601, 609, 1107n

Mexico, 577, 630

Miami Indians, 368

Michaux, André, 554

Mirabeau, Comte de, 985n

Miranda, Francisco de, 1119n

Missouri, 715–20, 724

Modern Griselda, The (Edgeworth), 702

Molinos, Jacques, 294

Monck, George, 472

Monnier, Jean-Joseph, 985n

Monocrats, 376, 380, 431

Monroe, James, xx, 213, 216, 234, 250, 363, 408, 411, 481, 517, 535, 614, 618, 627, 674, 788n
1808 election and, 653
Louisiana Purchase mission of, 576–81, 585
Spanish mission of, 621

Monroe, James,
(continued)
  TJ's correspondence
    with, 269, 271, 275,
    320, 373–74, 424,
    428–29, 442, 500,
    532, 536, 564,
    585–86, 653, 682,
    727, 937n, 949n
Monroe Doctrine,
  727–28
Montaigne, Michel de,
  421
Montesquieu, 156,
  682
Montgolfier, Jacques-
  Étienne, 947n
Montgolfier, Joseph-
  Michel, 947n
Montgomery, Richard,
  140
Monticello, xvii, xxiv,
  xxxi, 18, 20, 72,
  84, 88–94, 134,
  360, 424–25, 434,
  669–704, 719,
  752–53, 1145n–46n
  art and artifacts at,
    671–74
  British occupation of,
    206–8

building and
  rebuilding of, 70–71,
  89–91, 133–34,
  424–25, 852n
decor of, 671–75
entrance hall of, 671
family life at, 675–79
grandchildren at,
  676–78
Hemings family's move
  to, 93–94
Lafayette's visit to,
  729–30
library of, xxv, 134
pet birds at, 527, 669
porticles of, 677
public curiosity and,
  698–700
Randolph-Bankhead
  brawl at, 703
reading activities at,
  677–78
Sally Hemings's life at,
  347–48, 683–85
size of, 671
slaves at, 683–85,
  853n–54n
TJ's bedroom at,
  669–71
TJ's correspondence
  cabinet in, 680

TJ's happiness at, 679–81

Montmorin, Comte de, 985n, 986n

Monuments de la vie privée des douze Césars, 293

Monuments du culte secret des dames romaines, 293

Moore, Bernard, 62

Moore, Thomas, 569

Morocco, 270, 271

Morris, Gouverneur, 428, 497, 507, 549, 589, 986n

Morris, Robert, 1014n

Mount Vernon, 370, 385, 395, 754

Napoleon I, Emperor of France, 332, 542, 587, 612, 621, 622, 624, 645, 674

Louisiana Purchase and, 575–80, 583

National Assembly, French, 331–33, 356

National Gazette, 483

National Intelligencer, xxix, 518, 660, 706

Native Americans, **see** Indians

Navigation Acts, British, 41, 46

Nelson, Horatio, 603, 612, 622

Nelson, Hugh, 682

Nelson, Thomas, Jr., 148, 188, 189, 205

Netherlands, 230, 322

Neville, John, 430

New England, 128, 529, 532, 589, 652, 864n

Shays's rebellion in, 306, 463, 971n–72n, 984n

New Hampshire, 599

New Jersey, 149, 186, 242, 257, 495, 599, 902n

New Orleans, Battle of, xxxiii

New Testament, xxiv

Newton, Isaac, 26, 30, 352, 386, 674

New York, N.Y., 164, 319

TJ's sojourn in, 348, 352, 355, 360–62

New York Evening Post, 549, 608

New York **Gazette,**
1087**n**
New York State, xxxiv,
117, 149, 186, 315,
436, 470, 552, 586,
589, 599, 902**n**,
1083**n**
disunion movement in,
599–601
1800 election in, 488,
492
Nicholas, George, 936**n**
Nicholas, John, 479
Nicholas, Robert Carter,
123–24, 143, 184,
898**n**
Nicholson, Joseph, 494,
502, 509, 562
Nicolas, Wilson Cary,
586, 732–33, 1121**n**
Nootka Sound, 366–67,
644, 1001**n**
North, Lord, 885**n**
North Carolina, 361
Northwest Ordinance of
1787, 257
Northwest Territory, 368
**Notes on the State of
Virginia** (Jefferson),
14, 182, 234, 355,
911**n**, 944**n**, 964**n**

Nova Scotia, xxxiv, 252
nullification, idea of,
474–75

**Observations Relating
to the Influence of
Vermont and the
Territorial Claims
on the Politics of
Congress** (Madison),
230
Ogilby, John, 12
Ohio Company, 841**n**
Old Republicans
(Quids), 625,
1120**n**–21**n**
Olive Branch Petition,
130
Ontassete, Chief, 54
Order in Council, 423
Ordinance of 1784, 257
Orphan, The
(Otway), 65
Ossian, 89–90
Otis, James, 47
Otis, Samuel A., 500
Otway, Thomas, 65

Page, John, xxxvi, 35,
36–37, 58, 62, 71,
76, 113, 135, 139,

141, 143, 146, 161, 167, 463, 474, 513, 657, 852n, 910n, 912n, 927n–29n
  on Declaration of Independence, 161
  TJ's gubernatorial rivalry with, 189–91
Paine, Thomas, 47, 145, 175, 333, 374, 586–87, 674, 963n–64n, 985n, 1004n–6n, 1101n–2n
  TJ's visit with, 286
Paris, Treaty of, xxxv, 231, 253, 715, 958n
  provisions of, 241
  ratification of, 242–43
Parliament, British, 42, 43, 46–47, 59, 68, 101, 105, 287, 367, 803n, 840n, 865n–67n, 874n, 892n, 896n, 899n
Parton, James, 160, 684–85, 754
Passionate Sage: The Character and Legacy of John Adams (Ellis), 766

Paterson, William, 473, 476
Paul, Saint, 38, 550
Peale, Charles Willson, 618, 674
Pendleton, Edmund, 171, 184, 910n, 912n
Pennsylvania, 149, 239, 422, 492, 599, 902n
  1800 election in, 503–4
  excise tax rebellion in, 396–97
  Whiskey Rebellion in, 430–31
Pennsylvania Evening Post, 159
Pennsylvania Journal, or, Weekly Advertiser, 236
Petit, Adrien, 312
Philadelphia, USS, 603, 1110n
Philadelphia Gazette, 498
Philadelphia Mutiny, 958n
Philidor, François-André Danican, 545
Philips, Josiah, 195, 633, 922n

Philosophical Society for the Advancement of Useful Knowledge, 135

Philosophy of Jesus of Nazareth extracted from the Account of his Life and Doctrines as Given by Matthew, Mark, Luke and John, The (Jefferson), 711

Pichon, Louis-André, 529–30, 543, 549, 553–54, 559, 568, 765, 1082n, 1092n–93n

Pickering, John, 562

Pickering, Timothy, 456, 485, 492, 495, 589–90, 599–600, 618, 648, 652, 1108n

Pike, Zebulon, 617–18

Pilâtre de Rozier, Jean-François, 947n–48n

Pinckney, Charles Cotesworth, 490, 521, 610, 654, 695, 1038n, 1039n

Pinckney, Thomas, 448, 449, 490–91

Pinkney, William, 649–50

Plato, 334

Plumer, William, 594–96, 624, 632, 1105n–6n
  on Burr, 613

Plymouth colony, xxxii

Political Disquisitions (Burgh), 132

Political Observations (Madison), 436

Pope, Alexander, 113, 220

Poplar Forest (estate), 208, 663, 677, 702, 733

Preble, Edward, 674

press, freedom of the, 318, 477

Preston, William, 112, 925n

Price, Richard, 348

Priestley, Joseph, 530, 531, 583

primogeniture, 181

Princess Royal, HMS, 367

Principles of Surgery (Bell), 663

Proclamation of 1763, 841n

Prospect Before Us, The (Callender), 482, 605

Protestantism, 169

Prussia, 230, 316

Psalms, Book of, 735–36

Purdie, Alexander, 54

Purdie, Hugh, 371

Quasi-War with France, 456, 465, 529

Quids (Old Republicans), 625, 1120n

Quincy, Josiah, Jr., 684

Racine de Monville, François, 296

Raleigh, Walter, 69, 674

Ramsay, John, 183

Ramsey, Captain, 310–12

Randall, Henry, 28, 43, 55–56, 77, 360, 684, 699, 732–33, 752, 781n, 1174n

Randolph, Ann Cary, see Bankhead, Ann Cary Randolph

Randolph, Edmund, 214, 219, 231, 385, 847n, 1016n

Randolph, Edward, 9

Randolph, Henry, 8–9

Randolph, Isham, 8–9, 17

Randolph, James Madison, 623

Randolph, Jane Rogers, 9–10

Randolph, John, 9–10, 102, 135–36, 480, 494, 563, 798n, 868n, 896n, 898n, 1121n, 1126n–27n, 1139n
  TJ's break with, 624–25
  TJ's correspondence with, 135–38

Randolph, Mary Isham, 9

Randolph, Patsy Jefferson, 78–79, 100, 138, 170–72, 228–29, 240, 243, 343, 364, 373–74, 404–5, 426, 457, 470–71, 532, 568–73, 623, 662, 698, 703, 734, 741, 743, 949n

Randolph, Patsy
  Jefferson, (**continued**)
  children of, 457
  ferry incident and, 432
  marriage of, 346–47,
    993n
  Monticello sitting
    room of, 675
  Sally Hemings
    informally freed by,
    748–49
  with TJ in Paris, 260,
    265–67, 268–69,
    275, 279, 287, 289,
    311, 334
  TJ's correspondence
    with, 248–49, 505,
    512, 604, 611, 636,
    638, 786n, 996n
  TJ's grief for Patty
    Jefferson recalled by,
    214–15, 217–18
Randolph, Peter, 50
Randolph, Peyton,
    23–24, 33, 50, 111,
    123–24, 126, 140,
    171, 541, 812n,
    874n–75n, 886n,
    914n, 917n
Randolph, Richard, 9,
    404–5

Randolph, Thomas, 9
Randolph, Thomas
  Jefferson, 324, 426,
    459, 674, 684–85,
    701, 703, 725, 740,
    746–47, 781n, 1030n
Randolph, Thomas
  Mann, Jr., 346–47,
    370, 404, 485, 493,
    505, 523, 545, 573,
    581, 604, 637–38,
    644–45, 660, 701–3,
    741, 857n, 992n,
    1090n, 1125n–26n
Randolph, Thomas
  Mann, Sr., 13–14,
    437, 941n
Randolph, William,
    8–9, 13
Rapin (domestic), 528
Rapin-Thoyras, Paul de,
    12, 41–43
Rayburn, Sam, 759
Reagan, Ronald, 760–61
Reign of Terror, 332,
    349, 400
religion, freedom of, 177,
    182–84, 318
**Report on the Public
  Credit** (Hamilton),
  360

Republicans, 383, 422, 428, 436, 443, 457, 479, 524, 541, 551, 553, 460–61, 589, 592, 647, 728, 1020n–21n, 1037n, 1087n
Alien and Sedition Acts and, 467, 470, 479–80
1800 election and, 488, 501–2, 509, 659–60
Jay Treaty and, 439
Mazzei letter controversy and, 461
Quid faction of, 625–26, 1120n–21n
1796 election and, 446–49
TJ's assessment of, 439–41
TJ's presidency and agenda of, 559–61
War of 1812 and, 697
Resolution of the Freeholders of Albemarle County, 108
Restoration, 42
Revenge, USS, 642

Revere, Paul, 932n–33n
Revolutionary War, **see** American Revolution
Reynolds, James, 398
Reynolds, Joshua, 292
Reynolds, Maria, 398
Rhode Island, 241, 586, 599
Richmond **Examiner,** 472
Richmond **Recorder,** 557, 567–68
Rights of Man, The (Paine), 286, 374–75
Rights of the British Colonies Asserted and Proved (Otis), 47
Rind, Clementina, 111
Rind, William, 54, 111
Rittenhouse, David, 674
Robinson, John, 50
Rochefoucauld, Duc de la, 268, 457
Rochefoucauld, Duchess de la, 294
Rochon, Abbé, 282
Rodney, Caesar A., 493, 502, 604
Romain, Pierre-Ange, 948n
Romulus, 229

Roosevelt, Franklin D., 756, 758–59, 766, 768

Roosevelt, Theodore, 766

Royal Society, 30

Royle, Joseph, 54

Rules for Drawing the Several Parts of Architecture (Gibbs), 134

Rush, Benjamin, xx, 128, 150, 166–67, 522, 550, 556, 570, 650, 657, 680, 686–90, 694, 1041n

Rushworth, John, 105–7

Russia, 177, 230, 367

Rutledge, Edward, 445, 898n, 902n, 1033n, 1040n

Rutledge, John, 328, 367

St. Andrews Club, 481

St. Clair, Arthur, 368

St. Domingue, 267, 487, 644, 1057n

slave insurrection in, 380–81, 579–80

Salon des Échecs, 279

Samuel Howell v. Wade Netherland, 61, 75

San Ildefonso, Third Treaty of, 574–77

Scales, William, 510

Schuyler, Philip, 358, 488

"Secret Journal of Foreign Affairs" (Thomson), 230

Sedgwick, Theodore, 428

Senate, Kentucky, 475

Senate, U.S., 353, 428, 456, 497, 502, 524, 561, 637

Jay Treaty in, 439

Missouri statehood issue in, 715–17

Seven Years' War, 45, 103, 838n–39n

Sévigné, Madame de, xxv

Shackelford, Benjamin, 663

Shadwell (estate), xxxvii, 3, 15–18, 20, 54, 63, 64, 88, 99, 134, 763

destroyed by fire, 70–71

Shakespeare, William, 12, 15, 65, 71, 85

Shawnee Indians, 368

Shays, Daniel, 306

Shays' Rebellion, 306, 463, 984n

Shenstone, William, 57, 135

Shippen, Thomas, 283

Shippen, William, Jr., 57–58

Short, William, 250, 258–60, 309, 401

Siberia, 246–47

Sierra Leone Company, 488

Sieyès, Emmanuel-Joseph, 985n

Simcoe, John Graves, 378, 397

Simms, Charles, 446–47

Sinclair, John, 287

Six Nations of the Iroquois, 1046n

Skelton, Bathurst, 82

Skelton, John, 82

Skelton, Martha Wayles, see Jefferson, Martha Wayles Skelton

Skinner, Thomson J., 463

Skipwith, Henry, 273

Skipwith, Robert, 855n–56n

slaves and slavery, 184–85, 256, 569, 883n, 897n–98n

British threatened arming of, 120–21, 142, 1057n

Declaration of Independence and, 156–58, 185

expansion of, 257, 716, 720

Gabriel's insurrection and, 487–88

Haiti insurrection of, 380–81

Missouri statehood debate and, 715–16, 720

Northwest Ordinance of 1787 and, 257

relocation idea and, 488, 1057n–58n

St. Domingue insurrection and, 380–81, 579–80

sexual color line and, 83–84

three-fifths clause and, 451

Virginia legislation on, 855n

slave trade, 156–57, 185

Small, William, 23, 25–26, 113, 121, 182

Smith, Abigail Adams "Nabby," 269, 274, 275, 282–83

Smith, Adam, 26

Smith, Cotton Mather, 486

Smith, John Thomas, 292

Smith, Jonathan B., 374–75

Smith, Margaret Bayard, xxix–xxx, 53, 509, 519, 527–28, 539–40, 571, 594, 596–97, 620, 661–63, 679, 795n, 1062n, 1105n

Smith, Robert, 529

Smith, Samuel (general), 505–6, 508

Smith, Samuel (senator), 625

Smith, Samuel Harrison (publisher), xxix, 354, 374, 509, 518, 539–40, 574, 620, 660

Smith, William, Jr., 867n–68n

Smith, William S., 126, 279, 296, 411, 973n, 981n–82n

Society of Cincinnati, 254–56, 258, 429, 892n

Sophocles, 739

South Carolina, 149, 158, 193, 361, 448, 490, 492, 902n, 1038n

South Sea Company, 30

Spain, 230, 250, 349, 367, 378, 554, 574–75, 577, 621, 631, 727, 920n, 956n

Nootka Sound episode and, 366–68

Spanish Florida, 367–68, 575, 621, 839n, 903n, 1000n

Sparks, Jared, 711

Spectator, The, 15

speech, freedom of, 466

Spirit of the Laws (Montesquieu), 682

Stamp Act, British, 46–47, 59, 68, 106, 179, 576, 696, 829n

Fifth Resolution and, 48–52

Stanton, Lucia, 73

Stark, General, 724
State Department, U.S., 344, 382, 387
TJ's resignation from, 414–16
Sterett, Andrew, 546–47
Sterne, Laurence, 86, 215–16, 320
Stevens, Edward, 927n
Stiles, Ezra, 245, 971n
Story, Joseph, 543–44
Stuart, Archibald, 510
Stuart, Gilbert, 671, 672
Sugar Act, British, 46
Sullivan, James, 652–53, 1041n, 1138n
Summary View of the Rights of British America, A (Jefferson), 109–14, 118, 127, 170, 225, 877n
Supreme Court, U.S., 500–1, 543
Marbury decision of, 561–62, 1089n
Sweeney, George, 628
Swift, Jonathan, 12
Sydney, Lord, 314
System of Anatomy, A (Wistar), 617

Tacitus, 44, 620
Talleyrand, Charles-Maurice de, 580
Tammany Society of Washington, 669
Tarleton, Banastre, 203, 205–6, 423, 622, 728, 932n
Taylor, John, 447, 466, 476, 478, 548, 614, 647
Tazewell, Henry, 470
Tempest, The (Shakespeare), 71
Temple, John, 1008n
Tennessee, 444
Texas, 631
Third Treaty of San Ildefonso, 374–75
Thomson, Charles, 230, 290, 656, 662, 724, 957n
Thornton, Edward, 381, 544, 575
TJ assessed by, 619
Toussaint-Louverture, François-Dominique, 381
Towne, Benjamin, 159
Townley, Charles, 292
Townshend, Charles, 68

Townshend Acts, 68–69, 101, 837n

Trafalgar, Battle of, 622

Trail of Tears, 588

Transylvania College, 708

Treasury Department, U.S., 384, 387, 389, 410, 529

Treatise on Gardening by a Citizen of Virginia, A (Randolph), 135

Treaty of Aranjuez, 577

Treaty of Ghent, xxxiii, 697, 728

Treaty of Lancaster, 1046n

Treaty of Paris, **see** Paris, Treaty of

Tripoli, 270, 286, 546–47, 551, 603, 674, 1110n

Tripoli, 546

Trist, Eliza House, 229, 240, 244, 374, 679, 708

Trist, Nicholas, 741, 745–47, 1030n

Tristram Shandy (Sterne), 215–16, 320

Troup, Robert, 491, 548, 555, 1008n

Truman, Harry S., 756, 759, 768

Trumbull, John, 293, 294, 297, 350, 672, 674

Tunis, 270, 547

Turgot, Anne Robert-Jacques, 672–73

Tuscany, 230

Twelfth Amendment, 446, 602, 1037n

Tyler, John, 987n

United Netherlands, 316

United States, 423–24
    Barbary states crisis and, 270–71
    France's Quasi-War with, 456, 465, 529
    France's relations with, 177–79, 265–68, 400–2

Van Buren, Martin, xxi, 788n

Vancouver Island, 366

van der Werff, Adriaen, 320–21

Varina (estate), 993n

Vauguyon, Duke de la, 268

Venice Preserved (Otway), 65

Verling, William, 65

Vermont, 586, 599

Vermont Journal, 473

Vespucius, Americus, 672, 674

Virgil, 72, 416

Virginia, xxiii, 14, 65, 132, 166, 171, 186, 225, 247, 280, 313, 361, 374, 548, 600, 630, 654, 683, 829n, 865n, 872n–73n, 886n, 923n, 985n
British invasion of, 193, 199–206
and cession of western territory, 256
colonial society in, 10–11
Dunmore's campaign against, 116, 119–21, 140–42, 883n, 898n
economics issue in, 871n–73n
first recorded earthquake in, 99
Gabriel's slave uprising in, 487–88
gentry culture of, 723
Gunpowder Affair in, 116, 121–22
impetus for rebellion in, 104–5
inquiry on TJ in, 208–10, 213
Potomac River project of, 253–54
religious freedom in, 182–84, 762
Richmond named capital of, 198
slavery in, 185
slavery legislation in, 918n
Stamp Act debate in, 47–48
TJ as governor of, 189–94, 198, 446–47, 993n
Tory uprising in, 198

Virginia, University of, 706–8, 724, 760, 763, 1160n
appointments to, 708–10
founding of, 706–8

Virginia, University of, (continued)
religion issue and, 709–11
Virginia Company of Comedians, 65
Virginia Convention, 115, 141
Virginia Gazette, 54, 67, 81, 87, 228, 858n, 866n, 875n
TJ's runaway slave ad in, 72–73
Voltaire, 274, 673, 961n
Voyage Round the World (Anson), 12
Voyages from Montreal (Mackenzie), 554

Walker, Elizabeth Moore "Betsy," 61–65, 68, 83, 295, 568
Walker, John, 61–65, 68, 107–8, 682
Walker, Thomas, 62, 68, 111, 932n
Walpole, Horace, 293
Ward, Samuel, 127
War of 1812, xxxiii, 649, 693–97

Washington, George, xxi, xxii, xxxv, 74, 111, 127, 131, 132, 144, 164, 186, 209, 230–31, 327, 328, 334, 348, 357, 366, 370–72, 373, 376, 382, 385, 402–3, 405–7, 412–13, 421, 430, 433, 464, 509, 525, 526, 534, 542, 548, 553, 577, 589, 593, 614–15, 656, 674, 675, 691, 697, 754, 756, 765–66, 768, 875n, 883n, 888n, 1019n, 1036n, 1043n
at Adams's inauguration, 455–56
bust of, 280
death of, 482–84
draft Constitution and, 316–17
farewell address of, 445–46, 557
Hamilton on, 483
Jay Treaty and, 424, 437
Marshall's biography of, 725–26

Mazzei letter controversy and, 462

neutrality proclamation of, 408–9

postal service issue and, 387–88

reelection of, 399

TJ offered secretary of state position by, 343–46

TJ's correspondence with, 204, 254–56, 280–81, 320, 346–47, 394–95, 921n, 992n, 999n–1000n

TJ's relationship with, 350–52, 388–95, 442–43, 482–83

Washington, Martha, 188

Washington Federalist, xix

Wayles, John, 80–82, 83, 93, 102, 103, 527

Wayles, Martha Eppes, 80, 83

Weatherbourne, Henry, 13

Webster, Daniel, 731, 750

West Point, U.S. Military Academy at, 551

Whately, Thomas, 135

"What Is Enlightenment?" (Kant), 23

Whig Party, British, 42

Whiskey Rebellion, 430–31

Whitworth, Lord, 579

Wilkinson, James, 378, 555, 631, 634, 1132n

William and Mary, College of, 21–22, 62, 182, 247, 819n

William I (the Conqueror), King of England, 44

William III, King of England (William of Orange), 43–44, 769

Wilson, James, 157, 902n

Wilson, Woodrow, 751, 756

Wistar, Caspar, Jr.,
617
Wood, Gordon S.,
802n
Wright, Frances, 722
Wythe, Elizabeth, 172
Wythe, George, 24,
31–33, 47, 59,
72, 101–2, 113,
149, 171–72, 251,
424, 707–8,
844n, 1042n,
1125n
death of, 628–29

Xenophon, 334
XYZ affair, 464, 472,
564

York, Duke of, xxv
Yorktown, siege of,
xxxiii, 211, 936n

ABOUT THE AUTHOR

JON MEACHAM received the Pulitzer Prize for **American Lion,** his 2008 bestselling biography of Andrew Jackson. The author of the earlier **New York Times** bestsellers **Franklin and Winston** and **American Gospel,** Meacham is executive editor and executive vice president of Random House and a contributing editor of **Time**. Born in Chattanooga, he was educated at The University of the South. Meacham lives with his wife and three children in Nashville and Sewanee.

CHAPTER SIX

Anunciata was taking her three youngest children for an afternoon stroll in a quiet plaza when it happened.

With unusual religious zeal, Juan always closed the Havana Club on Sunday, giving his staff some well-deserved time off. Carmen had gone to the movies with her latest boyfriend, and Anunciata and her children were enjoying the charming square, with its tinkling fountain in the middle, and the bougainvillea adding bright splashes of purple as it climbed its way up the gray stone walls of the surrounding buildings.

Busy playing catch, chasing after his two younger brothers on the dusty grass, shrieking with laughter, Kristobel hadn't noticed the drunken tramp as he lurched toward his mother muttering under his breath. He didn't hear her answer:

"No, I have no money. Please go away—leave me alone."

He didn't see the filthy creature grab his mother's handbag from her frail wrist as he snarled, "*Putana*, give it to me. I know you have money. All of you *putas* have money on you."

It was only when Kristobel heard Anunciata's scream of protest that he turned to see the mad eyes of the derelict as he lunged at her, pushing her to the ground with all his force.

As she fell, the man spat at Anunciata, screaming, "Filthy *putana* bitch!" Then he turned, and bolted from the small peaceful square.

Anunciata shouted, "My bag, my bag, it's got all my money in it! Kristobel, go after him, please . . . Oh sweet Mother of God, he's got my money."

Kristobel chased the tramp on wiry thirteen-year-old legs, but the older man rapidly escaped, disappearing into the labyrinth of shabby back streets and alleys that bordered the square.

Despondent, Kristobel returned to the plaza, the image of the savage's evil face, long matted hair and beard etched in his mind.

A small crowd surrounded his mother, who was lying on the grass, wracked with coughing. Kristobel could see the worried expression of some of the women in the crowd and the frightened faces of his brothers.

Anunciata lay groaning, her white face contorted with pain. Drops of blood flecked the corners of her mouth, and as she suddenly convulsed with another bout of coughing, he saw with horror more blood staining the sparse grass in front of her.

"Call an ambulance, we must get this woman to a hospital at once!" The commanding voice came from a passerby, an American man in uniform, who spoke with the authoritarian air of a man who is used to being obeyed. An onlooker muttered that he would go and telephone for one.

"Mama, Mama, what is it? What's wrong?" Kristobel dropped to his knees, cradling his mother's head in his lap.

"Don't worry, my son," she croaked from bluish-white lips. "I'm all right—really I am—please don't worry."

The military man shook his head in pity and whispered something to the woman next to him who nodded sadly.

"I'm fine," said Anunciata as her body shook with another spasm of tubercular coughing. "Just fine, Kristobel." Weakly she spat into the white starched handkerchief that the major proffered.

"Did you see him? Did you see that bastard hit my mother?" Kristobel cried fiercely to the crowd.

Several of them nodded.

"Do you know him? Do you know who he is?" Kristobel's voice was filled with hatred. "I must find him—he has all our money, and now . . ." He looked at his mother, who, exhausted by her coughing spasm, had closed her eyes and was breathing shallowly. "It's all the money we have for the whole week," he said desperately. "If we don't have the money, our family won't eat."

The major quietly pressed a twenty-peseta note into Kristobel's hand, saying, "I hope that will be of some help. I'm very sorry about your mother, but I'm sure that she will be all right once she gets to the hospital."

"Thank you, *señor.*" Kristobel smiled with genuine gratitude.

"If my wife and I can be of any help at all, we are staying at the Casablanca Hotel," he said. "My name is Brown. Major Gordon F. Brown, United States Army, at your service."

"Thank you, *señor*, you are very kind." Kristobel stroked his mother's head tenderly. Her eyes were closed now and he saw the tiny blue veins on her eyelids and the faint pulse that beat in her left temple.

"Here comes the ambulance," said Major Brown, and with the organizational skill born of years of duty, he helped Anunciata and her sons into the back.

She lingered for three days. In between feverish bouts of coughing, Anunciata's burning eyes stared into those of her children, who had gathered around the narrow hospital bed to watch their mother die.

"You must take care of your brothers now, Kristobel, please," she whispered. "You are the head of the family now. Promise me you will look after them."

"I promise, Mama," he sobbed.

The somber major, accompanied by his wispy, pale wife, came to visit often, as did Juan and his portly spouse, Florinda.

When Anunciata finally died, surrounded by her few friends and her children, everyone wept when the doctor closed her eyelids with dispassionate thoroughness. As Kristobel held on to his mother's lifeless hand, he felt as though his own life had ended.

During their vigil at Anunciata's bedside, Florinda had become extremely attached to Kristobel's younger brothers, Pepe and Victor.

"Let them come and stay with us," she had begged Juan. "They are so young and they have no parents at all. I will look after them."

Juan grumbled, but nevertheless gave in. It would be nice for the motherly Florinda to have some children around now that their own were grown up. Only he would know that these were really his children. Now perhaps Florinda would stop smothering him and devote more of her time to those poor boys, who looked as if they could do with a good wash and a few square meals.

"I shall move in with Carlito," announced eighteen-year-old Carmen, hanging on to